ECONOMICS AND THE ENVIRONMENT

SEVENTH EDITION

ECONOMICS AND THE ENVIRONMENT

Eban S. Goodstein

Bard College

Stephen Polasky

University of Minnesota

WILEY

By this international commerce of geese, the waste corn of Illinois is carried through the clouds to the Arctic tundras, there to combine with the waste sunlight of a nightless June to grow goslings for all the land in between. And in this annual barter of food for light, and winter warmth for summer solitude, the whole continent receives as a net profit a wild poem dropped from the murky skies upon the muds of March.

—ALDO LEOPOLD

Vice President and Executive Publisher	*George Hoffman*
Executive Editor	*Joel Hollenbeck*
Content Editor	*Jennifer Manias*
Assistant Editor	*Courtney Luzzi*
Senior Editorial Assistant	*Erica Horowitz*
Director of Marketing	*Amy Scholz*
Assistant Marketing Manager	*Puja Katariwala*
Marketing Assistant	*Mia Brady*
Project Management Services	*Lavanya Murlidhar/Laserwords Private Limited*
Associate Production Manager	*Joel Balbin*
Production Editor	*Yee Lyn Song*
Cover Designer	*Alson Low*
Cover Credit	© *Gwen Schantz/Brooklyn Grange Rooftop Farm, www.brooklyngrangefarm.com*

This book was set in 10/12 Times Roman by Laserwords Private Limited and printed and bound by Edwards Brothers Malloy. The cover was printed by Edwards Brothers Malloy.

This book is printed on acid free paper.

Founded in 1807, John Wiley & Sons, Inc. has been a valued source of knowledge and understanding for more than 200 years, helping people around the world meet their needs and fulfill their aspirations. Our company is built on a foundation of principles that include responsibility to the communities we serve and where we live and work. In 2008, we launched a Corporate Citizenship Initiative, a global effort to address the environmental, social, economic, and ethical challenges we face in our business. Among the issues we are addressing are carbon impact, paper specifications and procurement, ethical conduct within our business and among our vendors, and community and charitable support. For more information, please visit our website: www.wiley.com/go/citizenship.

Evaluation copies are provided to qualified academics and professionals for review purposes only, for use in their courses during the next academic year. These copies are licensed and may not be sold or transferred to a third party. Upon completion of the review period, please return the evaluation copy to Wiley. Return instructions and a free of charge return mailing label are available at www.wiley.com/go/returnlabel. If you have chosen to adopt this textbook for use in your course, please accept this book as your complimentary desk copy. Outside of the United States, please contact your local sales representative.

Library of Congress Cataloging-in-Publication Data

Goodstein, Eban S., 1960-
   Economics and the environment / Eban S. Goodstein, Bard College,
Stephen Polasky, University of Minnesota. – Seventh Edition.
    pages cm
Includes index.
   ISBN 978-1-118-53972-9 (pbk.)

1. Economic development—Environmental aspects. I. Polasky, Stephen. II. Title.

   HD75.6.G66 2014
   333.7—dc23

                    2013022158

Printed in the United States of America

10 9 8 7 6 5 4 3 2 1

CONTENTS

PREFACE

This seventh edition of *Economics and the Environment* welcomes Dr. Stephen Polasky as a co-author, who brings to the text a reworked and stronger focus on natural resource economics and ecosystem services. This book was first published in 1992, as the Rio Earth Summit was concluding. Global warming had been brought to national and global attention only four years prior by James Hansen's famous congressional testimony. The first President Bush would soon sign the UN Framework Convention on Climate Change. At the time, CO_2 in the atmosphere stood at 356 parts per million.

Twenty one years later, CO_2 levels are at 400 parts per million and climbing. Climate change remains front and center, now understood less as an environmental problem than as a challenge to civilization. As in the first edition, global warming remains the topic that launches the book, and provides the framing example for a comprehensive look at environmental economics. With Steve's help, the book now provides a stronger resource and ecosystem processes lens for exploring climate change and other critical environmental issues.

The book retains the three interrelated advantages of its earlier incarnations: broad content; pedagogical clarity; and timely, well integrated examples. There are a few significant additions to content, several new end-of-chapter problems and exercises, and updated examples and information throughout.

A complete set of ancillary materials is available for adopters of *Economics and the Environment*. These resources can be found on the book's companion site at: www.wiley.com/college/goodstein.

- An Instructor's Manual containing suggestions for teaching from this book, sample exams, and chapter practice questions.
- PowerPoint Presentations for course lectures. In addition, electronic files for all the figures in the text are available in an Image Gallery.

Major changes to this edition include:

- The formerly separate chapters on Neoclassical and Ecological Economics have been reworked into two new chapters: The Sustainability Standard (Chapter 8) and Measuring Sustainability (Chapter 9). The discussion of the two perspectives is recentered around weak and strong sustainability. And in this edition, chapters on Measuring the Benefits of Environmental Protection (Chapter 6) and Measuring the Costs of Environmental Protection (Chapter 7) now precede the sustainability discussion.

- An all new chapter on Natural Resources and Ecosystem Services (Chapter 10) covers optimal non-renewable resource extraction; predictions about price paths; optimal renewable harvesting strategies; and the new economics involved in estimating the value of jointly produced ecosystem services.
- The discounting discussion has been reframed around the Ramsey equation, and it is made clear that discounting at a positive rate only makes sense if weak sustainability is assumed.
- The former chapter on benefit-cost analysis has been shortened and now appears as the concluding section to the chapter on the efficiency standard (Chapter 4).
- The former chapter on enforcement has also been shortened, and the material is included in the chapter covering the accomplishments and challenges of regulation (Chapter 14).
- Updated and in-depth discussions of California's new CO_2 emission trading and the EU ETS are provided.
- The Obama Administration's far-reaching impact on regulation and enforcement is discussed.

In terms of content, the book provides a rigorous and comprehensive presentation of the "standard analysis," including the property-rights basis of environmental problems, efficient pollution control, benefit-estimation procedures, and incentive-based regulation. However, *Economics and the Environment* also incorporates broader topics as separate chapters, notably, the ethical foundations of environmental economics, a focus on ecological economics and strong sustainability, a safety-based approach to controlling pollution, the ecological economic critique of economic growth, the potential for government failure, the promotion of "clean technology," and opportunities for sustainable development in poor countries.

The second major advantage of the book is pedagogical clarity. In contrast to other texts that work from a "topics" perspective—water, oil, forests, fish—*Economics and the Environment* is centered around four clearly focused questions:

1. How much pollution (or resource degradation) is too much?
2. Is government up to the job?
3. How can we do better?
4. How can we resolve global issues?

These questions are all introduced through a detailed case study of the "big" issue of the century—global warming. The first section of *Economics and the Environment* then proceeds to explore the explicitly normative question, "How much pollution is too much?" The tools of welfare economics and benefit–cost analysis are used to explore three possible answers. The first is the efficient pollution level. Here students are introduced to the fundamentals of benefit and cost estimation, and benefit-cost analysis. The second pollution standard is a safety standard, including questions of environmental justice, which in fact continue to drive much environmental policy. The advantages and drawbacks of safety as a goal are analyzed. Efficiency and safety are also contrasted in the context of the economic growth debate; students particularly enjoy Chapter 11, 'Is More Really Better?'

The third standard is sustainability, defined as an intergenerational equity constraint. In two new chapters, we explore weak (Neoclassical) and strong (Ecological) sustainability, and in the process consider natural capital measurement techniques, the logic of discounting, the importance of investing resource rents productively, substitution possibilities between manufactured and natural capital, the precautionary principle, and questions of long-run resource scarcity. Also new to the text this edition is a separate chapter focusing on "Resource Economics" (renewable and non-renewable resource management), the Peak Oil debate, and recent attempts by economists to model and value ecosystem services through ecological production functions.

Tying together this first, normative section of the book is a vital discussion that is missing from other texts: the utilitarian ethical basis for the normative analysis and its relation to an "environmental ethic." Many students come into an environmental economics course thinking that saving polar bears is important, without knowing exactly why they think so. The explicit welfare-based analysis in chapter 2 asks students to confront the assumptions underlying their own and others' worldviews.

The text fills a second major void through the second big question, "Is Government Up to the Job?" (Section 3) Most existing texts simply note that "government failure" is a potential problem when correcting for market externalities. In *Economics and the Environment*, the question of government's ability to effectively regulate pollution is carefully examined. The section begins with a discussion of the two primary obstacles to effective government action: imperfect information and the opportunity for political influence over government policy. It then provides a succinct review of existing legislation and accomplishments on air, water, solid and hazardous waste, toxic pollution, and endangered species. Part II ends with a discussion of the often neglected subject of monitoring and enforcement.

The third section of the book, "How Can We Do Better?" tackles the more positive aspects of pollution regulation. Two chapters are devoted to the theory and practical application of incentive-based regulation—marketable permits and Pigovian taxes. Real world analysis focuses on the technical challenges faced by permit systems (price volatility, hot spots) and the political obstacles to taxes. Appendices explore instrument choice under uncertainty, and incentive-compatible regulation. From here, the book examines an argument that attributes the root source of pollution to market failure in technological development rather than in the arena of property rights. We consider the view that the market often fails to generate incentives for investment in clean technology, as well as the feasibility of proposed solutions to this problem. In-depth discussion focuses on areas such as energy policy, pollution prevention, alternative agriculture, recycling, life-cycle analysis, and "green" labeling.

The final question that *Economics and the Environment* explores is: "How Can We Solve Global Issues?" Part IV focuses on global pollution and resource issues, and is centered around a definition and discussion of sustainable development. Topics covered include the preservation of natural capital; the economics of population control; rising per-capita consumption pressures; the relationship between poverty, sustainable development, and environmental protection in poor countries; international trade and the environment; and global pollution control agreements.

In sum, *Economics and the Environment* appeals to three groups of instructors. The first are economists who are simply looking for a clear and concise presentation of environmental and resource economics. The four-question format developed in the text provides a simpler and more useful pedagogical handle than is available in the "topics" approach followed by other authors. In addition, the book provides a wealth of examples as well as an explicit consideration of the government's role in environmental policy not available in competing works. Finally, the appendices cover advanced theoretical topics, ensuring that there is enough in-depth material to fill out a one-semester course.

The book will appeal also to those with an interest in expanding the scope of environmental and resource economics. *Economics and the Environment* moves beyond the standard analysis in five important areas. It provides a rigorous normative analysis of environmental goals; an in-depth evaluation of ecological economics and strong sustainability; serious attention to the potential for government failure in pollution control; substantial discussion of dynamic issues of path dependence and technological change; and a sophisticated presentation of sustainable development in poor countries. The book seeks to incorporate into a well-developed economic analysis ideas that have emerged in the environmental and ecological sciences over the past few decades.

Given this orientation, instructors in environmental studies courses will also find this text to be unusually user friendly. Chapters on measuring the value of nonmarket goods, cost-benefit analysis, markets for pollution rights, incentives for investment in appropriate technology, the governmental role in pollution control, population and consumption pressures, global bargaining, and conservation in poor countries provide accessible material for environmental studies courses with a social-science focus.

Ultimately, the test of any textbook comes in the classroom. *Economics and the Environment* was written for students. It addresses important questions raised in their lives and introduces them to the economist's view of some solutions.

A synthetic work such as this depends on the contributions of the hundreds of economists and environmental scholars working in the field. Some of their names appear in the list of authors cited at the end of this book; many important contributors were omitted because of the scarce resource of space. In addition, over the last twenty years, dozens of colleagues and anonymous reviewers have provided important comments and feedback. Many of their suggestions have found their way into the final version of this book. We are grateful to all who have contributed, and made this a more useful text. Final thanks to our editors Courtney Luzzi, Joel Hollenbeck, Production Editor Yee Lyn Song at John Wiley & Sons and Project Manager Lavanya Murlidhar at Laserwords Pvt Ltd.

INTRODUCTION

CHAPTER 1

FOUR ECONOMIC QUESTIONS ABOUT GLOBAL WARMING

1.0 Introduction

One of us recently had some surprise visitors to his environmental and natural resource economics class. It was alumni week at the college, and four members of the class of 1950, *back for their 60th reunion*, joined our discussion. We were talking about sustainability, and suddenly the day's lecture became very real. How has life really changed since these visitors left college in 1950? Have six decades of intervening economic growth—with per capita gross domestic product (GDP) more than tripling—made life better? Or have the costs of growth made things worse? Is economic growth sustainable? And over the coming decades, will your generation's quality of life rise or fall?

So imagine now: You are that older woman or man, heading to the classroom this week for your 60th class reunion. You are 80-something, and for you, it will be sometime in the 2070s. As you listen to the young professor at the head of the class talking about the latest theories, you sit back and reflect on the changes that you have witnessed in your lifetime. Maybe your story will go something like this:

> Over the 21st century, you lived through both deep recessions and economic booms, through wars and political upheavals. You experienced staggering technological breakthroughs, unprecedented droughts, sea-level rise that forced tens of millions from their homes, large-scale extinctions, and the outbreak of new diseases. Against this background, you and your classmates from around the world maintained a relentless focus: redesigning every city on earth, reengineering production processes, reimagining the global food system, reinventing transportation.
>
> World population grew from 6 to 8 to, eventually, 10 billion people, before it finally stabilized in 2063. And through a heroic effort, ramping up in

the 2020s, your generation managed to completely phase out fossil fuels, rewiring the entire planet with a new generation of renewable energy technologies and stabilizing the global climate.

At the end of the day, you shepherded both the human race and the remaining species on the planet through a critical bottleneck in human history, in which rising populations, aspiring to ever-higher levels of consumption, ran up against critical global resource shortages. Above all, you managed, by 2050, to roll back emissions of global warming pollution by 80% and stabilize the climate. In doing all this, you created tens of millions of jobs, helped lift billions of people out of poverty, and built a global economy that is truly sustainable.

Will that be your story?

We hope it will. And if so, you have a lot of work to do! Yours will be the "greatest generation" because you must guide the earth through this extraordinary half century. Your decisions will have profound consequences not only for you and your children but indeed for a thousand human generations to follow.

This book introduces you to economic concepts and tools that you will need to make the journey. We begin by framing economics in terms of four basic questions as they apply to the defining environmental—indeed, civilizational—challenge of your lifetimes: global warming.

1.1 Four Questions

Did you drive to school today? Or to work? Every mile you drove, you pumped around a pound of carbon dioxide (CO_2) into the air. This is a part of your small daily share of the more than 25 billion pounds people around the world contribute annually from the burning of carbon fuels such as coal, oil, natural gas, and wood. Carbon dioxide is a **greenhouse gas**—a compound that traps reflected heat from the earth's surface and contributes to **global warming**. Other greenhouse gases include nitrous oxide from natural and human-made fertilizers; methane gas emitted from oil and gas production and transport as well as from rice production and the digestive processes of cows and sheep; and chlorofluorocarbons (CFCs), once widely used for air conditioning, refrigeration, and other industrial applications.[1]

As a result of industrialization and the ensuing rapid increase in greenhouse gases in our atmosphere, the vast majority of climate scientists agree that the earth's surface temperature will rise over the next few decades. The extent of the warming is uncertain: low-end estimates suggest an increase in the earth's average surface temperature of 3 degrees F by the year 2100. The official high-end prediction from the UN's International Panel on Climate Change is 11 degrees over this time period. To put that number in perspective, during the last ice age, the earth's average surface temperature was only 9 degrees F colder than it is today.

The potential consequences of this warming range from manageable to catastrophic. The first major impact will be on patterns of temperature, flooding,

---

1. Chlorofluorocarbons also deplete the earth's protective ozone shield. This is a separate issue from global warming and is discussed in more detail in Chapter 22.

and drought, affecting **agricultural output**. As the planet heats up, it "forces" the hydrologic cycle, adding more moisture to the air, leading to both more extreme precipitation and flooding, along with increased temperatures, increased drought, and changed patterns of drought. More northerly regions may actually experience an increase in precipitation and yields, but the current grain belts of the United States, Australia, and central Europe will become drier and agricultural output in these regions will probably fall. The net global effect through the mid-century is expected to be, on balance, negative. It will be particularly harsh in many developing countries, which lack resources for irrigation and other adaptive measures. Tens of millions of people are likely to be at risk of hunger as a result of climate change.

Second, **natural ecosystems** will also suffer from climate change. The U.S. Environmental Protection Agency (EPA) has estimated that, by the year 2050, the southern boundary of forest ecosystems could move northward by 600 kilometers, yet forests can migrate naturally at a much slower pace. Several major vegetation models predict large-scale forest diebacks in, among other places, the southern and eastern United States and the Amazon Basin. Human and animal diseases and agricultural pests will also thrive in a warmer climate.

Major impacts in the ocean will occur not only because of warming waters that, for example, directly kill coral reefs but also because the oceans are absorbing large quantities of the CO_2 released by fossil fuel combustion. This in turn is leading to **ocean acidification**: the pH of the ocean has dropped markedly in the last century. As the ocean continues to acidify, life at the base of the ocean food chain could begin to die off. On both land and sea, massive disruption of ecosystems and widespread extinctions, affecting perhaps 30% or more of the life on the planet, are thus likely.

The third concern is the possibility of a **sea-level rise** as ice caps in Greenland and Antarctica begin to melt, and the warming ocean expands. An increase in sea level of 3 feet—well within the realm of possibility within your lifetimes—would flood many parts of Florida, Louisiana, Boston, and New York City as well as much of low-lying countries like Bangladesh and the Netherlands (unless they were protected by dikes). As many as 1 billion people live in areas that might be directly affected.[2]

The globe is very likely locked into a further warming of at least 3 degrees F over the next 100 years. This warming will have far-reaching human and ecosystem effects, but if contained would be a manageable event. A greater warming, however, not only would have a greater impact but also could result in truly **catastrophic outcomes**. One of these would be the collapse and melting of the Greenland and West Antarctic ice sheets, events that would, over the course of several hundred years, raise sea levels by 40 feet or more and inundate many of the world's major cities. Some scientists think that a warming of 4 degrees F or more would significantly raise the probability of this occurrence. Dr. James Hansen, NASA's chief climate scientist, stated in early 2006:

> How far can it go? The last time the world was three degrees [C] warmer than today—which is what we expect later this century—sea levels were 25m [75 feet!] higher. So that is what we can look forward to if we don't act soon....

---

2. IPCC (2007) details these impacts.

I think sea-level rise is going to be the big issue soon, more even than warming itself.... How long have we got? We have to stabilize emissions of carbon dioxide within a decade, or temperatures will warm by more than one degree [C]. That will be warmer than it has been for half a million years, and many things could become unstoppable.... We don't have much time left.[3]

A catastrophic collapse of the ice sheets is far from certain, but as Dr. Hansen suggests, decisions made in the next decade about reducing greenhouse gas emissions could have dramatic consequences lasting for tens of thousands of years.

Global warming is an environmental reality that presents stark choices. On the one hand, substantial, short-term reductions in the human contribution to the greenhouse effect would require substantial changes in Western energy use. In particular, our casual reliance on fossil fuels for transportation, heat, and power would have to be dramatically scaled back and new, clean energy sources developed. On the other hand, the consequences of inaction are potentially disastrous. By continuing to pollute the atmosphere, we may be condemning the next generation to even greater hardship.

This book focuses on the economic issues at stake in cases like global warming, where human actions substantially alter the natural environment. In the process, we examine the following four questions.

1. **How much pollution is too much?** Many people are tempted to answer simply: any amount of pollution is too much. However, a little reflection reveals that zero pollution is an unachievable and, in fact, undesirable goal. Pollution is a by-product of living; for example, each time you drive in a car, you emit a small amount of carbon dioxide to the air, thus exacerbating the greenhouse effect. The question really is, "At what level are the benefits of pollution (cheap transportation in the case we started with) outweighed by its costs?"

   Different people will answer this question in different ways, depending on their value systems: "costs" of pollution may be defined narrowly, as strictly economic, or they may be broadened to include ethical considerations such as fairness and the protection of rights. Costs may also be difficult to measure. Nevertheless, it is clear that a rough weighing of benefits and costs is a critical first step for deciding "how much is too much."

2. **Is government up to the job?** After resolving the first question, we must then rely on government to rewrite laws and regulations to control pollution. But is our government able and willing to tackle the tough job of managing the environment? The costs and mistakes associated with bureaucratic decision making, as well as the likelihood of political influence in the process, will clearly have an impact on government's ability to respond effectively to the challenge.

   The first Earth Day was April 20, 1970. Also that year, the U.S. Congress passed the first major pollution control initiative, the National Environmental Policy Act, which, among other things, created the EPA. Looking back over our 40-plus years of experience in regulating the environment, we have a

---

3. See Hansen (2006) and Hansen (2005).

record of both successes and failures to evaluate. Such an exploration can help us design policies to increase the effectiveness of the governmental response.

3. **How can we do better?** Suppose that as a society we decide on a particular target: for example, reduce carbon dioxide emissions to their 1990 level by 2020. Given the limitations that government might face, identified in the answer to the second question, how can we best achieve that goal? A long list of policies might be used: regulations, taxes, permit systems, technology subsidies (or their removal), research incentives, infrastructure investment, right-to-know laws, product labeling, legal liability, fines, and jail terms. Which policies will most successfully induce firms and consumers to meet the target?

4. **Can we resolve global issues?** Finally, regulating pollution within a single nation is a difficult task. Yet problems such as global warming transcend national boundaries. Brazilians say that they will stop cutting down and burning their rain forests to create crop and rangeland as soon as we stop driving gas-guzzling cars. (Although the United States has only 4% of the world's population, we account for over 19% of the greenhouse gases.) How can this kind of international coordination be achieved? Are economic development and environmental quality necessarily in conflict? And to what extent can the explosion in population growth and per capita resource use, which ultimately drive environmental problems, be managed?

Let us return to our discussion of global warming and see what type of answers we might develop to these four questions. Global warming is a consequence of what is known as the **greenhouse effect**. Solar energy enters the earth's biosphere in the form of visible and ultraviolet light from the sun. The first law of thermodynamics—energy can be neither created nor destroyed—requires that this energy go somewhere, and much of it is radiated back into the biosphere as infrared radiation or heat. The CO_2 and other greenhouse gases surrounding the earth let in the visible and ultraviolet light from the sun. Yet, like a blanket, these gases trap the reflected infrared radiation (heat) close to the earth's surface.

Until the present time, the naturally occurring greenhouse effect has been primarily beneficial. Without the true planet's blanket of water vapor, carbon dioxide, and other gases, the average temperature on earth would be about 91 degrees F colder—well below the freezing point. The problem we face today is the steady increase in human-made greenhouse gases, which began with the Industrial Revolution but dramatically accelerated after World War II. In less than two centuries, the thickness of the carbon dioxide blanket in the atmosphere has increased by more than 25%, rising from 280 parts per million (ppm) in 1880 to over 400 ppm today. Every year the blanket gets thicker by about 2 ppm. The question facing humanity is, how thick should we let this heat-trapping blanket grow? Should we try to hold it to 450 ppm? 550 ppm? 650 ppm? Or even roll it back to 350 ppm?

Is human-induced warming here yet? The earth's average temperature has risen more than 1 degree F over the last century, and the warming has accelerated in the last few decades. The years 2005 and 2010 tied for the hottest on record, and the last decade was probably the hottest in the last several thousand years. Back in 1995, the Intergovernmental Panel on Climate Change (IPCC), an organization of some 2,500 scientists operating under the auspices of the United Nations, made it official—the greenhouse effect is here. According to the IPCC, "the balance of evidence suggests that there is a discernible human influence on global climate." Since then, the evidence supporting human-induced warming has become much stronger.[4]

Today, scientists are virtually unanimous in their belief that further warming will occur, but the magnitude of the warming is difficult to predict. Nevertheless, we do have a range: recall 3–11 degrees F.

Uncertainty in predicting the degree of global warming is due primarily to the presence of **positive and negative feedback** effects. If it were necessary only to predict the impact of greenhouse gases on global temperature, the problem would be difficult enough. But changing temperatures will in turn affect many different parts of the earth and its surface, leading to either an acceleration of the warming (positive feedback) or a deceleration (negative feedback).

Two examples of the latter include the possibility that increasing cloud cover will reduce the amount of radiation entering the earth's atmosphere, or that higher rates of carbon dioxide will lead to higher rates of plant growth and thus more trapping of carbon dioxide. Negative feedbacks would clearly be welcome, but unfortunately, positive feedbacks appear just as likely, if not more so, to occur. For example, higher temperatures may generate widespread forest fires and forest dieback in regions like the Amazon; lead to the emission of methane and CO_2 currently trapped in frozen bogs and peat fields at high latitudes; expose heat-absorbing darker earth under ice shields; or reduce the capacity of ocean organisms to fix carbon dioxide in their shells. These positive feedbacks have led some researchers to believe that at some point, global warming will trigger a **runaway greenhouse effect**, in which the initial warming will feed on itself. Under this scenario, policymakers no longer face a continuum of temperature possibilities: a warming of somewhere between 4 degrees and 11 degrees. Instead, there are only two options; either hold warming to the low end, 4–5 degrees, or risk triggering positive feedback loops that quickly drive the planet's temperatures up by 9–11 degrees, the equivalent of a swing of ice-age magnitude, only in the opposite direction.

In the face of this uncertainty, what action should be taken to prevent or mitigate the consequences of global warming? Following the outline described, we can begin to tackle this daunting question piece by piece.

1.2 How Much Pollution Is Too Much?

First of all, where do we now stand on global warming emission targets? At the Earth Summit meeting in Rio de Janeiro back in 1992, attended by the leaders of more than 140 countries, the industrialized nations signed a pledge to "try" to stabilize greenhouse gas emissions at 1990 levels by the year 2000. However, this promise was not kept. In the United States, low energy prices and strong economic growth boosted greenhouse gas emissions by 19% between 1990 and 2009.

Faced with the failure of this voluntary approach, at a meeting in Kyoto, Japan, in 1997, the industrial countries of the world signed the **Kyoto global warming treaty**. The accord requires participating countries to reduce their emissions of greenhouse

---

4. See IPCC (1996) and IPCC (2007).

gases to around 5% below 1990 levels by 2012. Poor countries—including major emitters like India and China—were explicitly excluded under the reasoning that rich countries should shoulder the initial burden of developing clean-energy technologies like wind and solar power, making it affordable in the long run for the developing world to come on board. The treaty was ratified by the European countries, as well as Russia, Japan, and Canada, and entered into force in early 2005. All of these nations are taking implementation measures, though not all are likely to achieve the Kyoto targets. More on this in Chapter 21.

However, President Bush pulled the United States out of the Kyoto process, arguing that the country simply could not afford to tackle the global warming problem. Instead, he called for industry to take *voluntary* measures to reduce the rate of increase of emissions (not to reduce emissions themselves). In 2009 President Obama proposed U.S. cuts of around 17% by 2020, which would bring the nation back to 1990-level emissions, not quite achieving the Kyoto targets, ten years late. Was Kyoto the right short-term goal? Should emissions be reduced even further, as some European countries are already doing? Or, as Bush argued, should they not be reduced at all?

One way to answer this question is to use a benefit-cost framework. Quantifying the benefits and costs of reducing emissions is a difficult task, primarily because uncertainties loom very large in the case of climate change. On the benefits side, analysts are required to estimate the damages that will be avoided 100 years hence, by stabilizing CO_2 as it affects not only global agriculture and human health but also species extinction and biodiversity. Moreover, across the planet, some regions will gain and others will lose; impacts will be proportionally larger in poor countries and smaller in rich countries. Developing countries will be hardest hit because they tend already to be in warmer and drier parts of the planet—but more importantly, because they have fewer financial resources for adapting their agriculture or building sea walls.

Putting a monetary value on such benefits presents difficult issues, among them: How do we deal with uncertainty, and the possibility of cataclysmic change? How do we value damage to future generations? Can we measure the value of intangible or "priceless" benefits such as human suffering and death averted or forests saved? How do we weigh the fact that certain countries will lose more than others in the warming process? These are issues we explore in detail later in the book.

Nevertheless, and bearing in mind these large uncertainties, two prominent economists—Sir Nicholas Stern, former head of the World Bank, and William Nordhaus from Yale University—have recently offered very different perspectives on the net benefits of aggressively reducing global warming pollution. The two researchers start with different estimates of "business-as-usual" warming by 2100; that is, the warming that would occur in the absence of any laws or government policies requiring or subsidizing emission reductions. Stern explores a range of between 5 and 11 degrees F of warming from current levels, while Nordhaus focuses on a single warming estimate, a "best guess" of under 5 degrees F.

Stern's projections are that, unchecked, global warming would reduce global output of goods and services from 5 to 20%, and the higher end is more likely. (For a reference point, the Great Depression of the 1930s led to a reduction in U.S. GDP of 25%.)

Nordhaus is much more sanguine, arguing that by 2100, the impacts would be closer to a significant but much smaller 3% of world output.[5]

With such large damages, Stern's analysis calls for rapid cuts in emissions to hold global warming to the low end: 4 degrees F. This would require *global* reductions of 25% below 1990 levels by 2050. However, since emissions from India, China, and Brazil will keep growing for some time, this means 80% reductions by 2050 for the developed countries. Stern estimates that this policy would cost—in the form of reduced consumption—about 1% of global GDP per year by 2050, equivalent to about $540 billion (about half a trillion) in today's dollars.

Nordhaus, by contrast, calls for much smaller cuts of about 15% below business-as-usual, rising to 25% by 2050 and 45% by 2100. Because emissions will increase a lot under business-as-usual, relative to 1990 levels, Nordhaus is actually *recommending an increase* in global annual emissions of around 40% by 2050. Under Nordhaus's analysis, this policy of holding emissions down *relative to their unregulated state* would trim warming from a projected 5 degrees F increase to 4 degrees F. Nordhaus figures that the total benefits of this reduced warming will be $7 trillion while the costs will run $2 trillion, leaving society $5 trillion better off.

These are two very different policy prescriptions: "deep cuts" in emissions, versus "start slow, ramp up." But interestingly, both researchers arrive at similar answers to the "how much is too much" question: both recommend holding further global warming to the low end of 4 degrees F! Their big differences in recommended emission cuts instead reflect disagreement on three points: (1) how much warming will be generated by business-as-usual, (2) the costs of acting to slow climate change, and (3) the costs of inaction.

First, on the climate-warming side, Nordhaus sticks with a single "best guess" to back up his start-slow policy recommendation. If business as usual "only" leads to a 5 degrees F warming by 2100, it won't require as much in emissions cuts to get us back to 4 degrees. Stern, by contrast, is both less certain about the simple correlation between CO_2 buildup and future temperatures, and much more worried about the possibility of positive feedbacks and the unleashing of a runaway greenhouse effect of the kind discussed earlier. Stern takes seriously the possibility that business-as-usual will blow quickly past 5 degrees F, and push us beyond 10 degrees F, within your lifetimes. A 2009 Massachusetts Institute of Technology (MIT) study clearly supports Stern on this—it pushes the *median* projection of warming by 2100 under business as usual to a high-end, catastrophic 10 degrees F, with a one in nine chance that temperatures could rise as high as 12.5 degrees F.[6]

Second, Stern sees deep cuts in emissions as achievable at relatively low cost to the global economy: 1% of GDP. The Stern perspective is that energy efficiency and renewable energy technologies such as wind and solar electricity offer great promise for de-linking economic growth from fossil fuel use relatively quickly, thus achieving emission reductions cheaply. In important cases, emission reductions can even be

---

5. The discussion in these paragraphs is drawn from Stern (2006) and Nordhaus (2008). Ackerman and Stanton (2010) point out that Nordhaus's damage function implies that an increase in global temperature of 19 degrees C (34 degrees F) would be required to cut global GDP in half! Nordhaus is clearly a technological optimist.

6. Sokolov et al. (2009).

achieved at a profit, when initial investments in energy efficiency and renewable energy are offset by reduced spending on fossil fuels. Nordhaus, by contrast, does not believe in the potential of these low-cost alternatives. He reckons instead that Stern-level cuts would require, for example, more than a doubling of the cost of coal-fired electricity, cutting deeply into the growth of the global economy. More on this energy cost debate in Chapter 18.

Finally, Stern sees much bigger damages from global warming than does Nordhaus, even for the low end of 4 degrees F. There are three reasons for this. First, Stern includes more "nonmarket" costs of global warming—species extinctions, lost services provided by ecosystems, and negative impacts on human health. Second, Stern explicitly incorporates the fact that people in poor countries will bear the greatest costs of climate change. And finally, Stern puts more weight on the climate change costs borne by future generations than does Nordhaus. These are the issues—valuing nonmarket goods, human health, and ecosystem services; weighting for equity in benefit-cost analysis; and the appropriate discounting of future benefits and costs—that we take up later in the book. For now, recognize that Stern and Nordhaus are the leading economic voices in a deadly serious debate: is global warming a civilizational challenge demanding immediate and deep emission reductions, or is it simply another in a list of big problems, amenable to a go-slow fix?

Underlying the recommendations for only modest emission cutbacks is a belief that climate stability is important but not critical to the well-being of humanity. The argument is that people adapt to changing resource conditions. As emissions of greenhouse gases are regulated, the price of CO_2-based services will rise, and new low-CO_2 technologies will come on board, ensuring that greenhouse gas concentrations eventually stabilize. Moreover, the development of new agricultural techniques will ensure that food supplies are maintained even in the face of a changing climate, and sea walls can be built to hold back rising sea levels. In addition, agriculture in some regions will gain from a warmer, wetter CO_2-enhanced climate, and cold-related deaths will decline. Some analysts even envision the winners from climate change assisting those (mostly in poor countries) who lose out from sea-level rise and flooding. Clearly there will be significant losers from climate change, but on balance, it is believed that the quality of life for the average person in most countries can continue to rise even in the face of "moderate" climate change.

This mid-range benefit-cost perspective maintains that a near-term policy of CO_2 cuts below correct levels is too costly. Investing resources and person-power in reducing greenhouse gas emissions will divert investment from schools or health care, lowering living standards for future generations. Benefit-cost analysis is needed to obtain the right balance of investment between climate protection and other goods and services that people value.

It is critically important to recognize that virtually all economists conducting benefit-cost analyses of climate-change policy today agree that government action is needed immediately to cut emissions of global-warming pollutants. A recent survey of climate economists puts the number calling for action at 94%.[7] The debate is not over whether to require near-term emission reductions, but by how much. As noted earlier,

---

7. Holladay, Horne, and Schwartz (2009).

President Obama called for near-term reductions by 2020 of around 17% below 2006 levels, with much deeper 2050 targets of 80% reductions. Nordhaus (but not Stern) would be okay with the go-slow 2020 target, while Stern (but not Nordhaus) would be pleased with the ambitious 2050 goal. Perhaps over the coming decade, economists will be able to settle their debate on the appropriate goal for the next half century.

Note that the use of benefit-cost analysis by economists is implicitly endorsing an unstated ethical goal: control pollution only if the measurable monetary benefits of doing so are greater than the measurable monetary costs. This is one answer to the question, "How much is too much?" It is called an **efficiency standard** for pollution reduction.

However, there are ways of thinking about pollution standards other than through a narrow comparison of economic costs and benefits. First, there are issues of fairness: inaction on our part—though it may provide for somewhat higher incomes today, particularly for citizens in affluent countries—may condemn future generations, in particular those in already poor countries, to even greater hardship. Can we justify actions today that, for example, will destroy entire island nations and their cultures? A second answer to the question, "How much is too much?" emphasizes fairness. This is called a **safety standard**. Safety requires reducing pollution to (socially defined) "safe" levels, unless the costs of doing so are prohibitive.

Finally, there is the question of fundamental uncertainty regarding our impact on the planetary ecosystem. As we saw with Nordhaus, benefit-cost analysts typically assume an intermediate case of predictable damages, but of course, a worst-case scenario might emerge. In a related vein, can we even begin to put benefit numbers on things we know nothing about? For example, what would be the value to future generations of the unique genetic code that will be lost as species extinction accelerates? When uncertainties dominate benefit-cost analysis, it becomes a blunt, and sometimes misleading, tool. In the global warming case, a good number of economists argue that the future consequences of a destabilized climate are simply too uncertain—and potentially catastrophic—to justify making decisions based primarily on benefit-cost studies. In the face of this uncertainty, a third standard emerges—**ecological sustainability**. This standard requires protecting natural ecosystems from major changes—again, unless the costs of doing so are prohibitive.

The policies flowing from the safety and ecological sustainability standards are similar to Stern's: initiate a substantial reduction in emissions. Such a recommendation is strengthened by a final argument we explore in Chapter 10: that lost consumption from controlling CO_2 emissions in an affluent country like the United States really means very little over the long run. Because the happiness derived from consumption is in many ways a relative phenomenon, a general increase in income only accelerates the "rat race," leaving few better off in absolute terms. Put very simply, if fighting global warming reduces the level of U.S. GDP by 2% in 2050, then who would really care? Fighting global warming would only mean that we would all be getting slightly less rich together. Recall that real global GDP is expected by many economists to continue to grow at close to 2% per year, regardless of global warming. So the costs of stabilizing the climate would be that, as a world, we would need to wait until 2051 to be as rich as we otherwise would have been in 2050!

In response to these arguments put forward by safety and sustainability advocates, efficiency defenders would respond that aggressive global-warming actions will impose excessively high costs on the current generation, and by depressing current investment in capital goods, research, and education, reduce the welfare of future generations as well. The bottom line is that, regardless of whether formal benefit-cost analysis is involved, the public debate over global warming is framed in terms of costs and benefits. On one side, efficiency advocates will stress the measurable costs involved in reducing global warming and will advocate small reductions. On the other, proponents of safety and ecological sustainability will argue for major greenhouse gas cutbacks, focusing on uncertain but potentially devastating impacts on future generations.

The purpose of this book is not to sort out which answer is "correct," but rather to better understand the different positions. However, the first essential step in addressing any environmental problem is to decide, How much pollution is too much? Once this is resolved, it is then possible to move on to the second question.

1.3 Is Government Up to the Job?

For reasons explored further in this book, an unfettered free-market economy will produce too much pollution by almost anyone's standards. This suggests that government needs to step in and regulate market behavior in order to protect the environment. But government itself has its own limitations. Is government up to the job?

Two obstacles stand in the way of effective government action. The first is **imperfect information**. Regulators often have a hard time obtaining accurate information about the benefits and costs of pollution reduction. Benefits such as cancers reduced, visibility improved, and ecosystems salvaged are hard to measure and even harder to quantify. Costs are also hard to gauge accurately because they depend on the details of how an industry actually operates. Under these circumstances, even well-meaning bureaucrats may have a difficult time imposing regulations that achieve cost-effective control of pollution.

The second obstacle lies in the **opportunity for political influence**. How much impact do ideology and raw political power have in determining what types of pollution are regulated, which natural resources are protected, and which polluters are punished? Evaluating the importance of this problem requires a theory of governmental action. Economics, like all social sciences, is not a "value-free" pursuit. This is most apparent in political economy, where scholars of different political persuasions are in the business of analyzing government activity.

Traditional **conservatives** view governmental intervention as a necessary evil and argue for as limited a government role as is possible in all affairs, including environmental affairs. Conservatives argue that government legislators and regulators are self-interested individuals who desire to maximize their own well-being rather than wholeheartedly pursue their stated public mission. Such officials, in theory, seldom act in the public interest but instead serve special interests. Special interests include, for example, coalitions of particular businesses, environmental groups, women's or civil rights groups, or labor unions.

In contrast to this conservative view, **progressives** view government as capable of promoting an activist agenda to serve the general interest of the public. Like conservatives, progressives acknowledge the possibility of government failure. Yet in contrast to the conservative position, progressives argue that the problem with government involvement in the economy is not primarily the existence of pluralistic special interest groups but the dominance of big business and development interests in the legislative and regulatory process. For example, progressives point to well-financed lobbying by the fossil fuel industry as a major obstacle to the resolution of the global-warming issue.

As the next section illustrates, these different perspectives on the potential for effective government action will determine views on the best policies for dealing with global warming.

1.4 How Can We Do Better?

As noted, at Kyoto, many of the industrial countries committed themselves in principle to reducing global-warming pollution below 1990 levels. Carbon dioxide is the most important of the greenhouse gases, contributing about 60% of the total greenhouse effect. It is produced by the burning and decay of carbon-based materials: coal, oil, and plant matter. Given what we have just learned about the political economy of regulation, how do we set about controlling CO_2 emissions?

Government could take many possible actions to control carbon dioxide emissions. We can divide such measures into roughly three categories. First is **command-and-control regulation**, the current, dominant approach to environmental protection. Under command and control, government would regulate CO_2 emissions by mandating the adoption of particular types of CO_2 abatement technology on, for example, coal-burning power plants. Other types of technology would be required for automobiles, still others for natural gas plants.

As we shall see, command-and-control regulation has been widely criticized as centralized and inflexible, and thus, much more costly than necessary. Many economists have advocated a switch to **incentive-based regulation**. Incentive-based approaches set emission targets and leave it up to industry to figure out the best way to comply. Incentive-based regulation is called so because firms are provided with incentives to reduce emissions: a tax on pollution is one example and cap-and-trade systems (discussed later) are another.

Finally, government can intervene more directly to encourage the development and diffusion of new **clean technologies**. For example, government can force firms to meet energy-efficient design standards, such as building codes. Or government could promote clean technological change through its investment activities—for example, by favoring rail transport infrastructure over autos or providing research and development funding for solar energy. Which of these is the best method?

Of these three methods, economists of all stripes believe that incentive-based approaches, where feasible, are the best foundation to reduce pollution and resource degradation. There are two major policy tools: **pollution taxes** and **cap-and-trade** systems. To deal with U.S. CO_2 emissions, for example, a tax based on the carbon content of fuels (a carbon or CO_2 tax) would be one of the most effective policies we could use. By raising the price of "dirty" (carbon-intensive) fossil fuels, the marketplace would promote "clean" (lower carbon) fuels like renewable electric power.

The alternative approach, cap-and-trade, would place a cap on total U.S. CO_2 emissions. Then the government would auction off just enough permits to emit a ton of CO_2, so that the auctioned permits add up to the cap's total. Just like a CO_2 tax, cap-and-trade would also place a price on pollution, in turn raising the price of dirty fuels. (California is in the process of implementing a statewide cap-and-trade law for global-warming pollution.)

How high should the tax be? That depends on the underlying "how much is too much?" goal. Revisiting the Stern-Nordhaus debate from the previous section, to help achieve 80% reductions by 2050, Stern advocates prices with teeth—instituted now and rising fairly quickly to $50 per ton of carbon. Nordhaus, by contrast, recommends a relatively low carbon price of $7 per ton, rising to $25 per ton by 2050.

To put those numbers in perspective: a price of $7 per ton for carbon would raise gas prices by about 7 cents a gallon, and coal-fired electricity by around 3/4 of a penny per kilowatt-hour (kWh)—not really noticeable. But a $50 tax per ton of carbon would boost gas prices by $0.50 per gallon, and coal-fired power by around $0.05 per kWh—a significant increase in both gasoline and electricity prices here in the United States. These kinds of energy price increases—if not cushioned—could pose serious hardship, especially for low-income Americans who spend a disproportionate share of their monthly paychecks on gasoline, heat, and electricity.

How to ease the blow to consumers, and make this kind of policy politically possible? A CO_2 tax, or a government auction of CO_2 permits, would generate a lot of revenue. And to offset the problem of higher energy bills, much of this revenue could be rebated directly to taxpayers. One variant of a cap-and-trade system, dubbed "Sky Trust," would involve issuing one share of the total U.S. CO_2 quota, established by the government, to every woman, man, and child in the country.[8] A nongovernmental organization would then hold these shares in trust and, each year, auction them off to companies selling products that emit global warming pollution (oil refineries, electric power producers, etc.). For each ton of carbon dioxide emitted annually, a company would have to buy a 1-ton permit at auction. At the end of the year, each citizen would receive a check equal to his or her share of permits in the annual auction. Estimates put the likely dividend at more than $600 per person each year. And it appears that under a Sky Trust system, most Americans would actually be better off economically—that is, their dividend check would be larger than their increased energy bills. This would be a terrific way to make controlling global warming pollution a politically popular idea!

At the end of the day, putting a price on pollution—either through a tax or cap-and-trade—is the number one general recommendation from economists for protecting the environment. And done right, this kind of policy can actually benefit low- and middle-income consumers. But in the global warming case, pricing pollution alone will not be sufficient to achieve Stern-level cuts of 80% by 2050. To get there, Stern and other economists recommend direct government promotion of clean technologies.

Government could strengthen efficiency standards for fuel, lighting, and power; revamp the transport infrastructure; promote high-speed rail as a substitute for short plane flights; restructure zoning laws to encourage denser urban development; and increase investment in mass transit.

---

8. See Barnes (2001).

Finally, government-funded research and development (R&D) of new energy technologies, in particular those that utilize renewable, non-carbon-based sources, such as energy efficiency and solar, wind, and fuel-cell power, might be promoted. Significant carbon taxes combined with substantial government-sponsored R&D of clean-energy technologies and an aggressive approach to promoting efficient energy use is the route to achieving deep reductions in global warming pollution by 2050.

Conservative economists would be suspicious of government regulations mandating energy efficiency or government-funded R&D of clean-energy technologies. The question they would ask about such an agenda would be, can the government do a better job developing appropriate technologies than the market already does? First, conservatives would charge that the R&D pool is likely to become just another government pork barrel. Second, even granting efficient operation, some would maintain that government bureaucrats would have a hard time picking winners and determining which potential technologies are feasible, cost-effective, and environmentally benign.

Progressive economists would respond that existing government decisions such as energy tax breaks for fossil fuels, highway construction funds and other subsidies for auto transport, tax and zoning policies that encourage suburbanization, and high levels of poorly targeted R&D funding already constitute a de facto plan with major negative environmental and economic effects. The choice, therefore, is not between free markets and central planning but rather between myopic and farsighted government policy.

Progressives maintain that on energy policy, our market system (which is *already* affected by substantial government involvement) has failed miserably to deliver appropriate technology. Because private investors do not take into account the tremendous costs to society of carbon-based fuels, incentives do not exist to develop appropriate technologies. In addition, a network of vested interests, inappropriate government subsidies already in existence, and substantial economies of scale all justify government involvement. Due to the massive nature of the market failure, the argument is that picking winners would not be hard: among the obvious candidates are energy efficiency technologies, photovoltaic solar cells, and wind power, to name a few.

How can we do better? Most economists argue that a greater reliance on incentive-based approaches, such as pollution taxes or cap-and-trade systems, makes sense. Economists who hold a progressive viewpoint and/or who believe deep cuts in global warming pollution are needed argue that government also should take a more active hand in promoting the development and diffusion of clean technology.

1.5 Can We Resolve Global Issues?

Whether a government relies primarily on traditional regulatory mechanisms to achieve greenhouse gas reduction targets or also employs more incentive-based regulations and direct investment tools, its efforts will be in vain if other nations do not also reduce emissions. Global warming requires a global solution.

CO_2 reduction is what is known as a **public good**, a good that is consumed in common. This means, for example, that if the United States cuts back CO_2 emissions by 20%, the whole world benefits. Thus, since emission reduction is costly, each country would prefer to see the other cut back and then get a "free ride" on the other's action. Because every country is in this position, there is great incentive for signatories to a treaty to cheat on any agreement. One reason that nations are reluctant to commit to substantial carbon dioxide reductions is the fear that other countries will not comply, and thus their sacrifice will be meaningless in the long run.

However, economists would welcome being proven wrong in this logic. The fact that most developed countries are moving ahead with reductions in greenhouse gas emissions suggests that under a sufficient environmental threat, nations can work together to at least mitigate the impact of the free-rider problem. With global warming, however, a major long-run challenge will be bringing low-income countries into the process. Rapid economic growth (led by China), increasing energy use, and in places, accelerated deforestation are quickly increasing the share of global warming pollution arising in the developing world. (More on these issues in Chapters 18–20.) Some would argue that it is both unrealistic and unfair to expect these countries to sacrifice economic growth by reducing CO_2 emissions in exchange for uncertain environmental gains.

Yet economic growth in many poor countries has its own environmental costs and may prove **unsustainable**. The economic growth process is often rooted in exploitative colonial relationships that have encouraged the establishment of lopsided, resource-dependent economies. In the modern context, debt has replaced colonial status as the mechanism by which wealth flows from the poor to the rich. Deforestation, over-grazing, and massive pollution from mineral and oil development persist, reinforced by a network of government policies favoring local elite and multinational corporate interests, all occurring in an environment where common property resources are available for exploitation. When economic growth fails to compensate for natural resources depleted in the process, the economic development process is unsustainable; that is, growth today comes at the expense of future generations. (For a more careful definition of sustainable development, see Chapter 19.)

It is clear that the economic needs of the world's poor nations must be placed at the forefront of an effort to reduce global warming. In this fashion, global agreements to control greenhouse gas pollution are most likely to succeed. But it is also true that developing countries have more to lose from global warming because they have fewer resources to finance adaptive measures, from resettlement to irrigation to dike building. It is possible that by adopting a combination of energy efficiency and conversion to renewable energy sources (biomass, wind, and solar), poor countries can substantially slow the rate of growth of CO_2 emissions while at the same time promoting sustainable development, which in turn will lower population growth rates.

Is there a way to facilitate the development and transfer of this kind of technology by wealthy nations to developing countries? Fortunately, yes. A version of cap-and-trade has been suggested for resolving equity issues between the First and Third Worlds. Such a system would work in the following way: A successor to the Kyoto treaty would determine a worldwide greenhouse gas emission target and then assign each country a quota based, for example, on its total population.

Thus each person in the world might initially be permitted to make an equal contribution to global warming. But because the average Indian, for example, uses only 4% as much energy as the average American, Third World countries would have an excess supply of permits, while we in the First World would have an excess demand.

Because the permits are marketable, we would buy some from the poorer countries of the world to maintain our energy-intensive lifestyles. The funds generated could then be used to support the kind of investments in low-carbon energy—wind, solar, biofuels—that poor countries will require to develop. Moreover, because we would now be paying directly for our global warming, we would have the incentive both to conserve energy and to seek out new clean-energy technologies. (The Kyoto Accord includes a prototype of this kind of emissions trading system, in the form of the Clean Development Mechanism discussed in Chapter 21.)

Tradeable permit systems of this kind put a price on pollution. Within a country, companies that can now emit carbon dioxide for free would find pollution becoming expensive. This would give companies an incentive to reduce emissions and, more importantly, would encourage the development of clean-energy technologies, such as wind and solar power, and vehicles powered by fuel cells. At the international level, selling carbon dioxide permits provides the financial means for poor countries to leapfrog the period of fossil-fuel-intensive development and move straight to clean-energy options.

Of course, nothing comes without a price. Although under the system outlined both poor countries and average Americans would reap financial benefits from the sale of permits, rich-country customers (those same average Americans) would pay much of the price of pollution reduction in the form of higher prices for energy, cars, and manufactured goods, at least in the short run. As usual, the essence of the economic debate boils down to a comparison of benefits (reducing global warming) versus costs (higher prices for goods and services). Do the benefits of aggressive action to reduce greenhouse gas emissions outweigh the costs? At this point, the case remains open. Some economists say reduce a little; others say reduce a lot. This book gives you the tools you need to better understand the debate and make up your own mind.

1.6 Summary

This chapter has provided an introduction to the scientific issues surrounding the buildup of greenhouse gases in our atmosphere and the resultant global warming. But global warming is only one of the myriad environmental challenges posed by human activity. From the siting of landfills at the local level to regulations on chemical emissions from manufacturing plants that are issued by national governments to international agreements designed to preserve species diversity, the need for a public that is informed of the underlying scientific issues is great.

Environmental economists must also rely on scientific assessment of the dangers posed by environmental degradation to ourselves and our descendants. However, this book is *not* focused on specific environmental concerns arising from our economic activity. Instead, the point is to *illustrate the framework* that economists use for approaching pollution problems. For any such concern, from landfill siting to chemical regulation to loss of species diversity, three general questions must be answered:

1.   How much pollution is too much?
2.   Is government up to the job?
3.   How can we do better?

When, as is increasingly common, the issue is an international one, a fourth question must also be addressed:

4. Can we resolve global issues?

To this point, Chapter 1 has both outlined the questions raised and provided a sketch of the answers that arise when one grapples with the economics of environmental protection. As indicated, there is often lively debate among economists regarding the right answers. But what we do agree on is the centrality of these four questions. The rest of the book moves on to explain and explore a number of possible solutions. We hope that the reader will come away better equipped to address the local, national, and global environmental problems that we and our children will have to overcome in the 21st century.

APPLICATION 1.0

Setting Goals for Greenhouse Gas Pollution, Take One

The Kyoto Protocol requires that greenhouse gases be stabilized at a level that prevents "dangerous anthropogenic interference" with the climate system. In an effort to help define what this means, O'Neil and Oppenheimer (2002) relate certain physical effects to rising temperature:

- At 2 degrees F, we can expect "large-scale eradication of coral reef systems" on a global basis.
- At 4 degrees F, an irreversible process leading to the collapse of the West Antarctic Ice Sheet and a sea-level rise of 25 feet becomes significantly more likely.
- At 6 degrees F, the shutdown of the Gulf Stream leading to a sudden, dramatic cooling in Northern Europe and accelerated warming in the South Atlantic becomes significantly more likely.

The authors conclude that it is impossible to prevent a 2-degree warming. Based on the relationships, they call for holding global temperature increases to less than 4 degrees.

a. Is this an efficiency, ecological sustainability, or safety standard? Why?

APPLICATION 1.1

Setting Goals for Greenhouse Gas Pollution, Take Two

Estimating the economic costs of global warming is quite a difficult process. In a book examining the issue, Nordhaus and Boyer (2000) provided this disclaimer on page 98: "Attempts to estimate the impacts of climate change remain highly speculative. Outside of agriculture and sea-level rise the number of scholarly studies of the economic impacts of climate change remains small." Nevertheless, they undertook the process, as shown in Table 1.1.

TABLE 1.1   Impacts of Global Warming in the United States: 2.5 degrees C/5 degrees F (billions of 1990 dollars; benefits are positive while damages are negative)

Market Impacts	
Agriculture	−$ 4
Energy	0
Sea level	−$ 6
Timber	0
Water	0
Total market	−$10
Nonmarket Impacts	
Health, water quality, and human life	−$ 1
Migration	na
Human amenity, recreation, and nonmarket time	$17
Species loss	na
Human settlements	−$ 6
Extreme and catastrophic events	−$25
Total nonmarket	−$15
Total for Market and Nonmarket Sectors	
Billions of 1990 $	−$28
% of 1990 GDP	−0.5

Note: na = not available or not estimated.
Source: Nordhaus and Boyer (2000).

Nordhaus and Boyer find small negative impacts for agriculture (−$4 billion) and sea-level rise (−$6 billion); argue that warming is likely to yield significant benefits for outdoor recreation (in crude terms, more golf days; +$17 billion); and maintain that the biggest negative impacts of climate change are likely to come from destroying parts of historically or culturally unique human settlements such as New Orleans or Olympia, Washington (−$6 billion), or from catastrophic climate change (−$28 billion). Overall they find a negative impact of only 0.5% of GDP. (Notice that this figure leaves out the costs of species extinction—no accounting for coral reefs here.) The analysis that underlies calls for "small" taxes on carbon dioxide ($10 per ton).

a. Is this an efficiency, ecological sustainability, or safety standard? Why?
b. One might question the value of basing environmental decisions on data that are "highly speculative." How do you think Nordhaus defends drawing conclusions based on numbers like those in Table 1.1?

KEY IDEAS IN EACH SECTION

1.0 This book explores four key economic questions about the environmental challenges of the 21st century, starting with the civilizational challenge posed by climate change.

1.1 **Global warming**, arising from the accumulation of **greenhouse gases** and the resulting "carbon blanket," poses a potentially severe threat to human welfare and natural ecosystems. Changing rainfall patterns that accompany warming may lead to reductions in **agricultural output**, particularly in poor countries, and major changes in **natural ecosystems**, including accelerated species extinction and higher rates of disease. **Sea level** will also rise. Although scientists largely agree that *global warming is already a reality*, the magnitude of the warming will ultimately depend on **positive and negative feedback** effects. Economists need to answer **four questions** to address a problem like global warming.

1.2 The first question is, **How much pollution is too much?** With respect to global warming pollution, economist Stern argues for deep cuts; Nordhaus advocates a start-slow, ramp-up approach. Both analysts engaged in a comparison of the costs and benefits of action. How to weigh the two? There are three basic standards. An **efficiency standard** relies solely on benefit-cost analysis; **safety** and **ecological sustainability standards** argue for reducing pollution to much lower levels. This is fundamentally an ethical debate over the proper way to weigh both costs and benefits. Initial attempts to define an efficient level of global warming have also provoked a technical debate over to what extent and how fast we can adopt energy efficiency and other cleaner energy technologies.

1.3 Government action is necessary to reduce pollution in a market economy—but, **Is government up to the job?** Two basic obstacles to effective government action are **imperfect information** and the **opportunity for political influence**. **Conservatives** view environmental regulation as a necessary evil best kept at the absolute minimum; they believe that government action primarily serves special interests. By contrast, **progressives** see no way around an activist government role in environmental protection. From the progressive point of view, government failure results primarily from the influence of big business and development interests.

1.4 **Command-and-control regulation** is the dominant approach to pollution control today. In response to the question **How can we do better?** many economists have advocated adoption of **incentive-based** regulatory approaches, such as **pollution taxes** or **cap-and-trade**. Another option is the direct promotion of **clean technology** through actions such as R&D funding, infrastructure investment, zoning laws, and efficiency standards. Conservatives dispute the ability of government to achieve environmental goals by promoting clean technology.

1.5 **The final question of resolving global issues** often requires international agreement. Such agreements, in turn, face two major obstacles. The first of these is the **public good** nature of environmental agreements. Once an agreement is signed, the incentives to free-ride are great. Second, poor countries often cannot afford to invest in environmental protection. At the same time, they cannot afford not to; economic growth may lead to **unsustainable development**. In practice, this means funds to resolve global pollution problems must come from rich countries. A cap-and-trade system for controlling global CO_2 emissions (1) provides a way to fund poor-country efforts and, (2) provides rich countries with the right incentives to seek out less-polluting technology.

REFERENCES

Ackerman, Frank, Elizabeth Stanton, and Ramón Bueno. 2010. Fat tails, exponents, and extreme uncertainty: Simulating catastrophe in DICE. *Ecological Economics* 69(8): 1657–65.

Barnes, Peter. 2001. *Who owns the sky?* Washington, DC: Island Press.

Hansen, James. 2005. A slippery slope: How much global warming constitutes "dangerous anthropogenic interference"? *Climatic Change* 68: 269–79.

Holladay, J. Scott, Jonathan Horne, and Jason A. Schwartz. 2009. *Economists and climate change: Consensus and open questions.* Law Policy Brief No. 5. New York: Institute for Policy Integrity, New York University School of Law.

Intergovernmental Panel on Climate Change. 1996. *Climate change 1995: The science of climate change.* Oxford: Cambridge University Press.

———. 2007. *Climate change 2007—Impacts, adaptation and vulnerability.* Oxford: Cambridge University Press.

IPCC. *See* Intergovernmental Panel on Climate Change.

Jepma, Catrinus, and Mohan Munasinghe. 1998. *Climate change policy.* Cambridge: Cambridge University Press.

Nordhaus, William. 2008. *A question of balance: Economic modeling of global warming.* New Haven, CT: Yale University Press.

Nordhaus, William, and Joseph Boyer. 2000. *Warming the world: Economic models of global warming.* Cambridge, MA: Massachusetts Institute of Technology.

O'Neil, Brian, and Michael Oppenheimer. 2002. Dangerous climate impacts and the Kyoto Protocol. *Science* 296: 1792–93.

Sokolov, A. P., P. H. Stone, C. E. Forest, R. Prinn, M. C. Sarofim, M. Webster, S. Paltsev, et al. 2009. Probabilistic forecast for 21st century climate based on uncertainties in emissions (without policy) and climate parameters. *Journal of Climate* 22(19): 5175–204.

Stern, Nicholas Herbert. 2006. *The economics of climate change.* Oxford: Cambridge University Press.

HOW MUCH POLLUTION

IS TOO MUCH?

The first step in protecting the environment is setting a goal: How clean do we want it to be? There is no "right" answer to this question, but whatever answer we choose, implicitly or explicitly, the costs of clean up will be weighed against the benefits. Here we explore three different clean-up targets, each comparing costs and benefits in different ways: efficiency, safety, and sustainability. The focus is on both ethical and practical issues. We begin with a discussion of the utilitarian ethical framework that economists use and then explore two fundamental reasons why unregulated markets tend to produce too much pollution from *any* perspective. We then look carefully at the techniques that economists have developed to measure the benefits and costs of environmental protection, the strengths and limitations of benefit-cost analysis, and the broader relationship between growth in material consumption, resource depletion, and growth in well-being. How much is too much? This part of the book provides the tools to help you make up your mind.

CHAPTER 2

ETHICS AND ECONOMICS

2.0 Introduction

After reading the brief introduction to global warming, you are now more informed about the issue than 95% of the U.S. population. Suppose there was a presidential election tomorrow, and candidate A was supporting an efficiency standard. Based on the current benefit-cost analyses of reducing greenhouse gas emissions, he was advocating only a minimal carbon tax. Candidate B, by contrast, believed in an ecological sustainability standard and was pushing a much higher tax, combined with aggressive government action to promote clean technology. If you were a single-issue voter, for whom would you vote? Why?

If you voted for candidate A, you might have done so out of a concern for economic growth or jobs. You might even have reasoned that the economic slowdown brought on by increased regulation would actually penalize future generations more than the warming by reducing investment in education, capital, and new technology. If, on the other hand, you voted for candidate B, perhaps you did so because you thought it was unfair to punish our descendants for our wasteful consumption habits and that passing on to them a stable climate was more important than providing them with a new, improved form of breakfast cereal. You might also have thought that we have a moral duty to preserve the species of the earth. Finally, you might have reasoned that new jobs would be created in the process of controlling carbon emissions.

The question "How much pollution is too much?" is what economists call a **normative** issue—it focuses our attention on what should be, rather than what is. Some are tempted to dismiss normative or ethical questions by saying, "It's just a matter of opinion." But in fact, in our society, opinion matters. The underlying ethical viewpoints held by lawmakers, regulatory and industry officials, and voters fundamentally influence the making of pollution policy. Like most countries, the United States already has a system of laws and regulatory agencies responsible for controlling the amount of pollutants emitted by factories, offices, farms, cars, and in the case of cigarettes, even people's lungs. Are the current laws too strict (as many in industry maintain) or do they need tightening up (as environmentalists argue)?

Examining the ethical foundations of our own opinions will help us evaluate what is the "right" amount of pollution these laws ought to permit. Without a well-reasoned answer to this question, sensible environmental regulation becomes impossible.

In the first part of this book, we examine three different pollution standards: an **efficiency standard**, which carefully weighs benefits and costs; a **safety standard** emphasizing human health; and an ecological **sustainability standard**, which argues for the preservation of current ecosystems. Along the way, we explore the complex issues involved in measuring the costs and benefits of cleaning up our environment. Wrestling with this material probably will not change where you stand on the "growth versus environment" debate, but it should help you clarify why you think the way you do. This in turn will make you a more effective advocate of your position. And convincing others that your opinion is "better"—either more logical or more consistent with widely held social norms—is the basis for taking action to make our world a better place.

2.1 Utility and Utilitarianism

Economic analysts are concerned with *human* welfare or well-being. From the economic perspective, the environment should be protected for the material benefit of humanity and not for strictly moral or ethical reasons. To an economist, saving the blue whale from extinction is valuable only insofar as doing so yields happiness (or prevents tragedy) for present or future generations of people. The existence of the whale independent of people is of no importance. This human-centered (or anthropocentric) moral foundation underlying economic analysis is known as **utilitarianism**.

There are, of course, different perspectives. One such alternative is a *biocentric* view. Biocentrism argues that *independent of the utility of doing so*, people have a moral responsibility to treat the earth with respect. From the Native Americans to Henry David Thoreau and John Muir to Earth First! activism, this is an old and familiar idea in American culture. (Of course, a celebration of the unbridled exploitation of nature has also played a dominant role in American intellectual history.)[1] Aldo Leopold, considered by many to be one of the most influential environmental thinkers of the last century, stated it this way: "We abuse land because we regard it as a commodity belonging to us. When we see land as a community to which we belong, we may begin to use it with love and respect."[2]

As this quote suggests, many environmentalists are hostile to utilitarian arguments for protecting the environment. Indeed, an economic perspective on nature is often viewed as the primary problem, rather than part of the solution. The philosopher Mark Sagoff puts it this way:

> The destruction of biodiversity is the crime for which future generations are the least likely to forgive us. The crime would be as great or even greater if a computer could design or store all the genetic data we might ever use or need from the destroyed species. The reasons to protect nature are moral, religious and cultural far more often than they are economic.[3]

1. See Nash (1989) and Brown (1998).
2. See Leopold (1966).
3. See Sagoff (1995).

The focus on anthropocentric, utilitarian arguments in this book is not meant to discount the importance of other ethical views. Indeed, over the long run, nonutilitarian moral considerations will largely determine the condition of the planet that we pass on to our children and theirs. But economic arguments invariably crop up in short-run debates over environmental protection, and they often play pivotal roles.

Individual economists may in fact accept biocentrism as part of their personal moral code. However, in conducting their analysis, economists adopt a hands-off view toward the morality or immorality of eliminating species (or of pollution in general), because they are reluctant to impose a single set of values on the broader society. However, failing to make a judgment itself implies an ethical framework—and the moral philosophy underlying economics is utilitarianism.

Utilitarians have two hard questions to settle before they can apply their analysis to an issue like pollution. The first is, "What in fact makes people happy?" This is a difficult question; the great religions of the world, for example, each offer their own spiritual answers. Economists respond at the material level by assuming that the consumption of goods brings happiness or utility. *Goods* are defined very broadly to include any and all things that people desire. These include both **market goods**, such as tomatoes, ipods, and basketball shoes, and **nonmarket goods**, such as clean air, charitable deeds, or the view from a mountaintop. What makes something a good is a personal matter. Leon Walras, an economist who lived in the 1800s, puts it in this rather provocative way:

> We need not concern ourselves with the morality or immorality of any desire which a useful thing answers or serves to satisfy. From other points of view the question of whether a drug is wanted by a doctor to cure a patient, or a murderer to kill his family is a very serious matter, but from our point of view, it is totally irrelevant.[4]

One can express the positive relationship between consumption of goods and utility in a mathematical relationship known as a **utility function**. We can write a utility function for a person named Aldo on a given day as

$$\text{Utility}_{Aldo} = U_{Aldo}(\overset{+}{\text{\# of tomatoes}}, \overset{+}{\text{\# of ipods}}, \overset{+}{\text{\# of basketball shoes}},$$
$$\overset{+}{\text{lbs of clean air}}, \overset{+}{\text{\# of charitable deeds}}, \overset{+}{\text{\# of mountaintop views}}, ...)$$

where the ellipsis indicates all the other items Aldo consumes over the course of the day and the plus signs indicate that Aldo's utility rises as he consumes these goods. Another way to present Aldo's utility function is to compress all the goods he consumes into a consumption bundle, labeled X_A (the A is for Aldo), and write $\text{Utility}_A = U_A(X_A)$.

Now, the production of many of the market goods in his consumption bundle, X_A, also creates pollution, which Aldo doesn't like. So let us break out one element from Aldo's consumption bundle—P_A, the pollution to which Aldo is exposed. We can now write Aldo's utility function as $\text{Utility}_A = U_A(\overset{+}{X}_A, \overset{-}{P}_A)$, where the minus sign above the

---

4. See Walras (1954).

pollution variable reminds us that Aldo's utility declines as his exposure to pollution increases.

This utility function illustrates a key assumption underlying most economic approaches to environmental issues: A fundamental trade-off for human happiness exists between increased material consumption (economic growth) and environmental quality. Whenever P_A goes down (the environment is cleaned up), X_A goes down too (other consumption falls), and vice versa. Put another way, the opportunity cost of environmental cleanup is assumed to be slower growth in the output of market goods.

One additional assumption about this utility-consumption relationship is often made: **More is better**. That is, Aldo is always happier when given more stuff. This may seem implausible. Why should Aldo want more than one ice cream cone if he is already full? The standard reply is, he can give it to a friend (which would make Aldo happy) or sell it and use the money to buy something he wants.

As we shall see, the "more is better" assumption is a crucial one. On one hand, it provides substantial power to proponents of the efficiency standard. On the other hand, proponents of a safety standard argue that it incorrectly builds in a "bias" toward economic growth. Ignoring the additional pollution it creates, under the more-is-better assumption, growth *by definition* increases human happiness. We devote Chapter 11 of this book to a careful examination of this assumption. To the extent that more is *not* better, utilitarian arguments for protecting the environment at the expense of consumption growth become much stronger.

To summarize this section: In answer to the first question of what makes people happy, utilitarians argue it is consumption of market and nonmarket goods. The happiness trade-off between consumption and environmental quality can be conveniently expressed in the form of a utility function. A second and more controversial assumption often made is that, from the individual perspective, more of any such good always increases happiness. With this answer in hand, we can now move on to the second question facing utilitarians: How does one add up individual happiness into social happiness?

2.2 Social Welfare

If increases in consumption of both market and nonmarket goods make *individuals* happy, does this also mean that increases in individual consumption increase the overall welfare of a *society*? Answering this question involves incorporating issues of fairness and rights. How does one weigh a reduction in the happiness of one individual against an increase in the happiness of another? To make explicit their assumptions about fairness, economists often specify a **social welfare function**, which determines a "desirable" way of adding up individual utilities. In a society including Rachel (R), John (J), and many others ($\dots$), we can write:

$$SW = f(U_R(\overset{+}{X}_R, \overset{-}{P}_R), U_J(\overset{+}{X}_J, \overset{-}{P}_J), \dots)$$

where again, the plus signs indicate that social welfare rises as each individual gets happier.

One commonly used social welfare function is just the sum of individual utilities:

$$\text{SW} = U_R(\overset{+}{X_R}, \overset{-}{P_R}) + U_J(\overset{+}{X_J}, \overset{-}{P_J}) + \dots \tag{1}$$

The original 19th-century utilitarians believed this to be the correct form, arguing that the "greatest good for the greatest number" should be the guiding principle for public policy. They thought that to implement such a policy would require measuring utility in a precise way, and they devised elaborate methods for comparing the relative happiness derived from consumption by different individuals.

Unlike classical utilitarians, modern economists do not rely on direct measurements of utility. However, to determine the "correct" level of pollution from a social welfare perspective, we do need to weigh one person's consumption against another's. One social judgment we might make is that *additions* to consumption are valued equally by individuals. This is called an assumption of **equal marginal utility of consumption**, and it allows us to weigh the welfare impact of changes in patterns of consumption directly. For example, under this assumption, if your income goes up by a dollar and mine goes down by a dollar, social welfare will remain unchanged.[5]

Given this assumption and the specification of the social welfare function in equation (1), *increases* in each person's happiness receive equal weight—social welfare goes up at the same rate when the utility of either a millionaire (John) or a street person (Rachel) rises. In fact, social welfare could potentially rise as millionaire John was made better off at street person Rachel's expense! When utility is simply added up, no allowance is made in the social welfare function for issues of fairness in the distribution of income among those alive today.

Social welfare function—equation (1)—also provides no special protection for the well-being of future generations; under the simple adding-up specification, social welfare might rise if the current generation went on a consumption binge at the expense of our descendants. This would be true, provided that the increase in consumption today more than offsets the decrease in consumption tomorrow.

Finally, the social welfare function in equation (1) also assumes that pollution victims have no special rights. If, for example, Rachel lives downwind from John's steel factory and, as a result, suffers health damages of, let us say, $25 per day, this reduction in social welfare would be strictly offset by a gain in John's profits of $25. Equation (1) is thus "blind" to the distribution of the costs and benefits of economic events within the current generation, across generations, and between pollution victims and beneficiaries. All that matters for boosting social welfare is increasing net consumption of *both* market and nonmarket goods, regardless of who wins and who loses.

Equation (1) is in fact the "adding up" mechanism underlying an **efficiency standard** for pollution control. Under an efficiency standard, the idea is to maximize the **net benefits** (benefits minus costs) of economic growth, by carefully weighing the benefits (more consumption) against the costs (pollution and resource degradation). This is done without reference to who bears the costs or gains the benefits.

How can such a position be ethically defended? While pollution certainly imposes costs on certain individuals, efficiency advocates maintain that, over time, *most people*

---

5. The assumption of equal marginal utilities of consumption within the relevant range is implicit behind the efficiency standard and the Hicks-Kaldor test. See Kneese and Schulze (1985).

will benefit if the net consumption benefits from pollution control are maximized. Put in simple terms, lower prices of consumer goods for the vast majority (including necessities like food and energy) must be strictly balanced against protection of environmental quality and health.

The "blind" approach that efficiency supporters take toward the distribution of costs and benefits provides one extreme. By contrast, if Rachel is impoverished, we might assume that her marginal utility of income is *greater than* that of John; one dollar increases Rachel's happiness more than it increases John's. Then, in the interests of social well-being, we might well want to weigh increases in Rachel's consumption more heavily than those of the affluent.[6]

In practice, the strict efficiency standard for pollution control is often modified to include "fairness weights" in the social welfare function. In particular, as we discuss further in Chapters 8 and 9, a concern for fairness to future generations is often incorporated. For example, we might wish to employ a **sustainability rule** that says social welfare does not rise if increases in consumption today come at the expense of the welfare of our children. Suppose that Rachel (now an "average" person) is not yet born, while John (also an "average" person) is alive today, then our sustainable social welfare function would be written as

$$SW = w*U_R(\overset{+}{X}_R, \overset{-}{P}_R) + U_J(\overset{+}{X}_J, \overset{-}{P}_J) + \dots \qquad (2)$$

where w is a weighting number big enough to ensure that increases in John's consumption do not substantially penalize Rachel. Here, and unlike in equation (1), increases in happiness for the average individual today cannot come at the expense of future generations.

Finally, we bring Rachel back to the present, living downwind from John's steel factory. She is now exposed to air pollution, P_R. She consumes this pollution, but recall that it is an economic "bad" and so enters her utility function with a negative sign. Proponents of a **safety standard** will argue that in the interests of personal liberty, Rachel has a *right* to protection from unsolicited damage to her health. As a result they will weight very heavily the negative effect of pollution in her utility function:[7]

$$SW = U_R(\overset{+}{X}_R, w* \overset{-}{P}_R) + U_J(\overset{+}{X}_J) + \dots \qquad (3)$$

Now, social welfare rises substantially less with the production of steel than it does with less-polluting commodities. An extreme safety advocate, by choosing such a large value for the weighting number w, would essentially refuse to balance the benefits of the polluting steel process (cheaper steel, and all the products that steel contains) against the harmful impact of pollution.

The latter two specifications of the social welfare function—sustainability and safety—imply that a happy society is more than just the sum of its parts. Fairness

---

6. This in fact is the classical utilitarian argument for income redistribution. Rawls (1971) provides a contractual argument in favor of weighting the consumption of the least well off.

7. Equation (3) is a crude way of representing philosopher John Rawls's (1971, 61) lexicographic preference ordering that puts liberty of the person above material consumption. Kneese and Schulze (1985) specify the libertarian position as a decision rule requiring an actual Pareto improvement from any proposed social policy. Similarly, the w in equation (2) would be dichotomous: 1 for $U_J < U_R$ and equal to $1 + (U_J - U_R)/U_R$ for $U_J > U_R$.

criteria based on income distribution (both within and between generations) and personal liberty must be met as well. When the more-is-better assumption is relaxed in Chapter 11 of the book, we add yet another layer of complexity: because my happiness from consumption depends on your level of consumption in a variety of ways, happiness will depend on *relative* rather than absolute levels of material welfare. As a result, in order to correctly specify social welfare, certain "noncompetitive" consumption items such as environmental health will also be weighted in the social welfare function.

This section has illustrated three different forms for a social welfare function—efficiency, sustainability, and safety—each specifying how individual utility might be added up to equal social well-being. While these different social welfare functions may seem arbitrary, proponents of each will argue that, in fact, their vision reflects the "dominant viewpoint" in our society about the proper relationship between material consumption and social welfare.[8] Social welfare functions have the advantage of forcing advocates of utilitarian policies to precisely state and defend both their basic assumptions and the logic by which they reach their conclusions. As we proceed in this first part of the book, we shall see that the different pollution standards are defended ethically by making different assumptions about the proper form of both the utility and social welfare functions.

2.3 Summary

This chapter has provided an introductory discussion of the ethical foundations of economics. Economists maintain as a basic assumption that increases in material consumption of both market and nonmarket goods—including clean air and water—increase individual utility. Whether growth in material consumption, independent of fairness and rights, necessarily leads to an overall increase in *social* welfare depends on the form that is specified for the social welfare function. There is no "correct" social welfare function. But economists use social welfare functions to help clarify normative debates, including the one that concerns us: How much pollution is too much?

Three positions are often staked out in economic discussions regarding environmental protection. First, there are those who argue for a careful weighing of costs and benefits that pays no attention to the distribution of those costs and benefits. This is an efficiency position. Second, there are safety standard supporters, who maintain that people have a right to have their health protected from environmental damage, regardless of the cost.

The third position is sustainability, which argues for protecting the welfare of future generations. While the sustainability criterion is easy to state, we will find that there is much debate about what sustainability means in practice. This is because future generations are affected by our current decisions in complex ways. For example, will our grandchildren be better off if we leave them oil in the ground or if we exploit the oil deposits and invest the profits in developing new forms of energy? The answer to this question is not obvious.

Insofar as the debate about resources and the environment focuses on the welfare of people, it remains a utilitarian one and in the realm of economics. Again, this is

8. Arrow (1963) has analyzed the difficulties in democratically determining a social welfare function.

not to downplay the importance of noneconomic ethical views about the environment. However, the economic approach asks us to think clearly about the ways in which nature serves our social needs. By examining the ethical foundations of different views about the appropriate level of pollution, we can develop a better notion of why it is that we support either a modest or an aggressive position on slowing global warming.

APPLICATION 2.0

Social Welfare and Landfill Regulation

The U.S. Environmental Protection Agency (EPA) issues regulations covering the design and construction of landfills for municipal solid waste. Landfills can represent a threat to environmental health if toxic chemicals leach from the waste into surrounding ground or surface waters.

The current regulations require certain design, construction, and maintenance standards extending beyond the post-closure period, including, in most cases, installation of impermeable liners and covers and groundwater monitoring. The purpose of the regulations is to ensure safe containment of solid waste and to prevent future generations from having to bear cleanup costs from poorly disposed waste.

Even with the regulations, just under 10% of new landfills still pose what the EPA considers to be a "moderate" health risk for individuals who depend on contaminated groundwater: a greater than 1 in 1 million increase in the risk of contracting cancer. However, because so few people actually depend on groundwater within leaching distance of a landfill, the current regulations are predicted to reduce cancer by only two or three cases over the next 300 years. Potential benefits of the regulation not quantified by the EPA include increased ease of siting landfills, reduced damage to surface water, fairness to future generations, and an overall reduction in waste generation and related "upstream" pollution encouraged by higher disposal costs.

In aggregate, the regulations are expensive: about $5.8 billion, or around $2 billion per cancer case reduced. On a per household basis, this works out to an annual cost of $4.10 in increased garbage bills over the 20-year life of a landfill.

    a.   Using the concept of social welfare represented, respectively, by equations (1) and (3), explain why the EPA's landfill regulation is (a) too strict and (b) not strict enough.

APPLICATION 2.1

More on Landfills

Suppose that 100 people live around a hazardous waste dump. If the people continue to live there for 20 years, one of them will likely contract a painful, nonfatal cancer that will lead to $1 million in health-care costs, forgone wages, and pain suffering. Assume this is all the damage this waste will ever do (the waste loses its toxicity after 20 years).

The EPA has three choices:

    1.   Do nothing.
    2.   Clean up at a cost of $4 million.

3. Relocate the families at a cost to taxpayers of $1 million; fence off the property for 20 years.

    a. Rank the solutions in terms of efficiency. Explain your reasoning.

    b. Rank the solutions in terms of safety. Explain your reasoning.

KEY IDEAS IN EACH SECTION

2.0   **Normative** questions ask what *should* be rather than what is. Economic analysis of normative issues proceeds by clearly stating the underlying ethical assumptions.

2.1   The ethical foundation of economics is **utilitarianism**, a philosophy in which environmental cleanup is important solely for the happiness (utility) that it brings to people alive today and in the future. This philosophy is contrasted with a biocentric view, which values nature for its own sake. Economists assume that consumption of both **market goods** and **nonmarket goods** makes people happy. This relationship can be expressed in a **utility function**, in which pollution enters as a negative consumption element. A utility function assumes a fundamental trade-off between growth in consumption and improvements in environmental quality. Economists often make one further key assumption about the consumption-utility relationship: **more is better**.

2.2   To add up individual utility, economists use a **social welfare function**. In such a function, one might assume **equal marginal utility of consumption** so that social welfare is just the sum of individual happiness, regardless of the distribution of benefits within a generation, across generations, or between victims and polluters. This social welfare function underlies the **efficiency standard**, which seeks to maximize the **net benefits** from steps taken to protect the environment. Alternatively, one might want to weight the consumption of poor people more heavily than rich people, victims more heavily than polluters (**safety standard**), or adopt a **sustainability rule** ensuring that consumption today does not come at the expense of future generations. No social welfare function is "correct," but their use helps clarify the underlying assumptions in normative debates over the right level of pollution.

REFERENCES

Arrow, Kenneth. 1963. *Social choice and individual values.* New York: John Wiley.

Brown, Paul. 1998. Towards an economics of stewardship: The case of climate. *Ecological Economics* 26(1): 11–22.

Kneese, Alan V., and William D. Schulze. 1985. Ethics and environmental economics. In *Handbook of natural resource economics*. Vol. 1, ed. A. V. Kneese and J. L. Sweeney, 191–220. New York: Elsevier.

Leopold, Aldo. 1966. *A Sand County Almanac.* New York: Oxford University Press.

Nash, Roderick Frazier. 1989. *The rights of nature.* Madison: University of Wisconsin Press.

Rawls, John. 1971. *A theory of justice.* Cambridge, MA: Harvard University Press.

Sagoff, Mark. 1995. Carrying capacity and ecological economics. *Bioscience* 45(9): 610–19.

Walras, Leon. 1954. *Elements of pure economics.* Homewood, IL: Irwin.

CHAPTER 3

POLLUTION AND RESOURCE DEGRADATION AS EXTERNALITIES

3.0 Introduction

Any economy depends on the ecological system in which it is embedded in two fundamental ways, illustrated in Figure 3.1. First, human production and consumption processes rely on the environment as a **source** of raw materials; second, they also exploit the environment as a **sink** (or repository) for waste materials. Both sources and sinks form what economists call natural capital. **Natural capital** is the input that nature provides for our production and consumption processes. Pollution is the overuse of sinks; resource degradation is the overharvesting of sources. In this sense, pollution and resource degradation are flip sides of the same process, the excessive exploitation of natural capital.

What exactly do we mean by pollution? Consider three examples:

1. Tyler is eating in a smoky kitchen. Is he exposed to pollution?
2. Karen routinely comes in contact with low-level radioactive waste while working at a nuclear power plant. Is she exposed to pollution?
3. Myles is trying to get some sleep while his neighbor's sound system blares. Is he exposed to pollution?

For the purposes of this book, the correct answers are maybe, maybe, and yes. Economists define *pollution* as a **negative externality**: a cost of a transaction not borne by the buyer or seller. Pollution is termed an externality because it imposes costs on people who are "external" to the producer and consumer of the polluting product.

In the first case, what if Tyler is the one smoking? While the smoke is undeniably doing damage to Tyler's lungs, he may be aware of the damage and yet, balancing pleasure against risk, does not consider himself worse off. The second "maybe" is more difficult. Exposure to radioactive waste increases Karen's risk of cancer and is clearly a by-product of human activity. However, if she fully understands the risk to her health of performing the job, and yet shoulders it in exchange for a salary, then exposure to the waste is part of the bargain. That is, the exposure is not external to the transaction

FIGURE 3.1 Natural Capital: Sources and Sinks

between her and her employer. Under these circumstances, Karen would face a serious *occupational hazard*, which needs regulation on its own terms, but not a pollutant as we have defined it.[1] Finally, poor Myles is a clear-cut pollution victim. He is involuntarily being exposed to a negative by-product of his neighbor's listening experience.

From an economist's point of view, market systems generate pollution because many natural inputs into the production of goods and services—such as air and water—are "underpriced." Because no one owns these resources, in the absence of government regulation or legal protection for pollution victims, businesses will use them up freely, neglecting the external costs imposed on others. Coal-fired electric power production in the United States emits a variety of pollutants into the atmosphere, which in combination, lead to tens of thousands of premature deaths, asthma and other illnesses, and millions of lost work days. Economists have recently estimated that this cost to society runs around $0.04 per KWh of electric power produced by power plants, or more.[2] If power companies were forced to compensate the families of the victims for the damages they imposed (thereby **internalizing the externalities**), the firms would, in effect, be paying for the air quality they "used up." This, in turn, would raise the production costs of the firm. Air would no longer be underpriced. As a result, consumers would conserve on their use of electricity and firms would seek out ways to clean up their discharge.

Figure 3.2 provides a simple supply-and-demand analysis of the situation. Average electricity prices in the United States today, not including the external costs, are $0.08 per KWh. Note that the supply curve in the industry shifts up vertically by the $0.04 per KWh damage to internalize the costs. This leads to a somewhat lower final increase

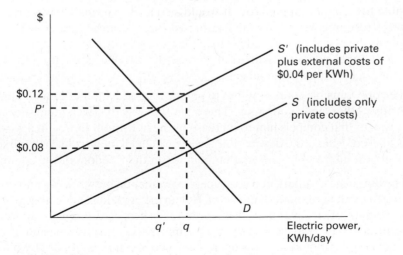

FIGURE 3.2 Social and Private Costs in the Electricity Market

---

1. These assertions require that Tyler and Karen *are indeed fully aware of the risks they face.*
2. Muller, Mendelsohn, and Nordhaus (2011).

in price than $0.04. (Assuming supply is not perfectly elastic and demand not perfectly inelastic). The diagram yields an immediate prediction. If all firms are forced to pay their full social costs of production, the competitive supply curve will shift up. The market price for electricity will be higher, and the quantity sold will be lower. The diagram indicates a general principle: it is difficult to reduce pollution without also reducing the supply of the polluting product.

Because the atmosphere is commonly owned and is thus a "free" good, electricity companies overexploit it, and many people downwind are exposed to a negative externality of the electricity production process. From an economic point of view, many pollution problems arise because environmental resources such as air, rivers, and groundwater are, by their nature, the heritage of humankind as a whole. The rest of this chapter takes a closer look at the implications of this common ownership.

3.1 The Open Access Problem

Many forms of natural capital, both sources and sinks, are not (and cannot be) privately owned. Because of this, pure free-market systems will generate too much pollution (or resource degradation) by any of the standards considered in this book—efficiency, safety, or sustainability. There are two related reasons for this: The first is the **open access problem**, which often arises when natural capital is commonly held. The second, addressed in the next section, is the public goods problem. The open access problem can be stated simply: if people weigh private benefits against private costs—as opposed to private plus external, or "social" costs—they will overexploit common resources when given open access.

This idea was popularized in the late 1960s by Garrett Hardin, who called it the "tragedy of the commons." He poses the problem facing a herder whose cattle forage on common land. Introducing one more cow onto the common grazing land would lead to a large private gain for this herder in the form of an additional animal available for sale or consumption. It would also lead to a small private loss, in that the degraded resource would provide less robust forage for the herder's existing animals. Of course the social cost would be much larger, given that most of the loss from the degraded rangeland is externalized and borne by other herders. But if the herder seeks to maximize his or her personal gain,

> The only sensible course for him to pursue is to add another animal to his herd. And another, and another .... Therein is the tragedy. Each man is *locked in* to a system that compels him to increase his herd without limit—in a world that is limited. Ruin is the destination toward which all men rush, each pursuing his own best interest in a society that believes in the freedom of the commons.[3]

Hardin suggests a stark and inescapable connection between common ownership of resources and their ultimate exhaustion. But, in fact, grazing and fishing grounds in most traditional societies have often been commonly held and managed quite sustainably for centuries. This was achieved by informal social constraints and traditions that prevented overexploitation. However, when such restraints break down as a result of "modernization" or population pressures, the open access problem emerges, and a tragedy of the commons is likely to result.[4]

---

3. See Hardin (1968).
4. See Bromley (1991) for a full discussion.

The open access problem explains not only why sources of natural capital such as grazing land are degraded but also why environmental sinks like the air are polluted. For example, a factory owner might install a low-cost technology that generates substantial air pollution, even though he and his family live nearby and will be exposed to the toxic materials. The owner captures the full benefits of the pollution (the profit from "low-cost" production), while his family bears only a small portion of the total risk.

In combination with vastly more efficient technology, open access also explains the dramatic decline in populations of commercial fish species over the last few decades. Close to half of America's fisheries and more than 70% of global fisheries are over-fished; the North Atlantic is estimated to contain only one-third of the biomass of edible fish that were present in 1950. Modern technology in the form of bottom trawling is also damaging habitat, essentially clear-cutting, and not replanting, the ocean floor.

Fisheries off the New England Coast have been particularly hard-hit. Landings of cod peaked in 1990 at 18,000 tons, and over the next eight years, that figure plummeted to only 1,000 tons as the fishery collapsed. Recovery has been very slow, and the government continues to reduce the limits on the fisheries. But even as the overall catch declined sharply, fishers were still opposing catch limits. Strapped with mortgages on expensive boats, fisherpeople said they could not afford the luxury of cutting back on their fishing effort. Indeed, perversely, the incentive for each boat was to employ more and more sophisticated technology to increase that owner's share of the dwindling stock.[5]

We can explore this overfishing issue further with the help of a hypothetical example. Suppose that fish cost a dollar a pound, and the marginal cost of running a vessel—including the fuel and salaries for crew and owner—is $250 per day, then the rational response for fishing boats is to continue to fish as long as, on average, the catch exceeds 250 pounds. Suppose that the long-run relationship between the number of vessels and the total catch per day in a New England bay is illustrated in Figure 3.3.

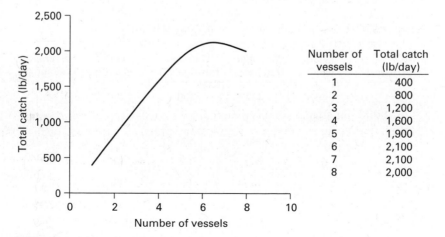

Number of vessels	Total catch (lb/day)
1	400
2	800
3	1,200
4	1,600
5	1,900
6	2,100
7	2,100
8	2,000

FIGURE 3.3 Vessels and Total Catch

---

5. Data on global catch are from Helvarg (2003). Cod fishery data are from National Marine Fisheries Service.

The catch level peaks at six boats, and after seven boats it drops off, reflecting fishing beyond a sustained yield level. If eight boats go out on a regular basis, then the breeding stock is harvested, and over time the population of fish declines.[6]

Given this information, consider the following:

PUZZLE

Part 1. If there were open access to the bay and seven boats were already fishing, would you fish in the bay?

Part 2. If you ran the government fisheries board, how many boats would you allow out if you wanted to maximize total profits from the bay?

SOLUTION

Part 1. The revenue for the eighth boat is $1 times the average catch of 250 pounds, or $250. You would earn a day's salary and cover costs if you went out, so it is worth it.

Part 2. Six is a common guess, but it is incorrect. Six maximizes *revenue*, but profit is revenue minus cost. Table 3.1 puts together some additional information to help answer this part. Note that Table 3.1 changes the focus from *total* revenues and *total* costs to *marginal* revenues and *marginal* costs—the addition to revenue and cost from sending out each additional boat.

To maximize the profit from the New England bay, additional boats should be sent out up to the point where the value of the addition to the total catch just exceeds the opportunity cost of sending out the boat. The fisheries board would stop at five boats, because the sixth would bring in only $200 in marginal revenue, less than enough to cover its costs of $250. The final column, labeled Marginal Profit (the extra profit from each additional boat), makes this clear: after five boats, losses begin to accumulate.

TABLE 3.1   Calculating the Profit-Maximizing Harvest

Number of Vessels	Total Catch (lb)	Marginal Catch (lb)	Marginal Revenue ($)	Average Catch (lb)	Average Revenue ($)	Marginal Profit ($)
1	400	400	400	400	400	+150
2	800	400	400	400	400	+150
3	1,200	400	400	400	400	+150
4	1,600	400	400	400	400	+150
5	1,900	300	300	380	380	+50
6	2,100	200	200	350	350	−50
7	2,100	0	000	300	300	−250
8	2,000	−100	−100	250	250	−350

---

6. This model is based on Gordon (1954).

Note that in addition to overfishing the resource, there is a second externality here. After four boats, some of the catch of the new entrants is *diverted from other boats*. When there is open access to the bay, however, individual fisherpeople don't recognize (but more importantly don't care) about these negative externalities imposed on the other boats; each bears only a small portion of the reduction in the total stock. Thus boats continue to go out even when the total catch, and total revenue in the industry, declines. As a result of open access, in New England and globally, a human and ecological tragedy is indeed unfolding.

Figure 3.4 develops a graphical analysis of the open access problem. Marginal revenue first stays constant and then falls, reflecting eventual declining marginal productivity as additional boats go out. Notice that the average and marginal revenue curves coincide for up to four boats, but once declining marginal productivity kicks in, the marginal revenue curve lies below the average revenue curve. (This decline is due to the mathematical relationship between marginal and average values: as long as the addition to revenue equals the average revenue, the average stays constant and equal to the marginal value. However, when additions to revenue fall below the average, the average is pulled down.) Finally, the constant marginal cost of sending out additional boats is represented by the straight line at $250.

Again, the figure tells us that private boats will go out as long as *average* revenue covers costs, even though the total profits earned in the industry are declining. Open access leads eight boats into the fishery. By contrast, the profit-maximizing catch level occurs where *marginal* revenue just exceeds marginal costs at five boats.

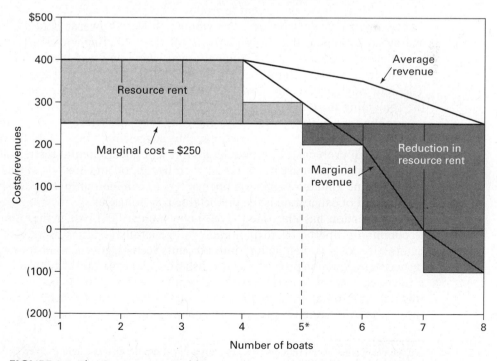

FIGURE 3.4 The Open Access Problem

The profit earned in the industry is displayed visually as the sum total of the difference between marginal revenue and marginal cost for each boat that goes out—the light-shaded area in the diagram.[7] The dark-shaded area in the picture shows the *reduction in profit* for the industry as a result of overfishing. For the sixth through eighth boats, the marginal revenue is *less than* the marginal cost, leading to a drop in industry-wide profits. Clearly, the total industry-wide profit is largest at five boats.

In Chapter 2 we learned that an efficient outcome is one in which the net benefits produced by the economy are maximized. Here, the efficient number of boats is five. This is true because in this example, where the price of fish (and thus the consumer) is unaffected by the small changes in supply, net social benefits are just equal to profits.

The picture also illustrates a key feature of markets that rely on scarce natural capital either as sources or sinks. *When natural capital is used efficiently, long-run economic profits will be earned by those who retain access to the resource.* It is precisely those profits that attract entry into the market and lead to overexploitation of the source or the sink. These long-run profits, generated by restricted access to natural capital, are called **resource rents**. Comparable to rents earned by landlords at choice properties, these are rents due to ownership of (or limited access to) scarce natural resources.

In our example, open access into the fishery leads to an outcome in which profits in the industry are competed entirely away. With eight boats, average revenue equals average cost, and all the boats just break even. But at the efficient level, where marginal revenue equals marginal cost, a substantial resource rent is earned. When we add up the difference between marginal revenue and marginal cost (marginal profit) for the first five boats, the resource rent turns out to be $650 per day.

In the New England case, economist Steven Edwards and biologist Steven Murawski estimated that fishing efforts off the New England coast would have to be reduced by about 70% to eliminate overfishing and achieve an efficient harvest. This in turn would generate a resource rent in the industry of about $130 million.[8] The rent might go to the government in the form of fees for fishing rights or to the remaining fishermen and women in the form of profits. Edwards calculated that government revenues from a fee system would be sufficient to compensate those boats put out of business due to restrictions, thus suggesting a politically feasible way out of this tough problem. Fisherpeople often resent governmental restrictions placed on access to fishing grounds; it is, after all, their livelihood and lifestyle at stake. However, without some kind of restraint on open access to **common property** resources, overuse to the point of exhaustion is the predictable consequence.

This section has illustrated three main points. First, when there is open access to common property, overexploitation will generally result as users will not take the externality costs of their actions into account. Second, government-imposed restraints on access to common property such as fisheries, clean air, and clean water will generate a resource rent, or long-run economic profit, for those who maintain access. Finally, this rent can sometimes be collected through taxes or fees and be used to reimburse those who lose out in the process of regulating and reducing access.

---

7. Technically, this is not profit but producer surplus, because the example ignores fixed costs. The language is chosen for ease of exposition.
8. See Tregarten (1992).

3.2 The Public Goods Problem

The open access problem may explain why there is a tendency for commonly held resources such as clean air and water or fisheries to be overexploited. But why does the government have to decide what to do about it? Instead, why don't the victims of negative externalities simply band together on their own to prevent pollution or overexploitation of resources? As we just noted, this was the response to environmental degradation of common grazing and fishing grounds in traditional societies. Informal social pressure and tradition were relied on to prevent overexploitation. The modern American equivalent would be to sue an offending company or individual for damages. Indeed, a few so-called **free-market environmentalists** have advocated eliminating many environmental regulations and then relying on lawsuits by injured parties to "internalize" externalities.[9]

However, such private remedies to environmental degradation run into what economists call the **public goods problem**. Public goods are goods enjoyed in common; a classic example, though a little dated, is the warning service provided by a lighthouse. Technically, economists describe public goods as "nonexcludable." Once the lighthouse is in operation, it is impossible to exclude any passing boat from utilizing the warning beacon provided by the lighthouse.[10]

The provision of public goods is a problem for the free market due to the existence of two factors: transactions costs and free riding. To illustrate, consider a good that is enjoyed in common—for example, the noise level after 11 p.m. in Myles' neighborhood. Now suppose that neighbor Tipper cranks her sound system. Myles could go to the considerable trouble of obtaining signatures from all of their neighbors, getting money from them to hire a lawyer, filing a lawsuit, and possibly obtaining a legal injunction requiring Tipper to turn it down. The costs of undertaking this action are known as **transactions costs**, and they are particularly high because of the public nature of the injury.

If Myles does undertake the effort, he will benefit not only himself but also the entire neighborhood. Some of the neighbors might refuse to help out and instead **free ride** on Myles' provision of the public good. Instead, Myles decides it's not really worth organizing a lawsuit and tosses and turns in bed, hoping that someone else will make the effort. The result is that the demand for a quiet evening in the neighborhood, although it may be considerable, doesn't get expressed. It is not possible for any one individual to overcome the transactions costs and the possibility of free riding to provide the public good of the lawsuit, although if Myles did, the social benefits might far outweigh the cost.

In most towns, the response to noise pollution is a government regulation called a nuisance law. With such a regulation in place, Myles can just call the cops, thus greatly reducing the costs associated with stopping the noise. More generally, if victims of pollution were to try to band together to protect themselves or seek compensation in the courts, they would face very high transactions costs. For most pollution problems, for example, good information about health risks, exposure routes, and emission sources are hard even for government officials to obtain. Given the costs of mounting

---

9. See the introductory and concluding essays in Greve and Smith (1992).
10. Pure public goods also have another characteristic: they are nonrival. This means that one boat's use of the lighthouse service does not reduce the value of that service to others.

a successful court case, the problems of free riding would be compounded. The general principle is that without government intervention in the form of pollution regulations, the public good of a safe environment will be undersupplied. This is not to say that no public goods will be supplied. Some will, but less than the amount that society collectively is willing to pay for.

To see this, consider another example: private contributions to purchase and preserve wetlands and other valuable ecosystems in the United States. The Nature Conservancy is an organization that currently solicits funds to do this. Suppose such an organization sends a mailing to Mr. Peabody and Mr. Massey saying it needs $50 per foot to preserve the last 100 feet of a prime Appalachian trout stream. Now Peabody would be willing to pay $30 per foot and Massey $40 per foot toward the effort, for a total of $70 per foot. Thus the monetary benefits of preservation exceed the costs by $20 per foot.

PUZZLE

Will the Nature Conservancy get enough in contributions to buy the land?

SOLUTION

Not necessarily. Peabody, figuring Massey will pay $40 per foot, may contribute only $10 per foot. Massey, following the same logic, will contribute only $20 per foot, for a total of $30 per foot. As a result, each will try to free ride off the other's provision of the 100 feet of public good, and sufficient funds will not be forthcoming.

We can approach this problem graphically, by examining the difference between the demand curve for a public good and a more conventional private good. In Figure 3.5A, let us assume that the trout stream is for sale to private individuals. Note that, for 100 feet of land, as discussed earlier, Peabody would pay $30 per foot and Massey $40, but now they do not have to share it. As you may recall from a previous course, the demand curve for a private good is the *horizontal* sum of the individual demand curves. At a price of $30 per foot, Peabody demands 100 feet while Massey demands 120 feet, so total demand equals 100 + 120, or 220 feet. In a market for private goods, consumers face a single price, and each person consumes as much as he or she wants to buy. Thus total demand is met.

By contrast, when goods are public, all consumers face a given public quantity and must decide how much to pay. In Figure 3.5B, the trout stream has become a public good; Massey and Peabody must share whatever is purchased. For 100 feet of land, we know their collective value is $70 per foot; following this logic, we can see that their total willingness to pay (or their demand) for any given amount of preservation is the *vertical* sum of the individual demand curves.

The true total demand for public goods is seldom expressed in the market, for two reasons. First, unlike the case for private goods, some third party must organize the

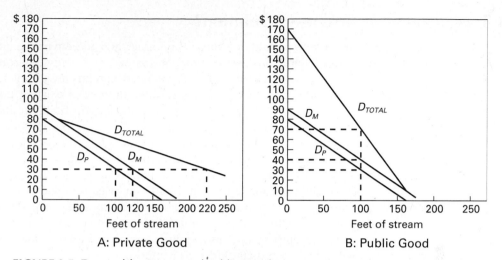

FIGURE 3.5 Demand for Private and Public Goods

collection of funds to pay for the public good or to initiate a lawsuit against a polluter. Myles would have to drag himself out of bed and go collect signatures on a petition from the neighbors to convince a judge to tell Tipper to be quiet. More generally, there may be large costs associated with proving highly contestable environmental damages in a court of law. As noted, the need to support such efforts raises the *transactions costs* — the costs associated with making a market deal — for public goods.

Second, in the case of public goods, individuals also have an incentive to *free ride* on the efforts of others. Though Massey and Peabody collectively value the land at more than its asking price, they may be unwilling to reveal their true preferences to a private agency or government collecting revenues to pay for the public good. Incentives to free ride are often dampened in small groups, where an individual can see his or her individual effort as "pivotal" to the success of the public effort, and/or the members carry a sense of group responsibility. However, such conditions are unlikely to hold for most pollution control efforts, thus making free riding a serious obstacle for nongovernmental attempts to provide such goods.

To summarize this section, in contrast to private goods, public goods are consumed in common. The true demand for public goods will not be satisfied in pure market economies due to high transactions costs and free riding. Free-market environmentalists advocate relying solely on the court system to internalize environmental externalities. Most economists, however, argue that, as a result of transactions costs and free riding, public goods such as clean air or water, rain forests, wilderness parks, and other environmental amenities will be undersupplied in a laissez-faire market system.[11] Thus there is a need for government to insure provision of these goods by protecting the environment through regulation.

---

11. Using the legal system to resolve externalities also involves very large administrative and transactions costs. For a general review of the economics of liability, see the symposium in the *Journal of Economic Perspectives* 5 (Winter 1991), especially the article by Menell (1991).

3.3 Is Sustainable Business a Solution?

In recent years, a new paradigm around economics and the environment has begun to emerge, the **sustainable business** movement. Instead of viewing environmental and social problems as unwanted costs to be externalized, can business firms look at them as potential profit opportunities? And within the confines of existing policies, laws, and regulations, can business effectively, dramatically, and profitably reduce pollution and resource degradation?

One example: In Troy, NY, two entrepreneurs have set out to eliminate Styrofoam from the face of the earth. Ecovative grows big blocks of fungus, the kind you see on logs in a forest, dries them, and then carves them up to make sculpted shipping sleeves, shipping peanuts, and even the equivalent of a foam insulation wall-board. Instead of a petroleum-based product that requires intensive mining and processing to produce, and on disposal, persists for tens of thousands of years, Ecovative's product grows in dark rooms at room temperature, and when it has served its purpose, the consumer can break it up and put it in their garden as compost.

Across the lifecycle of Styrofoam—from oil drilling to refining and manufacture, to transport and disposal—pollution problems (externalities) abound. A regulatory strategy to deal with each of these problems separately—typically end-of-pipe controls or end-of-life mandates—undoubtedly raises business costs for producing Styrofoam, and the price to the consumer for shipping and home insulation. What Ecovative, and hundreds of other green companies seek to do, is to innovate around those costs, developing inherently cheaper and cleaner solutions.

Pioneering business leaders began pursuing this strategy in the 1990s, and the sustainable business wave began to build in the 2000s. Three levels of cost-savings have been identified:

Risk Reduction. Firms that pro-actively reduce pollution reduce risk—risk of regulations, legal liability, and consumer backlash.

Resource Savings. Pollution is often a sign of waste. Firms that use water, energy, and raw materials more efficiently, also reduce emissions and will often save money.

Culture of Innovation. Firms that see it as part of their business to profitably solve their environmental problems create cultures that breed innovation.

Sustainable business has been widely hailed, and both start-ups and Fortune 500 companies have made progress pursuing this strategy. An emerging body of empirical evidence shows that environmentally leading firms are as profitable, if not more profitable, than less green competitors.[12] At the same time, however, many corporate efforts amount to little more than greenwash. At the end of the day, it is not clear how far the sustainable business movement can push. What is the scale of profitable reduction in ecological footprint that can be achieved without major changes in government regulations and policy?

We will look more closely at the opportunities for clean technology development in Chapters 18 and 19, and in Chapter 9, we will also explore the extent to which

---

12. See Sturmak and Krosinsky (2011).

firms pursuing sustainable business strategies can simultaneously reduce ecological footprint, cut costs, and increase profits—the so-called Porter hypothesis. But even if truly green companies can innovate and prosper, the vast majority of firms who are less focused on sustainable innovation can and do still raise profits the old-fashioned way, by overexploiting the commons and externalizing costs. This leads us back to the need for government policy to internalize externalities and create price signals that "tell the truth" about the real costs of production.

3.4 Summary

In this chapter, we have analyzed two different aspects of communal property that contribute to the degradation of the environment. First, the open access problem explains why individuals would knowingly damage a resource they depend upon; the benefits of exploitation are private while the costs are largely externalized. Second, the public goods problem explains, in part, why people cannot "buy" a clean environment, either by suing polluters or purchasing wilderness. Transactions costs are high and people tend to free ride on the efforts of others.

The recent rise of the sustainable business movement provides hope that, through innovation, business firms can find profitable solutions to some, and perhaps many, environmental and social challenges, particularly in conjunction with regulations that externalize internalities in the so-called dirty industries. The central point is that, generally, free-market forces do not provide the right incentives to ensure that adequate care is taken to protect our environment. Given this, what should our response be? As we have noted, a few have argued that externalities can be adequately internalized by means of private lawsuits. A second, more common response, which we examine in Chapters 17 and 18, is the call for development of more environmentally benign "clean" technologies that reduce pollution problems in the first place. However, the conventional response has been government regulation of pollution, which brings us back to our principal topic: How much is too much?

APPLICATION 3.0

Getting Government Out of Pollution Control?

An article in the business magazine *Forbes* blasts the U.S. Environmental Protection Agency for implementing ineffectual, expensive, and corrupt policies: "U.S. environmental policy is out of control, costing jobs, depressing living standards and being run by politicians, scheming business people and social extremists" (Brimelow & Spencer 1992, 67). I was actually not too surprised to find that politicians were running environmental policy; that is, after all, part of the job they were elected to do. Luckily, the article had a suggestion for eliminating our cumbersome pollution-control bureaucracy:

> There is an environmental policy suited to the American Way: The development of property rights and the common law of tort. The threat of litigation will discourage pollution, with the details worked out between private parties. For example, neighbors could use "nuisance law" to sue a malodorous factory.

Law students are taught in Environmental Law 101 that this approach didn't work, just as economics students are taught about "market failure"—the solution in both cases being government intervention. But modern scholarship suggests that the common law was indeed working until government intervened (67).

The *Forbes* article went on to cite Greve and Smith (1992) as a source of this "modern scholarship" that advocates free-market environmentalism.

a. Although the term *market failure* was not used in this chapter, we did indeed identify such a beast in the form of the public goods problem. And most economists do maintain that resolving pollution problems privately through lawsuits will result in too much pollution. Explain the two reasons why.

APPLICATION 3.1

Open Access and Logging

The following data refer to the number of logging operations working in a stretch of tropical rain forest. Excluding externalities, the private cost of a logging operation is $25,000 per week. Logs sell for $1 a piece. Fill in the chart below.

Number of Operations	Total Harvest (1,000 logs)	Average Harvest (1,000 logs)	Marginal Harvest (1,000 logs)
0	0		
1	40		
2	75		
3	105		
4	130		
5	150		
6	165		
7	175		
8	180		
9	182		

a. What is the number of logging operations in the forest that maximizes total profits in the industry (ignoring externalities)? How much *total* resource rent is generated at this level of harvest?

b. With open access to the forest, how many folks will wind up logging? With open access, will there be *any* resource rent earned by the loggers?

c. Which of the following are externalities associated with logging?
    _____ Loss of genetic material for medical or agricultural applications
    _____ Low wages for forestry workers

—— Release of carbon dioxide stored in the "carbon sink" of the forest
—— Building of roads by the companies to access timber

d. Suppose the total externalities associated with deforestation could be valued at $10,000 per operation. What is the efficient number of operators? What is the open access number of operators?

e. Suppose access to the forest is controlled by a (perfectly enforced) fee system. What (weekly) fee would have to be charged to ensure an efficient harvest level?

APPLICATION 3.2

Open Access and Paper Production

Surrounding the Great Lake are four paper mills, each producing 100 tons of paper per year. The paper is sold on the national market for $2 per ton, and including all the costs of production, costs for each firm are $1 per ton. Thus each firm earns a pure economic profit of $1 per ton. These paper mills require freshwater to operate and also produce a pollutant called gunk, which the mills dump into the Great Lake.

New paper mills can also locate on the Great Lake and produce at a base cost of $1 per ton. However, for each new paper mill that arrives, the water will become more polluted with gunk, and each firm will have to install a water treatment facility to obtain freshwater. This externality associated with new plants will raise the costs of paper production at all facilities, including the new one, by $0.15 per ton for each new mill.

a. Assume there is open access to the Great Lake. If paper mills will continue to locate as long as there is any economic profit to be earned, how many new mills will be built? How many mills maximize total combined profits for the paper producers? (Hint: Average revenue remains constant at $2. Create a table that compares average revenues with average and marginal costs as new firms locate around the lake.)

b. Draw a diagram of the marginal cost and marginal revenue curves with the number of mills on the horizontal axis. Assume that government regulation restricts lake access to the profit-maximizing number of firms. Show the resource rent earned by the mills that are allowed to operate.

c. Suppose that government regulation reduced the number of mills by one from the number that would have resulted given open access. Show that the increase in profits to the remaining firms (the resource rent) is sufficient to compensate the firm denied access for its lost profits.

APPLICATION 3.3

Demand Curves for Public Goods

Adam and Eve live on two sides of the Garden of Eden, a small suburban development. After they move in, an old PCB dump is discovered between their houses. If X total tons of PCBs are removed from the dump, Adam and Eve have a true willingness to pay (WTP) to finance a cleanup as follows:

$$\text{Adam's WTP} = 10 - X$$
$$\text{Eve's WTP } = 6 - X$$

a. Adam's WTP is higher than Eve's. Does this necessarily imply that Eve is less concerned than Adam about exposure to PCBs? Why or why not?

b. Draw one diagram illustrating the two individuals' demand curves for cleanup and the total demand for cleanup in the neighborhood. What is the total WTP for 3 tons of cleanup? For 4 tons?

c. If cleaning up 2 tons were to cost $12, is the WTP in this small community sufficient to finance it? What are the two potential reasons a voluntary cleanup might nevertheless fail?

KEY IDEAS IN EACH SECTION

3.0 **Natural capital** is the input that nature provides for our production and consumption processes. Pollution is the overuse of **sinks**; resource degradation is the overharvesting of **sources**. A **negative externality** is a cost of a transaction not borne by the buyer or seller. **Internalizing an externality** means forcing the source of the externality to bear the external costs imposed on others.

3.1 Negative externalities arise when there is **open access** to **common property** sources and sinks, such as air, water, or land. Traditional societies regulated access to common environmental resources using informal laws and restraints, but many of these have broken down. When access to natural capital is restricted, by either government action or private ownership, a **resource rent** is earned by those who retain access.

3.2 Is government regulation of the environment necessary to solve the open access problem? **Free-market environmentalists** believe that polluters should be left unregulated and victims should sue to ensure environmental quality. However, most economists argue that because a clean environment is a **public good**, the obstacles of high **transactions costs** and **free riding** mean that private negotiation in the courts would be inefficient (and also unsafe and unsustainable). Thus government regulation is needed to internalize environmental externalities.

3.3 **Sustainable businesses** focus on profitably reducing pollution and resource degradation within the structure of existing policies, laws, and regulations. Profits arise from three sources: risk reduction, resource efficiency, and continuous innovation. Beyond the problem of greenwashing, the larger question is how widespread are opportunities to achieve major improvements in environmental quality and earn profits doing so? And regardless, other firms currently still earn profits by externalizing environmental costs.

REFERENCE

Brimelow, Peter, and Leslie Spencer. 1992. You can't get there from here. *Forbes*, 6 July, 59–60.

Bromley, Daniel. 1991. *Environment and economy: Property rights and public policy*. Cambridge, MA: Blackwell.

Gordon, H. 1954. The economic theory of a common property resource: The fishery. *Journal of Political Economy* 62(2): 124–42.

Greve, Michael S., and Fred L. Smith. 1992. *Environmental politics: Public costs, private rewards*. Boulder, CO: Praeger.

Hardin, Garrett. 1968. The tragedy of the commons. *Science* 162(3859): 1243–4.

Helvarg, David. 2003. The last fish. *Earth Island Journal* 18(1): 26–30.

Menell, Peter S. 1991. The limitations of legal institutions for addressing environmental risks. *Journal of Economic Perspectives* 5(3): 93–114.

Muller, Nicholas Z., Robert Mendelsohn, and William Nordhaus. 2011. Environmental accounting for pollution in the United States economy. *American Economic Review* 101(5): 1649–75.

Sturmak, Bud, and Cary Krosinsky. 2011. "*On performance*" *in evolutions in sustainable investing*, ed. Cary Krosinsky. New York: Wiley.

Tregarten, Timothy. 1992. Fishermen find fewer fish. *The Margin* 7 (Spring).

4

THE EFFICIENCY STANDARD

4.0 Introduction

Economists sometimes point out that achieving a goal of zero pollution not only would be prohibitively expensive but, indeed, might well be counterproductive. The view is that we should balance the costs and benefits of pollution reduction and seek, in general, to achieve an efficient amount of pollution. The idea that any level of pollution is "efficient" strikes many people as a bit odd. This chapter thus begins by defining the efficient pollution level; then illustrates how marginal analysis can be used, both in principle and in practice, to identify the efficient pollution level; discusses the utilitarian ethical defense of the efficiency standard; and finally, reviews the challenges to real-world application of benefit-cost analysis.

4.1 Efficiency Defined

To understand what is meant by an efficient level of pollution, we need to look closer at the concept of efficiency. The term *efficient* in everyday parlance means a situation in which no resources are wasted. Economists use the term in a related but more specific way. The economic definition of efficiency was introduced by the Italian economist Vilfred Pareto in 1909 and is named in his honor.

Pareto-efficient situation: A situation in which it is impossible to make one person better off without making anyone else worse off.

When economists say an outcome is efficient, they almost always mean "Pareto efficient." We'll drop the Pareto most of the time as well, adding the modifier only when we want to remind the reader that we are using this specific definition.

The advantage of pursuing efficiency is that, conditional on the existing distribution of income, it makes the "economic pie" as big as possible. In fact, at the efficient outcome, the **net monetary benefits** produced by the economy are maximized. This means that the total of all benefits that can be given a monetary value, both human-made and those generated by nature, minus all costs of production, both private and external, will be as large as possible at the efficient point. How do we know this? By applying the definition of efficiency. If it were possible to make someone better off without making someone else worse off (meaning that we are at an *inefficient* point), we could always make the economic pie of net benefits bigger by moving toward efficiency.

The first point to make about efficiency is that it need not be fair. This is illustrated clearly in Figure 4.1, which shows two economic pies. Pie 2 is more efficient than Pie 1 because it is bigger—it maximizes the benefits to society *as a whole*. Yet Pie 2 is clearly much less fair than Pie 1. Both in absolute and relative terms, B is worse off with Pie 2. Thus, on its own, efficiency may not be useful as a guide to good social outcomes. (One of us recalls first learning about Pareto efficiency in my microeconomics class and asking the teacher if it would be possible to have an efficient slave society. The answer was yes—freeing the slaves might not be "efficient" because, in monetary terms, the masters might lose more than the slaves would gain.)

Yet whenever the economic pie is enlarged, it is *at least possible* for everyone to get a bigger slice in absolute terms. In Figure 4.1, a move from Pie 1 to Pie 2 could in *principle* provide both A and B bigger slices. Thus any move toward efficiency can in theory be a win-win situation. We have already considered one such case: By restricting fishing in New England, the government could generate enough resource rent to both compensate the fishers put out of business and allow the remaining boats to earn a decent living. Let us look at another such case involving the use of California's scarce water resources.

California is a semiarid state with a vast agricultural industry and rapidly growing urban centers. Water is scarce, and an unlikely coalition of corporate farmers and environmentalists have supported moving to an open market in water rights to increase the efficient use of existing supplies.[1] Farmers seek a profit from the sale of their water, while environmentalists are interested in forestalling the construction of ecologically disruptive new dams in the state.

To simplify a complex story, farmland in California comes endowed with rights to a percentage of water from a given reservoir; currently farmers use about 85% of the state's water. The price for agricultural water charged by state and federal governments is much lower than that for metropolitan use: one study puts the state

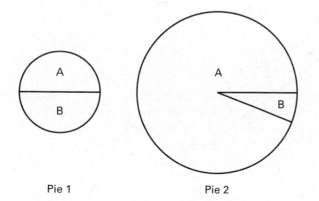

Pie 1   Pie 2

FIGURE 4.1 Pareto Efficiency versus Fairness

1. This analysis is drawn from Gomez-Ibanez and Kalt (1990). For current policy initiatives, see www.calfed.ca.gov.

price at $10 per acre-foot, while the urban price was $100 per acre-foot. This low price for agricultural water has resulted in such clearly inefficient but profitable uses as growing irrigated hay in Death Valley. This practice is inefficient because it shrinks the size of California's economic pie. The water could be used to produce output in other sectors of the economy with a higher monetary value—other less water-intensive crops, industrial products, or perhaps even green lawns (which raise the value of homes) in metropolitan areas. One study estimated that California's gross domestic product was about $5 billion lower than it would have been had water been allocated efficiently.[2]

We can analyze the situation by assuming the existence of two markets for water in California: agricultural and metropolitan, with no transfer in between. This situation is illustrated in Figure 4.2A. The state could move toward efficiency by combining the markets into one, as illustrated in Figure 4.2B, thus generating a single price of around $70.

One way to achieve this goal would be for the government bodies selling the water simply to raise the price to its market level, in this example, $70. One statewide initiative calling for a similar approach was defeated, not surprisingly, with heavy opposition from farm interests. Such an effort would clearly be efficient as the water not bought by farmers would be freed up for metropolitan use. However, it was thought to be unfair in the way it penalized farmers by changing the rules of the game midstream.

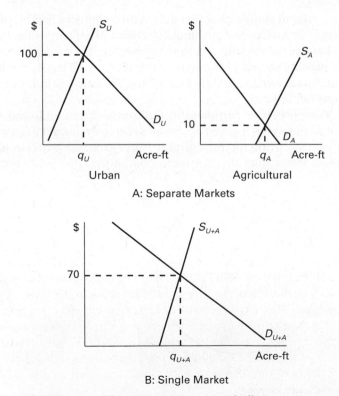

FIGURE 4.2 California Water Pricing and Efficiency

2. Cited in Gomez-Ibanez and Kalt (1990).

Yet, as is always the case when moving toward efficiency, a **Pareto-improving** alternative policy exists—one that actually does make everyone better off. In California, farmers could continue to purchase their old allotments at $10 but be allowed to resell them without restriction to the urban sector. In this case, the Death Valley farmer could continue to grow his/her hay but, by doing so, would be passing up substantial profit opportunities. By simply reselling his/her water, he/she could make $90 per acre-foot! Under this policy, farmers would gradually abandon inefficient farming practices and become "water tycoons." Reforms of this nature are now being sought in California.[3]

Either policy—a single price or subsidized prices with water marketing—would put a lot of farmers out of the farming business, and the California economy would shift toward greater production in the industrial and service sectors. Overall, economists would predict that the monetary value of California production would rise as water flowed into higher value uses. Thus *both policies are efficient*, though the first one is unfair in many ways. (It is worth noting that both policies would also encourage urban growth in California; many people consider such growth a problem in itself. Are green lawns in the suburban desert really an "efficient" use of water—that is, one that makes people happier overall? We take a closer look at the complex relationship between growth and social welfare later, in Chapter 11.)

One reason that economists like efficient outcomes is that, as in the California case, when moving from an inefficient outcome to an efficient outcome, it is at least possible to achieve a Pareto improvement that makes everyone better off without making anyone else worse off. This means that equity need not, in theory, be sacrificed when moving from a less to a more efficient outcome. More often, however, *there are almost always winners and losers* from any change in economic policy, even those that increase economic efficiency. As long as the gains to the winners are bigger than the losses to the losers, a move will be efficient. Keep in mind then, that efficiency and fairness are different notions. Efficient outcomes need not be equitable (or moral or fair), though they may be. At the same time, equitable outcomes need not be efficient, though they may be.

4.2 Efficient Pollution Levels

You may recall that we are supposed to be discussing the "right" amount of pollution. How does efficiency fit in here? Let's take the simplest example of pollution one can think of by following two workers, Brittany and Tyler, into their office in the morning.

They sit down at their desks, and Tyler pulls out a pack of smokes and lights up. Brittany hates cigarettes, but there's no rule against smoking in the office. Tyler's been smoking about five a day. Brittany is pretty desperate, so she considers a bribe. "How much would I have to pay you to smoke one less cigarette per day?" Tyler thinks it over. "One cigarette? I can put up with that for four dollars," he says. "Two per day?" she inquires. "That'll be tougher. You'd have to pay me six more dollars for that one." The third cigarette, it turns out, could be eliminated for a bribe of an additional $8. They keep at it, eventually developing Table 4.1.

---

3. This is the Hicks-Kaldor test for efficiency; for it to unambiguously improve welfare, the marginal utility of consumption must be equal across all parties. See Note 10.

TABLE 4.1 Marginal and Total Costs of Cleanup

Number of Cigarettes Reduced	Additional Payment Required per Reduced Cigarette	Total Payment Required
1	$ 4.00	$ 4.00
2	$ 6.00	$10.00
3	$ 8.00	$18.00
4	$10.00	$28.00
5	$12.00	$40.00

The table reveals that, due to his addiction, Tyler is increasingly reluctant to give up each additional cigarette. Indeed, even after receiving a total of $28 for the first four, he would have to receive *an additional $12* to quit smoking altogether.

Brittany has her own notion of the benefits of pollution reduction in the office. Getting rid of the first cigarette is essential to making the environment tolerable: she'd be willing to pay $10 to do so. Eliminating the next cigarette would make a big improvement but is not absolutely necessary. It's worth $8. Her private benefit schedule for cigarette reduction is illustrated in Table 4.2.

The benefits of additional pollution reduction decline for Brittany as the number of cigarettes smoked falls, because the health damage and discomfort she experiences also decline. Thus she's willing to pay only $2 to get rid of the last cigarette, perhaps because she can take her daily coffee break (choose your poison) when Tyler chooses to light that one up.

Note that we're focusing on reducing cigarettes (units of pollution) one at a time. Economists call this **marginal analysis**. The last unit of pollution reduced is called the **marginal unit**; the costs (to Tyler) of reducing that unit are called the **marginal costs**, and the benefits (to Brittany) from reducing that unit are called the **marginal benefits**. Comparison of marginal costs with marginal benefits will help us zero in on the efficient level of pollution.

To help us determine the efficient level of cigarette reduction, Figure 4.3 graphs the marginal costs and benefits of giving up cigarettes. On the horizontal axis we have the number of cigarettes reduced per day; on the vertical axis, dollars. Because marginals represent *changes* in total values as we move from one unit to the next, it is conventional to graph marginal values between the units on the X axis. For example, the marginal cost of the fourth cigarette reduced is $10. Because this is the change in

TABLE 4.2 Marginal and Total Benefits of Cleanup

Number of Cigarettes Reduced	Additional Willingness to Pay per Cigarette Reduced	Total Willingness to Pay
1	$10.00	$10.00
2	$ 8.00	$18.00
3	$ 6.00	$24.00
4	$ 4.00	$28.00
5	$ 2.00	$30.00

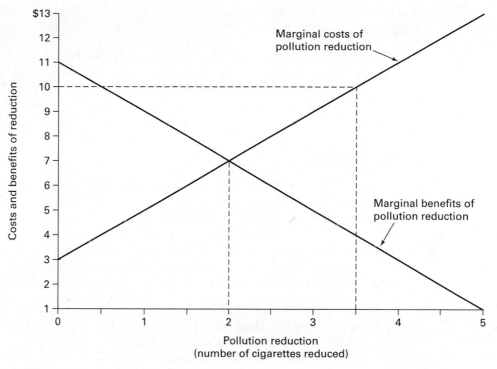

FIGURE 4.3 Marginal Costs and Benefits of Cleanup

total cost as we move from three to four cigarettes reduced, you will notice that the $10 value is graphed halfway between 3 and 4.

The curve labeled "Marginal costs of pollution reduction" illustrates the cost to Tyler of giving up additional cigarettes. It slopes upward, reflecting that the first cigarette smoked can be given up at low cost by Tyler, although he would have to be mightily bribed to give up smoking altogether. The curve labeled "Marginal benefits of pollution reduction" reflects the value to Brittany of a progressively less smoky environment. It slopes downward because the health risk and discomfort from breathing secondary smoke decreases as the number of cigarettes is decreased.

You can probably guess where the efficient level of pollution reduction is going to be. (*X* marks the spot.) Indeed, two cigarettes reduced is the efficient number. Why? Because *at any other level of pollution, both parties can be made better off by trading.* To see this, consider the following:

PUZZLE

Tyler, who loves to smoke, would puff his way through five cigarettes a day if he were in the office by himself. Tyler is a selfish individual and he has the right to smoke as much as he wants. Would he continue smoking five cigarettes if Brittany were around?

SOLUTION

The answer is no. Tyler is willing to give up one cigarette for $4, and Brittany is willing to pay him $10 to do so. Thus he can make up to $6 in "profit" by accepting the initial bribe. Similarly, Tyler will accept $6 for the next cigarette, and Brittany would pay up to $8 to get him not to smoke it. Thus he can earn an additional profit of up to $2 by reducing the second cigarette. Finally, Brittany would pay Tyler only $6 to reduce the third cigarette, and that would be less than the $8 necessary to get him to give it up. Thus Brittany will pay Tyler to eliminate two cigarettes, and *both* will be better off than if Tyler smoked all five.

Clearly Tyler would not give up the second-to-last cigarette: Brittany would have to pay Tyler $10 to get him to give it up, and it is worth only $4 to her in increased comfort and safety. Only for those cigarettes where the marginal cost curve (Tyler's required compensation for reducing pollution) lies below the marginal benefit curve (Brittany's willingness to pay for pollution reduction) will Tyler be better off by striking a deal with Brittany than by smoking.

This example is worth close study (or, as we tell our students, this one will be on the test). To make sure you follow it, take a minute to explain to yourself why it is that, *at any level of pollution other than three cigarettes smoked (or two reduced), both parties can be made better off through a trade*. Three cigarettes smoked is the efficient level of pollution, because only at three cigarettes is it impossible to make one party better off without making the other worse off.

Here is an outcome that, while efficient, would strike many people as being unfair. Why should Brittany have to pay Tyler not to slowly poison her? This question is, as we will see, crucial in the discussion of a safety pollution standard. But efficiency defenders respond that the issue of whether polluters have a right to pollute or victims have a right to prevent pollution should not necessarily be settled in the victim's favor. While agreeing that fairness is an important issue, they feel ultimately that it is a matter of value judgment and thus lies outside the realm of economics.[4] But as we will see, the efficiency standard, in fact, has its own basis in "value judgments."

A more consistent defense of the efficiency standard is that, because efficient outcomes maximize the monetary size of the total pie, consistently pursuing efficient outcomes does, on balance, benefit most people over time. While Brittany might lose out from this level of cigarette pollution, she will benefit from efficient regulation elsewhere. For example, she may get lower priced strawberries if pesticide use is regulated at an efficient and safe, as opposed to a more stringent and costly, level.

In this section, we have employed marginal analysis to identify the efficient pollution level—where the marginal benefits and costs of pollution reduction are equal. At any other level of pollution, it is *possible* to make all parties better off

---

4. In textbook neoclassical theory, of course, equity and efficiency are the two normative criteria that should drive policy. However, in practice, some environmental economists look only at efficiency. See Bromley (1990) for a discussion.

by moving toward efficiency. This section has also illustrated that efficient outcomes need not accord with standard notions of fairness. We now move on to consider the relationship between a marginal analysis of pollution reduction and one based on total costs and benefits.

4.3 Marginals and Totals

As noted, focusing on marginal costs and marginal benefits allowed us to isolate the efficient pollution level. This section digresses for a moment to illustrate the relationship between marginal and total cleanup costs and the marginal and total benefits of cleanup. The bottom panel of Figure 4.4 reproduces the marginal relationships in Figure 4.3 while the top panel graphs the total costs of cleanup (to Tyler) and the total benefits (to Brittany).

Both sets of curves illustrate the same information. The *total* costs of pollution reduction rise at an increasing rate, generating a curve that is bowed upward; another way of saying this is that the additional or *marginal* cost of each cigarette given up rises. Similarly, the *total* benefits of cleanup rise at a decreasing rate, producing a downward-bowed curve; thus, the *marginal* benefits of pollution reduction are falling.

How can we move from one set of curves to another? The marginal cost curve represents the change in total costs. Thus, as the figure illustrates, the marginal cost of the first cigarette reduced, $4, is just the change in the total cost curve between 0 and 1 cigarette reduced. Similarly, the marginal benefit of the fifth cigarette reduced, $2, is the change in the total benefits curve between four and five cigarettes reduced. The marginal curves graph the total change in y for a one-unit change in x. But this is just the "rise" over the "run" of the total curve. Thus the marginal curves graph the slopes of the total curves.[5]

Moreover, the area *under* the marginal cost curve equals the total cost. For example, the marginal cost of the first cigarette reduced, $4, plus the marginal cost of the second, $6, equals the total costs of two cigarettes reduced, $10. But $4 is just the area under the marginal curve between 0 and 1, while $6 is the area under the curve between 1 and 2. We use this relationship often in the chapters ahead.

Finally, note that *the efficient pollution level does not occur where total costs equal total benefits* (at four cigarettes reduced). At this point, because total benefits and costs are equal, the net monetary benefits to "society" are zero. Instead, the efficient level occurs where the total benefit curve lies farthest above the total cost curve. Here, the net monetary benefits to Brittany and Tyler combined are maximized. At the point where total benefits and costs are equal, we know we have reduced pollution "too much" under an efficiency standard. At this point, the *marginal* costs of reduction exceed the *marginal* benefits, given the conventional shapes of the benefit and cost curves.[6]

To summarize, the relationship between the marginal and total benefit and cost curves is a straightforward one. The marginal curves graph the change in the total curves or, equivalently, their slope. The upward slope of the marginal cost of reduction curve thus reflects total pollution control costs, which rise at an increasing rate. Similarly, the downward slope of the marginal benefit of reduction curve results from an assumption

---

5. For those students with a calculus background, the marginal curve graphs the derivative of the total curve.
6. In important cases, the curves may not be shaped this way. See Application 4.2 at the end of this chapter.

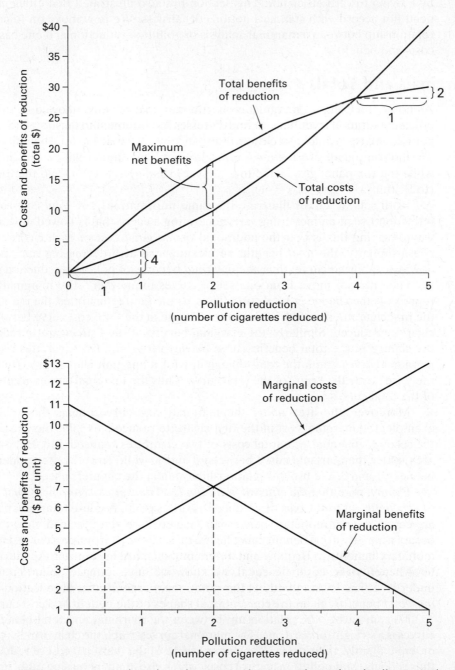

FIGURE 4.4 Marginals and Totals Compared: Costs and Benefits of Pollution Reduction

that the total benefits of reducing pollution increase at a decreasing rate. Controlling pollution to a level at which the total benefits of reduction equal the total costs results in too much control from an efficiency perspective.

4.4 The Coase Theorem Introduced

One interesting aspect of the efficiency perspective is that, under certain circumstances, whichever way initial rights over pollution are granted, the efficient level of pollution doesn't change! To see this, think for a minute about a situation in which Brittany is granted the right to ban smoking in the office. Will she do so?

Upon referring to Figure 4.3, we can see that the answer is no. If Tyler were willing to give up his last cigarette for $12, he would enjoy smoking that cigarette more than, say, $11.99 in cash. Thus he should be *willing to pay up to that amount* to be able to smoke it! Brittany, on the other hand, is now in the position of taking bribes, and her marginal benefit curve indicates she would rather have $2 than a smoke-free environment. So the two can strike a deal on the first cigarette. Similarly, because Tyler values the second at up to $10, and Brittany will sell him a "smoking right" for anything over $4, there is room to deal. Finally, Tyler would pay $8 for the third cigarette, and Brittany would accept (though she would be making only $2 in profit, it is still profit!). Notice that they would not go on to four cigarettes though, because Tyler would pay only $6 for it, and Brittany would demand $8.

We have just shown that, for a simple case of pollution reduction uncomplicated by transactions costs and free riding (discussed in the last chapter), the efficient outcome is independent of whether pollution is legal. If polluter and victim can bargain easily and effectively, private negotiation should arrive at the efficient outcome regardless of who has the initial right to pollute or prevent pollution. This result is known as the **Coase theorem**, after the Nobel Prize–winning economist Ronald Coase.[7]

Some have interpreted the Coase theorem to imply that from an efficiency perspective it does not matter who has to pay for pollution—victims or polluters. Either way, one arrives at an efficient solution. (Of course, on fairness grounds most would argue that polluters should generally have to pay for damages.) However, as Coase himself recognized, the theorem holds only under highly limited circumstances.

In fact, efficiency is generally better served under a **polluter-pays principle**. This is true for two reasons. The first of these is the public good inherent in pollution cleanup, as discussed in the last chapter. In real-world settings, a single polluter typically affects a broad community. Requiring polluters to pay for the privilege of polluting is more likely to generate an efficient outcome than does a policy that legalizes pollution and requires victims to pay polluters to reduce emissions. Having the polluter pay reduces the free riding and transactions costs associated with the latter policy.

More importantly, the assignment of liability has significant long-run effects. If Brittany paid Tyler not to smoke, she would very likely soon find all the smokers in the office moving their desk close to hers! More generally, if firms are given the right to pollute (or are subsidized to reduce pollution), their costs will be lower. In the long run, this practice encourages entry into the market and creates more pollution.[8]

---

7. See Coase (1960).
8. See Mohring and Boyd (1971).

For example, when taxpayers at large pay for the construction of landfills, households and firms have little long-run incentive to minimize their production of garbage. On the other hand, if landfill construction costs are financed by "pay by the bag" disposal fees, waste producers have an incentive to modify their long-run waste production strategies.

As we will see later, the Coase theorem is quite useful when analyzing the initial distribution of permits in a marketable permit system. For now, though, this example illustrates clearly the claim not only that zero pollution levels are expensive (poor Tyler suffers severe nicotine withdrawals) but also that a solution more efficient than banning exists in which all parties are made better off.

To review this section, the Coase theorem demonstrates that in the absence of transactions costs and free riding, the efficient pollution control level can be achieved through negotiation regardless of who has the legal right to pollute or prevent pollution. In the real world, however, efficiency is generally best served by following a polluter-pays principle. This is true both because of transactions costs and free riding, and because long-run incentives for entry into the polluting industry are reduced when the polluter pays.

4.5 Air Pollution Control in Baltimore: Calculating the Efficient Standard

To give you a feel for how the efficiency standard might be applied in practice, let us look at a study that estimated the marginal benefits and marginal costs of reducing suspended particulate emissions in Baltimore under the current type of regulation.[9] Suspended particulates are small particles of ash or soot emitted as a by-product of burning fossil fuels for power or transport. They contribute to respiratory ailments, some of which are fatal; they also soil clothing and buildings and reduce visibility. Figure 4.5 graphs the estimated marginal costs and benefits of different total suspended particulate (TSP) standards.

The marginal cost curve has the same shape as that in Figure 4.3; reducing particulate emissions becomes increasingly costly. To move from a standard of 110 to 109 parts per million (ppm) would cost about $3 million, while tightening the standard from 95 to 94 ppm would cost an additional $16 million. This is because under the regulations in Baltimore, source types with relatively low costs of reduction must trim their emissions first. To meet tougher standards, facilities facing higher control costs must also reduce emissions.

The marginal benefit curve, on the other hand, is relatively flat. Unlike the cigarette case, the additional benefits of reduction do not decrease as the pollution level falls. Instead, the authors of the study assume that tightening the standard from 110 to 109 ppm yields roughly the same benefits—reduced death, sickness, and soiling and improved visibility—as moving from a standard of 100 to 99 ppm. They estimate these benefits to be around $10 million for each one-unit decrease in the particulate standard.

To arrive at this monetary figure for benefits, the authors value each life saved at $2 million, each lost workday at $100, and each restricted activity day at $25. Monetary benefits were also estimated for soiling and visibility. Chapter 6 discusses the means by

---

9. See Oates, Portney, and McGartland (1989).

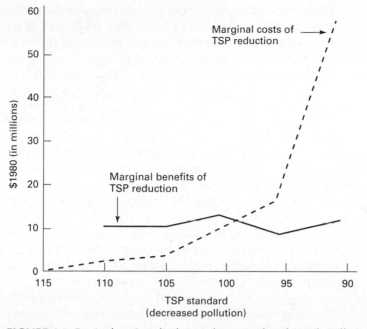

FIGURE 4.5 Particulate Standards in Baltimore: Identifying the Efficient Pollution Level
Note: For ease of presentation, the marginal benefit curve is not shown in full.
Source: Wallace E. Oates, Paul R. Portney, and Albert M. McGartland, "The Net Benefits of Incentive-Based Regulation: A Case Study of Environmental Standard Setting," *American Economic Review* 79, no. 5 (1989): 1233–42, fig. 2. Reprinted by permission.

which environmental economists attempt to estimate dollar values for these "priceless" elements of our lives. But to preview briefly, as suggested by the smoking example, economists generally measure the benefits of pollution reduction based on society's willingness to pay for that reduction. The benefits of less smoke in the office were measured precisely by Brittany's willingness to pay for fewer cigarettes. Although this willingness-to-pay approach has problems we will explore in detail later, it captures the basic idea of trade-offs between a cleaner environment and all other goods.

The efficient standard occurs at about 98 ppm. With a looser particulate standard, the additional benefits from reducing pollution up to 98 ppm would be greater than the additional costs. However, moving to a standard tighter than 98 ppm would entail additional costs exceeding the additional value of the benefits. Thus net monetary benefits—the estimated value of clean air enjoyed by citizens of Baltimore minus the cleanup costs borne by Baltimore firms (and ultimately, to some extent, Baltimore consumers)—are maximized at the efficient standard.

4.6 The Ethical Basis of the Efficiency Standard

Let us look one last time at the cigarette example and use our utility and social welfare functions to clearly focus on the ethical assumptions underlying the efficiency standard. First, there are no "equity" weightings: Tyler and Brittany's utilities count equally in overall social welfare. Second, no distinction is made between the utilities of pollution victims and beneficiaries—Tyler's need for cigarettes holds just as much weight as Brittany's need for clean air. Together these conditions imply that the social welfare function underlying the efficiency standard looks like this:

$$\text{SW} = U_{Tyler}(\overset{+}{\#Cigs_T}, \overset{+}{\$_T}) + U_{Brit}(\overset{-}{\#Cigs_T}, \overset{+}{\$_B})$$

Note the negative sign over Tyler's cigarette consumption in Brittany's utility function. Cigarettes are a "bad," not a "good," for her and so lower her utility. The social welfare function clearly illustrates the value judgments underlying the efficiency standard. By treating victims and beneficiaries equally, efficiency proponents do not acknowledge a "right" to protection from harmful pollutants.

Recall that, as we have stressed, the efficiency standard does not require that losers be compensated, even though this is possible. Suppose that company policy originally banned smoking in the office, but the office manager then decreed Tyler could smoke three cigarettes a day and offered Brittany no compensation in return. *This is still an efficient outcome* because in dollar terms, the gain to Tyler is greater than the loss to Brittany.

It is worth stressing this point because many textbooks refer to the efficient standard as "optimal" or "socially optimal." But unless, as economists, we are prepared to make judgments about who should win and who should lose in our society, efficient pollution control outcomes are not optimal for society. Rather, they simply balance the costs and benefits of pollution reduction at a level where net *monetary* benefits are maximized.[10]

Because a move to efficiency almost always creates losers as well as winners, such a move is not "socially optimal." Rather, the best defense of efficiency is that over time *most people* (*not* just polluters) eventually reap net benefits from a move toward more efficient pollution standards. In concrete terms, most of us are *both* consumers of goods whose prices are raised by environmental regulation and beneficiaries of cleaner air and water. Efficient regulation, according to its proponents, is the best way to balance these two concerns.

4.7 Real-World Benefit-Cost

To this point, this chapter has looked at the efficiency standard, and benefit-cost analysis, in theory. In the real world, benefit-cost studies currently play an important, but not dominant, role in U.S. environmental regulation. Air, water, and hazardous waste are primarily regulated under a safety standard, and cost considerations play

---

10. If overall happiness or social welfare is somehow maximized by such a policy, it must be the case that *additions to income must generate equal increases in happiness for the two people*, or in economists' terms, the two must have the same **marginal utility of income**. This, in turn, would imply that because the dollar gain to Tyler exceeds the dollar loss to Brittany, the happiness gain to Tyler also exceeds the happiness loss to Brittany. Thus there is an overall gain in total happiness by a move toward efficiency, regardless of whether Brittany is compensated. For the efficiency standard to maximize social welfare, the assumption of equal marginal utilities of income must be true in general: a dollar must yield equal happiness to a millionaire or to a street person. However, this is highly unlikely. Thus we must conclude that, *on its own terms*, the ethical basis of the efficiency standard is a bit murky. This point is made in Kneese and Schulze (1985). Bromley (1990) also discusses the normative basis of the efficiency standard.

a relatively minor role. For example, the Clean Air Act requires air standards that protect human health, while the Clean Water Act sets as its final goal zero discharge into navigable waters, and an intermediate target of "fishable and swimmable waters." In neither case are compliance costs mentioned.

And so, for example, in 1997, the EPA passed a regulation to tighten smog standards for which its own estimated costs ($600 million to $2.5 billion) exceeded the measurable benefits ($100 million to $1.5 billion). Why did it do so? It did so for reasons of safety. Despite the negative benefit-cost picture, the regulations were expected to save lives and allow more people to exercise safely outside.[11] In fact, the courts have ruled that the air and water protection statutes, along with national hazardous waste legislation, explicitly prohibit benefit-cost tests for new regulations. On the other hand, pesticides, insecticides, and other toxic substances are regulated under an efficiency standard. Chemicals and pesticides cannot be banned unless the benefits of doing so are (roughly) shown to exceed the costs.

However, even for the safety statutes, the EPA is required to conduct formal benefit-cost analyses of any new regulation expected to cost more than $100 million. These benefit-cost studies, known as **regulatory impact analyses (RIAs)**, are prepared for new safety standard regulations, such as the ozone tightening done in 1997, even though their results cannot legally determine the regulatory decision. Why do them then? Under a safety standard, the agency is still directed to select "the regulatory alternative maximizing net benefits from those alternatives within the scope of the law." In our terminology, the EPA is supposed to examine several different options and, among all the options that achieve a safety goal, pick the most efficient.[12]

The major distinction between benefit-cost in theory, and in practice, is the presence, sometimes overwhelming, of uncertainty in the estimation of costs and benefits. As we will see in the next two chapters, it can be quite difficult to put a dollar value on the benefits and costs of a proposed environmental policy. In fact, rather than Figure 4.6, a realistic MC-MB diagram might look like Figure 4.7. Here the MC of pollution reduction lie in the range between the two thick lines, and MB within the range between the two thin lines. This generates a wide band of potentially efficient outcomes instead of a single point. This presence of significant uncertainty, in turn, creates the potential for political influence in the benefit-cost process, as no particular outcome can be labeled "efficient."

Given that conservatives often push hardest for the use of benefit-cost tests, many environmentalists view benefit-cost analysis as merely a political tool for rolling back environmental gains, in part by burying the regulatory process under a mound of paperwork. And at its worst, benefit-cost analysis is indeed used as an excuse to gloss over hard moral choices and provide a rubber stamp for preconceived notions about the right course of action.

However, at its best, a benefit-cost study clarifies the decision-making process. A **good benefit-cost** study follows accepted procedures for estimating benefits and costs, provides a clear statement of all assumptions, points out uncertainties where they exist,

---

11. From "Clintonites Debate" (1997).
12. For an extensive evaluation, see Harrington et al. (2009). The quote from the executive order is cited in Fraas (1984).

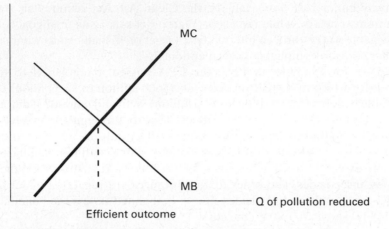

FIGURE 4.6 Efficient Outcome with Certain Costs and Benefits

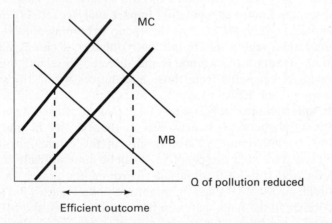

FIGURE 4.7 Efficient Outcomes with Uncertain Costs and Benefits

and suggests realistic margins of error. Good benefit-cost contrasts with bad benefit-cost (those studies that violate these basic requirements). The latter are commonly sighted in offices in Washington, DC, and in state capitals. Partisan think tanks often hire researchers to generate benefit-cost analyses in support of their favored policies. Like most tools, the benefit-cost methodology can be used for good or for evil.

One advantage of benefit-cost analysis, according to its advocates, is that it substantially reduces political influence in the policy arena. A naive claim in its favor is that benefit-cost analysis "allows the numbers to speak for themselves." In reality, if one tortures the numbers sufficiently, they will often confess to the analyst's viewpoint. The real advantage of benefit-cost analysis is that it places limits on the type of data torturing that can go on. For example, an economist may set out to prove that more stringent regulations of landfills are desirable on efficiency grounds. Within admittedly broad limits, however, his/her benefit and cost estimates are constrained by the methodology we will outline in the next two chapters. It may well be that the numbers simply cannot credibly support his/her case.

How elastic are the bounds within which good benefit-cost studies must stay? This section explores three ways in which political influence affects the benefit-cost process: the hard numbers problem, agenda control, and paralysis by analysis.

Benefit-cost studies can often provide decision makers with a false sense of precision. This is known as the **hard numbers illusion**. The apparently "hard" numbers in a summary table for a benefit-cost study are often quite soft when uncertainty and incomplete benefit coverage are factored in. Yet decision makers are often not interested in "uncertainty" and incompleteness; they want an answer, and often one that supports their particular political agenda.

Political influence also shows up subtly in its impact on natural and social scientific debates. Corporate interests have used their resources in trying to **control the scientific agenda** by funding conferences and targeting research in certain areas. For example, the American Paper Institute and the Chlorine Institute have aggressively funded and promoted research downplaying the health effects of dioxin, a chemical used in these industries. The difference between the perspectives of industry, government, and academic scientists is reflected in a poll showing that 80% of the first group, 63% of the second group, and only 40% of the last group believed that a threshold existed below which exposure to cancer-causing agents was risk-free.[13] Even academic scientists, however, must often obtain research funding from industry.

Finally, when an efficiency test is enshrined as law, opponents of regulation can resort to the legal system and exploit the uncertainty in the process to delay or block the implementation of regulations. This is known as **paralysis by analysis**. One major environmental statute that requires regulations to pass an efficiency test is the Toxic Substances Control Act (TSCA).

Under TSCA the EPA tried for over ten years to phase out the remaining uses of asbestos, a mineral product well known to cause lung cancer. The two big users left were in cement pipe and automobile brakes. In the early 1990s, an appeals court rejected the EPA's proposed phaseout of these products on several grounds. Although the EPA had in hand what it thought was a good benefit-cost study showing a substantial surplus of benefits over costs, the court ruled that the EPA (1) had not adequately considered less-costly alternatives, (2) had not adequately evaluated the environmental dangers of substitute products (non-asbestos brakes and piping), and (3) had not followed proper procedures for public comment on the dangers of asbestos.

Without dwelling on the merits of the case, it should be evident that trying to "prove" in a court of law that any regulatory decision not only has positive net benefits (benefits greater than costs) but also is the *most* efficient option (maximum net benefits) is a virtual impossibility. As a result of this decision, some have concluded that the provision for banning existing substances under TSCA is essentially unworkable.[14]

Clearly, benefit-cost analysis cannot pinpoint the efficient pollution level with the accuracy suggested by diagrams like Figure 4.6. And given the uncertainties, politics influences the benefit-cost process, just as it would any alternative decision-making tool. A recent report harshly critical of benefit-cost analysis concluded: "Cost-benefit analysis cannot overcome its fatal flaw: it is completely reliant on the impossible attempt to price the priceless values of life, health, nature and the future ... Cost-benefit analysis

---

13. See Ackerman (2008) and Greider (1992).
14. Revesz and Livermore (2008, 97).

has not enriched the public dialogue; it has impoverished it, covering the topic with poorly understood numbers rather than clarifying the underlying clashes of values."[15]

Despite this, however, benefit-cost analysis methodology does provide a "consensus" framework for helping to judge the balance between measurable benefits and costs. There is such a thing as good benefit-cost. However, the only way to make sure that the good benefit-cost is carried out is to assure adequate review of the study and opportunities for appeal by the affected parties. Given the technical nature of benefit-cost methodology, some have suggested that the government provide funds to community groups and others who seek to challenge government studies. And legal standards that mandate efficiency are a poor idea on their own terms. Benefit-cost is just not capable of identifying efficient outcomes with a precision that can stand up in court.

4.8 Summary

The efficiency approach puts the question of "how much pollution?" in a marginal cost, marginal benefit framework. In principle, we can replace "cigarettes reduced" with "pollution cleanup" in Figure 4.3, and the diagram will show us the efficient amount of global-warming pollution, nitrous oxide, sulfur dioxide, CFCs, dioxin, DDT, waste oil, particulates, heavy metals, litter, nuclear waste, or PCBs that "should" be in the environment. Of course, to make this approach operational, one needs to estimate a *dollar figure* for both the costs and benefits of reducing each unit of pollution. The benefit figure will include quantifiable savings such as those on medical care. But, as in the Baltimore case, it also must take into account less easily calculable benefits such as human lives saved and cancers avoided.

But why should any pollutant be in the environment? Society is willing to suffer pollution because it is an essential by-product of some good or service that people desire and because cleanup is not free. In Figure 4.8, the "supply curve" for pollution cleanup is just the marginal cost of reduction curve; it shows the increasing cost to society of eliminating additional units of pollution. This cost will be determined by the technology available for controlling the pollutant. The curve, for example, would shift down (toward the *x*-axis) if cheaper ways of reducing pollution were discovered.

Society, on the other hand, clearly has a demand for pollution reduction. The "demand curve" for cleanup is the marginal benefits of reduction curve; it illustrates the increasing damages inflicted on people or the environment as the amount of cleanup decreases. The location of the curve depends on a variety of factors, such as the number of organisms (including people) affected, weather conditions, and defensive measures taken by those affected. In the Baltimore case, for example, the curve would shift up (away from the *x*-axis) if more people moved into the city.

The efficient quantity of pollution from the production of a desired product will occur just at the point where the additional costs of reduction are equal to the additional benefits of reduction. Any more reduction, and the additional monetary costs borne by members of society exceed the additional monetary benefits; any less, and net social monetary benefits can be gained.

As our discussion of the open access and public good problems in the last chapter made clear, economists do not think that free markets generate the efficient amount of pollution. In the cigarette example, we saw that self-interested private parties, through

---

15. From Heinzerling and Ackerman (2002; 20, 33).

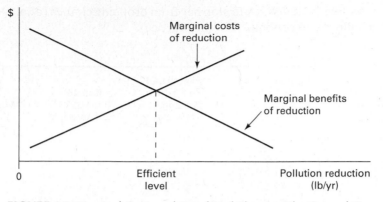

FIGURE 4.8 Marginal Costs and Benefits of Cleanup: The General Case

their own negotiation, might arrive at the efficient level of pollution. But this was a rather special example, featuring perfect information about costs and damages, clearly defined property rights, zero transactions costs, and no free riding. In the real world, "markets for pollution" seldom develop naturally, and a more likely outcome in an actual office would be an inefficient one. In the 1970s the open access outcome would have meant complete pollution—five cigarettes per day; a safety-based regulation banning smoking completely is likely these days.

This chapter has employed the notion of marginal costs and marginal benefits associated with pollution reduction to illustrate how one might identify an efficient level of pollution. We have also seen that a move to more efficient pollution control almost always generates winners and losers, and because the losers are seldom compensated, such a move cannot be considered socially optimal. The best ethical defense of efficiency is thus that, because it maximizes the size of the measurable economic pie, over time "most" people will benefit from more efficient pollution control. Finally, in the real world, benefit-cost tests are not a primary driver behind most U.S. environmental regulations, which tend to be safety based. When benefit-cost is used as a basis for action, however, the primary challenge for economists is to provide sufficiently certain estimates of benefits and costs for practical guidance. When uncertainty looms large, and the efficient outcome is not clear, then benefit-cost analysis can become a politicized tool via mechanisms such as hard numbers illusion, agenda control, and paralysis by analysis. In the next two chapters, we explore the methods that economists in fact use to estimate the benefits and costs of environmental and resource protection, with more or less precision.

APPLICATION 4.0

Ronald and His Daughter

The living room floor at Ronald Coase's house is common property. His daughter, Joan, really likes to drop clothing items on the living room floor; Ronald hates this form of littering. If Joan is left to do as she wishes, she will drop ten items of clothing per week. The following table indicates Ronald's total willingness to pay (WTP) to stop this littering—or, alternatively, his willingness to accept (WTA) continued littering.

It also shows Joan's total WTA to stop her from dropping clothes (or alternatively, her WTP to be allowed to continue with the practice).

Clothes Dropping Reduced (items/week)	Ronald's Total WTP for Cleanup ($/week)	Joan's Total WTA for Cleanup ($/week)	Ronald's Marginal WTP ($/item/week)	Joan's Marginal WTA ($/item/week)
0	$0.00	$0.00	—	—
1	$1.00	$0.02		
2	$1.80	$0.08		
3	$2.50	$0.15		
4	$3.00	$0.25		
5	$3.40	$0.40		
6	$3.70	$0.70		
7	$3.90	$1.10		
8	$4.00	$1.60		
9	$4.05	$2.20		
10	$4.07	$2.90		

a. Fill in the marginal columns, and identify the efficient cleanup level. At the efficient cleanup level, what are the net benefits to the family? What are the net benefits to the family if the floor is completely clean?

b. Graph the marginal costs and marginal benefits of cleanup.

c. Suppose that Joan initially has the right to dump as many clothes as she likes (and dad has to pick up—as is the case for a small child). If there are no transactions costs associated with bargaining between dad and child, what would Coase predict to be the outcome, and how, specifically, would we get there? (Hint: It has to do with bribery.)

d. As Joan grows up, dad decides to flip the property rights. Joan no longer has the right to dump her clothes in the living room. Ronald has the authority to penalize Joan (by withholding allowance) if she dumps any clothes. Assuming no transactions costs, what would Coase predict to be the outcome; and how, specifically, would we get there? (Hint: Coase would be a weird dad, because he would … do what?)

APPLICATION 4.1

Marginals and Totals

The following graph illustrates the marginal costs and benefits of reducing emissions of benzene from year 2005 levels in a chemical factory. Currently, the firm is not reducing any emissions at all.

a. Suppose that state regulators tell the firm it must reduce emissions by 20 lbs per day from zero. On the graph, illustrate *the areas* that show (1) *the total benefits* of reduction; (2) *the total costs* of reduction; and (3) the *total net benefits* of reduction. Approximately, what are these values?

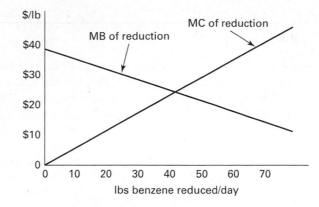

b.   If, after achieving a reduction of 20 tons per day, firms then had to increase their reduction further from 20 to 21 lbs per day, what is the approximate *marginal* benefit? *Marginal* cost? Increase in net benefit?

c.   Suppose it was discovered that the benzene emissions, in addition to doing harm via air pollution to people, were also contaminating the river. How would this affect the picture and the efficient cleanup level?

APPLICATION 4.2

More on Efficient Smoking

These smoking problems are a little silly but are good at illustrating some basic lessons about efficiency. So, this time, Groucho and Harpo work together in the same office. Groucho smokes; Harpo hates smoke. Groucho currently smokes 12 cigars per day. He faces marginal costs of reducing smoking (withdrawal pains) equal to x, where x is the number of cigars reduced. In other words, the cost of giving up the first cigar is $1, the second, $2, and so forth. Harpo receives marginal benefits (reduced discomfort and risk of cancer) equal to $(12 - x)$ from Groucho reducing the number of cigars smoked.

It is possible to rent a clean-air machine that reduces smoke in the air by 50% for $10 per day. It is also possible to relocate Groucho in a different office so Harpo would not have to breathe any smoke at all for $40 per day.

a.   Draw a diagram showing the marginal costs and marginal benefits of pollution reduction; put the number of cigars reduced on the horizontal axis. Use this diagram to determine the efficient number of cigars reduced if machine rental or relocation is not allowed.

b.   Suppose that the clean-air machine is installed. What is the efficient number of cigars reduced now? [Hint: The marginal benefits of reduction fall to $(6 - x/2)$.]

c.   Recall that Groucho begins by smoking 12 cigars a day. Is it more efficient to rent the machine or relocate Groucho to another room?

d.   This problem has no transactions costs or free riding. The Coase theorem says that, in this kind of simple example, the efficient outcome should be achieved through negotiation even if Harpo has the power to banish Groucho to another office *at Groucho's expense*. Explain why.

APPLICATION 4.3

The Stray Cow Problem

Rancher Roy has his ranch next to the farm of farmer Fern. Cattle tend to roam and sometimes stray onto Fern's land and damage her crops. Roy can choose the size of his herd. His revenues are $6 for each cow he raises. The schedules of his marginal cost of production (MCP) and the damage each additional cow creates (marginal cow damage, or MCD) are given.

No. of Cattle	MCP ($)	MCD ($)
1	3	1
2	3	2
3	4	3
4	5	4
5	6	5
6	7	6

Farmer Fern can choose either to farm or not to farm. Her cost of production is $10, and her revenue is $12 when there are no cattle roaming loose. For each additional cow, her revenue is reduced by the amount in the MCD column.

To answer the following questions, you need to figure out four things: the profit-maximizing number of cows for Roy to own, his profits, whether Fern will farm, and what her profits will be. Remember that efficient outcomes maximize the net monetary benefits to both parties; in other words, total ranching plus farming profits. Finally, a diagram won't help for this problem.

a. What will be the outcome if there is no liability (Roy does not pay for any damages caused)?
b. What will be the outcome if Roy is liable for damages?
c. What is the efficient outcome (the outcome that maximizes total profits)?
d. Suppose it is possible to build a fence to enclose the ranch for a cost of $9. Is building the fence efficient?
e. Suppose the farmer can build a fence around her crops for a cost of $1. Is building this fence efficient?

APPLICATION 4.4

End-of-the-Pipe Control versus Pollution Prevention

The marginal cost of reduction curve illustrated in Figure 4.5 assumes a particular approach to reducing pollution, often called end-of-the-pipe control. In other words, when we draw that upward-sloping MC curve, we assume that firms respond to regulation by maintaining the same basic production technology but adding on scrubbers or filters to clean up their emissions. Under these conditions, rising marginal costs of reduction are quite likely.

However, suppose that firms radically overhaul their production technology, so that they completely eliminate emissions. This is known as a "pollution prevention" strategy. An example might be a jeweler, who in the face of regulation adopts a closed-loop production system. This is one in which all mineral waste products are recovered from recycled wastewater and then reused. What would the marginal cost of reduction diagram look like in this case?

a. Specifically, assume that reducing metal pollution by the first 1% required the installation of a $100,000 recycling system, but that the marginal cost of further reduction was zero. Draw the marginal cost of reduction curve.

b. Let the marginal benefit of reduction curve be equal to $(30,000 − 1/3 ∗ x)$, where x is the percentage reduction in pollution (ranging from 0% to 100%). In this case, is installation of the recycling system efficient? What is the efficient cleanup level?

APPLICATION 4.5

Efficient Regulation of Drinking Water

When setting standards for lead in drinking water, the EPA considered three options illustrated in Table 4.3. The symbol µg/l stands for micrograms (millionths of a gram) per liter. Standard A, the most strict standard, would require municipal systems (small and large in size) to take action if lead levels were greater than 5 µg/l; B relaxed the action level for small municipal systems to 15 µg/l; and C set a standard for both small and large at 15 µg/l.

The EPA undertook a benefit-cost analysis of the proposed standards as part of a Regulatory Impact Assessment. The final results are reproduced in Tables 4.4 and 4.5. (Note, there are eight questions listed. Questions 5–8 follow some additional text.)

1. What are the net benefits of the three options? Which option is the most efficient? Is there a conflict between safety and efficiency here?

2. The marginal benefit of option A ($5,192) in the fourth line of the table is derived from the total benefit values listed in the first line of the table. How is this number calculated?

TABLE 4.3   Proposed Action Levels for Lead Leached from Solder

Option	System Type	Action Level µg/l
A	Small	5
	Large	5
B	Small	15
	Large	5
C	Small	15
	Large	15

Source: U.S. Environmental Protection Agency (1991a).

TABLE 4.4 Summary Benefit-Cost Results, Lead Solder ($ millions)

	Option		
	A	B	C
Total benefits	$68,957	$63,757	$24,325
Total costs	$ 6,272	$ 4,156	$ 3,655
B/C ratio	11.0	15.3	6.7
Marginal benefits	$ 5,192	$39,400	$24,325
Marginal costs	$ 2,117	$ 500	$ 3,655
Marginal B/C ratio	2.5	78.8	6.67

Note: Figures are based on 20-year life, 3% discount rate. Monetary figures are in 1988 dollars.
Source: U.S. Environmental Protection Agency (1991).

TABLE 4.5 Annual Estimated Benefits of Reducing Lead in Drinking Water ($ millions)

	Option		
	A	B	C
ADULT MALES			
Hypertension			
Cases reduced/yr	685,302	635,199	246,479
Value	$ 430	$ 399	$ 155
Heart Attack			
Cases reduced/yr	884	818	315
Value	$ 884	$ 818	$ 315
Stroke			
Cases reduced/yr	657	609	235
Value	$ 657	$ 609	$ 235
Death (heart disease)			
Cases reduced/yr	672	622	240
Value	$1,680	$1,555	$ 599
CHILDREN			
Treatment cost reduced	*	*	*
Additional education reduced	$ 2	$ 2	$ 2
Lowered IQ			
Children no longer affected	205,221	188,313	68,133
Value	$ 942	$ 864	$ 313
IQ <70			
Children no longer affected	784	738	325
Value	$ 40	$ 38	$ 17
TOTAL	$4,635	$4,286	$1,635

*Less than $1 million. Monetary figures are in 1988 dollars.
Source: U.S. Environmental Protection Agency (1991).

3. The marginal benefits and costs for option C are measured relative to a no-regulation baseline. Are the MB > MC for option C? Option B? Option A? Does this result contradict your answer to part 1?
4. Option B has the biggest benefit/cost ratio. Does this contradict your answer to part 1?

Lead is a well-known neurotoxin. Some credit lead in drinking water to contributing to the downfall of the Roman empire! Lead also has additional health impacts. Table 4.6 illustrates the impacts the EPA tried to take into account. However, the agency was able to quantify and include in the benefits line of the table less than half of these impacts (marked with an *).

Given this, and the myriad uncertainty associated with the benefits it did measure, the EPA authors "assume," based on "professional judgment," that the "true" benefit measure could be up to two times as high, or 70% below, the actual value their estimation procedure generated. The EPA argued that there was a similar uncertainty band around their estimate costs. To better reflect this uncertainty, the EPA included Figure 4.9 in the analysis.

5. Given the uncertainty, do all three options pass a test such that B > C?
6. Given the uncertainty, can one really tell if option A is more efficient than B? How about option A relative to C?
7. Does the table showing the final results of the benefit-cost analysis illustrate the "hard numbers illusion"?
8. If you were in charge of deciding, would you pick option A or B? Why?

TABLE 4.6 Health Costs of Lead Exposure

MEN (age group)
* a. Hypertension (adult)
* b. Heart disease, stroke, and death (ages 40–59)
   c. Possible item b. (ages 20–40; >59)
   d. Cancer

WOMEN
   e. Possible hypertension, heart disease, stroke, and death
   f. Fetal effects from maternal exposure, including diminished childhood IQ, decreased gestational age, and reduced birth weight
   g. Possible increases in infant mortality
   h. Cancer

CHILDREN
   i. Interference with growth
* j. Reduced intelligence
   k. Impaired hearing, behavioral changes
   l. Interference with PNS development
   m. Metabolic effects, impaired heme synthesis, anemia
   n. Cancer

---

*Items the EPA was able to consider directly.
Source: U.S. Environmental Protection Agency (1991).

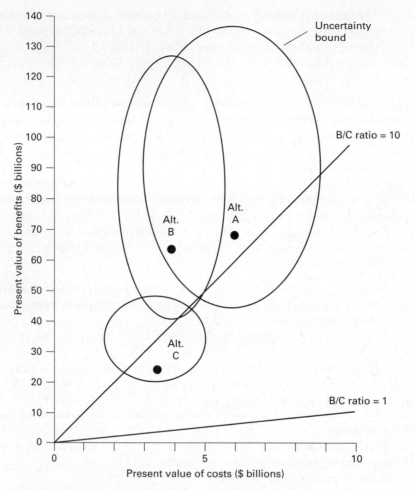

FIGURE 4.9 Uncertainty of Benefit-Cost Estimates for Corrosion Control
Source: U.S. Environmental Protection Agency (1991a).

KEY IDEAS IN EACH SECTION

4.0   The efficiency standard argues for a careful balancing of the costs and benefits of pollution control.

4.1   *Efficiency* is defined as **Pareto efficient**. Pareto-efficient outcomes maximize the measurable **net monetary benefits** available to a society. Thus in any move toward efficiency, it is always *possible* for the winners to compensate the losers, a so-called Pareto improvement. However, compensation is not required for efficiency, so efficient outcomes are not necessarily fair.

4.2   **Marginal analysis**, which compares the **marginal costs** of pollution reduction against its **marginal benefits**, is used to pinpoint the efficient pollution level. At any point other than the efficient level, both polluter and victim can *potentially* be made better off through negotiation.

4.3   The marginal curves graph the change in the total curves. The area under the marginal cost (benefit) curve equals the total costs (benefits). At the point where total costs and benefits are equal, net benefits are zero and pollution has been "overcontrolled" from an efficiency perspective.

4.4   The **Coase theorem** states that *in the absence of transactions costs and free riding*, private negotiation will arrive at the efficient pollution level, regardless of whether victims have the right to impose a ban or polluters have the right to pollute. In the real world, however, the **polluter-pays principle** leads to a more efficient outcome as it generally reduces transactions costs and free riding and does not distort the incentives for entry into the market.

4.5   The case of air pollution in Baltimore illustrates how the efficiency standard might be applied in practice.

4.6   The efficiency standard weights the utility of all individuals equally: rich and poor, current and future generations, and victims and polluters. Thus outcomes are efficient even if the increased consumption by one group comes at the expense of another. This means that any individual move toward efficiency does not clearly increase social welfare. Nevertheless, efficiency can best be defended by arguing that, over time, most people will benefit in their role as consumers if efficiency is pursued at every turn.

4.7   Benefit-cost tests are not required for most U.S. environmental regulations, which are generally safety based. However, all major regulations must still undergo a benefit-cost analysis called a **Regulatory Impact Assessment (RIA)**, with the intent of identifying, from the universe of safe options, *more* efficient outcomes. The key challenge for economists is to provide sufficiently certain estimates of benefits and costs. If there is major uncertainty, and the efficient outcome is not clear, then benefit-cost analysis can become a politicized tool via mechanisms such as **hard numbers illusion**, **agenda control**, and **paralysis by analysis**.

REFERENCES

Ackerman, Frank. 2008. *Poisoned for pennies*. Washington, DC: Island Press.

Bromley, Daniel. 1990. The ideology of efficiency: Searching for a theory of policy analysis. *Journal of Environmental Economics and Management* 19(1): 86–107.

Coase, Ronald. 1960. The problem of social cost. *Journal of Land Economics* 3 (October): 1–44.

Gomez-Ibanez, Jose A., and Joseph P. Kalt. 1990. *Cases in microeconomics*. Englewood Cliffs, NJ: Prentice Hall.

Heinzerling, Lisa, and Frank Ackerman. 2002. *Pricing the priceless: Cost-benefit analysis of environmental protection*. Washington, DC: Georgetown Environmental Law and Policy.

Kneese, Alan V., and William D. Schulze. 1985. Ethics and environmental economics. In *Handbook of natural resource economics*, ed. A. V. Kneese and J. J. Sweeney. Vol. 1. New York: Elsevier.

Mohring, Herbert, and J. Hayden Boyd. 1971. Analyzing "externalities": "Direct interaction" versus "asset utilization" frameworks. *Economica* 38: 347–61.

Oates, Wallace E., Paul R. Portney, and Albert M. McGartland. 1989. The net benefits of incentive-based regulation: A case study of environmental standard setting. *American Economic Review* 79(5): 1233–42.

Revesz, Richard L., and Michael A. Livermore. 2008. *Retaking rationality: How cost-benefit analysis can better protect the environment and our health*. Oxford: Oxford University Press.

———. 1991a. *Final regulatory impact analysis of national primary drinking water regulations for lead and copper*. Washington, DC: U.S. EPA, Office of Drinking Water.

———. 1991b. *Addendum to the regulatory impact analysis for the final criteria for municipal solid waste landfills*. Washington, DC: U.S. EPA, Regulatory Analysis Branch, Office of Solid Waste.

CHAPTER 5

MEASURING THE BENEFITS OF ENVIRONMENTAL PROTECTION

5.0 Introduction

The efficiency framework discussed in the last chapter appears to give us a very precise answer to the question: Are we polluting too much? Yes, if the marginal benefits of reduced pollution (both today and in the future) exceed the marginal costs of reduction. However, determining the efficient pollution level requires that we first devise accurate measures of both the benefits and costs of decreased pollution.

The benefits of pollution control can be divided into two categories: **market benefits** and **nonmarket benefits**. For example, cleaning up a river may lead to increases in commercial fish harvests, greater use of tourist services, and fewer medical expenses and days lost at work due to waterborne diseases. Measuring these market benefits in dollar terms is a natural approach.

However, economists have also devised methods for measuring nonmarket benefits. In our example, these would include increased recreational use of the river (boating, swimming, fishing), the enjoyment of greater species diversity in the river, and a reduction in premature death due to diseases contracted from bad water. Nonmarket benefits are measured by inferring how much money people *would be willing to pay* (or accept) for these benefits if a market for them did exist.

Complicating the measurement of nonmarket benefits is the need to estimate the *risk* associated with industrial pollutants. For example, consider the case of polychlorinated biphenyls (PCBs), industrial chemicals widely used until the late 1970s as lubricants, fluids in electric transformers, paints, inks, and paper coatings. PCB-contaminated waste dumps remain fairly widespread throughout the country today.

PCB exposure is related to developmental abnormalities in people and causes cancer in laboratory animals. However, the risk to humans from exposure to low levels of PCBs is not precisely known and can only be determined to lie within a probable range. The need to estimate, rather than directly measure, both nonmarket benefits and risk means that benefit measures for pollution reduction are necessarily fairly rough.

By a similar token, the direct costs of reducing pollution can be measured in terms of the increased expense associated with new pollution control measures and additional regulatory personnel required to ensure compliance. However, indirect costs resulting from impacts on productivity and employment can only be inferred.

The next two chapters take a close look at methods of measuring and comparing the benefits and costs of environmental cleanup. The principal conclusion is that benefit-cost analysis is far from a precise science. As a result, pinpointing the "efficient" pollution level can be achieved only within broad boundaries, if at all.

5.1 Use, Option, and Existence Value: Types of Nonmarket Benefits

The nonmarket benefits of environmental protection fall into three categories: use, option, and existence values. **Use value** is just that value in use. Returning to our river example, if people use a clean river more effectively for swimming, boating, drinking, or washing without paying for the services, then these are nonmarket use values.

An environmental resource will have **option value** if the future benefits it might yield are uncertain and depletion of the resource is effectively irreversible. In this case, one would be willing to pay something merely to preserve the option that the resource might prove valuable in the future. In certain cases, option value may actually be negative; that is, people may value a resource today less than its expected future use value. However, in many important environmental applications, option value will be positive.[1]

Finally, economists have indirectly included moral concerns about environmental degradation, including empathy for other species, in their utilitarian framework under the heading **existence value**. For example, if a person believed that all creatures had a "right" to prosper on the planet, then he or she would obtain satisfaction from the protection of endangered species, such as the spotted owl or the right whale, even if these species had no use or option value. The desire to leave an unspoiled planet to one's descendants (a bequest motive) also endows species or ecosystems with an existence value.

As an example of the potential importance of existence value, a survey-based study estimated that Wisconsin taxpayers were willing to pay $12 million annually to preserve the striped shiner, an endangered species of tiny minnow with virtually no use

---

1. I focus here on option value arising from supply uncertainty, which seems most applicable to resource issues. Freeman (1985) shows that supply-side option value will be positive if supply is assured. If a project delivers supply only with a positive probability, a positive sign for option value will be more likely the greater the uniqueness of the resource. But option value is usually brought up only in the context of unique resources. To illustrate a case in which supply-side option value will actually be negative, consider a resource with perfect substitutes, such as a dollar bill. A risk-averse individual would have to be paid to accept a fair lottery to preserve a dollar bill for possible future use.

or option value. As we will see, the results of this type of study must be interpreted with care. However, results do seem to indicate a substantial demand for the preservation of species for the sake of pure existence.[2]

The **total value** of an environmental resource is the sum of these three components:

Total value = Use value + Option value + Existence value

5.2 Consumer Surplus, WTP, and WTA: Measuring Benefits

Having defined the types of benefits that nonmarket goods generate, the next step is measurement. The benefit measure for pollution reduction that economists employ is the increase in **consumer surplus** due to such a reduction. Consumer surplus is the difference between what one is willing to pay and what one actually has to pay for a service or product. A simple illustration: Suppose that it is a very hot day and you are thirsty. You walk into the nearest store perfectly willing to plunk down $1.50 for a small soft drink. However, you are pleasantly surprised to discover the price is only $0.50. Your consumer surplus in this case is $1.00.

To illustrate how one would apply the consumer surplus concept to an environmental good, let us return to the example we employed in Chapter 3, in which Mr. Peabody has a private demand for the preservation of a trout stream in Appalachia. This demand may be based on his expected use, option, or existence value, or a combination of all three. His demand curve is illustrated in Figure 5.1.

Initially, 10 acres of stream have been preserved. Assume Mr. Peabody did not pay for this public good. Nevertheless, he still benefits from it. His consumer surplus from

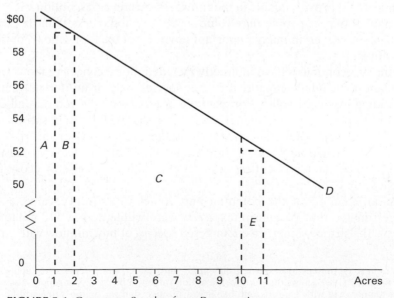

FIGURE 5.1 Consumer Surplus from Preservation

---

2. Boyle and Bishop (1987).

the first acre preserved is his willingness to pay ($60), less the price ($0), or $60. We can portray this consumer surplus graphically as the area A, lying below the demand curve and above the price (zero) for the first unit. Similarly, for the second acre, he is willing to pay about $59, which is also his consumer surplus as the good has a zero price. Consumer surplus from this unit is represented graphically as area B. Peabody's *total* consumer surplus from the initial 10 acres is represented graphically by the entire area $A + B + C$.

Now suppose that a nature preservation society buys an extra acre of stream land. The benefits of this action for Peabody will be his increase in consumer surplus, area E. But this is just the price he is willing to pay for a 1-acre increase! For small increases in the stock of a public good enjoyed at no charge by consumers—such as trout streams or clean air or water—*the price that people are willing to pay is a close approximation to the increase in consumer surplus that they enjoy.*

This analysis suggests that one can measure the benefits of environmental improvement simply by determining people's **willingness to pay** (**WTP**) for such improvement and adding up the results. However, WTP is not the only way to measure consumer surplus. An alternate approach would be to ask an individual his or her minimum **willingness to accept** (WTA) compensation in exchange for a degradation in environmental quality. In our example, Peabody could be persuaded to give up the 11th acre of stream in exchange for a little more than $52.[3]

In theory, WTP and WTA measures are both good approximations to the change in consumer surplus from a small change in a public good such as environmental quality. Economists predict that WTA will be a bit higher than consumer surplus, because individuals are actually made a bit richer when they are compensated for damage. On the other hand, WTP should be a bit lower than consumer surplus, as people will be made poorer if they actually have to pay for environmental improvement. However, the differences should not, in theory, be large as the income changes involved are not big.

Interestingly, however, the evidence does not support this prediction. What kind of evidence? Over the last few decades, economists have conducted many experiments in which the subjects were asked what they would pay for a wide array of both market and nonmarket items—a coffee mug, a hunting license, or improved visibility in the Grand Canyon, for example. A different pool of subjects would then be asked what they would be willing to accept in compensation to give up the mug, the license, or a haze-free day on the canyon rim. Even for everyday items like coffee mugs, WTA values are typically higher than WTP. And for nonmarket goods, like preserving land from development, WTA values are typically seven times as high as WTP.[4]

How can we explain the divergence between WTP and WTA benefit measures? One possibility is that, for psychological reasons, people are more willing to sacrifice to maintain the existing quality of the environment than they are to improve environmental quality beyond what is already experienced. People may adopt the *status quo* as their reference point and demand higher compensation to allow environmental degradation than they are willing to pay for making improvements. If this hypothesis,

3. In this example, I use WTP for improvement from the status quo and WTA for degradation to the status quo, where the status quo is 10 acres. These are, respectively, compensating and equivalent variation measures. One can also use WTP for improvement to the status quo and WTA for degradation from the status quo.
4. Horowitz and McConnell (2002).

known as **prospect theory**, is correct, it would reshape our marginal benefit curve for pollution reduction as illustrated in Figure 5.2. Here, the marginal benefits of reduction rise dramatically just inside current levels of pollution.[5]

A second explanation for the divergence between WTP and WTA is based on the degree of substitutability between environmental quality and other consumption goods. Consider, for example, a case in which people are asked their WTP and WTA to reduce the risk of cancer death for members of a community from air pollution. A substantial reduction in the risk of death is something that, for many people, has few good substitutes. Nevertheless, a person whose income is limited will be able to pay only a certain amount for such a guarantee. On the other hand, because good substitutes for a reduced risk of death cannot be purchased, the compensation necessary for accepting such a risk might well be very large, even greater than the individual's entire income.

Some have argued that this "no good substitutes" argument is of limited value in explaining the measured discrepancy between WTP and WTA. Can it really be true, for example, that a stand of trees in a local park has no adequate substitute for people in the community? Appendix 5A and Chapter 11 both take up in more detail the degree to which environmental goods and more common consumption items might actually substitute for one another in the provision of utility.

Regardless of the explanation, the WTA-WTP disparity is clearly important as economists try to place a value on improved or degraded environmental quality. The standard practice in survey research is to use WTP, on the basis that WTA measures are too hard to estimate reliably. But the right measure to use probably depends on the underlying property rights. If we think of common property resources such as clean air and water as belonging to "the people," then WTA compensation for their degradation would appear to be the more correct measure of pollution damages.

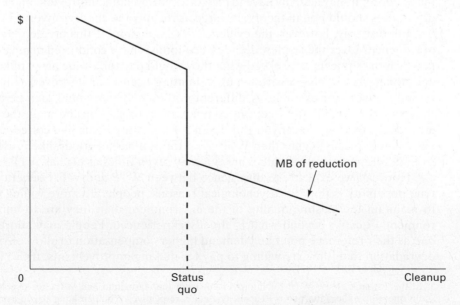

FIGURE 5.2 Prospect Theory and Marginal Benefits of Cleanup

---

5. Kahneman and Tversky (1979).

Both hazardous waste and oil spill legislation explicitly vest the public with rights to a clean environment by giving them the right to compensation for damages. Under this kind of property rights regime, WTP is clearly the wrong measure and will generate underestimates of the underlying resource value.[6]

Using either WTP or WTA as benefit measures generates one additional concern. Rich people, by the simple virtue of their higher incomes, will be willing to pay more for environmental improvement and will require more to accept environmental degradation. In other words, using WTP or WTA to assess the benefits of identical pollution control steps in rich and poor areas will lead to a higher benefit value for the wealthy community. As we see later, the ethical dilemma posed by this measurement approach shows up strongest when comparing WTP and WTA for reduction in the risk of death or illnesses between rich and poor countries.

5.3 Risk: Assessment and Perception

The first step in actually measuring the benefits of pollution reduction is to assess the risks associated with the pollution. As noted in the introduction, this can be a difficult process. Information on health risks comes from two sources: epidemiological and animal studies. Epidemiological studies attempt to evaluate risk by examining past cases of human exposure to the pollutant in question. For example, in the case of PCBs, developmental abnormalities such as lower birth weights, smaller head circumference, and less-developed cognitive and motor skills have been found in three separate communities of children whose mothers suffered substantial exposure. There is also limited evidence of a link between occupational exposure to PCBs and several types of cancer.

In animal studies, rats and mice are subjected to relatively high exposures of the pollutants and examined for carcinogenic effect. PCBs have been found to generate cancers in animal studies. The combined epidemiological and animal evidence has led the U.S. Environmental Protection Agency (EPA) to label PCBs as probable human carcinogens.

Due to concern about PCB (and other industrial pollutant) contamination of the Great Lakes, researchers undertook an evaluation of the risk of eating Lake Michigan sport fish.[7] In this case, as in any risk assessment, it is necessary to estimate the number of cancers likely to happen from different levels of exposure. From animal studies, the number of extra tumors generated as a result of high exposure to PCBs is known. Translating this information to a human population requires two steps: first, the cancer incidence from high levels of exposure among animals must be used to predict the incidence from low levels, and, second, the cancer rate among animals must be used to predict the rate among people.

The assumptions made in moving from high-dose animal studies to low-dose human exposure constitute a **dose-response model**. A typical model might assume a linear relationship between exposure and the number of tumors, use a surface-area scaling factor to move from the test species to humans, and assume constant exposure for 70 years. Such a model would generate a much higher estimated risk of cancer for humans than if a different model were used: for example, if a safe threshold exposure

6. Arrow et al. (1993); Bromley (1995); Knetsch (2007).
7. Glenn et al. (1989).

to PCBs were assumed, if a scaling factor based on body weight were employed, or if exposure were assumed to be intermittent and short-lived.

The point here is that risk assessments, even those based on large numbers of animal studies, are far from precise. Because of this imprecision, researchers often adopt a *conservative modeling* stance, meaning that every assumption made in the modeling process is likely to overstate the true risk. If all the model assumptions are conservative ones, then the final estimate represents the upper limit of the true risk of exposure to *the individual pollutant*. Even here, however, the health risk may be understated due to synergy effects. Certain pollutants are thought to do more damage when exposure to multiple toxic substances occurs.

Bearing this uncertainty in mind, the study estimated that, due to high levels of four industrial pollutants in the Great Lakes (PCBs, DDT, dieldrin, and chlordane), eating one meal per week of Lake Michigan brown trout would generate a conservative risk of cancer equal to almost 1 in 100. That is, for every 100 people consuming one meal per week of the fish, at most, one person would contract cancer from exposure to one of these four chemicals. The study concluded as well that high consumption levels would likely lead to reproductive damage. There are, of course, hundreds of other potentially toxic pollutants in Lake Michigan waters. However, the risks from these other substances are not well known. For comparison, Table 5.1 lists the assessed mortality risk associated with some other common pollutant exposure, along with other risks, and one should recognize that all these estimates come with some uncertainty.

The risk figures in Table 5.1 show the estimated number of annual deaths per 10,000 people exposed. Thus, around five Californians out of 10,000 each year die as a result of exposure to particulate air pollution. Avid peanut butter fans will be disappointed to learn that it contains a naturally occurring carcinogen, aflotoxin. However, one would have to eat four tablespoons per day to raise the cancer risk to eight in one million.

The Scientific Advisory Committee of the EPA has ranked environmental hazards in terms of the overall risk they present for the U.S. population. The committee's results are presented in Table 5.2. The overall risk from a particular pollutant or environmental problem is equal to the product of the actual risk to exposed individuals multiplied by the number of people exposed. Thus, topping the EPA's list are environmental problems likely to affect the entire U.S. population—global warming, ozone

TABLE 5.1   Annual Mortality Risks

Event	Annual Risk of Death
Car accident[1]	1.4 per 10,000
Police killed by felons[2]	1.0 per 10,000
Particulate air pollution, California[3]	5.0 per 10,000
Radon exposure, lung cancer[4]	0.6 per 10,000
Peanut butter (4 tablespoons/day)[5]	0.008 per 10,000 (8 per million)
Cigarette smoking[6]	15 per 10,000

Source: Calculated from [1] National Safety Council (2010); [2] Johnson (2008); [3] American Lung Association (2009); [4] U.S. Environmental Protection Agency (2010); [5] Wilson and Crouch (1987); [6] National Cancer Institute (2010).

TABLE 5.2   Relative Risks as Viewed by the EPA

Relatively High Risk
   Habitat alteration and destruction
   Species extinction and loss of biodiversity
   Stratospheric ozone depletion
   Global climate change

Relatively Medium Risk
   Herbicides/pesticides
   Toxics, nutrients, biochemical oxygen demand, and turbidity in surface waters
   Acid deposition
   Airborne toxics

Relatively Low Risk
   Oil spills
   Groundwater pollution
   Radionuclides
   Acid runoff to surface waters
   Thermal pollution

Source: U.S. Environmental Protection Agency (1990).

depletion, and loss of biodiversity. The relatively low-risk problems are often highly toxic—radionuclides, oil spills, and groundwater pollutants—but with exceptions like the BP oil blowout in 2010, they affect a much more localized area.

Risks of equal magnitude do not necessarily evoke similar levels of concern. For example, although risks from exposure to air pollution in California cities are somewhat smaller than risks from cigarette smoking, as a society we spend tens of billions of dollars each year controlling the former and devote much less attention to the latter. As another example, airline safety is heavily monitored by the government and the press, even though air travel is much safer than car travel. The acceptability of risk is influenced by the degree of control an individual feels he or she has over a situation. Air pollution and air safety are examples of situations in which risk is imposed upon an individual by others; by contrast, cigarette smoking and auto safety risks are accepted "voluntarily."

Other reasons that the public perception of risk may differ substantially from the actual assessed risk include lack of knowledge or distrust of experts. Given the uncertainty surrounding many estimates, the latter would not be surprising. Either of these factors may explain why the public demands extensive government action to clean up hazardous waste dumps (1,000 cancer cases per year) while little is done to reduce naturally occurring radon exposure in the home (5,000 to 20,000 cancer deaths per year). The issue of imposed risk may also factor in here. However, to the extent that lack of knowledge drives public priorities for pollution control, education about risks is clearly an important component of environmental policy.[8]

---

8. Cancer mortality is from Gough (1989). For extended discussions of these issues, see Kammen and Hassenzahl (1999).

Finally, economists do know that people in general are **risk averse**; that is, they dislike risky situations. Risk aversion explains, for example, why people buy auto theft insurance even though, on average, they will pay the insurance company more than the expected risk-adjusted replacement value of their vehicle. By purchasing insurance, people are paying a premium for the certain knowledge that they will not face an unexpected loss in the future. Risk aversion also partially underlies the option value placed on a natural resource.

If people are risk averse, then we should expect them to give extra weight to measures that avoid environmental disasters. Much of the concern over issues such as global warming and nuclear power probably arises from risk aversion. It seems sensible to many people to take measures today to avoid the possibility of a catastrophe in the future, even if the worst-case scenario has a relatively low probability. Indeed, if people are quite risk averse, this becomes another reason for choosing a safer rather than a more efficient standard for pollution cleanup, or an ecological rather than a neoclassical standard for protecting natural capital.

5.4 Measuring Benefits I: Contingent Valuation

With the risk of additional pollution established, the final step in estimating the benefits of changes in environmental quality is to obtain actual value measures. One might think that the most straightforward way of assessing benefits would be simply to ask people their WTP or WTA. Economists do use survey approaches for measuring the benefits of environmental protection; these are called **contingent valuations** (CVs) because the survey responses are "contingent" upon the questions asked. However, interpreting the results from CV studies is far from a straightforward process.

An example: Johnson (1999, 2003) looked at the WTP of residents of Washington State to accelerate cleanup of leaking underground storage tanks at gasoline stations. Doing so would protect groundwater from contamination. Phone surveyors obtained basic background information about the respondents, including their estimated monthly expenditures on gasoline, their levels of concern about environmental risk, and their general positions on environmental issues. After providing some details about the benefits of the proposed cleanup policy, surveyors asked:

> "If you had the opportunity, would you vote to require oil companies to begin tank overhaul immediately if it were on the ballot right now?"

After obtaining a response of yes, no, or don't know, the surveyor then introduced a "price" for the cleanup policy:

> When deciding whether to support the measure, people are usually concerned not just about the environmental issue at hand, but also with how much it will cost them. ... Suppose [that to pay for the cleanup], you had to spend $X [amount varied randomly among respondents] more per month over the next 18 months on gas, over and above $Y, your previously reported monthly household gasoline expenditures that you currently spend. In this situation, do you think the measure would be worth the groundwater reserves that would be protected?

Note that the surveyors reminded people how much they were spending on gas per month ($Y) when they asked the respondents for their additional WTP for the cleanup,

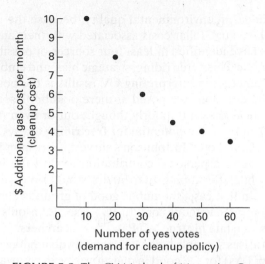

FIGURE 5.3 The CV Method of Measuring Consumer Surplus

so that the respondents would think hard about opportunity cost. And as one would expect, the introduction of a personal cost to the cleanup policy significantly reduced the number of yes votes—and higher costs led to more and more no votes. By varying the amount that people were required to pay in the survey (and also by statistically controlling for factors such as income differences between respondents and preexisting pro-environment sentiment), Johnson was able to construct a "demand curve" for the cleanup that looked something like the one in Figure 5.3.

Here is a quick puzzle.

PUZZLE

What is the approximate gain in consumer surplus to the individuals in the sample if the cleanup in fact occurs and costs $4 per person?

SOLUTION

The first 10 folks get approximately $10 − $4 = $6; the next 10 get about $8 − $4 = $4; the folks from 20 to 30 get $6 − $4 = $2 each; from 30 to 40, the respondents get $4.50 − $4 = $0.50; the next batch, from 40 to 50, have a WTP equal to the cost, so they neither gain nor lose; and the final batch of folks—from 50 to 60—are made a little worse off by the policy because their WTP is less than the cost: $3.50 − $4 = −$0.50. Multiplying through by 10 for each group gives a net gain in consumer surplus from cleanup equal to $60 + $40 + $20 + $5 + $0 − $5 = $120.

The contingent valuation survey approach to eliciting WTP and consumer surplus is easy to understand in principle. However, interpreting the results from a CV study is anything but straightforward. As with any survey, the answers given depend heavily on the way the questions are presented. This is especially true of surveys attempting to elicit true WTP (or WTA) for changes in environmental quality, because the respondents must be made to recognize the actual dollar costs associated with their answers. Contingent valuation researchers have identified at least four sources of possible errors in their survey estimates: hypothetical bias, free riding, strategic bias, and embedding bias.

The first possibility that emerges in interpreting CV results is the possibility of a **hypothetical bias**. Because the questions are posed as mere possibilities, respondents may provide equally hypothetical answers—poorly thought out or even meaningless. Second, as we discussed in Chapter 3, the potential for **free riding** always exists when people are asked to pay for a public good. In Johnson's survey, if a respondent thought a yes vote would in effect require a personal contribution toward the leaking tank cleanup, he might vote no while still hoping that others would vote yes—and that others would pick up the bill. In that case, the public good of groundwater protection would be provided to the free rider without cost. In this case, Johnson's respondent would have an incentive to understate his true WTP to CV researchers.

In contrast, **strategic bias** arises if people believe they really do not have to pay their stated WTPs (or forgo their WTAs) for the good in question, say groundwater cleanup. Suppose, for example, the respondent thought that a big oil company would ultimately pick up the tab, and gas prices wouldn't rise as much as the stated hypothetical price. Under these circumstances, why not inflate one's stated WTP? This would be a particularly good strategy if the respondent thought that larger WTP values in the survey results (as expressed through a higher percentage of yes votes) would lead to a higher likelihood of mandated protection for the groundwater.

Finally, the most serious problem with CV surveys is revealed by an observed **embedding bias**. Answers are strongly affected by the context provided about the issue at stake. This is particularly evident when valuation questions are "embedded" in a broader picture. In the case of the striped shiner mentioned in the introduction to this chapter, Wisconsin residents may well have felt differently about the shiner if they had first been asked their WTP to protect the Higgins' eye pearly mussel, another endangered species. In this case, preservation of the one species is probably a good substitute for preservation of the other. That is, by stating, on average, a WTP of $4 to protect the shiner, Wisconsin residents in fact may have been willing to commit those resources to preserving a species of "small water creatures."[9]

On the other hand, might Wisconsinites, via their commitment to the shiner, be expressing a desire to preserve the broader environment or even to obtain the "warm glow" of giving to a worthy cause? The interpretation of CV responses is quite difficult in the face of this embedding bias. In one experiment, researchers found that median WTP to improve rescue equipment decreased from $25 to $16 when respondents were first asked their WTPs to improve disaster preparedness. When respondents were first asked their WTPs for environmental services, their WTPs for disaster preparedness, and then their WTPs for improving rescue equipment and personnel, estimates fell to $1. Which of these estimates is the "true" WTP for rescue equipment?[10]

Johnson's groundwater study was in fact designed to tease out how much the context in which CV studies are presented can influence WTP answers. In the version

---

9. Bishop and Welsh (1992) make this point.
10. Knetsch and Kahneman (1992).

you read earlier, respondents were asked their WTPs if oil companies were forced to do the cleanup. A different version substituted gas stations and added the following caveat: "Most gas stations are independently owned, and have small profit margins because they are very competitive. Even though they *advertise* well-known brands of gas made by the major oil producers, most gas stations are not owned by the oil companies themselves." Johnson also randomly varied the percentage of the total cleanup costs that respondents were told these businesses (either big oil companies or small gas stations) could pass on to consumers in the form of higher prices.

Johnson found that people were more willing to vote to pay higher gas prices for the tank-repair policy if they thought businesses were also paying their fair share. And this effect was much stronger if big oil companies were paying for the cleanup than if the regulation was going to be imposed on small, independent gas stations. Her conclusion was that the perceived fairness of the policy strongly influenced individual WTP. This reinforces the point that, depending on the context in which CV studies are presented, answers can vary widely.

The embedding problem in particular has generated a tremendous amount of research attention. Based on this research, CV advocates argue that in most studies, respondents in fact vary their answers in a predictable fashion to changes in the scope or sequence of questions posed. This means that a well-designed survey—one focusing on the particular policy proposal at hand—can provide solid, replicable information, at least for WTP. But such high-quality studies can be expensive. CV analyses of the damages caused by the Exxon Valdez oil spill, for example, cost a reported $3 million.

In addition, such ambitious efforts are relatively rare. A generally favorable review of CV analyses concluded that "it is still quite difficult to obtain data from CV surveys which are sufficiently reliable and valid to use for policy purposes, and that the dangers of attempting to draw conclusions from poorly conceived or executed studies are great." Most CV results must therefore be carefully reviewed for potential biases before they are accepted as reasonable estimates of true WTP or WTA.[11]

Despite these criticisms, the CV approach is increasingly being used by economists, policymakers, and courts. This is because it provides the *only available means* for estimating nonmarket benefits based primarily on **existence value**, such as the benefits of preserving the striped shiner. These existence benefits are potentially quite large. In the case of the Exxon Valdez oil spill in Alaska, CV estimates of damages were on the order of $30 per household, for a total of $3 billion. This is roughly three times what Exxon actually paid out in damages.[12]

CV is called a "stated preference" approach to eliciting nonmarket values, because people are asked to state their preferences in surveys. We now turn to two other methods that rely instead on the "revealed preference" of consumers. These approaches impute a price tag for the nonmarket value of a resource from the demand or "revealed preference" of consumers for closely related market goods. As we will see, because revealed-preference methods depend on the actual use of the nonmarket good by consumers, they can pick up use and option value, but not existence value.

---

11. Quote is from Mitchell and Carson (1989, 15). Alberini and Kahn (2006) discuss the state of the art.
12. From "Value of Intangible Losses" (1991).

5.5 Measuring Benefits II: Travel Cost

The first of these market-based approaches to estimating nonmarket values is known as the **travel-cost method**. This approach is used to measure the benefits associated with recreational resources, such as parks, rivers, or beaches. The basic idea is to measure the amount of money that people expend to use the resource (their "travel cost"). By relating differences in travel cost to differences in consumption, a demand curve for the resource can be derived and consumer surplus estimated.

A simple case is illustrated in Figure 5.4. Assume that 1,000 people live in each of three concentric rings, areas A, B, and C, surrounding a national forest. All these people are identical in terms of their income and preferences. People in area C live farthest from the forest and face travel costs of $50 to use the resource for a day; they take only one trip per year. Folks in area B must pay $25 to visit the forest; they take six trips per year. Finally, area A people can wander in for free, and they do so 15 times per year.

We can use this information to derive the demand curve shown in Figure 5.4, which plots the relation between travel cost and visits. With this demand curve in hand, total consumer surplus can be determined from the following formula:

$$
\begin{aligned}
\text{Total Consumer Surplus} &= \text{Area A surplus} + \text{Area B surplus} + \text{Area C surplus} \\
&= 1{,}000 \text{ people} * (d + e + f) \\
&\quad + 1{,}000 \text{ people} * [(d + e) - 6 * 25] \\
&\quad + 1{,}000 \text{ people} * (d - 50)
\end{aligned}
$$

The 1,000 people living in area A get a huge amount of surplus—the entire area under the demand curve, or d + e + f in surplus from their 15 trips, and they have no travel costs. Area B residents receive d + e, but have to pay $25 in travel costs for each of their six trips. Finally, note that the folks from area C get very little net surplus (d − 50). They take only one trip and are almost indifferent toward going and not going.

Of course, in the real world, people are not identical—they have different incomes, tastes, and opportunity costs for travel. How do economists deal with these complications when applying the travel-cost method?

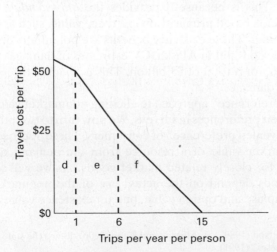

FIGURE 5.4 Demand Curve Derived from Travel-Cost Data

A study on the recreational benefits of Florida beaches for tourists provides a good example. The authors surveyed 826 tourists leaving Florida by plane or car and obtained information on days spent at the beach and expenses incurred to use the beach, including hotel/motel or campground fees, meals, travel to and from the beach, and access fees and other beach expenses. They also gathered data on initial travel costs in and out of the state, length of stay, age, income, and perception of the crowds and parking conditions at the beaches. Their basic hypothesis was that, holding all the other factors constant, lower beach expenses would lead tourists to spend a greater number of days at the beach.[13]

Using a statistical technique called multiple regression analysis, the authors were able to control for all other factors and isolate the impact of beach expenses on consumption. They found that demand was price inelastic, and a 10% increase in "price" led to only a 1.5% decrease in time on the beach, all other things being equal. The average tourist spent 4.7 days on the beach, incurring an estimated daily expense of $85. With this information, the study estimated consumer surplus for all 4.7 days to be $179, for an average per day of $38. With 70 million tourist days per year, the authors calculated that Florida's beaches yield a flow of value to tourists equal to $2.37 billion annually.

Evaluating the reliability of a travel-cost study boils down to determining how good a job the authors have done controlling for "other factors" that might affect recreation demand. For example, the beach study has been criticized because it did not control for the opportunity cost of the tourists' time. An extreme example shows why this might affect their result: Suppose an idle playboy and a heart surgeon, in all other respects identical, were two of the tourists surveyed. Suppose further that hotel prices were lower in the area visited by the playboy, and he was observed to stay longer in the area and visit the beach more frequently. The incorrect inference would be that the lower prices caused the higher number of visits when, in fact, the surgeon simply could not afford to stay away from work.[14]

Another important external factor for travel-cost analysis is the presence of alternative recreational opportunities. In Figure 5.4, for example, suppose that some folks who lived in area C had access to a second, equally close forest. In that case, they might choose to travel to the original forest only every other year, thus shifting the observed demand curve in and reducing the measured surplus for all groups, C, B, and A. But the existence of this second, more distant forest would in fact have little impact on the actual surplus gained by folks in area A from visits to the original forest. The travel-cost method has been extended to address this type of issue as well.[15]

5.6 Measuring Benefits III: Hedonic Regression

Like the travel-cost approach, the final method used for valuing nonmarket resources estimates benefits from observed market behavior. This method, **hedonic regression**, uses the change in prices of related (complementary) goods to infer a WTP for a healthier environment. The word *hedonic* means "pertaining to pleasure"; a hedonic regression estimates the pleasure or utility associated with an improved environment.

---

13. From Bell and Leeworthy (1990).
14. Shaw (1991) makes this point.
15. This is accomplished using random utility models. See the discussion in Freeman (1993).

As in the travel-cost method, regression techniques are used to hold constant factors that might be causing prices to change other than a degradation in environmental quality.

A good application of the hedonic regression method evaluated the damages arising from PCB contamination of sediments in the harbor of New Bedford, Massachusetts. The presence of PCBs was first made public in 1976; by 1983, about one-half the residents were aware of the pollution. Researchers attempted to measure the damage suffered in the community by examining the decline in real estate prices associated with the presence of this hazardous waste.

Their first step was to gather data on 780 single-family homes that had been sold more than once. The authors' approach was to examine the relative decline in prices for those homes whose repeat sales spanned the pollution period, using regression techniques to control for home improvements, interest rates, the length of time between adjacent sales for the same property, property tax changes, and per capita income in New Bedford. Assuming that knowledge of the pollution was widespread by 1982, houses located closest to the most hazardous area, where lobstering, fishing, and swimming were prohibited, had their prices depressed by about $9,000, all other things being equal. Homes in an area of secondary pollution, where bottom fishing and lobstering were restricted, experienced a relative decline in value of close to $7,000.

Multiplying these average damage figures by the number of homes affected, the authors conclude that total damages experienced by single-family homeowners were close to $36 million. This estimate does not include the impact on renters or on homeowners in rental neighborhoods. Based on the results from this and other studies, firms responsible for the pollution have since paid at least $20 million in natural resource damage claims.[16]

As with the travel-cost method, the key challenge in a hedonic regression study lies in controlling for other factors that may affect the change in the price of the related good. The following section illustrates this difficulty when hedonic regression is used in its most controversial application: valuing human life.

5.7 The Value of Human Life

The most ethically charged aspect of benefit-cost analysis is its requirement that we put a **monetary value on human life**. I recall being shocked by the notion when I first learned of it in a college economics class. And yet, when we analyze the value of environmental improvement, we clearly must include as one of the most important benefits reduction in human mortality. If we seek to apply benefit-cost analysis to determine the efficient pollution level, we have no choice but to place a monetary value on life. Alternatively, if we adopt a safety standard, we can merely note the number of lives an action saves (or costs) and avoid the direct problem of valuing life in monetary terms.

And yet, because regulatory resources are limited, even the safety standard places an implicit value on human life. In the past, the U.S. Department of Transportation generally initiated regulatory actions only in cases where the implicit value of life was

---

16. Mendelsohn et al. (1992).

$1 million or more, the Occupational Safety and Health Administration employed a cutoff of between $2 million and $5 million, while the EPA used values ranging from $475,000 to $8.3 million.[17] Courts also are in the business of valuing life when they award damages in the case of wrongful death. In the past, courts have often used the discounted future earnings that an individual expected to earn over his or her lifetime. This approach has some obvious flaws: it places a zero value on the life of a retired person, for example.

Efficiency proponents argue that the best value to put on life is the one people themselves choose in the marketplace. Hedonic regression can be used to estimate this value. By isolating the wage premium people are paid to accept especially risky jobs—police officer, firefighter, coal miner—it is possible to estimate a willingness to accept an increase in the risk of death, and implicitly, the value of a life.

For example, we know from Table 5.1 that police officers face about a one in 10,000 chance of being killed by felons. Suppose that, holding factors such as age, work experience, education, race, and gender constant by means of regression analysis, it is found that police officers receive on average $700 more per year in salary than otherwise comparable individuals. Then we might infer that, collectively, police officers are willing to trade $7 million (10,000 police times $700 per officer) for one of their lives. We might then adopt this figure of $7 million per life for use in estimating the environmental benefits of reducing risk and thus saving lives.

Note that this is not the value of a specific life. Most individuals would pay their entire income to save their own life or that of a loved one. Rather, the regression attempts to measure the amount of money the "average" individual in a society requires to accept a higher risk of death from, in our case, environmental degradation. For this reason, some economists prefer to call the measure the "value of a statistical life" instead of the "value of a life." I use the latter term because the lives at stake are indeed quite real, even if they are selected from the population somewhat randomly. An overall increase in mortality risk *does* mean that human lives are in fact being exchanged for a higher level of material consumption.

Even on its own terms, we can identify at least three problems with this measure. The first is the question of *accurate information:* Do police recruits really know the increased odds of death? They might underestimate the dangers, assuming irrationally that it "won't happen to me." Or, given the prevalence of violent death on cop shows, they might actually overestimate the mortality risk. The second problem with this approach is *sample selection bias.* Individuals who become police officers are probably not representative of the "average" person regarding their preference toward risk. People attracted to police work are presumably more risk seeking than most.

A third problem with applying this measure to environmental pollution is the *involuntary nature of risk* that is generated. In labor markets, people may agree to shoulder a higher risk of death in exchange for wages; however, people may require higher compensation to accept the same risk imposed upon them without their implicit consent. Polluting the water we drink or the air we breathe is often discussed in terms of violating "rights"; rights are typically not for sale, while labor power is. We will

17. From "Putting a Price Tag on Life" (1988).

explore the issue of a "right" to a clean environment later, when we evaluate the safety standard in Chapter 7.

Hedonic regression researchers have attempted to control for these factors as best they can. Reviews of wage-risk studies suggest that the median value for a statistical life in the United States or other wealthy countries is around $7 million. By contrast, studies conducted in Bangladesh put the value there at only $150,000. This huge discrepancy again reveals the moral choices implicit when using a consumer surplus (WTP or WTA) measure of value: because poor people have less income, they will be willing to accept riskier jobs at much lower wages. This means that reductions in the risk of death emerge in this benefit-cost framework as much less valuable to them.[18]

Using hedonic measures to value life thus raises a basic question: to what extent are labor market choices to accept higher risk really "choices"? Consider the following recent description of 12-year-old Vicente Guerrero's typical day at work in a modern athletic shoe factory in Mexico City:

> He spends most of his time on dirtier work: smearing glue onto the soles of shoes with his hands. The can of glue he dips his fingers into is marked "toxic substances ... prolonged or repeated inhalation causes grave health damage; do not leave in the reach of minors." All the boys ignore the warning.[19]

Vicente works at his father's urging to supplement the family income with his wages of about $6 per day.

From one perspective, Vicente does choose to work in the factory. By doing so, he respects his father's wishes and raises the family standard of living. However, his alternatives are grim. Vicente's choices are between dying young from toxic poisoning or dying young from malnutrition. In important respects, Vicente's choices were made for him by the high levels of poverty and unemployment that he was born into.

Similarly, the "choice" that a worker in a First World country makes to accept higher risks is also conditioned by general income levels and a whole variety of politically determined factors such as the unemployment rate and benefit levels, access to court or regulatory compensation for damages, the progressivity of the tax structure, social security, disability payments, food stamps and welfare payments, and access to public education and health-care services. All these social factors influence the workers' alternatives to accepting risky work. By utilizing a hedonic regression measure for the value of life, the analyst implicitly is either endorsing the existing political determinants of the income distribution or assuming that changes in these social factors will not affect the measure very much.

Valuing life by the "acceptance" of risk in exchange for higher wages reflects the income bias built into any market-based measure of environmental benefits. The hedonic regression method values Vicente's life much less than that of an American worker of any age simply because Vicente's family has a vastly lower income. Proponents of this approach would argue that it is appropriate, because it reflects the real differences in trade-offs faced by poor and rich people. We will explore this issue further when we discuss the siting of hazardous waste facilities in Chapter 7.

---

18. From Viscusi (2004); Khanna and Chapman (1996).
19. From "Underage Workers" (1991).

The point here is to recognize this core ethical dilemma posed by using hedonic regression to determine a value of life.

5.8 Summary

This chapter discussed the methods that economists use for valuing the nonmarket benefits of environmental quality. The focus has been on problems with such measures. Consider the questions an analyst has to answer in the process of estimating, for example, the benefits of PCB cleanup:

1. Is consumer surplus a good measure of benefits, especially when valuing life?
2. Which measure should be used: WTP or WTA?
3. How reliable is the risk assessment?
4. How broad a scope of benefits should be included?
5. How precise and reliable are the benefit measures?

There simply are no generally accepted answers to any of these questions. A good benefit analyst can only state clearly the assumptions made at every turn and invite the reader to judge how sensitive the estimates might be to alternative assumptions.

Despite their many uncertainties, however, nonmarket estimates of environmental benefits are increasingly in demand by courts and policymakers. As environmental awareness has spread, claims for natural-resource damages are finding their way into courts more and more frequently. One important court decision confirmed the right to sue for nonuse-value damage to natural resources and explicitly endorsed the contingent valuation methodology as an appropriate tool for determining existence or option value.[20] In addition, policymakers require benefit estimates for various forms of benefit-cost analysis. As we discussed in the previous chapter, all new major federal regulations have been required to pass a benefit-cost test when such tests are not prohibited by law.

In an ambitious article in the journal *Nature*, an interdisciplinary group of scientists attempted to put a value on the sum total of global ecosystem services—ranging from waste treatment to atmospheric regulation to nutrient cycling.[21] They concluded, stressing the huge uncertainties involved, that ecosystems provide a flow of market and nonmarket use value greater than $33 trillion per year, as against planetary product (world GDP) of $18 trillion!

The authors use many of the tools described in this chapter. In justifying their effort, they state, "although ecosystem valuation is certainly difficult and fraught with uncertainties, one choice we do not have is whether or not to do it. Rather, the decisions we make as a society about ecosystems imply valuations (although not necessarily in monetary terms). We can choose to make these valuations explicit or not … but as long as we are forced to make choices, we are going through the process of valuation."[22]

Ultimately, economists defend benefit measures on pragmatic grounds. With all their flaws, the argument goes, they remain the best means for quantifying the

---

20. From Kopp, Portney, and Smith (1990).
21. From Costanza et al. (1997).
22. Ibid., 258.

immense advantages associated with a high-quality environment. The alternative, an impact statement like the EIS to be discussed in Chapter 10, identifies the physical benefits of preservation in great detail but fails to summarize the information in a consistent or usable form.

At this point, benefit analysis is a social science in its relative infancy; nevertheless, it is being asked to tackle very difficult issues and has already had major impacts on public policy. Thousands of environmental damage studies have been completed in the last two decades. Perhaps the wealth of research currently under way will lead to greater consensus on acceptable resolutions to the problems identified in this chapter.

APPLICATION 5.0

A Travel-Cost Example

Now it is time for your first consulting job as an environmental economist. The Forest Service would like to know whether it should set aside some national forestland, previously slated to be logged, for hiking. You are helping with a travel-cost analysis to estimate the benefits of setting aside the land.

Survey data have been gathered from 500 hikers who visited a forest in a neighboring state. Using a statistical technique called regression analysis, you have controlled for differences in income, employment status, age, and other important factors that might affect the number of hiking trips taken. Taking these factors into account, you have developed the following relationship:

Cost to Get to Hiking Areas ($)	Hiking Trips per Person per Year
20	8
40	6
80	2

1. Graph the demand curve for hiking trips as a function of the "price"—the travel cost.
2. Based on demographic information about the people living in the vicinity of the proposed park, you have estimated that 50,000 people will take an average of four hiking trips per year. For the average person, calculate (1) the consumer surplus for a single visit to the new park; (2) the total consumer surplus for an average visitor (*Hint:* the area of a triangle is $1/2[B * H]$); and (3) the total expected consumer surplus per year from the proposed park.

APPLICATION 5.1

Calculating the Value of Life

In your second consulting job, you have been trying to estimate the WTA risk on the part of workers. You have gathered data on a variety of blue-collar occupations ranging from clerical work to truck driving to coal mining. Controlling for age, gender, education, work experience, and race, you have uncovered the following relationship:

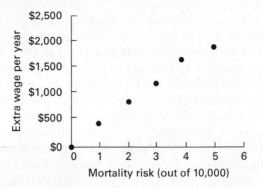

1. What is your estimate of the "value of a statistical life"? What does this mean?
2. Why might this value be a poor estimate of the value placed on lives saved from pollution reduction (give three reasons)?

APPLICATION 5.2

Plover Protection

For consulting job 3, suppose you are analyzing the use value of a public beach. Controlling for income, age, preferences, and everything else that might affect beach visits, you have gathered the following data:

Travel Cost ($)	Number of Day Trips/Yr
0	40
20	20
39	1
40	0

1. If there are 1,000 people in each of the three travel-cost categories $0, $20, and $39, what is the approximate total consumer surplus arising from day trips to this beach?
2. Your boss needs help evaluating a decision to close this particular beach in order to preserve habitat for an endangered seabird, called a plover, that inhabits only this stretch of beach. From a CV study, you know that U.S. citizens are WTP $1,500,000/yr to preserve the plover. Based on your analysis and your understanding of the usefulness and limitations of these benefit analyses, do you conclude that protecting the plover is efficient? Argue both sides. (This answer requires at least four paragraphs!)
3. Under the Endangered Species Act, could your analysis have any legal bearing on the decision to protect the plover?

APPLICATION 5.3

Benefit-Cost Controversy

When taken to its extreme, the logic of benefit-cost analysis can generate some strange conclusions. In one case, researchers wanted to determine the value that mothers placed on their children's lives. In Indiana in 1985, parents were not fined for failure to have car seats for infants and toddlers, though they were legally required. Also, some parents would not take the time to fasten car seats correctly. Two economists reckoned that this behavior (failure to purchase or correctly use car seats) on the part of the mothers raised the risk of death to their children by 0.0004, or 4 out of 10,000, from birth to age 4. They collected data on 190 people (all women) leaving a shopping mall with their kids; only 33% either had a car seat or were using it correctly.[23]

The authors calculated that properly hooking the kids in would take about 69 hours over four years. They hypothesized that the opportunity cost of women's time would be an important determinant of whether car seats were installed or properly used. And using a statistical model, they in fact concluded that controlling for (some) other factors, moms with a higher opportunity cost to their time (generally, a higher forgone wage) were statistically less likely (though not at a high level of confidence) to install or properly use a car seat.

From this, they calculated that a wage increase equal in value to about $2.40 per hour would, all other things equal, induce a mom to forgo installing or properly using a car seat—all this leading finally to the following estimated value of a child's life:

$2.40 per hour saved * 69 hours saved per mom/0.0004 lives lost
per mom = $418,597 per life lost

Note that this number is well below the $7 million figure used by the EPA for adults, even accounting for inflation since the time of the study.

1. Does this conclusion make sense to you? If not, why not?

APPLICATION 5.4

Rethinking the Value of Life

In the political tug-of-war over benefit-cost analysis, some economists have argued that rather than value human lives saved as a result of regulation, we should instead value "life years." The reasoning here is that many regulations that protect, for example, air quality, have the effect of extending the lives of older people—so it is primarily old folks who benefit from pollution control.

So rather than use a figure of $7 million per life for 10,000 lives saved, the idea would be to use $7 million * 5/80, figuring that the regulations, on average, extend the lives of a sample of old folks from ages 75 to 80. This new accounting of course would lead to many fewer regulations in passing a benefit-cost test, and so it was advocated by conservative politicians. When the George W. Bush administration proposed a move

---

23. From Carlin and Sandy (1991).

toward using life years saved in benefit-cost analysis, it was widely attacked as a "senior death discount," and the proposal was quickly withdrawn.[24]

   a.   From within the framework of economics, can you imagine why other economists object to this change in valuation from lives saved to life years saved? In particular, can you think of two reasons why a 75-year-old might value (be willing to pay) more to reduce risk and live an additional year than would a teenager?

   b.   That said, and ignoring the 5/80 fraction, are you persuaded by the general logic that a regulation that saves the lives of a 75-year-old should show up with measured benefits relative to a regulation that saves the lives of 40-year-olds? Why or why not?

KEY IDEAS IN EACH SECTION

5.0   There are both **market and nonmarket benefits** to environmental protection. Market benefits are measured at their dollar value; a value for nonmarket benefits must be estimated using economic tools.

5.1   The **total value** of an environmental benefit can be broken down into three parts: **use**, **option**, and **existence values**.

5.2   Economists consider the benefits of environmental protection to be equal to the **consumer surplus** gained by individuals through such environmental measures. For a freely provided public good, like clean air or water, a consumer's **willingness to pay (WTP)** for a small increase in the good or **willingness to accept (WTA)** a small decrease should be a good approximation to consumer surplus gained or lost. In actuality, however, measured WTA is almost always substantially greater than measured WTP. **Prospect theory** provides one explanation for the difference; a second explanation depends on the closeness of substitutes for the good in question.

5.3   Environmental risks must be estimated by means of epidemiological or animal studies. The estimated risk to humans varies depending on factors such as the assumed **dose-response model**. The risk to the population at large from an environmental hazard depends on both the toxicity of the pollutant and the number of people or animals exposed. Public perceptions of relative risk often differ from those based on scientific risk assessment. Among other factors, this may be due to a distrust of scientists, as well as **risk aversion**.

5.4   The first approach used for estimating nonmarket benefits is based on survey responses and is known as **contingent valuation (CV)**. CV studies are controversial due to the possibility of **free riding**, and **strategic**, **hypothetical**, and **embedding biases**. However, CV is the only available approach for estimating benefits of environmental protection based primarily on **existence value**.

---

24. See Revesz and Livermore (2008, 77–84).

5.5 Another approach for estimating nonmarket benefits is the **travel-cost method**, used principally for valuing parks, lakes, and beaches. Researchers construct a demand curve for the resource by relating information about travel cost to the intensity of the resource use, holding all other factors constant.

5.6 The final method of measuring the nonmarket benefits of environmental protection is known as **hedonic regression**. This approach estimates the benefits of an increase in environmental quality by examining the change in the price of related goods, holding all other factors constant.

5.7 Hedonic regressions that rely on the wage premium for risky jobs are used to place a **monetary value on human life**. This is often necessary if benefit-cost analysis is to be used for deciding the right amount of pollution. This is a gruesome task; yet, even if regulators do not explicitly put a dollar value on life, some value of life is implicitly chosen whenever a regulatory decision is made. As a market-based measure, hedonic regression assigns a higher value of life to wealthier people, because their WTP to avoid risks is higher. This poses an obvious moral dilemma.

REFERENCES

Alberini, Anna, and James Kahn. 2006. *Handbook on contingent valuation.* Northampton, MA: Edward Elgar.

American Lung Association. 2009. *State of the air.* http://www.lungusa.org/about-us/publications/.

Arrow, Kenneth, Robert Solow, Edward Leamer, R. Radner, and H. Schuman. 1993. Report of the NOAA panel on contingent valuation. *Federal Register* 58(10): 4201–614.

Bell, Frederick, and Vernon Leeworthy. 1990. Recreational demand by tourists for saltwater beach days. *Journal of Environmental Economics and Management* 18(3): 189–205.

Bishop, Richard C., and Michael P. Welsh. 1992. Existence value and resource evaluation. Unpublished paper.

Boyle, Kevin J., and Richard C. Bishop. 1987. Valuing wildlife in benefit-cost analysis: A case study involving endangered species. *Water Resources Research* 23: 942–50.

Bromley, Daniel. 1995. Property rights and natural resource damage assessments. *Ecological Economics* 14(3): 129–35.

Costanza, R., R. d'Arge, R. de Groot, S. Farber, M. Grasso, B. Hannon, K. Limburg, et al. 1997. The value of the world's ecosystem services and natural capital. *Nature* 387(6630): 253–59.

Freeman, A. Myrick III. 1985. Supply uncertainty, option price, and option value. *Land Economics* 61(2): 176–81.

———. 1993. *The measurement of environmental and resource values: Theory and methods.* Washington, DC: Resources for the Future.

Glenn, Barbara S., J. A. Foran, and Mark Van Putten. 1989. *Summary of quantitative health assessments for PCBs, DDT, dieldrin and chlordane.* Ann Arbor, MI: National Wildlife Federation.

Gough, Michael. 1989. Estimating cancer mortality. *Environmental Science and Technology* 8(23): 925–30.

Horowitz, J., and K. McConnell. 2002. A review of WTA/WTP studies. *Journal of Environmental Economics and Management*, 44: 426–47.

Johnson, Kevin. 2008. Police deaths plummet in first half of '08. *USA Today*, 10 July, Page 1.

Johnson, Laurie. 1999. Cost perceptions and voter demand for environmental risk regulation: The double effect of hidden costs. *Journal of Risk and Uncertainty* 18(3): 295–320.

———. 2003. Consumer versus citizen preferences: Can they be disentangled? Working paper, University of Denver.

Kahneman, Daniel, and Amos Tversky. 1979. Prospect theory: An analysis of decisions under risk. *Econometrica* 47(2): 263–91.

Kammen, Daniel, and David Hassenzahl. 1999. *Should we risk it?: Exploring environmental, health, and technological problem solving.* Rutherford, NJ: Princeton University Press.

Khanna, Neha, and Duane Chapman. 1996. Time preference, abatement costs and international climate change policy: An appraisal of IPCC 1995. *Contemporary Economic Policy* 13(2): 56–66.

———. 2007. Biased valuations, damage assessments, and policy choices: The choice of measurement matters. *Ecological Economics*, 63: 684–89.

Knetsch, Jack, and Daniel Kahneman. 1992. Valuing public goods: The purchase of moral satisfaction. *Journal of Environmental Economics and Management* 22(1): 57–70.

Kopp, Raymond J., Paul R. Portney, and V. Kerry Smith. 1990. Natural resource damages: The economics have shifted after *Ohio v. United States Department of the Interior*. *Environmental Law Reporter* 20: 10127–31.

Mendelsohn, Robert, Daniel Hellerstein, Michael Huguenin, Robert Unsworth, and Richard Brazee. 1992. Measuring hazardous waste damages with panel models. *Journal of Environmental Economics and Management* 22(3): 259–71.

Mitchell, Robert Cameron, and Richard T. Carson. 1989. *Using surveys to value public goods: The contingent valuation method*. Washington, DC: Resources for the Future.

National Cancer Institute. 2010. *FactSheet*. www.cancer.gov/cancertopics/factsheet/Tobacco/cessation.

National Safety Council. 2010. http://www.nsc.org/news_resources/Documents/nscInjuryFacts2011_037.pdf.

Putting a price tag on life. 1988. *Newsweek*, 11 January, 40.

Shaw, W. Douglas. 1991. Recreational demand by tourists for saltwater beach days: Comment. *Journal of Environmental Economics and Management* 20: 284–89.

Underage workers fill Mexican factories, stir U.S. trade debate. 1991. *Wall Street Journal*, 8 April.

U.S. Environmental Protection Agency. 1990. *Reducing risk: Setting priorities and strategies for environmental protection*. Washington, DC: U.S. EPA.

———. 2010. *What's your EnviroQ?* www.epa.gov/epahome/enviroq/index.htm#lungcancer.

Value of intangible losses from Exxon Valdez spill put at $3 billion. 1991. *Washington Post*, 20 March.

Viscusi, W. Kip. 2004. The value of life. In *New Palgrave dictionary of economics and the law* (2nd ed.) New York: Palgrave Macmillan.

Wilson, Richard, and E. A. C. Crouch. 1987. Risk assessment and comparisons: An introduction. *Science* 236: 267–70.

APPENDIX 5A

WTA and WTP Redux

In Chapter 5, we noted that there is a large and persistent gap between people's estimated WTP for environmental cleanup and their WTA compensation in exchange for environmental degradation. Two explanations have been offered for this. The first is prospect theory: people form an attachment to the status quo, and thus feel less strongly about cleanup than they do about degradation. A second explanation flows from conventional economic theory. It turns out, as this appendix shows, that when goods have few substitutes, WTA *should* be higher than WTP. We also review here the results of an interesting experiment that tried to sort out whether observed WTA-WTP disparities are best explained by this "no good substitutes" argument, or prospect theory, and think a little more about why it matters.

5A.1 An Indifference Curve Analysis

Because this appendix is optional,[1] we are going to assume that you recall perfectly how indifference curve analysis works from a previous course and jump right into the diagrams. Figure 5A.1 shows my (Eban's) indifference curve map for standard quarters and one of the state quarter series, the one with Wyoming on the tails side. The curves are drawn in a straight line, implying that, to me, the goods are perfect substitutes, with a (marginal) rate of substitution of 1:1. I am not a coin collector, I just like money. So I am equally as happy with four standard quarters and one Wyoming quarter as with one standard and four Wyomings.

---

1. This presentation follows Hanneman (1991) and Shogren et al. (1994).

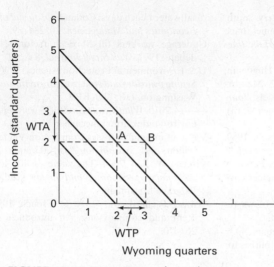

FIGURE 5A.1 WTA-WTP: Perfect Substitutes

Now suppose I am at point A (2, 2). What is my *maximum* WTP to get one more Wyoming and move to point B (3, 2)? The answer is illustrated by the distance marked WTP in the diagram; if I paid $0.25 to get to B, I would be just as well off as I was at A—paying anything less makes me better off. Therefore, $0.25 is my *maximum* WTP.

Let's change the rules. Suppose I am still at point A (2, 2). What is my *minimum* WTA to give up a chance to move to B (3, 2)? To be equally happy as I would have been at B, I need to be given income until I am on the same indifference curve as B. But that is the distance marked WTA on the diagram—again one standard quarter or $0.25. When goods are perfect substitutes, WTA and WTP should be identical.[2]

In Figure 5A.2, the trading gets more serious. I am now confronted with a choice of spending money to reduce my risk of death: let's say I can do this by laying out additional dollars each month on pesticide-free organic vegetables. On the horizontal axis, the risk of death gets more severe as we move toward the origin. For the purposes of illustration, let us also say that each additional $1 per month spent on pesticide-free veggies reduces my extra risk of dying by one out of a million.

Note that these indifference curves are not straight lines; instead, they have the conventional bowed-in shape. The slope of the indifference curves decreases as risk levels decrease, reflecting a decreasing rate of marginal substitution. At high levels of risk I am willing to trade a lot of income to reduce risk a little. But as my risk level decreases, I am less willing to accept cash in exchange for further safety. Put another way, at high risk levels, cash is not a good substitute for risk reduction.

As the diagram shows, when goods are not perfect substitutes, WTA will tend to be higher than WTP—a lot higher when the indifference curves are steeper, indicating poor substitutability. If I start at point A (with $250 per month and a four out of a million increased risk of death by pesticide consumption), then my *maximum* WTP to move to an excess risk of three out of a million is the line segment labeled WTP—equivalent

2. Ignoring small income effects.

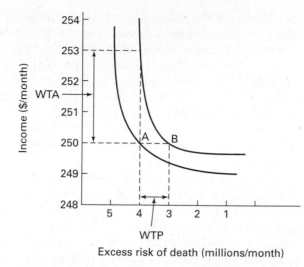

FIGURE 5A.2 WTA-WTP: Poor Substitutes

to $1. By contrast, my *minimum* WTA compensation to stay at an excess risk level of four out of a million is illustrated on the income axis. To be just as content as I would have been at point B, I would have to be given enough cash to get me out to the higher indifference curve, or $3. It is apparent from this diagram that WTA will generally be bigger than WTP, and the difference increases as one moves along the horizontal axis toward the origin and higher risk levels.

5A.2 Prospect Theory or Substitutability?

A group of researchers had fun trying to sort out the explanation—prospect theory or poor substitutes—for the observed differences between WTA and WTP by doing experiments with a panel of college students. In the first experiment, the panel members were given an initial endowment of $3 and a small piece of candy. The researchers then conducted a series of trials to find out how much students would be WTP to upgrade to a brand-name candy bar. In an alternate series of experiments, different students were given the cash and the candy bar and then asked their WTA cash to downgrade to the small piece of candy.[3]

The second experiment raised the ante: students were given $15 and a food product like a conventional deli sandwich, which of course bears a low risk of a possible infection from pathogens such as salmonella. Students were then asked how much they would pay to upgrade to a stringently screened food product with a very low risk of infection. In addition to hearing a bit about the symptoms of salmonella infection, they were also provided with the following sort of information: "The chance of infection of salmonellosis is one in 125 annually. Of those individuals who get sick, one individual out of 1,000 will die annually. The average cost for medical expenses and productivity losses from a mild case of salmonella is $220."

---

3. From Shogren et al. (1994).

In the last stage of the experiment, the researchers flipped the property rights. This time, they gave the students the screened food product and the $15 and then asked their WTA cash to downgrade to the conventional product. (In both cases, of course, the students actually had to eat the sandwiches!) Each subject participated in either both WTP experiments or both WTA experiments, but no individual was involved in WTP *and* WTA sessions. Finally, each of the 142 participants sat through several trials to allow them to gain experience with the experimental procedure.

In the candy bar experiment, WTA and WTP quickly converged very close to the market price of $0.50. However, for risk reduction, WTA remained well above WTP, even after 20 repeated trials. For exposure to salmonella, the mean WTA was $1.23, twice the WTP of $0.56. The authors concluded that this experiment, along with subsequent work, provides support for a "no good substitutes" explanation of the WTA-WTP discrepancy, as opposed to one based on prospect theory. Do you agree?

Advocates of prospect theory might respond that candy bars or other low-value items do not provide a good test of the two theories: people are not likely to become attached to a candy bar or a coffee mug in the same way that they might become attached to a grove of trees in a local park. In this sense, the two explanations begin to converge. People are attached to the status quo because there are no good substitutes for environmental degradation from the status quo!

Regardless of the explanation, this experiment also illustrates that the choice of WTP or WTA in some sense flows naturally from the assignment of property rights. If people own the conventional sandwich, then it makes sense to ask their WTP to upgrade; if they own the superior sandwich, then it is natural to ask their WTA to downgrade.

REFERENCES

Hanneman, Michael. 1991. Willingness to pay and willingness to accept: How much can they differ? *American Economic Review* 81(3): 635–47.

Shogren, Jason, Seung Y. Shin, Dermot Hayes, and James Kliebenstein. 1994. Resolving differences in willingness to pay and willingness to accept. *American Economic Review* 84(1): 255–70.

MEASURING THE COSTS OF ENVIRONMENTAL PROTECTION

6.0 Introduction

When the Environmental Protection Agency tightened the national air-quality standard for smog (ground-level ozone), the agency developed official cost estimates for this regulation ranging from $600 million to $2.5 billion per year. Where do numbers like this come from?[1]

On the face of it, measuring the costs associated with environmental cleanup appears substantially easier than measuring benefits. One can simply add up all the expected expenditures by firms on pollution-control equipment and personnel, plus local, state, and federal government expenditures on regulatory efforts, including the drafting, monitoring, and enforcing of regulations. This **engineering approach** to measuring cost is by far the most widespread method in use.

However, because engineering cost estimates are often *predicted* costs, they require making assumptions about future behavior. For example, cost estimates may assume full compliance with pollution laws or assume that firms will adopt a particular type of pollution-control technology to meet the standards. To the extent that these assumptions fail to foresee the future accurately, engineering cost estimates may be misleading on their own terms. In a famous case of getting it wrong, the EPA overestimated the costs of sulfur dioxide control by a factor of two to four; "credible" industry estimates were eight times too high.[2]

Moreover, from the economic point of view, there are additional problems with the engineering approach. Economists employ a measure of cost known as **opportunity cost**: the value of resources in their next best available use. Suppose the new smog laws

1. From "EPA Plans" (1997).
2. See Harrington, Morgenstern, and Nelson (1999).

lead to engineering costs of $2 billion per year. If as a society we were not devoting this $2 billion to pollution control, would we be able to afford just $2 billion in other goods and services? More? Less? The answer to this question provides the true measure of the cost of environmental protection.

Engineering cost estimates will overstate true social costs to the extent that government involvement (1) increases productivity by increasing the efficiency with which available resources are used, forcing technological change, or improving worker health or ecosystem services, and/or (2) reduces unemployment by creating "green jobs."

On the other hand, engineering cost estimates underestimate true social costs to the extent that government involvement (1) lowers productivity growth by diverting investment and/or (2) induces structural unemployment. This chapter first examines EPA estimates of economy-wide engineering costs, along with an example of the potential costs of reducing global-warming pollution. We then consider the degree to which these estimates overstate or understate the "true" costs of environmental protection. We end with a final look at the benefit-cost analysis and its role in generating more efficient environmental protection.

6.1 Engineering Costs

Engineering cost estimates require the use of accounting conventions to "annualize" capital investments—in other words, to spread out the cost of investments in plant and equipment over their expected lifetimes. Table 6.1 provides EPA estimates of the historical "annualized" engineering costs of pollution control in the United States since the major federal programs were initiated in the early 1970s.

The figures in Table 6.1 for 1990 to 2000 are estimated and assume full compliance with pollution-control regulations. Fixed capital costs for each year are determined by depreciating on a straight-line basis and assuming firms pay a 7% interest rate on funds borrowed to finance the investment.

The table shows historical annual pollution-control expenditures for four categories of pollutants—air, water, land, and chemicals—as well as an "other" category including unassigned EPA administrative and research expenses. The costs listed cover all direct compliance and regulatory expenses for pollution control, including investments in pollution-control equipment and personnel, the construction of municipal water treatment plants, and the bill your family pays to your local garbage collector. (Note that these costs are not identical to the costs of environmental regulation: even without regulations, the private sector would undertake some amount of sewage treatment and garbage disposal!)

As a nation, we are indeed devoting greater attention to pollution control. Over a period of 25 years, total spending rose from $43 billion to more than $260 billion. Perhaps more significantly, pollution control as a percentage of GNP rose from less than 1% in 1972 to 2.1% in 1990 to more than 2.8% by 2000. Thus pollution control more than doubled its claim on the nation's resources.

The next big step in pollution control for the United States, and the rest of the world, is attacking global warming. Figure 6.1 provides one very detailed engineering-cost assessment of reducing global-warming emissions at a global level. On the vertical axis, the figure shows the marginal costs in $ per tonne of CO_2e (CO_2 "equivalents" or CO_2 plus other greenhouse gases) reduced from a variety of measures and technologies

TABLE 6.1   U.S. Annualized Pollution Control Costs (2005 $ billion)

Type of Pollutant	Year			
	1972	1980	1990	2000
AIR				
Air	$12.9	$28.8	$ 45.1	$ 71.5
Radiation	$ 0.0	$ 0.2	$ 0.7	$ 1.5
WATER				
Quality	$14.9	$37.3	$ 63.5	$ 93.4
Drinking	$ 1.3	$ 3.2	$ 5.6	$ 10.7
LAND				
Waste disp.	$13.7	$22.2	$ 40.5	$ 61.9
Superfund	$ 0.0	$ 0.0	$ 2.8	$ 13.1
CHEMICALS				
Toxics	$ 0.1	$ 0.7	$ 0.9	$ 2.0
Pesticides	$ 0.1	$ 0.8	$ 1.6	$ 2.8
OTHER	$ 0.1	$ 1.5	$ 2.7	$ 3.7
TOTAL	$43.3	$94.6	$163.6	$260.3
% of GNP	0.9	1.6	2.1	2.8

Note: Both the costs and GNP shares from 1990 to 2000 are estimated.
Source: Carlin (1990).

that are either already available today or are near commercialization. On the horizontal axis, the figure illustrates the total reduction in gigatons of CO_2e per year achieved by taking these steps.

A gigaton is equal to a billion tons of avoided carbon dioxide emissions—also equivalent to what has been called one "wedge." To stabilize global warming at the low end (4 degrees F warming, with the CO_2 blanket at 450 ppm) would require cutting emissions by the full 38 wedges of CO_2 listed, all by 2040 or so. This, in turn, would require implementing the full suite of technologies in the diagram, or a comparable set.[3]

First note that the researchers argue that the first 12 gigatons can actually be gotten at negative cost—these measures would save businesses and households money. So, for example, the very first bar is labeled "Lighting—switch residential to LED." LED (light-emitting diode) sources use about half the energy of compact fluorescent (CFL) bulbs, and about one-tenth that of a conventional incandescent lamp. Making the switch to LED would save consumers $120 in reduced energy costs for every ton of emissions reduced. Close to the zero dollar point at 12 gigatons reduced, small-scale hydro is still below the line (just barely profitable), while the next category, reducing slash-and-burn agriculture in tropical rain forests, rises above the line (costs a little, but not much). Finally, at the high end, capturing carbon emitted from existing coal plants and sequestering it underground (coal CCS retrofit) is estimated to cost about $55 per ton, while similar sequestration and storage of carbon from old natural gas plants (gas CCS rerofit) is the most expensive option considered, weighing in at about $75 per ton.

---

3. A 38 CO_2 wedge strategy would be roughly equivalent to a 12- to 14-wedge carbon approach, as described in Romm (2009).

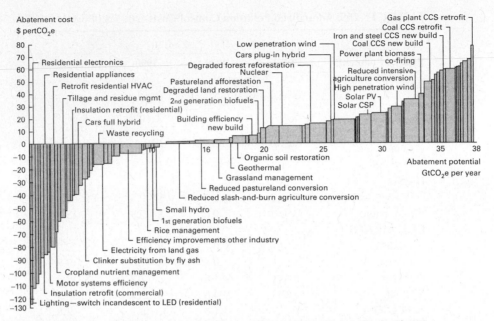

FIGURE 6.1 Global GHG Abatement Cost Curve Beyond Business-as-Usual, 2030
Source: Beinhocker et al. (2008) and Romm (2008).

Overall, the annual cost estimate for reducing 38 gigatons a year by 2030 is around 1% of global GDP—currently about $500 billion. (Quick Puzzle: How would you calculate this *total cost* from the marginal cost curve in Figure 6.1? See Application 6.1.) Assuming that the United States does aggressively attack global warming, then over the next decade we might expect the annual engineering costs of pollution control to rise by 1% point, from around 3% of U.S. GDP to about 4%. The question we seek to answer in the rest of the chapter is this: Do these engineering estimates understate or overstate the true social costs of environmental protection?

6.2 Productivity Impacts of Regulation

Undoubtedly, the biggest unknown when it comes to estimating the costs of environmental protection is its impact on *productivity*. Productivity, or output per worker, is a critical economic measure. Rising productivity means the economic pie per worker is growing. A growing pie, in turn, makes it easier for society to accommodate both the needs of a growing population and the desire for a higher material standard of living.

Between 1974 and 1995, productivity growth in the United States averaged only 1%, well below the 3% rate the American economy experienced in the 1950s and 1960s. And because growth is a cumulative process, the small changes in productivity had dramatic long-run effects. If, rather than declining after 1974, productivity growth had continued at its 1950 to 1970 rate of 3%, GDP in 2007 would have been several trillion dollars greater than it actually was!

Although productivity growth rebounded after 1995, some have charged that environmental regulations specifically were a major contributor to the productivity slowdown. By contrast, others have argued that pollution-control efforts can *spur* productivity growth by forcing firms to become more efficient in their use of resources and adopt new and cheaper production techniques. As we will see, this debate is far from settled. But because productivity growth compounds over time, the impact of regulations on productivity—whether positive or negative—is a critical factor in determining the "true" costs of environmental protection.

First, let us evaluate the pro-regulation arguments. Theoretically, regulation can improve productivity in three ways: (1) by improving the short-run efficiency of resource use; (2) by encouraging firms to invest more, or invest "smarter" for the long run; and (3) by reducing health-care or firm-level cleanup costs, which then frees up capital for long-run investment.

You can see an example of the short-run efficiency argument clearly in Figure 6.1. The economists who estimated the cost curve for attacking global-warming pollution believe they have identified hundreds of billions of dollars of waste in the global economic system. Tremendous cost-savings could be gained immediately, if firms (and households) would only adopt already existing, energy-efficient technologies—more efficient lighting, cooling, heating, and mechanical systems. These savings in turn would free up capital for productive investment in other sectors of the economy. However, other economists are suspicious that these so-called free lunches are actually widespread, arguing on theoretical grounds that "there ain't no such thing." Why would competitive firms ignore these huge cost-saving opportunities if they really existed? Chapter 19 is devoted to a discussion of energy policy and the free-lunch argument. For now, recognize that should regulation force firms to use energy more cost-effectively, greater output from fewer inputs, and thus an increase in productivity, will result.

The second avenue by which regulation may increase productivity is by speeding up, or otherwise improving, the capital-investment process. The so-called Porter hypothesis, named after Harvard Business School Professor Michael Porter, argues that regulation, while imposing short-run costs on firms, often enhances their long-run competitiveness.[4] This can happen if regulation favors forward-looking firms, anticipates trends, speeds investment in modern production processes, encourages R&D, or promotes "outside the box," nonconventional thinking.

For example, rather than installing "end of the pipe" equipment to treat their emissions, some firms have developed new production methods to aggressively reduce waste, cutting both costs and pollution simultaneously. In this case, regulation has played a **technology-forcing role**, encouraging firms to develop more productive manufacturing methods by setting standards they must achieve. More broadly, as was discussed in Chapter 3, the whole sustainable business movement is predicated on solving environmental problems, profitably, and achieving superior business performance by reducing risks, improving resource efficiency, and developing innovative substitutes for polluting products and processes. A number of studies have supported the Porter hypothesis, finding that firms known for environmental leadership are no less profitable, and often are more profitable than the average for their industry.[5]

---

4. From Porter and van der Linde (1995), Goodstein (1999), and Ambec et al. (2011).
5. Sturmak, Bud, and Cary Krosinsky. 2011. *"On performance" in evolutions in sustainable investing*, ed. Cary Krosinsky. New York: Wiley.

Finally, the third positive impact of regulation on productivity flows from the health and ecosystem benefits that arise from environmental protection. In the absence of pollution-control measures, the U.S. population would have experienced considerably higher rates of sickness and premature mortality. In addition, firms that rely on clean water or air for production processes would have faced their own internal cleanup costs. These factors would have reduced productivity directly and also indirectly because expenditures on health care and private cleanup would have risen dramatically. This spending, in turn, would have represented a drain on productive investment resources quite comparable to mandated expenditures on pollution control.

Productivity may also be dampened in a variety of ways. First, regulation imposes direct costs on regulated firms; these costs may crowd out investment in conventional capital. Second, a further slowdown in new investment may occur when regulation is more stringent for new sources of pollution, as it often is. Third, regulation will cause higher prices for important economy-wide inputs such as energy and waste disposal. These cost increases, in turn, will lead to reductions in capital investment in secondary industries directly unaffected by regulation, for example, the health and financial sectors of the economy.

Finally, regulation may frustrate entrepreneurial activity. Businesspeople complain frequently of the "regulatory burden" and "red tape" associated with regulation, including environmental regulation. Filling out forms, obtaining permits, and holding public hearings all add an additional "hassle" to business that may discourage some investment.

However, despite the chorus of voices attacking regulation as one of the main culprits in explaining low levels of American productivity growth, evidence for this position is not strong. On balance, federal environmental regulations primarily put in place in the 1970s and 1980s reduced measured productivity in heavily regulated industries somewhat; yet, such effects account for only a small portion of the total productivity slowdown. Moreover, in the absence of regulation, productivity would have fallen anyway due to increased illness and the subsequent diversion of investment resources into the health-care field. Finally, there is scattered evidence for productivity improvements arising from regulation, following both the Porter hypothesis and the energy-efficiency lines of argument. Rolling back environmental laws to their 1970 status, even if this were possible, would at best make a small dent in the problem of reduced U.S. productivity and might easily make things worse.[6]

Nevertheless, due to the large cumulative effects on output of even small reductions in productivity growth, minimizing potential negative productivity impacts is one of the most important aspects of sensibly designed regulatory policy. As we shall see in Chapters 15 and 16, regulations can be structured to better encourage the introduction of more productive, and lower cost, pollution-control technologies. Bottom-line: long-run productivity impacts are important, and economy-wide, it is hard to assess their overall impact—either in direction or magnitude. Thus the true cost of existing or proposed environmental clean-up measures can be hard to assess—yet another challenge to benefit-cost-based decision making.

6. See the review in Goodstein (1999) as well as Boyd and McClelland (1999), Xepapadeas and de Zeeuw (1999), Morgenstern, Pizer, and Shih (1997), Ambec et al. (2011), and Graff Zivin, and Neidell (2011).

6.3 Employment Impacts of Regulation

Is environmental protection (1) a "job killer," (2) a "green jobs" engine, or (3) neither of these? Many people do believe there may, in fact, be a serious **jobs versus environment trade-off**. In one poll, an astounding one-third of respondents thought it somewhat or very likely that their own jobs were threatened by environmental regulation![7]

Much of this perception is due to overheated political rhetoric. A case in point was that of the 1990 Clean Air Act Amendments, which regulated both sulfur dioxide emissions from acid rain and airborne toxic emissions from factories. In the run-up to the legislation, economists employed by industry groups predicted short-term job losses ranging from "at a minimum" 200,000, up to a high of two million, and argued that passage of the law would relegate the United States to "the status of a second-class industrial power" by 2000.

Now despite apocalyptic forecasts like this, the law passed. Did jobs drop as much as predicted—or even anywhere close? Between 1992 and 1997, a period in which substantial reductions in SO_2 emissions were achieved—an average of 1,000 workers per year were laid off nationwide as a direct result of the Clean Air Act Amendments, for a total of 5,000 jobs lost nationwide. In an economy that was losing two million jobs from non-environmental causes in a normal year, this was a very small number, and it was far, far below the "minimum" forecast of 200,000.

Over the last four decades, economists have looked closely at the employment impacts of environmental protection. Four lessons stand out clearly:

- **No economy-wide trade-off**: At the macro level, gradual job losses are at least matched by job gains.
- **Green job growth**: Spending on environmental protection (versus spending in other areas that are more import or capital intensive) can boost net job growth when the economy is not already at full employment.
- **Small numbers of actual layoffs**: Direct job losses arising from plant shutdowns due to environmental protection are very small: about 2,000 per year in the United States.
- **Few pollution havens**: Pollution-intensive firms are not fleeing in large numbers to developing countries with lax regulations.

ECONOMY-WIDE EFFECTS

Widespread fears of job loss from environmental protection need to be understood in the context of a "deindustrialization and downsizing" process that became increasingly apparent to U.S. citizens during the 1980s and 1990s. Over the last couple of decades, the United States lost millions of manufacturing jobs, due primarily to increased import competition both from First World nations and newly industrializing countries. At the same time, U.S. manufacturers increasingly began turning to offshore production, investing in manufacturing facilities in low-wage countries rather than at home. High-paying manufacturing jobs were once the backbone of the blue-collar middle class in the United States. Has environmental regulation contributed to this dramatic shift away from manufacturing and over to service employment? The surprising answer is no.

---

7. Goodstein (1999), 5.

On the one hand, stringent pollution regulations might be expected to discourage investment in certain industries, mining and "dirty" manufacturing in particular. This will contribute to **structural unemployment**, most of which will disappear in the long run as displaced workers find new jobs elsewhere in the economy. In essence, regulation cannot "create" long-run unemployment; instead, it will contribute to a shift in the types of jobs that the economy creates. Indeed, today, several million jobs are directly or indirectly related to pollution abatement in the United States.[8]

This notion of job shifting should be familiar to you from the first week of your Econ 100 class, in which you undoubtedly saw a diagram that looked something like the one in Figure 6.2. This production-possibilities frontier (or transformation curve) shows how the economy has shifted from 1970 to 2014. If regulation were to have caused widespread unemployment, the economy would have moved from point A to point C.

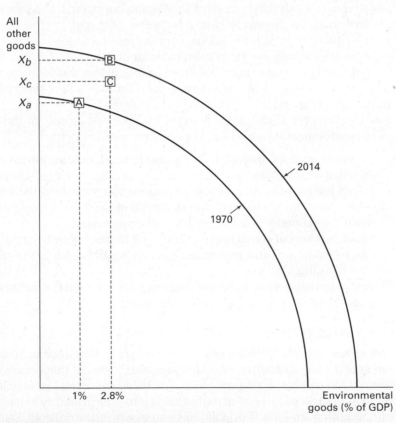

FIGURE 6.2 A Jobs-Environment Trade-Off?

8. By "directly and indirectly," I include multiplier effects. For example, a complete accounting of jobs in the aluminum recycling industry needs to include workers in the steel industry who make the machines to recycle aluminum, as well as workers who make the equipment to make the steel to make the aluminum recycling machines, and so on. Economists use input-output models to capture all these indirect effects. The U.S. Environmental Protection Agency (1995) provides an employment estimate of 2 million.

However, again referring to your Econ 100 class, you know that until the 2008 recession, the U.S. economy was operating very close to full employment: at point B. Indeed, the Federal Reserve Board raised interest rates several times during the last 20 years to try to cool down the economy, by *raising* the unemployment rate. Over the past two decades, the constraint on economy-wide job growth has been the inflationary fears of the Federal Reserve, not an economy devoting 2.8% of output to environmental protection.

What kinds of jobs are generated by environmental spending? In fact, environmental protection provides employment heavily weighted to the traditional blue-collar manufacturing and construction sectors. Figure 6.3 illustrates this point, providing an estimated breakdown of the composition of nonagricultural jobs directly and indirectly dependent on environmental spending with comparative figures for the economy as a whole.

While only 20% of all nonfarm jobs were in the manufacturing and construction sectors, 31% of employment generated by environmental spending fell in one of these categories. By contrast, only 12% of environment-dependent jobs were in wholesale and retail trade, finance, insurance, or real estate, compared to 29% for the economy as a whole. And despite criticisms that environmental regulation creates jobs only for pencil-pushing regulators, less than 12% of environmental employment was governmental, as compared to an economy-wide government employment rate of 17%.

How can we account for these results? Environmental protection is an industrial business. The private sector spends tens of billions of dollars on pollution-control plants and equipment and on pollution-control operations ranging from sewage and solid waste disposal to the purchase and maintenance of air pollution-control devices on

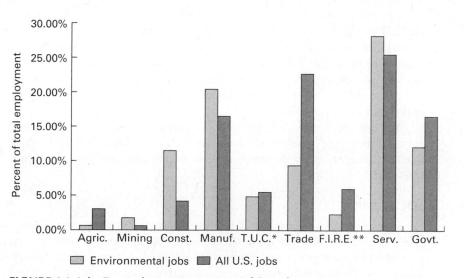

FIGURE 6.3 Jobs Dependent on Environmental Spending
* Transportation, utilities, and communication.
** Finance, insurance, and real estate.
Source: Author's calculations from U.S. Environmental Protection Agency (1995) and *Employment and Earnings*, Washington, DC: U.S. Department of Labor. Data are from 1991.

smokestacks and in vehicles. Federal, state, and local governments spend billions more on the construction of municipal sewage facilities. In addition, a very small percentage of all environmental spending supports the government's direct regulation and monitoring establishment. The bulk of environmental spending thus remains in the private sector, generating a demand for workers disproportionately weighted to manufacturing and construction and away from services. This is not to say that environmental spending creates only high-quality, high-paying jobs. But it does support jobs in traditional blue-collar industries.

GREEN JOBS

Of course, the several million jobs in the environmental industry are not net jobs created. If the money had not been spent on environmental protection, it would have been spent elsewhere—perhaps on health care, travel, imported goods, or investment in new plants and equipment. This spending, too, would have created jobs. In the long run, the level of economy-wide employment is determined by the interaction of business cycles and government fiscal and monetary policy. However, in the short run, and locally, where we spend our dollars does matter for regions facing structural unemployment. As a rule, money spent on sectors that are both more labor-intensive (directly and indirectly) and have a higher domestic content (directly and indirectly) will generate more American jobs in the short run. Environmental spending is often either labor-intensive or has a high domestic content.

To illustrate, a recent study examined a "green stimulus" package recommendation for the Obama administration that called for $100 billion of spending over two years on (1) retrofitting buildings to improve energy efficiency, (2) expanding mass transit and freight rail, (3) constructing a "smart" solar-powered electrical grid, and (4) investing in wind power and second-generation biofuels. The authors estimated that total jobs created would be 1.9 million. By contrast, if the money had simply been rebated to households to finance general consumption, only 1.7 million jobs would have been created. And if the $100 billion was spent on offshore drilling? Only 550,000 jobs would have resulted. Again, "green" wins here because relative to the two alternatives, the proposed policies lower imports of energy, rely on domestically produced inputs, and/or are more labor-intensive.[9]

Bottom line: most of the time, if you hear a sentence that begins with "All economists agree," you should head for the door. But in this case, there is agreement that at the economy-wide level *there is simply no such thing* as a **jobs-environment trade-off**.

LOCAL IMPACTS

Of course, this knowledge will not be comforting to the manufacturing or mining worker who *has* lost his or her job due to regulation. Short-run, structural unemployment impacts from environmental regulation (or any other cause) should not be minimized. **Plant shutdowns** cause considerable suffering for workers and communities, particularly for older workers who find it difficult to retool. Moreover, the disappearance of high-wage manufacturing jobs is indeed cause for concern. Yet, fears of such

---

9. Pollin et al. (2008).

effects from pollution-control efforts are liable to be greatly overblown as industry officials can gain politically by blaming plant shutdowns due to normal business causes on environmental regulations. Keeping this in mind, based on employer responses, the U.S. Department of Labor has collected information on the causes of mass layoffs (greater than 50 workers). Table 6.2 presents this data, covering 75% of all layoffs at large employers and 57% of all manufacturing plants.

On average, according to employers' own estimates, environmental regulation accounted for less than one-tenth of 1% of all mass layoffs nationwide. In the survey, *seven plants per year* closed primarily as a result of environmental problems. If we double the figures to account for the remainder of manufacturing jobs, on average, 2,000 lost positions per year could be partially attributed to environmental regulation. Supporting this survey data, one very detailed study looked at a set of chemical and manufacturing plants (of all types) in heavily regulated southern California and then compared them with similar plants in the rest of the country. The study found

TABLE 6.2   Sources of Mass Layoffs

Reason for Layoff	Layoff Events			People Laid Off		
	1995	*1996*	*1997*	*1995*	*1996*	*1997*
Total, all reasons	4,422	5,692	5,605	926,775	1,158,199	1,103,146
Environment related*	**9**	**7**	**5**	**2,816**	**1,098**	**541**
Automation	6	14	9	4,284	5,522	2,117
Bankruptcy	78	103	80	20,144	21,247	21,637
Business ownership change	120	167	121	28,482	46,425	25,141
Contract cancellation	103	87	61	18,700	19,269	11,813
Contract completion	459	557	759	100,289	124,506	175,572
Domestic relocation	63	76	76	11,059	11,323	15,241
Financial difficulty	249	263	153	58,473	56,749	39,634
Import competition	51	72	66	8,527	13,684	12,493
Labor-management dispute	20	32	32	3,370	14,119	16,149
Material shortages	19	21	14	2,666	2,821	1,705
Model changeover	17	18	18	7,589	6,799	5,716
Natural disaster	7	16	5	2,117	3,599	892
Overseas relocation	14	26	38	3,713	4,326	10,435
Plant or machine repairs	31	23	19	3,867	5,169	2,362
Product line discontinued	20	35	45	4,392	6,037	9,505
Reorganization within company	384	578	482	86,331	115,669	78,324
Seasonal work	1,688	2,173	2,434	385,886	488,398	499,331
Slack work	515	831	656	78,514	112,313	90,382
Vacation period	66	69	92	14,221	11,844	13,499
Weather-related curtailment	87	97	63	10,619	9,802	8,652
Other	253	266	211	42,153	55,265	39,821
Not reported	163	161	166	28,563	22,215	22,184

*Includes environmental- and safety-related shutdowns.
Source: U.S. Bureau of Labor Statistics, Local Area Unemployment Statistics Division.

no decrease in employment at existing California plants, and no effect on California jobs from increased bankruptcies or decreased investment. Indeed, the authors conclude: "In contrast to the widespread belief that environmental regulations cost jobs, the most severe episode of air quality regulation in the United States probably created a few jobs."

That said, in individual cases, such as the restrictions imposed on the timber industry to protect the old-growth forest in the Pacific Northwest, or clean-air requirements faced by the Appalachian high-sulfur coal industry, local unemployment has been exacerbated by environmental regulation. Several thousand jobs were lost regionally over a few-year period of time. And beyond numbers, many of the jobs lost were relatively "good" union, high-paying ones, and reemployment opportunities for some workers also were quite limited. These negative effects should not be ignored, and they can be partially alleviated through government job-retraining programs or bridge financing to retirement.

POLLUTION HAVENS

The number of actual layoffs due to environmental regulation is clearly much smaller than is generally believed. As noted earlier, one-third of the entire U.S. workforce perceived a threat to their jobs from environmental protection measures! In reality, 40 times more layoffs resulted from ownership changes than from environmental measures.[10] However, rather than shutdowns, one might expect *new* investment to occur in poorer countries with less strict pollution regulations. How serious is this problem of flight to the so-called pollution havens?

In their survey of 25 years of research on this issue, Jaffe and colleagues (1995, 133) conclude: "Studies attempting to measure the effect of environmental regulation on net exports, overall trade-flows, and plant location decisions have produced estimates that are either small, statistically insignificant, or not robust to tests of model specification." In other words, despite looking hard, economists initially found precious little evidence to suggest that the competitiveness of U.S. manufacturing firms has been hurt by environmental regulation. More recent evidence, however, has renewed debate about the degree to which dirty industry has slowly migrated offshore. By looking carefully at the few U.S. industries that face high regulatory costs, and controlling for high shipping costs often associated with commodities produced by dirty industry, a pattern is emerging that shows a slow change in the composition of trade in pollution-intensive products that favors middle-income countries.[11]

This pollution-haven effect is not readily apparent, nor universal. For example, with its close proximity to the United States, the maquiladora region of northern Mexico would be a logical candidate to become a pollution haven. Yet a comprehensive look at investment in the area confirms that environmental factors are, in general, relatively unimportant. Industries with higher pollution-abatement costs are not overrepresented in the maquiladora area, although those with higher labor costs are. At this point, we can conclude that the direct costs associated with pollution control have not been

10. The Department of Labor figures presented here are consistent with a variety of other surveys covering the 1970s and early 1980s, including one that incorporated small businesses. See Goodstein (1999).
11. Recent research that "unmasks" a pollution-haven effect is summarized in Brunnermeier and Levinson (2004).

a primary factor in influencing plant-location decisions. As with other firms, highly polluting industries are relocating to poor countries; the reason, however, is typically low wages.

Why have the effects not been greater? First, pollution-control costs are a small portion of total business costs; and second, costs are only one factor influencing business-location decisions. In addition to costs, factors as diverse as access to markets and the quality of life are important components of business-location decisions. Market size, wages, tax rates, political stability, access to the European market, and distance to the United States are some of the primary determinants of U.S. investment abroad. Finally, much pollution-control technology is embedded in modern plant designs. This means that a chemical factory built by a multinational corporation in South China will, in fact, look a lot like one built in West Virginia. Given these factors, most U.S. direct foreign investment continues to be in developed countries with environmental regulations comparable to our own.[12]

This section has established that, first, economy-wide, net job loss has not resulted from environmental protection, as many, if not more, new jobs have been created than have been lost. At the national level, debates that assume a job versus the environment trade-off are thus based on pure myth. Second, gross job loss due to environmental protection has been surprisingly small. Approximately 2,000 workers per year have been laid off in recent years, partially as a result of regulation. Finally, the flight of U.S. manufacturing capital overseas appears to be driven much more by wage differentials than stringent environmental rules. Despite these facts, the fear of job loss remains widespread, as indicated by the poll results cited earlier. Much of the political resistance to environmental protection remains motivated by such fears.

Generally, the jobs issue is overstated in discussions of environmental protection. Large numbers of jobs are, typically, neither gained nor lost, when new regulations come into force. As a result, while types of jobs will slowly shift as a nation devotes more resources to environmental protection, this shift does not add to the dollar costs, or increase the dollar benefits, from environmental protection.

6.4 General Equilibrium Effects and the Double Dividend

The last important area in which there may be "hidden" costs (or benefits) of regulation lies in what economists call **general equilibrium (GE) effects**. These effects of regulation are felt throughout the economy, as opposed to effects felt in the specific regulated sector (partial equilibrium effects).

To make this issue concrete, suppose you were working at the EPA and trying to figure out the cost of a new air quality regulation on coal-burning power plants. To simplify matters, first assume that there are 100 coal plants nationwide and each would install scrubbers, costing $100 million apiece. In that case, the estimated cost of the regulation would be $10 billion (100 plants * $100 million). Yet, even ignoring other compliance options (like switching to low-sulfur coal), this would be only a partial equilibrium estimate.

In fact, the higher cost for electricity would reduce electricity demand, as people conserved more. Hence, utilities would probably retire rather than retrofit some of the

---

12. Mexico study is by Grossman and Krueger (1995).

coal plants, leading to lower overall costs. Taking into account the general equilibrium effects in the electricity market, the real costs of the regulation would be lower than your partial equilibrium estimate. Of course, you would also want to calculate impacts throughout the economy of higher electricity prices. Probably the most significant general equilibrium effect runs through the so-called double dividend hypothesis. The idea here is that a pollution tax can have two beneficial effects on the economy. The first impact is to internalize the externality, so that firms and consumers stop over-consuming "dirty" goods. The second impact flows through beneficial use of the tax revenue. For example, suppose carbon tax revenues were used to cut payroll taxes on labor. This would encourage firms to hire more workers. By shifting taxes from "good things" to "bad things," pollution fees could lower the overall cost to the economy of cleaning up the environment.

While the double-dividend idea is intuitively appealing, some economists have questioned the size, and even the existence of the effect. This is because a pollution tax on coal emissions, for example, raises the costs of unrelated goods and services (e.g., medical services from a hospital that depends on coal-fired electricity). Higher prices for goods and services can then feed back to reductions in consumption, and potentially, *reduced* labor supply.

Piling up these kinds of inter-related, theoretical interactions can quickly cause one's head to spin. General equilibrium effects are hard to comprehend, or to assess definitively, because they are quite complicated. And from a policy perspective, precisely because these general equilibrium costs (and benefits) are so deeply hidden, no one besides (a few) economists currently care much about them. Nevertheless, these indirect costs—if they could be reliably measured—are as real as the more obvious direct ones. The take-home message of this section is, again, that a careful reckoning of environmental protection costs can be as difficult as developing good benefit measures.

6.5 A Final Look at Benefit-Cost Analysis

We will end this chapter with a real-world look at a recent EPA benefit-cost effort, a 2011 Regulatory Impact Analysis completed in support of rules that require coal-fired electric utilities to reduce mercury emissions. (Read why this regulation was delayed for *40 years* before coming into force in Chapters 12 and 17!). Here we reproduce the Executive Summary, Table 6.3, and the RIA punchline from the first paragraph. (PM 2.5 refers to particulate matter of 2.5 microns or larger in size).[13]

> This rule will reduce emissions of Hazardous Air Pollutants (HAP), including mercury, from the electric power industry. As a co-benefit, the emissions of certain PM2.5 precursors such as SO_2 will also decline. EPA estimates that this final rule will yield annual monetized benefits (in 2007$) of between $37 and $90 billion. The great majority of the estimates are attributable to co-benefits from 4,200 to 11,000 fewer PM2.5-related premature mortalities. The monetized benefits from reductions in mercury emissions, calculated

---

13. The complete RIA is available at http://www.epa.gov/ttn/ecas/regdata/RIAs/matsriafinal.pdf. The benefit figures presented here were estimated discounting at a rate of 3%, a process we will discuss in Chapter 8. The agency also used a 7% discount rate, generating slightly lower benefit numbers, which are omitted for ease of exposition.

TABLE 6.3   Summary of the EPA's Estimates of Annualized Benefits, Costs, and Net Benefits of the Final MATS in 2016 (billions of 2007$)

Description	Estimate
Costs	$9.6
Benefits	$37–$90+ "B"*
Net benefits	$27–$80+ "B"*

*"B" represents unquantified benefits. See the related discussion.

only for children exposed to recreationally caught freshwater fish, are expected to be $0.004 to $0.006 billion in 2016 using a 3% discount rate and $0.0005 to $0.001 billion using a 7% discount rate. The annual social costs, approximated by the compliance costs, are $9.6 billion (2007$) and the annual monetized net benefits are $27 to $80 billion. The benefits outweigh costs by between 3 and 1 or 9 and 1 depending on the benefit estimate and discount rate used. There are some costs and important benefits that EPA could not monetize, such as other mercury reduction benefits and those for the HAP other than mercury being reduced by this final rule. Upon considering these limitations and uncertainties, it remains clear that the benefits of the MATS are substantial and far outweigh the costs. Employment impacts associated with the final rule are estimated to be small.

There is a lot of complexity in this paragraph, but from what we have learned in the last two chapters, we are ready to tackle it piece by piece. Note first that the benefits and costs are "annualized"—Table 6.3 reports expected benefits and costs of cleaning up on a yearly basis, instead of the sum of all benefits and costs over time. More on this to follow.

Costs. The EPA took a "simple" approach to measuring costs: "Total social costs are approximated by the compliance costs." To get at this, EPA used detailed models of the oil- and coal-fired electricity generating sectors to estimate the direct costs of installing pollution control equipment; the number of older plants liable to shut down; and the costs imposed on electricity users from slightly higher electricity prices. The agency also included monitoring, reporting, and recordkeeping costs. Note there is NO uncertainty bound reported for costs: the EPA felt comfortable with the $9.6 billion per year cost estimate.

That said, and hitting the themes of this chapter, at the end of the Executive Summary the EPA notes:

Compliance costs are used to approximate the social costs of this rule. Social costs may be higher or lower than compliance costs and differ because of preexisting distortions in the economy, and because certain compliance costs may represent shifts in rents. [What we called General Equilibrium impacts]

Analysis does not capture employment shifts as workers are retrained at the same company or re-employed elsewhere in the economy.

Technological innovation is not incorporated into these cost estimates. Thus, these cost estimates may be potentially higher than what may occur in the future, all other things being the same.

These cost uncertainties highlight the difference between engineering cost estimates of compliance and the true social opportunity cost. And as always, there is a lot of wiggle room for partisan attacks on the EPA's methodology: industry critics of the mercury rule argued that compliance costs, and costs to industries affected by higher electricity prices, could be three times as high as the EPA asserted.[14]

Costs were annualized using a 6.15% discount rate: this means that $9.6 billion is the annual cost to firms and electricity users for around 20 years. For example, if electric utility firms borrowed the money upfront to pay the total cost of all the new equipment, they needed to cut emissions in year 1, they would have to pay $9.6 billion in principal and interest for about 20 years to pay off the initial cost.

Benefits. The RIA acknowledges HUGE uncertainty here. First, the range of $37–$90 billion reflects only *two* benefits: reductions in cognitive impacts on children exposed to mercury from eating fish and reductions in premature death and sickness from a "co-benefit" of the mercury rules: reductions in tiny particles (PM2.5) that cause respiratory illnesses and heart disease. In fact, 99% of the measured benefits were from this second category and had nothing to do with direct reductions in mercury!

In particular, the EPA concluded that the regulations, per year, would result in "510 fewer mercury-related IQ points lost as well as avoided PM2.5-related impacts, including 4,200 to 11,000 premature deaths, 4,700 nonfatal heart attacks, 2,600 hospitalizations for respiratory and cardiovascular diseases, 540,000 lost work days, and 3.2 million days when adults restrict normal activities because of respiratory symptoms exacerbated by PM2.5. We also estimate substantial additional health improvements for children from reductions in upper and lower respiratory illnesses, acute bronchitis, and asthma attacks."

The 510 IQ points gained annually by children were calculated by (1) estimating contaminated fish consumption and mercury exposure and (2) assuming a dose-response function by which decreased mercury exposure leads to higher IQ. The IQ increase from less contamination was in turn valued at $4–$6 million, based on an estimated increase in net life-time earning less the cost of remedial schooling. (Imagine the uncertainty in each of these steps!) The reductions in mortality of 4,200 to 11,000, again based on scientific models, and using a statistical value of life of $8 million for each death averted, weighed in at $34 to $87 *billion*. The additional health benefits identified earlier—reduced sickness, lost workdays, and restricted activity days—rounded out the additional $3 billion in annual benefits. A general point to be drawn here: reductions in premature mortality tend to generate the largest regulatory benefits.

Is mercury reduction itself only valued at $4 to $6 million annually? No. That's where the "+B"—representing un-quantified benefits—in Table 6.3 comes in. The RIA lists 3 full pages of benefits that the EPA did not even try to quantify, with the following categories:

- Reduced incidence of mortality from exposure to ozone
- Reduced incidence of morbidity from exposure to ozone, SO_2 and NOx
- Reduced visibility impairment
- Reduced climate effects

---

14. See ALEC's Utility Maximum Achievable Control Technology Rule Policy Guide, http://www.alec.org/publications/epas-regulatory-train-wreck-2/utility-mact-rule/.

- Reduced effects on materials
- Reduced effects from PM deposition (metals and organics)
- Reduced vegetation and ecosystem effects from exposure to ozone
- Reduced effects from acid deposition
- Reduced effects from nutrient enrichment
- Reduced vegetation effects from ambient exposure to SO_2 and NOx

For mercury, unquantified benefits for human health included other neurologic effects beyond IQ loss (e.g., developmental delays, memory, behavior); cardiovascular effects; and genotoxic, immunologic, and other toxic effects. Neither did the study attempt to quantify the value of improved fish and wildlife health from reduced mercury exposure nor the benefits to commercial and recreational fishing and hunting.

Why did the EPA list but not quantify all these additional benefits? In part, because it is hard and expensive to do so. And in part, because the health co-benefits of PM2.5 were so large, that without quantifying all the other impacts, and in spite of large uncertainties, the rule clearly passes a benefit-cost test. That said, without the PM2.5 co-benefits, it is unlikely that mercury reductions alone would have justified the regulation from a benefit-cost perspective.

Jobs. The RIA concludes that employment impacts of the rule in the regulated sector itself will be small. In fact, the EPA estimates small net job increases to be more likely, giving a range of −15,000 to +30,000. At the same time, the study estimated that short-term, manufacturing and installing the required pollution control equipment would create 46,000 jobs. Of course, these job gains would need to be balanced against jobs slowly lost as a result of higher electricity prices outside of the regulated sector, or slowly gained as low-mercury electric generation capacity came on line. Consistent with the discussion earlier in this chapter, jobs created or lost to environmental regulation are generally not large enough in number to determine policy.

In this section, we have brought some of our recently gained knowledge to bear in helping us understand how the EPA uses benefit-cost analysis. Again, in real-world application, especially on the benefits side, uncertainty will always loom large. In spite of that, when regulations will save a lot of lives, we can often assert with some confidence that benefits do exceed costs.

6.6 Summary

This chapter has explored different ways to evaluate the costs of environmental protection. Engineering cost data are much easier to obtain than nonmarket benefit information; as a result, the EPA has been able to put a price tag of close to 3% of GDP on our federal, state, and local pollution control efforts.

However, even on their own terms, engineering cost estimates are only as good as their predictions regarding, for example, compliance and control technologies. More significantly, engineering estimates do not generally incorporate indirect effects, such as negative or positive productivity impacts, or general equilibrium effects. On the productivity front, the overall costs of protecting the environment will be lower if firms respond to regulations by better managing risk, becoming more resource efficient, and investing in new areas of profitable innovation, replacing polluting products and processes. Also, environmental protection can lower economy-wide health costs. On the flip side, increasing end-of-the-pipe control costs can eat up funds for investment, and cause prices to rise for industries that depend on dirty goods, with a similar effect. Red-tape and regulatory delay can also slow investment and innovation. On balance, the net, economy-wide impact on productivity has probably been small. Nevertheless, small declines in productivity growth have big long-run effects and should be a primary concern in regulatory design.

On the employment front, environmental regulation has not led to any net job loss in the economy; there is simply no evidence of a long-run "jobs versus the environment" trade-off. Instead, regulation has led to a shift in the types of jobs. Rather surprisingly, regulation-induced employment is heavily weighted to manufacturing and away from services. And when green spending is more domestic-content or labor-intensive, it can lead to net employment growth in the creation of "green jobs." Gross job losses partially due to environmental protection in the 1990s were on the order of 1,500 to 2,000 per year. Finally, there is little evidence to support widespread capital flight to "pollution havens."

Environmental policy can change prices throughout the economy, altering firm and consumer behavior. In particular, if pollution taxes or permit auction revenues are used to cut other taxes, then the emerging double-dividend can lower the overall cost to the economy of achieving environmental or resource protection.

Due to these three different indirect effects, the "true" social cost of regulation (its opportunity cost) may vary widely from engineering cost estimates. This point again highlights the relative imprecision of benefit-cost analysis for determining the "efficient" pollution level. We ended this chapter with a look at a real-world benefit-cost analysis at the EPA. Mercury regulations were expected to cost, on an annual basis, $9.6 billion, and generate benefits ranging from $37 to $90 billion, plus "B," unquantified benefits. This case illustrates that big benefits emerge for regulation expected to significantly reduce premature deaths. Also, while the study is careful to highlight uncertainty on the benefits side, it also illustrates something of a **hard numbers illusion** on the cost side. In part, this is the EPA seeking to defend the rule from industry attacks. In spite of the lack of an official uncertainty bound, industry groups still put the possible cost of the regulations at three times the EPA's estimate, and characterize the rule as the most expensive in the history of regulation.

The last three chapters have explored in much detail the first answer to the question: How much pollution is too much? Efficiency advocates argue that environmental policy measures must pass a benefit-cost test, and indeed, weighing the costs against the benefits of clean-up, deliver the maximum net dollar benefits to society. To do this, of course, one needs to be able to measure with some accuracy, both the dollar benefits and dollar costs of environmental protection. We have seen that this task can be quite difficult. So even assuming that efficiency is indeed the correct ethical goal for environmental clean-up, there is an open question as to how well we can effectively implement it. Next we turn our attention to an alternate answer to the How Much is Too Much question, an answer that underlies most current U.S. policy: The Safety Standard.

APPLICATION 6.0

The Importance of Productivity

Two well-known economists, William Baumol and Alan Blinder, have stated that, in the long run, "nothing contributes more to reduction of poverty, to increases in leisure, and to the country's ability to finance education, public health, environmental improvement and the arts" (1991, 356) than the rate of growth of productivity.

1. Define *productivity*.
2. See if you can verify Baumol and Blinder's very strong claim ("*nothing* contributes more ...") through the following exercise. Assume GDP in the United States is $10 trillion and that the labor force remains constant in size and fully employed. Estimate the value of GDP in one year's time if productivity growth is 3%. What if it were only 2%? How much will GDP fall in two years' time if productivity growth remains at 2% rather than 3%? In three years?
3. Why might environmental regulation reduce productivity growth?
4. Why might it increase productivity growth?
5. Even if, on balance, environmental regulation has not reduced productivity growth, are negative productivity impacts from regulations something we should still worry about?

APPLICATION 6.1

Jobs and the Environment

In 2009, the conservative Heritage Foundation called the global-warming cap-and-trade bill being debated in the U.S. House a "jobs destroyer" and published an analysis claiming that the law, if passed, would increase unemployment by an average of 1 million jobs a year for the coming few decades.[15]

1. Based on the information presented in this chapter, would a global-warming law be likely to cause an economy-wide drop in the number of U.S. jobs? Why or why not?
2. Are U.S. workers in particular industries likely to lose their jobs partially as a result of the law? If the impact of the global-warming cap was comparable to past episodes of new regulations, about how many workers per year would be likely to face layoffs? How might the blow to these workers be cushioned?
3. Again, based on past experience, is it likely energy-intensive industries would start to migrate abroad in large numbers as a result of the global-warming law? If not, what might keep them at home?

---

15. Beach et al. (2009).

4. In the Heritage Foundation analysis, how do you think the authors get such big job-loss numbers? You have to guess at this one, because the answer is not in the text.

APPLICATION 6.2

Calculating the Total Costs of Climate Control

Referring to Figure 6.1, what is the approximate *total cost* of achieving 38-gigaton reductions in carbon dioxide equivalents, below the 2030 baseline? *Hint:* The answer has to do with the area of two triangles.

APPLICATION 6.3

What's Wrong with This Picture?

As an aide to Governor Blabla, you are given the task of recommending whether the state should locate a low-level nuclear waste facility in a rural county. The nuclear industry provides you with a cost-benefit study it has conducted, and it contains the following information:

COST-BENEFIT SUMMARY FOR PROPOSED WASTE FACILITY

Prepared by the Center for the Objective Study of Nuclear Issues

Conclusion: The project will result in net benefits of $3 billion, with a benefit-cost ratio of 13. While these figures, of course, depend on the assumptions of the study, the very large net benefit figure, along with the extraordinarily high benefit-cost ratio, both indicate that the project will remain attractive under most plausible assumptions. We therefore strongly recommend initiating the proposal.

Assumptions:

1. Discount rate of 10%
2. Principal costs:
   a. Worker exposure
   b. Risk of accidental exposure during transport
   c. Reduction to zero of the land value at the storage site
   d. Construction and maintenance
3. Principal benefits:
   a. Reduced exposure at current temporary storage sites
   b. Job creation—1,000 temporary, 200 permanent jobs

    c. Extends life of existing nuclear power plants by ten years
        i. Lower electricity costs for consumers
        ii. Saves 7,000 jobs
    d. Increased profits for local service industries
4. Risk assessment:
    a. Exposure/fatality assumptions from the U.S. Department of Energy
    b. Probability of fatal exposure due to transport accident: 1/100,000,000 miles (Source: U.S. Department of Energy)
    c. Value of a statistical life: $1 million

1.   Do you believe the report?
2.   See if you can find six separate concerns with the study.

KEY IDEAS IN EACH SECTION

6.0   The standard method of estimating the costs of environmental protection, simply adding up direct compliance and regulatory expenses, is called an **engineering approach**. Economists, however, would like to measure the **opportunity cost** the value of goods and services forgone by investing in environmental protection. Opportunity costs include three indirect effects: productivity impacts, employment impacts, and general equilibrium effects.

6.1   In 2000, the United States spent about $260 billion on pollution control measures, measured in engineering terms. Between 1970 and 2000, environmental protection expenditures jumped from less than 1% to more than 2.8% of GNP, more than doubling their claim on the share of the nation's resources.

6.2   The productivity slowdown of the 1970s has been partially blamed on environmental regulation. The main argument is that regulatory expenses divert investment from new plants and equipment. Several economic studies indicate that a small portion of the slowdown (less than 10%) may be due to environmental protection measures. However, this does not take into account possible positive impacts on productivity growth from more efficient resource use, **Porter hypothesis** effects, or a healthier population and resource base. Nevertheless, even small negative effects on productivity growth can impose large costs in the long run.

6.3   This section reviews the employment impact of environmental regulation and makes four main points. First, at the economy-wide level, environmental protection has *not* generated a **jobs-environment trade-off**. Moreover, investment in **green jobs** can lead to net job growth in some cases. Third, extrapolating data from a large sample of employer responses, gross job loss from **plant shutdowns** due to environmental regulation was about 1,500 to 2,000 workers per year during the 1990s. Therefore, little **structural unemployment** can be attributed to regulation. Finally, it appears that in only a few cases have U.S. firms invested in **pollution havens** primarily to avoid environmental regulations.

6.4   A final source of hidden costs and benefits for measures to protect the environment and the resource base arises from **general equilibrium** effects. Such impacts arise as regulation alters prices, not just for the regulated commodity, but throughout the economy, causing firms and consumers to change their behaviors. The major general equilibrium impact of pollution taxes or for government auctioned permits under cap and trade, works through the **double dividend hypothesis**, in which pollution tax or permit revenues are used to cut taxes on labor leading to greater levels of employment.

6.5   The benefit-cost analysis (**regulatory impact statement**) done by the EPA for mercury control from power plants highlights the uncertainty associated with estimating benefits, and illustrates the **hard numbers illusion** with respect to costs. The RIA also affirmed the general point that jobs effects—both positive and negative—associated with environmental policy measures are small, and tend to balance each other out.

REFERENCES

Ambec, Stefan, Mark A. Cohen, Stewart Elgie, and Paul Lanoie. 2011. *The Porter hypothesis at 20 can environmental regulation enhance innovation and competitiveness?* Discussion paper 11-01. Washington, DC: Resources for the Future.

Baumol, William, and Alan Blinder. 1991. *Macroeconomics: Principles and policy.* New York: Harcourt Brace Jovanovich.

Beach, William, David Kreutzer, Karen Campbell, and Ben Lieberman. 2009. Son of Waxman-Markey: More politics makes for a more costly bill. Heritage Foundation, WebMemo 2450, 18 May.

Beinhocker, Eric, Jeremy Oppenheim, Ben Irons, Makreeta Lahti, Diana Farrell, Scott Nyquist, Jaana Remes, et al. 2008. *The carbon productivity challenge: Curbing climate change and sustaining economic growth.* London: McKinsey Global Institute.

Boyd, Gale, and John McClelland. 1999. The impact of environmental constraints on productivity improvement in integrated paper plants. *Journal of Environmental Economics and Management* 38(2): 121–42.

Brunnermeier, Smita B., and Arik Levinson. 2004. Examining the evidence on environmental regulations and industry location. *Journal of Environment & Development* 13(1): 6–41.

Carlin, Alan. 1990. *Environmental investments: The cost of a clean environment, Summary.* Washington, DC: U.S. EPA.

EPA plans to tighten pollution rules. 1997. *Wall Street Journal,* 6 June, A16.

Goodstein, Eban. 1999. *The trade-off myth: Fact and fiction about jobs and the environment.* Washington, DC: Island Press.

Goulder, Lawrence, and Ian Parry. 2000. Green tax reform and the double dividend. *AERE Newsletter* 20(1): 9–13.

Graff Zivin, Joshua, and Matthew J. Neidell. 2011. The impact of pollution on worker productivity NBER working paper no. 17004, Issued in April.

Grossman, Gene M., and Alan B. Krueger. 1995. Economic growth and the environment. *Quarterly Journal of Economics* 110(2): 353–77.

Harrington, Winston, Richard Morgenstern, and Peter Nelson. 1999. Predicting the costs of environmental regulation. *Environment* 41(7): 10–14.

Jaffe, Adam B., Steven R. Peterson, Paul R. Portney, and Robert N. Stavins. 1995. Environmental regulation and the competitiveness of U.S. manufacturing: What does the evidence tell us? *Journal of Economic Literature* 33(1): 132–63.

Morgenstern, Richard, William Pizer, and Jhih-Shyang Shih. 1997. *Are we overstating the real costs of environmental protection?* Discussion paper 97-36-REV. Washington, DC: Resources for the Future.

Pollin, Robert, Heidi Garrett-Peltier, James Heintz, and Helen Scharber. 2008. *Green recovery: A program to create good jobs and start building a low-carbon economy.* Amherst: University of Massachusetts Political Economy Research Institute.

Porter, Michael, and Claas van der Linde. 1995. Toward a new conception of the environment-competitiveness relationship. *Journal of Economic Perspectives* 9(4): 97–118.

Romm, Joe. 2009. How the world can (and will) stabilize at 350 to 450 pmm. ClimateProgress Blog, posted 26 March.

———. 2008. McKinsey 2008 research in review: Stabilizing at 450 ppm has a net cost near zero. ClimateProgress Blog, posted 29 December.

U.S. Environmental Protection Agency. 1995. *The U.S. environmental protection industry: A proposed framework for assessment.* Washington, DC: U.S. EPA, Office of Policy Planning and Evaluation.

Xepapadeas, Anastasios, and Aart de Zeeuw. 1999. Environmental policy and competitiveness: The Porter hypothesis and the composition of capital. *Journal of Environmental Economics and Management* 37(2): 165–82.

THE SAFETY STANDARD

7.0 Introduction

In Chapters 4–6, we explored the logic of controlling pollution at an efficient level. The efficiency approach emphasizes trade-offs—pollution control has opportunity costs that must be weighed against the benefits of environmental protection. This is not, however, the kind of language one hears in everyday discussions of pollution control. Instead, pollution is more generally equated with immoral or even criminal behavior, a practice to be stamped out at all costs. In this chapter, we explore the pros and cons of a safety standard that, like much popular opinion, rejects a benefit-cost approach to decisions about the "correct" amount of pollution.

The **safety standard** springs fundamentally from fairness rather than efficiency concerns. Recall that the efficiency standard makes no distinction between victims and perpetrators of pollution. Instead, efficiency weighs the dollar impact of pollution on victims' health against the dollar impact on consumers' prices and polluters' profits. Each is considered to have equal say in the matter, based on the reasoning that in the long run most people will benefit as consumers from the larger pie made possible via efficient regulation. Advocates of a safety approach, on the other hand, contend that our society has developed a widespread consensus on the following position: People have a right to protection from unsolicited, significant harm to their immediate environment. Efficiency violates this right and is thus fundamentally unfair.

Curiously, there is also an efficiency argument to be made in favor of relying on safety standards. We know that the efficiency standard requires that the costs and benefits of environmental regulation be carefully measured and weighed. However, as we saw in Chapters 5 and 6, many important benefits of protection are often left out of benefit-cost analyses because they cannot be measured. Moreover, as discussed in Chapter 11, material growth in our affluent society may primarily feed conspicuous consumption, fueling a rat race that leaves no one better off. If the measured costs of protection are overstated by this rat-race effect, while the benefits are understated because they cannot be quantified, then safe regulation may in reality meet a benefit-cost test. Having said this, however, safety is more often defended in terms of basic rights rather than on efficiency grounds.

7.1 Defining the Right to Safety

There is a saying that the freedom to wave your fist ends where my nose begins. In a similar vein, many Americans believe that the freedom to pollute the environment ends where a human body begins. Preventing positive harm to its citizens is the classic liberal (in modern parlance, libertarian) justification for governmental restraint on the liberties of others. At the extreme, permitting negative externalities that cause discomfort, sickness, or death might be looked upon as the equivalent of permitting the poisoning of the population for material gain.

The safety standard can thus be defended as necessary to protect **personal liberty**. Viewed in this light, we require that pollution should be reduced to levels that inflict "minimal" harm on people. What constitutes minimal harm is, of course, open to debate. In practice, the U.S. Environmental Protection Agency (EPA) appears to consider risks below 1 in 1 million for large populations to be acceptable or "below regulatory concern." On the other hand, the EPA and other federal agencies tend to take action against risks greater than 4 in 1,000 for small populations and 3 in 10,000 for large populations. Risks that fall in between are regulated based on an informal balancing of costs against benefits and statutory requirements. Regulators pursuing safety are thus expected to take technological and economic factors into account, but to make continual progress, reducing to "minimal" levels damage to the environment and human health.[1]

Based on this real-world experience, for the purposes of this book, we can define **safety** as a mortality risk level of less than 1 in 1 million; risks greater than 1 in 10,000 are **unsafe** and risks in between are up for grabs. (For comparison, police officers bear a risk of about 1 in 10,000 of being killed on the job by a felon.) Cancer risks are the most common health risks that are quantified this way.

Of course, many other health risks besides cancer are associated with pollution, such as impacts on the immune, nervous, and reproductive systems. However, the risks in these areas are much harder to quantify, and as yet there is no social consensus, as reflected in a judicial record, about exposure levels. Because noncancerous, nonfatal health risks are not well understood, and because cancer risks can be estimated only with a substantial margin of error, the safety standard can be quite nebulous. As a result, the precise definition of safety must often be determined on a case-by-case basis through the give and take of politics. (As we saw in Chapter 4, pinning down the efficient pollution level can be quite difficult as well!)

Despite this uncertainty, however, a safety standard in fact remains the stated goal of much environmental policy. As we explore further in Chapter 13, the basic antipollution laws covering air, water, and land pollution require cleanup to "safe" levels, period. There is no mention of a benefit-cost test in the legislation. Similarly, the

---

1. For a more extended discussion, see Goodstein (1991).

international climate agreement calls for nations to prevent "dangerous" disruption of the climate.

Ultimately, however, cost considerations *must* play a role in the political determination of safe pollution levels. Attainment of "objectively" safe standards in some areas would be prohibitively expensive. Indeed, while U.S. courts have thrown out regulatory standards for safety legislation based solely on benefit-cost analysis, at the same time they have allowed costs of attainment to be considered as one factor influencing the stringency of regulation. They also have interpreted *safe* to mean not the absence of any risk, but the absence of "significant" risk. On the other hand, the courts have not allowed costs to be a factor in the determination of significant risk.

Accepting that some danger to human health is inevitable does not require abandoning the safety standard. For example, it is commonly accepted that we have a right to live free from violent behavior on the part of our neighbors. Now this right, like most others, is not enforced absolutely: we are willing to fund police departments, the court system, the construction of new jails, educational and job programs, and drug rehabilitation centers only to a certain level. Moreover, poor people receive much less protection than wealthy people do. Ultimately, the decision about how much violence to live with is a political one, influenced but not solely determined by willingness to pay.

One could characterize this approach as declaring the protection of all individuals from violent crime to be a societal right and then backing away from such a goal on a case-by-case basis in the face of rising cost. This results in a substantially different standard than would determining the police departments' homicide budget based on a benefit-cost analysis. In particular, the former approach generally results in less violent crime. Returning to environmental concerns, a safety target of a maximum 1 in 1 million cancer risk may not always be economically feasible. But relaxing a safety standard that is too costly is quite different from adopting an efficiency standard.

In the real world, the safe level will certainly be influenced by the associated sacrifices in consumption. Nevertheless, safety advocates would argue that in the arena of environmental protection, costs are not, and should not be, a dominant factor in people's decision-making process.

Survey research seems to find widespread support for this claim. Most Americans consistently agree with statements like "protecting the environment is so important that requirements and standards cannot be too high, and continuing improvements must be made regardless of the costs."[2] This is a strong position. Efficiency proponents suggest that it represents softheaded thinking, and if the remark is taken literally, obviously it does. But a less harsh interpretation of this survey data is that people feel that, because *current levels* of pollution significantly affect human health and well-being, cleanup is justified regardless of the cost within the relevant range of possibilities.

To illustrate, one study asked residents of a Nevada community about their willingness to accept annual tax credits of $1,000, $3,000, and $5,000 per person in exchange for the siting of a potentially dangerous hazardous waste facility nearby. Contrary to the author's expectations, increases in the rebate had no measurable impact on approval of the facility. The results were "consistent with a threshold model of choice, whereby individuals refuse to consider compensation if the perceived risk falls

---

2. See WSJ Online (1991).

in the inadmissible range. For those respondents where the risk was perceived to be too high, the rebates offered were not viewed as inadequate, but as inappropriate … most of the Nevada sample viewed the risks as inherently noncompensable … ."[3]

Behavior such as this suggests that one important benefit of environmental protection—the right not to be victimized—is unmeasurable. Casting this argument in terms of our social welfare function, in the interests of personal liberty, safety advocates put very strong weights on injuries to human health arising from pollution. To illustrate, let us return to our Chapter 4 example, in which Brittany and Tyler were wrangling over smoking in the office. To a safety advocate, the social welfare function might look like this:

$$SW = U_{Tyler}(\overset{+}{\#Cigs_T}, \overset{+}{\$_T}) + U_{Brit}(\overset{-}{w * \#Cigs_T}, \overset{+}{\$_B})$$

where the weight w given to the negative impact of smoke on Brittany is a very big number, one that may well justify banning smoking altogether.[4]

Should smoking be banned in public places under a safety standard? This is a question for voters and courts to decide. One feature of the safety standard is its imprecision. No right is absolute, as rights often come in conflict with one another, and the political arena is where the issue is ultimately decided. What the safety standard maintains is that in the absence of a "compelling" argument to the contrary (which may include, but is not limited to, cost of attainment), damage to human health from pollution ought to be minimal. Individuals have a right to be free from the damage that secondary smoke inflicts.

7.2 The Safety Standard: Inefficient

The first objection to the safety standard is that it is, by definition, inefficient. Efficiency advocates make the following normative case against safety: Enshrining environmental health as a "right" involves committing "too many" of our overall social resources to environmental protection.

As a result of pursuing safe levels of pollution, regulators and voters have often chosen pollution control levels that may be "too high" based on a benefit-cost or efficiency standard. Consider, for example, the air toxics provision of the Clean Air Act Amendments, designed to control the emission of hazardous air pollutants. When the law was passed in 1990, the EPA estimated that at 149 industrial facilities nationwide, cancer risks to the most exposed local residents from airborne toxics were greater than 1 in 10,000; at 45 plants, risks were greater than 1 in 1,000. The law required firms to impose control technology that, it was hoped, would reduce risks to below the 1 in 10,000 level.

While the costs and benefits of the legislation were difficult to pin down precisely, economist Paul Portney estimated that when the program was fully phased in, total

---

3. See Kunreuther and Easterling (1992).
4. Kneese and Schulze (1994) formalize a libertarian social welfare function as one in which a Pareto improvement must actually take place for a policy to increase social welfare. The safety standard discussed here is not this restrictive.

costs would be $6 to $10 billion per year (about $60 to $100 per household). He also estimated that total benefits would be less than $4 billion per year ($40 per household). Thus, "If these estimates are even close to correct, Congress and the President ... [shook hands] on a landmark piece of legislation for which costs may exceed benefits by a substantial margin."[5]

In other cases besides air toxics, pursuing safety undoubtedly generates a high degree of inefficiency. For example, consider the EPA's regulations for landfills mentioned in Application 2.0. In this case, even with the new regulations, just under 10% of landfills will still pose what the EPA considers to be a "moderate" health risk for individuals who depend on contaminated groundwater: a greater than 1 in 1,000,000 (but less than 1 in 10,000) increase in the risk of contracting cancer. However, because so few people actually depend on ground-water within leaching distance of a landfill, the new regulations were predicted to reduce cancer by only two or three cases over the next 300 years. Potential benefits of the regulation not quantified by the EPA include increased ease of siting landfills, reduced damage to surface water, fairness to future generations, and an overall reduction in waste generation and related "upstream" pollution encouraged by higher disposal costs.

In aggregate, the regulations are expensive: about $5.8 billion, or approximately $2 billion per cancer case reduced. On a per household basis, this works out to an annual cost of $4.10 in increased garbage bills over the 20-year life of a landfill. An efficiency proponent would say that it is simply crazy (horribly inefficient) to spend so much money to reduce risk by so little. The $4.10 per year per household is an unjustified tax.

The landfill and air toxics cases both illustrate a more general point: regulations that protect small groups of people from risk will almost always be inefficient, because even relatively high risks will not generate many casualties. Here is a classic situation in which efficiency and fairness (measured as equal risk protection for small and large groups) conflict. Economists, perhaps due to their professional training, are often efficiency advocates, so one will often find economists leveling normative criticisms at safety-based environmental protection laws. Economists are not wrong to level efficiency criticisms at safety standard environmental legislation; in some cases, particularly when marginal benefits of further regulation are very close to zero, the argument may be quite convincing. It is, however, important to remember that economists have no special authority when it comes to proscribing what the appropriate target of pollution control *should be*.[6]

Efficiency criticisms of safety are most persuasive when they suggest that an *actual* improvement in quality of life for the affected people will result from a move from safety to efficiency. One group of economists, for example, argue: "Since there are a variety of public policy measures, both environmental and otherwise, which are capable of preventing cancer at much lower costs [than the $35 million per life saved from

---

5. Portney (1987). The report is discussed in Greider (2006). In the same article, Portney (1987) argued that the acid rain provisions of the Clean Air Act would also be very inefficient. However, Burtraw et al. (2007) have since shown that the acid rain program is in fact easy to justify on efficiency grounds. Measurable benefits (mostly from reduced death and sickness and improved visibility) will exceed the costs under virtually any set of assumptions. Indeed, the estimated benefits for the acid rain program alone range from $23 to $26 billion—well above Portney's original speculation of $14 billion for the *entire* legislative package. But Portney's characterization of air toxics control as inefficient probably remains valid.
6. Bromley (1990).

pesticide regulation], we might be able to reduce the cancer rate through a reallocation of resources [i.e., by relaxing pesticide regulations]."[7]

The problem with this line of reasoning is that the resources freed up from less stringent pesticide regulation, to the extent they are properly estimated, would reemerge as higher profits for pesticide manufacturers and lower food prices for consumers. They would *not* likely be channeled into other "public policy measures" to improve environmental health. Thus only a potential and not an actual Pareto improvement would emerge by relaxing pesticide regulations to achieve efficiency gains.

7.3 The Safety Standard: Not Cost-Effective

The second, and perhaps most telling, criticism leveled at the safety standard is its lack of **cost-effectiveness**. A cost-effective solution achieves a desired goal at the lowest possible cost. In pollution control, this goal is often defined as "lives saved per dollar spent." The cost-effectiveness criticism is not that safety is a bad goal per se, but that it gives no guidance to ensure that the maximum amount of safety is indeed purchased with the available resources. If safety is the only goal of pollution control, then extreme measures may be taken to attack "minimal" risk situations.

For example, the EPA, following its mandate from the Superfund legislation, has attempted to restore to drinking-level purity the groundwater at toxic spill sites. Tens of millions of dollars have been spent at a few dozen sites on such efforts, yet cleanup to this level has proven quite difficult. Marginal costs of cleaning rise dramatically as crews try to achieve close to 100% cleanup. Critics have argued that rather than restoring the water to its original safe drinking quality, the goal should be simply to contain the contaminants. EPA's limited resources could then be redirected to preventing future spills.

More generally, economist Lester Lave points out that children have about a 5 in 1 million chance of contracting lung cancer from attending a school built with asbestos materials. This is dramatically less than the threat of death from other events in their lives, and Lave suggests that if our interest is in protecting lives, we would do better spending money to reduce other risks, such as cancer from exposure to secondary cigarette smoke, auto accidents, or inadequate prenatal nutrition and care.[8]

A safety proponent might argue in response that devoting more resources to *each* of the first three problems would be a good idea. And in fact, the limits to dealing with them are not fundamentally limited resources, but rather a lack of political will. More generally, a safety advocate would respond that Lave's comparison is a false one, as funds freed up from "overcontrol" in the pollution arena are more likely to be devoted to increasing consumption of the relatively affluent than to saving children's lives. Taxpayers do put a limit on governmental resources for dealing with environmental, traffic safety, and children's welfare issues. Yet safety proponents ultimately have more faith in this political allocation of funds than in an allocation based on a benefit-cost test.

That said, it is clear that the politically determined nature of the safety standard can also set it up to fail from a cost-effectiveness perspective. Determining "significant

7. Cropper et al. (1991).
8. See Lave (1987).

harm" on a case-by-case basis through a political process is a far from perfect mechanism in which money and connections may play as large a part as the will of the electorate regarding environmental protection.

Chapter 12 of this book, which examines the government's role in environmental policy, also considers measures to correct this kind of government failure. For now, safety proponents can respond only by saying that imperfect as the political process is, voting remains the best mechanism for making decisions about enforcing rights. Moreover, as we will see, the benefit-cost alternative is certainly not "value free" and is arguably as subject to influence as the political process itself.

Ultimately, however, given the limited resources available for controlling pollution, safety alone is clearly an inadequate standard for making decisions. Requiring regulatory authorities to ensure a safe environment may lead them to concentrate on eradicating some risks while ignoring others. To deal with this problem, the so-called risk-benefit studies can be used to compare the cost-effectiveness of different regulatory options. The common measure used in this approach is lives saved per dollar spent. This kind of cost-effectiveness analysis can be a useful guide to avoid an overcommitment of resources to an intractable problem. However, adopting a cost-effective approach does not mean backing away from safety as a goal. Rather, it implies buying as much safety as possible with the dollars allocated by the political process.

To summarize the last two sections, critics charge safety standards with two kinds of "irrationality": (1) inefficiency, or overcommitment of resources to environmental problems, and (2) lack of cost-effectiveness in addressing these problems. Criticism (1) is fundamentally normative and thus is a subject for public debate. In this debate, benefit-cost studies can be useful in pointing out just how inefficient the pursuit of safety might be. Criticism (2), however, does not question the goal of safety. Rather it suggests that blind pursuit of safety may in fact hinder efforts to achieve the highest possible level of environmental quality.

7.4 The Safety Standard: Regressive?

The final objection to a safety standard is based on income equity. Safety standards will generally be more restrictive than efficiency standards; as a result, they lead to greater sacrifice of other goods and services. Quoting efficiency advocate Alan Blinder: "Declaring that people have a 'right' to clean air and water sounds noble and high-minded. But how many people would want to exercise that right if the cost were sacrificing a decent level of nutrition or adequate medical care or proper housing?"[9]

Blinder is worried that a fair number of people will in fact fall below a decent standard of living as a result of overregulation. While such dramatic effects are unlikely, given the level of hunger, poverty, and homelessness in our society, it is possible that stringent environmental standards are something poor people may simply not be able to afford. Currently, compliance with pollution regulations commits more than $200 billion of U.S. gross domestic product (GDP). Suppose that by moving from a safety

---

9. See Blinder (1987, 138).

standard to an efficiency-based standard we spent $30 billion less on environmental improvement. Would the poor be better off?

The first issue is: Who ultimately pays the hypothetical extra $30 billion for pollution control? It does appear that because much pollution is generated in the production of necessities—basic manufactured goods, garbage disposal, food, drinking water, electric power, and transport—the cost of environmental regulation is borne unevenly. In general, pollution control has a **regressive** impact on income distribution, meaning that the higher prices of consumer goods induced by regulation take a bigger *percentage* bite of the incomes of poor people than of wealthier individuals.

As an example, one study looked at the impact of proposed taxes on global warming pollution. A carbon dioxide tax of $70 per ton would increase expenditures on energy by the bottom 10% of households by 11%, but increase expenditures by only 5% for the top 10% of families. At the same time, because they consume so much more, rich people would pay a lot more in absolute terms from the carbon tax: $1,475 versus $215 per person.[10] This kind of regressive pattern is fairly typical and extends economy-wide to the general impact of pollution-control measures.

On the other hand, while poor and working-class people may pay a higher proportion of their income, they also generally benefit more from pollution control than the relatively wealthy. In the case of air pollution, for example, urban rather than suburban areas have been the primary beneficiaries of control policies. The effects are further magnified because those in the lower half of the income distribution have a harder time buying their own cleaner environment by way of air and water filters and conditioners, trips to spacious, well-maintained parks, or vacations in the country. Dramatic evidence of the exposure of low-income people to air pollution comes from the autopsies of 100 youths from poor neighborhoods in Los Angeles. According to the pathologist, "Eighty percent of the youths had notable lung abnormalities ... above and beyond what we've seen with smoking or even respiratory viruses.... It's much more severe, much more prevalent."[11]

One area where there is a clear link between not only income but also race and pollution exposure is in the location of hazardous waste facilities. Table 7.1 reports on recent research exploring the demographics of the neighborhoods surrounding the nation's 413 hazardous waste facilities. As one moves closer to a facility, the population clearly becomes significantly less wealthy, and also much less white. This pattern has also been documented for exposure to toxics from manufacturing plants, air pollution from motor vehicles, and other pollutant pathways. In most studies, race does appear as an important, independent factor explaining pollution exposure.[12]

An important question emerges from this data: do polluting industries locate in poor and minority communities, taking advantage of less effective political resistance and/or cheaper land? Or do low-income people choose to locate close to hazardous facilities because rents are cheaper there? One analysis looked specifically at five hazardous waste sites in the Southern United States. Researchers found that in the

10. Boyce and Riddle (2008, table 7).
11. See Mann (1991).
12. See Bullard et al. (2007) for a review of this literature.

TABLE 7.1   Race, Poverty and Hazardous Waste Facilities

	Within 1 km	Between 1 km & 3 km	Between 3 km & 5 km	Beyond 5 km
Percent people of color	47.70%	46.10%	35.70%	22.20%
Percent poverty rate	20.10%	18.30%	16.90%	12.70%
Mean household income	$31,192	$33,318	$36,920	$38,745

Source: Bullard et al. (2007, table 7).

location decision, firms were able to deal with a predominantly white political power structure that was able to disregard the needs of a disenfranchised black majority. A survey of the African American neighbors of the five toxic facilities revealed substantial majorities who felt that the siting process had not been fair. And in four of the five communities, a clear majority disagreed with the statement that the benefits of the facilities outweighed the costs; the community was split in the fifth case.[13]

Regardless of the causes, the inequities in pollution exposure are now clearly documented and have been dubbed **environmental racism**. They have also sparked political engagement demanding stronger enforcement of safety-based laws called the environmental justice movement. As a result, some of the staunchest advocates of strong, safety-based regulations have emerged from low-income and minority communities.

Because poor, working-class, and minority people, relative to their income, both pay more for, and receive more from, pollution control, it is difficult to evaluate its overall distributive impact. Thus one cannot conclusively argue whether pollution control imposes net benefits or net costs on the lower half of the income distribution. Nevertheless, in important cases such as a carbon tax to slow global warming, which would raise the price of necessities, distributional issues need to be weighed carefully. Here, as noted in Chapter 1, economists have recommended that much of the revenue raised from the tax be rebated as tax cuts disproportionately to those in the lower half of the income distribution.

Beyond the issue of distributional effects, efficiency critics of the safety standard point out correctly that the additional costs imposed on society are real. It is certainly possible that the money saved under an efficiency standard could, as Blinder implies it will, be used to fund basic human needs: nutrition, adequate medical care, and housing. However, safety proponents might argue in response that the funds would more likely be funneled into consumption among the middle and upper classes.

The last three sections have looked at criticisms of the safety standard—inefficiency, potential for cost-ineffectiveness, and the charge of regressive distributional impacts. All have some merit. And insofar as safe regulations are regressive in their net effect, safety advocates lose the moral high ground from the claim that their approach is "fairer" than efficiency. Yet, as we have seen, the alternative efficiency standard is open to its own criticisms. Perhaps no issue dramatizes the differences between these two standards better than the disposal of hazardous wastes.

---

13. Bullard (1991, 86–95).

7.5 Siting Hazardous Waste Facilities: Safety versus Efficiency

In an infamous internal memorandum to his staff, Lawrence Summers—then chief economist at the World Bank and most recently economic adviser to President Obama—wrote: "Just between you and me, shouldn't the World Bank be encouraging more migration of the dirty industries to the [less developed countries]? ... I think the economic logic behind dumping a load of toxic waste in the lowest-wage country is impeccable and we should face up to that." The memo, leaked to *The Economist* magazine, stirred considerable controversy. Brazil's environment minister, responding to Summers's blunt analysis, said, "It's perfectly logical but perfectly insane," and called for Summers's dismissal from the Bank.

Summers, in a letter to the magazine, maintained that his provocative statements were quoted out of context. "It is not my view, the World Bank's view, or that of any sane person that pollution should be encouraged anywhere, or that the dumping of untreated toxic wastes near the homes of poor people is morally or economically defensible. My memo tried to sharpen the debate on important issues by taking as narrow-minded an economic perspective as possible."[14] This "narrow-minded" view is what we have characterized as the efficiency perspective. However, we also know that the efficiency perspective—in this case, trade in waste—can be defended both morally and economically, as it provides *an opportunity* for making *all* parties better off. The morality of the trade depends on the degree to which this promise is fulfilled.

Disposing of waste—hazardous, radioactive, or even simple nonhazardous municipal waste—has become an increasingly vexing and expensive problem. Such "locally unwanted land uses" (**LULUs**) impose negative externality costs on their immediate neighbors, ranging from the potential hazards of exposure to decreased land values, for the benefit of the broader society. This is true even when very expensive protective measures are undertaken to reduce expected risk. For someone with a waste dump in his or her backyard, an "adequate" margin of safety means zero risk. By definition, communities do not want LULUs for neighbors, and the wealthier (and better organized) the community, the higher the level of safety the community will demand.

Because the benefits to the broader society of having toxic facilities are great, one possible solution to the problem of siting is to "compensate" communities with tax revenues, generated by the facility, that would pay for schools, hospitals, libraries, or sewer systems. Poorer communities of course would accept lower compensation levels; thus, to reduce disposal costs, some (including Summers), have argued that government policy should promote this kind of "trade" in LULUs. Should poor communities (or countries) be encouraged to accept dangerous facilities in exchange for dollars? The dumping controversy provides a classic example of the conflict between the efficiency and safety positions on pollution control. Both sides maintain that their policy promotes overall social welfare.

First, let us consider the logic of the efficiency position. Summers defends his trade-in-toxics stance on two counts. First, if the physical damages to pollution rise as it

14. Summer's quotes are from Let them eat pollution. 1992. *The Economist*, 8 February, 66; and Polluting the poor. 1992. *The Economist*, 15 February, 6. Environment minister's quote is from *In These Times*, 8 March 1992.

increases, then pollution in cleaner parts of the world will do less physical damage than comparable discharges in dirty areas. In other words, Summers assumes the standard case of decreasing marginal benefits of cleanup. As he puts it: "I've always thought that underpopulated countries in Africa are vastly underpolluted," relative to Mexico City or Los Angeles.

Summers's second point is that people "value" a clean environment less in poorer countries. In his words: "The concern over an agent that causes a one-in-a-million change in the odds of prostate cancer is obviously going to be much higher in a country where people survive to get prostate cancer than in a country where the under-five mortality is 200 per thousand." This difference in priorities shows up in the form of a much lower monetary value placed on all environmental amenities, including reduced risk of death. Thus trading waste not only reduces the physical damage to the environment but also results in (much) lower dollar damages measured in terms of the fully informed willingness of the community to accept the waste. Firms will be able to dump their waste at a lower cost, *even including compensation costs*, thus freeing up resources to increase output and raise the gross global product.

Figure 7.1 presents a graphical analysis of Summers's position. Due to lower incomes (and lower population densities in some cases), the poor country has a marginal benefit of cleanup schedule lying below that of the rich country. In addition, because current pollution levels are relatively low in the poor country (PC_1 versus

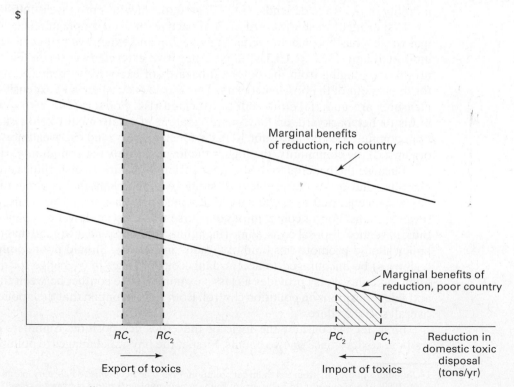

FIGURE 7.1 Efficiency and Toxic Trade

RC_1), the marginal benefits of cleanup are also low relative to the rich country. Transferring 10% of the waste from the rich country to the poor country reduces monetary damages (in the rich country) by the shaded area and increases damages (in the poor country) by the hatched area. Overall, *monetary* damages from the pollution have been reduced by the trade.

Clearly there will be winners and losers in such a process. The winners include those in wealthy countries no longer exposed to the waste, those around the world who can buy products more cheaply if output is increased, firm managers and stockholders who reap higher profits (assuming imperfect competition), and those in the poor countries who obtain relatively high-wage work at the dump sites or benefit from taxes levied against the dumping firms. The losers will be those poor-country individuals—alive today and as yet unborn—who contract cancer or suffer other diseases contracted from exposure, and those who rely on natural resources that may be damaged in the transport and disposal process.

Because dumping toxics is indeed efficient, we know the total monetary gains to the winners outweigh the total monetary loss to the losers. Thus, in theory, the winners could compensate the losers, and everyone would be made better off. A higher risk of cancer in poor countries from exposure to waste might be offset by reduced risk of death from unsafe drinking water if, for example, revenues from accepting the waste were used to build a sewage treatment facility. In practice, however, complete compensation is unlikely. Thus, as we saw in Chapter 4, toxic dumping—like any efficient strategy—is not "socially optimal"; it can only be defended on utilitarian grounds if, over time, the great majority of the population benefits from the action. Summers clearly believes it is in the interests of the people of poor countries themselves to accept toxic wastes.

The first response to this argument is, what kind of world do we live in when poor people have to sell their health and the health of their children merely to get clean water to drink? Shouldn't there be a redistribution of wealth to prevent people from having to make this kind of Faustian bargain? But an efficiency defender might note that socialist revolution is not a current policy option. Given that rich countries or individuals are not likely to give up their wealth to the poor, who are we to deny poor people an opportunity to improve their welfare through trade, if only marginally?

A more pragmatic response to the Summers argument is that, in fact, most of the benefits from the dumping will flow to the relatively wealthy, and the poor will bear the burden of costs. The postcolonial political structure in many developing countries is far from democratic. In addition, few poor countries have the resources for effective regulation. One could easily imagine waste firms compensating a few well-placed individuals handsomely for access while paying very low taxes and ignoring any existing regulations. In fact, as we noted earlier, a similar process may well explain the racial disparities in toxic site locations in the United States.

The basic criticism of the efficiency perspective is that the *potential* for a Pareto improvement is an insufficient condition to increase overall welfare. This is especially apparent in the case of international trade in toxics, where the benefits are likely to accrue to the wealthy in both rich and poor countries while the costs are borne by poor residents of poor countries. By contrast, we expect pollution policy to *actually increase* the welfare of most of those affected by the pollution itself.

On the other hand, safety proponents face a difficult issue in the siting of LULUs. A politically acceptable definition of safety cannot be worked out, because a small group bears the burden of any positive risk. Nobody wants a LULU in *his* or *her* backyard. As a result, compensation will generally play an important role in the siting of hazardous facilities. And firms and governments will tend to seek out poorer communities where compensation packages will be lower. Yet there are at least two preconditions for ensuring that the great majority of the affected population in fact benefit from the siting. The first of these is a government capable of providing effective regulation. The second is an open political process combined with well-informed, democratic decision making in the siting process.

The siting of a LULU presents a case in which the important insight of efficiency proponents—that something close to a Pareto improvement is possible—can be implemented. But to do so requires that the enforceable pollution standard be quite close to safety. It also requires an informed and politically enfranchised population.

7.6 Summary

In the last four chapters, we have wound our way through a complex forest of arguments to examine two different answers to the question, "How much pollution is too much?" Table 7.2 summarizes their features.

The first standard, efficiency, relies heavily on benefit-cost estimates. In theory, it requires precise calculation of *marginal* benefits and costs, and leads to maximization of the net monetary benefits to be gained from environmental protection. In practice, as we shall see later, benefit-cost analysts can only roughly balance benefits and costs. The efficiency standard requires a belief that intangible environmental benefits can be adequately measured and monetized. This in turn sanctions a "technocratic" approach to deciding how much pollution is too much.

TABLE 7.2   Comparing Efficiency and Safety

1. SOCIAL GOAL

EFFICIENCY:	Marginal benefits equal marginal costs
SAFETY:	Danger to health and environment "minimized"

2. IMPLIED SOCIAL WELFARE FUNCTION

EFFICIENCY: $SW = U_A(\overset{+}{X_A}, \overset{-}{P_A}) + U_R(\overset{+}{X_R}, \overset{-}{P_R}) + U_T(\overset{+}{X_T}, \overset{-}{P_T}) + \ldots$

SAFETY: $SW = U_A(\overset{+}{X_A}, \overset{-}{w * P_A}) + U_R(\overset{+}{X_R}, \overset{-}{w * P_R}) + U_T(\overset{+}{X_T}, \overset{-}{w * P_T}) + \ldots$
Weights; $w > 1$

3. ADVANTAGES AND DISADVANTAGES

EFFICIENCY:	Maximizes measurable net monetary benefits; relies heavily on assumptions of benefit-cost analysis
SAFETY:	Seems to be consistent with public opinion; often cost-ineffective and may be regressive

By contrast, the safety standard ignores formal benefit-cost comparisons to pursue a health-based target defined by an explicitly political process. In theory, under a safety standard, regulators are directed to get as close to a 1 in 1 million cancer risk as they can while also pursuing more nebulous noncancer safety goals, all conditional on the funds allocated to them by the political system. In practice, regulators often back away from safety when faced with high compliance costs.

The social welfare function for the safety standard relies on a liberty argument, putting heavy weights on the welfare reduction from pollution. Consequently, as illustrated in Figure 7.2, a stricter pollution standard is called for than is implied by the efficiency standard. Efficiency proponents attack the "fairness" defense of safety with the charge that it is regressive, but this claim is hard to either verify or refute in general.

One point not highlighted in Table 7.2 is that the choice between the two standards does not affect the long-run employment picture. As discussed in the last chapter, the more stringent safety standard may result in slightly more short-run structural job loss; yet it also creates more jobs in the environmental protection industry. *The real trade-off is between increased material consumption and increased environmental quality.*

Beyond concerns of fairness, choice between the safety and efficiency standards also depends on a key assumption: more is better. Recall that the underlying premise of benefit-cost analysis is that modern societies are made better off as income and consumption rises. But, what real benefits would we gain from the increased consumption that is sacrificed by tighter environmental controls? If benefit estimates leave out much that is hard to quantify, or if increased material consumption just feeds a rat race that leaves no one any happier, then safety may be "more efficient" than efficiency! We explore this idea later in the book.

Before that, however, the next three chapters consider a problem we have so far left off the table: sustainability. How should we incorporate the interests of future generations into environmental protection measures taken today?

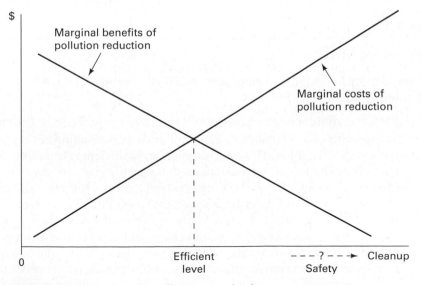

FIGURE 7.2 Costs, Benefits, Efficiency, and Safety

APPLICATION 7.0

Controlling Air Toxics

As noted in this chapter, one of the Clean Air Act Amendments passed by the U.S. government in 1990 was designed to control the emission of hazardous air pollutants. The EPA released a publication that year, estimating that at 149 industrial facilities nationwide, cancer risks to the most exposed local residents from airborne toxics were greater than 1 in 10,000; at 45 plants, risks were greater than 1 in 1,000.

The air toxics law required firms to impose control technology that, it was hoped, would reduce risks to below the 1 in 10,000 level. After the control technologies are installed, a follow-up risk analysis will be conducted to see if further control is necessary to further reduce any unsafe exposure. While the legislation did not require risk reduction to the 1 in 1 million level, that remains the long-run target.

1. Clearly, air toxics control is justified on safety grounds. Suppose that total benefits of the legislation just matched total costs, at $5 billion annually. Would air toxics control be justified on efficiency grounds?
2. Also as noted, one economist in fact criticized the legislation from an efficiency perspective. He put estimated total costs at $6 to $10 billion per year and total benefits at $0 to $4 billion per year (Portney 1987). The air toxics legislation attacks some fairly significant risks. How can the estimated benefits be so low (as low as zero)?
3. Suppose the air toxics regulations raised household expenditures on gasoline (due to extra controls on oil refineries) by an average of $20 per year. If millionaire Mary and janitor Jane each paid the extra $20, in what sense is the impact of the legislation regressive?

APPLICATION 7.1

Arsenic and Water Do Mix?

Consider the following statement published on the website of the AEI-Brookings Joint Center for Regulatory Studies:

> EPA's analysis of its new arsenic rule estimates annual costs of $210 million and benefits of $140 million to $200 million ... with resulting net costs of $10 million to $70 million. This clearly signals an inefficient rule, but recent analysis by the Joint Center estimates that true net costs are closer to $190 million per year. ... Beyond the high costs of the rule, Burnett and Hahn (the authors of the Joint Center study) raise the possibility that implementation of the rule could actually result in a net *loss* of lives. The high costs of the rule would reduce funds available to individuals for health care. The long latency period associated with arsenic-related cancers means that reduced funds for health care could result in a net increase of health risk, on the order of about 10 lives per year.

The difficulty of justifying the EPA's arsenic standard with cost-benefit analysis demonstrates clearly that this rule should be withdrawn ("Drinking Water," 2006).

1. How do you know that the EPA has chosen a safe rather than an efficient standard?
2. In arguing for a move toward efficiency, how do Burnett and Hahn utilize the idea of a Pareto improvement? Describe how they see such an outcome arising.
3. Does a Pareto improvement seem plausible in this case? Why or why not?

KEY IDEAS IN EACH SECTION

7.0 This chapter defines and then critically examines a **safety standard** for pollution control. Safety standards are defended primarily on fairness grounds. However, if unquantified benefits are large and/or the true costs of protection are overstated due to "rat race" effects, then safe regulations may be more efficient than those passing a conventional benefit-cost test.

7.1 Safety standards are defended on **personal liberty** grounds. A political consensus has developed that environmental cancer risks less than 1 in 1 million are considered **safe**, while risks greater than 1 in 10,000 are generally **unsafe**. There is no consensus on whether risks lying in between are safe. A precise safety standard cannot yet be defined for noncancer risks or ecosystem protection. In these areas, safe levels are determined politically on a case-by-case basis.

7.2 The first criticism of the safety standard is that it is often *inefficiently* strict. This is a normative criticism and is thus a proper subject for political and moral debate.

7.3 The second criticism of the safety standard is that it fails to give sufficient guidance to ensure **cost-effectiveness**. Cost-effectiveness is often measured in dollars spent per life saved. If regulators pursue safety at every turn, they may devote too many resources to eradicating small risks while ignoring larger ones. This problem can be alleviated by using **risk-benefit analysis**. The cost-effectiveness criticism is not that too many resources are being devoted to environmental protection, but rather that these resources are not being wisely spent.

7.4 The final criticism of the safety standard is that it might have a **regressive** impact on income distribution. While poor people do pay a higher *percentage* of their income for pollution control than do rich people, the poor, working-class, and minority communities also benefit disproportionately. (The greater exposure borne by minorities is referred to as **environmental racism**.) Thus the overall impact of environmental regulation on income distribution is uncertain. Moreover, it is not clear that freeing up resources from environmental control would in fact lead to increases in well-being among the poor.

7.5 The siting of a **LULU** is used to compare and contrast efficiency and safety standards for pollution control. In such a case, efficiency is a hard standard to implement because it ignores fairness issues. Thus something like a safety standard is generally enforced. If a basic level of "safe" protection is afforded through effective regulation, however, Pareto-improving compensation schemes can result in some movement toward efficient regulation.

REFERENCES

Blinder, Alan. 1987. *Hard heads, soft hearts*. New York: Addison-Wesley.

Boyce, James, and Matthew Riddle. 2008. Cap and dividend: How to curb global warming while promoting income equity. In *Twenty-first century macroeconomics: Responding to the climate challenge*, ed. Jonathan Harris and Neva Goodwin, 191–222. Cheltenham and Northampton, U.K.: Edward Elgar.

Bromley, Daniel. 1990. The ideology of efficiency: Searching for a theory of policy analysis. *Journal of Environmental Economics and Management* 19(1): 86–107.

Bullard, Robert D. 1991. *Dumping in Dixie: Race, class and environmental quality*. Boulder, CO: Westview.

Bullard, Robert, Paul Mohai, Robin Saha, and Beverly Wright. 2007. *Toxic wastes and race at twenty: 1987–2007*. Cleveland, OH: United Church of Christ.

Burtraw, Dallas, Alan Krupnick, Erin Mansur, David Austin, and Deidre Farrell. 1998. Reducing air pollution and acid rain. *Contemporary Economic Policy* 16(4): 379–400.

Cropper, Maureen L., William N. Evans, Stephen J. Berardi, Marie M. Ducla-Soares, and Paul R. Portney. 1991. *The determinants of pesticide regulation: A statistical analysis of EPA decisionmaking*. Discussion paper CRM 91-01. Washington, DC: Resources for the Future.

Burnett, Jason, and Robert Hahn. 2006. Drinking water standard for arsenic. AEI-Brookings Joint Center for Regulatory Studies. www.aei-brookings.org/admin/authorpdfs/page.php?id = 54.

Goodstein, Eban. 1994. In defense of health-based standards. *Ecological Economics* 10(3): 189–95.

Greider, William. 1992. *Who will tell the people? The betrayal of American democracy*. New York: Simon & Schuster.

Kneese, Alan V., and William D. Schulze. 1985. Ethics and environmental economics. In *Handbook of natural resource economics*. Vol. 1, ed. A. V. Kneese and J. L. Sweeney. New York: Elsevier.

Kunreuther, Howard, and Douglas Easterling. 1990. Are risk benefit trade-offs possible in siting hazardous facilities? *American Economic Review* 80(2): 252–56.

Lave, Lester. 1987. Health and safety risk analyses: Information for better decisions. *Science* 236: 297.

Mann, Eric. 1991. *L.A.'s lethal air*. Los Angeles: Labor Community Strategy Center.

Portney, Paul. 1990. Policy watch: Economics and the Clean Air Act. *Journal of Economic Perspectives* 4(4): 173–82.

WSJ Online. 2005. Nearly half of Americans cite "too little" environment regulation. *Wall Street Journal*, 13 October. http://online.wsj.com/public/article/SB112914555511566939.html.

THE SUSTAINABILITY STANDARD

8.0 Introduction

The Iroquois Indians are said to have lived under a traditional directive to consider the impact of their decisions on the next seven generations. What kind of world are we leaving to our children, our grandchildren, as well as our great-great-great-great-great grandchildren? In this chapter and the next two, we move beyond our efficiency versus safety debate over pollution-control standards and consider these long-run impacts. In the process, our focus shifts from allowable standards for pollution to questions of the maintenance of environmental quality and natural resources over the long term.

Many current decisions involving pollution and the environment have long lasting impacts. A pollutant that has long-term consequences is called a **stock pollutant**. Each one of us carries in the fat cells of our bodies residues of the pesticide DDT, even though it was banned from use in this country in the early 1970s. Chlorofluorocarbons released into the atmosphere contribute to ozone depletion for decades. Certain types of high-level nuclear waste retain their toxicity for tens of thousands of years. And current CO_2 emissions from burning oil, natural gas, and coal will continue warming the planet for more than 100 years. In contrast, **flow pollutants** do their damage relatively quickly and are then either diluted to harmless levels or transformed into harmless substances. Examples include smog, noise, and heat pollution.

People also modify the environment through the use of **natural resources** and the exhaustion of **environmental sinks**. Natural resources are inputs into the economy—both renewable (water, wood, fish, and soil) and nonrenewable (minerals, oil, and the genetic code in species). Exploiting natural resources at rates faster than they regenerate will reduce resource stocks, making them less available for future generations. As long as the rate of extraction of *renewable* resource stocks is balanced by regeneration, resource use will not reduce future availability. However, any use of *nonrenewable* resources reduces their stock. For example, extracting oil and burning it reduces the stock of oil that remains. Economists refer to natural resource stocks, environmental quality, and the ability of the environment to assimilate pollutants as

natural capital. Changes in natural capital are one important way in which current decisions affect the future.

But current decisions also affect future generations through other channels. Since the start of the Industrial Revolution in the late 1700s and early 1800s, scientific discoveries, new technologies, and new ways of doing things have led to rapid economic growth. Innovations have transformed sectors of the economy such as health care (vaccines, pharmaceutical drugs, and X-rays), transportation (automobiles, high-speed trains, and jet airplanes), food production (synthetic fertilizers, pesticides, and high-yield crop varieties), and communications (television, cell phones, and Internet). Building new industrial plants and machinery (**manufactured capital**) or increasing the level of education and experience of workers (**human capital**) have made the global economy more productive. Establishing trust among members of society or having functioning institutions (**social capital**) is also important for economic productivity. Increases in various forms of capital have led to large improvements in standards of living for many (but not all) people over the past 200 years. But these improvements have also come at a cost in the form of pollution and declines in natural resource stocks as noted earlier.

The main question of this chapter is what do all of these changes mean for the future? Due to the dramatic increase in the pace of environmental, social, and technological change, it is difficult for us today to predict what the future will look like 100 or 200 hundred years from now. Just imagine what someone living in the 1800s would think if they were to be suddenly transported to modern day and see cities with 10 million people, computers, cell phones, and airplanes for the first time. Yet thinking about the next seven generations requires us to try to think through the long-term consequences of current actions.

We start here by defining sustainability generally, and then we'll quickly see how achieving sustainability in practice requires determining the extent to which increases in manufactured, human, or social capital can substitute for lost natural capital. This in turn will help determine whether "growth" in the economy is actually leading to increases in human welfare—or, put another way, whether investments in other forms of capital at the expense of natural capital loss are really making us better off.

If, on one hand, growth is making us better off, then we can explore how best to trade-off investments between preserving natural capital and expanding manufactured capital, through a modified form of benefit-cost analysis that brings future benefits and costs of today's actions into the equation. If, on the other hand, natural capital is unique and irreplaceable, and has no manufactured, human, or social capital substitute, what policies can we put in place so that development decisions protect much of our remaining natural capital and ensure sustainability? This chapter and the next are the hardest conceptual chapters in the book—they get us deep into a debate between neoclassical and ecological economists—so buckle your seat belts.

8.1 Sustainability: Neoclassical and Ecological Approaches

Most people accept that we have a responsibility to manage the environment and the planet's natural resources to provide future generations with a high quality of life: the idea of **sustainability**. The most commonly used definition of sustainability comes from a report by the World Commission on Environment and Development (1987), or

Brundtland Commission, named for former Norwegian Prime Minister Gro Harlem Brundtland, the Commission Chair. The Bruntland Commission defined sustainable development as "development that meets the needs of the present without compromising the ability of future generations to meet their own needs." Economists find it difficult to precisely define "needs" and generally think instead about well-being. So, in economics, sustainability is typically defined as follows.

> A sustainable economy is one in which the well-being of a typical (median) member of all future generations will be higher, or at least the same, as the well-being of the typical member of the current generation. Put another way, sustainability means non-declining utility for the typical member of all future generations.[1]

While the definition is precise, putting it into operation is controversial. Every time we drive our car, and burn up a gallon of petroleum, aren't we in fact impoverishing future generations by depriving them of access to this amazing gift from nature, this unique, nonrenewable, high-energy fuel? How can oil consumption possibly be sustainable? Well, it *might* be sustainable if, at the same time, technology is advancing to provide future generations alternative energy sources (solar and wind) that can provide a comparable energy supply at roughly the same price. The idea here is that we do not need to sustain any particular resource as long as we can find alternatives that provide equal or better outcomes. Up to a point, manufactured, human, or social capital can substitute for natural capital in improving human welfare. Whether we have reached that point is the key question.

If substitution is still generally possible, then achieving sustainability does not require that *any particular form* of capital to be conserved. This definition of sustainability, known as **weak sustainability**, requires only that the overall capital stock— manufactured, human, social, and natural—needed to support a high quality of life is maintained. For example, weak sustainability would be achieved in food production if increases in manufactured capital, in the form of manufactured fertilizers and pesticides, can replace the loss of natural soil nutrients and pest control. In other words, weak sustainability can be achieved even with the loss of natural capital as long as other forms of capital are adequate substitutes.

Two inputs are **substitutes** in production if one input can replace the other and keep production levels the same. (If you have taken intermediate microeconomics, let your mind drift back to a smooth, bow-shaped *isoquant*; now recall how two inputs such as capital and labor can be substituted for each other while keeping the total output level the same.)

Weak sustainability also does not imply that the same mix of products needs to be produced. It may also be possible to substitute in consumption as well as production, if increased consumption of one good replaces the loss of another and keeps people equally satisfied. (Again, if you have taken intermediate microeconomics, think about an indifference curve where good X can be substituted for good Y and achieve the same level of utility.) If people are happy to substitute video games and amusement

---

1. This is the standard economic definition of sustainability, see Pezzey (1992). For recent critiques, see Bromley (2007) and Howarth (2007).

parks for spending time in nature, the loss of natural areas does not necessarily reduce satisfaction from recreation and tourism. As a case in point, consider the number of tourist visits in Florida. In 2010, approximately 17 million people visited Disney World's Magic Kingdom while less than 1 million visited Everglades National Park.

Knowing whether the economy is on a path to satisfy weak sustainability is not easy. As we have seen, material growth often comes at the expense of environmental quality. Judging whether the future is better with improvements in some areas and declines in others requires making value judgments about whether the gains really do outweigh the losses. And not all people have the same values. While the typical person might be willing to have more Disney Worlds and less Everglades, the avid bird watcher or nature lover may be made worse off were this to happen. Of course, in judging sustainability, it is really the value judgments of future generations that count. Would future generations consider themselves better off with the world we give them as compared to the world as it is now? If we give them more material goods but more pollution, or more video games and amusement parks but fewer chances to walk in nature, will they think that is a good trade? Because they are not here yet to ask we cannot know for sure.

Such difficulties have led some economists to take a different tack to assessing sustainability. Rather than focus on an overall measure of well-being, **strong sustainability** requires maintaining the total stock of each form of capital (natural, manufactured, human, and social). In particular, strong sustainability focuses on measures of natural capital. Declines in natural capital violate strong sustainability regardless of whether there are increases in manufactured, human, or social capital. Strong sustainability tends to emphasize irreplaceable assets, those things for which there is no substitute. If a forest or wetland were lost, how could all of the complex set of ecological functions that occur in such systems be replaced? At least some components of natural capital may be essential in that they constitute the life-support system for humans and other species. People need oxygen to breathe but we can't manufacture oxygen in the volumes required; we depend on trees and other plants to produce oxygen as a by-product of photosynthesis. If all plants went extinct people would soon follow.

Irreplaceable assets may also refer to uniqueness. In the 1960s, the U.S. Bureau of Reclamation contemplated constructing a dam on the Colorado River that would have flooded part of the Grand Canyon. The dam was never built, in large part because critics pointed out that the Grand Canyon was unique and there was no adequate compensation for its loss.

Discussions around weak and strong sustainability have divided economists into two broad groups: neoclassical and ecological. (For purposes of argument, we draw very sharp distinctions between these two groups, but in reality, many economists have one foot in both camps.) **Neoclassical economists** tend to view natural and other forms of capital as substitutes in production. They also tend to be technological optimists, believing that as resources become scarce, prices will rise, and human innovation will find high-quality substitutes, lowering prices once again. Neoclassical economists also tend to view nature as highly resilient; pressure on ecosystems will lead to steady, predictable degradation, but no surprises. This view of small (marginal) changes and smooth substitution between inputs is at the heart of the neoclassical tradition in economics.

From a broader perspective, neoclassical economists generally believe that the global spread of market-based economies provides a powerful foundation for achieving a sustainable future. While still seeing a need for government regulations to control pollution and resource depletion, neoclassical economists generally believe that as markets spread, living standards around the globe will continue to increase. This, in turn, will lead to declining population growth rates and to demands for increased environmental protection that will keep environmental degradation within an acceptable range. This is not to say that neoclassical economists believe there are no trade-offs, only that sustainability is most likely to be achieved through a well-functioning and properly regulated market system.

By contrast, **ecological economists** argue that other forms of capital cannot be used to substitute for natural capital; natural capital is essential and irreplaceable (L-shaped isoquants for microeconomics fans). Ecological economists emphasize the fundamental importance of nature as a critical and irreplaceable support system on which the economy is built: the economy is a wholly owned subsidiary of nature. Ecological economists view the global ecosystem in which our economy is embedded as fragile, in the sense that accumulating stresses may lead to catastrophic changes in the system itself. For example, climate change from unchecked global warming or increased ultraviolet exposure from unchecked ozone depletion could radically alter the natural environment.

Ecological economists also worry about sudden and abrupt changes in nature that might lead to catastrophic problems. For example, climate change may lead to disintegration of ice sheets in Greenland and the Antarctic, leading to rapid rise in sea levels, or abrupt changes in ocean currents and weather patterns. Of course, ecosystems are subject to catastrophe all the time—for example, when lightning causes a fire in a forest. Catastrophe, when severe enough, in fact forms grist for the mill of evolution by favoring individuals within species better adapted to new conditions. So nature itself is not threatened. "Saving the planet" is not the issue. But preserving conditions that support human life and well-being is the issue.

Local and global **ecosystem services**—water purification, nutrient cycling, regional climate regulation, waste processing, soil stabilization, pest and disease control, and crop pollination—provide a critical foundation for our economic well-being. Ecological economists argue that our economy depends in countless, often subtle ways on the complex web of services provided by our natural environment *as it exists today*. As a result, major environmental changes brought on by the stress of doubling and then redoubling population and consumption levels could lead to very large and sudden declines in human welfare.

Ecological economists also tend to be technological pessimists. They view recent rapid increases in living standards as a temporary phenomenon made possible only by the unsustainable use of natural capital. This ongoing degradation of natural capital will likely lead human well-being to decline. New innovations may not save us as they often have unintended consequences that result in increased pollution and resource depletion thereby intensifying sustainability problems.

In contrast to neoclassical economists, ecological economists consider current patterns of globalization and economic growth to be unsustainable and that further ecological pressure in the form of population and consumption growth intensifies the problems and is likely to lead to disaster. While not hostile to the spread of markets or to incentive-based approaches to resolving environmental problems, ecological economists see the need for an expanded role for government in aggressively protecting our dwindling stock of natural capital.

We will return to the debate between the views of neoclassical and ecological economists in Chapter 9 where we discuss how to measure sustainability and what the empirical record indicates. The remainder of this chapter develops the fundamental building blocks for thinking about sustainability—the allocation of resources and changes in capital stocks through time. We begin by considering the treatment of future versus present benefits and costs and the role and meaning of discounting.

8.2 Future Benefits, Costs, and Discounting

In this section, we think about how to value benefits reaped by future generations that result from our actions today. Consider the following:

PUZZLE

Would you prefer to receive $100 in real purchasing power this year or next year, or are you indifferent? By "real purchasing power," we mean that if you opt to take the money next year, you will be compensated for any inflation. Assume you don't "need" the money any more this year than next.

SOLUTION

This one requires a little business acumen. It's better to take the money up front, put it in the bank, and earn interest. As a result, you will have more "real purchasing power" next year than this year. For example, suppose the interest rate on a savings account is 3%, and there is no inflation. If you put $100 in the bank this year, next year you would have $103 to spend.

Now, stop to think about where exactly did that extra $3 come from? It came from the bank, obviously. (When asked why he robbed banks, the famous bank robber Willie Sutton is reported to have said "because that's where the money is"). But where did the bank get the extra $3? The bank loaned out your money to a businessperson (or to the government) who in turn invested it in productive real assets: machines, buildings, roads, and schools. A year later, thanks to your saving effort, and other people's ingenuity and labor, the economy as a whole was capable of producing 3 more dollars worth of stuff. At the national level, this year-to-year increase in productive capacity leads GDP to grow on average around 2 to 3% per year. This growth is the ultimate source of profits, interest, and wage increases.

This puzzle illustrates a crucial point: investment is productive. As a result, at least from an individual's point of view, $100 today is worth more than $100 next year or $100 fifty years from now. From a social point of view as well, resources today are worth more than same resources in the future because resources today can be invested to yield more resources in the future.

How does this observation relate to the environment? Consider a simplified example: a decision today to clean up a hazardous waste site costing taxpayers $1.3 million. If we fail to clean up, then in the year 2050, one individual (call her Joanne) who lived close to the site will contract a nonfatal cancer, thus imposing costs on Joanne—including medical bills, lost wages, and pain and suffering—equivalent to $1.5 million. Assume this is the only damage that the waste will ever do. Further assume that Joanne will feel fully compensated if paid $1.5 million. In other words, that she is indifferent between not having cancer and contracting cancer plus receiving compensation of $1.5 million. (Whether monetary compensation can really substitute for good health is an important question, and one that is similar to the debate over strong versus weak sustainability and how easy it is to find adequate substitutes.) With these assumptions, the issue on the table is this: should we spend $1.3 million this year to prevent $1.5 million in damages in 40 years' time?

An efficiency advocate would argue no. To see why, consider the following response: We could more than compensate the future pollution victim for the damage done by setting aside money today that would be available for Joanne's health care and compensatory damage payments in 40 years. However, we wouldn't need to put aside $1.3 million. We could put a much smaller amount of money in the bank today, and by earning interest, it would grow over time to equal $1.5 million. In fact, $1.5 million in 2053 is equivalent to only $459,000 banked today (2013) at a 3% real (inflation-adjusted) rate of interest. Putting money aside into a bank account specifically to compensate future generations for pollution damages or depletion of natural capital is known as posting an **environmental bond**.

The Alaska Permanent Fund, which sets aside money from current oil revenues for the benefit of current and future generations of Alaska residents, provides one example of a real-world environmental bond. A second example is a bottle deposit. Currently, ten U.S. states require a refundable deposit of five to ten cents per can or bottle of soda or juice purchased. If you choose to throw your container out the window of your car, the deposit money is then available for cleanup. (The deposit also provides an incentive for third parties to clean up the mess.) On a larger scale, mining companies and generators of hazardous waste sometimes must post bonds sufficient to allow regulatory agencies to assure reclamation if the property is abandoned.

The potential for posting an environmental bond offers us a rationale for spending less on prevention today than the full value of the damage we inflict in future generations. When future benefits are not weighted as heavily as current benefits, we say that the future benefits have been **discounted**. The basic rationale behind discounting is that *because investment is productive*, resources on hand today are more valuable, both to individuals and to society as a whole, than are resources available at a later date.

The figure of $459,000 mentioned earlier is known as the **present discounted value** (PDV) of $1.5 million paid or received in the year 2053. Formally, the PDV of $X received in T years is the amount of money one would need to invest today to receive $X in T years, at a specified rate of interest, or **discount rate**, r. We use the term interest rate to refer to the rate at which money increases going into the future, and discount rate as the rate at which future values are decreased to find an equivalent present value. But they are identical concepts. There is a simple formula for calculating the value of a future benefit in terms of today's dollars. If the discount rate is r, then the present discounted value of X received in T years is

$$PDV = \$X/(1 + r)^T$$

In the case just described,

$$PDV = \$1.5 \text{ million}/(1.03)^{40} = \$459,000$$

Let us consider a real-world private investment decision to see how discounting works.

8.3 An Example of Discounting: Lightbulbs

A recent technological innovation has the potential to dramatically reduce electricity use throughout the world. It may lead to lessened reliance on fossil and nuclear fuels and, thus, substantial improvements in environmental quality. The product is the humble lightbulb. New light emitting diode (LED) lightbulbs can replace standard incandescent bulbs, generate a similar quality of light, use around one-sixth of the electricity, and last around 40 times as long. So what's the catch? The up-front investment is substantially higher. Each LED bulb costs $30 to $40, compared with an initial cost for a standard incandescent of around $1.

Suppose you are the physical plant manager at a new hotel with 1,000 light fixtures and have to decide whether investing in these new bulbs is a good idea. How do you proceed? The first step is to marshal the information that you have on the costs and benefits of the two options over their lifetimes. This is done in Table 8.1.

The numbers in Table 8.1 consider a simplified problem with a four-year time horizon. Suppose that the initial investment to buy 1,000 LED bulbs is $40,000 and for 1,000 incandescent bulbs is $1,000. Now because LED bulbs last 40 times as long, assume that the LED bulbs last for four years so there is a one-time expense of $40,000 in year 1. Assume that incandescent bulbs have to be replaced 10 times each year. That means that every year there is an investment cost of $10,000 for incandescent bulbs. Suppose that the electricity bill for LED bulbs is $500 per year and for incandescent bulbs is $3,000. We also assume, as we will throughout the book, zero inflation (or, alternatively, that the figures are inflation-adjusted to reflect real purchasing power). On the face of it, buying LED bulbs appears to be a good idea as it leads to savings of $10,000 over the four years.

TABLE 8.1   Cash Outlays for Investing in Lighting

Option	Year				Total
	1	2	3	4	
LED bulbs	$40,500	$500	$500	$500	$42,000
Incandescent bulbs	$13,000	$13,000	$13,000	$13,000	$52,000
Savings from LED bulbs	−$27,500	$12,500	$12,500	$12,500	$10,000

Unfortunately, choosing between the options is not that simple. The reason: the LED bulbs require an extra initial investment in the first year. If instead of buying LED bulbs you bought the incandescent bulbs you could take the money saved in year 1 and put it in the bank and earn interest. At reasonable interest rates you might still do better investing in LED bulbs. But at a high enough interest rate you will actually do better with incandescent bulbs.

Things have suddenly become more complex. Fortunately, there is a simple way out: calculate the PDV of the net savings from investing in LED bulbs. The PDV will tell you how much, in today's dollars, investment in LED bulbs saves over incandescent bulbs. To calculate the PDV of the investment, simply apply the formula for each year and add up the values:

$$PDV = -27{,}500/(1 + r)^0 + 12{,}500/(1 + r)^1 + 12{,}500/(1 + r)^2 + 12{,}500/(1 + r)^3$$

Table 8.2 provides the relevant calculations. How do we interpret the numbers in the table? Consider $9,391.43, the number in the fourth-year column and the 0.10 discount rate row. This is the PDV of $12,500 received in four years when the discount rate is 10%. In other words, one would need to bank $9,391.43 today at a 10% interest rate to have $12,500 on hand in four years. If the interest rate were 0.00 (the first row), then one would have to have the full $12,500 on hand today to have $12,500 four years from now.

The last column of the table illustrates that if the interest rate is zero, the LED bulbs do save $10,000. However, as the interest rate climbs to 5% and 10%, the investment looks less attractive but overall is still a good deal. However, when the interest rate rises to 20%, the LED bulbs become the more expensive option. With this high interest rate, it is better to save the money upfront on the initial investment and earn interest while paying out larger sums in electricity and investment costs in later years. The main lessons to be learned here are that the higher the discount rate, (1) the less important are benefits earned down the road and (2) the more important are initial expenses.

Private for-profit decision makers, such as hotel managers, do not have to decide what discount rate to use when comparing future benefits with present costs. Businesses seeking to maximize profits should use the market rate of interest on investments of similar risk, that is, their opportunity cost of capital. A rate of 5%, 10%, or 20% will be determined in the financial marketplace. This begs the question of how markets determine interest rates, which is discussed in the next section. However, government policymakers do not need to rely on the market interest rate. Instead they must

TABLE 8.2   PDV of Savings from LED Lightbulbs Varies with the Discount Rate

Discount Rate	Year				Total
	1	2	3	4	
0.00	−$27,500	$12,500	$12,500	$12,500	$10,000
0.05	−$27,500	$11,904.76	$11,337.87	$10,797.97	$6,540.60
0.10	−$27,500	$11,363.64	$10,330.58	$9,391.43	$3,585.65
0.20	−$27,500	$10,416.67	$8,680.56	$7,233.80	−$1,168.98

choose a discount rate for analyzing policy decisions such as deciding how much stock pollution to allow. What is the right discount rate for public choices, such as the cleanup of hazardous waste sites or the level of legal carbon dioxide emissions? After we understand the factors that influence market interest rates, we can consider the right choice for social decision making.

8.4 Savings, Investment, and Market Interest Rates

Private sector discount rates—or equivalently, market rates of interest—are determined by the aggregate investment and savings decisions of individuals, businesses, and governments, much the same way that market prices are determined by the choices of producers and consumers. In fact, the discount rate really functions like a price; it determines the relative value of future benefits and costs compared with present benefits and costs, just as prices determine the relative values of various products.

A simple way to understand what determines an interest rate, say the interest rate paid on savings accounts in banks, is through supply and demand analysis in the **market for "loanable funds."** Figure 8.1 illustrates.

The supply of loanable funds is determined by bank deposits—money in individual and business savings accounts that, in turn, form the basis for loans by banks. The supply curve slopes up, because, in order to induce people to save more, and consume less, people must be offered a higher price or return for their savings. What are the motivations for saving? People save money to purchase goods and services in the future, primarily for retirement. It is a bit of a puzzle that people do not save more of their income—the U.S. savings rate is typically 5% or less. Part of the reason has to do with what economists call **positive rate of time preference**: the well-known desire to consume more today, regardless of the consequences for tomorrow. Positive time preference may have a biological basis. Our hunter-gatherer ancestors did not have secure means of saving, and a good meal today might be the best strategy to ensure genetic survival. Regardless of whether the basis is cultural or biological, a positive rate of time preference is a clear deterrent to savings. As a result, advanced

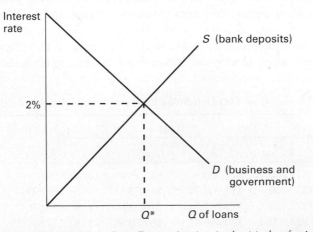

FIGURE 8.1 Interest Rate Determination in the Market for Loanable Funds

capitalist countries all have forced savings programs such as social security to overcome a natural tendency for people to save too little for retirement. This positive rate of time preference also partially explains why higher interest rates are needed to induce people to save more.

On the other side of the market, the demand curve for loanable funds reflects the opportunities for productive investment projects in the economy—in manufactured, natural, human, or social capital. It slopes down, reflecting the idea that, at any given moment there are limited opportunities for the high rate of return investments that can pay a high interest rate, but more opportunities for low rate of return investments, supporting payback to lenders at a lower interest rate. (Formally, this reflects declining marginal productivity of capital). At equilibrium in the market—in this diagram, 2%—the marginal dollar invested by borrowers will generate real gains to borrowers at the same rate demanded by savers needed to supply the dollars for investment. (In markets with risky investments, the supply curve for savings will shift up to the left, raising the interest rate that savers will require to provide their dollars to investors or governments.)

The underlying point here is that market interest rates, equivalently, discount rates, will be determined by two key factors. First is the rate of return on investment, which is the rate at which the economy is able to make real gains through productive investment in all forms of capital. Higher productivity will shift the demand curve for loans out, thus raising the interest rate. Second is the rate of time preference—the premium that savers must be offered to induce them to save and keep them from consuming part of their income today. A higher rate of time preference will shift the supply curve of savings in, also raising interest rates.

8.5 The Social Discount Rate and Dynamic Efficiency

Understanding how savings and investment decisions interact to generate market discount rates also provides the key to understanding discounting for social decisions. We can now tackle the question as to what discount rate a government *should* choose for analyzing decisions about how much to spend to clean up hazardous waste sites, how much to regulate emissions of greenhouse gases, or how fast to use up natural resource stocks.

In 1928, a young mathematician named Frank Ramsey wrote a paper that sought to answer the question of how much of a country's income should be saved and invested to maximize the present value of benefits to the nation over time. John Maynard Keynes (of Keynesian macroeconomic fame) who was a contemporary of Ramsey said the paper was "one of the most remarkable contributions to mathematical economics ever made, both in respect of the intrinsic importance and difficulty of its subject..." (Keynes 1933). Though it was not written about environmental issues, Ramsey's analysis is directly relevant to addressing the question of the determination of the discount rate to use in analysis of environmental issues such as climate change, stock pollution, and natural resource use. What is perhaps all the more remarkable for someone who made central contributions to the analysis of issues involving the long-term consequences of policies, and who has had such a lasting influence on economics, is that he died at the young age of 26.

Ramsey derived the discount rate that should be used in order to maximize the present value of net benefits over time to society as a whole. Though the mathematics that Ramsey used in his analysis are a bit beyond what can be presented here (he used the "calculus of variations," which could be thought of as calculus on steroids), the logic of the result mirrors what we learned from the supply and demand analysis of interest rate determination discussed in the previous section. The Ramsey equation breaks the discount rate (r) into two distinct components.

$$r = \delta + \eta g.$$

The first component is the rate of time preference, which we will label as δ (*delta*). If $\delta = 2\%$, then out of pure "short-sighted" desire to consume more today than in the future, people would discount future consumption at that rate. With a 2% rate of time preference, they would trade $100 five years from now for somewhat less money today. To be precise, $\$100/(1 + 0.02)^5 = \$90.57$.

The second component of the discount rate comprises two terms, η (*eta*) and g. The term g refers to the growth rate of the economy. If $g > 0$, the economy is growing and people in the future will generally be richer and able to consume more than people today. The term g also captures the idea discussed in the previous section. The higher the payoff of productive investment g, the higher is the opportunity cost of forgoing that investment, the more valuable dollars are today, and thus, the higher is the discount rate.

The term η refers to the elasticity of the marginal utility of consumption. Economists often assume there are "declining marginal benefits" of consumption: that is, a dollar to a wealthier individual or economy is worth less than a dollar to a poorer individual or economy. So, if people will be wealthier in the future and consume more then, they will tend to have low marginal benefits from additional consumption.[2]

To address environmental and resource issues, we must modify Ramsey's model. Rather than have g represent the rate of growth of the economy, we have to consider it as the rate at which productive investment is paying off in terms of *real increases in human welfare*. We will look more at this issue in the next chapter, where we will see that GDP growth is generally not a good measure of real increases in well-being.

To get some sense of what the Ramsey formula implies for the discount rate we can plug in reasonable values for the rate of time preference, the economic growth rate, and the elasticity of the marginal utility of consumption. The rate of time preference for individuals is usually taken to be positive (sooner is better than later in terms of enjoying benefits) but generally felt to be fairly low, so let's say 1%. The long-term growth rate of the U.S. economy has been between 1 and 3%, so let's say 2%. Estimates

---

2. A faster growing economy leads to the use of a higher discount rate—not only because investment is more productive but also because wealthier people value the extra future income less. The term η captures this effect. If η is > 1 (marginal benefits are declining), then as g gets bigger, the discount rate rises by even more than g.

Think about it in the following way. Chances are good that you are currently a student (or why else are you reading this book?). Students often do not have a lot of money. But good students like yourself are likely to have more money in the future when you are gainfully employed in a good paying job (hopefully). What would it take to make you want to give up current consumption when you are relatively poor in order to get more consumption in the future when you are likely to have a lot more income? Most people would say they need a really high rate of return to give up current consumption under those conditions.

for the elasticity of the marginal utility of consumption generally center around 2. In this case, the social rate of discount would be

$$r = \delta + \eta g = 1\% + 2 * 2\% = 5\%$$

However, others have argued that the social discount rate should be far lower. First, some economists have argued that the rate of time preference for society as a whole should be 0. The famous economist A. C. Pigou (1920; of "Pigouvian tax" fame) thought a positive rate of time preference was the result of a "faulty telescopic facility" and Frank Ramsey (1928) thought that a positive rate of time preference, which means that future generations count less than the present generation, was "ethically indefensible." On the growth side, some ecological economists have argued that long-term economic growth is doubtful, largely because of declining environmental quality and limited natural resources. Also, it is not clear whether growth, as conventionally measured, is actually improving human well-being today, an issue we explore in Chapters 9 and 11. If long-term economic growth ceases, then $g = 0$ and the second term in the Ramsey equation would also be 0. So, without a positive rate of time preference and no long-term growth in per capita human welfare, the social discount rate should be 0!

For now, assume the neoclassicals are right, that g is positive. It is easy to get lost in the math of discounting, but pause for a minute to recognize one very important fact: if g in the Ramsey equation is greater than zero, then our economy is by definition, (weakly) sustainable! That is because g is defined as the rate of growth of human well-being, and if it is positive going forward, this means that people's welfare, on average, is going up. This reflects, again, neoclassical optimism about the ability of manufactured capital to substitute for natural capital. In the next chapter, we will look at some data to assess this assumption.

That said, neoclassicals admit that *in individual cases*, businesses can "overexploit" natural capital, leading to inefficiently high damages for future generations. That is, pumping stock pollutants into the air or water, or depleting a natural resource can impose greater damages on current and future generations than the benefits gained by current and future generations from exploiting the resource. How can this be avoided? If the economy is indeed weakly sustainable, then the neoclassical "best" policy to maximize net benefits across generations is to make decisions to use up natural capital through an appropriately adjusted benefit-cost lens. So, whether we should protect natural capital, clean up a hazardous waste site, or take action on climate change depends on whether the benefits of doing so exceed the costs (the efficiency standard).

When costs and benefits occur at different times, discounting is used to put everything into a common framework of present value, and achieve what is known as **dynamic efficiency**. Under the dynamic efficiency approach, an action is justified if the present value of the benefits from the action exceeds the present value of the costs. Of course, this is true only if *all* costs and benefits (market and non-market) to *all* people (current and future generations) are included. This approach, in theory, appropriately weighs the trade-offs between protecting natural capital and investing in manufactured, social, or human capital.

In the earlier example of the hazardous waste site with cleanup costs of $1.3 million now and benefits of $1.5 million in 40 years, the present value of the costs ($1.3 million) exceed the present value of the benefits ($459,000) when using a 3% discount rate. Therefore, it wouldn't make sense to clean up the waste site. The $1.3 million could be better used for some other form of investment that has a higher rate of return or to generate current benefits. In fact, with suitably high discount rates, say, because the current generation has many opportunities for productive investment in human or manufactured capital, the dynamic efficiency rule might cause us to choose to do very little investment in hazardous waste cleanup, or not take action on climate change, or protection of natural capital. This is the argument often made in many fast-growing developing countries, where raising living standards often trumps pollution concerns.

This section has highlighted the importance of the long-term economic growth rate, and the assumed rate of time preference, for determining the proper social discount rate—a key parameter in using cost-benefit analysis when the costs and benefits of the action under scrutiny extend out over time. Unfortunately, because there is no agreement among economists over the values of the rate of time preference, or the long-term economic growth rate, there is also no agreement over the proper social discount rate that should be used. The right discount rate to use—particularly with respect to whether g is actually greater than zero—is a major divide between more "ecological" and more "neoclassical" economists. In many ways, the choice gets back to the degree of substitutability between human-made and natural capital, and the prospects for welfare improvements from economic growth. We will return to questions of accurately measuring long-run growth, and the correlation between growth and happiness, in Chapters 9 and 11. For now, recognize that this lack of agreement is critical as it has major consequences for recommendations about environmental policy, as we see in the next section.

8.6 Discounting Climate Change

The choice of the discount rate can have a major influence on benefit-cost conclusions for policy. This is especially true in cases like climate change, where the really large benefits of today's emission reduction policies will not begin to be seen for 50 or even 100 years. As illustrated in Table 8.3, high rates of discount reduce the present value of future benefits dramatically. Even huge benefits 100 years from now are worth next to nothing even when a discount rate as low as 5% is applied. A future benefit of $1 million falls to only $6,738!

Indeed, it was the choice of discount rate that was largely responsible for the dramatic differences in policy recommended by economist Nicolas Stern on one hand, and Willaim Nordhaus on the other, that we discussed in Chapter 1. Recall that Stern's benefit-cost analysis recommended 80% cuts in global warming pollution in developed countries by 2050, while Nordhaus called for allowing global emissions to grow by 40%—a lot, but still below the business-as-usual trajectory. Stern's analysis assumed a "low" discount rate of 1.4%, while Nordhaus opted for a much higher discount rate of 5.5%. Stern used the Ramsey equation to justify his discount rate. He assumed that the rate of time preference was near zero (0.1%) and the growth rate of the economy was 1.3% while the value of the elasticity of marginal utility was 1. These assumptions imply that the discount rate should be:

$$r = \delta + \eta g = 0.1\% + 1 \times 1.3\% = 1.4\%.$$

TABLE 8.3   The present value of $1 million in 100 years

Discount Rate (%)	Present Value ($)
0	1,000,000
1	367,879
2	135,335
3	52,033
5	6,738
10	45.40
20	0.01

Nordhaus believed that the correct discount rate to use was the market rate of return on manufactured capital investment, which is much higher, somewhere around 5 to 6%. Similar to the example in the last section, Nordhaus was able to get a discount rate of 5 to 6% by assuming higher values parameters in the Ramsey equation, 1.5% for the rate of time preference, 2% for the long-term economic growth rate, and 2% for the value of the elasticity of marginal utility.

The different discount rates mean that the same future damages—say, $100 billion of damages in 2100—show up very differently in the different economists' analyses. At the 1.4% rate (Stern), the $100 billion is still reduced significantly to $29.3 billion, but discounted at 5.5% (Nordhaus), the damages fall to only $0.95 billion—a huge difference. Given this it is no surprise that Stern recommends much more aggressive action than does Nordhaus.

So who is right in this debate? From our perspective, it depends on the social opportunity cost of capital, which in turn depends on the elements in the Ramsey equation: what should be assumed about the long-term growth rate of economic well-being (g) (and the rate at which marginal benefits decline with income)? And does, or should, "society" even have a positive rate of time preference? Overall, what is the real rate of return on alternative investments in education, health care, and the economy more generally into which society could put its resources, rather than into rewiring the global energy system to stabilize the climate? Is it 5%? Or 1%? Or zero? Again, more on the empirical evidence in the next chapter.

8.7 Ecological Economics, Strong Sustainability, and the Precautionary Principle

We began this chapter by thinking about the long-term consequences of current actions on the environment and future generations. Just as there are two ways of thinking about how much pollution is too much, the efficiency standard and the safety standard, there are also two ways of thinking about long-term consequences: weak sustainability and strong sustainability.

We have seen that neoclassical economists typically assume weak sustainability, and recommend cost-benefit analysis, with discounted future costs and benefits, to avoid penalizing future generations in *individual cases* of resource depletion or stock pollution. By contrast, ecological economists believe that in many important instances, natural capital cannot be substituted for manufactured capital, and strong sustainability must be pursued. Ecological economists thus reject the key underlying assumption of benefit-cost analysis—that substitution is possible—and argue instead that natural capital stocks must be maintained. But obviously, not all natural capital can be protected—some forests will be converted to agriculture, some oil will be burned, and some copper will be mined. How should society prioritize?

A famous baseball player and announcer, Yogi Berra, once said "It's tough to make predictions, especially about the future." At the beginning of the chapter we began with the Iroquois directive to think about the impacts on the next seven generations. We noted that with the dramatic pace of environmental, social, and technological change, it is difficult to predict what the future will look like 100 or 200 hundred years from now. Thinking about future impacts and sustainability brings us face to face with uncertainty.

The underlying question from the ecological perspective is this: to what extent, if any, can we afford to further run down the existing stock of natural capital? The concept of sustainability was originally used in the context of a specific resource. For example, a "sustained yield" of timber can be generated when the harvest rate does not exceed the growth rate of new forest. Ecological economists have raised this idea to the economy-wide level by making the following proposal:

Precautionary Principle: Never reduce the stock of natural capital below a level that generates a sustained yield of services unless good substitutes are currently available for the services generated. When in doubt, conserve.

The precautionary principle is often invoked in debates over the introduction of new chemicals. But what is the "stock of natural capital" that is potentially endangered by unknown chemical effects? The absorbtive capacity of the human body! A second example: when European nations rely on the precautionary principle to restrict the introduction of genetically engineered crops, they are doing so to protect natural capital services embodied in traditional agriculture from, for example, the potential development of "superweeds."

The first thing to note about the precautionary principle is that it is like a commandment—it says, "Thou shalt protect natural capital without good substitutes" *regardless of the cost* of doing so. In other words, under the presumption that future generations will benefit from protecting resources, the precautionary principle requires that the current generation make potentially large sacrifices on behalf of generations to come. In the case of genetically engineered crops, for example, by restricting development in this area—and thus preserving human health from potential degradation by, for example, new allergies—we may face higher prices for food. Like a safety standard, at some point, the costs of protecting natural capital might simply become so high that political support for the precautionary principle can disappear.

Given this caveat, to apply the precautionary principle we first need to address what we mean by the "yield" of a resource. The important aspect of natural capital from our utilitarian perspective is not the capital itself: that is, the oil, the old-growth forest, or the clean air. Rather, the important feature is the flow of services from that capital: inexpensive transportation, biodiversity resources and wilderness experiences, and environmental health.

To determine the availability of substitutes requires focusing on **uniqueness** and **uncertainty** combined with **irreversibility**. First of all, do the services provided by the natural capital in question currently *have* substitutes? Each day, for example, more than a hundred species of plants or animals are destroyed because of tropical deforestation. The primary use value from this natural capital is its medicinal and genetic properties; currently, an average of one in four pharmacy purchases contains rainforest-derived compounds. Suppose that of the millions of species alive in the forest, only one contains a chemical compound effective in curing many types of cancer. In such a case, clearly that species and the rain forest that harbors it are unique natural capital.

A question closely related to uniqueness is the *technological potential* for substitution. Each species, for example, represents a unique DNA blueprint that has evolved over millions of years. While we may be able to imagine substitutes for rainforest products generated by advanced technology, are such options feasible within the relevant time frame? In cases of unique natural capital—where good substitutes do not now, or will not soon, exist for the services flowing from the natural capital being destroyed—the stock should be protected, according to the precautionary principle.

It is possible, of course, that species extinction can proceed for some time at the current rate with no loss of unique medicinal or genetic value for humans. The remaining (millions) of species may provide an adequate resource base for developing medicines and biotechnologies on a sustained-yield basis. But they may not. This example highlights another issue that arises in attempting to apply our sustainability criterion: the uncertainty of benefits flowing from natural capital. The genetic resources of the rain forest may yield tremendous improvements in health care and agricultural productivity, or they may prove relatively fruitless. In the case of the rain forest, beyond the major loss of pharmaceutical material, the ultimate consequences of destroying so vast an ecosystem are essentially unknowable. Similarly, as we saw in the introductory chapter, the atmosphere may be able to absorb current emissions of greenhouse gases with manageable changes in global temperature, but alternatively the real possibility of major catastrophe exists.

While there is substantial uncertainty about the potential yield of some natural capital, decisions to degrade capital stocks such as rain forests or the atmosphere are often irreversible. Once these resources are depleted, they can be restored only at great cost, if at all. Uncertainty combined with irreversibility provide what is known as an option value to natural capital (discussed further in Chapter 6). That is, preservation of the stock is valuable merely to keep our options open. The greater the uncertainty and the more severe the irreversibility, the more caution should be exercised in the exploitation of natural capital. We look now at how the precautionary principle plays out in the real world.

8.8 Strong Sustainability in Practice: Endangered Species, EIS, and Reach

There is currently only one major piece of U.S. legislation that mandates strong sustainability: the Endangered Species Act. We will review the functioning of the act in Chapters 13 and 14, but for now, recognize that the act requires the preservation of species designated as endangered, regardless of the cost. The rationale is consistent with our analysis above: species extinction is irreversible, and in many cases, species carry unique cultural and scientific value.

Beyond endangered species, the National Environmental Policy Act (NEPA), requires a "light" version of the precautionary principle for many development decisions in the United States. One section of the 1970 act required that government agencies prepare an **environmental impact statement (EIS)** for "legislation or other major federal actions significantly affecting the quality of the human environment." The statement must include

1. any adverse environmental effects that cannot be avoided should the proposal be implemented;
2. alternatives to the proposed action;
3. the relationship between local short-term uses of man's environment and the maintenance and enhancement of long-term productivity; and
4. any irreversible and irretrievable commitments of resources that would be involved in the proposed action should it be implemented.[3]

The law also requires that public comments be solicited in the drafting of the impact statement. More than half the states have subsequently adopted their own versions of the EIS to assist them in their decision making.

The basic philosophy behind the EIS is that the government should identify potential adverse environmental impacts of its actions and recommend superior alternatives. Further, by opening up the process to public comment, much broader perspectives on the likely effects can be incorporated into the decision-making process. As a planning tool, the EIS has had its share of success stories. When it works well, it encourages agency officials to respond to the environmental concerns of the public—environmentalists, developers, workers, and citizens—and hammer out an ecologically sound compromise on development issues.

However, even on its own terms, the process has its faults. The rather nebulous charge to identify adverse negative effects has led to a situation in which "the usefulness of the NEPA process to decision makers often is weakened by a persistent tendency to overload NEPA documents with a voluminous amount of irrelevant or highly technical data. No one wants to read such documents: not public citizens, not members of public interest groups, not judges, and certainly not decision-makers."[4] More importantly, there is no process by which "superior alternatives" are judged, nor effective procedures to ensure post-project compliance with the recommended mitigation measures is assured. Finally, the EIS process imposes costs on both government and the private sector. From an industry perspective, the EIS provides an opportunity for environmentalists to drag out the permitting process, engaging in what is known as **paralysis by analysis**.

A major precautionary-based decision faced the Obama administration in the spring of 2013. Secretary of State John Kerry was being asked to block a proposed pipeline that would have carried "tar-sands" petroleum from mining operations in northern Canada to refineries in Houston. Following a legally contested EIS process,

---

3. See Glasson et al. (2005).
4. The quote is from Bear (1987, 74). See Glasson et al. (2005).

and large-scale protests in Washington, Kerry had to decide if the pipeline ran contrary to U.S. national interests. The question: would the pipeline would enable large-scale development of Canada's oil sands, leading to another major new source of carbon dioxide pollution which in turn would accelerate global warming?

The EIS is one direct government regulation that seeks to encourage the precautionary principle. In the past, the neoclassical assumption has often held sway. Generally, the exploitation of natural capital would lead to increases in human welfare over time, and conservationists were forced to prove the reverse in order to slow the rate of resource depletion. The EIS has shifted some of that burden of proof to developers.

The most recent effort to implement precautionary regulation has occurred through the European Union's system of chemical regulation, REACH (registration, evaluation, and authorization of chemicals). Unlike chemical policy in the United States, the European system requires chemical manufacturers to carry out health and environmental safety tests prior to introducing new chemicals. The approach is comparable to the system of testing required for new drugs in the United States. REACH allows EU governments to restrict chemicals that pose unacceptable risks to health or the environment, either through risk management measures, partial bans, or complete bans. Again, following precautionary principle logic, regulation has shifted the burden of proof of safety to the manufacturers. Finally, REACH's cost burden was reasonable, allowing this precautionary approach to make it through the EU legislative process (Ackerman 2005).

Applying the precautionary principle means augmenting market decisions in cases where endangered resources are unique, risks are high, or impacts are irreversible. These can be rather tame governmental regulations, such as the EIS, or much more aggressive regulations like REACH, which, from a conservative perspective, begin to look like dreaded "ecosocialism." The ecological economics view undoubtedly requires much stronger government intervention then we commonly observe to promote sustainability.

8.9 Summary

Like the Iroquois Indians, we can recognize our ability to alter the welfare of our descendants dramatically, both for good and for bad. In the material sphere, we clearly have a responsibility to endow future generations with the productive capital—natural, human, manufactured, and social—sufficient to generate a quality of life at least comparable to our own. However, the means of achieving this goal of sustainable development remain subject to intense debate.

All economists share a common definition of sustainability: non-declining welfare for the typical member of all future generations. This chapter examines two ways to think about the goal. Neoclassical economists start with two underlying assumptions: (1) created capital can generally substitute for natural capital in production and (2) technological progress will uncover these substitutes as natural capital becomes scarce. These two assumptions imply that we are not "running out of resources." In general, neoclassical economists believe that with well-functioning and properly regulated market economies, "weak sustainability" is more or less assured.

Neoclassicals do recognize that, in particular cases, future generations can be made worse off by decisions to "overexploit" resources and environmental sinks. They thus advocate the use of cost-benefit analysis for actions that run down the stock of natural capital, in order to build up other kinds of capital: manufactured, human, or social. This kind of analysis, if it includes *all* future costs and benefits, and discounts them at the rate prescribed by the Ramsey formula, is designed to ensure that net benefits will be maximized over time—that is, to ensure dynamic efficiency.

If manufactured capital can indeed substitute for natural capital, then maximizing the overall size of the economic pie for future and current generations, *if the pie is growing*, can be done using the tools of benefit-cost analysis and discounting. Yet, even within the neoclassical framework, discounting for social decision making remains controversial. Economists do not agree on the appropriate discount rate for society as a whole. And this is critical, especially for projects yielding benefits more than a couple of decades out. In those cases, small changes in the discount rate chosen to evaluate a proposal can dramatically alter the outcome of a benefit-cost test.

In contrast to the neoclassical view, ecological economists argue that, in many instances, natural capital does not find adequate substitutes in manufactured, human, or social capital. For unique resources or sinks, where decisions that degrade the natural capital stock are irreversible, ecological economists argue for the application of the precautionary principle. Similar to a safety standard, the precautionary principle demands as much protection for resources and sinks as is politically feasible, rather than attempting to identify some efficient level of continued degradation. Ecological economists argue, for example, that there is no good substitute for global climate stability. Further degradation of the atmosphere's ability to safely store carbon dioxide is likely to lead to widescale and extended human suffering. At the same time, the costs of a phase-out of fossil fuels over the next few decades are manageable—the obstacles are not technical or economic, rather political. Therefore governments should act much more aggressively to address the problem if we are to avoid catastrophic climate change.

In arenas ranging from chemical pollution to affordable energy and water supplies to biodiversity and agricultural potential, ecological economists are not optimistic about the prospects for sustainability under the current trajectories of population and consumption growth. The only solution will be a shift to precautionary policies by government, and the widespread adoption of sustainable business practices (discussed in Chapter 3) by businesses.

As we have seen, a neoclassical benefit-cost approach (Stern) can reach the same aggressive policy conclusion about action on climate change as does an ecological, precautionary approach. But neoclassical economists can also reach a "go sort of slow" conclusion (Nordhaus), again depending significantly on the choice of discount rate.

Peering 200 years into the future, the neoclassical vision is fairly optimistic on sustainability. In fact, by asserting that g in the Ramsey model will continue to be 1, 2, or 3% per year going forward for decades to come, neoclassical economists *traditionally assume that weak sustainability is assured*. Why? Market systems, they say, given the proper government regulation of environmental sinks and sources, will induce the technological innovation necessary to overcome any widespread shortages of natural capital. However, failure over the last decade by many national governments to cut global warming pollution *at all*—even at the go-slow levels recommended by Nordhaus' benefit-cost analysis—is tempering that optimism.

Ecological economists, meanwhile, are downright gloomy about sustainability for the global economy. They argue that absent a major sea-change in both government policy (in the direction of precautionary principles) and business practice (in the direction of sustainability), the prospects for the seventh generation could be quite challenging. In the next chapter, we look more closely at attempts to measure sustainability at the level of individual resources and sinks, and at the economy-wide level. We will also examine the challenges faced in implementing the precautionary principle. This exploration will shed additional light on the ecological-neoclassical debate.

APPLICATION 8.0

Thinking Sustainability

From an economic point of view, sustainability is about maintaining a high quality of life for future generations. To see how difficult this problem is to address, try to answer the following questions: From a quality of life viewpoint, point would you rather have been born in 1930, 1960, or 1990? Assume that you would have been born in the same country and region, but that you don't know your parents' income, or your gender or race, ahead of time. If you prefer 1990, this may suggest we have been on a sustainable track until now. Does it also imply that we are currently on a sustainable track? If you prefer an earlier year, what unsustainable decisions did your parents' or grandparents' generations make?

APPLICATION 8.1

Dynamic Efficiency, Equality, and Sustainability

Suppose Pandora is deciding how to dispose of some hazardous waste. She can contain it safely at a cost of $175 or bury it in the local landfill. If she chooses the second option, in ten years' time the stuff will have seeped out enough to permanently ruin the vineyard of Bacchus, who lives next door to the landfill. The vineyard has a value to him in ten years of $450 (i.e., he'd sell it then for $450). This is the only damage the hazardous waste will ever do. Assume there is no inflation.

1. What is the present value of $450 in ten years at a discount rate of 10%?
2. In the absence of regulation, Pandora is likely to bury the stuff and save $175. If the interest rate is 10%, is it *efficient* for Pandora to bury her waste in the landfill? To answer this, discuss how Bacchus could maximize his utility if he had the legal right to prevent the dumping (and was not an ardent environmentalist). What does this say about the relative size of the total net monetary benefits under the two alternatives? How do total net benefits relate to efficiency?
3. Could the use of an environmental bond satisfy a fairness problem if it exists?
4. Is burying the waste sustainable from a neoclassical point of view? Why or why not?

APPLICATION 8.2

The Onceler Considers Replanting

The Onceler has clear-cut a forest of Truffula trees and is considering replanting. If he replants, in 40 years he will have another stand of trees to harvest, and he will earn an (inflation adjusted) resource rent of $10 million. Replanting costs $1 million each year for 3 years. Onceler's opportunity cost of capital is a mutual fund investment paying 6%.

1. Fill in the chart to determine if replanting is profitable.

Year	Cost ($)	Benefit ($)	Discounted Cost ($)	Discounted Benefit ($)
0	1 m	—		
1	1 m	—		
2	1 m	—		
40	—	10 m		
TOTAL				

2. If the Onceler does replant, then the Brown Barbaloots, Swamee Swans, and Humming Fish will come back due to the improved habitat. Beginning in 40 years, their populations will recover sufficiently to generate a flow of benefits (people enjoy recreating among these creatures) equal to $1 million per year forever. What discount rate should the neoclassical Department of Sustainability use to evaluate replanting today? Fill in the following chart to evaluate whether replanting and clear-cutting, replanting and not clear-cutting, or not replanting is potentially sustainable.

Year	Replant Cost ($)	Replant Benefit Harvest ($)	Replant Benefit Recreation ($)	Discounted Cost ($)	Discounted Benefit Harvest ($)	Discounted Benefit Recreation ($)
0	1 m					
1	1 m					
2	1 m					
40		10 m	1 m			
41			1 m			
42			1 m			
43			1 m			
44			1 m			
45			1 m			
46			1 m			
47			1 m			
48			1 m			
...						
TOTAL						

3. Suppose in this example that the benefits of clear-cutting and not replanting outweighed the costs. What must be true for that decision to be economically sustainable?

KEY IDEAS IN EACH SECTION

8.0   We reduce the stock of natural capital available for future generations in two ways: first, via the emission of **stock pollutants**, which exhaust **environmental sinks**; and second, through the exploitation of **natural resources**, both renewable and nonrenewable. (**Flow pollutants** have no long-term impact.) Natural capital, along with **manufactured**, **human**, and **social capital**, comprises the basis for producing goods and services needed for human well-being. This chapter shows that a sustainable economy depends on the degree to which increases in manufactured capital, in particular, can substitute for reductions in the stock of natural capital.

8.1   This section defines **sustainability** as "non-declining utility" for the typical member of all future generations. Achieving **weak sustainability** does not require that any particular form of capital be preserved, reflecting the core belief of **neoclassical economists** that, practically speaking, manufactured capital can generally substitute for natural capital to produce the goods and services people need: we are not "running out of resources (or sinks)." **Strong sustainability**, by contrast, requires that many forms of natural capital (as well as human, social, and manufactured) must be preserved, if not enhanced, in order to protect the well-being of future generations. Advocated by **ecological economists**, strong sustainability as a goal is based on the assumption that manufactured capital is not generally a good substitute for natural capital.

8.2   To compare costs and benefits across time, economists rely on a process called **discounting**. Discounting reflects **the time value of money**: because investment is productive, society (and individuals) are better off having dollars today, as they can be productively invested to increase the size of the economic pie for tomorrow. The **present discounted value** of $X received in T years at a discount rate of r, is the amount of money you would have to have today to put in the bank at that interest rate, to have on hand, $X in T years.

8.3   The use of present value calculations for private benefit-cost analysis is illustrated in the lightbulb example. A higher **discount rate**—in this case, the market interest rate—means a lower present discounted value. High discount rates thus mean that current costs and benefits are weighed much more heavily than those occurring in the future. Private decision makers use market rates of interest or profit for making decisions. But when social decisions are being made, a different discount rate is often chosen.

8.4   The section illustrates how market interest rates are set in **markets for loanable funds**. One factor that affects the supply of loanable funds (deposits in savings accounts) is

positive time preference. A higher time preference will lower savings, and thus raise market interest rates. On the demand side, the availability of higher rate of return investments will shift the demand for loans out by business and government investors, also raising market interest rates. Higher rates of return on investments occur when there are higher rates of growth for the economy. Thus both time preference and higher economic growth rates will tend to raise interest rates—which, for businesses and consumers, are used as discount rates to evaluate alternative investments.

8.5   **The Ramsey equation** is the basis for determining **the social discount rate**—the rate used by government when setting policies about pollution control and resource degradation. We focus on two key determinants: again, the rate of time preference (δ) and also the rate of growth of the human well-being (g, note: different than the rate of growth of the economy). As there is no widespread agreement on the magnitude of either of these two factors, the choice of discount rate is often controversial. Because neoclassical economists assert that g is positive, they, in fact, assume the economy is (weakly) sustainable. Under these circumstances, it is possible to under- *or* overinvest in protecting natural capital, so benefit-cost analysis (with discounting) is needed to determine the right trade-off between investing in protection of natural capital versus creation of other types of capital. If used properly, benefit-cost analysis will ensure **dynamic efficiency**: maximizing the net benefits to future and current generations in decisions to use up, or protect, natural capital.

8.6   Nordhaus and Stern both use benefit-cost analysis in two different efforts seeking to identify the dynamically efficient level of global warming pollution reduction, reaching very different conclusions. Again, this is because of different assumptions about the value for the parameters of the Ramsey equation, leading to very different discount rates, leading to very different assessments of the benefits of pollution control 50 to 100 years out.

8.7   Under weak sustainability, benefit-cost analysis with discounting can guide decisions to protect, or not protect, natural capital. By contrast, achieving strong sustainability requires applying the **Precautionary Principle**. Similar to a safety standard, the Precautionary Principle requires the maximum politically feasible protection for natural capital. In assessing which resources to protect under this standard, **uncertainty**, **irreversibility**, and **uniqueness** all factor in.

8.8   Examples of applications of the Precautionary Principle include the U.S. Endangered Species Act, and to a lesser extent, the **Environmental Impact Statement (EIS)** process required under NEPA. The EIS requires negative environmental impacts and superior alternatives to be identified if federal agencies are involved in a project, but has little ability to ensure precautionary outcomes. The European Union's recent chemical regulation, REACH, is the latest example of a precautionary regulation.

REFERENCES

Ackerman, Frank. 2005. The unbearable lightness of regulatory costs. *Fordham Urban Law Journal* 33: 1071–96.

Bear, Dinah. 1987. Does NEPA make a difference? In *Environmental Impact Assessment*, Nicholas A Robinson (Ed.). Albany, NY: New York Bar Association.

Bromley, Daniel. 2007. Environmental regulations and the problem of sustainability: Moving beyond market failure. *Ecological Economics* 63: 676–83.

Glasson, John, Rika Therivel, and Andrew Chadwick. 2005. *Introduction to Environmental Impact Assessment*. London: Taylor & Francis.

Howarth, Richard. 2007. Towards an operational sustainability criterion. *Ecological Economics* 63: 656–63.

Keynes, John Maynard. 1933. Frank Plumpton Ramsey. In *Essays in Biography*. London: Macmillan and Co.

Pezzey, John. 1992. Sustainability: An interdisciplinary guide. *Environmental Values* 1(4): 321–62.

Pigou, Arthur. 1920. *The Economics of Welfare*. London: Macmillan and Co.

Ramsey, Frank. 1928. A mathematical theory of savings. *The Economic Journal* 38: 543–59.

The World Commission on Environment and Development. 1987. *Our Common Future*. New York: Oxford University Press.

CHAPTER 9

MEASURING SUSTAINABILITY

9.0 Introduction

Over a broad range of metrics, over the past 200 years, human well-being has shown dramatic improvements. This is true even as the population has risen from less than 1 billion in 1800 to over 7 billion today. Economist Gale Johnson of the University of Chicago summarized the trends over the past two centuries: "the improvement in human well-being goes far beyond the enormous increase in the value of the world's output. The improvements are evident in fewer famines, increased caloric intakes, reduced child and infant mortality, increased life expectancy, great reductions in time worked, and greatly increased percentage of the population that is literate" (Johnson 2000). The average person today is much richer, better fed, and lives much longer than his or her ancestors. Life expectancy (the age to which the average person lives) at present, even in the poor countries, far exceeds life expectancy in the richest countries in 1800. For example, life expectancy was 65 years in India in 2000 while it was just 36 years in England in 1800. The gains have been dramatic. In India, life expectancy was a mere 23 years in 1900.

Why have living standards gone up so dramatically despite limited natural resources and increased population? Economists point to human ingenuity as the key factor. New products, new methods of producing goods using fewer inputs, and discovery of abundant low-cost resources to replace scarce natural resources have meant that resource constraints seem to be less important now than in the past. The key questions for this chapter are whether this trend has continued in recent decades, and will it continue in the future?

We have already explored the theoretical basis for optimism (neoclassical economics) and pessimism (ecological economics) in which a key difference between the two is the view on whether manufactured, human, or social capital can more than offset for losses of natural capital. The neoclassical side believes that ingenuity will continue to prevail. Ecological economists, while acknowledging past accomplishments of growth, argue that the economics of our current "full planet" are fundamentally different than what was possible in an era of low population and low per capita consumption.

Increasingly, ecological economists argue, growth is being achieved at the expense of future generations. We have fueled the current boom by eating through our natural capital, using up nonrenewable resources such as oil and other fossil fuels and increasing levels of pollution. Climate change, extinction of species, degradation of ecosystems, depletion of natural resources, increases in toxic waste, and high levels of air and water pollution, all indicate declines in critical natural capital that will harm the well-being of future generations. Herman Daly, a leading ecological economist, summarized the view of many ecological economists about the current economic growth paradigm: "Humankind must make the transition to a sustainable economy—one that takes heed of the inherent biophysical limits of the global ecosystem so that it can continue to operate long into the future. If we do not make that transition, we may be cursed not just with uneconomic growth but with an ecological catastrophe that would sharply lower living standards" (Daly 2005).

The views of neoclassical and ecological economists sketch out a very different view on future prospects. So who is right?

Two prominent academics, an economist and an ecologist, decided to take a very nonacademic approach to proving who was right: they made a bet. In 1980, economist Julian Simon and ecologist Paul Ehrlich bet on whether the price of five metals (chrome, copper, nickel, tin, and tungsten) would increase or decrease between 1980 and 1990 (Tierney 1990). Simon, representing the view of many neoclassical economists, argued that prices of natural resources would fall over the decade of the 1980s because technological progress and new discoveries would make natural resources less important despite increases in population and economic growth. Ehrlich, representing the view of many ecological economists, argued that prices of natural resources would rise because increased demand from population growth and rising per capita consumption would run smack into the constraints imposed by the limited supply of these resources.

Who won the bet? We'll answer that question at the end of the chapter. Before then, however, we'll examine the larger context of debates over sustainability. We'll start our discussion of what the future holds by looking back to the past, discussing the historical roots of debates about sustainability. We will then turn to questions of how to assess sustainability. What are the right yardsticks to judge whether the economy and the environment are on a sustainable or unsustainable trajectory? We will also review some of the evidence about whether current trends are sustainable or not. And then we'll return to the bet.

9.1 Malthus and Ecological Economics

In 1798, Reverend Thomas Malthus wrote a book entitled *An Essay on the Principle of Population* that has given the economics profession a bad name ever since (Malthus 1798). Malthus laid out a simple proposition with a dire and seemingly inescapable outcome. Assuming (1) that the food supply grows *arithmetically* (increasing at a constant rate of, say, 10 million tons of grain per year) and (2) that a healthy population grows *geometrically* (doubling every 30 to 50 years), the prospects for long-run human progress are dim. Eventually, Malthus argued, population growth would outstrip the food supply, leading to increasing human misery, famine, disease, or war. This in turn would provide a "natural" check on further population growth.

This **Malthusian population trap** is illustrated in Figure 9.1. As population grows geometrically, and the food supply increases only arithmetically, available food per person declines. Eventually, the lack of food limits births and increases deaths halting or even reversing population growth. Malthus was one of the first modern economists, and this, his most famous work, led to economics being labeled "the dismal science." (You, of course, may have other reasons for thinking of economics as dismal.)

Malthus's theory should sound familiar. Ecological economists in fact trace their lineage back to Malthus and are sometimes called **Neo-Malthusians**. Malthus's theory emphasizes the limits imposed by natural resources. Food production is limited by land availability. It also gives little scope for new knowledge or technological improvements to increase food production.

But surely, wasn't Malthus wrong? Since the time that Malthus wrote his book human population has indeed grown rapidly. But instead of mass starvation, food production has grown even more rapidly. To date, we have indeed avoided a Malthusian fate because of impressive technological developments in the fields of agriculture, health care, and birth control.

These technological advances have challenged Malthus's basic assumptions. First, it need not be the case that agricultural output grows only arithmetically. From about 1950 through the 1980s, the **Green Revolution** in agriculture resulted in greatly increased yields for major crops around the world. The Green Revolution brought new, hybrid forms of wheat, rice, and corn seeds that produced much higher yields per acre than did conventional seeds. The results were dramatic. From 1950 to 1984, world

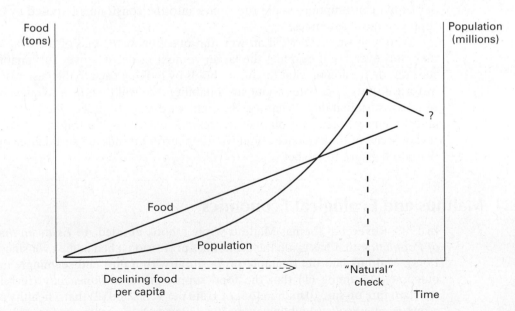

FIGURE 9.1 The Malthusian Population Trap

grain output increased by a factor of 2.6. Over the same period, world population roughly doubled.

Since the mid-1980s, as Green Revolution technologies began to show diminishing returns, grain yields have continued to increase, but more slowly. As Figure 9.2 shows, and contrary to Malthus's prediction, total per capita food production is still rising, meaning that output is running ahead of population growth.

Malthus's second assumption, that population always increases geometrically, also has not held. Excluding immigration, developed countries have very low population growth rates—often *below* zero. The availability of effective birth control, not foreseen by Malthus, has meant that families are able to control their "natural" reproductive tendencies given the desire. As we shall see in Chapter 20, for a variety of reasons, as countries develop economically, most households in fact do opt for small families. The very good news here is that, despite the tremendous momentum behind population growth—we are adding 80 million people a year to the planet—by 2050, many demographers believe that the planet's population will stabilize at between 9 and 10 billion people.

Still, "only" 3 billion more people is a huge number. It is, for example, three times more people than were alive at the time that Malthus warned about population pressures outstripping food supply. Will the year 2050 bring with it widespread food shortages? Provided that population does stabilize around 9 to 10 billion, there will likely be enough land to grow the food we need. In fact, there are large gains that remain by applying modern agricultural technology more broadly in many low-income countries where yields remain far below potential yield. Closing the "yield gap" so that all land currently growing crops achieved yields equal to the best producing land given the same climate conditions could increase food production by more than 50% (Foley et al. 2011). In addition, advances in biotechnology, genetically modified organisms, and other new technology may boost yields still further.

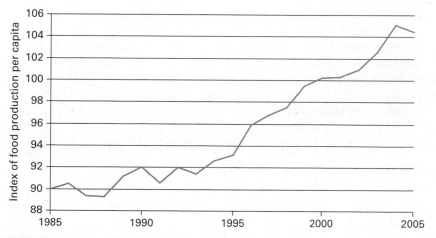

FIGURE 9.2 Global Food Production per Capita, Year 2000 = 100

Source: Food and Agriculture Organization of the United Nations (FAO). 2006. FAOSTAT Online Statistical Service. Rome: FAO. http://apps.fao.org.

Ecological economists point out that, beyond simply acres of land, there are other ways in which resource constraints matter. Agriculture requires massive quantities of fresh water, energy, fertilizers, and pesticides. Runoff from modern farming practices is the main source of water pollution through much of the world. For example, the increase in use of fertilizers to grow corn and other crops in the U.S. Midwest has increased the flow of nutrients flowing out of the Mississippi River resulting in a large increase in the "dead zone" in the Gulf of Mexico. The dead zone is created when algae blooms fed by excess nutrients decay and deplete the water of oxygen required to maintain fish and other marine life. And climate change threatens to disrupt weather patterns in the world's main agricultural regions. Drought or excessive heat can damage crops. In the hot dry year of 2012, corn production in the United States fell by over 1.5 million bushels compared to 2011 despite more corn being planted. Ecological economists are quick to point out that just because food production has increased faster than population in the past is no guarantee that it will continue to do so in the future.

And it is not just a matter of basic grain production keeping up with population. Rising affluence has resulted in changing diets that increase the demand for food production per person. As people get richer they consume a lot more meat. Over the last 15 years, global meat consumption has more than doubled. And meat production requires a good deal more agricultural output than just directly consuming the grain. Grain-fed beef requires 7 pounds of grain to produce 1 pound of meat. Meat production is responsible for an astounding 15 to 25% of global warming emissions worldwide. Meat production also requires large quantities of fresh water. On a per kilogram basis, compared to soy protein, production of meat protein requires 6 to 20 times as much fossil fuel. Finally, as petroleum prices rise over time (see the peak oil discussion later in this chapter), and affluence increases, the demand for biofuels will also rise, leading to "food versus fuel" conflicts. Ecological economists worry that the end result is a world of extremes: rising food prices combined with an epidemic of obesity in the developed parts of the world and large increases in the percentages of people facing poverty, malnutrition, and hunger in poor countries and communities.

Malthus was truly the forerunner of ecological economics. He captured the sense in which fundamental limits on natural capital place a bound on supply, which when combined with rising demand from a continually growing population, eventually lead to an unsustainable outcome. Though his prediction of decline in available food per capita has not been borne out, at least to date, echoes of his logic continue in modern debates over sustainability.

9.2 Modern Debates: Limits to Growth and Planetary Boundaries

Much of the concern about sustainability has shifted from a more narrow focus on food availability to a much broader set of issues involving the state of the environment and its ability to support an expanded human population in the future. Is natural capital being degraded in ways that threaten future prosperity?

Let's start with an analogy. Salmon fisheries in the Pacific Northwest have collapsed, and many are on the verge of extinction. The reasons for this are complex, but clear-cut logging has played an important role. In an old-growth forest, fallen conifers create dams, which in turn develop spawning pools; different types of hardwood trees—maple and later alder—provide food for insects upon which young salmon smolts feed. Large trees throughout the watershed protect streams from devastating debris flows during heavy rains. Slowly these trees have been removed and replaced by a much less diverse second-growth forest, thus destroying the resilience of the ecosystem. Now, catastrophic events like mud flows, once a part of stream rejuvenation, scour and destroy the salmon habitat.

Ecological economists claim, essentially, that we are doing to ourselves what we have done to the wild salmon; in complex and perhaps unknowable ways, we are dismantling the delicate physical and biological structure that underlies the resilience of the ecosystems on which we depend. This in turn dramatically increases our economic vulnerability to any large-scale ecosystem shifts that we may induce.

Modern ecological economics was launched, in part, by an influential 1972 book entitled *The Limits to Growth* that in many ways extended Malthusian logic to a broader set of issues about whether the earth could sustain an ever-expanding human population and economic activity (Meadows et al. 1972). The book argues that "If the present growth trends in world population, industrialization, pollution, food production, and resource depletion continue unchanged, the limits to growth on this planet will be reached sometime within the next one hundred years. The most probable result will be a rather sudden and uncontrollable decline in both population and industrial capacity." However, the authors went on to state that this future was not predestined. An intelligent shift in direction could alter these trends and achieve "ecological and economic stability that is sustainable far into the future." But achieving this shift in direction would require major changes in the way the economy is organized and reductions in consumption. Many of the authors involved in the first book went on to publish follow-up books, such as the 1993 book entitled *Beyond the Limits* (Meadows et al. 1993), that provided evidence that global society had gone even further down an unsustainable path.

More recently, a group of natural scientists defined a set of "planetary boundaries," which if crossed could have disastrous consequences for humanity (Rockström et al. 2009). They identified several global boundaries that have already been crossed: climate change, biodiversity loss, and excess nitrogen flows, and others that are in danger of being crossed in the near future. Like arguments by Malthus and *Limits to Growth*, the main thrust of this article was that unless humanity changed course it was headed toward a crash.

Neoclassical economists, for reasons you should now be familiar with, have generally been highly critical of *Limits to Growth* and planetary boundaries. William Nordhaus noted, in a review of *Limits to Growth*, that the approach assumed "There is no technological progress, no new discovery of resources, no way of inventing substitute materials, no price system to induce the system to substitute plentiful resources for scarce resources" (Nordhaus 1973, p. 1158). Inclusion of any or all of these factors makes the future considerably less bleak. Nordhaus was also critical of the lack of data and specific equations used in the modeling approach. Paul Krugman was much more blunt in his assessment of *Limits to Growth*, "the study was a classic case of garbage-in-garbage-out" and he claimed that the authors "didn't know anything about the empirical evidence on economic growth or the history of past modeling efforts…"(Krugman 2008).

Back on the other hand, the most comprehensive review of the state of the environment was provided by the Millennium Ecosystem Assessment, which involved more than 1,300 scientists including some economists. The Millennium Ecosystem Assessment emphasized the essential role of ecosystem processes and biodiversity in supporting human well-being. A central concept of the Millennium Ecosystem Assessment was **ecosystem services**, the benefits that people receive from nature. The range of ecosystem services includes provisioning services such as food, energy, and clean water; regulating services such as carbon sequestration, water purification, pollination, and disease and pest control; and cultural services such as recreation and ecotourism. The Millennium Ecosystem Assessment documented a widespread decline in biodiversity and degradation of many ecological processes. The loss of natural capital has led to a reduction in supply of many important ecosystem services. In fact, the Millennium Ecosystem Assessment found that the majority of ecosystem services were in decline, including virtually all of the regulating and cultural services (Millennium Ecosystem Assessment 2005).

But how can the majority of ecosystem services be declining at the same time as there are big gains in human well-being (recall the evidence from economist Gale Johnson quoted near the start of this chapter)? If ecosystem services are declining shouldn't that translate into a decline in well-being? Not necessarily. First, not all ecosystem services are in decline. It may be that the really important services, like food production, are increasing and this more than makes up for declines in other services. Second, technological advances have made well-being less dependent on natural capital. Third, there may be time lags between declines in natural capital and declines in standards of living. A recent review found some evidence in support of all three of these explanations (Raudsepp-Hearne et al. 2010).

It can be hard to wrap your brain about such weighty questions as whether the global system is on a crash course or whether everything is just fine. Economists are hands-on types, and if we can't measure something, we find it hard to talk about it. In concrete terms, how do we know if we are achieving sustainability or not? You might have gathered from the fact that there have been persistently held and widely divergent views about sustainability that it is difficult to find conclusive evidence one way or the other. Sustainability, it turns out, is a difficult thing to measure. Most of the existing measures of the state of the economy or the state of the environment capture only a part of what is needed for a complete measure of sustainability.

The next two sections explore empirical approaches to measuring sustainability and the strengths and weaknesses of these various approaches. One set of approaches builds from the foundation of strong sustainability that requires that we maintain stocks of natural capital. These approaches focus on biophysical measures of natural resources and environmental quality. Ecological economists tend to emphasize these types of measures of sustainability. A second set of approaches builds from the foundation of weak sustainability that requires that we maintain human well-being so that the typical person in the future is no worse off than the typical person living today. These approaches focus on measures of income and wealth (the aggregate value of all capital stocks). Neoclassical economists tend to emphasize these types of measures of sustainability.

9.3 Measuring Strong Sustainability: Impacts and Footprints

Back in 1971, two scientists—Paul Ehrlich and John Holdren (now President Obama's Science Advisor)—presented an influential method for thinking about environmental problems. Their approach is now called the **IPAT equation:**

$$\text{environmental Impact} = \text{Population} * \text{Affluence} * \text{Technology}$$

The IPAT relation suggests that we think about three main causal factors underlying environmental problems: population growth, growth in consumption per person (affluence), and the damage per unit of consumption inflicted by the available technology.

   The IPAT equation also points broadly toward solutions: addressing both overpopulation and overconsumption and improving technology to reduce the environmental damage per unit of production ("clean technology"). To make the equation more concrete, consider the global emissions of carbon dioxide from cars circa 2013:[1]

$$\mathbf{I} = \qquad \mathbf{P} \qquad\qquad \mathbf{A} \qquad\qquad \mathbf{T}$$

$$CO_2 \text{ emissions per year} = \{7 \text{ billion people}\} \times \frac{\{0.1 \text{ cars}\}}{\{\text{person}\}} \times \frac{\{5.4 \text{ tons } CO_2\}}{\{\text{car per years}\}}$$

$$= 3.8 \text{ billion tons } CO_2/\text{year}$$

Now, get set for some depressing mathematics. By the year 2050, global population is estimated to increase to approximately 9 to 10 billion people, or about a 40% increase from current levels. Affluence (the number of cars per person) is likely to more than quadruple as people in China, India, Brazil, and many other current middle and low-income countries become wealthier. The IPAT equation tells us that, holding technology constant, CO_2 emissions from autos would thus rise by a factor $1.4 * 4 = 5.6$. Alternatively, to keep CO_2 emissions constant, technology would have to advance so that each auto could reduce emissions to roughly one-sixth the current level. That is quite a tall order. Then recall that to stabilize the stock of CO_2 in the atmosphere we must actually *steeply reduce CO$_2$ emissions* rather than merely keep them constant.

   So are we doomed? Is it possible to reduce emissions while population and affluence are increasing? Yes, if technology changes fast enough. In the United States, for example, emissions of SO_2 and other air pollutants have fallen since 1970 despite increases in population and economic growth. For CO_2 emissions and cars, it may also be possible. We could, for example, develop electric cars fueled by solar power, thereby reducing CO_2 emissions to very low levels. But the IPAT equation has much broader implications. Consider the environmental impacts of the almost sixfold increase in mining, oil drilling, food production, timber production, and manufacturing needed to support a larger and more affluent population. Even the production of so many electric vehicles and solar power facilities would have environmental impacts. Or consider

---

1. See Ehrlich and Holdren (1971). Estimates courtesy of the American Council for an Energy Efficient Economy.

the impacts on the natural environment if road construction expands along with auto use.

The IPAT equation is useful to get a handle on environmental impacts and the potential ways to reduce environmental impacts. In particular, it gives us guidance to the scale of substitution from manufactured capital that would be needed to keep from degrading natural capital. However, it doesn't necessarily tell us about the relative scarcity of natural capital stocks critical for maintaining human well-being. To measure sustainability, ecological economists therefore favor the use of *physical measures of natural resource stocks and ecosystem resilience weighed against population and consumption pressure.*

Put another way, ecological economists look at the current value for "I" in the IPAT equation, assess trends in P, A, and T, and from that, make a judgment about the need for government to take further action to reduce I. Recall that from an ecological point of view the only way to ensure that future generations are not penalized by our actions is to hand down a stock of natural capital that largely resembles our own—particularly if the natural capital has uncertain value or its degradation is irreversible. This means, for example, on the global-warming and ozone-depletion fronts, our current impacts are not sustainable. This follows because everybody agrees that, unchecked, these effects will lead to large-scale, negative changes in the global environment. (Of course, some neoclassical economists argue that we could adapt to climate change, and therefore do not *necessarily* need to stop it.)

Ecological economists have looked to ecological studies to find other signs of "limits to growth." For example, Vitousek et al. (1997) calculated that humans now appropriate, directly or indirectly, 40% of the "net primary production," which is a measure of the amount of increase in plant biomass fueled by the conversion of sunlight into chemical energy via photosynthesis. Net primary productivity is a good measure of the productivity of ecosystems. In other words, humans consume close to half of the useful output of ecosystems presently. From the ecological point of view there is no substitute for photosynthesis! Projecting trends forward "If we take this percentage as an index of the human carrying capacity of the earth; and assume that a growing economy could come to appropriate 80% of photosynthetic production before destroying the functional integrity of the ecosphere, the earth will effectively go from half to completely full during the next... 35 years." (Rees and Wackernagel 1994, p. 383). Considering that this statement was written almost 20 years ago that doesn't leave much time.

Let's pause for a:

PUZZLE

The authors of the previous quote are applying the IPAT equation and assuming that the combined effect of increasing population and consumption will lead to a doubling of the human appropriation of biomass in 35 years. What are they "forgetting," and why are they forgetting it? Another way to phrase the question is this: How would a neoclassical economist respond to this dire prediction, and how would a ecologically minded author reply?

SOLUTION

The neoclassical response is that this "limits to growth" approach is forgetting technology and price responses: as land becomes scarce prices will rise and induce adoption of best management practices to close "yield gaps" and advances in biotechnology and plant breeding, all of which will boost yields per acre to compensate for the growth in P (population) and A (affluence). History provides some comfort here. Despite increases in food production, for example, New England now has a much greater forest cover than it did in the mid-1800s. And as we discussed earlier, food production has more than outpaced population growth since the time of Malthus.

The ecological economic reply is that history provides little guidance for assessing the impact of continued geometric economic growth. While technology may have been able to accommodate the last 200 years of increase on an initially "empty" planet to 6 or 7 billion people and their consumption needs, there are few remaining frontiers and no promise that we can continue to have "green revolutions" to boost yields. We are now facing a 35-year doubling of food production from population increase and diet shifts toward meat consumption on an already crowded planet. Yes, technology will improve, but ecological economists argue that constraints on available land and on cheap energy pose a fundamental, relatively short-term problem. Therefore, "forgetting" technology is justified. We will return to this core area of disagreement again at the end of the chapter.

Another example of an ecological accounting of sustainability relates to freshwater use. Humans now use about 54% of the surface-water runoff that is geographically accessible. New dam construction could increase accessible runoff by 10% over the next 30 years, but the population is expected to increase by 45% over the same period. Of course, other technological possibilities exist; chief among them are increases in the efficiency of water use. However, ecological economists would argue that freshwater prices are likely to increase substantially over the next few decades and that adequate substitutes are unlikely to be forthcoming (Postel, Daly, and Ehrlich 1996).

More fundamentally, however, ecological economists following the IPAT logic would have us consider the broader ecological impacts of significant increases in the demand for water. Dam construction in remote areas, for example, often has high ecological externality costs. Water conflicts throughout the world are already driving many freshwater creatures to the brink of extinction and beyond, destroying industries and livelihoods in the process. Some have argued that water wars between nations will soon follow. Beyond the "simple" question of access to cheap water, ecological economists believe that resource scarcity will lead us to fundamentally damage many of the ecosystems on which our economic and cultural lives depend.

In addition to IPAT, ecological economists sometimes rely on a different measure of strong sustainability: the **ecological footprint**. The ecological footprint summarizes in a single number the various constraints of land, water, and environment that we have just discussed. In particular, the ecological footprint of a community (or nation) calculates how much land and water area is needed to provide the resources for production and for assimilation of wastes for that community. It is relatively easy to calculate the land area needed to grow food or timber. But it is harder to calculate the land or water area needed for other types of production or for the assimilation of waste.

For example, how does the ecological footprint compute the land area needed for energy use from fossil fuels? Clearly there is some land use for coal mines, oil drilling platforms, and refineries, but this direct use of land is relatively small. As we have seen, fossil fuel use is a major contributor of CO_2 emissions that increase global warming. The ecological footprint asks how much area devoted to growing forests it would take to sequester the same amount of CO_2 as is released by burning fossil fuels. This amount of area for waste assimilation, which keeps the stock of CO_2 in the atmosphere constant, is then added to area needed for production to get a total area needed for energy production and consumption.

When the sum total of all area needed for production and waste assimilation is added together for the global economy, ecological footprint calculations indicate that we currently need about 1.5 earths to accommodate all the demands over time. Obviously we have only one earth, so any ecological footprint measure over 1 indicates we are living unsustainably. The ecological footprint provides a quick summary metric of how far the global economy is living beyond what can be supported on a long-term sustainable basis. Of course, as in IPAT, improvements in technology that improve resource efficiency lower the ecological footprint for a given level of population and consumption.

To see the difficulty that the sustainable development challenge poses to global society consider Figure 9.3. This figure plots how various countries fare in terms of their ecological footprint calculated at the national level and considering a widely used measure of human well-being, the **human development index** (HDI). The HDI includes measures of per capita income, education levels, and life expectancy. The HDI for each country is scored relative to the highest country score so that HDI varies between 0 and 1. Most of the countries with a high HDI are high-income, developed countries like the United States, Canada, Australia, and many European countries. Norway has the highest score (0.94). Countries with low HDI are primarily low-income countries in Africa and Asia that also have relatively poor education systems and low life expectancy. The Democratic Republic of Congo has the lowest score (0.29).[2]

The ideal situation is to have a high HDI, indicating a high level of human well-being, but a low ecological footprint. To be sustainable, the ecological footprint should lie to the left of the vertical line at 2.1 hectares per person, the level that would yield a global ecological footprint equal to 1 (so that we only need one earth to support all of the demands of the global economy). No country has an HDI greater than 0.9 and an ecological footprint below 2.1. To achieve sustainable development all countries in the world would achieve this. Even Cuba which appears to be doing relatively well in Figure 9.3, has an HDI score below 0.8 (0.78) according the *Human Development Report 2011*.

While the ecological footprint has the advantage of being simple to present, its critics think that the approach is overly simplistic and that it does not produce meaningful results. How can one really represent all of the dimensions important for

---

2. HDI by country are reported in the United Nation's Human Development Report 2011.

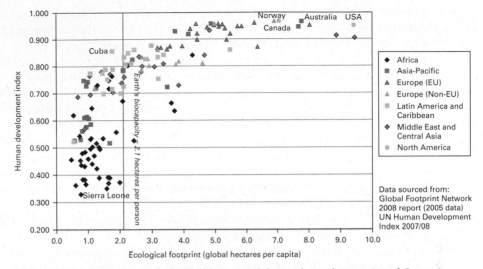

FIGURE 9.3 Measuring Human Well-being and the Ecological Footprint of Countries

sustainability and convert them into the land or water area needed? For example, absorbing CO_2 into forests requires a large land area and contributes greatly to the ecological footprint. If, instead, CO_2 were captured and stored underground as is done in carbon capture and storage (CCS) projects, then the land area needed for fossil fuel use would be greatly reduced. Using CCS might then make it appear that we are more sustainable. But CCS introduces other problems. It is costly to do and there are fears that the CO_2 will not remain trapped underground but will eventually leak back into the atmosphere. As we will see in the next section, the question of whether it is possible to summarize sustainability in a single number is also a central issue on measures of income and wealth favored by neoclassical economists.

In this section, we have seen that in judging whether our use of natural capital is sustainable, ecological economists rely on physical measures of resource stocks and the absorption capacity of environmental sinks. If natural resources have no good substitutes on the horizon, and rapidly growing demand is a large portion of current supply (water, energy supplies, and net primary productivity), then our use is unsustainable. If the absorptive capacity of environmental sinks is exceeded, leading to long-term alterations in the environment from stock pollutants (ozone-depleting CFCs, and carbon dioxide), then our use of those sinks is unsustainable. Again, as the focus here is on protecting individual stocks of natural capital—absorptive capacity of the atmosphere, particular forests or fisheries, and regional water supplies—the policy objective is to ensure strong sustainability.

9.4 Measuring Weak Sustainability: Net National Welfare and Inclusive Wealth

Neoclassical economists take a different approach to sustainability. In line with notions of weak sustainability, they are less interested in the trends of any particular element of natural capital (or human, manufactured, or social capital) and more interested in whether the sum total of capital assets is capable of supporting improved well-being. If different types of capital are, in general, substitutes then the decline in any particular type of capital can be offset by increases in other types of capital.

In this section, we discuss two neoclassical measures of weak sustainability. The first, **Net National Welfare (NNW)**, attempts to measure, on an annual basis, the "real" well-being of society's members. If well-being is rising, our economy is, by definition, sustainable—at least to the current date. The second approach, **inclusive wealth (IW)**, focuses on the capital stock side, but seeks to capture the total value of *all forms* of capital (human, manufactured, social, and natural). Increases in IW would indicate that the economy is sustainable, while decreases indicate that it is unsustainable. (If you have taken accounting, NNW is something like a national (or global) income statement, while IW is more like a national (or global) balance sheet, focusing on the value of the national capital stock.)

We start this exploration in sustainability accounting with a look at the standard macroeconomic metric of economic performance: gross domestic product or GDP. GDP is a national-level measure of the final value of all goods and services produced and consumed in the market each year; it also equals the income earned and spent by consumers. GDP is a reasonable measure of market activity. But GDP is a bad measure of sustainability—whether the typical person is better off in the long run. GDP has at least four well-known problems in regard to sustainability.

1. *GDP fails to include the value of nonmarket goods and services.* Housework, child care, and volunteer work are three biggies. But the main problem with GDP from a sustainability perspective is that it does not include many ecosystem services. Improving air or water quality, seeing wildlife or a beautiful view, improving recreational opportunities, all may generate benefits but much of the value of these benefits will not be reflected in the economic accounts. Some value may be included, at least indirectly. For example, improved water quality in a lake may result in improved fishing, swimming, and boating, drawing more people to the lake and thereby increasing sales at local businesses and increasing property values of lakefront homes. We have already discussed ways to measure values of nonmarket benefits in Chapter 5.

2. *GDP fails to exclude costs incurred in reducing harmful activities.* A true measure of welfare needs to account for the fact that raising GDP imposes costs on society. These include externalities: the direct health and productivity costs of pollution and congestion, borne by third parties. Sometimes these externality costs show up as what are called defensive expenditures—money spent to protect oneself from a deteriorating environment or loss of ecosystem services. Examples include increased doctor visits, water purifiers, and cell phones (to make traffic jams tolerable). When defensive expenditures boost final consumer demand, the GDP measure perversely increases even though people are clearly not better off! The costs of growth also include increased spending on internalized externalities. These include the direct costs to industry and government of pollution control and cleanup (more than $225 billion per year in the United States). Here again, GDP counts on the positive side of the ledger expenditures on pollution abatement and cleanup. Thus, after the giant BP oil spill in the Gulf of Mexico in 2010, the cleanup money spent by

the company translated into a big boost to regional consumer spending, and thus GDP.

3. *GDP fails to account for the depreciation of the capital used up in production.* One quick way to boost current income is to spend down capital. For example, unsustainable fishing effort can boost current harvest and incomes earned from fishing, but it does so at the cost of loss of future income because it has depleted the fish stock. Similarly, not spending money on upkeep of machinery can increase current income but at the cost of much higher expenses for repairs and replacements in the future. The U.S. government publishes an adjusted GDP measure, called net national product (NNP), which takes into account the depreciation of manufactured capital. However, our main concern here is the lack of similar accounting for the **depreciation of natural capital**—sources and sinks—used up in the production of GDP.

4. *GDP reflects the experience of the "average" but does not account for distribution or equity concerns.* GDP is reported on a per capita basis, showing the *mean* (average) value for a society. Average income doesn't tell you much about how the poorest people in society are doing (or the richest). Average income does not take into account income distribution or equity. For this, a better measure is *median* income. In the United States, for example, since 1980, GDP per capita has risen substantially, but the median income of the typical family has barely budged. How is this possible? Virtually all of the GDP gains from growth have flowed to the top 20% of families. An increasing fraction of very high–income people has raised the average income, but not the income of the typical (median) person. Note that when Bill Gates walks into a room full of people, the "average" person is suddenly a millionaire, even though no one except Bill Gate has that much income! For sustainability, which addresses equity of well-being across generations, equity within the current generation may also be an issue of concern.

To build a measure of sustainability we need to adjust GDP to account for the four problems mentioned above. One way to do this is to build a measure **NNW**. Currently, there is no universally agreed-upon approach to this kind of environmental/economic accounting. However, because such a measure would be quite valuable, economists have focused a lot of attention on calculating NNW.[3]

In principle, NNW can be defined as the total annual output of both market and nonmarket goods and services minus the total externality and cleanup costs associated with these products, minus the depreciation of capital, both natural and human-made, used up in production. Figure 9.4 shows the arithmetic.

The first step in calculating NNW is to augment GDP with nonmarket consumption—the value of leisure time, nonmarket work such as housecleaning and child care, and the value of capital services, such as owner-occupied housing. From augmented GDP, one then subtracts both market and externality costs associated with economic growth from GDP. These range from obvious pollution-control expenses to the increased congestion costs of commuting to work to increased spending on

3. Nordhaus and Kokkenberg (1999); the special issue on green accounting of *Environment and Development Economics, vol. 5,* nos. 1 and 2 (February–May 2000), World Bank, 2006.

NNW = Total Output – Costs of Growth – Depreciation

= GDP + nonmarket output
  – externality costs
  – pollution abatement and cleanup costs
  – depreciation of created capital
  – depreciation of natural capital

Note: This countrywide measure of NNW must be adjusted to reflect changes in income distribution, because sustainability requires that the *typical* person be no worse off.

FIGURE 9.4 Calculating Net National Welfare

health care due to environmental damage. Economists have developed a variety of techniques for estimating the costs of both pollution control and environmental damage. We explored these methods in detail in Chapters 5 and 6.

As a last bit of arithmetic, one must subtract a depreciation fund—the amount of money necessary to replace the capital, both natural and created, used up in the production of GDP and to provide for a growing population. Included in this fund would be depreciation of machines, plants, equipments, and physical infrastructure as well as much government investment in human capital, such as spending on education and health care. The depreciation of human-made capital is relatively straightforward, but how does one value nonrenewable resources used up in production? Calculating the "right" depreciation rates for lost topsoil, species extinctions, or exhausted petroleum reserves is difficult, controversial, and the subject of the next section.

The formula in Figure 9.4 gives a value for NNW on a national basis. But a final adjustment for changes in income distribution may be required. Rather than look at the average (or per capita) NNW, we may also want to consider what is happening to the distribution of income, and in particular whether the poorest and most vulnerable in society are seeing their lives improve or not.

Figure 9.4 gives us what we want, at least in principle—a way to measure sustainability. Our NNW figure incorporates both the (positive) material and (negative) environmental features of economic growth. Under the neoclassical assumption that reductions in environmental quality can be remedied through use of new technologies or increases in human or manufactured capital, subtracting the environmental costs of growth from the material benefits makes sense. If, overall, income that accounts for the value of all goods and services and that has been properly adjusted for depreciation is increasing through time we have achieved economic sustainability, at least to the present date.

NNW seeks to measure sustainability directly: are people becoming better off over time? OK, so the important question: Is NNW in the United States, for example, actually rising? Or is it falling? More on that in Section 9.6. Before looking at the empirical data, let us consider a second approach to measuring sustainability: Inclusive Wealth or **IW**. Rather than focus on outcomes, IW looks at the health of the underlying productive potential of the economy. IW is defined as the value of all capital stocks including human capital, manufactured capital, natural capital, and social capital. The idea behind IW is that if we leave future generations with greater overall wealth, then they will have the means to be better off. However, if we deplete wealth, future generations will be unable to match current standards of living.

In principle, the value of a capital asset is equal to the present value of the flow of net benefits that it creates. For example, how valuable is it to own an apartment building? Suppose the building has 10 apartments and each apartment rents for $1,000 per month, or $12,000 per year. In total the apartment building generates $120,000 in rental payments per year. If upkeep of the building were $20,000, the owner would earn $100,000 (rental payments minus upkeep expenses: $120,000–$20,000) from owing the building. Suppose the discount rate is 5% and the building is going to last for 20 years. Using the present value calculations discussed in Chapter 8, we can find that the present value of the apartment building is equal to:

$$PV = 100,000 + \frac{100,000}{1 + 0.05} + \frac{100,000}{(1 + 0.05)^2} + \cdots + \frac{100,000}{(1 + 0.05)^{19}}$$

$$= \$1,308,532$$

We can calculate the value of other assets in a similar manner. What is the value of agricultural land? It is the present value of the profits from growing crops. What is the value of an oil deposit? It is the present value of the profits from the extraction and sale of oil. What is the value of an education? It is the present value of the increase in lifetime earnings.

Actually, education may be worth more than simply the change in lifetime earnings. Education may lead people to be more informed and more involved citizens and so increase social capital, or it may increase one's ability to appreciate art or nature and so increase well-being quite apart from increased earnings. Education in this sense delivers many "positive externalities" that would need to be included in an appropriate measure of IW. Similarly, the measure of IW from a farm would need to subtract from the stream of profits negative externalities on, for example, stream health, from pesticide run-off. These points bring us squarely back to one of the problems faced in adjusting GDP to come up with NNW: how to properly account for nonmarket goods and services.

With this background, we can think about how to measure IW. In principle, we need to know two things:

1. The amount of each capital stock: K_j, for $j = 1, 2, \ldots, J$ types of capital stock. For farmland, for example, K would be measured in acres; for factories, it could be measured in dollars.

2. The value of a unit of each type of capital stock. We saw earlier that this value is just the present value of future profits derived from the capital stock, adjusted for externality costs and benefits. We will define V_j as the value of a unit of capital stock j.

Then, IW is the sum of the value of all capital stocks:

$$IW = V_1 K_1 + V_2 K_2 + \cdots + V_J K_J = \sum_{i=1}^{J} V_j K_j$$

So to calculate IW we would attempt to sum the value of all forms of human capital (education and experience, etc.), manufactured capital (apartment buildings, machinery, industrial facilities, infrastructure, etc.), natural capital (oil and mineral deposits, the state of ecosystems that generate ecosystem services, etc.), social capital (social institutions, organizations, trust, etc.). As with NNW, actually measuring IW is a tall order (we'll have more to say on this in Section 9.6). But the advantage of this approach is that for sustainability we just need to know whether IW is increasing or decreasing. Holding all the values (V_js) fixed, we would achieve sustainability if for every capital stock that declined by a unit, there was an equally or more valuable capital stock that was increasing by a unit.

This highlights the task of understanding how to think about depreciation (decline) of natural capital: in the United States, we are "using up" *725 million gallons of oil a day*. What are we providing future generations in exchange? Once we have explored this issue, we can come back to the main question of what the evidence tells us about whether we are achieving sustainability in Section 9.6.

9.5 Natural Capital Depreciation

Any human-made capital good has a relatively fixed useful life before it wears out; a pizza delivery truck, for example, may last for five years. Each year, then, we say the truck has "depreciated" in value. Depreciation is a measure of how much of the truck is used up each year in the delivery process, and depreciation must be subtracted from the firm's income statement, thus lowering net profits. As a society, how should we also value the loss of natural capital—such as oil, timber, or species diversity—that we use up in production? We need to know this number in order to adjust GDP to arrive at our measure of weak sustainability: NNW. We also need to know it to value changes in the national capital stock, to calculate IW.

Let's begin answering this question with a:

PUZZLE

Suppose that Mr. Bill has an oil field containing 100 barrels of oil on his property.

He can hire a firm from a neighboring town to pump his oil at a total economic cost of $1 per barrel—but because it is scarce, the price of oil is $2 per barrel, well above cost.[4] Scarcity of the oil means that Mr. Bill can earn a **resource rent** of $1 per barrel from its production. Resource rents develop when, due to absolute scarcity of resources, prices get bid up above the total economic cost of production (see Chapter 3). They are thus a form of economic profit.

If all the oil is produced and sold today:

1. How much will Mr. Bill's *net* income (economic profits) rise for the year?
2. If Mr. Bill spends all the income on a big night out (leaving his family at home), how much worse off are his children?
3. If Mr. Bill's family were the sole residents of the country of Billsville, how much would Billsville's GDP rise?
4. How much would Billsville's NNW rise?
5. What would happen to Billsville's IW?

---

4. Total economic costs include interest payments on borrowed capital and a "normal" profit for any equity financing. See any introductory microeconomics textbook for more on this concept.

The big question addressed by the Billsville situation is this: to what extent does GDP overstate true NNW or IW as a result of the current generation running down the stock of natural capital? We are seeking a way to measure the wealth that we of the current generation are taking away from future generations by using up scarce natural capital.

SOLUTION

Economic profits are equal to total income ($200) minus total economic costs ($100), or $100. This is just the resource rent. If Mr. Bill blows the money on a consumption binge, his children are also worse off by the value of the resource rent or $100 (not $200, because they too would have to pay $100 to get the oil out of the ground). Thus *none* of this increased income can be devoted to Mr. Bill's consumption and still be sustainable. He needs to invest the entire $100 of resource rent in created capital to replace his natural capital and thus ensure that his children are not being made worse off by his action.[5]

Billsville's GDP also rises by $100, the increase in net income. Mr. Bill now has the option of going on a shopping spree at the local Target. But, Mr. Bill *cannot* increase his consumption out of the oil profits (the resource rent) *without* penalizing his kids. Thus NNW does not rise at all! And, reflecting the loss in the value of natural capital, IW actually falls by $100. Applying this Mr. Bill logic in the real world to the U.S. oil industry, government analysts have estimated that in the past U.S. GDP has overstated real NNW by between $23 billion and $84 billion.

Note in this example that Mr. Bill is not necessarily punishing his kids by draining the oil today. If he invests the resource rent productively, his kids may well be better off than if he were to leave them the untapped field. Investing resource rents will pay off, especially if, due to technological change, natural resource prices may actually fall in the future. Neoclassical economists, again reflecting an underlying technological optimism, often urge early exploitation of resources for precisely this reason. Ignoring the cost of extraction, if oil prices are rising in percentage terms at less than the going rate of interest (true, on average, over the last 50 years), Bill's family will clearly be better off if he develops the field today *and* invests the resource rents. Then IW would recover, and in fact, more than completely replace the lost resource rent.

The oil-rich state of Alaska has actually pursued such an approach, diverting some of its oil tax revenues into the so-called Permanent Fund. Earnings from this giant investment fund (over and above the amount reinvested to keep the fund intact) are paid out annually to all Alaskans and total around $1,000 per person per year. Alaska has also invested in a lot of created capital—roads, telecommunications, and a better educated population. The fund and the greater stock of created capital may not fully compensate

---

5. This is not strictly true if real interest rates exceed the real rate of growth of oil prices. In such a case, Bill could use a small portion of the profits to finance his own consumption and, utilizing the power of compound interest, not make his children any worse off.

future generations of Alaskans for the depletion of the resource. Nevertheless, it does suggest how the current generation can directly substitute created wealth for natural wealth, thus making resource depletion sustainable in economic terms.

The Mr. Bill puzzle provides a **depreciation rule** for natural capital: *depreciation equals the measured value of the resource rent.*[6] The resource rent, not the full market value of the resource, is what future generations are losing by our exploitation of natural capital. It is also exactly the amount that needs to be saved and invested (e.g., in a permanent fund or in education, productive infrastructure, or research and development) if resource depletion is to be sustainable—that is, to avoid reducing IW immediately, and NNW over the long run.

Resource rent is earned when people cut down forests; harvest fish, wildlife, or medicinal products; use up groundwater; or develop a mine. Figure 9.5 illustrates how to calculate the resource rent from a supply-and-demand diagram—in this case, for tropical hardwoods. The long-run supply curve (as you surely recall from an introductory course) reflects the full cost of production. As prices rise, higher cost producers are induced to enter the market. The last producer to enter, at Q1, just breaks even. Area *A*, between the supply curve and the price, thus shows the resource rent earned by firms in the hardwood industry. Area *A* is the value lost to future generations from our decision to harvest today.[7]

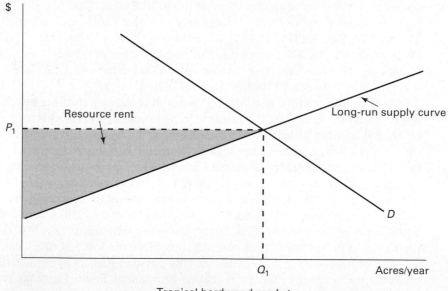

FIGURE 9.5 Measuring Resource Rent

---

6. Solow (1992) develops this point and also provides the inspiration for the puzzle; see also Nordhaus and Kokkelenberg (1999).
7. This is true so long as today's prices reflect a fair intergenerational allocation of wealth. For more on this topic see Howarth and Norgaard (1990).

In summary, Mr. Bill's world illustrates how resource rent is the correct measure for depreciation of natural capital. This in turn allows us, in principle, to correctly measure NNW (annual well-being) and Inclusive Wealth (the value of society's total capital stock). If properly measured NNW or IW rise over time, we can confidently say that society would be better off, because increases in material welfare would not be coming at the expense of future generations. In Mr. Bill's case, draining the oil field leads to no increase in NNW, and would decrease IW, to properly reflect the fact that he has depleted a valuable asset. Yet development led to an increase in GDP by $100.

The year the field is drained Bill received benefits, but at the cost of potentially leaving his family with less wealth and income for the future. The difference between GDP and NNW or IW is that the NNW and IW both account for resource depletion and show what must be "saved" and productively invested in order to ensure sustainability—and this amount is exactly the resource rent. This savings can take the form of investment in created capital (putting the money into a college fund). However, if the current generation is too consumption oriented and refuses to invest (Mr. Bill blows the income on a big night out), the savings gap would have to be made up by setting aside some natural capital for preservation, thus lowering GDP. Mr. Bill's children should cancel the development order rather than let him head off to town with the proceeds.

This section has addressed an important technical issue: How can we measure progress toward sustainable development? From a neoclassical perspective, both NNW and IW properly account for depletion of natural resources: NNW subtracts resource rents from GDP and IW measures the change in value of resource stocks by subtracting off the value of resources used up in the current period. In addition, we have seen that it is possible to penalize future generations by consuming, rather than investing, resource rents. Both neoclassical and ecological economists agree that resource-depleting development decisions that finance pure consumption and not investment are unsustainable.

9.6 Are We Achieving Sustainability?

We started this chapter by noting that neoclassical and ecological economists tend to have very different views about the future with neoclassical economists tending to be the optimists and ecological economists tending to be the pessimists. In thinking about future environmental impact, neoclassical economists emphasize improving technology (T in the IPAT equation) to reduce impacts, while ecological economists emphasize increasing population and affluence (P and A in the IPAT equation) leading to increased impacts. Ecological economists fear that such impacts will lead to erosion of vital natural capital that will eventually lead to a potentially dramatic decline in future human well-being. What does the evidence suggest? Is the optimism of the neoclassical economists justified? Or are the ecological economists correct in being pessimistic without some major changes in current behavior?

One way to address these questions is to look at measures of NNW and IW and see whether they are increasing or decreasing. Unfortunately, NNW and IW require making judgment calls about components of these indexes for which there is often insufficient or missing data. If different experts make different judgments that are each valid, and they arrive at different conclusions then we cannot sort out in a "scientific way" whether our economy is sustainable. In some ways, this situation should be obvious. People have very differing opinions about whether the typical person is made better off or worse off with economic growth. These differing opinions reflect an underlying complexity that makes NNW and IW very difficult to measure.

However, there have been several attempts to measure NNW and IW and these attempts can tell us something about the prospects for achieving sustainability. One of the main values in calculating NNW or IW is to see whether growth in GDP serves as a good proxy for growth in real social welfare. Two early attempts by neoclassical economists estimated growth rates for NNW of 0.5 to 1%. The studies showed no clear correlation between growth in GDP and growth in NNW in the United States (Nordhaus and Tobin 1972; Zolatas 1981). Both studies, in fact, looked at GNP, a closely related measure to GDP. For example, one study found that the rate of growth of NNW dropped by more than 50% after 1947; at the same time, growth of GDP accelerated. From this we can conclude that the popular perception of GDP as a measure of economic welfare may well be misguided.

The most ambitious recent attempt to calculate NNW has been undertaken by a California think tank called Redefining Progress. Table 9.1 illustrates how their measure, called the Genuine Progress Indicator or GPI, was developed for the year 2004. It follows, more or less, the formula identified earlier in the chapter:

$$NNW = GDP + nonmarket\ output$$
$$- \text{externality and cleanup costs}$$
$$- \text{depreciation of natural capital}$$
$$- \text{depreciation of created capital}$$

The GPI subtracts $1.9 trillion from GDP for pollution and cleanup costs, and the largest amount comes from climate change. Costs arising from short-term environmental impacts (air, water, and noise pollution and household abatement expenditures) total approximately $200 billion. The GPI also deducted for depreciation of natural capital. From the prior section, you should have an idea of the right way to estimate the value of the natural capital depreciated: the lost wetlands and used up renewable and nonrenewable resources. In principle, researchers at Redefining Progress should use as a measure the resource rent yielded through the development of these resources. For wetlands, one would need to recognize that much of the *in situ* value (or rent) takes the form of nonmarket services. The researchers estimated that over $2 trillion of natural capital was used up in 2000, including $53 billion in loss of services from wetlands, $50 billion from old-growth forests, and $1,761 billion in nonrenewable resources.

Finally, the GPI also subtracts a category of "Other Social Costs," including the use of "equity weights" that adjust the social welfare function for increased inequality as well as the costs of underemployment and lost leisure time. In 2000, GPI researchers concluded that while GDP equaled $6.2 trillion (in 1996 dollars), the GPI was only $2.6 trillion. It is worth stressing that this is only one estimate of an adjusted GDP; many controversial assumptions go into constructing such an index, but the GPI does illustrate in principle how researchers go about trying to calculate NNW.

TABLE 9.1 The 2004 Genuine Progress Indicator
(billions of 2000 dollars)

GDP*	$7,588
NONMARKET OUTPUT	
Housework and parenting	+2,542
Volunteer work	+130
Value of education	+827
Value of highway services	+743
Other	+11
EXTERNALITY AND CLEANUP COSTS	
Household abatement	−21
Water pollution	−120
Air pollution	−40
Noise pollution	−18
Ozone depletion	−478
Long-term global warming damage	−1,182
DEPRECIATION OF NATURAL CAPITAL	
Wetlands	−53
Farmlands	−263
Nonrenewable resources	−1,761
Old-growth forests	−50
DEPRECIATION OF CREATED CAPITAL	388
OTHER COSTS OF GROWTH	
Commuting and auto accidents	−699
Unequal income distribution	−1,260
Underemployment	−176
Net foreign borrowing	−254
Loss of leisure time	−401
Other	−360
GPI	**$4,419**

*The GPI actually starts with the Personal Consumption category of GDP
(omitting government spending, business spending, and net exports). But for
ease of exposition, and to keep the relationship consistent with the presentation
in the chapter, I label personal consumption as GDP. In fact, GDP in 2004 was
$10.7 trillion.
Source: Talberth, Cobb, and Slattery (2006).

Beyond just the simple magnitude of the GPI, Figure 9.6 shows how the growth
rate in per capita GDP compared with that of the estimated GPI. During the 1950s and
1960s the two grew at roughly the same rates. During the 1970s GPI growth slowed
dramatically, it turned negative in the 1980s, and it recovered a bit during the 1990s.
The downturn in GPI in the 1970s and 1980s was due primarily to stagnating median
family incomes, growing income inequality, nonrenewable resource exhaustion, and
long-term environmental damage. The 1990s recovery reflected a rise in real wages

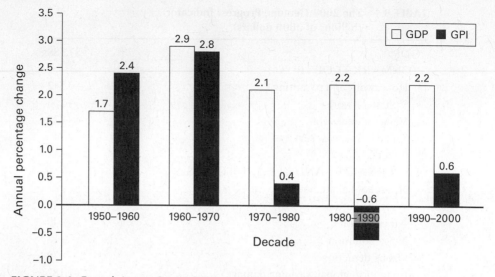

FIGURE 9.6 Growth in per Capita GDP versus per Capita GPI
Source: Talberth, Cobb, and Slattery (2006).

for the median household, a slowdown in the growth of inequality, and a drop in the rate of loss of natural capital—farmlands, wetlands, old-growth forests, and mineral resources.[8]

Consistent with the earlier findings, Figure 9.6 illustrates that there is no clear correlation between growth in GDP and growth in GPI. GDP growth therefore appears to tell us little about trends in overall welfare. Finally, the average rate of growth of per capita GPI over the entire period was 1.1%; since 1970, it has been 0.1%. To conclude, from the limited evidence available, the average historical rate of growth of NNW in the United States appears to be 1% or less over the long term.

There have been several attempts by neoclassical economists to estimate changes in IW as an indicator of whether we are achieving sustainability. The World Bank (2006) estimated "genuine savings," which is a measure of the change in IW. When genuine savings is positive it means that the value of IW in the country is increasing. While they find that genuine savings on average across all countries is positive, there are some notable exceptions. Some countries report gains in GDP but negative genuine savings (Figure 9.7). Countries such as Angola and Nigeria that sell oil and other resources but fail to reinvest show healthy growth in GDP while they are lowering the wealth of the nation and damaging future prospects.

Recently a group of researchers attempted an in-depth analysis of changes in inclusive wealth of five countries, the United States, China, Brazil, India, and Venezuela (Arrow et al. 2012). Following similar techniques as used by the World Bank (2006), the researchers estimated changes in the value capital stocks including human capital,

8. See Talberth, Cobb, and Slattery (2006). The GPI can be accessed on the web at www.redefining progress.org.

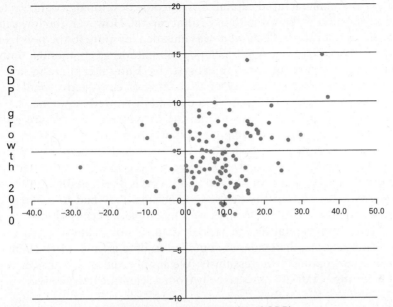

FIGURE 9.7 Genuine Savings versus the Percentage Change in GDP Growth in 2003
Source: World Bank 2005 (printed on p. 45 of World Bank 2006).

manufactured capital, and natural capital. With the exception of Venezuela, IW (which they called comprehensive wealth) increased in these countries (Table 9.2). However, in all countries the rate of growth of IW per capita was lower than the rate of growth of GDP, reinforcing the pattern found in other studies that GDP growth tends to overestimate improvement over time because it fails to adjust for depreciation of natural capital.

For most countries the value of natural capital made up a small portion of total wealth. In the United States in the year 2000, for example, the value of natural capital was 6.7% of total capital value. The low percentage for the value of natural capital is due in part to the fact that the United States is a developed country with large wealth

TABLE 9.2   Inclusive Wealth versus GDP Growth for Five Countries 1995–2000

Country	Per capita inclusive wealth growth rate	Per capita GDP growth rate
United States	1.70	2.93
China	5.63	7.60
Brazil	0.14	0.50
India	2.70	3.99
Venezuela	−2.94	−1.20

Source: Table 3 in Arrow et al. (2012, p. 343).

in human and manufactured capital. Low-income developing countries tend to have a higher proportion of their wealth in natural capital. However, the low calculated value for natural capital also reflects what was included, or more to the point, excluded from the calculations. Natural capital included oil, natural gas, minerals, timber, land, and the value of carbon sequestered in ecosystems. Natural capital did not include other aspects of environmental quality or the status of ecosystems, omissions that many ecological economists would argue could result in skewed numbers.

The evidence to date seems to indicate that NNW and IW are growing in most countries but that each is growing more slowly than growth in GDP. One reason the NNW and IW grow more slowly than GDP is that NNW and IW properly account for depreciation of natural capital, which is ignored in GDP. Whether this evidence is really proof of achieving sustainability, however, is questionable. The authors of these reports are well aware of the heroic assumptions they had to make to generate the estimates, and the fact that the analysis is incomplete because it fails to include many aspects of natural capital due to lack of data. Unfortunately, given the state of the science and the data, the evidence compiled to date is unlikely to change the mind of either die-hard optimists or pessimists. We simply cannot yet answer the question of "are we getting better off" persuasively from a scientific perspective.

9.7 Discounting, Sustainability, and Investing for the Future

The rate of growth of NNW—if we knew it with confidence—would help answer the question of the underlying sustainability of the economy. It is also a critical data input into the discounting process. In the last chapter, we explored the logic of discounting, and learned that the Ramsey equation provided guidance as to the right choice of discount rate for maximizing social costs and benefits over time:

$$r = \delta + \eta g.$$

One of the key parameters here is g, defined as the rate of growth of well-being for the typical individual. This, in fact, is just the rate of growth of NNW, which, as we saw in the last section, is likely less than 2% for the United States, and may even be below zero. Assuming a low rate for social time preference (δ), this evidence suggests that low discount rates (0–2%) are appropriate for evaluating long-run costs and benefits as they apply to development decisions that run down the stock of natural capital in developing countries like the United States. What discount rates are in fact used by the government in the United States? A recent EPA analysis of climate change costs and benefits used rates ranging from 3 to 5% (US EPA/NHSTA 2009). The UK government has used a lower rate of 1.4% for assessing climate change impacts (Stern 2007).

At the same time, the evidence above suggests that g is higher for rapidly growing developing countries like China. Here, investment in manufactured capital has a higher real rate of return in terms of raising people out of poverty, increasing life expectancy, and expanding opportunities for schooling, and thus the growth of the human capital stock. To some degree, this justifies less focus on preserving natural capital. And yet, in some areas of China, extremely severe water and air pollution is clearly compromising the ability of manufactured capital investment to improve well-being. Moreover, as

Chinese consumption of fossil fuels rises to meet per capita levels found in the United States, Japan, and Europe, the resulting massive increase in global warming pollution is compromising the potential for long-run global sustainability.

Decision makers in the private sector often have shorter time horizons than do government agencies. Companies often require profit rates on the order of 15% or more to initiate an investment. Few private sector firms invest in projects with paybacks longer than seven years; most have a time horizon shorter than five years. *This is a very important point.* Along with open access to common property (Chapter 3), **high market discount rates** explain why many of our decisions today might be unsustainable. Due to high discount rates, we fail to make many long-lived investments that could benefit our descendants.[9]

People sometimes wonder why private energy companies and other investors—knowing that oil is a finite resource—don't pour resources into R&D for alternative fuels such as biodiesel or hydrogen fuel cells. Won't these sectors provide high profits? Maybe. But the problem is that the profits will not come for a decade or more. And private investors evaluate projects using high market discount rates, which reflect the private opportunity cost of their capital. The fact that energy companies can make a 20% rate of return on conventional investments in oil properties means that they can earn their investment back in five years. Access to these high market rates of return gives market actors very short time horizons.

Why are required profit rates so high, if society is benefiting at a much lower rate overall from these investments? First, these high required returns reflect only the private benefits of investment and fail to account for the external costs of growth. Second, some of these profits are coming from resource rents, and do not reflect any depreciation of natural capital used up in production. And finally, as we saw in Chapter 8, high returns are required to induce people to save and invest their income, rather than consume it today. Partly this is due to positive time preference and partly to the risk inherent in investment: investors are not confident that firms will even be around beyond five years out, and so require short-term paybacks.

And this returns us once again to the neoclassical-ecological debate. In spite of high private sector discount rates, neoclassical economists think that we are still making *enough* investments in manufactured, human, and social capital to ensure sustainability. They argue that because of rapid technological progress, NNW is nevertheless still rising (though not as fast as possible). As a result, our descendants will still be better off than we are, despite our shortsightedness. Ecological economists, by contrast, argue that these two fundamental economic problems—open access to common property and high market discount rates—have already led to unsustainable exploitation of natural capital. In other words, they maintain, our failure to invest in protecting natural capital has already begun to impoverish our descendants.

---

9. Low discount rates are not always "pro-environment." Any undertaking with high up-front costs and a long stream of future benefits will look better with a low discount rate. Huge dams may thus be favored by low discount rates, as people will enjoy the cheap electricity and recreational opportunities for decades. The point here is that using market discount rates of 15 or 20% dramatically undercounts the benefits that future generations reap from current investment—whether those benefits are low-cost energy from hydro plants or a cleaner environment.

9.8 The Ecological-Neoclassical Debate in Context

In many respects, the debate between ecological and neoclassical economists over sustainability reflects the same underlying issues as the differences between the safety and efficiency camps. Both ecological economists and safety proponents view environmental protection as a special commodity that should not be traded off for more of "everything else." Safety proponents privilege a clean environment on the grounds of individual liberty and the right to be free of assaults on the body; ecological economists argue that, in general, natural capital has no good substitutes for which it can be traded. Both groups reject benefit-cost analysis, arguing that the benefits of protection cannot be adequately captured, and both groups therefore rely on physical, not monetary, measures of their underlying goals: safety and sustainability.

Note that in advocating for strict standards, both safety proponents and ecological economists make utilitarian arguments: Environmental protection is *good for people* because the society-wide opportunity cost of protection is relatively low. Moreover, we have not, to this point, questioned the underlying assumption that more is better. If increasing material affluence in fact does not lead to greater well-being, a hypothesis we explore in Chapter 11, then the "low opportunity cost" case for the safety and ecological positions is strengthened.

Efficiency advocates and neoclassical economists respond that the safety and ecological positions are too extreme. They insist there are trade-offs and that we can pay too much for a pristine environment. Resources and person-power invested in reducing small cancer risks or preserving salmon streams, for example, are resources and people that then cannot be invested in schools or health care. Benefit-cost analysis is needed to obtain the right balance of investment between environmental protection and other goods and services. Moreover, in the sustainability debate, neoclassical economists argue that history is on their side: Malthusian predictions have been discredited time and time again.

The problem with all of these early predictions, as with Malthus's original one, was that they dramatically underestimated the impacts of changing technologies. Looking just at the P and the A and essentially ignoring the T (technology) in the IPAT relation has not, in the past, proven to be justified. Neoclassical economists point to these failed predictions to support their basic assumption that natural and created capital are indeed good substitutes—we are not "running out" of natural resources or waste sinks.

Ecological economists respond that history is not a good guide for the future. Two hundred years after the beginning of the Industrial Revolution, accumulating stresses have begun to fundamentally erode the resilience of local and global ecosystems upon which the economy ultimately depends. Indeed, ecological economists have largely shifted their 1970s concerns about running out of nonrenewable minerals and oil to other resources: biodiversity, fresh water, environmental waste sinks, and productive agricultural land. While ecological economists stretching back to Malthus have indeed done their share of crying wolf, this does not, of course, mean the wolf won't come.

We can illustrate the debate between ecological and neoclassical economists over the scarcity of one specific form of natural capital: topsoil. David Pimentel is an ecologist and prominent member of the International Society for Ecological Economics. Along with several coauthors, he published an article in the journal *Science* claiming that topsoil losses cost the United States some $27 billion per year in reduced agricultural productivity (Pimental et al. 1995). This is a big number—about a quarter of total U.S. farm output.

In a stinging response, neoclassical economist Pierre Crosson accused Pimentel et al. of ignoring evidence contrary to their position (Crosson 1995). Crosson himself had earlier published an estimate of agricultural losses due to erosion at closer to $500 million per year—smaller than Pimentel's by a factor of 50. Two other studies ignored by the Pimentel et al. (1995) article backed Crosson's position.

So, are we running out of topsoil? Not being soil scientists we are not going to settle this debate for you here. (A great term paper topic!) But one point to take away is this: The I in the IPAT equation—in this case, productivity declines from topsoil loss—arising from a given level of population, a given level of demand (affluence), and a given type of technology can be quite hard to pin down. A second point: we do know that *unless* more environmentally friendly agricultural techniques are developed, this impact will quickly grow in the face of a 50% increase in P, and at least a doubling of A.

And indeed, this point is one that Crosson himself makes explicit. His position is that productivity declines due to topsoil erosion, while real, will be dwarfed by the expected three- to fourfold increase in world food demand over the next 50 years (Toman and Crosson 1991). And in the area of world food supply, while there are some optimists that see ever increasing yields as keeping up with increasing demand, even many neoclassical economists are worried about the ability of the food system to cope, especially in light of potential climate change and trying to end problems of hunger among the nearly 1 billion people who are chronically undernourished.[10] Even if we are not destroying our stock of topsoil as rapidly as Pimentel argues, the logic of IPAT and the ghost of the Reverend Malthus still hang over our shoulders as we consider the world's food prospects.

9.9 Summary

This chapter started by describing a famous bet between optimistic economist Julian Simon and pessimistic ecologist Paul Ehrlich. Simon and Ehrlich wagered on the price trends of five nonrenewable metals from 1980 to 1990. Simon predicted that metal prices would fall as human ingenuity would find ways to use more available, cheaper materials and essentially make resources more abundant while Ehrlich predicted prices would rise as demand from increasing population and affluence ran up against limited supply. Who won the bet?

Simon did. Prices for all five metals declined in the 1980s. Metal prices declined because new metal deposits were discovered, more efficient mining and refining methods were introduced, and other cheaper materials replaced metals. For example, telephones up to the 1980s relied on copper wires to transmit signals but now we use fiber-optic cables and wireless technology and have no need for copper wires.

So does this mean that the optimists are correct and the pessimists are wrong? Not necessarily. Had they made the bet in 2000, Ehrlich would have been the easy winner.

---

10. See Chapter 10 in World Resources Institute 2009.

The price of virtually all commodities, including most metals, climbed rapidly between 2000 and 2010. For Ehrlich this may have just been a case of bad timing.

But more to the point, the central questions about sustainability are broader questions of whether human actions are undermining ecosystem services and a wider spectrum of natural capital—from fresh water to planetary temperature to biodiversity, more so than just whether metal prices are rising or falling. As long as the population and consumption continue to grow, the logic of relentless pressure on resources and sinks remains, and indeed, accelerates. Asked whether the bet settled anything, Paul Ehrlich responded "Absolutely not...I still think the price of those metals will go up eventually, but that's a minor point. The resource that worries me the most is the declining capacity of our planet to buffer itself against human impacts. Look at the new problems that have come up: the ozone hole, acid rain, global warming... If we get climate change and let the ecological systems keep running downhill, we could have a gigantic population crash" (Tierney 1990).

So what is to be done? How do we decide if our use of resources and the environment is sustainable or not? Achieving strong sustainability involves an application of IPAT at the resource level: is growing impact (I) causing resource levels to decline? If so: invoke the precautionary principle and take more aggressive policy measures to protect natural capital. Strong sustainability can also be assessed at the community or national level using footprint analysis. This provides some guidance as to the fit between aggregate resource use and sink exhaustion and the level of consumption in a society.

Weak sustainability can be assessed in two ways. The first is via Net National Welfare, arrived at by adjusting GDP to develop a direct assessment of rising or declining welfare. This requires adding into GDP nonmarket production, subtracting out the costs of growth and natural capital depreciation, and adjusting for changes in income distribution. The second method is to measure Inclusive Wealth, a monetary valuation of the total capital stock: natural, manufactured, human, and social. If IW is rising, then the society has the capacity to continue to provide a comparable or rising standard of living to its citizens.

A key concept to understand here is depreciation of natural capital. We illustrate that when an oil field is developed, a forest cut down, or a fishery harvested, society's income (NNW) is unchanged: we are trading the resource rent embodied in the resources in or on the ground, or in the ocean, for a comparable pile of cash. At the same time, however, the value of society's capital stock (IW) declines by exactly the amount of the resource rent. Whether, over time, society's capital stock will recover and rise, and NNW will ultimately increase, depends on whether the resource rent is productively invested in replacement forms of capital.

Empirical estimates of NNW and IW are quite complex and quite recent, and require much professional judgment about which there is still little consensus. Are these measures increasing or decreasing? We do not know with any confidence. The neoclassical/ecological debate about current economic sustainability cannot yet be settled scientifically. However, studies do consistently show that the growth rate of both measures is less than the growth rate of GDP. In the United States, the measured growth of NNW is likely less than 2%, and may be less than zero.

The growth rate of NNW feeds back into the social discount rate, via the Ramsey equation. Assuming a low rate of time preference, developed countries should therefore use a rate of discount of 0–2% for resource depleting decisions, in order to maximize benefits and costs across time. Higher rates can be justified in rapidly developing countries, where the high productivity of investment in manufactured and human capital is leading to rapid rates of poverty alleviation, access to education, expanding civil liberties, lengthening life spans, and real increases in human well-being.

Private sector discount rates are much higher: typically 15% or more. This means that private sector actors have very short time horizons. Typically, investments must pay back in five years or less. This helps explain why private businesses and citizens fail to make many long-lived investments that will pay off in the mid to distant future: from technology investments in solar to low-input farming methods to household investments in weatherization or efficient appliances. Along with open access to common property, high market discount rates represent the two fundamental economic challenges to economic sustainability.

Let us end this conversation with a roadmap for a sustainable future. How can we really meet the needs of 9 to 10 billion people in a world of limited resources? Where, ultimately, should policy be taking us? Here, the sustainable business movement, discussed at the end of Chapter 3, can provide some guidance. Paul Hawken, a businessman and author of an influential book called the *Ecology of Commerce* (Hawken 1995) has offered a vision of a transformed economy in which business practices mimic natural systems. He offers three principles:

No Energy Crisis: Like nature, businesses need to run on abundant "solar income" (direct sunlight, wind power, and biomass) as opposed to "solar wealth" (fossil fuels) that is both nonrenewable and polluting.

No Pollution: In nature, "all waste is food." This means closed loop production systems, in which wastes from one production process become inputs into another. Ultimately, pollution disappears.

No Systems Too Big to Fail: Nature promotes and thrives on diversity, creative destruction, and system resilience. Crony capitalism, in which large business controls government to promote its interests, leads to fragile and unproductive systems.

An interesting example of ecological design is the so-called living machine—a series of pools, supporting a complex artificial wetland, that digests human waste and turns raw sewage into fresh drinking water. The ecological perspective seeks to expand this metaphor of the closed loop—where waste from one sector is food for another—to the macroeconomy at large. When our business systems have learned to mimic natural systems, then we can see our way to a just and prosperous future.

As promised, the last two chapters have been conceptually challenging, and also, we hope, intellectually exciting. This debate between ecological and neoclassical economists is perhaps the fundamental question of our time: without dramatic changes to our business as usual trajectory, will human progress continue, or are we undermining the foundations of that progress? Is more intelligent and more incentive-based regulation sufficient to insure sustainability (the neoclassical view)? Or must government play a much more aggressive role in protecting natural capital, promoting

TABLE 9.3 Four Normative Standards for Environmental Quality

Standard	Rule	Implementation
1. EFFICIENCY	MB of reduction = MC of reduction	Benefit-cost analysis
2. SAFETY	Health risk < 1 in 1 million	Risk assessment
3. NEOCLASSICAL SUSTAINABILITY	Discount future at rate of growth of NNW; invest all resource rents	Benefit-cost analysis
4. ECOLOGICAL SUSTAINABILITY	Protect natural capital	Weigh resource stock against population and consumption growth

clean technology, encouraging less resource-intensive consumption, and helping slow population growth rates (the ecological view)? These different policy suites are the subject of Parts III and IV of the book.

This chapter draws our discussion of different standards for pollution control and resource degradation to a close. Table 9.3 provides a summary of the four different approaches. The first two, efficiency and safety, focus on standards for pollution control. The second two, weak and strong sustainability, are standards for the protection of natural capital. The concepts blend into each other when protecting natural capital (e.g., the CO_2 absorptive capacity of the atmosphere) also requires controlling pollution. And if the economy is indeed weakly sustainable, then resource protection decisions can be made using a dynamic efficiency criterion, that is, benefit-cost analysis with discounting using a rate derived from the Ramsey equation.

We now leave our discussion of standards to focus in the next chapter on specific economic tools for natural resource management. We then conclude the first part of the book—How Much Pollution is Too Much?—with one final, critical "big" discussion: does money really buy happiness?

APPLICATION 9.0

A Growth Parable[11]

Suppose that a bacterium lives in a test tube and the bacterial population doubles every minute, so that at the end of one minute there are two, at the end of two minutes there are four, and so on. Suppose also that at the end of 15 minutes, the food supply runs out.

1. How many bacteria will be around at the end of 15 minutes?
2. How many bacteria will be around at the end of 14 minutes?
3. When will half of the food be used up?
4. What percentage of the food will be left at the end of 13 minutes? Do you think that, after 13 minutes, "Joe Average" bacterium would be easily persuaded that a food crisis was at hand?
5. Suppose, despite your answer to question 4, that at the beginning of the 13th minute the bacteria do get a wake-up call. They begin a crash scientific program,

11. Thanks to Dennis Palmini for suggesting this problem, which he adopted from Perry (1994).

putting the best bacterial minds to work on growing more food. Success! By the beginning of the 14th minute, the bacteria manage to quadruple the remaining food supply. How much time do they buy themselves?

6. Is there a difference between these bacteria and people that might give us some hope for our long-run survival? If so, is it likely to work through P, A, or T?

APPLICATION 9.1

Running Out of Salmon?

At the same time that wild salmon are threatened with extinction across the planet, salmon is now widely available and relatively cheap in U.S. supermarkets. The reason? The explosive growth of salmon farming.

a. Would an ecological economist see low salmon prices in grocery stores as evidence that she or he must convert to neoclassicism? The answer must of course be "no." In your answer, requiring a little Internet research, be sure to discuss (1) ecological costs of salmon farming, (2) values that are lost with the extinction of wild salmon that cannot be replaced with farmed salmon, and (3) long-run prospects for sustainability of salmon farming.

APPLICATION 9.2

Mining and Economic Development

One economic development paradox receiving recent research attention has been the "dismal" economic performance of many mineral-dependent countries in the Third World. On average, they have fared very poorly: per capita GDP has actually fallen in three-quarters of the 15 countries studied, and they have accumulated some of the highest relative debt levels in the world.

This poor performance is in many ways surprising: In principle, economic rent from mineral production can be used for investment in other sectors of the economy, thus spurring economic growth. One author explains this apparent contradiction partially as a result of unproductive investment of the economic rent. "Rents lost through waste and needlessly high production costs contribute nothing to economic growth. The same holds true for rents spent on current consumption or rents captured and expatriated by foreign interests. Even those rents that are invested can retard economic growth if they are used unwisely" (23).[12]

1. If per capita GDP had risen in these mineral-dependent countries, would they necessarily have achieved "sustainable development"? Why or why not?

---

12. Tilton (1992) also identifies two other factors: "distortions" such as wage inflation and currency appreciation induced by mineral booms, and the slow pace of mineral development arising from investor insecurity. From a sustainability perspective, however, and given the potential for waste and distortions, a slow pace of mineral development may ultimately turn out to be a plus. This will be less true if mineral prices fall in relative terms. See also Sachs and Warner (1999).

2. Does the evidence presented suggest that countries are better off not developing their mineral wealth?

KEY IDEAS IN EACH SECTION

9.0   This chapter focuses on sustainability assessment: how could we tell if we are running out of resources and waste sinks? And are we?

9.1   Ecological economics' intellectual lineage can be traced back to Malthus and his **population trap**; ecological economists are sometimes called **neo-Malthusians**. Malthus was "wrong," thanks in large measure to the **Green Revolution** in agriculture. However, gains from the Green Revolution have recently tapered off. Ecological economists share the Malthusian view that population (and consumption) pressures lead initially to steady, and eventually catastrophic, declines in human welfare.

9.2   Modern ecological economics was launched with the publication of *Limits to Growth* in 1972, and more recent work on planetary boundaries. Ecological economists differ from Malthus in that they have broadened the drivers from population to include consumption, and the resource constraint from land to a whole suite of **ecosystem services**.

9.3   Ecological economists use the **IPAT equation** to identify particular forms of natural capital in need of more aggressive protection, to insure strong sustainability. They employ **physical measures of resource stocks or pollution impacts weighed against population and consumption pressure** as their measure of sustainability. If demand for resources without good substitutes is a large portion of current supply, then our use is unsustainable (e.g., water). If the absorptive capacity of environmental sinks is exceeded, leading to changes in ecosystems from stock pollutants, then our use of those sinks is unsustainable (e.g., CO_2 in the atmosphere and oceans). Ecological economists also employ **footprint analysis** to assess sustainability at the economy-wide level. It is a challenging goal to achieve both a high **Human Development Index** rating and a low footprint.

9.4   Weak sustainability is measured in two ways: **Net National Welfare (NNW)**, which adjusts GDP to get a better measure of annual well-being, and **Inclusive Wealth (IW)**, which seeks to assess the total value of a society's capital stock: natural, manufactured, human, and social. If either measure is falling over time, the economy is unsustainable. A key challenge in developing either measure is properly accounting for external costs and benefits, and the **depreciation of natural capital**.

9.5   The **depreciation rule** for natural capital is that depreciation equals the value of the **resource rent** generated through resource-depleting activities. When an oil field is developed, for example, GDP rises by the value of the rent, but NNW does not change: society has traded oil in the ground for cash in hand. At the same time, IW falls by the value of the rent. For IW to rise, and for NNW to eventually grow, these resource rents must be productively invested in alternative forms of capital. The Alaska **Permanent Fund** provides an example.

9.6   So, are things getting better or worse? Unfortunately, the science is not settled. However, NNW and IW growth rates are generally lower than GDP growth rates; in the United States, the number is probably less than 2% and could be less than zero. In high-growth developing countries, NNW and IW are both higher, reflecting a higher opportunity cost for protecting natural capital: investment in these countries is yielding high rates of poverty reduction and improvements in education, for example.

9.7   The rate of growth of NNW not only determines whether an economy is weakly sustainable, it also should help determine, through the variable g in the Ramsey equation, the discount rate that maximizes net benefits in a benefit-cost analysis of environmental or resource protection projects. If the social rate of time preference is low, then in developed countries, appropriate discount rates for projects with long-term benefits and costs, should thus approximate g—lying below 2%. The U.S. EPA currently uses a value of 3% for climate change damages. Market discount rates are typically much higher, at 15% or more. This means that market actors have very short time horizons—typically five years or less. **High market discount rates** are thus a critical factor that could undermine the level of investment in natural capital protection, and in manufactured capital substitutes, needed to insure sustainability.

9.8   Finally, the safety-efficiency debate over pollution standards is similar in nature to the ecological-neoclassical debate over natural resource exploitation. Both safety proponents and ecological economists argue that human society as a whole is best off protecting environmental quality at a high level *regardless of the trade-offs*. Ecological economists make this case by arguing that natural and created capital are not good substitutes in production. Neoclassical economists counter that trade-offs are real, because perceived resource limits can be overcome via technology. The topsoil debate illustrates that these issues are not easy to resolve.

REFERENCES

Arrow, Kenneth J., Partha Dasgupta, Lawrence H. Goulder, Kevin J. Mumford, and Kirsten Oleson. 2012. Sustainability and the measurement of wealth. *Environment and Development Economics* 17(3): 317–53.

Crosson, Pierre. 1995. Soil erosion and its on-farm, productivity consequences: What do we know? RFF discussion paper 95-29. Washington, DC: Resources for the Future.

Daly, Herman E. 2005. Economics in a full world. *Scientific American* 100–7.

Ehrlich, Paul R., and John P. Holdren. 1971. Impact of population growth. *Science* 171: 1212–7.

Foley, Jon, Navin Ramankutty, Kate A. Brauman, Emily Cassidy, James Gerber, Nathan D. Mueller, Christine O'Connell, et al. 2011. Solutions for a cultivated planet. *Nature* 420: 337–42.

Hawken, Paul. 1995. *The Ecology of Commerce*. New York: Harper.

Howarth, Richard B., and Richard B. Norgaard. 1990. Intergenerational resource rights, efficiency and social optimality. *Land Economics* 66(1): 1–11.

Johnson, D. Gale. 2000. Population, food and knowledge. *American Economic Review* 90(1): 1–15.

Krugman, Paul. 2008. Conscience of a Liberal Blog, *New York Times*, April 22, 2008.

Malthus, Thomas. 1798. *An Essay on the Principle of Population*. London: printed for J. Johnson.

Meadows, Donella H., Dennis L. Meadows, Jorgen Randers, and William W. Behrens, III. 1972. *The Limits to Growth*. New York: Universe Books.

Meadows, Donella H., Dennis L. Meadows, and Jorgen Randers. 1992. *Beyond the Limits*. White River Junction, VT: Chelsea Green Publishing Company.

Millennium Ecosystem Assessment. 2005. *Ecosystems and Human Well-Being*. Washington, DC: Island Press.

Nordhaus, William D. 1973. Measurement without data. *Economic Journal* 83: 1156–83.

Nordhaus, William, and James Tobin. 1972. *Economic Growth*. New York: Columbia University Press.

Nordhaus, William, and Edward Kokkenberg, eds. 1999. Nature's Numbers: Expanding the national Economics Accounts to Include the Environment. Washington, DC: National Academy Press.

Pimental, David, C. Harvery. P. Resosudarmo, K. Sinclair, D. Kurz, M. McNair, S. Crist L. Shpritz, L. Fitton, R. Saffouri, and R. Blair. 1995. Environmental and economic costs of soil erosion and conservation benefits. *Science* 267: 1117–23.

Postel, Sandra L., Gretchen C. Daily, and Paul R. Ehrlich. 1996. Human appropriation of renewable fresh water. *Science* 271: 785–8.

Raudsepp-Hearne, Ciara, Garry D. Peterson, Maria Tengö, Elena M. Bennett, Tim Holland, Karina Benessaiah, Graham K. MacDonald, and Laura Pfeifer. 2010. Untangling the environmentalist's paradox: Why is human well-being increasing as ecosystem services degrade? *BioScience* 60(8): 576–89.

Rees, William E., and Mathis Wackernagel. 1994. Ecological footprints and appropriated carrying capacity: Measuring the natural capital requirement of the human economy. In *Investing in Natural Capital: The Ecological Approach to Sustainability*, A. Jansson, M. Hammer, C. Folke, and R. Constanza (eds.), pp. 362–91. Washington, DC: Island Press.

Rockström, Johan, Will Steffen, Kevin Noone, Åsa Persson, F. Stuart Chapin, III, Eric F. Lambin, Timothy M. Lenton, et al. 2009. A safe operating space for humanity. *Nature* 461: 472–5.

Solow, Robert. 1992. An almost practical step toward sustainability. Washington, DC: Resources for the Future.

Stern, N. H. 2007. *The Economics of Climate Change*. Cambridge: Cambridge University Press.

Talberth, John, Clifford Cobb, and Noah Slattery. 2006. *The Genuine Progress Indicator, 2006*. San Francisco: Redefining Progress.

Tierney, John. 1990. Betting the planet. *The New York Times Magazine*, December 2, 1990.

Toman, Michael, and Pierre Crosson. 1991. Economics and sustainability: Balancing trade-offs and imperatives. Discussion paper ENR-91-05. Washington, DC: Resources for the Future.

United Nations Development Program. 2011. *United Nation's Human Development Report 2011. Sustainability and Equity: A Better Future For All*. New York: United Nations.

US EPA/NHTSA (National Highway Traffic Safety Administration). 2009. Proposed Rulemaking to Establish Light-Duty Vehicle Greenhouse Gas Emission Standards and Corporate Average Fuel Economy Standards. Docket No. EPA-HQ-OAR-2009-0472/NHTSA-2009-0059.

Vitousek, Peter M., Harold A. Mooney, Jane Lubchenco, and Jerry M. Melillo. 1997. Human domination of earth's ecosystems. *Science* 277: 494–9.

World Bank. 2005. *World Development Indicators 2005*. Washington, DC: World Bank.

World Bank. 2006. *Where is the Wealth of Nations? Measuring Capital for the 21st Century*. Washington, DC: World Bank.

World Resources Institute. 2009. *Earth Trends Data Bank*. http://earthtrends.wri.org.

Zolatas, Xenophon. 1981. *Economic Growth and Declining Social Welfare*. New York: New York University Press.

CHAPTER 10

NATURAL RESOURCES AND ECOSYSTEM SERVICES

10.0 Introduction

You may be reading this book from the comfort of your apartment, or perhaps in a coffee shop, library, or office. Wherever you are, surrounded by human-made things, it is easy to think that we are not dependent on natural capital. But think more deeply. Your chair is made from wood or metal and covered with cloth or leather. Your building is heated or air conditioned by the combustion of fossil fuels; or nuclear power, which uses uranium as a fuel source; or renewable energy like wind or solar power. You likely drove to your current location in a gasoline-powered car or bus, assembled from various metals, rubber, and plastic made from oil or other hydrocarbons. The cell phone that you carry around contains small amounts of beryllium, cadmium, cobalt, copper, lead, mercury, nickel, palladium, silver, and zinc. Though many economics textbooks depict production as being dependent on capital, by which it is usually meant manufactured capital (industrial plant and equipment), and labor, we are, in fact, utterly and totally dependent on natural resources.

The previous two chapters have focused on sustainability as the goal of our economy. As we have seen, an important determinant of whether society is achieving sustainability is whether we are leaving the next generation suitable capital stocks, including stocks of natural resources. (Note: by stocks in this chapter, we mean physical stocks of resources—trees, minerals in the ground, and fish in the ocean—not stocks as pieces of paper representing ownership in a company). Here, we dive deeper into economic issues surrounding our use of natural resources.

"Natural Resources" comprise a huge category, including all of the raw materials that sustain human well-being that are not directly made by humans. All manufactured capital, as well as all final goods and services, ultimately depend on some sort of natural resource, which is one form of "natural capital." Natural capital also includes ecological processes that underlie the provision of ecosystem services. In this chapter, we will explore the economics of three broad classes of natural capital: nonrenewable resources, renewable resources, and ecological processes undergirding ecosystem services.

Nonrenewable resources are resources in fixed supply like oil, coal, or minerals. Over the long arc of geologic time, millions of years, more oil or coal will be produced, so in a sense these resources are really very slowly renewing resources. But for practical purposes, at least in thinking about things over the next 1,000 years, we have the oil and coal supply that we have, and nature will produce no more. **Renewable resources**, by contrast, are biological resources for which there is a natural growth function. Fish, game species, trees, fruits, and grains, all will grow back after harvesting as long as we are intelligent enough to leave some stock and not cause extinction.

Traditionally, "Resource Economics" focused only on these first two categories: renewable and nonrenewable resources. The third category, **ecosystem services**, broadens "natural resources" to the more modern conception we have been using in the book to this point, natural capital. Ecosystem services are benefits that people obtain from nature. These include benefits from the use of renewable and nonrenewable resources and also go well beyond these. Ecosystem services also include benefits generated by ecological processes such as when ecosystems filter out pollutants to provide clean drinking water or sequester carbon in plant material that reduces the amount of CO_2 in the atmosphere. To understand the economic management of these ecosystem services, we must also understand the underlying **ecosystem processes** that deliver these services.

The Millennium Ecosystem Assessment (2005) defined four categories of ecosystem services:

Provisioning Services: the products obtained from ecosystems that include nonrenewable resources (oil, coal, and minerals) and renewable resources (fish, game, and timber).

Regulating Services: the benefits derived from ecological processes controlling the flows of water, carbon, nutrients, and energy through ecosystems including filtering nutrients or pollution to provide clean drinking water, pollination services that increase crop productivity, or disease and pest control.

Supporting Services: the underlying support systems or "natural infrastructure" that allows everything to continue to function.

Cultural Services: the nonmaterial benefits derived from nature including ecotourism, recreation, and spiritual inspiration.

Unlike much of natural resource economics, managing ecosystems to provide for ecosystem services requires us to think about joint production of multiple ecosystem services and potential tradeoffs among services, unintended consequences of actions that affect ecological processes, and the particular locations and spatial patterns of those ecological processes that produce ecosystem services.

In the last two chapters, we evaluated sustainability as the central goal for managing natural capital. In this chapter, we focus a closer lens on the economics of resource management to help achieve this goal.

10.1 Nonrenewable Resources and the Hotelling Model

The formula for success according to billionaire J. Paul Getty, the founder of Getty Oil and one of the richest people in the world during his lifetime, was to "rise early, work hard, and strike oil." There is good reason why oil is sometimes called "black gold." In 2010, global oil consumption was around 87 million barrels per day. At prices of around $100 per barrel that means that $8.7 billion was spent to buy oil every day! That sums to more than $3 trillion per year.

Oil has such value because of its uniquely high energy content as a fuel, and its useful chemical structure for plastics and chemical production. It fuels transportation for cars, trucks, buses, ships, and airplanes. Often the roads themselves are made of oil products (asphalt). Oil is used for heat and to make electricity. Oil is the primary ingredient for a variety of chemicals ("petrochemicals"). The modern economy simply could not function without oil. To use the words of former president George W. Bush "America is addicted to oil" (and other countries are too).

But oil is a finite resource. There is only so much of it in the ground. And we are using it up at a rapid pace. How will oil be allocated to meet both current demands as well as future demands when there is only a limited supply of it? Will we run out of oil at some point? And will oil become so expensive in the future as we begin to deplete supplies that future generations will be penalized?

To answer questions about production and price of oil and other nonrenewable resources, economists typically start with a simple model, developed by Harold Hotelling (1931). Hotelling had a basic insight about how a firm that owned a nonrenewable resource like oil would choose to use its stock to maximize its profits. For Hotelling, owning a resource stock was an investment. Firms would choose to hold onto the resource stock if it offered a competitive return and would sell it off if it didn't. If a firm were to sell its oil deposits now and put the money in a bank, it would earn interest. But oil in the ground doesn't earn interest. Oil in the ground doesn't seem to earn any return. So why would anyone hold onto oil deposits?

Oil in the ground does become more valuable if its price increases. In order to get firms to be willing to save some of their resource stock until the future, prices of nonrenewable resources like oil must rise over time. Hotelling showed that in market equilibrium the rate of return on the resource stock (the percentage increase in resource rents earned) would equal the rate of return on alternative investments (the interest rate). This will provide an incentive for firms to save some (not all) of the resource for later periods, a process known as profit-based conservation. More importantly, rising prices will signal to investors that there are profit opportunities in developing substitutes.

We can see the basic logic of the Hotelling model using an example involving the production and sale of a nonrenewable resource over time. Suppose that 100 tons of a brand-new mineral is discovered in the country of Billsville and that Billsville is the only place on earth with this mineral. The president, Mr. Bill, modestly names this new resource Billite. To keep things simple, assume that Billite can be produced at no cost (it is easy to collect and requires no refining). The Billite industry is also a competitive with lots of small producers that take prices as given.

Investors can earn a 10% interest (or "discount") rate elsewhere in the economy. Assume that the inverse demand curve for Billite is the same in both periods: $P_t = 260 - q_t$, where P_t is the price in period t, and q_t is the total quantity demanded in period t. For simplicity, we are going to assume there are only two periods, so that all the Billite must be sold either in the first or second period. (The logic can be extended to a model with many periods). Then, the setup for a given period is illustrated in Figure 10.1. If all the Billite were sold in period 1, it would fetch a price of $160 per ton. But clearly, firms will not sell it all in the first period, but rather hold some stock for sale in the second period, which could get a price as high as $260. Holding stock until the second period would raise the price in the first period as well.

PUZZLE

How much Billite would be produced in the first period and in the second period? And what will be the price for Billite in periods 1 and 2?

Any principles of economics textbook will tell you that perfectly competitive firms will produce where price equals marginal cost. When price exceeds marginal cost a firm can increase profit by increasing production. But trying to boost production so that price equals to marginal cost, which here is assumed to be 0, would require selling 260 units of stock in a period. Of course, there are only 100 units in total so this isn't possible. Even with competitive firms, price will not be driven down to marginal cost and firms that own stocks of Billite will earn some profit. This profit arises because the resource is scarce relative to demand, and so—as we discussed back in Chapter 3—we call this profit a **resource rent**.[1]

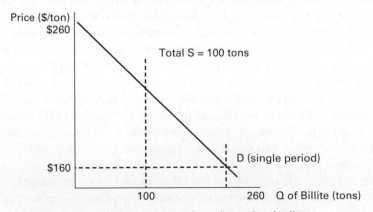

FIGURE 10.1 Annual Demand and Total Supply of Billite

---

1. Resource rents also occur for desirable properties with limited supply such as property located in midtown Manhattan or beachfront property in Southern California.

Back to the puzzle. How much Billite will be produced and sold in period 1 and how much will be produced and sold in period 2? First, recognize that firms will produce and sell all of their Billite at some point because doing so generates profit and leaving it unsold does not. Therefore, we know that total sales over the two periods will equal the amount of stock: $q_1 + q_2 = 100$ (or $q_2 = 100 - q_1$). Because producers face downward sloping demand, it seems reasonable to think that they will divide the stock evenly between the two periods. That way they sell 50 units in each period and receive a price for each unit of $210(260 - 50 = 210)$, in both periods.

However, this is not a profit-maximizing outcome. Consider that a firm that sells one unit in period 1 can invest its proceeds and by the end of period 2 will have $231 = 210 * (1 + 0.1)$. This is better than waiting to sell the unit in period 2 and only getting $210, so there will be pressure to sell more in period 1 and less in period 2. Stated another way, the present value of the sale of a unit of Billite in period 1 is $210 while the present value of the sale of a unit of Billite in period 2 is only $210/(1 + 0.1) = 190.91$. This pressure to sell more in the first period and less in the second period will cease only when firms earn the same amount regardless of whether they sell in period 1 or 2. This occurs where the period 1 price, P_1, and the discounted period 2 price, $P_2/(1 + r)$, are equalized:

$$P_1 = P_2/(1 + r)$$

With a small bit of algebra, we can rearrange this expression and find that the percentage increase in price of the resource stock is equal to the interest rate:

$$P_1(1 + r) = P_2$$
$$P_1 * r = P_2 - P_1$$
$$r = (P_2 - P_1)/P_1$$

This is **Hotelling's rule**, which in words says that the percentage increase in the resource price $((P_2 - P_1)/P_1)$ will equal the interest rate (r).

We are getting closer to answering our puzzle: how many units sold in each period? We know it is not 50/50, and that the quantity sold will be greater in the first period (lowering the first period price) and lower in the second period (increasing the second period price). How much higher and lower? One approach would be guess and check: Try 51/49, 52/48, and see which combination solves Hotelling's rule and equalizes the discounted prices in each period. Instead, let's solve for the answer algebraically.

Using Hotelling's rule and the inverse market demand curve ($P_t = 260 - q_t$) for each period we can solve for the amount that will be sold in each period:

$$r = (P_2 - P_1)/P_1$$
$$0.1 = [(260 - q_2) - (260 - q_1)]/(260 - q_1)$$
$$0.1(260 - q_1) = q_1 - q_2$$

We can also use the fact that total sales over the two periods will equal the amount of stock: $q_1 + q_2 = 100$ or $q_2 = 100 - q_1$:

$$26 - 0.1\,q_1 = q_1 - (100 - q_1)$$
$$126 = 2.1\,q_1$$
$$q_1 = 60$$

Period 2 quantity will be $q_2 = 100 - 60 = 40$. So our final quantities that maximize profit across both periods are 60/40. With this distribution, no firm has an incentive to mine and sell more Billite in one period or less in another.

Moving on to prices: Price in period 1 will be $P_1 = 260 - q_1 = 200$. Price in period 2 will be $P_2 = 260 - q_2 = 220$. Note that discounted period 2 price just equals period 1 price $(220/1.1 = 200)$.

Figure 10.2 provides a useful way to show the results of this example. In Figure 10.2, the total width of the figure is 100 units, which represents the total amount of Billite available. We measure Billite produced in the first period starting with 0 on the left and increasing by moving to the right. We measure Billite produced in the second period starting with 0 on the right and increasing by moving to the left. By construction, then, any point along the horizontal axis represents a division of the 100 units of Billite produced between periods 1 and 2 $(q_1 + q_2 = 100)$.

Similarly, we plot the demand for Billite in period 1 (line starting at 260 on the left and sloping downward) and in period 2 (line starting at 260 on the right and sloping upward). Note that without consideration of discounting, the demand curves cross at 50 units produced in each period and at a price of $210 per unit. However, as we noted earlier, what producers really care about is equalizing discounted price: $P_1 = P_2/(1 + r)$. Discounted period 2 demand is the lower of the upward sloping lines. As shown, discounted prices are equalized when $q_1 = 60$ and $q_2 = 40$ so that period 1 price is $200 and period 2 price is $220, which when discounted at 10% equals $200.

Figure 10.2 looks almost identical to Figure 4.3 in Chapter 4, which shows the efficient level of pollution reduction. Figure 4.3 shows the marginal benefits of pollution reduction, which is a downward sloping line showing that it is less beneficial to further reduce pollution, the more pollution has already been cleaned up. Figure 4.3 also

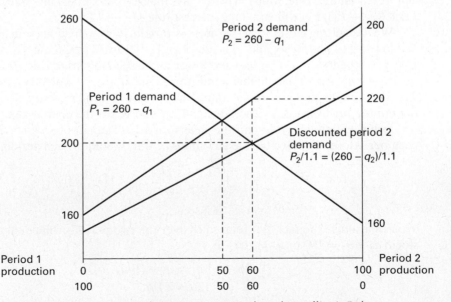

FIGURE 10.2 Resource Use between Two Periods and Hotelling's Rule

shows the marginal cost of pollution reduction, which is an upward sloping line in pollution reduction showing that it is increasingly expensive to reduce pollution, the more pollution is cleaned up. This diagram is similar. Using more Billite in period 1 generates a marginal benefit to the producers (profit from sale), which is represented by the downward sloping demand curve in Figure 10.2. However, the more that is used in period 1, the less that can be used in period 2. There is, therefore, a cost of using more Billite in period 1, which is the loss of use in period 2. The marginal cost of increasing period 1 production is thus equal to discounted demand curve in period 2. The efficient amount of production in periods 1 and 2 occurs where MB = MC, which is where discounted prices are equal: $P_1 = P_2/(1 + r)$.

This two-period example illustrates a couple of fundamental points. First, as long as the supply of the nonrenewable resource is limited and scarce relative to demand, those who own resource stock will earn a positive resource rent. In the simple example, owning a unit of Billite is worth $200 (in present value terms). Second, with a positive interest rate the price of the nonrenewable resource will increase through time. Hotelling's rule says that rates of returns on holding the resource equals the rate of return on an alternative investment. An increase in price is how a positive rate of return for holding the resource stock is generated. Third, if demand is constant across periods, as was assumed in this simple example, then a rising price means falling consumption through time. Here more was produced and sold in period 1 (60) than in period 2 (40). The higher the discount rate, the more attractive the forgone alternative investments, the faster the stock will be depleted, and the faster the price will rise. Again, steadily rising prices are the trigger for firms to invest in potential substitutes.

Following Hotelling's rule is also dynamically efficient. Dynamic efficiency is achieved when the resource stock is allocated over time in a way that maximizes the present value of its use. When discounted prices across periods are equal there is no way to reallocate sales between periods and increase returns. This result should, perhaps, not be surprising given that the market is competitive and producers have perfect information. However, there often is the feeling that the market outcome is causing resources to be depleted too quickly. Such a conclusion will occur if there is pollution associated with resource use. Then, just like we showed before, there will be too much of the activity associated with pollution generation (and this is a real concern with use of oil and other fossil fuels that are associated with greenhouse gas emissions and climate change, as well as local air pollution). But without a pollution externality or other distortions, the market will allocate nonrenewable resources efficiently across time.

The basic Hotelling model can be extended far beyond the simple example shown so far, with just two periods and no cost of production. Suppose that the nonrenewable resource can be produced at a constant marginal cost of $c per unit. The resource rent from production and sales of the nonrenewable resource in this case is price minus marginal cost: $R = P - c$. What firms care about is the rent, not just the price. At market equilibrium (where firms do not shift production from one period to another) the discounted resource rent will be equated across time:

$$(P_1 - c) = (P_2 - c)/(1 + r).$$

So, for example, suppose that in the case of Billite, the marginal cost of production was $42 per unit. In this case, discounted marginal rents will be equalized when:

$$(P_1 - c) = (P_2 - c)/(1 + r)$$
$$(260 - q_1 - 42) = (260 - q_2 - 42)/(1.1)$$
$$(218 - q_1) * 1.1 = 218 - (100 - q_1)$$
$$q_1 = 58$$

With a higher cost than before, the amount of first period production falls and second period production increases. One way to think about how this occurs is that discounting means that firms want to push costs into the future and this delays production somewhat. In general, an increase in cost, or a fall in demand, will cause resource rent to decline. Lower resource rents tend to lead toward more equal distribution of production over time.

The basic Hotelling logic holds for a model with a large number of time periods. With constant marginal costs of production, in any period in which the resource is produced and sold, the discounted rent (price – marginal cost) is equalized across all t time periods.

The resulting prices and quantity produced through time are shown in Figure 10.3 for the case where the demand curve at time t is $q_t = a - P_t$, and there is constant marginal cost of production of c per unit. When price rises to the **choke price** (a) then quantity demanded falls to zero (demand is choked off). This occurs when the resource stock is exhausted at time T.

As shown in Figure 10.3, there is a time when the resource stock is exhausted (date T in the figure). In the run up to date T, price is gradually increasing and demand is gradually falling until the choke price is reached and no one demands the nonrenewable resource anymore. What does this mean in terms of sustainability?·

Implicit in this model is that there are substitutes for the nonrenewable resource. As oil becomes increasingly scarce, its price will rise, inducing firms to search out and develop new technologies that serve similar functions at lower cost or that use the existing oil with much greater efficiency. For example, solar, wind, and biomass technologies may power hydrogen fuel-cell or battery-powered vehicles and provide heat and electricity as oil stocks are depleted. Markets can act as one powerful social

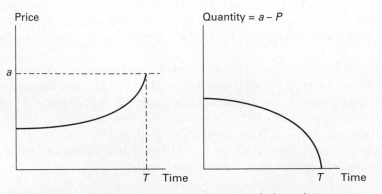

FIGURE 10.3 Hotelling Price and Production Path through Time

mechanism for replacing one form of natural capital with other forms of capital. Consumer behavior may also shift. There is a shift toward smaller more fuel-efficient cars during periods of high oil prices (and a shift toward monster trucks when prices are low). Driving habits are also sensitive to oil prices. People will take fewer trips and generally drive less when gasoline prices are high.

In fact, if oil prices go too high (approaching the choke price) then oil is likely to be priced out of the market almost entirely. Eventually solar-powered electric cars would be cheaper than oil if oil prices continue to increase. Solar/battery powered cars can be thought of as a **backstop technology** that provides a readily available and renewable substitute for the nonrenewable resource. Having a backstop technology such as solar power would put an upper bound on oil prices.

But aren't some resources irreplaceable? This question gets us back to the neo-classical/ecological debate of the previous two chapters. Oil is among the most unique nonrenewable resources, with its high energy content and wide variety of uses that do not have readily available low-cost substitutes. A sudden restriction in oil supplies, given our "addiction," would no doubt cause a large contraction in the economy and a substantial decline in standards of living, unless we have adequate energy substitutes. This reason is enough for putting large-scale research and development efforts into developing alternative renewable energy supplies. But before oil literally runs out, Hotelling's model predicts that price will begin to rise significantly to reflect its scarcity. The price increase will trigger a more serious search for substitutes. And if price gets too high, oil may price itself out of the market as consumers find cheaper alternatives.

Can we rely on Hotelling's predictions of rising resource prices to alert us to looming shortages? We first turn to the empirical evidence across a range of commodities, and then return to the question of "Peak Oil."

10.2 Testing the Nonrenewable Resource Model

Do nonrenewable resource prices tend to rise and quantities tend to fall as suggested by the Hotelling model? Throughout the 20th century the real price of natural resources, controlling for inflation, was relatively flat or even somewhat downward trending (recall "The Bet" from Chapter 9 in which the prices of five metals fell quite significantly during the 1980s). A comprehensive study examined the real prices for six minerals (aluminum, copper, lead, nickel, tin, and zinc) for the period 1967 to 2001 (Krautkraemer 2005). Despite some ups and downs, the overall trend in prices was downward during this period. An earlier study by Barnett and Morse (1963) found declining extraction costs for natural resources, except for timber, which of course is a renewable rather than nonrenewable resource, for the period from 1870 to 1958. Until quite recently, natural resources did not seem to be showing signs of greater scarcity as time went on.

Two possible explanations may account for the lack of upward movement in prices of nonrenewable resources through time. First, looking forward at available supply-and-demand conditions, consumers or firms may not have seen long-term shortfalls of these basic commodities within a relevant time frame—say 20 years. So even though there will be scarcity of the resources some time in the future, it is still too far off for it to factor into either consumer or firms' behavior (Krautkraemer 1998). The second explanation relates to cost reductions. As mining and processing technology steadily advances, lower grade ores can be mined cost-effectively. This effectively shifts the supply curve down and out, further reducing any imminent scarcity.

A dramatic example of the impacts of new technology on resource availability and prices is the effect of hydraulic fracturing, or "fracking," and natural gas in the United States over the past several years. Hydraulic fracturing is a process by which water is injected under high pressure to open small fractures in the underlying rock formations. These fractures allow oil and natural gas to flow more freely. Some types of rock, notably shale, have been known for some time to contain large quantities of oil and natural gas. However, prior to fracking there was no economic way to recover the oil and natural gas because it was too tightly locked up in the surrounding rock. With the advent of fracking techniques, these oil and gas deposits became commercially viable.

Fracking has led to a boom in production in the United States, particularly for natural gas production and also for oil. Between 2007 and 2011, natural gas production in the United States increased by over 25% from 23.5 billion cubic feet in 2006 to 29.8 billion cubic feet in 2012.[2] The rapid increase in supply has resulted in dramatic declines in natural gas prices from a high of over $10 per thousand cubic feet in 2008 to less than $2 per thousand cubic feet in April and May of 2012.[3] The increased supply and lowered prices have been a boon to U.S. industries and consumers that rely on natural gas. There are, however, concerns about the environmental impacts of fracking, which include the potential for ground water contamination from both natural gas and injected chemicals used in fracking, pollution of surface waters when wastes are not properly handled, air pollution, and emissions of CO_2. How to regulate fracking to minimize the environmental harm is the subject of on-going debates.

Other than natural gas, however, prices for natural resources *have* been increasing in recent years. Large increases in demand from rapidly developing countries like China and India have pushed up prices for a wide range of natural resources, everything from mineral and energy prices, to food prices (Figure 10.4). It might be that Hotelling was just ahead of his time. In the 20th century, new discoveries of resource stocks and new technologies seemed to more than offset the resource depletion effect. It may be that the 21st century, a period with few unexplored areas to find new resources and rapidly increasing demand, will be the time period when the predictions of Hotelling for increasing prices of resources will at last be correct. Case in point: Peak Oil?

10.3 "Peak Oil"

In 1956, M. King Hubbert, a geoscientist working for Shell Oil, presented a paper at a meeting of the American Petroleum Institute predicting that production of oil in the continental United States would peak in the late 1960s or early 1970s. Starting with Hubbert, a number of analysts have tried to predict the time of **peak oil**, when oil production hits its high and starts to decline. At the time that Hubbert first made his

2. U.S. Energy Information Administration. U.S. Natural Gas Gross Withdrawals. http://www.eia.gov/dnav/ng/hist/n9010us2A.htm.
3. U.S. Energy Information Administration. U.S. Natural Gas Wellhead Price. http://www.eia.gov/dnav/ng/hist/n9190us3m.htm.

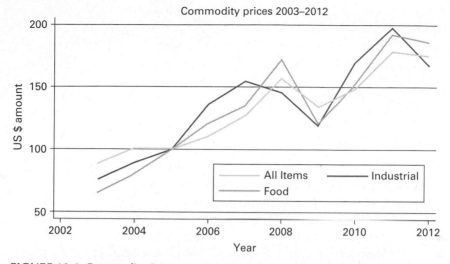

FIGURE 10.4 Commodity Prices 2003–2012
Source: IMF Data and Statistics, http://www.imf.org/external/np/res/commod/Table1.pdf.

prediction about peak oil in the United States many in the oil industry thought this was nonsense. At that time production was steadily climbing and many thought it would continue to climb for a long time. In fact, though, U.S. oil production peaked in 1970 at 9.6 million barrels per day. It steadily declined from the peak until it reached a low of 5 million barrels per day in 2008. However, since then it has climbed back up a bit, though nowhere near the high of 1970, in large part due to fracking technology that was discussed earlier.

In 1974, Hubbert also predicted that world oil production would peak in 1995. He was far less successful on this prediction than on his first one. In fact, world oil production has continued to increase (Figure 10.5) and is now close to 90 million barrels per day. But many observers are worried that peak oil is not all that far off. Consider this 2008 press release from a major oil company.

> World demand for oil and gas will outstrip supply within seven years, according to Royal Dutch Shell.

The oil multinational is predicting that conventional supplies will not keep pace with soaring population growth and the rapid pace of economic development. Jeroen van der Veer, Shell's chief executive, said in an e-mail to the company's staff this week that output of conventional oil and gas was close to peaking. He wrote: "Shell estimates that after 2015 supplies of easy-to-access oil and gas will no longer keep up with demand."[4]

At some point, rising demand will run into the physical reality of limited supply. So in some sense peak oil shouldn't be controversial. The real question is when we will hit peak oil, not whether we will hit peak oil. Is peak oil going to happen by 2015 or will production continue to climb for several more decades? Like Shell, the

---

4. Shell Oil (2008).

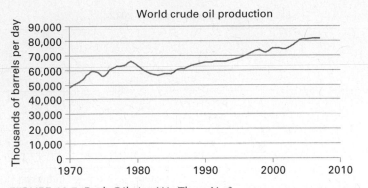

FIGURE 10.5 Peak Oil: Are We There Yet?
Source: US EIA, International Energy Statistics,
http://www.eia.gov/cfapps/ipdbproject/IEDIndex3.cfm?tid=5&pid=53&aid=1.

World Resources Institute sees a peak soon, sometime before 2014.[5] Others, however, continue to see production increases. For example, the International Energy Administration recently predicted that surging oil production would make the United States the largest oil producer, overtaking Saudi Arabia by 2020 and energy independent by 2030.[6] Leonardo Maugeri, a researcher at Harvard, predicts that world oil production will increase to over 110 million barrels per day by 2020 (Maugeri 2012).

When it does occur, peak production will take place against a backdrop of ever-rising demand. With stagnant or declining production, oil prices must rise. At the peak, the world will not have "run out of oil"; we will, however, run out of cheap new oil. In fact, we may have seen the first real signs of this over the past few years. Oil prices have shot up over the past few years (Figure 10.6). They have remained at or above $100 per barrel for several years, far above the historical average price.

Until very recently, however, there was little evidence that oil prices have reflected any long-run scarcity. In Figure 10.6, the real price of oil was flat throughout much of the 20th century. The figure reveals several big jumps in oil prices resulting from political economic events. In the mid 1970s and early 1980s, the OPEC oil cartel used its monopoly power to increase price; and in 1990, the Gulf War created great uncertainty about short-run oil supplies. The early OPEC price increases did have their predicted impact on energy use. Overall oil consumption in developed nations declined dramatically during the early 1980s as firms and consumers adopted efficiency measures, but after 1985, consumption rose again. However, the oil price run-up that began in 2002, following the war in Iraq and fueled by two decades of explosive growth in China and India, eventually sent prices to their highest level ever. With the onset of the global recession in 2008, prices fell, along with demand—though perhaps tellingly, not back to their early 2000 levels. And as the global economy has recovered, oil prices have climbed again.

No one knows exactly when peak oil will occur; however, *sometime* in the next 5 to 30 years, production is very likely to peak, and oil prices may rise substantially over

---

5. MacKenzie (2000).
6. IEA (2012).

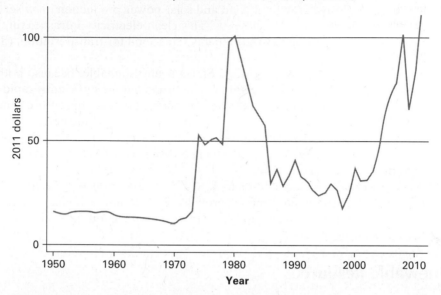

Crude oil prices 1950–2011 (dollars per barrel)

FIGURE 10.6 Oil Prices 1950–2012 (2011 Dollars per Barrel)

where they are today. It may well be that the large and easy deposits of oil have already been found and exploited. Firms will have to drill deeper, in more remote areas, go further offshore into deeper water, or tap smaller, less productive fields. Producing oil in these conditions is more expensive. Petroleum products can also be derived from more abundant but highly polluting and more expensive sources like tar sands, shale, and coal.

Let us pause to summarize. Hotelling predicted that markets will signal scarcity through prices that rise steadily at a rate more or less equal to interest rates in the economy. In spite of their fundamentally limited supply, this has not been true of oil prices, until recently. One critical reason is that very few market participants have good information about the true size of total global petroleum reserves. We also don't know what breakthroughs in energy technology may occur 5, 20, or 50 years from now that would vastly change the outlook for oil. As a result, Peak Oil might happen soon with very little warning, with rapidly rising prices, and with potentially crippling economic impacts or it might happen well in the future with a steady run-up in prices, incentivizing new technology, and making the transition manageable. There is no way to know for sure.

Ignoring the major environmental impact of oil production and consumption, are we penalizing future generations by depriving them of a supply of cheap oil? Until 2002, as there had been no long-run upswing in prices, private investors in the United States were not investing heavily in energy technology. That has begun to change with the increase in prices. However, in many other countries where, due to taxes, oil and gasoline prices are much higher, market forces are working more successfully to promote the development of substitute technologies. For example, in Denmark and

Germany, high electricity prices and an aggressive government tax credit program have led to the explosive growth of wind and solar power production, now serving upward of 20% of the countries' total needs. This clean electricity infrastructure could form the foundation of a system to sustainably replace oil for transportation. (See Sharman 2005.)

However, oil use in the United States is unsustainable, because both prices and government R&D funding levels are too low to encourage sufficiently rapid deployment of substitutes. Given this, the ecological economists argue that future generations will be penalized in the form of higher prices for transportation and petrochemical products such as plastics. (More significantly, fossil fuel combustion poses long-term threats to the resilience of the regional and global ecosystems in the form of urban air and water pollution and global warming.)[7]

We will take a much closer look at U.S. energy policy in Chapter 19. For now, this tour of the Hotelling model provides a basic understanding of the economics of nonrenewable resources, and how markets with good information should signal scarcity.

10.4 Renewable Resources

Many important natural resources are renewable resources whose supplies are not fixed but grow ("renew") over time. Fish in the ocean, game species, and forests are biological resources that regenerate and grow, as long as they are not harvested to extinction. Even water supplies are renewable because rain and snow replenish supplies. Unlike nonrenewable resources such as oil or metals, renewable resources can be harvested and used in a sustainable manner. A **sustainable harvest** is one that does not exceed natural growth so that the renewable resource stock increases or remains the same.

We represent the fact that renewable resources grow with a **growth function**, which expresses growth in new units per period as a function of the size of the existing resource stock. If there are 100 fish currently and in the next period there will be 120 fish, we would say that growth is 20 fish. The growth function tells how much the resource stock will increase (or decrease) in the next period starting from any given level of stock in this period. Typically, the growth of the resource stock will depend on the current size of the stock. For example, as the number of fish increase there are fewer food resources to go around and the birth rate and survival rate of the fish decline. This common feature of growth functions for biological resources is known as **density-dependent growth**.

An example of a density-dependent growth function for a fishery is shown in Figure 10.7. (A similar function might apply to forests or livestock.) The X axis shows the size of the original stock (Total Fish at the start of a given period). The Y axis shows the growth in the stock (New Fish in the next period) as a function of the original stock. The growth function shown in Figure 10.7 reaches a maximum at the stock level labeled S_{MSY}, where MSY stands for **maximum sustainable yield**. Growth falls to zero when the resource stock rises to carrying capacity, K. At this point, competition for

---

7. Daly (1996, p. 83).

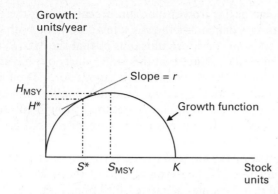

FIGURE 10.7 Growth Function, Maximum Sustainable Yield, and Optimal Harvest

food and other resources reduces the birth rate to the level of the death rate. Growth is also zero when there is no resource stock (fish that are extinct do not reproduce!).

When the resource stock is at S_{MSY}, harvest could be set at maximum sustainable yield, shown as H_{MSY} (harvesting all the growth in the stock each year) in Figure 10.7. Maximum sustainable yield, H_{MSY}, is just equal to the natural growth in the stock and so the stock size will remain at S_{MSY} if that number of fish is harvested each year. Managing the renewable resource stock in this way in fact maximizes the amount of harvest that can be done in a sustainable manner.

But will renewable resources be harvested in this manner? Not if firms seek to maximize profits. We will show that profit-maximizing firms sometimes reduce stock below S_{MSY}.

To understand questions about the rate of harvest of renewable resource in a market economy we need to consider the incentives of resource users. Just like in the Hotelling model for nonrenewable resources, a renewable resource harvesting firm should think about the resource stock as an investment. Unlike oil in the ground, however, fish left in the ocean or trees left in the forest grow and this will factor into the resource firm's decision about how much to harvest. The growth of the resource means that saving the resource stock will offer a positive return even when the price is not increasing. If the growth of the resource is fast enough it will make holding onto the resource more valuable than harvesting it right away. However, if the resource growth is too slow it may be more profitable to harvest everything right now.

To provide more detail on how much competitive firms would harvest and how much of the resource stock would be conserved, let's return to the country of Billsville. Along the coast of Billsville there are numerous mudflats with a species of clam. Suppose that each portion of each mudflat is owned by an individual clam-harvesting firm. That firm gets to decide how many clams to harvest in period 1 and how many clams to harvest in period 2.

Clams left in the mudflat at the end of period 1 grow in size and reproduce. Let $G(S)$ represent the growth function of clams, which depends on the current number of clams (S). As in Figure 10.7, assume that the more clams there are currently, the lower the growth rate (the amount of growth per unit of existing clams: $G(S)/S$), and at some point growth actually starts to decline back towards zero. We can define the **marginal**

growth (MG(S)) as the change in the growth function. Because both the growth rate and the change in the growth rate depend on the stock level we write both variables as a function of the stock. In fact, some basic calculus tells us that the MG(S) is the slope of the growth function in Figure 10.7. Note that this slope starts out big and positive, and then declines up to the top of the curve, where it equals zero. Then as we move beyond the sustained maximum yield, the growth becomes smaller, indicated as MG (the slope of the curve) turns negative. As you move out to K, growth falls back toward zero. At the point K, the carrying capacity for clams is reached, and growth simply stops.

To summarize, the growth of the stock starts at zero, tops out at the maximum sustained yield, then declines to zero. The growth rate of the stock starts out high, decreases, reaches zero, and then becomes negative, until finally, at K, growth itself is zero.

Suppose the stock of clams for an individual firm at the beginning of period 1 is S_1 and the first period harvest is H_1. This means that $S_R = S_1 - H_1$ clams remaining after harvest. It is the remaining clams (S_R) that can grow and reproduce for the second period. The number of clams at the beginning of period 2 after growth has occurred is equal to $G(S_R)$:

$$S_2 = S_R + G(S_R).$$

As period 2 is the last period, the firm will sell all remaining clams in period 2: $H_2 = S_2$. Suppose it costs c per unit to harvest clams, the price of clams in periods 1 and 2 is P_1 and P_2, respectively, and the interest rate is r. By harvesting a unit of clams in period 1, the firm can earn profits off that unit of Π_1:

$$\Pi_1 = P_1 - c.$$

On the other hand, by saving that same unit of clams and letting it grow, the firm will have $1 + $ MG units of clams in period 2.[8] The value to the firm of saving a unit of clams from period 1 and harvesting the additional clams in period 2 (Π_2) is equal to:

$$\Pi_2 = (P_2 - c) * (1 + \text{MG}).$$

Of course, if the firm waits to sell clams until period 2 it must discount the value to get the present value. Just as in the Hotelling model, if $\Pi_1 > \Pi_2/(1 + r)$, the firm will wish to harvest all its clams now. On the other hand, if $\Pi_1 < \Pi_2/(1 + r)$, the firm will save all of its clams and harvest them in period 2. In equilibrium, however, the discounted returns will be equal, so setting the two equal allows us to derive the equivalent of Hotelling's rule for renewable resources:

$$P_1 - c = \frac{(P_2 - c) * (1 + \text{MG})}{1 + r}$$

As noted earlier, renewable resource prices do not have to be rising to ensure that some stock is preserved over time. Even with constant prices there is still an incentive to conserve some of the stock because of its growth. Suppose that prices are indeed

---

8. Note that saving clams beyond the point where MG turns negative (e.g., the maximum sustained yield) is a bad idea, because additional clams saved start to reduce the productivity of the entire system. Saving one more clam means you will get back less than a clam in the next period!

constant: $P_1 = P_2$. When $P_1 = P_2$, then $P_1 - c = P_2 - c$. This means, from the equation above, that $\frac{(1+MG)}{1+r} = 1$, or simply, that MG = r. This relation is known as the **golden rule of growth**.

The golden rule tells the resource manager to keep increasing the harvest until the growth rate of the stock (MG) is driven down to r. Or if the harvest is so high that the growth rate (MG) is less than r, to cut back on the harvest and allow stock to increase, until MG equals r. In equilibrium, the returns to investment in the resource must be equal to the rate of return elsewhere in the economy to achieve dynamic efficiency. For renewable resources with constant prices, the return on investment for the resource is equal to the marginal growth. The return on investment elsewhere in the economy is simply the interest rate, r.

Returning to Figure 10.7, the golden rule of growth is satisfied when stock is S^*. At this level of stock, MG = r, which is shown by noting that the slope of the growth function at S^* equals the interest rate, r. The rule characterizing how much to harvest and how much stock to conserve holds with multiple periods as well. In each and every period, the profit maximizing firm should conserve S^* units of clams and harvest H^*, which is the natural growth of the clams at S^*.

Finally, note that this is a sustainable harvest because it maintains a constant population of clams at S^*. In other words, if you harvest at a rate H^*, you are taking away exactly all the growth of the stock generated from S^*: so year after year, assuming no shocks to the system, the population will neither shrink nor grow.

Let's pause to summarize: So far we've talked about harvests that generate the maximum sustained yield and the profit maximizing yield. If interest rates are positive, note that the model predicts that the profit-maximizing yield will be less than the sustained yield. Why?

Time for a

PUZZLE

How can it be the case that the profit-maximizing yield is less than the maximum sustained yield?

For this puzzle let's use a specific growth function often used in studying renewable resources, called the logistic growth function. The equation for the logistic growth is:

$$G(S) = g * S * (1 - S/K)$$

where S is the resource stock, K is the carrying capacity, and parameter g is called the intrinsic growth rate (which is constant). If you graph this function, it is similar to the picture in Figure 10.7, in that the maximum sustained yield occurs when the stock is half the carrying capacity, or when $S = K/2$. With logistic growth, the marginal growth rate (the slope of the $G(S)$ function, we need calculus for this one) turns out to be:

$$MG(S) = g(1 - 2S/K)$$

Note that, as in our discussion above, the marginal growth rate starts out high and positive (if S is small relative to K), then, when S is half of carrying capacity

($K/2$), the change in the growth rate falls to zero. Beyond that point, the marginal growth is negative as the system productivity falls.

Here we will assume that $K = 100$ and $g = 1$. Figure 10.8 gives the growth for various levels of stock between zero and the carrying capacity of 100 with these parameter values. The maximum sustained yield occurs when $S = 50$. The maximum sustained harvest is 25.

In the golden rule of growth we will set MG(S) = r. We'll assume that clam harvesters face a high interest rate: $r = 20\%$. The stock level that satisfies the golden rule of growth and maximizes present value of harvest is $S = 40$ (MG(S) = r means that $1 - 2S/100 = 0.2$, which is true for $S = 40$). For $S = 40$, sustainable harvest is 24.

Now surely harvesting 25 is better than harvesting 24 so why isn't the maximum sustained harvest the optimal harvest?

Stock size	Growth
0	0
10	9
20	16
30	21
40	24
50	25
60	24
70	21
80	16
90	9
100	0

FIGURE 10.8 Natural Growth for Various Levels of Renewable Resource Stock

SOLUTION

The reason that the maximum sustained yield does not generate the highest present value of profit from harvesting has to do with discounting and when the harvester gets revenue.

Suppose the clam harvesting firm started with a stock of 50 clams. If the firm harvested according to maximum sustained yield it would harvest 25 clams every period. If the firm could literally sell clams from now to eternity and $r = 20\%$, the present value of clam harvests is

$$V = (P - c) * 25 + \frac{(P - c) * 25}{1.2} + \frac{(P - c) * 25}{(1.2)^2} + \frac{(P - c) * 25}{(1.2)^3} + \cdots = 150(P - c)$$

If the firm instead follows the golden rule of growth it will harvest 35 clams in the first period (25 of natural growth plus 10 more so the resource stock falls from 50 to 40). From that point forward, the firm will harvest 24 clams. The present value of clam harvests following this rule is

$$V = (P - c) * 35 + \frac{(P - c) * 24}{1.2} + \frac{(P - c) * 24}{(1.2)^2} + \frac{(P - c) * 24}{(1.2)^3} + \cdots = 156(P - c)$$

The firm gets to have a bonus of extra harvesting in the initial period when there is no discounting and this more than makes up for the loss of the harvest of one clam per period in all future periods.

Put another way, the intuition of the golden rule goes like this:

1. If MG(S) is greater than r, then the firm is better off growing the stock to a larger size, and profiting off the larger future harvest. This in turn will drive MG(S) down to r.
2. If MG(S) is less than r, then the firm is better off liquidating some of the stock, selling it and banking the interest. This in turn will drive MG(S) up to r.

This puzzle shows that discounting was the key factor explaining the difference between the maximum sustained yield and the harvest satisfying the golden rule of growth that maximized the present value of returns. Indeed, if the discount rate were zero, then the golden rule of growth harvest and the maximum sustained yield would be identical. Both rules would set the resource stock at the point of maximum growth (this can be seen in Figure 10.7) as the point at which the slope of the growth function is zero (i.e., where MG(S) = r = 0).

But what about the other extreme? What if the discount rate is really high or the resource is very slow growing? In 1973, mathematical biologist Colin Clark wrote a paper entitled "Profit Maximization and Extinction of Animal Species" (Clark 1973). In this article, Clark showed that for very slow growing species, or very impatient harvesters, the profit-maximizing solution was to harvest the stock to zero—to deliberately cause extinction! The logic of this unsavory outcome is quite straightforward. The resource-harvesting firm earns more money by harvesting the resource and investing the money in higher yield alternative assets rather than conserving the slow-growing (low-return) species. Clark's main point here was NOT to advocate for harvesting to extinction. He was showing the inexorable logic of profit maximization and what it might mean for species.[9]

Several important factors might prevent such a dire outcome from ever occurring. First, as a species gets rarer and harvests decline, its price will tend to rise (remember scarcity rent discussed earlier). The anticipation of future high prices might be enough

---

9. In the same vein, high discount rates in the Hotelling model will lead to extraction patterns heavily biased toward the present, and by extension, rapid run-ups in resource prices.

to get some resource stock owners to conserve. Second, species often have value independent of harvest. Most people like panda bears and giraffes place great value on their existence even though they have no harvest value. Many species have **existence value**, which is literally a value that people have for the continued existence of the species. If existence value is high enough and resource owners can be paid for existence value it will never be profit maximizing to cause extinction. Generally speaking, private owners of renewable and nonrenewable resources are incentivized to engage in some level of **profit-based conservation**, and not immediately liquidate the resources they own.

Extinction pressure may come through another route—open-access resource harvesting that leads to "the tragedy of the commons" (see Chapter 3). Suppose that instead of clams, Billsville was famous for "Billfish" that swim in the ocean off the coast. And suppose that anyone who wants to can go and catch fish. As long as there is a profit from catching fish someone will go and catch more fish. There is no incentive for any individual fisherman (or fisherwoman) to conserve the fish stock because someone else will catch the fish. In the case of open access it is as if there was an infinitely high discount rate because no individual can afford to think about the future. As long as it remains possible to profitably harvest a species even as it gets very rare, then the species will be hunted or fished to extinction.

10.5 Renewable Resource Policy: Fisheries and Endangered Species

As discussed in Chapter 3, the solution for tragedy of the commons is to set some type of limit on harvest. Fisheries with functioning quota systems that limit harvests have generally been successful at sustainable management while those that have not generally seen overfishing and large declines in stock abundance (see Costello, Gaines, and Lynham 2008).

The standard regulatory recommendation for fisheries management from economists is a form of a cap-and-trade system called an **individual transferable quota** or **ITQ**. (For more on the generic pros and cons of marketable permits, see Chapters 16 and 17.) The basic idea is that a fisheries board sets a total allowable catch (TAC), preferably at the efficient level, but definitely at or below the maximum sustained yield. Then each fisher receives a permit allowing a certain percentage of the TAC, equivalent to a specified tonnage of fish. These quotas can then be bought and sold, but at the end of the season, a fisher needs to be in possession of enough quotas to cover his or her total catch, or else face a stiff fine. How are ITQs distributed? They can be auctioned by the government, or they can be given away to existing fishers on a "grandfathered" basis; that is, fishers receive an allocation based on their catch history.

The advantage of ITQs over rigid allowances is the flexibility built into the system. If a boat is having a particularly good season, the owner can purchase or lease additional quota from vessels not having as much luck. And over the long run, more efficient fishers can buy out less efficient operators. Some have criticized ITQ for this kind of impact. ITQ systems encourage the departure of small operators, leaving more efficient boats (sometimes giant factory trawlers) a larger share of the market. While this may lead to a lower cost industry, it also leads to consolidation in an industry traditionally hosting small, independent producers.

A variety of practical problems are inherent in the implementation of any kind of fisheries regulation, including ITQs. Generic problems include political influence over fisheries boards, leading to excessive TAC levels, and difficulty monitoring mobile sources like fishing boats. The so-called bycatch—fish accidentally caught for which boats don't have permits—is also a problem. Bycatch is often dumped overboard to avoid fines—a wasteful process. New Zealand has been our major laboratory for ITQs; most of the nation's fisheries have adopted the system. The results have been generally positive. While some small fishers have exited, they were the unprofitable ones to begin with.

Researchers have found that "the industry started out with a few big players (especially vertically integrated catch and food processing companies) and many small fishing enterprises, and it looks much the same today. The size of holdings of the larger companies, however, has increased." In other words, small producers generally managed to survive, but big producers have gotten bigger. Fish populations have either stabilized or improved under the ITQ system, and fishers have altered their practices to avoid bycatch and stay below permitted levels. And finally, the total value produced by the fishery more than doubled between 1990 and 2000.[10]

ITQ systems are one way to overcome the open-access problem. A second way is to assign individual property rights in ocean resources to fish farmers. **Aquaculture**—the commercial raising and harvesting of fish in ocean environments over which fishers are granted exclusive rights—is an old industry with its roots in oyster farming. But in recent years the industry has expanded into freshwater species such as catfish and tilapia and ocean-raised salmon and shrimp. The U.S. industry more than doubled in size between 1985 and 2000.[11]

Aquaculture has the potential to significantly decrease pressure on natural fisheries as well as boost the productivity of the oceans. However, as currently practiced, aquaculture generates significant negative externalities, including the impact on the immediate ocean environment from fish waste, heavy metals, pesticides, and antibiotics. In addition, fish feed for the carnivorous species such as salmon is often harvested unsustainably in the open ocean; approximately one-third of the world's total annual ocean catch is currently used for fish food! And finally, aquaculture can destroy local habitats. For example, many of Thailand's mangrove swamps—shoreline stabilizers—have been cut down and converted to shrimp farms.[12]

In a world likely to be inhabited by more than half as many people by 2050, our ocean commons need to be maintained as an important source of both food and biodiversity. Effectively managing and restoring fisheries is a critical task. Some combination of ITQ management for open-ocean fisheries (combined with regulations protecting habitat) and sustainable aquaculture must provide the answers.

One point worth stressing is that there is large uncertainty about the likely future level of many resource stocks. The populations of many species are subject to great

---

10. See Sanchirico and Newell (2003).
11. Fisheries Statistics and Economics Division, U.S. National Marine Fisheries Service (www.nmfs.gov).
12. See Goldberg (2001) and Nash (2001).

variability. Disease outbreaks or unfavorable weather (drought, flood and extreme cold or heat) can result in sudden large population reductions. Even seemingly minor environmental changes have led to large changes. Fish populations in particular are subject to high year to year variability in "recruitment," the number of fish born that survive to maturity. Trying to maintain a steady harvest policy, such as maximum sustained yield or the golden rule of growth harvest, in the face of highly variable populations is likely to lead to trouble. For example, suppose that unfavorable environmental conditions lead to growth being reduced by 50%. Keeping harvest at maximum sustained yield set under normal circumstances will result in harvests that greatly exceed natural growth. The stock level will then fall. With lower stock, growth will be reduced. If harvest levels are maintained this will cause further stock declines leading to a vicious downward spiral.

Highly variable resource stocks should cause resource managers to continually adjust harvest levels to try to maintain stocks at desired levels. In fact, some work on fisheries with variable recruitment has shown that the optimal management policy is to aim for a constant population size in which harvests expand in good years and contract in poor years to match growth.[13] But this places a lot of burden on getting accurate information and often puts managers at odds with harvesters who don't want to be told to cut back on harvests. And there is often political pressure to keep harvest rates up even when there is evidence that the stock is falling, which intensifies the problem of declining resources.[14]

When future conditions are highly uncertain, it is often not possible to make decisions about harvest rates and conservation in the same way as when there is certainty about what the future holds. For example, if fish harvesting quotas are set assuming an average year but it turns out to be a very poor year, the quota may greatly exceed what is sustainable. This fact has led some economists to advocate what is called a **safe minimum standard** (**SMS**) for threatened resources with uncertain future value. SMS advocates argue that unique resources should be preserved at levels that prevent their irreversible depletion, unless the costs of doing so are "unacceptably" high.[15] The SMS is thus another version of the precautionary principle. In a fisheries context, the SMS sometimes takes the form of setting aside **Marine Protected Areas** for species recovery.

Figure 10.9 illustrates the basic idea behind the SMS. The horizontal axis shows the current stock of a renewable resource, in this case, mating pairs of spotted owls in a forested area. The S-shaped line relates the stock of owls alive today to the stock of owls around next year, graphed on the vertical axis. So, for example, if there are seven pairs alive this year, there will be five pairs alive next year, thus implying that the natural death rate exceeds the birth rate. Carrying this logic further, if there are 5 pairs next year, there will be only 2.5 pairs the year after that, and so on, to extinction. Points on the 45-degree line reflect stable populations, because the number of owls in the next period is the same as in current period.

---

13. See Reed (1979) and Costello, Polasky, and Solow (2001).
14. See Ludwig, Hilborn, and Walters (1993) for an assessment of the problems of managing renewable resources with uncertainty.
15. Bishop (1978) introduced the "unreasonable cost" constraint. Both he and Ciriacy-Wantrup (1968) argue as well that the costs of preservation are, on a society-wide basis, likely to be low.

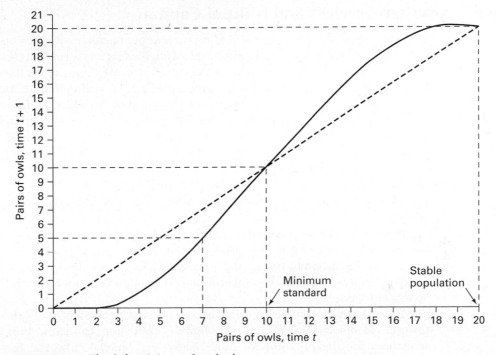

FIGURE 10.9 The Safe Minimum Standard

The point where the S curve first crosses the 45-degree line (10 pairs) is called the minimum standard (MS); any fewer owl pairs than the MS, and the species begins to decline in numbers, eventually slipping into extinction. With more pairs than the MS, however, the species will recover, as a given stock this period produces a larger stock next period, and so on. Eventually, the population size will stabilize at 20 pairs. (Extra credit question: Why does the S curve bend back down and not keep rising?)

The SMS lies somewhere to the right of the MS—say 12 or 14 pairs—at the point where the resource can be guaranteed to recover on its own. Getting too close to MS would allow some bad outcome to push the spotted owl below MS and put the owl on the road to extinction.

The SMS argument is often applied to endangered species. Each species has highly unique biological properties as well as uncertain future genetic value; and *Jurassic Park* aside, species extinction is irreversible. Moreover, endangered species often serve as **indicator species** for threatened ecosystems. Thus, saving the spotted owl in the Pacific Northwest means saving a complex and biodiverse old-growth forest ecosystem. Especially considering their role as indicators, endangered species clearly merit protection under a precautionary principle approach.

In fact, as we noted in the last chapter and will explore further in Chapter 13, endangered species legislation is the one major national law currently on the books that reflects ecological sustainability as an underlying goal. The law states that natural capital in the form of species must be protected from extinction, regardless of the cost.

10.6 Ecosystem Services and Natural Capital

Economic analysis of renewable and nonrenewable resources focuses on the rate of use of particular resource stocks. This type of analysis is clearly relevant for such things as fish harvested commercially, oil lifted from the ground, or metals mined. But the ways in which the natural world contributes to human well-being are much broader than just the supply of these resources. Ecosystem processes filter pollution, pollinate crops, regulate climate, improve soil fertility, and provide numerous other ecosystem services on which human well-being depends. In this section, we consider the much broader issue of managing ecosystems to supply a wide range of ecosystem services rather than managing for one specific resource.

Ecosystem management differs from specific resource management for three main reasons: joint production, unintended consequences, and the importance of spatial analysis.

Ecosystem management involves **joint production** of multiple ecosystem services. For example, a forest not only produces timber but also provides habitat for game species, stores carbon to reduce the amount of CO_2 in the atmosphere, filters air and water pollutants, and prevents soil erosion. There often are important tradeoffs among ecosystem services.

Ecosystems are complex, interconnected systems. Ecosystem management directed toward one objective, like increasing timber production, can cause **unintended consequences** for the provision of other ecosystem services, like the loss of habitat for forest-dwelling species. Minimizing the unintended consequences of management actions requires first understanding how ecosystems function. How might cutting trees for timber in a particular location affect the ecological process in the forest? For example, will timber harvests lead to increased soil erosion that will cause buildup of silt in nearby streams that can affect fish and other aquatic life? Gaining this type of understanding is primarily a question for environmental scientists.

But minimizing unintended consequences also requires providing incentives so that decision makers, be they private landowners, firms, or government agencies, take proper account of the consequences on the multiple ecosystem services affected by their decisions. For example, if cutting trees near streams leads to water quality problems then there may be a need for either regulation that mandates a buffer along streams or incentives that make it costly to cut trees near streams without taking precautions for water quality concerns. The task of designing regulations or incentives falls in the lap of environmental economists, often working closely with environmental scientists.

Ecosystem management for ecosystem services also puts a premium on **spatial analysis**. Much of economics ignores *where* things happen. But for ecosystem services *where* is often the crucial question. There is great variability in ecosystems because of differences in climate, soil, and other environmental variables so that ecosystem services are only provided in certain locations and not others. Forests grow only where there is adequate moisture and suitable temperatures. Deserts occur in places with little rainfall. The location of ecosystems in relation to the location of people is also an important determinant of the value of ecosystem services. For example, coastal wetlands absorb the energy from waves and reduce the risk of flooding further inland. If coastal wetlands protect towns or cities further inland, the value of coastal protection services will be high. But if no one lives near the wetland then there is little value from coastal protection. Some ecosystem services require close proximity of different elements. For example, the ecosystem service of pollination depends on having close proximity of pollinators, which often require natural habitat, and agricultural fields that have crops that need pollination. For all of these reasons, ecosystem management for ecosystem services requires spatial analysis that addresses questions of where things occur.

Analysis of ecosystem services is relatively new in economics. The vast majority of the work by economists on ecosystem services has happened since the publication of the Millennium Ecosystem Assessment in 2005, and much of this has happened in just the past couple of years. One influential article completed prior to 2005 addressed the question of the economic value of conserving intact ecosystems (Balmford et al. 2002). This analysis compared the benefits of services generated by relatively intact natural ecosystems versus the benefits of services generated from systems that had been heavily modified by human uses.

The authors compared "reduced impact logging" to "conventional logging" in Malaysia; "reduced impact logging" to "plantation conversion" in the Cameroon; "intact mangrove" ecosystems to shrimp farming in Thailand; "intact wetlands" in Canada to intensively farmed lands; and "sustainable fishing" to "destructive fishing" in coral reef ecosystems in the Philippines. The study included the value from a wide range of services, such as the value of timber harvesting, crop production, fisheries, water supply, hunting and gathering activities, recreation, carbon sequestration, and protection of endangered species. In all of the five cases analyzed, the value of ecosystem services generated by a relatively intact natural ecosystem exceeded the value from heavily modified ecosystems. Plantation forestry in Cameroon actually had negative net benefits (operation costs exceeded the benefits) and was only possible to carry out because of government subsidies.

Making the comparison across alternative ecosystem management requires knowing the level of service provision for each ecosystem service under each alternative. Estimates of service provision can be generated by looking at data for both intact and modified systems or by using **ecological production functions**. Production functions in economics predict the output of final goods that can be made with a certain amount of inputs (labor, machinery, and raw material). Ecological production functions predict the provision of ecosystem services (output) given the state of the ecosystem (input). Ecological production functions are useful for predicting how ecosystem service provision will change if the ecosystem is altered, either because of climate change, land use change, or changes in management.

A recent study of ecosystem service provision by Nelson et al. (2009) used ecological production functions combined with economic valuation to show the impact of alternative land use scenarios on ecosystem service provision in the Willamette Basin in the state of Oregon. The study used a model called InVEST (Integrated Valuation of Ecosystem Services and Tradeoffs) to predict how land-use change under three scenarios (business-as-usual, development, and conservation) would affect carbon sequestration, flooding, water quality (phosphorus loadings), erosion, biodiversity conservation, and the combined market value of timber production, agricultural crop production, and housing development.

Applying the InVEST model, Nelson and colleagues quantified the amount of increase in ecosystem services under the conservation scenario compared to the other two scenarios. The conservation scenario preserved more natural areas compared to the other two scenarios and resulted in greater provision of ecosystem services. The only exception to this outcome was that the combined market value from timber, agriculture, and housing was lower under the conservation scenario. If landowners are only paid for market values they will tend to prefer either the business-as-usual or development scenarios. However, for society as a whole, the value of the other ecosystem services makes the value of the conservation scenario higher than either of the other two scenarios. Nelson and colleagues showed that providing payments even for only one ecosystem service, sequestering carbon, would be enough to make the conservation scenario generate higher value to landowners compared to the other scenarios. In this case, instituting a scheme for carbon payments would provide enough incentive for landowners to conserve more land, which would generate higher payments to landowners and would also be good for species conservation (Figure 10.10).

Many of the benefits generated by more intact ecosystems come from public goods. Private landowners or firms generally do not capture these benefits. Often they are better off converting land to realize private benefits even though this may result in loss of the benefits from public goods. For example, a farmer who drains a wetland to

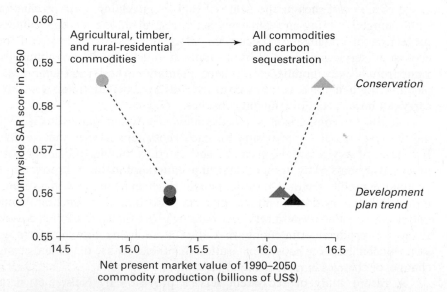

FIGURE 10.10 The value of marketed commodities and biodiversity conservation under the conservation, development, and plan trend (business-as-usual) scenarios. Without paying for ecosystem services there is a tradeoff between biodiversity conservation and values for landowners (illustrated by the circles). With payment for carbon, values for landowners and biodiversity conservation are higher under the conservation scenario (illustrated with the triangles).

Source: Nelson et al. (2009)

plant crops can generate profit from selling the crops. Protecting the wetland does not generate income for the farmer, even though it provides habitat for ducks and other species, filters nutrients to provide cleaner water downstream, sequesters carbon, and regulates the flow of water. The farmer will typically choose to drain the wetland. Preserving the wetland to provide for public goods requires providing the farmer with incentives to do so.

One direct way to provide such incentives is to institute a program of **payment for ecosystem services (PES)**. In a PES program, landowners who agree to certain land use or management practices that generate ecosystem services are paid for doing so. For example, municipal water supply agencies in Quito, Ecuador and in New York City have targeted payments to landowners in watershed areas that supply water for these cities. A properly designed PES will result in payments being sufficiently attractive so that the landowners are better off with conservation, and cities are better off because they get clean water more cheaply than having to build expensive water treatment plants to clean up polluted water. New York City was able to forestall the construction of an expensive water filtration system by instituting programs to protect watersheds in the Catskill Mountains that are the source of drinking water for the city. PES expenditures to date—paying farmers to adopt best management practices for livestock and towns and households to upgrade their sewage and septic systems—have been far less than the cost of building and operating a water filtration system.

The values of ecosystem services can be large and if properly taken into account could lead to many changes in ecosystem management. There is huge interest at present in finding out how economic decisions affect the provision of ecosystem services and whether society would benefit from greater protection of specific ecosystems. Such information can be important in evaluating the costs and benefits of local or regional projects. Such information is also important in calculating national-level accounts of net national welfare or inclusive wealth (see Chapter 9).

10.7 Summary

This chapter has looked more deeply into the economics of nonrenewable and renewable resources (traditional resource economics), and the much more recent analyses focused on the economic value of ecosystem services. Resource economics provides guidance for firms interested in maximizing profits from the resources they control. And assuming that firms follow that advice, resource economics makes predictions about how firms will conserve, or exploit, resource stocks.

The key to resource economics comes from understanding that holding resources is a form of investment. If nonrenewable prices (or more technically, resource rents) are rising more slowly than the rate of interest, the Hotelling model shows that it makes economic sense for holders of resources to develop more of the stock today instead of holding it for the future. This way, they can make money now and bank the money at a higher rate of interest. This in turn reduces supply in the future, and raises prices (and resource rents) in the future. Ultimately, prices in equilibrium will have to rise at the rate of interest to stop this kind of arbitrage. The reverse logic also holds: persuade yourself what you should do if prices are rising more rapidly than the rate of interest.

Following this logic, the model concludes that in a world of perfect foresight, competitive firms should allocate stocks of nonrenewable natural resources in such a manner that prices rise sufficiently to ensure that the resource rent increases at close to the rate of interest. The observed failure of resource prices to rise over the last 40 years may reflect either no imminent shortage or, in the case of oil, imperfect information about the size of global oil reserves, in part driven by differing assessments about the pace of technical change allowing the exploitation of lower grade fuel deposits.

Concerns about peak oil can thus best be understood as concerns about the failure of the Hotelling model's predictions to come true. If prices fail to rise steadily well in advance of hitting the peak, then there are no strong market signals driving the development of substitute technologies. In that case, a global economy addicted to oil would suffer through an extended period of painful withdrawal. And indeed, if at that time, clean substitutes for oil are not yet available, it is not clear if a crippled global economic system would then be able to deliver them.

Similar to nonrenewable resource markets, conserving renewable resources for future harvest is a form of investment. However, here things are complicated by the fact that renewable resources grow naturally over time. The Golden Rule in this case tells resource managers to shift their harvesting practices (either decreasing or increasing them) so that the marginal growth rate of the resource stock (the change in the growth rate) is just equal to the rate of interest.

Here again, high discount rates will drive higher rates of near-term exploitation (and smaller optimal stocks) as firms seek to derive near-term gain, and bank those gains. If the interest rate is high enough, or resource growth is slow enough, the cold-blooded, profit-maximizing strategy would be to drive the resource to extinction and invest the profits from liquidation elsewhere in the economy. Again, economists do not endorse this idea. We just note that it is the logic of profit maximization in a renewable resource market.

In general, in both nonrenewable and renewable markets, resource owners do have some profit-based incentive for conservation, driven either by the prospect of rising prices or the growth of the underlying resource. Open access—when ownership of resources is not defined—can be thought of as a resource situation with very high discount rates. If one actor restrains from catching fish (or lifting oil or water out of a common underground pool) he or she receives very little benefit in the future, as the catch (or oil or water) will be scooped up by a competitor. Thus profit-based incentives for conservation are undermined.

In the real world, growth functions for some resources are not typically as well-defined or stable as the inverted U shape we have illustrated here. Fisheries managers, for example, typically set TAC levels to sustain species, not necessarily at the profit-maximizing level. ITQs can improve efficiency and help managers keep their fisheries within the TAC. In cases when conditions are highly variable and there is some risk of allowing unsustainable catch, a SMS can be imposed; in the fisheries context this might involve the creation of Marine Protected Areas to support sufficient breeding stock to ensure recovery of the species. The SMS is an application of the precautionary principle.

Finally, economists, working with environmental scientists, have only recently begun to model the complex ecosystem processes which generate ecosystem services. These services include provisioning, regulating, supporting, and cultural services. Ecosystem processes typically involve joint production of multiple services; managing the system for one services, such as timber production, and have unintended consequences on the provision of other services, such as carbon sequestration. In addition, ecosystem services must be studied from a spatial perspective. The magnitude and type of services generated by an ecosystem will vary as a result of differences in underlying earth system characteristics: geology, hydrology, micro-climates, and more.

The last three chapters have explored the economic impacts of decisions taken today on the well-being of future generations, to assess the underlying goal of sustainability. The goal is easy to understand conceptually—we want to maintain or improve the quality of life for the typical member of generations to come. However, we have seen that putting it into practice requires judgments about the degree to which manufactured, social, and human capital can offset reductions in natural capital in the production of goods and services critical to human well-being. We now leave this conversation and turn to one final debate: what does economic growth really buy us? If we get richer, do we get happier? And if not, then why "pave paradise to put up a parking lot"?

APPLICATION 10.0

The mineral unobtainium is a valuable nonrenewable resource with a total estimated supply of 74 million tons. Suppose that the inverse demand curve for the unobtainium in each of the two periods is $P_t = 200 - 2Q_t$, where Q_t is quantity in time period t measured in millions of tons and P is the price in time period t. The discount rate is 10%.

a. Use Hotelling's rule to solve for the amount of unobtainium produced in period 1 and in period 2, and the price for unobtainium in periods 1 and 2.

b. Suppose that a new discovery of a large unobtainium ore deposit adds to the supply so that now there are 95 million tons rather than 74 million tons. Use Hotelling's rule to solve for the amount of unobtainium produced in period 1 and in period 2, and the price for unobtainium in periods 1 and 2. How does your answer for production and price compare to that in (a)? Explain the economic intuition for these changes.

c. Now suppose that the interest rate falls from 10 to 5% and that supply is 95 million tons. Use Hotelling's rule to solve for the amount of unobtainium produced in period 1 and in period 2, and the price for unobtainium in periods 1 and 2. How does your answer for production and price compare to that in (b)? Explain the economic intuition for these changes.

APPLICATION 10.1

There is a fish species that grows according to logistic growth:

$$S_{t+1} = S_t + g * S_t * \left(1 - \frac{S_t}{K}\right)$$

where S_t is the number of fish in period t, S_{t+1} is the number of fish in the next period $(t + 1)$, K is natural carrying capacity (maximum fish population), and g is the intrinsic growth rate. Assume that $g = 1$ and $K = 500$. Assume that the price of fish in the market is \$10 per fish. For simplicity assume that it costs \$5 per fish to harvest fish. Assume the discount rate is 10%.

    a.   If in period t there are 200 fish, how many fish will there be in the next period, $t + 1$? What is the growth of the fish population where growth equals $S_{t+1} - S_t$?

    b.   Plot the growth of the fish population as a function of current fish population by solving for $S_{t+1} - S_t$ for values of $S_t = 0, 50, 100, 150, 200, 250, 300, 350, 400, 450$, and 500.

    c.   Using your answer to (b), at what level of population does growth reach its highest point? Note that this is the maximum sustained yield population level. How much growth is there at this level of population? Note that this is the maximum sustained yield. How much profit would harvesters make if they harvested the maximum sustained yield?

    d.   What happens to growth if the population is at carrying capacity $(S_t = K)$? What happens to growth if, for some reason, the population temporarily exceeded carrying capacity?

    e.   For logistic growth, the Marginal Growth Function is $MG(S_t) = g * \left(1 - \frac{2S_t}{K}\right)$. Use the golden rule of growth to find the level of stock that maximizes the present value of harvest. How does this level of stock compare to the maximum sustained yield level of stock? How does the level of harvest compare?

    f.   Now suppose that the discount rate is zero. Use the golden rule of growth to find the level of stock that maximizes the present value of harvest. How does this level of stock compare to the maximum sustained yield level of stock?

APPLICATION 10.2

The county of Greenlandia has four regions. Information for the four regions is shown in Table 10.1. Suppose there are three types of land use: (1) agriculture, (2) managed forestry and (3) conservation to maintain native habitat. As a land manager, you must choose a land use for each of the four regions (note: you can choose different land uses in the different regions). You are interested in the following objectives: (1) carbon sequestration, (2) water quality, (3) agricultural production, (4) timber production, (5) forest birds, and (6) grassland birds. Consider the following simple "models" of provision of ecosystem services and biodiversity conservation:

    •   Carbon: 100 units of carbon in native forest, 70 units of carbon in managed forest, 50 units of carbon in native prairie, and 20 units of carbon in agriculture.

TABLE 10.1 Information about Greenlandia

Region (1)	Region (2)
Native habitat type: prairie	Native habitat type: forest
Agricultural productivity: high	Agricultural productivity: low
Forest productivity: low	Forest productivity: high
Water quality impact: high	Water quality impact: low
Region (3)	**Region (4)**
Native habitat type: forest	Native habitat type: forest
Agricultural productivity: high	Agricultural productivity: low
Forest productivity: high	Forest productivity: low
Water quality impact: high	Water quality impact: low

- Water quality: native habitat (forest or prairie): 100 units of water quality in high impact zones and 50 units of water quality in low impact zones; managed forests: 60 units of water quality in high impact zones and 30 units of water quality in low impact zones; agriculture: 0 units of water quality in either zone.
- Agricultural production (occurs only on land put into agricultural production): 100 units of production in high agricultural productivity zones and 20 units of production in low agricultural productivity zones.
- Timber production (occurs only on land put into managed forest): 100 units of production in high timber productivity zones and 20 units of production in low timber productivity zones.
- Forest birds: 100 units for native forest habitat, 50 units for managed forest, and 0 units for prairie or agriculture. If a forest unit shares a border (corners do not count) with agriculture then the forest bird score is reduced by 50%.
- Grassland birds: 100 units for native prairie, 20 units for agriculture, and 0 units for native forest or managed forest.

a. What is the land use plan you would choose if you were trying to maximize the score for forest birds? For this land use plan, what is the score for each of your objectives (carbon, water quality, agricultural production, timber production, forest birds, and grassland birds)?

b. What is the land use plan you would choose if you were trying to maximize the score for grassland birds? For this land use plan, what is the score for each of your objectives (carbon, water quality, agricultural production, timber production, forest birds, and grassland birds)?

c. Suppose that private landowners wish to maximize the market value of production from their land and suppose that each unit of agricultural production is worth $2 and each unit of timber production is worth $1 (i.e., they wish to maximize 2 * agricultural production + 1 * timber production). What would each land owner choose to maximize their market returns? For this land use result, what is the score for each of your objectives (carbon, water quality, agricultural production, timber production, forest birds, and grassland birds)?

d. Suppose that we instituted a "payments for ecosystem services" program. If landowners are paid $1 for each unit of carbon and $1 for each unit of water quality, what would each landowner choose if they were interested in maximizing their sum of market returns (2 * agricultural production + 1 * timber production) and payments for ecosystem services? For this land use result, what is the score for each of your objectives (carbon, water quality, agricultural production, timber production, forest birds, and grassland birds)?

e.   Suppose we expanded the "payments for ecosystem services" program so that it also paid landowners $1 for each unit of forest birds and $1 for each unit of grassland birds. Now what would each landowner choose if they were interested in maximizing their sum of market returns (2 * agricultural production + 1 * timber production), payments for ecosystem services, and bird conservation? For this land use plan, what is the score for each of your objectives (carbon, water quality, agricultural production, timber production, forest birds, and grassland birds)?

KEY IDEAS IN EACH SECTION

10.0   Traditional resource economics focused on **nonrenewable** and **renewable** resources. More recent analysis has recognized that natural capital also includes the **ecosystem processes** that underlie **ecosystem services**. These services include provisioning, regulating, supporting, and cultural services.

10.1   The **Hotelling rule** illustrates that in competitive markets, a profit-maximizing equilibrium will occur in which the resource rents generated from scarce, nonrenewable resources will rise at the rate of interest. A **choke price** is defined as the price at which demand falls to zero: the choke price reflects the existence of a **back-stop technology** to which users switch at a given price.

10.2   Hotelling predicts that markets will signal scarcity with steadily rising prices, providing incentives and time for firms to invest in substitutes. This was not true for nonrenewable resources until 2000, but since then, prices for most commodities, including oil, have risen. (The exception is natural gas, where new "fracking" technology has unexpectedly increased global reserves.) Prior to 2000, most resource markets were not signaling scarcity, but now appear to be.

10.3   Historically, individual oil fields exhibit an inverted U shape for production. Hubbert predicted the same would be true for regional and global oil supplies. The challenges to assessing the timing of global **peak oil** include poor information about the size of the existing oil stocks, and disagreement about technological change that might make exploitation of currently marginal oil sources economic. As a result, we do not know if peak oil will occur soon and suddenly, causing large-scale disruption, or gradually and manageably.

10.4   Renewable resources can be characterized by a **growth function** relating the growth in a given period to the size of the stock at the beginning of the period. Growth functions sometimes display **density-dependent growth**. A **sustainable harvest** is one in which the size of the stock does not decline over time, and the **Maximum Sustainable Yield** is the largest possible sustainable harvest. For renewable resources, the **Golden Rule**

of Growth tells profit-maximizing managers to adjust their harvests up or down so that the **marginal growth rate** MG(S), is equal to the interest rate. If the discount rate is high enough or the growth rate low enough, profit maximization can lead to liquidation of the resource, and investment of the resource rents elsewhere. Generally, however, both renewable and nonrenewable resource owners do have incentives for **profit-based conservation**.

10.5   In fisheries, **Total Allowable Catch (TAC)** levels are set to try and control open-access and ensure sustainability of the fishery. **Individual Transferable Quotas (ITQs)** can reduce the problem of excessive capitalization: too many boats chasing a set number of fish. **Aquaculture** also helps solve the open-access problem, but has its own environmental challenges. **Safe Minimum Standard (SMS)** management is used for threatened and endangered species, where stock levels ensuring species recovery are required. SMS is thus an application of the precautionary principle.

10.6   **Ecosystem services** are provided by underlying **ecological processes**. The flow from processes to services is modeled using an **ecological production function**. Ecosystems typically produce **joint outputs**; focusing management attention to optimize the production or harvest of a single output can lead to **unintended consequences** in terms of reduction in other outputs. Finally ecological production functions vary across geographies, requiring a focus on **spatial analysis**. Ecosystem service modeling is quite recent, but the results suggest that the value of intact ecosystems can be higher than the value of individual commodity production that degrades the ecosystem. One way to preserve the services is through **payment for ecosystem services (PES)** policies.

REFERENCES

Balmford, Andrew, Aaron Bruner, Philip Cooper, Robert Costanza, Stephen Farber, Rhys E. Green, Martin Jenkins, et al. 2002. Economic reasons for conserving wild nature. *Science* 297: 950–53.

Barnett, Harold J., and Chandler Morse. 1963. *Scarcity and growth: The economics of natural resource availability*. Washington, DC: Johns Hopkins University Press.

Bishop, Richard C. 1978. Endangered species, irreversibility, and uncertainty: The economics of a safe minimum standard. *American Journal of Agricultural Economics* 60(1): 10–8.

Ciriacy-Wantrup, S. V. 1968. Resource conservation: Economics and policies. 3rd ed. Berkeley: University of California Press.

Clark, Colin. 1973. Profit maximization and the extinction of animal species, *Journal of Political Economy* 81: 950–61.

Costello, Christopher, Steven Gaines, and John Lynham. 2008. Can catch shares prevent fisheries collapse? *Science* 321: 1678–81.

Costello, Christopher, Stephen Polasky, and Andrew Solow. 2001. Renewable resource management with

environmental prediction. *Canadian Journal of Economics* 34(1): 196–211.

Daly, Herman. 1996. *Beyond growth: The economics of sustainable development*. Boston: Beacon Press.

Goldberg, R. J., M. S. Elliot, and R. L. Taylor. 2001. *Marine aquaculture in the United States*. Arlington, VA: Pew Oceans Commission.

Hotelling, Harold. 1931. The economics of exhaustible resources. *Journal of Political Economy* 39: 137–75.

International Energy Agency (IEA). 2012. *World energy outlook 2012*. Paris: International Energy Agency.

Krautkraemer, Jeffrey. 1998. Nonrenewable resource scarcity. *Journal of Economic Literature* 36(4): 2065–107.

Krautkraemer, Jeffrey. 2005. Economics of natural resource scarcity: The state of the debate. Discussion paper 05-14. Washington, DC: Resources for the Future.

Ludwig, Donald, Ray Hilborn, and Carl J. Walters. 1993. Uncertainty, resource exploitation, and conservation: lessons from history. *Science* 260: 17, 36.

MacKenzie, James. 2000. *Oil as a finite resource: When is global production likely to peak?* Washington, DC: World Resources Institute.

Maugeri, Leonard. 2012. *Oil: The next revolution*. Discussion paper 2012-10, Belfer Center for Science and International Affairs. Cambridge, MA: Kennedy School of Government, Harvard University.

Millennium Ecosystem Assessment. 2005. *Living beyond our means: Natural assets and human well-being*. Washington, DC: Island Press.

Nash, Colin, ed. 2001. *The net-pen salmon farming industry in the Pacific Northwest*. Seattle, WA: Northwest Fisheries Science Center.

Nelson, Erik, Guillermo Mendoza, James Regetz, Stephen Polasky, Heather Tallis, D. Richard Cameron, Kai M. A. Chan, et al. 2009. Modeling multiple ecosystem services, biodiversity conservation, commodity production, and tradeoffs at landscape scales. *Frontiers in Ecology and the Environment* 7(1): 4–11.

Reed, William. 1979. Optimal escapement levels in stochastic and deterministic harvesting models. *Journal of Environmental Economics and Management* 6: 350–63.

Sanchirico, James, and Richard Newell. 2003. Catching market efficiencies. *Resources* 150: 8–11.

Sharman, Hugh. 2005. Why wind power works for Denmark. *Civil Engineering* 158: 66–72.

Shell Oil. 2008. World demand to outstrip supply. *Press Release*, 25 January. http://royaldutchshellplc.com/2008/01/24/the-times-shellchief-fears-oil-shortage-in-sevenyears/.

IS MORE REALLY BETTER?
CONSUMPTION AND WELFARE

11.0 Introduction

What were your grandfather and grandmother doing in 1955, when they might have been in their early twenties? Were they in college? Or working? If they were in school in the United States, then they had, on average, about 30% of your income. Put another way, in inflation-adjusted terms, for every $100 you spend a week, they spent only $30. What did that mean? They grew up in small houses without air conditioning; were very unlikely to own a car, a record player, or a typewriter; probably had never flown on a commercial airplane; hardly ever ate out in restaurants; seldom traveled away from their home city; had no Tylenol, Advil, or allergy medications (just aspirin); obviously, no smartphone, Internet, cable subscription, or ipod. Do you think you are happier than they were? If not, why not? If so, how much? A little? A lot? Are we making progress? Or are we a society mired in "overconsumption"?

Within the benefit-cost efficiency framework, there is simply no room for the concept of overconsumption. The whole point of doing a benefit-cost study, after all, is to ensure that we do not sacrifice too much consumption in pursuit of environmental quality. From an efficiency perspective, our generation's increase in consumption over what our parents enjoyed clearly reflects progress.

How then can overconsumption be viewed as an environmental problem? First, consumption (or affluence) crops up in the IPAT equation from Chapter 9:

$$\text{environmental Impact} = \text{Population} * \text{Affluence} * \text{Technology}$$

IPAT suggests that one of the three main causes of environmental decline is the growth in the consumption of material goods. Why? From an ecological perspective, pessimism is in order about the possibility for technological progress to keep up with the pace of consumption (and population) growth. Thus, for ecological economists, the fact that consumption levels are high and growing gets translated into overconsumption as a serious environmental problem. Efficiency advocates, by contrast, are technological optimists and so do not view consumption itself as a serious issue.

If, as ecologicals believe, technological progress cannot offset the environmental impact of a quadrupling of consumption over the next 50 years, then this is one sense in which overconsumption is indeed a major environmental issue. But this chapter focuses on a second argument against high consumption. It does so by questioning a key assumption of the efficiency standard and benefit-cost analysis: "More is better."

Recall that our target of an efficient outcome was defined as one in which it is impossible to make one person better off without making someone else worse off. In practice, *better off* means "having more goods." We should remember that goods can include environmental amenities, such as hikes in the mountains, nice views, or clean air, but these are considered by benefit-cost economists as simply goods that are literally exchangeable for hair conditioners, air conditioners, or video games. They are exchangeable because having more of one of these goods means having less of another. This in turn means they can ultimately be valued in monetary terms, if only indirectly, along the lines spelled out in Chapter 5.

But what if more isn't really better? If material gain in fact does not lead to greater happiness, then efficient outcomes do not really increase welfare. If more isn't better, then the trade-off identified by benefit-cost analysis—more environmental protection means less of all other stuff—loses much of its force, and safety or ecological sustainability goals make more sense. Finally, if more isn't better, then it is certainly fair to say that society is "overconsuming" resources.

11.1 Money and Happiness

One crude but accurate way to state the more-is-better assumption underlying benefit-cost analysis is that "money buys happiness." Does it? According to Jesus, Buddha, Poor Richard, and a recent fortune cookie, the answer is no. However, let's take a look at the more scientific findings of survey researchers on this issue.

For more than five decades, researchers have been asking groups of people about the relationship between income and happiness in their lives. The results of many studies in America and Western Europe reveal a strikingly similar conclusion: money does buy happiness, but it does so at a decreasing rate. Table 11.1 shows the results from a recent survey of 900 working women from Texas. Note that for comparison, median family income in the United States is about $50,000. These figures are typical of those found in most other studies and illustrate what has been called the **Easterlin paradox**: Rising income is clearly correlated with increased life satisfaction only up to around the median income level. It is well documented that rich people are not much happier than middle-class folks.[1]

Moreover, among Western countries, people in wealthier nations often report being less happy than those in poorer ones. Ireland, for example, with two-thirds of the per capita income of the United States, ranks consistently higher on the life-satisfaction scale.[2] And the percentage of the U.S. population reporting themselves to be "very

---

1. Easterlin (1974), Layard (2005), Kahneman and Krueger (2006).
2. There are substantial intercountry differences. The French, for example, claim to be much less happy than the Dutch. Researchers conclude that this in part reflects social norms about reporting life satisfaction.

TABLE 11.1   Income and Reported Happiness

Income ($)	Percent "Very Happy" (%)
< 20K	22
20K–49K	30
50K–89K	42
> 90K	43

Source: Kahneman et al. (2004).

happy" has remained roughly constant since the 1950s, despite personal consumption expenditures per capita having more than doubled.[3]

Why is it that money doesn't buy much happiness, and only does so up to a point? We consider two answers to this question, the first rooted in the psychology of consumption, the second in the material realities of modern life.

11.2 Social Norms and the Rat Race

Here is the famous economist Adam Smith, writing in the year 1759:

> From whence, then, arises that emulation which runs through all the different ranks of men, and what are the advantages which we propose by that great purpose of human life which we call bettering our condition? To be observed, to be attended to, to be taken notice of with sympathy, complacency, and approbation are all the advantages which we can propose to derive from it. It is the vanity, not the ease or the pleasure which interests us.[4]

If 250 years ago, Smith could declare that people sought to improve their material condition primarily for "vanity" as opposed to the "ease or pleasure" (utility) that came with increased consumption, imagine what he would conclude today, when individuals below the poverty line are, along many dimensions, richer than were the upper classes of Smith's era?

An 11-year-old friend recently reported to his mother that he wanted a pair of brightly colored, baggy pants manufactured by a company called Skidz. These pants were retailing for $54, and so his mother was a bit reluctant to buy him the pants. She offered to make him a pair that looked and felt identical, figuring she could do that for as little as $10. "No way," said her son. The homemade pair would not have the Skidz label on the back and that was really what made them *cool*. She asked him if he really wanted her to spend $44 for a label, and he said without hesitation, "Yes."

In our affluent society, access to food and shelter sufficient for *basic* survival is widely, though not universally, available. Under these circumstances, much consumption of goods and services takes on a profoundly "social" character. The utilitarian value of the Skidz pants—their warmth, comfort, and cheerfulness—was much less

3. Layard (2005).
4. Smith (1759, 70).

important to my friend than the idea that they were "way cool." Along the same lines, the pleasure felt by the owner of an expensive sports car lies not only in the excitement of fast driving but also, and perhaps more importantly, in the image of a fast-driving man the car provides to both the owner and others.

The social norms that we satisfy through our consumption are established in the communities in which we seek membership and recognition. The type of community may range from a romantic community of two to the nuclear or extended family, from a circle of friends to a neighborhood, or from a religious or ethnic group to a union or professional organization, but the need to belong to at least one of these groups is a powerful motivating force. Critics of growth argue that much of our consumption—from the clothes we wear to the food we eat to the cars we drive—is geared not only or even primarily to attain physical warmth, nourishment, comfort, or transportation but rather to attain membership and recognition in one of these communities.

The point here is *not* to pass a value judgment on this process in which we all participate. Rather, the idea of consumption norms simply explains the observation that money fails to buy much happiness. On one hand, greater income increases access to intrinsically useful goods and services. On the other, as people grow wealthier, the expectations of the community rise, and keeping up with social consumption norms becomes more costly.

One can divide the social motives for consumption into three rough categories: bandwagon, snob, and Veblen effects.[5] **Bandwagon effects** refer to a desire to consume something because others are as well, in order to conform to a social norm. Television commercials frequently play on the bandwagon effect. McDonald's ran a campaign advertising "Food, Folks, and Fun." The message was clear: come on down and join the party, and incidentally, you can eat here too.

At the same time, Burger King was trying to set itself off from the crowd with its slogan: "Sometimes, You Gotta Break the Rules." The appeal here was to the **snob effect**—the desire to do or consume something because others aren't. The snob effect is usually attributed to those buying expensive products to differentiate themselves from the common herd. But the sentiment may also be exploited, as in the Burger King case, to sell the humble hamburger. Or to take another example, it can be seen in the college professor who takes pride in driving a beat-up car to show that he, unlike the rest of the world, does not care about material goods. The desire for Skidz pants expressed by my young friend showed both bandwagon and snob influences—they were cool both because cool people were wearing them and because uncool people were not.

The words *bandwagon* and *snob* are perhaps poorly chosen, because they have rather negative connotations. But the desire to join in and the desire to be different in fact reflect quite normal, universal, and important social drives. For example, the desire to "get ahead" in any pursuit—sport, music, science—reflects both the snob effect (get ahead of one's peer group) and the bandwagon effect (become like those who are already ahead).

---

5. Leibenstein (1950). Bagwell and Bernheim (1996) explore the microfoundations of Veblen-type consumption decisions in a signaling context.

The final social motive underlying consumption is named for Thorstein Veblen, an economist who argued that status could often be achieved in our society through the open display of wealth, what he termed "conspicuous consumption."[6] The **Veblen effect** is the purchase of expensive goods to illustrate to the community that the owner is a person of "substance"—that is, someone with money and the power that money brings. Its purpose is to elicit envious statements such as "He wears a Rolex" or "She drives a BMW" or "He belongs to the High Society Country Club." Part of the "coolness" of Skidz pants was certainly their high price—wearing them said to the rest of the kids in the class: "My parents have got the power to get me what I want, even if it costs a lot of money." While the Veblen effect is related to the snob effect, the two are not identical. Veblen goods hold appeal primarily because their expense denotes membership in a certain social class; as noted, the definition of a snob good varies from consumer to consumer and need not involve expensive goods.

To the extent that material consumption is not geared to utilitarian functions but is rather a means to an end of satisfying social needs for membership and status in a community, it is not surprising that attaining more material goods fails to increase happiness to any significant degree. Among both poor and rich, bandwagon and snob effects will greatly influence the degree of satisfaction obtained from consumption. Whether it is the right smart-phone to impress your friends, the right bike for joining a motorcycle gang, the right T-shirt to wear to a party, the right beer to serve at a cookout, the right restaurant to please your sweetheart, the right suit to keep your job, the right school for your children, or the right street address to get into a particular golf foursome, membership and recognition in the community is an important by-product of consumption. As people get wealthier, "basic" needs multiply; in other words, it costs more to satisfy social norms.

Having said that, it is clear that many people do *want* more material things. Indeed, survey research reveals that "getting ahead" in terms of income is clearly correlated with increases in reported life satisfaction. While rich people are on average only a bit happier than poor people, people who have *recently* gotten richer are much more satisfied with their lives than people who have *recently* gotten poorer. Social satisfaction from consumption apparently requires not just keeping up but getting ahead of "the Joneses." *Exceeding* the consumption norms established by one's peer group, family, and personal expectations appears to be the material route to happiness.[7]

However, while getting ahead may make sense from the individual perspective, competitive consumption is a strategy that yields much smaller benefits to individuals when pursued at a society-wide level. If everyone is racing for entry into the next-highest social group, it becomes much harder to get there, and for every winner in the race, there will be losers. Moreover, everyone now needs to run harder just to stay in the same place.

The common name for this kind of situation is a **rat race**. The two distinguishing features of a rat race are that (1) everyone would be better off if the race was canceled and (2) given that everyone else is racing, each person is better off trying to win.

---

6. For a more recent reformulation, see Bagwell and Bernheim (1996).
7. These ideas are developed further in Daly (1987), Schor (1991), and Layard (2005).

This situation can be analyzed through the so-called prisoner's dilemma model. (Suggestion: stall your class by asking your professor to explain the name "prisoner's dilemma.") Figure 11.1 illustrates the situation facing two students, Arnold and Maria, who have been asked to bring soft drinks to a party. Each student can choose to bring either Coca-Cola or budget cola. For the purposes of argument, assume that the quality of the products are identical—blindfolded, people on average don't prefer one to the other. (Suggestion: stall your class by bringing in supplies for a demonstration taste test.) But Coke, given its large advertising budget, has developed some name recognition.

Suppose that the initial social norm among the students is to drink the budget brand. If both parties then go for the budget brand, nobody is embarrassed by bringing a product perceived to be cheap. As a result, the utility of both students is ten. This is clearly preferred to an outcome in which the social norm is to buy Coca-Cola—as the quality is the same, and the cost is higher. As a result, the Coke-Coke outcome yields utility of only eight to each student.

But in this setup, it will be hard to maintain budget-budget choices as the social norm. Consider what happens if Arnold goes budget while Maria shells out for Coke. Maria receives (subtle) praise for exceeding the social norm, so her utility rises to 12, while Arnold is (quietly) shamed and finds his utility falling to 7. The same holds true in reverse if Maria buys budget while Arnold goes with Coke.

Though both parties would prefer the budget-budget outcome, both have strong incentives to "cheat" on any informal agreement to maintain the budget-brand social norm. If on one hand Maria chooses budget, Arnold can gain at Maria's expense by exceeding the social norm and going for Coke. If on the other hand Maria exceeds the norm, Arnold is better off defending himself by doing the same. Regardless of what choice Maria makes, Arnold is better off choosing Coca-Cola, and vice versa.

An interesting study identified a real-world prisoner's dilemma operating in professional organizations. The authors found in a survey of legal firms that attorneys are "overworked" in the sense that they would like to trade increases in income for time off. But publicly, lawyers are afraid to admit their desire for shorter hours, fearing that this will signal to partners that they are unproductive (even if they are not). As a result, the social norm for hours worked is too high—everyone would be made better

		Maria	
		Coke	Budget
Arnold	Coke	$U_M = 8$ $U_A = 8$	$U_M = 7$ $U_A = 12$
	Budget	$U_M = 12$ $U_A = 7$	$U_M = 10$ $U_A = 10$

U_M = Maria's utility
U_A = Arnold's utility

FIGURE 11.1 The Rat Race as a Prisoner's Dilemma

off if a lower standard workweek could be agreed on and enforced. This change in norms would scale back the rat race, lowering both incomes and material consumption while raising leisure time.[8]

By framing the rat race as a prisoner's dilemma, we can see how social consumption norms get ratcheted upward. A rat race often emerges whenever people send social signals through their consumption or workplace behavior, and especially when bandwagon, snob, or Veblen effects dominate the motives underlying the desire for more material goods. And, if the social satisfaction obtained from material gain is indeed dependent on surpassing one's neighbors, economic growth simply cannot quench the social desires that people attempt to satisfy through increased consumption.

11.3 Positional Goods and Consumption Externalities

One reason that money does not seem to buy much happiness is the social psychology of consumption. However, another reason is rooted in the realities of modern-day growth. A paradox of our affluent society is that, even as we grow wealthier, access to certain goods becomes more and more difficult. Consider the recent "housing bubble." Any market in which speculation can take root is based on inelastic supply, at least in the short run. And so, in the early 2000s, investors who had been burned in the tech bubble on the stock market turned to housing. Paradoxically, though, the rapid run-up in some urban and suburban housing prices occurred at the same time that many other urban neighborhoods featured boarded-up buildings and high vacancy rates. So the shortage driving the bubble was clearly not one of housing units, but rather of units in a "desirable" neighborhood: prosperous, safe, with access to good schools, and within easy commuting distance of jobs and amenities.

Housing in desirable neighborhoods is a good for which long-run supply is very inelastic, and in these neighborhoods, investors felt safe watching housing values skyrocket. The price run-up seemed simply the continuation of a long-term trend. One effect of the massive "suburbanization of America" that has been occurring over the last 50 years has been an increase in the price of housing within the commuting shadow of all major cities. At the same time, these areas developed many of the urban problems that people were attempting to leave behind: increasing congestion, traffic jams, longer commuting time, higher crime rates, and in general a lower quality of life for residents. Simultaneously, citizens left behind in the inner city have seen their communities deteriorate drastically as members of the middle class fled to the suburbs, shrinking the tax base of the cities.

Driving this process has been increased private demand for "better housing." While many individuals did get such housing, the social outcome was less positive. The limited supply of this good in the suburbs was rationed through both higher prices and increased congestion. Concurrently, property values in the cities plummeted, and the quality of life for many residents there has become increasingly desperate.

---

8. Landers, Rebitzer, and Taylor (1996). The authors frame their argument in a signaling context. The key assumptions are that the pool of professionals reap spillover benefits from having more productive team members, and that long hours are a signal for high productivity. For more on overwork, see Schor (1991) and Application 11.0.

Two economic concepts help explain this phenomenon: positional competition and consumption externalities.

Goods with a fixed or inelastic long-run supply, such as uncrowded suburbs within an easy commute to the city, are referred to as **positional goods**. **Positional competition** is the competition for these goods. Some simple examples of positional goods are 50-yard-line Super Bowl tickets, Rembrandt paintings, or spacious seaside vacation homes. Less obvious examples include commuter highways, slots in prestigious four-year colleges, creative work, jobs with status and authority, green space in the city, accessible wilderness, and clean air and water.

As people grow wealthier, the demand for these positional goods increases. In the face of this growing demand, some rationing scheme is necessary. For privately owned goods, say football tickets, the price rises to eliminate the excess demand and clear the market. For many **public goods**, however, the price mechanism is ineffective. Here the rationing takes place through congestion, for example, as seen in traffic jams.

Higher relative prices for positional goods combined with increasing congestion in their consumption have generated a degradation in the quality of life for many people. At the same time, the per capita consumption of TVs, dishwashers, smartphones, fast-food outlets, computers, pain relievers, and a million other commodities has increased. To obtain access to many of the goods that people took for granted only a generation ago, we must either pay a higher proportion of our income or accept a degradation in quality. This is not to say that economic growth has been on balance negative. The point is that increased positional competition generates an important and often unrecognized cost of economic growth.

Positional competition has been compared to a concert hall. If the individuals in the front row stand up to get a better view, then everyone in the entire arena has to stand. Eventually, everyone is uncomfortably up on their tiptoes, but no one can see any better than they could while sitting down! Once again, getting ahead makes sense from an individual perspective, but the social result is to leave everyone worse off.

Positional competition often generates **consumption externalities**. These are benefits and costs of consumption not borne by the consumer—in the example provided earlier, blocking a neighbor's view. Or consider the private decision to commute by car. Although it may save 20 minutes of the driver's time, it also contributes to traffic jams because it reduces the speed at which others can get to work. More generally, the cumulative effect of thousands of private decisions to move to the suburbs is to introduce many of the problems of the city: increasingly depersonalized communities, deteriorating schools, rising crime rates, and environmental degradation.

Consumption externalities are important in other markets besides housing. An individual's decision regarding educational attainment has important externalities, both positive and negative. On one hand, there is such a clear social benefit to having a populace able to read and write that all agree the government must subsidize and indeed mandate a basic education. On the other hand, advanced education is in many respects a type of positional competition. One's decision to obtain a master's degree in business administration increases one's chance of getting a scarce "prestige" job, but at the same time decreases the chances of those without the degree. "Credentials inflation"—the competitive process by which degree requirements for entry into a given career are ratcheted upward—is a negative consumption externality.

Pure positional competition is what economists call a **zero-sum game**. For every person who gains access to a positional good, someone else must give it up. As positional goods become more important in our economy, increases in income channeled into this competition fail to be translated into overall increases in human welfare. This holds doubly true when consumption decisions bear important negative externalities, as in the case of housing and advanced education.[9] These two factors help explain the paradox that although individuals act rationally to increase their wealth, collectively we fail to grow much happier.

11.4 Welfare with Social Consumption

It is useful to recast the arguments of the preceding section into our utility/social welfare function framework. To do so requires that we divide up each individual's consumption bundle into **competitive** and **noncompetitive** elements, X^c, X^{nc}. The former contains (1) rat-race items—those that bring utility primarily because their consumption involves exceeding social norms; (2) positional goods; and (3) goods with significant negative consumption externalities. The noncompetitive bundle includes everything else: goods consumed primarily for their intrinsic utility (taste, warmth, relaxation); leisure time spent with family and friends; physically or intellectually challenging activities; and many environmental goods such as clean air, water, and health.

In practice, this competitive-noncompetitive distinction may be a difficult one to make. Under which category does bike riding fit? The biking experience itself is very noncompetitive, and yet some of the pleasure serious enthusiasts feel for the sport is driven by competitive social norms—wearing the latest clothing or owning the most up-to-date machine. Yet, in principle, it is possible to sort out the consumption components that are fashion- or status-driven from the consumption components of the sport itself.

By doing so, we can rewrite Aldo's utility function (from Chapter 2) as

$$U_A = U(\overset{+}{X_A^{nc}}, \overset{+}{X_A^c}, \overset{-}{X_{NA}^c})$$

The last term, X_{NA}^c, stands for the competitive consumption bundle of all people who are not Aldo (NA); the negative sign above X_{NA}^c indicates that Aldo's happiness *decreases* as the social consumption of others goes up. Aldo still gets happier by increasing his consumption of both noncompetitive (X_A^{nc}) and competitive goods (X_A^c); more remains better for Aldo as an individual. But his overall happiness now depends on the consumption levels of his peer group.

There are two lessons to be learned from this form of the utility function. The first is that economic growth that increases the supply of competitive consumption goods need not increase happiness (though it may). Every time one person gets ahead, a new standard is set for the community. Indeed, competitive consumption goods are often sold by making people who don't buy the product feel worse off! (Consider, for

---

9. Of course, advanced education can have positive consumption externalities as well. Improvements in technology resulting from advanced training are the most obvious example.

example, the typical deodorant campaign that exploits insecurities about being left out and unhappy.)

The second lesson is that, under this form of the utility function, increases in the stock of noncompetitive consumption goods unambiguously raise social welfare. Many, if not most, environmental "goods"—human health, appreciation of natural beauty, respect for both human and nonhuman life—are primarily noncompetitive. One person's enjoyment of his health does not "raise the standard" that others must aspire to. Similarly, land set aside for parks is land not available for private development as part of status-enhancing positional competition. Thus a case can be made for weighting these items more heavily than material consumption in a social welfare function.

What are the economic implications of all this? When relative consumption becomes important, three conclusions emerge. First, taxes on the consumption of status goods become efficient; they increase overall well-being by discouraging excessive work effort and increasing leisure. They also reduce unnecessary production and thus pollution. Second, people tend to overvalue increases in private consumption (given the negative externalities imposed on others) and undervalue noncompetitive public goods and improved environmental quality. Thus willingness-to-pay measures need to be adjusted upward to reflect the true increase in well-being generated by a cleaner environment. In the case of global warming, for example, researchers estimate that the efficient tax on carbon dioxide is 50% higher than that yielded by conventional benefit-cost analysis.[10]

Finally, in economies where status goods are important, GDP growth fails to capture real increases in social welfare on yet one more ground. As discussed in Chapter 9, economists have in fact made several attempts to construct a social welfare index that reflects some of the disamenities of economic growth. The idea is to adjust our basic measure of economic growth—GDP—to better capture the "true" trend in social welfare over the last few decades. If you turn back to Table 9.1, you will find a description of the Genuine Progress Indicator, or GPI.

GPI proponents claim to have uncovered a dramatic slowdown in improvements in the average quality of life over the last few decades, while GDP continued to rise at a steady pace. The GPI does this in part by accounting for the negative consumption externalities arising from positional goods discussed in this chapter. For example, in addition to the conventional externality costs, the researchers deduct from augmented GDP the costs of urbanization, increased commuting time, and auto accidents. They also subtract the rising price of land.

Yet for purposes of the index, the GPI researchers accept the conventional assumption that more is better. According to the GPI authors: "Our calculus of economic well-being has failed to take into account that happiness is apparently correlated with relative rather than absolute levels of wealth or consumption. Having more is less important than having more than the 'Joneses.' Yet in the absence of any way to quantify this sense of relative well-being, we have ignored this important finding in our index, just as others have."[11] If they had devised such a measure, it seems likely

---

10. These points are made by Brekke and Howarth (2002).
11. From Daly and Cobb (1989, 415).

that net national welfare would have increased even less than they estimated over the past 30 years, despite the tremendous growth in GDP.

To summarize, if social norms drive much material consumption, and positional goods and consumption externalities are relatively important in the economy, a strong utilitarian argument can be made for environmental protection. The happiness trade-off between environmental protection and economic growth is not as great as it seems.

11.5 Controlling the Impact of Consumption

A society in which consumption becomes the primary means of achieving social status is known as a **consumer culture**. The reasons for the advance of the consumer culture in rich countries are complex, including factors as diverse as the increasing mobility of both workers and jobs and the subsequent breakdown in community, increasing exposure to television and advertising, and a decline in the moral influence of religion, which traditionally preached an antimaterialistic message.

Some people have argued that as environmental awareness spreads, people in wealthy countries can be persuaded to abandon their affluent lifestyles and begin, for example, riding bikes to work. Yet the advance of the consumer culture appears to be pervasive and very deep-seated. One sees it best through a comparison of generational attitudes. I (Eban) admit to being a bit shocked when I asked my 6-year-old niece why she wouldn't let me cut the huge L.A. Gear tag off her new tennis shoes. "That's what makes them cool," she said. My young niece's strong brand identification—the shoes made her happy *because* of the label—was the result of a shift in marketing strategy by clothing firms. When we (Steve and Eban) were small, firms marketed children's clothes to their parents, and the emphasis was on rugged and practical. Now Saturday morning cartoons are filled with clothing ads targeted directly at children, and the emphasis is on beauty and status. Our parents, of course, had much less exposure to marketing and find our attachment to many of our family gadgets a bit puzzling.

Thus, even if you believe that high levels of consumption in affluent countries are a major environmental threat, it is hard to imagine making much headway against the consumer culture via moral arguments alone. This section discusses three potential *economic* instruments for reducing consumption: **consumption taxes**, **mandated European-style vacations**, and the **regulation of advertising**.

Many economists have argued for non-environmental reasons that the U.S. consumption rate is too high, or equivalently, that the national savings and investment rate is too low. During the 1980s, national savings declined from around 8% to 2.4% of net national product and by 2000 had actually gone negative, while the foreign debt skyrocketed. The argument is made that for the last two decades, we have been financing current consumption at the expense of investment in created capital, which portends a decline in living standards. Nordhaus makes, in effect, a non-environmental sustainability argument for reducing current consumption.

The policy response called for has been an increase in taxes (income or sales) to reduce consumption and increase savings and investment. The ultimate purpose, however, is to *boost* consumption in the future. This is clearly not the policy goal proposed here. Yet, if the revenues from such a tax were invested in the generation of new, clean technologies, such as those discussed in Chapters 17 and 18, this kind of policy could achieve the goal of reducing the environmental *impact* of consumption. This would be true even if consumption levels themselves had only temporarily declined.

Alternatively, taxes could be used to divert resources away from consumption in rich countries to sustainable development efforts in poor countries. Funds could be used for a variety of purposes: from debt relief to family planning to land reform or resource protection efforts to transferring clean energy and manufacturing technologies to poor countries.

As a final point, in rich countries, social consumption theory has a rather startling implication: beyond an initial adjustment period, in which people lowered their expected consumption levels, a shift of resources from current consumption to investment or development assistance would not reduce overall social happiness or welfare.

Put in more practical terms, suppose that income taxes in the United States were raised gradually in a progressive fashion, so that ultimately the highest group faced a marginal tax rate of 50%, while poor Americans maintained the same tax rate. Suppose as well that the additional money raised was diverted to investment in environmental technology: to the training of scientists and engineers and to research and development. Social consumption theory says that in the long run, on average, people would be just as content. (Incidentally, wealthy Americans did pay a 70% marginal tax rate or higher throughout the 1950s, 1960s, and 1970s.) The problem with this theory, of course, is that there is an initial adjustment period in which people are dissatisfied. Given this, the political prospects for new taxes to promote sustainability—either environmental or economic—are challenging.

It is sometimes argued that high levels of consumption are necessary for a modern economy to operate and that a reduction in consumption would lead to high levels of long-run unemployment. Not necessarily. Reduced consumption can be accommodated if increased savings are channeled into domestic investment for long-run sustainability: in clean technology and human capital development.

Alternatively, one very sustainable way to reduce consumption without boosting unemployment significantly is to **mandate European-style vacations**. In Western Europe, employers are required by law to provide workers with at least four weeks paid vacation plus several days of paid holidays, and almost all countries have paid family leave as well. By contrast, one in four Americans has no paid vacation or holidays, and very few Americans get paid parental leave.[12] The way Europeans finance these vacations and holidays, in effect, translates into lower hourly wages—Europeans accept slightly slower economic growth and consumption in exchange for more leisure time.

Beyond boosting savings rates and increasing leisure time, a final possible strategy for controlling consumption is to regulate advertising. For such a strategy to make sense, one must first make the case that advertising in fact raises aggregate consumption levels. It is possible that advertising merely causes people to switch brands, leading to no overall increase in consumption. On the other hand, in the United States, we receive massive exposure to advertising. Indeed, TV might be thought of as the church of the 21st century. By the time the typical American reaches college, he or she will

---

12. Ray and Schmitt (2007).

have spent three to four hours a week watching TV ads, about 100,000 of them in all.[13] These advertisements all preach a variation of the same underlying social message: satisfaction through purchase. Such a constant propaganda barrage may well induce us to consume more than we otherwise would.

Assuming that advertising does have a major positive impact on overall consumption, effective regulation of advertising remains a difficult task. From an economic point of view, advertising has an important function—fostering competition by providing consumers information about the availability, quality, or price of a product. Advertising can be thought of as a useful product itself, the production of which generates a negative externality, in the same way that paper production generates water pollution. Regulation should focus on controlling the negative externality—the promotion of consumer culture—rather than the product itself.

One way this has been traditionally accomplished is through the regulation of advertising on children's television. The government sets limits on the number of minutes per hour that can be devoted to advertising and has in the past prohibited the mixing of advertisements and entertainment. Sweden, for example, bans commercial ads targeted at children under age 12.[14]

Another way to sort out "good" commercials from "bad" ones is by medium. Ads in the print and radio media have a harder time exploiting emotional weaknesses to develop brand identification than do television ads. They thus tend to provide much more useful information about price, quality, and availability. Local and trade-specific advertising also tend to be more information intensive than national advertising does. Perhaps reflecting the limited economic usefulness of national television advertising, many European countries have commercial-free television. (They finance the production of TV programs with tax dollars.)

In the United States, one possible policy measure would be to institute a "pollution tax" on national TV advertising. As with any tax, such a measure would cause firms to shift resources away from television to other media, or out of advertising altogether.

In the long run, any successful attempt to rein in the growth of per capita consumption in rich countries will require a broad social movement that challenges the consumer culture and its values head on—a discussion well beyond the scope of this book.[15] With their high tax rates, generous vacation requirements, and controls on advertising, Western European countries like Sweden or Germany demonstrate both the possibility for partial cultural transformation toward sustainability and the limits of a strategy targeted at restraining consumption. For example, although Europeans have much smaller global warming footprints than do most Americans, they still have a large impact on the planet. The average German is responsible for around 11.9 tons of CO_2 each year; the average American, 22.5. The global average is 5.6.[16]

At the end of the day, controlling the growth of "A" in the IPAT equation is possible through government policy—but doing so is an incremental process involving cultural changes much deeper than can be generated by simple legislation. Economic

13. Layard (2005).
14. Layard (2005, 143).
15. See, for example, Daly and Cobb (1989), Schor (1991), and Layard (2005).
16. World Resources Institute (2009).

analysis does provide us with some useful insights, however. First, policies of shared sacrifice may in fact lead to little reduction in overall welfare, if the happiness derived from consumption is relative. If this view is widely held, it suggests that people will more likely accept a tax increase to reduce their consumption for a "good cause," such as their children's welfare. Second, reducing consumption in rich countries need not lead to an increase in unemployment. Rather, labor and other resources can shift into production of goods for consumption in poor countries or into investment in clean technologies. Finally, a common proposal to restrict the advance of consumer culture, regulation of advertising, must be approached carefully because of the economic benefit—information—that advertising can generate.

11.6 Summary

The central metaphor behind benefit-cost analysis and the efficiency standard is a perceived environment-growth trade-off. More environmental protection in the form of regulations, bans, and red tape means higher costs and ultimately fewer "goods" for consumers. Why should everyone be forced to have a pristine environment, regardless of the cost?

Overconsumption critics respond in two ways. First, ecological economists argue that technology is increasingly less capable of providing substitutes for natural capital, and that the long-run costs of "business-as-usual consumerism" are much higher than efficiency advocates envision. Second, some economists have questioned the fundamental assumption that more is better, which underlies the defense of efficiency. Because much of the satisfaction derived from consumption is social rather than intrinsic in nature, and because of the negative externalities in the competition for positional goods that growth engenders, the benefits of economic growth are much smaller than conventionally measured.

If the more-is-better assumption underlying efficiency analysis is often simply wrong, then the case for pursuing safety or ecological sustainability instead is strengthened. When more isn't better, "efficient" outcomes aren't really efficient—that is, welfare enhancing. As a result, stricter safety or ecological sustainability standards *may actually be more efficient* than an approach grounded in conventional benefit-cost analysis.

The global impact of consumption growth is becoming larger as more and more people look to material consumption to satisfy social needs for membership and status in a community—the advance of consumer culture. Three policies were explored for controlling the growth of consumption. The first was a tax whose proceeds were used to finance either investment in clean technology or increased consumption in poor countries. An important point is that declines in consumption in rich countries need not reduce overall employment; instead, they can represent a shift of resources including labor into other productive sectors. However, as social consumption theory predicts, tax policies lower utility in the short run and are thus very difficult to sell politically.

The second policy would be to mandate extensive paid vacation; this would reduce work and output, leading to somewhat lower overall consumption in exchange for greater leisure time. And the final policy involved regulating advertising, on the grounds that it promotes the growth of an unsustainable consumer culture. The danger here is that advertising can play a useful economic function, providing information and promoting competition. One possibility would be a "pollution tax" on national television advertising, which tends to be heavy on emotional appeal and low on information content.

This chapter concludes the first part of the book, and our discussion of how much pollution is too much. At one end of the spectrum we have considered efficiency as a target. In learning about the efficiency standard, we explored the tools that economists have developed to measure environmental protection benefits and costs, and the use of benefit-cost analysis. We have also examined the logic of promoting efficiency over time (dynamic efficiency) through discounting, granting the neoclassical assumption that technological progress will offset all resource shortages and that, as a consequence, human welfare will continue to rise.

At the other end of the spectrum, we have considered two stricter standards: safety and ecological sustainability. Both these approaches reject benefit-cost analyses and argue for protecting the environment "regardless of the cost." But in evaluating these approaches, we learned that there really is no such thing as a free lunch; ultimately trade-offs do emerge, even if they are not as severe as neoclassicals believe.

So how much is too much? This ultimately is a values question and cannot be resolved by economics alone, but the goal of the first 11 chapters has been to provide the information and analytical tools you need to better resolve the question in your own mind. In the next presidential election, global warming is likely to be an important issue. Whether you support a candidate speaking for an efficiency, a safety, or an ecological sustainability standard for carbon dioxide emissions, you now have a better understanding of the issues at stake in your decision.

APPLICATION 11.0

Overworked Americans

In the United States, the flip side of increasing consumption over the last 30 years has been increasing hours of work. The increase in hours of work is surprising first because it goes against historical trends: until 1940, the length of the workday fell continuously, and workers gained additional vacation time. This forward progress has continued in most European countries, which have strong unions. U.S. manufacturing employees now work almost two months per year longer than their German or French counterparts.

The increase in work hours is also surprising because economists assume that leisure is a normal good: as people get richer, they should consume more of it. Instead, leisure appears to be an inferior good. Since 1948, U.S. output per worker has more than doubled. In other words, we could consume at the level of our parents in early adulthood, and *take every other year off*. Instead, we work a little harder and consume more than twice as much.

1. Economist Juliet Schor identifies two chief culprits behind the increased workweek: hiring incentives and the lack of a strong union movement to push

for shorter hours. As far as incentives go, even though employers must, by law, pay time and a half for overtime, they seem to prefer this to hiring new employees. Why do you think this might be?

2. Among salaried and professional employees, Schor argues that increased competition has led to a natural upward progression in hours spent at the office. The monster workweek experienced by young doctors is becoming common for corporate lawyers, accountants, architects, and other professionals. In an increasingly competitive environment, "'enough' is defined not by some pre-existing standard like the length of the workday, but by the limits of human endurance" (Kanter, as cited in Schor 1991, 70). Some economists respond that there is nothing wrong with this lengthening of the workweek. If people didn't like it, they could just quit and choose less demanding jobs that offer more leisure and result in less consumption. Do you agree?

APPLICATION 11.1

McMansion on the Canyon

Consider the following social welfare function:

$$SW = U_a(X_a^{nc}, X_a^c, X_{\sim a}^c, P_a) + U_b(X_b^{nc}, X_b^c, X_{\sim b}^c, P_b) + U_d(X_d^{nc}, X_d^c, X_{\sim d}^c, P_d) + \dots$$

where:

$$X = \text{consumption bundle}$$
$$P = \text{pollution}$$
$$nc = \text{noncompetitive}$$
$$c = \text{competitive}$$
$$a, b, d = \text{people}$$
$$\sim a, \sim b, \sim d = \text{all other people besides } a, b, d$$

1. Place positive and negative signs above all the terms in the function, illustrating whether they increase or decrease each person's utility.
2. Will an overall increase in the level of *noncompetitive* consumption always increase social welfare?
3. Let X_b^c be a new house overlooking a canyon. Let P be the reduction in scenic beauty experienced by the community. Finally, let $X_{\sim b}^c$ be the status impact on folks who are not b arising from the new McMansion. Assume that the positive increment to individual utility for individual b of an increase in X_b^c equals $10,000 in consumer surplus and that the negative status increment to other people is −$500. Assume also that a one-unit increase in X_b^c produces one unit of P, which further causes a −$1,000-unit impact on utility for everyone exposed. In a world of five people (including Mr. b), what are the private benefits to Mr. b of consuming one more unit of X_b^c? What are the external costs of a one-unit increase in X_b^c? What will be the net increase in SW of a one-unit increase in X_b^c?

4.   What parts of the development decision in question 3 would a conventional benefit-cost analysis capture? What would it miss?

KEY IDEAS IN EACH SECTION

11.0   This chapter explores the idea of "overconsumption." The argument is that in affluent countries, continued economic growth does not in fact buy much happiness, while compromising the natural resource base and critical ecosystem services.

11.1   The **Easterlin paradox** refers to survey data showing that increases in income boost reported happiness only slightly, and only to about the median income level.

11.2   One way to explain the Easterlin paradox is that satisfaction from consumption depends on one's consumption relative to social norms. Social consumption patterns are influenced by **bandwagon**, **snob**, and **Veblen effects**. When people attempt to obtain happiness by competing in consumption levels, the process often degenerates into a self-defeating **rat race**, which can be modeled as a **prisoner's dilemma**.

11.3   **Positional competition** is competition over goods with a limited long-run supply, or **positional goods**. Private positional goods are rationed by their increasingly high price; **public goods** are rationed by congestion. Competition over pure positional goods is a **zero-sum game**. Negative **consumption externalities** are often generated through positional competition.

11.4   This section illustrates how the utility function changes in the presence of social consumption and positional goods. Goods must be divided into **competitive and noncompetitive consumption** bundles. While more of everything is still better at the individual level, externalities generated by others' consumption now depress each person's utility. It is thus no longer true that increases in society-wide consumption must increase happiness.

11.5   A **consumer culture** is one in which the primary means of achieving social status is via material consumption. Three economic policies for reducing the spread of consumer culture are **consumption-reducing taxes**, **mandated European-style vacations**, and the **regulation of advertising**. However, economic tools can change attitudes only if they are part of a much broader cultural movement.

REFERENCES

Bagwell, Laurie Simon, and Douglas Bernheim. 1996. Veblen effects in a theory of conspicuous consumption. *American Economic Review* 86(3): 329–48.

Brekke, Kjell Arne, and Richard B. Howarth. 2002. *Status, growth and the environment: Goods as symbols in applied welfare economics*. Northampton, MA: Edward Elgar.

Daly, Herman E. 1987. The economic growth debate: What some economists have learned but many have not. *Journal of Environmental Economics and Management* 14(4): 323–36.

Daly, Herman E., and John J. Cobb Jr. 1989. *For the common good*. Boston: Beacon Press.

Easterlin, Richard. 1974. Does economic growth improve the human lot? Some empirical evidence. In *Nations and households in economic growth: Essays in Honor of Moses Abramovitz*, ed. Paul A. David and Melvin W. Reder. New York: Academic Press.

Kahneman, Daniel, and Alan B. Krueger. 2006. Developments in the measurement of subjective well-being. *Journal of Economic Perspectives* 20(1): 3–24.

Kahneman, Daniel, Alan B. Krueger, David A. Schkade, Norbert Schwarz, and Arthur A. Stone. 2004. A survey method for characterizing daily life experience: The day reconstruction method. *Science* 306(5702): 1776–80.

Landers, Renee, James B. Rebitzer, and Lowell J. Taylor. 1996. Rat race redux: Adverse selection in the determination of work hours in law firms. *American Economic Review* 86(3): 349–72.

Layard, Richard. 2005. *Happiness: Lessons from a new science*. New York: Penguin Press.

Leibenstein, Harvey. 1950. Bandwagon, snob and Veblen effects in the theory of consumers' demand. *Quarterly Journal of Economics* 64: 183–207.

Ray, Rebecca, and John Schmitt. 2007. *No vacation nation*. Washington, DC: Center for Economic Policy Research.

Schor, Juliet B. 1991. *The overworked American*. New York: Basic Books.

Smith, Adam. 1759. *The theory of moral sentiments*. New York: Augustus M. Kelly.

World Resources Institute. 2009. Climate Analysis Indicators Tool. http://cait.wri.org/.

IS GOVERNMENT

UP TO THE JOB?

The first part of this book focused on an explicitly normative question: how much pollution is too much? We analyzed several possible answers to that question—efficiency, safety, and ecological sustainability—from both ethical and practical points of view. Having set a goal, at least in our own minds, we can now consider how to get there. As it turns out, we have one primary vehicle: government. From Chapter 3, we know that private markets generate too much pollution from both efficiency and safety perspectives. Thus it is up to government to devise policies that modify market behavior and reduce pollution.

Government has a variety of tools at its command to attack the pollution problem, ranging from regulations and bans to pollution taxes and marketable permit systems to subsidy policies and infrastructure and R&D investments. But before discussing policy details, we first need to consider a more central question: is government up to the job?

In recent years, many people have become skeptical of government's ability to accomplish positive goals. This increased distrust may well have been fueled by the rising number and severity of problems we now expect government to resolve: providing security against terrorism, shoring up disintegrating families, tackling violent crime and drug abuse, reducing unemployment, poverty, homelessness and hunger, controlling inflation, providing worker training and retraining, ensuring the safety of consumers and workers, and protecting the environment. As we have demanded more from government, we have perhaps become more aware of its limitations.

This part of the book provides an overview of governmental efforts to control pollution. This chapter begins by developing a theory of government action that highlights two primary issues: the information-intensive nature of environmental regulation and the potential for political influence in the regulatory process. In light of this theory, Chapter 13 reviews the major environmental legislation and Chapter 14 evaluates regulatory accomplishments and constraints, including a look at the vital, yet often overlooked, component of environmental regulation: enforcement and compliance.

The conclusions reached in this part of the book may seem harsh. At their best, regulators marshal the available information about environmental impacts and control costs and lurch in a steady, yet cumbersome, manner to define and achieve an environmental goal: "efficiency," "safety," or "sustainability." At their worst, regulators become partners in a corrupt process where backdoor deals are struck with disregard for environmental consequences. More generally, legislating, drafting, and enforcing regulations is a complex, tedious affair, the outcome of which bears the stamp of the various organized interests likely to be affected. In general, interests with more resources have more influence.

Just as markets fail to deliver many desirable social goals, including a clean environment, so too does government have its own failings. It would be naive to think otherwise. The point of this section is to isolate and identify these problems so that government policies to promote a cleaner planet can become more successful. Is government up to the job of crafting sensible and effective policy to protect the environment? This is really a rhetorical question. If it is not, we had better make it so. It is the principal tool we have.

12

THE POLITICAL ECONOMY OF ENVIRONMENTAL REGULATION

12.0 Introduction

In 1970, the U.S. Congress passed the Clean Air Act, declaring it the law of the land that the air breathed by Americans should provide "an adequate margin of safety...requisite to protect the public health." Yet early in the 21st century, some tens of millions of people in the United States are still exposed on occasion to ground-level ozone (smog) concentrations considered dangerous; air toxic emissions at some industrial facilities still remained high enough to impose cancer risks greater than 1 in 1,000 to surrounding residents.

Is this evidence of government failure? Some would turn these figures around, saying instead, "look how far we have come." Many cities now meet the ozone standard that didn't in 1970; more significantly, consider how many *would* be failing today if we had not taken the measures we have. In the next few chapters, we look in more detail at the overall impact of regulation, which can be viewed as a glass half empty or half full. However, many would still argue that 40 plus years is a long time to wait for a law to be enforced.

What lies behind this slow progress? Scientific uncertainty as to an "adequate margin of safety"? High compliance costs? Other priority areas at the Environmental Protection Agency (EPA)? Insufficient funds allocated to the EPA by Congress? Industry influence over legislators and regulators? All of these factors have played a role. The point here, however, is simply to illustrate that passing a law is only the first step in the long process of changing market behavior.

Economists have identified two main obstacles that stand in the way of effective government action to control pollution. The first is the highly **imperfect information** that regulators possess. To begin with, regulators are never given a clear-cut goal. For most pollutants, it is difficult, if not impossible, to define "safe" emission levels in purely scientific terms. Thus a political definition of safety, based on technical information, must be worked out. More generally, the available risk assessments give only rough, if any, indications of health risks, and cost estimates can be equally unreliable. Moreover, regulators must often turn for information to the very sources they seek to regulate. Thus, as we shall see, many economists have focused on improving regulators' access to information as a crucial strategy for improving regulation.

However, ultimate uncertainty about the "facts" means that any decision to promote safety or efficiency, while informed by the technical merits of the case, will also leave substantial room for bureaucratic discretion. With the opportunity for discretion comes the opportunity for **political influence**. Government officials clearly have motivations other than fulfilling the letter of the law: these include career building or satisfying ideological preferences, for example. Given the existence of bureaucratic discretion, industry and environmental groups deploy substantial resources to affect elections, government legislation, and regulatory decisions.

This chapter begins by detailing the generic process of environmental regulation and then goes on to explore, in some detail, the obstacles presented by poor information and political influence. Finally, we consider briefly what lessons the disastrous environmental policies followed by the former Soviet Union hold for Western market-oriented democracies. Chapter 13 then provides a more detailed overview of the major environmental laws now in effect.

12.1 The Process of Environmental Regulation

Today, the level of ozone concentration in the air (known as the ambient pollution level) officially designated by the government as providing an "adequate margin of safety" is 0.08 parts per million (ppm). Where did this particular environmental regulation, and thousands of others like it, come from? The history of a regulation such as ozone control is a three-step process.

STEP 1. U.S. CONGRESS PASSES BILL

Of course, step 1 doesn't come out of nowhere. First, there must be a generally perceived environmental problem. Next, some enterprising congressperson or congressional aide decides to make the problem a top issue. Then legislation is drafted, and industry and environmental lobbyists line up support for and against and try to insert friendly amendments. Finally, legislation is passed, and the president signs on.

Even though this first step takes several years, the legislation is usually not very specific. Because of compromises struck between various parties, the language of the bill is often purposefully vague or even contradictory. All this leads to step 2.

STEP 2. EPA DRAFTS REGULATIONS

Congress usually delegates to the EPA the hard work of figuring out the exact meanings of terms such as *safety, prudent,* and *reasonable balance.* The EPA tries to translate the bill's language into actual regulations, specifying either allowable levels of emissions or of ambient pollution.

As we saw in Chapter 4, the process of creating a major new regulation requires the EPA to generate a regulatory impact analysis, a technical document that includes extensive documentation of both the scientific basis for its decision and its likely economic impact, including compliance costs. Yet the EPA most often has only limited information about the environmental impacts of pollutants and the technologies available for their control. Thus, during the process of drafting regulations, the agency asks for comments from industry and environmental groups. Before the regulations can become law, they must also officially go through several rounds of public comment, to which the agency is legally required to respond. Thus interest groups are formally incorporated into the decision-making process.

Part of this is self-defense on the EPA's part—many decisions the agency makes are appealed, or one side or the other will sue. Former EPA administrator William Ruckelshaus estimated that 80% of the EPA's rules were subsequently challenged in court.[1] For example, in the late 1970s, the ozone standard mentioned previously was revised upward from 0.08 to 0.12 ppm under the threat of industry lawsuits, and this revision itself was challenged in court by both industry and environmentalists. In 1997, after again being sued by environmentalists and in the light of new scientific evidence, the EPA tightened the standard back to the original 0.08 ppm.

This information-gathering and public-comment phase can take a couple of years when it proceeds smoothly. Generally, however, Congress fails to appropriate enough money for the EPA to do all its tasks, and certain regulations are moved to the back burner. Finally, the president's staff in the Office of Management and Budget (OMB) reviews the new regulation and may send it back to the EPA with recommended revisions.

Typically, the EPA regulations provide general guidelines for industries and municipalities to follow. However, the implementation details are left to step 3.

STEP 3. STATE GOVERNMENTS IMPLEMENT AND ENFORCE REGULATIONS

The EPA often requires state governments to submit plans detailing how they intend to achieve the agency's goals. In the ozone case, for example, the state agency would need to tell the EPA what measures it intended to take to control emissions from vehicle tailpipes and stationary sources such as petroleum refineries in order to come into compliance with the 0.08-ppm ambient air standard. Failure to do so would theoretically result in the EPA mandating certain measures, although it might just result in more delay. Thus the hard economic choices are often left to state officials. Enforcement, too, is primarily a state function, although the EPA does have its own enforcement division to supplement state efforts.

There are three major points to be taken from this brief review of the legal process. First, even when it operates on schedule, drafting regulations is a cumbersome and time-consuming process. Because information about benefits and costs is highly

---

1. From Bryner (1987, 117).

imperfect and not widely available, legislators and regulators have provided many opportunities for affected parties to explain their positions.

In this process, the United States has adopted a **judicial model of regulation**. The EPA is expected to adhere to strict procedural guidelines for accepting and addressing comments and must build a quasi-legal case for each major regulation it issues. Even under ideal circumstances, regulators gather their information in a forum where both sides are doing their best to obscure, rather than clarify, the underlying issues. This process tends to exaggerate differences over scientific and economic issues rather than generate a consensus position the agency can accept as the "truth."

Moreover, those interested in stalling regulations have ample opportunity to do so merely by flooding regulators with extraneous information. For example, several feet of shelf space was required to hold more than 1,200 comments, all of which required responses, that the EPA received on a single proposal.[2] "Paralysis by analysis" is a frequent outcome.

Finally, the regulatory process can be influenced at dozens of points. Here is only a partial list of opportunities for interested parties to shape the final outcome: drafting of initial laws or insertion of amendments; discussions with high EPA officials or mid-level technicians involved in the agency's day-to-day work; formal and informal public comments; limiting or enlarging the budget that Congress and state legislators provide for regulatory agencies to do their work; meeting with the president's oversight agency in the OMB; influencing state implementation plans and state enforcement mechanisms; suing in court for changes once regulations have finally been put into place; and, finally, bargaining with enforcement officials over compliance.

Given the complex nature of the regulatory task, regulators *must* turn to industry and private groups for information about the potential benefits and costs of regulation. Moreover, because Congress itself has no way of knowing whether the EPA is making wise decisions, following our familiar system of checks and balances, the regulatory process itself has been consciously opened up to all interested parties. A complex, legally binding decision-making process (the judicial model) has been put in place to prevent abuse of power by regulatory bureaucrats. Yet the politics of information gathering itself has often yielded regulatory gridlock.

12.2 Regulation under Imperfect Information

The EPA was founded in 1970 as an independent agency within the executive branch of government. It now employs more than 17,000 people in 10 regional offices and Washington, DC, and has an annual budget of more than $7 billion. The agency is required to develop, implement, and enforce regulations under dozens of different laws. The EPA has many ongoing projects and responsibilities, including the regulation of tens of thousands of water pollution sources and hazardous waste dumps, hundreds of thousands of stationary air pollution sources, millions of automobiles, and hundreds of new chemicals and pesticides introduced each year.

To accomplish these tasks, the EPA is obviously provided only limited resources. Thus the agency has to determine priorities—not all of its regulatory functions can be

---

2. From Jenkins, Kopits, and Simpson (2009).

performed adequately without spreading personnel too thin. As a result, in virtually all of its decisions, the agency gathers or generates less than full information about the problem before acting.

The extent of this information gap was revealed by a joint EPA-Amoco study of benzene air pollution at an Amoco oil refinery in Virginia. The agency had issued regulations to control benzene emissions from wastewater ponds at refineries. These regulations, based on research done in 1959, proved dramatically far off base. When the joint study project was completed, ponds were discovered to be polluting at a level 20 times lower than predicted. The real benzene pollution problem arose on the loading docks, where fuel was pumped into barges.

Amoco eventually constructed a $41 million treatment system to deal with pollution from the ponds. Meanwhile, much more extensive pollution from the loading docks, which could have been controlled for $6 million, went unregulated and unabated.[3] How could such a situation develop? In general, before writing a regulation, the EPA has neither the staff nor the legal right to conduct the kind of intensive examination of an industrial facility that it eventually did in the Amoco case. Usually, the agency can sponsor only limited research of its own; as a result it must turn to industry, environmental groups, or university researchers for much of its data.

In addition to relying on outdated or poor information, the EPA must also contend with a **reporting bias** when it turns to industry for information about compliance costs. To illustrate the problem, suppose the EPA seeks to regulate a pesticide thought to contaminate groundwater. The agency is considering a ban on the use of a pesticide in high-risk counties. As discussed in the next chapter, pesticides are regulated under an efficiency standard—Congress has directed the EPA to weigh benefits against costs in this case. Figure 12.1 illustrates our efficiency standard diagram.

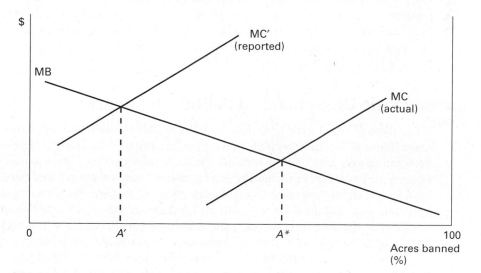

FIGURE 12.1 Regulation with Imperfect Information

3. See "What Really Pollutes?" 1993.

The true marginal benefits and costs of the ban are reflected by the curves labeled MB and MC. If the EPA had access to this information, efficiency would require a ban applying to A^* acres. However, suppose the EPA must rely on agrichemical company sources for information about how much it will cost farmers to switch over to alternative pest-control methods. Industry has a clear incentive to lie and overstate the cost (MC/). If the industry does so, and the EPA uses the industry estimates, the agency will ban $A/$ acres, an inefficiently low number.

There are two responses to reporting bias. The first is to improve the **in-house analytic capability** of the agency. While the EPA will never have the resources to fund all the research it needs, concentrating on training and retaining technical personnel is a basic aspect of improved regulation. However, political developments can work against this goal. For example, following the general trend toward privatization of services, much of the EPA's technical work has been contracted out to private consulting firms. The ostensible motive was to save money (a goal that, in fact, has often proved elusive), but the net result was to reduce the agency's technical capabilities. Reliance on contractors reached the point, according to some critics, that the agency could not even evaluate whether contract work was being performed well. Moreover, many of the consulting firms also depend for their livelihoods on contracts from industries regulated by the EPA. Reducing outside contracting would help build up the EPA's technical expertise and reduce conflicts of interest.

The second approach to the information problem is to rely on the so-called incentive-compatible regulation. Regulation designed to elicit truthful information is called incentive-compatible because the *incentive* for the regulated party is *compatible* with the regulatory goal. Using the mix of tools at their command, regulators can, in fact, do better than is illustrated in Figure 12.1. As we discuss more fully in Appendix 15B, it turns out that if regulators were to control pesticide use by taxing rather than banning it, then firms would have an incentive to *understate* rather than overstate their control costs. In Appendix 15B, we also find that an appropriate mix of taxes and marketable permit systems (discussed more fully in Chapters 15 and 16) can help provide just the right incentives for truth telling.

12.3 Bureaucratic Discretion and Political Influence

Regardless of the degree to which the EPA is able to hone its information-gathering and evaluation abilities, regulatory issues will never be resolved in a clear-cut manner. The ambiguous and often contradictory goals provided by Congress, as well as the underlying uncertainty in scientific and economic analyses, ensure that bureaucrats will retain substantial **discretion** in regulatory decision making. Because regulatory decisions impose substantial costs on affected industries, businesses will devote resources to influence the discretion that regulators exercise (in ethical, questionably ethical, and unethical manners) just as they devote resources to minimizing labor or energy costs.

In addition, simply because a business lobbies for regulatory relief does not mean that the relief is unjustified. It remains true that industry has the best knowledge about the likely impact of regulation and that bureaucrats have the power to arbitrarily impose substantial burdens on firms for reasons that are not obvious. Thus the ability of industry (and environmental groups) to lobby regulators is not necessarily a bad thing.

The problem is that legitimate access can become transformed into undue influence. This section considers factors that motivate bureaucrats to stray from "doing their job."

Environmental regulators are expected by the public to pursue their congressionally mandated goals of efficiency or safety in pollution control. However, like all other people, they have personal interests to consider. To the extent they are able, bureaucrats are likely to use their positions to satisfy three types of goals: agency building, external career building, and job satisfaction.

Many observers of bureaucracy (both governmental and corporate) have argued that a primary goal of managers is **agency growth**. Protecting and enlarging the agency budget, of course, can make the agency more effective in doing its primary job, but it also provides more perquisites (new computers, travel, opportunities for promotion, etc.) and prestige for agency personnel. A bias toward unwarranted growth may lead to "overregulation" (especially from an efficiency point of view) as the agency personnel engage in new activities to justify greater funding. On the other hand, it may just lead to wasted money.

The second factor that regulators keep in mind is **external career building**. I (Eban) once interviewed for a job in the Antitrust Division of the U.S. Justice Department. The typical career track, I was told, involved working at Justice for five years, at which point one's salary topped out. Most people then went on to work for law firms or economic consulting firms that *defended* companies from antitrust suits. This so-called revolving door between industry and its regulators is widespread. EPA employees need to keep in mind future career options when making tough regulatory decisions.

While there are some jobs in environmental organizations or academic institutions, most private-sector jobs for people with experience in the EPA, and virtually all the high-paying ones, are in private industry. Thus the potential for conflict of interest clearly exists. More significantly, in the struggle to define exactly what the public interest really is, top policymakers are often clearly aware of the industry position as they are on intimate terms with many from that side of the aisle. They may be less aware of what it is like to live next to a hazardous waste dump.

This leads us to the third bureaucratic motivation that might influence regulatory policy: **job satisfaction**. Are bureaucrats likely to use their discretion to draft and enforce aggressive or meek laws? Three factors come to play here: **ideology**, **power**, and the **quiet life**. First, regulators with either an environmental or free-market ideological bent may satisfy their own personal preferences for more or less regulation. Second, regulators may impose harsh restrictions on industry because it provides them with power and authority. Conservatives have often charged that the EPA is staffed by power-hungry environmental zealots. And on the face of it, it seems more likely that persons attracted to a job in the EPA would be sympathetic to environmental concerns.

Yet the political appointees who run the EPA are more likely to come through the revolving door from industry and to share a deregulatory philosophy, especially if appointed by a conservative president. Probably the most jaw-dropping example of bureaucratic discretion was the decision during the George W. Bush years to allow the widespread practice of "mountaintop removal" to mine coal in Appalachia. In this practice, companies literally blow the tops off of mountains to get at the underlying coal. They then dump the debris in surrounding areas, including on top of streams.

Over the last two decades, close to a thousand miles of streams in Appalachia have been buried by mine waste.

Mountaintop removal clearly runs counter to a regulatory mandate in 1983 that required mining companies to avoid mining activities within 100 feet of a stream, and it also appears to be a clear violation of Clean Water Act statutes that require protecting surface-water quality. But exercising their bureaucratic discretion, both the Office of Surface Mining and the Army Corps of Engineers regularly provided permits for the dumping of mine waste, especially from 2000 to 2008. For much of this time, the permitting process was overseen by a former coal-industry lobbyist who had been appointed to the job by President Bush.[4]

One final factor that probably helped this process along is the desire on the part of agency personnel for "a quiet life." The road to advancement within a bureaucracy is often to avoid antagonizing outside interests and to proceed with caution when doing so. The outcome is an emphasis on procedure over substance. This generates a substantial bias toward the status quo. One Former EPA employee maintains that EPA officials are more interested in keeping their heads low than in sticking their necks out. Because industry is highly concerned with the process of drafting the details of regulations, mid-level bureaucrats often find themselves in day-to-day contact with industry officials. Here, "in addition to real and hinted at job opportunities," EPA officials become aware that "people who cooperate with the lobbyists find that the lobbyist will lobby for their advancement with upper management. Those who don't cooperate will find the lobbyists lobbying for their heads."[5]

This section has identified three potential goals beyond their legislative mandate that bureaucrats might pursue: agency growth, external career building, and job satisfaction. Growth suggests, if anything, a tendency toward overregulation; career building would lead to underregulation; and job satisfaction might generate either. As a result, it is not possible to identify an a priori bureaucratic bias. However, it is worth keeping in mind that bureaucrats are people too. Like anyone else, they take pride in a job well done—serving the public interest as they see it.

12.4 Who Wins the Influence Game?

The answer to this question, of course, depends on whom you ask. Environmentalists would point to 20 or 30 years of delay in enforcing the Clean Air Act; industry would respond that the laws themselves make unrealistic demands. Rather than answer this question outright, we can identify the resources available to the two sides and the arenas in which the parties tend to prevail.

The two types of resources in the political world are **votes** and **dollars**. In general, environmentalists are better at martialing voting support, while industry has greater monetary resources at its command. Tough environmental laws command broad public support in the polls, even when the opportunity cost of higher prices is explicitly factored in. Thus environmentalists have a large natural political constituency. Moreover,

---

4. Broder (2007).
5. Quote is from Sanjour (1992, 9).

among the public, environmentalists are a more trusted source of information about environmental issues than are either industry or government officials.

This advantage is translated into influence in the crafting of national environmental protection legislation. Ten major national environmental organizations (Sierra Club, National Wildlife Federation, National Audobon Society, Environmental Defense Fund, Natural Resources Defense Council, Wilderness Society, Nature Conservancy, Greenpeace, Ducks Unlimited, and World Wildlife Fund) represent over 10 million members. These groups hire experts to analyze the benefits and costs of new policies, lobbyists to spread this information and promote environmental legislation, and lawyers to sue government agencies. The combined annual policy analysis, lobbying, and legal budgets of these groups runs into tens of millions of dollars—a substantial sum, but much less than the resources that industry can bring to bear. However, environmental dollars often have greater leverage among many legislators due to the votes they represent as well as to a higher perceived level of credibility.

It is fair to say that in the past, environmentalists have won substantial gains in drafting and passing national environmental protection laws. This is reflected in the general tendency of environmental law to set safety rather than efficiency standards for pollution control as well as in the passage of substantial environmental legislation under conservative Presidents Bush (senior) and Reagan.

Due to their ability to mobilize voters, grassroots environmental movements have also done well at the local level, particularly in blocking the siting of new facilities (power plants, landfills, incinerators) and, in some cases, promoting alternatives such as recycling. Environmentalists have also had some success leveraging their voting power at the state level (California, Wisconsin, New York) and have also faced severe challenges in states traditionally dominated by particular industries (Louisiana, oil, gas, and chemicals; and Kentucky, coal).

This has been evident in the recent fight over climate legislation. In early 2009, the fossil fuel industry was outspending environmental lobbyists ten to one. On advertising, the ratio was three to one: industry spent $76 million on ads in the first four months of the year, and environmental groups, including Al Gore's Alliance for Climate Protection, the Environmental Defense Fund, and the Sierra Club, countered with $28 million in the same period. At the same time, seven key Democratic lawmakers on the House committee deciding the initial shape of the legislation each received more than $100,000 from oil and gas, coal, and electricity companies during the 2008 election cycle.[6]

Besides the fossil fuel industry, a few of the dozens of other major industry trade groups with a strong lobbying presence in Washington include the Chemical Manufacturers Association, the Fertilizer Institute, the American Paper Institute, and the Chlorine Institute. In addition, most of the large chemical, petroleum, and manufacturing firms maintain their own Washington staffs and/or hire DC law firms to lobby on their behalf.

Dollars can be used to buy a number of things useful for influencing the regulatory debate: technical studies, lobbying staff, the promise of future jobs, access to legislators and regulators, and votes (through advertising).

---

6. Goldenberg (2009).

As I have stressed, control over information is a crucial aspect of regulation. Thus the ability to hire "experts" to conduct **technical studies** of benefits and costs is an important channel of influence. A good example was the "full court press" launched by industry against the EPA's proposed technological standard for injection of hazardous wastes into deep wells. The Chemical Manufacturers Association, along with many of its members—Monsanto, CYRO Industries, Dow, DuPont, BP Chemicals, Celanese, Cynamid, and ARCO—met repeatedly with mid-level EPA officials, providing them with data about the cost of the new proposals as well as warnings of plant shutdowns. Some of the lobbyists threatened political repercussions if the agency did not respond. According to one EPA official, "We were attacked on a technical basis—the kind of case they felt they could make in a lawsuit if we didn't yield. Industry argued there would be huge costs if we went forward with the proposed rule. Depending on who you listened to, it was the end of the world."

The EPA's final rule was ultimately watered down substantially. The point here is not whether the company's claims were correct, which they may have been. Rather, in the information war surrounding the impact of the regulation, environmentalists did not have the resources to bring much expert testimony to bear. Moreover, even if they had access to information about costs, environmental groups did not have the **staff** capacity of the chemical companies. Dozens of industry lobbyists repeatedly delivered the same message to mid-level EPA officials, as well as to presidential staff. In this particular case, there is evidence that pressure from a close presidential adviser influenced the final EPA decision.[7]

Money buys information, lobbying and legal staff, and **access** to politicians and regulators. Out-and-out bribery—I'll contribute $5,000 to your campaign if you vote against bill X—is not common in the United States, though it is not unknown. Instead, the more money one contributes to a political campaign (or party), the more often one gets to meet with the politician or his or her appointees at the EPA to make one's case known. In an information war, where all sides can make a "reasonable" case on the surface, access is easily translated into influence. Industry has not been able to translate its dollar advantage into many clear-cut victories at the legislative level. Tough environmental laws remain on the books. However, industry is much more effective in using its resources to dilute the impact of these laws. Through the revolving door of domination of information generation and delivery, large legal staffs, and superior access to politicians and political appointees, industry probably wins more often than it loses in all of the steps subsequent to the passage of laws. From the public-comment phase in the drafting of regulations by the EPA, through the implementation and enforcement of these laws by state officials, through the budgeting of resources to these agencies, through the opportunity for court challenges and through bargaining over and compliance, industry has many opportunities to influence how the ultimate regulatory process will work.

Washington lawyer Lloyd Cutler, whose firm has represented many corporate clients, put it this way: "It would be wrong to think that corporations are on top or ahead. They feel very put upon or defeated. It's true that they manage to survive and deal and push things off—they feel the added costs of regulation exceed the benefits

---

7. See Greider (1990, 138–40).

[editor's note: an efficiency perspective!]—but they would say the notion that they now control or dominate the health and safety agencies is just crazy." Still, Cutler explained, "It's harder to pass a law than to stop one. On the whole, I would say the professional lobbyists and lawyers prefer to live in this world where there are so many buttons to push, so many other places to go if you lose your fight."[8]

Given this balance of power—environmentalists with the edge in the national legislative arena, business dominant in the regulatory sphere—an unfortunate dynamic develops. Environmentalists, anticipating that laws will be weakened on implementation, try to push through Congress very stringent, sometimes unachievable goals. Industry, galvanized by this threat, pours more resources into mitigating the regulatory impact.

There are many potential solutions to the problem of bureaucratic discretion and political influence; several are explored later in this book. At this point, we focus on the potential for political reform of the regulatory process itself.

12.5 Political Reform of Regulation

Efforts at gaining political influence are often a form of the positional competition discussed in the previous chapter. In such a zero-sum, or negative-sum, game, the gains of one party can come only at the expense of another. Under these circumstances, a natural tendency is to overinvest resources in unproductive competition. This situation can be analyzed through the prisoner's dilemma model, last seen in our Chapter 11 discussion of the rat race. Figure 12.2 illustrates the situation in a hypothetical regulatory decision about an emissions standard.

Each side must decide how many lobbyists to deploy. If neither group lobbies, then a standard of 4 ppm will be set. Note that an identical result will occur if both sides send a lobbyist—the extra efforts cancel one another out. If environmentalists don't lobby and industry does, then a loose standard of 6 ppm will result. If, on the other hand, industry doesn't lobby and environmentalists do, a strict standard of 2 ppm will emerge.

What is the likely outcome of this kind of setup? If there is no agreement to restrict lobbying, environmentalists must assume that industry will lobby (and vice versa for

		Environmentalists	
		Don't lobby	Lobby
Industry	Don't lobby	4 ppm	2 ppm
	Lobby	6 ppm	4 ppm

FIGURE 12.2 A Zero-Sum Lobbying Competition

8. From Greider (1990, 134).

industry). Thus each side will choose a lobbying strategy for defensive purposes, even though the same outcome could be achieved at lower cost. Moreover, the process is likely to escalate into a full-blown "lobby race" as each side tries to forestall the other from gaining an advantage.

An agreement to limit lobbying seems in the interests of both parties. If cheating on such an agreement were easily observable, the agreement would be self-enforcing: If industry observed environmentalists cheating, it could simply retaliate by sending in its own lobbyist. However, if cheating is not easily detectable, as is the case in lobbying, the agreement will break down as each side cheats to protect itself from the possibility that the other will cheat!

The prisoner's dilemma model implies that cooperation rather than competition might be in everyone's best interest. How might this insight actually be applied in the regulatory arena? One approach is to adopt a **corporatist model of regulation**. Here, regulations would be explicitly decided in a bargaining context between representatives of "corporate" groups—the EPA, private firms, and environmental organizations. In exchange for being included at the table, all the groups would have to agree to abide by and support the final outcome. The EPA would thus be given much more flexibility in determining policy and be insulated from subsequent lawsuits. In essence, the corporatist model accepts that "a few big interests" determine the details of government environmental policy and provides a more efficient forum for them to do so.

European countries have adopted a more corporatist approach to regulation than we have in the United States. The fruits of corporatism can be seen in efforts by the Netherlands; since 1989 the Dutch government has instituted a series of "environmental covenants" with different industries. These covenants are voluntary agreements among government regulators and industry to reduce specific pollutants by specified amounts, and once signed, they have the force of a contract under civil law.[9]

However, it is not clear how well corporatist regulation really works, nor whether it can be successfully translated to the United States. Corporatism requires trimming back general public access to decision makers and is often perceived as a restriction of democracy. Who, for example, gets a seat at the table? Indeed, some believe that the environmental movement has already been split between the "conservative" DC-based national groups and more "radical" grassroots organizations and that the latter have accused the former of selling out to industrial interests. Moreover, the national groups have few members from working-class or minority communities, which have their own environmental interests.

Unlike European countries (and Canada), the United States does not have a strong labor or social-democratic political party to counterbalance the political influence of business. Partly for this reason, Americans have been much more distrustful than Europeans of placing discretionary decision-making power in the hands of government bureaucrats. In the United States, it is not clear that the national environmental groups, which are unaccountable to the voters—or indeed, the EPA, have the power to represent and enforce the public's general interest in environmental protection. Thus many people would oppose trading in the restrictions imposed on bureaucratic

---

9. See Arentsen, Bressers, and O'Toole (2005).

discretion under the current judicial regulatory model for a more goal-oriented, but less open, corporatist model.

If excess resources are indeed being devoted to influencing the political process, a straightforward economic response would be to raise the cost by eliminating the status that lobbying now holds as a **tax-deductible business expense**. More generally, **campaign finance reform** could serve to reduce efforts by all sides to gain advantage. Unfortunately, given the benefits to incumbent politicians of the existing system, genuine campaign finance reform has proven quite difficult to achieve. Finally, moving more responsibility for regulation to the state level, a policy known as **environmental federalism**, would both bring issues closer to those affected and reduce the influence of Washington-based interests. The case against such environmental federalism is that competition between states for business will lead to lower overall levels of environmental protection. The seriousness of this latter problem remains unclear.[10]

Political reform of the regulatory process might occur through a move away from a judicial to a corporatist model, by reducing the role of money in politics by raising the cost of lobbying or campaign finance reform, or through decentralization. However, while potentially helpful, none of these reforms would fundamentally challenge the underlying problems of imperfect information and political influence in the regulatory process. Indeed, these two issues have led some to despair over government's ability to stem the process of environmental decline. As an extreme example of government failure, we turn briefly to the experience in the former Communist nations.

12.6 Better Information, More Democracy

The environmental consequences of limited information and lack of political account-ability were made clear after the fall of the Berlin Wall in 1989, when the frightening conditions in the former Communist regimes became public. Driven to industrialize at all costs and despite official laws mandating strict environmental protection, officials in the state-owned industries proceeded to raise the level of poison in the land, water, and air to fatal degrees. Commenting on the widespread use of highly toxic pesticides such as DDT; the contamination and exhaustion of agricultural water resources; urban centers with air pollutants typically five times above legal levels; rivers and seas filled with untreated agricultural, industrial, and human waste; and death and disease from the Chernobyl nuclear accident and military nuclear wastes, one set of authors con-cluded: "When historians finally conduct an autopsy on the Soviet Union and Soviet Communism, they may reach the verdict of death by ecocide."[11]

What lessons can we learn from this story? Traditional conservatives have argued that the lesson is a simple one: "free-market economics, good; government involvement in the economy, bad." Yet, with the Soviet model of a centrally planned economy discredited, the environmental problems the globe faces are now generated primarily by market economies and market-driven growth. Thus the traditional conservative lesson provides us with only limited guidance. Clearly, governments can create environmental disasters that rival, if not exceed, those generated by private economic actors. Yet, in capitalist countries, government is *not* the primary source of environmental problems.

---

10. See the discussion in Oates (2001).
11. From Feshbach and Friendly (1992, 1).

Instead, as both world population and economic activity continue to grow, the Soviet story is best viewed as a cautionary tale: without an *effective* governmental process forcing economic actors to pay for the externalities they impose on others, ecocide is a future that may await many countries, if not the entire globe.

Most economic comparisons between communism and capitalism have focused on the market versus private ownership distinction. Yet, in capitalist countries, environmental degradation is the result of factors *external* to market transactions. A **demand for environmental protection** can be expressed only through government action. Thus the key issue is the responsiveness of the political system to this kind of demand.

Given this, the political distinction between Western countries and the former USSR—democracy versus totalitarianism—is probably more relevant to environmental concerns than the market versus state ownership distinction. When scientists or environmentalists in the Soviet Union attempted to bring information forward, they did so only at personal risk and generally found themselves cut off from any effective means of communication. Whenever economic decision makers can insulate themselves from those exposed to pollution—either through control over information or suppression of dissent—externalities are unlikely to be accounted for by the political system.

For example, one need not look to the Soviet Union to find governmental abuses of the environment. Many of the worst hazardous waste sites in our country resulted from U.S. military programs, shrouded in Cold War secrecy. At the Hanford nuclear site in eastern Washington, for example, the U.S. Department of Energy has created a gargantuan waste problem, the extent of which is only now becoming clear after 50 years of tight information control. The cleanup at Hanford, if indeed it goes through, is expected to cost at least $60 billion—more than the entire Superfund program directed at civilian dumps. In the United States, however, the potential for this kind of environmental abuse by the government has been largely reigned in by mandated public scrutiny of major decisions: the environmental impact statement process described in Chapter 9.

Consider another example. Agricultural workers in many poor, market-oriented countries employ the same environmentally destructive agricultural techniques so decried in the Soviet Union. These include the widespread use of pesticides, such as DDT, that have been banned in developed countries. Farmworkers and their families who bear the brunt of the environmental costs in these countries have neither access to information about alternatives nor sufficient political power to challenge the marketing efforts of the firms that profit from the sale of these chemicals. (Indeed, farmworkers in our own country have much less influence over environmental policy than suburban professionals who provide the core support for major environmental groups.)

Both **access to information** and the practice of **effective and widespread democracy** are thus necessary ingredients for successful environmental policy. Without them, citizens cannot translate their demand for environmental protection into a reality. Absent substantial pressure from those affected, government will have neither the power nor the inclination to force economic decision makers—whether state bureaucrats, managers of private corporations, or ordinary citizens—to internalize the external environmental costs generated by their actions.

Part IV of this book explores how this prescription of knowledge and power might be applied in poor countries to address problems ranging from population growth to conservation. Here, in the United States, a general trend toward accountability has been embodied in environmental law, ranging from the EIS to requirements for public hearings in the regulatory process to more recent innovations such as the **Toxics Release Inventory**. In 1986, after a chemical factory in Bhopal, India, exploded, killing and maiming thousands, the U.S. Congress passed the Emergency Planning and Community Right-to-Know Act. The act required companies to publicly report on their releases of 450 chemicals suspected or known to be toxic, many of them unregulated.

The Toxics Release Inventory provides self-reported data on chemical releases on a plant-by-plant basis across the country. This information is now on the Web at www.epa.gov/tri; you can go there and check out emissions from a plant in your neighborhood! The TRI has a variety of goals, but an important one has been to make industry decision makers more accountable to the communities in which they operate. The TRI has spawned a variety of community-based, nonregulatory efforts to reduce chemical emissions. It provides a good example of how expanded information and effective democracy can serve to internalize externalities associated with economic production.[12] (For more on the TRI, see Chapters 13 and 14.)

What, then, are the environmental lessons from communism? Given that government action is needed to force market actors to account for external costs, the experience of the former USSR teaches that *"unaccountable* government intervention is bad."* When government uses its authority to silence its critics or distort and control information flows, or when those on the receiving end of environmental externalities have little real power, government failure in the environmental arena is likely. Strict environmental laws, without a vigilant, informed citizenry, are hollow laws.

12.7 Summary

This chapter has provided an introduction to the political economy of regulation. The regulatory process begins with national legislation. The EPA then translates the law into specific regulations. Finally, state governments implement and enforce the guidelines developed by the EPA. The United States has adopted a judicial model of regulation in which the EPA is required to go through a formal and elaborate process of information gathering and public hearings and must establish a quasi-legal basis for its major regulatory actions. The judicial model is designed to limit abuse of authority by regulatory bureaucrats but can be easily exploited to generate regulatory gridlock.

From an economic point of view, the primary obstacle to effective regulation is imperfect information. Regulators have only limited resources with which to gather information on the costs and benefits of a proposed rule and so must often turn to the very sources they regulate for information about the problem. This sets up a reporting bias problem: how can regulators be sure the information they receive is correct? One way is to train and retain qualified technical personnel within the regulatory agency. Another way is to design regulatory policy to minimize incentives for distortion.

Regardless of how much good information the agency collects, however, bureaucrats are still left with substantial discretion in interpreting how environmental laws

---

12. See Fung and O'Rourke (2000).

are to be implemented. Consideration of bureaucratic interests—agency building, personal career building, and job satisfaction—reveal no necessary bias toward over- or underregulation. Yet discretion raises the problem of political influence.

Who wins and who loses in the influence game? Due to their superior ability to mobilize votes, environmentalists sometimes make substantial gains in the legislative arena, while given their monetary advantage, industry tends to come out ahead in the regulatory process. The big loser from this adversarial structure is public faith in the rule of law. Public disenchantment with the EPA is a serious problem as an effective and respected regulatory agency is the principal tool we now have for controlling market externalities.

The prisoner's dilemma model suggests that competition between environmentalists and industry to influence bureaucrats leads to an inefficiently high level of lobbying and lawsuits. One suggested response to this problem has been to replace the judicial model of regulation, which imposes many legal restrictions on the EPA's behavior, with a corporatist model that gives the EPA much more discretion. Corporatism could potentially foster a more cooperative spirit between industry and environmentalists and is more widespread in Europe. Critics of corporatism argue, however, that in the U.S. context, where the government bureaucracy is relatively weak, corporatism amounts to a sellout to industry interests.

More straightforward ways of reducing lobbying include eliminating its tax-exempt status and instituting campaign finance reform. Environmental federalism would also help reduce the influence of Washington, DC–based interests but might lead to interstate competition to weaken standards.

Many have argued that the collapse of the Soviet Union demonstrates the ecological superiority of market-based economic systems over centrally planned systems. Environmental disaster in the former USSR certainly confirms that state socialism is not the answer to environmental problems. But the problem remains: market-based economic systems have the potential to ultimately generate ecocide on a level comparable to that of communism.

The relevant lesson from the former USSR is that a lack of effective democracy will doom well-meaning government environmental initiatives to failure. Economic decision makers—whether state planners or private managers—will take external environmental costs into account (internalize them) only if those who bear the costs have the political power to force internalization. Nurturing effective democracy, in turn, requires both empowering citizens and providing access to information. The Toxics Release Inventory is a good example of this in the United States.

This chapter has focused on the obstacles that the information-intensive regulatory process has encountered in attempts to achieve its legislative target—efficiency, safety, or sustainability in pollution control. The potential solutions discussed here have focused on procedural or political reforms such as better information gathering, a move to corporatism, campaign finance reform, and right-to-know laws.

By contrast, Part III of this book focuses on economic reforms of the pollution control process. Chapters 15 and 16 explore one option: a system of regulation that relies on *economic incentives*, requiring less information and fewer bureaucratic decisions. A second possibility is discussed in Chapters 17 through 19. Rather than reform the regulatory process itself, instead refocus government pollution control policy on the promotion of clean technology, which reduces pollution in the first place. A final, and more optimistic view is that, despite the many problems with the regulatory process, overall it has worked surprisingly well. We take up this line of argument in the next two chapters.

APPLICATION 12.0

Corporatist Solutions?

To implement portions of the 1990 Clean Air Act, the EPA adopted a distinctly corporatist approach—negotiating the regulatory details with representatives from industry, the states, and big environmental groups.[13] Agreement was reached by representatives of these generally hostile groups on regulations designed to encourage the use of the so-called clean fuels. Industry benefited by having gasoline content standards set on an average basis rather than for every gallon of fuel. This provision reduced costs substantially. Environmentalists won a favorable resolution of an ambiguity that Congress had left in the law about the maximum allowable vapor pressure for fuels.

1. As the price for participation, all of the parties to the agreement pledged not to sue the EPA over its final clean-fuel regulations. Assume the agreement to sue is not legally binding. What incentives do the parties at the table have to abide by their promise not to sue?

2. The *New York Times* reports that all parties involved were happy with the clean-fuels decision, calling it a win-win solution. Relabel the prisoner's dilemma diagram in Section 12.5, using the strategies "negotiate" and "negotiate and sue" and the payoffs "average gas content" or "per gallon gas content" (for industry) and "strict vapor emissions" or "lax vapor emissions" (for environmentalists). Does the diagram illustrate, in principle, that all parties can be made better off by making an enforceable pledge not to sue?

3. Despite the apparent success of the clean-fuels negotiations, the EPA has made little headway in encouraging other corporatist endeavors. At the time of this particular deal, the Consensus and Dispute Resolution Staff at the agency had succeeded in getting agreements in only 12 out of 600 cases. Why might corporatist strategies be hard to implement in the United States?

4. In fact, not everyone was happy with the agreement. One critic of the corporatist approach, Stephen Viederman, put it this way: "'Where you stand,' according to Miles Law, 'depends on where you sit.' Who comes to the table is undeniably central to what is decided at the table.... The good news [about the clean-fuels decision] was a broader participation in rule-making, with the views of business and industry balanced by other groups" ("Who Comes to the Table" 1991). Based on the criticisms of corporatism discussed in Section 12.4, what do you think Viederman's bad news might be?

---

13. This problem is drawn from information reported in "U.S. Agencies Use Negotiations" (1991).

APPLICATION 12.1

The Power of Information

Head to www.epa.gov/tri, read the *TRI Overview*, and then find out about the toxic releases for several plants in your zip code, or one nearby. Do you find that the information is reported in an understandable form? Do you get any sense of the relative risk of exposure from the toxic releases reported? What has been happening to the reported releases over time? These data are self-reported by the companies. Do you trust its accuracy? If you were concerned about the health risk posed by the toxic releases in your neighborhood, what would you do about it?

KEY IDEAS IN EACH SECTION

12.0   This chapter discusses two primary obstacles to effective government regulation of pollution: **imperfect information** and the opportunity for **political influence**.

12.1   The "generic" regulatory process has three steps: (1) passage of a law by Congress and the president, (2) drafting of regulations by the EPA, and (3) implementation and enforcement by state officials. The United States currently relies on a **judicial model of regulation**, which reduces bureaucratic discretion and also can lead to regulatory gridlock.

12.2   The first obstacle facing regulators is highly imperfect information. Because the agency has so many tasks, it often drafts rules based on inadequate or poor data. In addition, the agency must deal with a **reporting bias** when it turns to outside groups for information. Two ways to address this problem are to improve **in-house analysis** and rely on **incentive-compatible regulation**.

12.3   Imperfect information gives rise to **bureaucratic discretion** in drafting and enforcing regulations. Bureaucratic motivations include **agency building**, **external career building** (influenced by the **revolving door**), and **job satisfaction**. Job satisfaction, in turn, can depend on **ideology**, the exercise of **power**, and the maintenance of a **quiet life**.

12.4   Where there is bureaucratic discretion, there is the opportunity for political influence. Political resources wielded by environmental groups and industry include **votes** and **dollars**. Dollars are useful for buying (1) **technical studies**, (2) lobbying **staff**, (3) **access** to decision makers, and (4) votes. This book argues that environmentalists win more often at the legislative stage of the regulatory process while industry wins more often at all subsequent stages.

12.5   The prisoner's dilemma model suggests that competition for political influence is a zero-sum game leading to an overinvestment in lobbying. Political reforms that might reduce this wasted effort include adopting a **corporatist model of regulation**, moving toward more **environmental federalism** and **campaign finance reform**, and eliminating the **tax-deductible status** of lobbying. The first two policies, however, are not without costs; the latter two have proven politically quite difficult.

12.6   The Communist experience illustrates the potential for massive government failure in the regulatory process. Such failure is most likely when citizens are unable to express their political **demand for environmental regulation**. Doing so requires both **access to information** and **effective and widespread democracy**. The **Toxics Release Inventory** is a good example of government action to encourage such trends in the United States.

REFERENCES

Arentsen, Maarten, Hans Th. A. Bressers, and Laurence J. O'Toole Jr. 2005. Institutional and policy responses to uncertainty in environmental policy: A comparison of Dutch and U.S. styles. *Policy Studies Journal* 28(3): 597–611.

Broder, John. 2007. Rule to expand mountaintop coal mining. *New York Times*, 23 August, Page 1.

Bryner, Gary C. 1987. *Bureaucratic discretion*. New York: Pergamon.

Cleaning up. 1990. *The Atlantic*, October.

Feshbach, Murray, and Alfred Friendly Jr. 1992. *Ecocide in the USSR*. New York: Basic Books.

Fung, Archon, and Dara O'Rourke. 2000. Reinventing environmental regulation from the grassroots up: Explaining and expanding the success of the toxics release inventory. *Environmental Management* 25(2): 115–27.

Goldenberg, Suzanne. 2009. Barack Obama's key climate bill hit by $45M PR campaign. *Guardian*, 12 May, Page 1.

Greider, William. 1990. *Who will tell the people? The betrayal of American democracy*. New York: Simon & Schuster.

Jenkins, Robin, Elizabeth Kopits, and David Simpson. 2009. Policy monitor—The evolution of solid and hazardous waste regulation in the United States. *Review of Environmental Economics and Policy* 3(1): 104–20.

Oates, Wallace. 2001. *A reconsideration of environmental federalism*. Discussion paper 01–54. Washington, DC: Resources for the Future.

Sanjour, William. 1992. *What EPA is like and what can be done about it*. Washington, DC: Environmental Research Foundation.

U.S. agencies use negotiations to pre-empt lawsuits over rules. 1991. *New York Times*, 23 September.

What really pollutes? Study of a refinery proves an eye-opener. 1993. *Wall Street Journal*, 29 March.

Who comes to the table? 1991. New York: Jessie Smith Noyes Foundation.

13

AN OVERVIEW OF ENVIRONMENTAL LEGISLATION

13.0 Introduction

Perhaps the most striking aspect of the U.S. national environmental regulation is its brief history. As recently as 45 years ago, the United States had *no* major federal legislation controlling the discharge of pollutants into the air and water, *no* national regulations covering the disposal of hazardous waste onto land, *no* process for reviewing new chemicals, only a limited procedure for registering new pesticides, and *no* protection for endangered species.

Before 1970, the states had sole responsibility for pollution-control activities, but even at the state level, serious efforts at environmental protection have only a short history. Oregon initiated the first statewide air pollution control effort in 1952; only California had mandated tailpipe emission standards for cars by 1970. In the late 1950s and 1960s, as national attention began focusing on environmental problems, the federal government passed a variety of laws encouraging such decentralized efforts to regulate air and water pollution. These laws sponsored research on the health effects of pollution, provided resources for technical assistance and mechanisms for resolving cross-boundary disputes, and put informal pressure on U.S. automakers to reduce vehicle emissions.

On April 20, 1970, Americans celebrated Earth Day for the first time. Also that year, motivated by increasing public awareness, dissatisfaction with slow state regulatory efforts, and little improvement in the pollution performance of U.S. cars, the U.S. Congress struck out on a different, centralized environmental road. The Clean Air Act (CAA) amendments of 1970 embraced a new philosophy in which minimum standards for air pollution control for the entire nation would be set in Washington. During the remainder of the decade, a similar approach was adopted for water pollution, solid and hazardous waste disposal, and chemical and pesticide registration.

New pollution laws continued to pass at the federal level through the early 1990s, but over the last two decades, the legislative pendulum has swung back to the states. Because the federal government has been slow to regulate emissions of carbon dioxide

(CO_2), the principal global-warming pollutant, states on the East and West coasts have begun imposing their own statewide restrictions on carbon dioxide.

By historical standards, environmental protection efforts are still in their childhood. Nevertheless, environmental protection is growing up fast. As detailed in Chapter 6, the share of national output devoted to the environment has increased from about 1% to more than 2.8% over the last 40 years. This chapter provides an overview of national legislation in five areas: air pollution, water pollution, hazardous waste, toxic substances, and endangered species.

With this background laid, in the next chapter we move on to consider the actual accomplishments of this legislation, criticisms of regulation, and an evaluation of the prospects for future regulatory success.

13.1 Cleaning the Air

The original CAA, passed in 1963, focused on federal assistance to the states. Major amendments to the CAA occurred in 1970, 1977, and 1990 and have shaped the national regulatory framework.[1] The CAA (as amended) mandates a safety standard. Standards are to be set to "provide an **adequate margin of safety** … to protect the public … from any known or anticipated adverse effects associated with such air pollutants in the ambient air." Congress explicitly ruled out a consideration of costs and benefits in the attainment of this goal. Yet, as we saw in Chapter 7, completely safe levels of many pollutants, short of zero discharge, do not exist. One of the difficulties the EPA has had in implementing the CAA has been in hammering out a politically acceptable definition of safety.

The CAA distinguishes two types of air pollutants. First are the so-called criteria (or common) air pollutants: particulates, sulfur dioxide, carbon monoxide, nitrogen oxide, ground-level ozone (smog), and lead. All these pollutants generate a variety of respiratory and heart-related problems, some contribute to cancer, and lead also causes neurological diseases. Ground-level ozone, better known as smog, should not be confused with ozone in the upper atmosphere. Ground-level ozone is a harmful pollutant, while the ozone layer surrounding the earth provides a shield protecting us from dangerous ultraviolet rays. Similarly, carbon monoxide (CO)—the fatal gas that accumulates in a closed garage when the car is running—should not be confused with carbon dioxide. Carbon dioxide, which is the major contributor to global warming, is also emitted from cars but does not directly harm human health.

In addition to the criteria pollutants, Congress was also concerned about other less common air pollutants, which are also carcinogenic or interfere with reproductive, immune, or neurological systems. These pollutants, now called **hazardous air pollutants** or **air toxics**, are also regulated under a safety standard, but in a different manner than the criteria pollutants.

For the criteria pollutants, Congress directed the EPA to develop **National Ambient Air Quality Standards (NAAQS)**. **Ambient air quality** refers to the average quality of air in a particular region. Each criteria pollutant was to be given a primary standard, designed to protect human health, and a secondary standard that focused on protecting

---

1. Portney (2000) provides a good, detailed discussion of air pollution policy.

TABLE 13.1 Primary NAAQS for Criteria Air Pollutants

Pollutant	Averaging Time	Concentration Level	
		ppm	$\mu g/m^3$
Particulate matter (PM10)	Annual	—	50.0
	24-hour	—	150.0
Sulfur dioxide	Annual	0.030	80.0
	24-hour	0.140	365.0
Carbon monoxide	8-hour	9.000	10.0
	1-hour	35.000	40.0
Nitrogen oxide	Annual	0.053	100.0
Ozone	8-hour	0.008	—
Lead	Max quarterly	—	1.5

Source: Portney (2000, Table 4.2), who cites as his source the Office of Planning and Standards, *National Air Quality and Emissions Trend Report*, Research Triangle Park, NC: U.S. EPA, 1998.

wildlife, visibility, and ecological systems. Table 13.1 lists the primary NAAQS for the six criteria pollutants.[2]

The NAAQS are minimum standards, uniform around the country. In other words, regardless of the variation in compliance costs, all regions are expected to meet the NAAQ levels of air quality. If they desire, states are allowed to impose stricter standards.

What about areas already cleaner than the NAAQS? The 1977 CAA amendments set up a three-tiered system designed to prevent the significant deterioration of air quality. National parks and other scenic areas were designated Class I, in which air quality was to be maintained at the current level. Most areas were put into Class II, in which some deterioration was allowed. In the remaining areas, Class III, air quality was allowed to fall to the level of the NAAQS, but not below.

Once the NAAQS were set, each state was required to develop a **state implementation plan** detailing how emissions from both **stationary sources** (factories, power plants) and **mobile sources** (cars, trucks, airplanes) would be controlled to meet the ambient standards. To do this, state environmental officials first had to divide their territory into the so-called air quality control regions, geographic areas sharing similar air pollution problems. The plan would then provide an implementation strategy for each region.

For stationary sources, the EPA requires states to use what is known as **technology-based regulation**. For all new sources, the states must mandate the type of pollution technology required for new plants. These New Source Performance Standards (NSPS) require firms to install the "best technological system of emissions reduction" commercially available at the time the standards are set. Note that NSPS technology may not be sufficient to achieve the NAAQ standard; it is simply supposed to represent a serious effort to get there.

---

2. Only sulfur dioxide has a secondary standard tighter than the primary standards. Carbon monoxide has no secondary standard; for particulates, nitrogen oxide, ozone, and lead, the secondary standard is identical to the primary standard. See Portney (2000).

State regulators are also supposed to define even more stringent technology-based regulation for sources wishing to locate in areas that have not achieved the NAAQ standards (**nonattainment areas**). Such firms must use the lowest achievable emission rate (LAER) technology. Those wishing to locate in Class I (pristine) areas are theoretically required to achieve yet another standard, the best available control technology (BACT). In practice, there is often little difference between NSPS, LAER, and BACT.

Until 1990, states were not required to impose technology-based regulations on existing sources. However, the 1990 CAA amendments require the states to define and impose RACT, reasonably available control technology, on existing sources in nonattainment areas. RACT, BACT, LAER, NSPS—these acronyms seem bewildering upon introduction, and in fact, the actual regulatory process is quite tortured. The legal struggle to define what these different terms mean for individual industries has been one of the primary battlegrounds in the information war discussed in the previous chapter.

There are several major, ongoing exceptions to the technology-based regulation of stationary sources common under the CAA. Authorities in the Los Angeles area and the northeastern United States have created incentive-based "cap-and-trade" programs designed to provide firms with substantial flexibility in achieving targets for emissions of criteria pollutants. The 1990 CAA amendments also provided for a similar flexible system to control acid rain that created a nationwide trading program capping sulfur dioxide and nitrogen oxide emissions from power plants. These alternative incentive-based approaches will be explored in detail in Chapters 15 and 16.

To control emissions of criteria pollutants from mobile sources, the CAA has put most of the burden on auto manufacturers, requiring several rounds of reductions in vehicle emissions for new cars. This policy, however, has been criticized as a cost-ineffective strategy for achieving the NAAQS, because it builds in equally high costs for auto consumers in both clean and dirty areas. In other words, rural residents wind up paying for cleanup they may not need, in the form of higher priced cars. The EPA has also required nonattainment areas to use more closely targeted programs, including vehicle-inspection programs and the sale of reformulated (lower polluting) fuels. In addition, as we discuss further in Chapter 18, California has implemented a low-emission vehicles program in an attempt to meet the NAAQ standard.

To summarize: For the criteria pollutants, the regulatory process is now well advanced and progress has been made on several fronts, though problems remain. By contrast, the air toxics case illustrates regulatory gridlock at its extreme. Under the 1970 CAA statute, the EPA was instructed to identify and regulate hazardous air pollutants, defined as substances "which may reasonably be anticipated to result in an increase in mortality or an increase in serious, irreversible, or incapacitating reversible illness."[3] As with the criteria pollutants, the CAA established "an ample margin of safety" as the regulatory target.

Over the next 20 years, the process went into a deep stall. The EPA argued that a literal interpretation of the CAA's safety mandate would require a zero-discharge

---

3. This discussion of the air toxics program draws from Robinson and Pease (1991), who also provide the quote from the 1970 CAA.

standard, effectively banning dozens of valuable industrial chemicals. Unwilling to take such a severe step, the agency chose to ignore the problem and regulated only a couple of air toxics during the 1970s. Environmentalists sued the agency, arguing that bans were not necessary; instead, high levels of (expensive) controls should be imposed on products without substitutes. A compromise along these lines was developing in the late 1970s but collapsed with the election of President Reagan in 1980, who had campaigned on a deregulatory agenda.

During the first half of the decade, the EPA chose to "study the problem." However, by the late 1980s, pressure was building for action: the 1984 explosion of a chemical plant in Bhopal, India, and the congressionally mandated release of plant-by-plant chemical emissions (the TRI discussed in Chapter 12) prodded the EPA into a study revealing that cancer risks from air toxics in 205 communities around the country exceeded 1 in 1,000.

The impasse was finally addressed in the 1990 CAA. The 1990 amendments adopt technology-based regulation, requiring the EPA to specify MACT (maximum achievable control technology) for different sources emitting 189 air pollutants presumed to be hazardous. The EPA can add or delete substances from this list. MACT was not supposed to achieve an "ample margin of safety" immediately, because Congress mandated that it be selected with some consideration of attainment cost. However, once MACT had been put in place, additional control measures would be required to reduce any residual cancer risk to a level of at least 1 in 10,000 for the most exposed population, with an ultimate risk target of 1 in 1 million for the population at large. The EPA has since issued dozens of MACT regulations and initiated several of the follow-up industry-level risk analyses.[4]

Up through 2012, however, certain pollutants continue to slip through the regulatory cracks; airborne mercury (primarily from coal-fired power plants) was the most egregious offender. Originally considered an air toxic, mercury escaped regulatory attention until 2000, when MACT rules were finally proposed by the Clinton administration. But the Bush EPA decided to reject the Clinton proposals and reclassified mercury as a criteria pollutant—enabling the agency to propose less strict regulations that also featured a cap-and-trade component (more on this in Chapter 16). Several states then sued the Bush EPA over this decision, and in 2008, the courts determined that the EPA had acted improperly in declaring mercury a nontoxic air pollutant. The Obama administration dropped the Bush plan, and in 2012, mercury regulation using MACT command-and-control techniques was finally being put into place.

To summarize, for air toxics, it took 20 years of stalled progress and contentious litigation until, in 1990, policymakers finally took the bull by the horns and defined clearly what was meant by "an ample margin of safety." With some very notable exceptions like mercury, the process of regulating air toxics is now well under way. The 1990 CAA amendments, however, addressed only stationary sources of hazardous air pollutants. Only 20% of air toxics are in fact emitted by stationary sources that fall under the purview of the amendments. Thus, air toxic emissions from small and mobile sources remain uncontrolled under current legislation.[5]

---

4. Morgan Lewis (2004, 16).
5. Portney (2000).

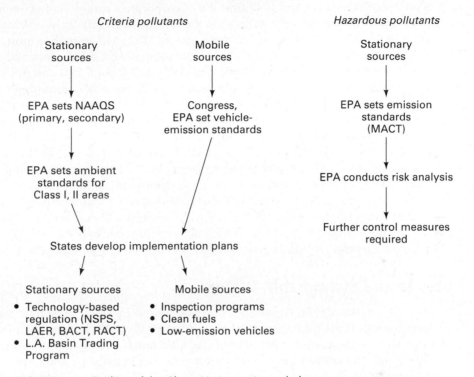

FIGURE 13.1 Outline of the Clean Air Act as Amended

Figure 13.1 provides a general outline of the CAA amendments. To summarize: The CAA sets a general goal of "safety" for the two categories of criteria and hazardous pollutants. Emissions of the criteria pollutants are regulated with the intent to achieve an ambient air quality standard within each air quality control region. By contrast, hazardous pollutants must meet emission standards ultimately designed to reduce cancer risks to the most exposed to *at least* 1 in 10,000. Finally, both programs are technology based. With a few exceptions, regulators decide on particular pollution-control technologies that firms are then required to adopt.

The CAA plays one final, critically important regulatory role. In 2007, the U.S. Supreme Court ruled that carbon dioxide and other greenhouse gasses should be considered criteria air pollutants, potentially harmful to human health and the environment. This opened the door to EPA regulating CO_2, and in 2009, the EPA concluded that greenhouse gas pollution did indeed constitute a threat to human health and welfare.

Given that CO_2 is a global pollutant, and stabilizing the climate is far outside the reach of any U.S. government agency, how did the EPA interpret their mandate under the CAA— to provide a safe level of air quality? Essentially, step-by-step: requiring BPT regulations, first for new sources, later for existing sources.

Under the Obama administration, the government has taken two major steps to reduce greenhouse gas pollution. First, corporate average fuel economy (CAFE) standards were increased for the first time in decades. By 2016, average fleet fuel economy is required to reach 35.5 mpg, and by 2025, 54.5 mpg. For more on this, see Chapter 17. And second, the EPA has begun to propose a set of command-and-control standards for major emitters—plants that emit more than 25,000 tons of CO_2 per year. The first proposed standard was unveiled in 2012, essentially requiring that any *new* coal-fired power plant produce no more CO_2 than a comparably sized natural gas plant. This effectively rules out the construction of new coal plants that do not intend to capture and sequester their carbon.

Following Obama's re-election in 2012, the next step for the EPA will be the regulation of greenhouse gas emissions from already existing power plants and industrial sources. This step will be much more controversial, and faces strong political opposition, particularly from "Tea Party" conservatives. Interestingly, in the utility sector, states might be able to comply with any new CO_2 reduction requirements by joining the Northeastern states "Regional Greenhouse Gas Initiative" (RGGI), which is an existing cap-and-trade system for carbon dioxide. More on this in Chapter 16.

13.2 Fishable and Swimmable Waters

The first national water pollution law was passed in 1899. Its simple intent was to prevent industries from disrupting navigation by literally clogging rivers and streams with sludge, sawdust, or fiber. There was little national activity beyond this until the 1950s and 1960s, when the federal government began assisting and encouraging states to develop their own pollution standards. In 1972, however, Congress opted for a centralized strategy with the passage of the **Federal Water Pollution Control Act (FWPCA)**. In combination with the **Clean Water Act** of 1977, this legislation provides our basic water pollution framework.[6]

FWPCA laid out an ambitious safety-based goal: the achievement of **fishable and swimmable waters** by 1983. However, the legislation set its sight beyond this charge, which we might consider a reasonable safety standard as defined in Chapter 7 (the elimination of "significant" risk). FWPCA, in fact, called for the elimination of all risks—zero discharge of pollutants into navigable waters by 1985. Needless to say, this last goal has not been met. Finally, the act prohibits the discharge of "toxic materials in toxic amounts," another ambiguous phrase that has provided grist for the regulatory lawyers' mill.

Individual states are left to draft their own water-quality emissions guidelines. For consistency with the FWPCA, they must be sufficiently strict to allow swimming and some types of fishing. However, states are free to draft stricter regulation, for example, to protect water habitat or undeveloped rivers.

The approach used to achieve state water-quality targets is in many ways similar to the regulation of air toxics described in the previous section. In 1972, Congress envisioned two initial rounds of technology-based controls. The EPA was directed to determine the best practical technology (BPT) and a more stringent best available

6. The next few paragraphs are based on the more detailed discussion in Freeman (2000).

technology (BAT) so that all industrial dischargers could have the technologies installed by 1977 and 1983, respectively. The timetable proved too stringent, however, and was amended in 1977.[7] It took until 1988 for the EPA to issue all (save one) of its BAT regulations. Once BAT is in place, the EPA has the authority to impose a third round of even more stringent (better than the best!) technology-based controls on sources contributing to the pollution of lakes or streams that have yet to achieve state ambient quality standards.

Besides installing BPT and then BAT (or BAT alone for newcomers), each discharger must hold a permit that specifies his or her legal pollution emission level. State agencies are generally responsible for the permitting process and for enforcing compliance. The process does not always run smoothly. In the mid-1990s, the states of Alaska and Idaho together had a backlog of more than 1,000 permit applications.[8]

One of the major sources of water pollution is improperly treated sewage. As a result, a principal component of federal clean-water legislation has been the provision of **grants to municipalities** for the construction of sewage facilities. From 1965 to 1991, close to $100 billion in federal dollars were committed for this purpose. While the increased federal spending displaced spending by state and local authorities, overall federal aid did *accelerate* the pace of sewage treatment. In addition, financing sewer projects with federal tax dollars proved less regressive than local financing. However, because the federal aid came in the form of large grants, local incentives to carefully monitor construction costs were reduced and costs inflated.

Finally, federal clean-water legislation has focused primarily on stationary point sources of pollution (factories and sewage plants). However, **nonpoint water pollution** (runoff from storm sewers in urban areas and from farms and construction sites) has always been an important source of water pollution. For the last 20 years, siltation, nutrient and pesticide loading from agricultural runoff, has in fact been the primary source of pollution affecting our streams, rivers, and lakes. Nitrate pollution from fertilizer is one of these serious problems, leading to major "deadzones" at the mouth of the Mississippi River, in the Chesapeake Bay, and elsewhere.

The federal clean-water legislation puts responsibility for regulating nonpoint pollution on the states; the 1987 Water Quality Act requires states to develop the so-called best management practices to control runoff from industrial and agricultural sites. Progress in this area has been slow because the diverse nature of the nonpoint problem makes centralized, technology-based regulation infeasible.

Two ways to control nonpoint water pollution are to (1) reduce runoff and (2) reduce the volume of pollutants available to be mobilized, a "pollution-prevention" strategy. As an example of the latter, farmers have begun adopting the so-called conservation-tillage practices, which leave stubble in fields to reduce runoff. In addition, a variety of measures have been introduced that reduce overall pesticide use. We look more closely at some of these steps in Chapter 18. Finally, the EPA has experimented with permit trading between point and nonpoint sources. Under these experimental schemes, point sources can pay nonpoint sources to reduce pollution as an alternative to installing point-source technology controls.[9]

---

7. An additional technology category, best conventional technology, was also added here (Freeman 2000).
8. See "The EPA" (1998).
9. Details on the pilot programs can be found at www.epa.gov/owow/watershed/trading/.

Other water quality issues include controlling the loss of wetlands from both pollution and drainage. Wetlands are managed under a "no net loss" directive by the Federal Army Corps of Engineers, through the authority of the Clean Water Act. Finally, the recent emergence of "fracking" technology for use in recovering natural gas (see the discussion in Chapter 18) has led to an upsurge of concern about potential groundwater contamination. Groundwater itself is largely unprotected, coming under regulatory control only when there is a threat of contamination of drinking water.

13.3 Hazardous Waste Disposal on Land

The 1970s was the decade of air and water pollution legislation. In the 1980s, concern shifted to land disposal of hazardous waste. Although the initial law covering hazardous waste disposal, the **Resource Conservation and Recovery Act** (RCRA, pronounced RICK-ra), was passed in 1976, actual regulation did not get under way until 1980 and accelerated when the law was amended by Congress in 1984.[10] RCRA is concerned with current disposal practices. The second major piece of hazardous waste legislation deals with abandoned dump sites. The Comprehensive Environmental Response, Compensation, and Liability Act (CERCLA, better known as **Superfund**) was passed in 1980 and amended in 1986.

What exactly is hazardous waste? One inclusive definition is any substance that poses a potential, substantial threat to human health or the environment. However, resolving what this means has proved a thorny problem. The EPA has developed a **RCRA list** of several hundred substances and waste flows deemed to be hazardous, based on criteria such as ignitability, corrosivity, reactivity, and toxicity. However, certain materials—oil-drilling muds and mine tailings—were granted immunity from hazardous waste regulation under RCRA. Some states, such as California and Washington, have instituted more stringent definitions that effectively double the volume of substances regulated as hazardous.[11]

A typical hazardous waste dump will include many substances known or suspected either to be carcinogenic or to have adverse effects on reproductive, immune, or neurological systems. While hazardous waste thus clearly poses a potential threat to human health and the environment, what are the actual risks? This is a very contentious topic. Most exposure to waste occurs when chemicals leach out of dumps in rainwater or into the air in vaporous form. However, because the number of people living in close proximity to the dumps is small, and because residents come and go, it is difficult to establish whether elevated levels of disease sometimes found by such dumps occur by chance or as a result of exposure to water. Moreover, because many wastes are quite long-lived, long-term effects that are difficult to predict must be factored in.

Love Canal, formerly a suburb of Niagara Falls, New York, is the best-known example of a hazardous waste dump. From 1942 to 1953, the Hooker Chemical and Plastics Corporation (now Occidental Chemical) buried millions of pounds of chemical wastes encased in metal drums in the abandoned canal. Hooker then sold the site to

---

10. RCRA also authorizes the EPA to regulate a variety of nonhazardous wastes. These include wastes at municipal landfills as well as hazardous industrial wastes exempted from official designation as "RCRA hazardous wastes," for example, oil-drilling muds or incinerator ash.
11. See Jenkins, Kopits, and Simpson (2009).

the city for $1 as a possible location for an elementary school. A suburban housing development soon grew up around the area. However, the drums rusted, and liquid waste began to pool on the surface and seep into people's basements. In 1978, after growing concern by residents over reported health effects—ranging from the loss of fur on pets to birth defects and breast cancer—and the detection of high levels of chemicals in some homes, the state of New York ordered the area immediately around the dump evacuated.

Love Canal is probably the most extensively studied hazardous waste site in the world, yet many questions remain about possible health effects. The New York State Department of Health did find roughly double the expected rate of low-birthweight babies in a low-lying area adjacent to the dump during the period of active dumping, as well as a statistically significant increase in babies born with birth defects after the chemicals were dumped. Another study found that children who had lived in the canal area were shorter and weighed less than a control group.[12]

The Love Canal case illustrates first that improperly handled hazardous waste can pose a real health threat. Second, it shows that establishing the full extent of adverse health effects is quite difficult. One government-sponsored scientific review panel, charged with assessing public concern that hazardous waste poses a serious threat to public health, concluded only that such concern could be neither confirmed nor refuted.[13]

Nevertheless, because of the limited routes of exposure, and the small numbers of people living in the close vicinity of dumps, many have argued that hazardous waste is unlikely to pose a national health threat comparable to that of air and water pollution. Following this line of reasoning, the EPA's Science Advisory Panel did not list hazardous waste as a primary concern for ecological, welfare, or health risks (see Table 5.1). At Love Canal, after the dump had been capped with a layer of clay, the streams cleaned up, and other remedial action taken, the New York State Department of Health commissioner concluded in 1989 that some homes in the area could be safely reoccupied.[14]

However, despite official assessments that downplay the overall risk from hazardous waste, the public remains quite concerned. Partly, this has to do with a disagreement over the normative goal of environmental policy. Under a safety standard, the fact that the numbers at risk of exposure are small does not lessen concern. Concern over hazardous waste also has to do with the visibility of victims. While tracing a birth defect directly to a neighboring waste dump is difficult, it is easier than linking it to smokestack emissions a hundred miles away. Finally, the public remains wary of scientific risk assessment; given the current state of knowledge about possible effects of hazardous waste, such skepticism might be warranted.

The volume of hazardous waste is significant. Each year, American industry and households generate about 40 million tons that fall under RCRA regulation; much of the remainder is disposed of through liquid discharges regulated by the Clean Water Act. Household hazardous waste takes the form of used motor oil, house paint,

---

12. See Brown (1989) and Jenkins et al. (2009).
13. See National Research Council (1991, 1).
14. See Brown (1989).

pesticides, and batteries. The bulk of waste, however, is produced by industry, and about 2% of industrial sources produce 95% of the total.[15]

What happens to all this waste? Common disposal methods include surface impoundment, landfilling, injection into deep underground wells, direct or indirect discharge into surface waters, incineration, and treatment. However, under the presumption that disposal on land posed the greatest long-term environmental threat from hazardous waste (and given that discharge into water and air was already regulated), the 1984 RCRA amendments built in a strong **bias against land disposal**. The legislation essentially puts the burden of proof on firms to demonstrate that the disposal method is indeed safe.[16] Deep-well injection, incineration, recycling, and water discharge are thus likely to become the most common disposal methods in the future.

The regulatory framework for hazardous waste disposal under RCRA has a three-part focus. First, as noted, the EPA has been required to designate which substances are to be deemed hazardous. RCRA then requires cradle-to-grave tracking of such wastes. When hazardous waste is shipped, it must be accompanied by a manifest stating its origin and intermediate stops. This manifest system was designed to discourage illegal dumping, though its effect on this process is unclear.

Finally, RCRA requires that facilities that treat, store, or dispose of hazardous wastes are to be regulated under a safety standard. To accomplish this goal, RCRA imposes location restrictions and requires personnel training, groundwater monitoring, closure and post-closure plans, and adequate insurance coverage. Under RCRA, facilities can also be forced to clean up old dump sites under their jurisdiction in order to receive a permit. However, the stringency of regulations varies from program to program. As we saw in Chapter 12, the EPA's final regulatory standards for deep-well injection of wastes (finalized in 1989) were successfully challenged as too onerous by the chemical industry.

RCRA governs the current disposal of wastes. By contrast, CERCLA, or Superfund, provides a mechanism for cleaning up abandoned dump sites. Superfund takes its name from what was originally a large pool of money collected by the government in the form of taxes on the chemical and petroleum industries and a general corporate environmental tax, supplemented by personal income tax revenues, used to finance dump cleanups. However, the industry taxes were abolished in the mid-1990s, and the Superfund is largely exhausted. As a result, cleanup efforts around the country have slowed significantly due to lack of funding.

Superfund also provides another more controversial funding mechanism. Any party that disposed of waste in a particular dump, legally or not, can be sued by the government to finance the entire cost of the cleanup. This system, known as **strict, joint, and several liability**, was put in place as a way to fund cleanups without spending additional government dollars. If the government could find one responsible party, the theory went, that party would then have the incentive to uncover other dumpers. However, the system has developed into a legal morass. Rather than bear what are potentially tremendous cleanup costs, firms have devoted resources to suing one another and the government over who will pay what share. Detroit automakers,

15. See Sigman (2000).
16. See Jenkins et al. (2009).

for example, sued more than 200 parties, including the Girl Scouts, to contribute to one Michigan cleanup.[17]

Given this situation, the legal costs of Superfund can be quite high. As a percentage of cleanup costs, legal fees and other transaction expenses range from 23% to 31%; about $8 billion could be saved from currently designated Superfund sites if retroactive liability provisions were eliminated and cleanup was financed solely out of the trust fund.[18]

The liability system under Superfund does have one attractive efficiency feature: waste *generators*, not just disposal facility operators, are held strictly responsible for the ultimate fate of their waste; this policy clearly provides a powerful incentive for careful management practices today. **Fear of future liability** under Superfund has spurred manufacturers both to seek methods for reducing their use of hazardous chemicals and to take greater care in their disposal practices. Moreover, Superfund liability applies to a broader spectrum of potentially hazardous materials than does RCRA regulation.

In addition, some fear that weakening the retroactive liability provisions under Superfund in order to reduce legal costs may send the wrong signal to industry about government's future intent to force polluters to pay. Retroactive liability also encourages private parties to initiate cleanups of non-Superfund sites.

Beyond high legal costs, Superfund has been bedeviled by other problems, including site selection, costly cleanup efforts, and resolving the "How clean is clean?" issue. By 2011, from a universe of some 40,000 dump sites nationwide, the EPA had designated around 1,500 as high-priority Superfund sites. More than 1,120 sites had been cleaned up to varying degrees. Average per site cleanup cost estimates range from $27 million to $50 million. Total cleanup costs for the currently designated sites alone are estimated to run to at least $51 billion. Congress has long considered major changes to the Superfund program; as of 2012, however, no revision had been undertaken.[19]

Superfund also authorizes the EPA to conduct emergency action at sites where immediate risks to the public or the environment are present. From 1980 to 2000, the agency had undertaken remedial emergency action at more than 3,200 sites. More than 40,000 people were evacuated from their homes, and close to 90% eventually returned. Alternative water supplies had been provided to 200,000 people. Emergency removals continue: EPA annually oversees hundreds of evacuations associated with hazardous chemical spills and releases.[20]

13.4 Chemicals and Pesticides

So far, this chapter has given a brief review of the legislation governing the disposal of wastes into the air and water and onto the land. The government has also passed two laws that share the ostensible goal of restricting the use of environmentally dangerous products in the first place. The Federal Insecticide, Fungicide and Rodenticide Act (**FIFRA**) and the Toxic Substances Control Act (**TSCA**, pronounced TOSS-ka) provide a mechanism for the EPA to review both new and currently marketed

---

17. See "The Toxics Mess" (1992).
18. Sigman (2000) and Probst and Portney (1992).
19. Cleanup progress is from Jenkins et al. (2009); cost estimates are from Probst and Portney (1992).
20. See Superfund Emergency Response website: www.epa.gov/oem/content/er_cleanup.htm; Sigman (2000).

pesticides and chemicals, respectively, for their environmental impact. The agency can then recommend restrictions on such products, *if* they can be justified on a benefit-cost basis. Thus, unlike the other major pollution statutes just described, FIFRA and TSCA direct the EPA to pursue an explicit balancing of costs and benefits in the regulatory process. **Efficiency** rather than safety is the intended goal.

FIFRA was originally passed by Congress in 1947 to protect farmers from fraudulent claims by pesticide manufacturers. Amendments in 1964, 1972, 1978, and 1988 have provided the legislation with an environmental mandate. Under FIFRA, all new pesticides must be registered with the EPA; to obtain approval for major new ingredients, manufacturers must conduct and submit scientific studies of an agent's toxicity. This can be an expensive and time-consuming process. According to an industry source, registering a major new ingredient will cost between $5 million and $7 million in scientific studies and take as long as five years.[21] The EPA is then expected to weigh the benefits of approving the new pesticide (lower costs to farmers and, ultimately, food prices for consumers) against the environmental costs.

If evidence accumulates that an *existing* pesticide is harmful, the EPA can institute a benefit-cost analysis of the product and, depending on the findings, limit or restrict its use. This so-called special review process entails a lengthy, trial-like procedure. Finally, under the 1972 amendments, the EPA was required to reregister hundreds of existing pesticides that had already been registered without environmental analysis. However, until 1988, when it was forced to do so by Congress, the EPA took no action on this front.

The EPA's cost-benefit analyses under FIFRA have been subject to criticism, primarily on the benefits side. In theory, pesticide benefits should be measured as the net increase in consumer surplus from lower food prices, plus any change in growers' and manufacturers' profits. Ironically, if pesticides boost yields, farmers as a group may be worse off as crop prices fall and demand is unresponsive to price decreases (inelastic). In the agricultural case, one also needs to subtract additional subsidy payments to farmers who report an increase in yields. To do this properly, one would need good estimates of the pesticide's effectiveness relative to the next best alternative, the price responsiveness of demand (elasticity) for different crops in question, and good input and output price data.

This information is generally hard to get. In fact, for pesticide registration, the EPA has often done no benefits estimation at all. Instead the agency relies on the manufacturer's willingness to expend money on the registration process as evidence that the project will yield some benefit. The EPA in fact does not even require any evidence that the pesticide is effective; thus, it cannot even begin a formal benefit analysis. As a result, the process for new pesticides looks only at risks and is essentially a "loose" safety standard.[22]

Under the special review process for existing pesticides, the agency does engage in benefits analysis, but the available information is often poor. Thus the quality of the benefits assessment varies from study to study. One analysis found that numerical

---

21. See Shapiro (1990).

22. See Shistar, Cooper, and Feldman (1992) for a fuller discussion. Cropper et al. (1991) report maximum accepted risks in the special review process of 1.1 in 100 for applicators, 3.1 in 100,000 for mixers, and 1.7 in 10,000 for mixers.

benefit estimates were available for only 167 of the 245 food-use decisions studied in the special review process.[23]

The researchers also looked at the political economy of the special review process and found that regulators did in fact respond to the information presented in the benefit-cost analyses. Pesticide uses were more likely to be canceled as the associated health and environmental risks increased. At the same time, higher estimated costs of cancellation reduced the likelihood that such an action would be taken.

The authors also found substantial evidence for political influence. Comments by environmentalists (often concerned about protecting marine life) dramatically increased the likelihood of restriction, while comments by growers and academics (primarily representing industry) had the opposite effect. Environmentalists commented on 49% of the decisions and growers and academics commented on 38% of the decisions. On any particular decision, the combined influence of the latter group outweighed that of the former. Of course the influence of the pesticide manufacturer, involved throughout the process, was important but could not be independently identified.[24]

This brief discussion of the benefit-cost process under FIFRA highlights several points made in Chapter 12. First, information about the benefits and costs of regulation is not easy to obtain. Second, regulators must often turn to regulated firms to obtain access to the information that is available. Third, lobbying resources and political orientations matter; special review decisions were clearly affected by the presence of industry and environmental advocates. Finally, lobbying is not the only thing that matters. In controlling for the presence of industry and environmental advocates, regulators did respond to their legislative mandate of weighing costs against benefits.

The legislation governing toxic chemicals, TSCA, was passed in 1976. Like FIFRA, TSCA requires the EPA to review all new chemicals and gives the agency the authority to restrict the use of existing chemicals. However, TSCA gives the government much less leverage than does FIFRA.

There are currently over 80,000 synthetic chemicals used in industrial processes in the United States. Under TSCA, for existing chemicals, the EPA must go through a formal legal procedure, which can easily take more than two years, merely to require testing. A similar legal process is then necessary to justify, on a benefit-cost basis, any proposed restrictions on the chemical. For new chemicals, the EPA must be notified 90 days prior to manufacture. However, no scientific data need to be included with the notification. The agency then uses the premanufacture period to review the chemical. Because most of the new chemicals are not accompanied by substantial test data, the EPA must rely on toxicity comparisons with similar compounds.

If the EPA does determine that the new product may pose an unreasonable health risk, the agency can prohibit manufacture of the chemical until the manufacturer provides sufficient data to make a final decision on the product. Otherwise, the product is presumed safe. The EPA reviews around 700 new chemicals each year.

As of 2009, the EPA had requested tests on more than 540 new and existing chemicals and had issued regulations to ban or limit the use of only five chemicals. However,

---

23. Cropper et al. (1991).
24. Cropper et al. (1991).

the EPA has used the threat of regulation to reach agreements with manufacturers, such as restrictions on occupational exposure, for a greater number of chemicals.

As discussed in Chapter 4, the EPA's ten-year effort to restrict asbestos use under TSCA was thrown out by the courts for failing to meet a rigorous efficiency standard. Because TSCA places a much higher legal burden of proof on the EPA than does FIFRA, there has been substantially less regulatory activity under the former statute. And by strong contrast, chemical regulation in the European Union requires companies to submit test data proving the safety of new chemicals before they are manufactured.[25]

While TSCA regulates the *use* of chemicals, an information-based law appears to have had a much bigger impact on U.S. chemical *emissions*. In 1986, after a chemical factory in Bhopal, India, exploded, killing and maiming thousands, the U.S. Congress passed the Emergency Planning and Right-to-Know Act. The act required companies to report on their releases of 450 chemicals suspected or known to be toxic—many of them unregulated at the time. The so-called Toxics Release Inventory (TRI), mentioned briefly at the end of Chapter 12, provides self-reported data on chemical releases on a plant-by-plant basis across the country.

The TRI data first went public in 1989 and proved to be startling: industry was emitting nearly 5 billion pounds of chemicals of various toxicities, mostly substances that were either unregulated or under legal limits. In the face of public relations pressures generated by the TRI list, many big chemical firms adopted pollution prevention programs.

The TRI numbers provide evidence of success. Overall, releases of the 17 most toxic chemicals fell by 51% from 1988 to 1994, and firms with more public exposure reduced emissions the most.[26] Unlike all the other laws discussed in this chapter, the TRI did not mandate emission reductions or indeed have any particular goal other than informing the public about emissions. Its success suggests that preventing pollution at industrial plants, either through recycling or source reduction, is relatively inexpensive.

13.5 Endangered Species Protection

The **Endangered Species Act (ESA)** is our one piece of ecologically motivated environmental legislation. The law, passed in 1973, requires protection of a certain type of natural capital—species—regardless of the cost. The rationale for the law is strictly anthropocentric: "These species ... are of aesthetic, ecological, educational, historical, recreational and scientific value to the Nation and its people."[27]

The strict implications of the law became apparent in the mid-1970s, when a University of Tennessee law school student filed suit and successfully halted the construction of a nearly completed $110 million dam. The reason? A new species of fish called the snail darter had been discovered downriver. Upset by the successful lawsuit, Congress created the so-called God Squad—an appointed committee with the authority to overrule ESA decisions on efficiency grounds.

25. Stephenson (2009).
26. Davies and Mazurek (1997), Videras and Alberini (2000), and Arora and Carson (1996).
27. As cited in Jost (1996).

Ironically, the God Squad concluded that the dam in fact didn't make sense even on benefit-cost terms. Finally, Congress overrode the God Squad and authorized construction by a special act of legislation. A new population of snail darters, meanwhile, had been discovered elsewhere; and in 1984, the status of the fish was upgraded from "endangered" to "threatened."

Under the ESA, federal agencies are required to list animals and plant species considered to be **endangered** or **threatened** (likely to become endangered). Recovery plans for these organisms must be developed and then **critical habitat** designated. Once this had been done, both public and private actors must refrain from damaging this habitat. (Technically, the act prohibits "taking" of a listed species, and the Supreme Court has ruled that this includes damaging their habitat.) Both the listing and habitat designation decisions are supposed to be purely scientific and involve no consideration of economic costs or benefits.

Currently, there are approximately 1,350 listed species—75% endangered and 25% threatened. Some 4,000 other species are potential candidates for listing. The scientific basis for deciding which critters and plants to list is far from precise; both larger and perceived "higher" life-forms are more liable to get listed, and there is little consistency in the scientific justifications across listings. In the past, ten feathered or fuzzy species (eight birds, one bear, one panther) have accounted for more than half of all federal expenditures on recovery.[28]

These expenditures are not large: The government spends about $80 million a year on listing and recovery, or about the cost of a few miles of interstate highway.[29] However, the ESA has been embroiled in controversy because, its critics allege, it imposes large economic costs on private landholders. Recall that the statute prohibits all actors—public and private—from disturbing the critical habitat of a listed species. This means, in practice, that should an endangered animal be discovered on your property, then you might not be able to develop that land—no matter how much you paid for it.

Now, from an economic perspective, markets should be able to adapt readily to this kind of situation. If such surprise discoveries happened often, then people would start paying attention to them. One might even expect potential property buyers to demand "ESA surveys" before they buy land. Indeed, such surveys are routine now for uncovering the presence of hazardous waste. The fact that we don't see a market for ESA surveys suggests the problem is fairly isolated. And the data bear this out. From 1987 to 1991, the U.S. Fish and Wildlife Service engaged in 2,000 formal consultations on development proposals under the ESA; 18, less than 1%, were blocked.[30] And in an analysis of two recent endangered species actions involving fish protection on the Colorado and Virgin rivers, the authors found very small impacts on employment and income; for some areas the impacts were positive, for others negative. In no case did impacts rise above three-tenths of 1% change from the baseline forecasts.[31]

Nevertheless, the ESA, like all regulations, imposes costs on the private sector, and in certain cases, these costs have been large and dramatic. Perhaps the best-known

---

28. Schwartz (2008), Metrick and Weitzman (1996), Jost (1996), and Easter-Pilcher (1996).
29. See Jost (1996).
30. See Schlickeisen (1996).
31. Berrens et al. (1998).

case involves protection of the spotted owl in the old-growth forests of the Pacific Northwest. While a far cry from the disaster predicted by critics, owl protection beginning in 1994 has meant that a few thousand timber jobs lost in the 1990 recession have not reappeared. (As noted in Chapter 6, this case, along with high-sulfur coal mining, represents by far the most severe local jobs-environment trade-off found in the United States.)

However, the overall Pacific Northwest economy performed quite well through the mid-2000s and had very low unemployment rates. Many area economists attributed the robust growth of the non-timber economy largely to the high quality of life—including protected forests—found there.[32] Finally, one benefit-cost study found that the nation-wide willingness to pay (WTP) for owl preservation exceeded the costs, implying that owl preservation met the standard of ecological sustainability as well as efficiency.[33]

Beyond high and/or unfairly distributed compliance costs, the ESA has received two other types of criticism. The first is economic. The ESA is all stick and no carrot; in its current format, it gives landowners no incentive to go beyond the letter of the law. (Indeed, some have argued that it provides an opposite, perverse incentive. Upon discovering an endangered critter, landowners might be tempted to "shoot, shovel, and shut up." True, but the penalties upon being caught are very high!)

The second criticism is biological. The ESA's focus on species rather than ecosystems distracts attention from the primary task—preserving biodiversity. Too much energy can be devoted to saving a single species while a rich ecosystem goes down the tubes. (This is similar to the criticism that the safety standard provides no guide to cost-effectiveness.) As a result, interest has turned to the identification and preservation of the so-called hot spots—ecosystems rich in threatened or endangered biodiversity. Despite these criticisms, however, a National Academy of Sciences review of the ESA was generally favorable.[34]

13.6 Summary

This chapter has provided a brief look at the existing structure of national environmental protection legislation. Table 13.2 provides a summary. The three statutes governing disposal on land and in the air and water have as their goal the achievement of a safe and clean environment, irrespective of the cost. In fact, costs do enter through the back door, in decisions about the resources the EPA can devote to each area and in the specific regulations that emerge to implement the laws. However, the clear intent of the legislation is to target environmental cleanup at a level much higher than efficiency would dictate.

By contrast, the two statutes governing the introduction of new pesticides and chemicals seek explicitly to balance the costs and benefits of environmental protection, in an attempt to achieve something like efficient regulation. (Chemical *emissions* have also been affected by the public relations pressure generated from the TRI.) Finally,

---

32. See Power (1996).
33. See Haigne, Vincent, and Welle (1992).
34. See National Research Council (1995).

TABLE 13.2   Principal Resource Protection Laws

Resource or Pollutant	Major Legislation	Standard
Air	Clean Air Act (amended, 1990)	Safety
Water	FWPCA; Clean Water Act	Safety
Land	RCRA: new sites, CERCLA (Superfund): old sites	Safety
Pesticides	FIFRA	Efficiency
Chemicals	TSCA	Efficiency
Species	ESA	Ecological sustainability

the ESA is our only major statute that explicitly seeks ecological sustainability as a goal.

Given this background, we turn now to an evaluation of the successes and failures of this impressive regulatory structure.

APPLICATION 13.0

Time to Regurgitate

1. Give some examples of technology-based regulation.
2. Give some examples to show how safety-based legislation can be inefficient.
3. Give some examples to show how efficiency-based legislation can be unsafe.
4. Give an example in which ecological sustainability-based legislation also happens to lead to an efficient outcome.

KEY IDEAS IN EACH SECTION

13.0   This chapter reviews the major federal environmental laws and their accomplishments in five areas: waste disposal (1) in the air, (2) in the water, and (3) on land; (4) the regulation of new and existing pesticides and chemicals; and (5) protection of endangered species.

13.1   The **Clean Air Act** and its amendments require regulation to achieve an **adequate margin of safety**. Two types of pollutants, **criteria (common)** and **hazardous air pollutants (air toxics)**, are regulated differently. The EPA sets **National Ambient Air Quality Standards (NAAQS)** for criteria pollutants and a health-based standard for air toxics. States must develop **implementation plans** to bring both **stationary** and **mobile sources** into compliance with standards. **Nonattainment areas** face special requirements. In all cases, the EPA relies on **technology-based regulation**, specifying particular types of technology firms must use (e.g. NSPS, LAER, BACT, RACT, and MACT). Recently, the CAA has begun to target global warming pollution.

13.2 Water-quality regulation, under the **Federal Water Pollution Control Act** and the **Clean Water Act**, also has safety as its target, mandating **fishable and swimmable waters**. Technology-based regulation (BPT, BAT) is employed. The government has invested directly, through **grants to municipalities**, for sewage treatment plants. Difficult-to-regulate **nonpoint sources** are now the major contributors to water pollution.

13.3 Two statutes deal with hazardous waste disposal on land, and both require a **safety standard**. The **Resource Conservation and Recovery Act (RCRA)** has created the **RCRA list**, a variety of substances that must be disposed of in a controlled manner. RCRA has a built-in **bias against land disposal** of hazardous waste. Assessing the actual health risks from hazardous waste dumps such as the one at **Love Canal** is difficult. Nevertheless, in contrast to popular opinion, the EPA's science advisory board views hazardous waste as a relatively low-priority environmental problem. **Superfund** is the second hazardous waste statute, and it deals with existing dumps. Cleanups are financed through public funds and by means of **strict, joint, and several liability**. While the latter has led to high legal costs, **fear of future liability** may have had a positive effect on current disposal practices. Superfund has been bedeviled by high costs, uncertain benefits, and slow progress.

13.4 The statutes regulating new and existing pesticides (**FIFRA**) and chemicals (**TSCA**) are based on an **efficiency standard**. Both laws have a registration and screening process for new substances, and both provide for **special review** of existing substances. Benefit-cost analysis to support efficient regulation under these laws is often sketchy to nonexistent. Many more regulatory actions have been taken under FIFRA than TSCA because the burden of proof under the former lies more with industry and less with the EPA. The **Toxic Release Inventory (TRI)**, taking an information-based approach, has proved an effective weapon to promote the reduction of chemical emissions.

13.5 The **Endangered Species Act (ESA)** seeks ecological sustainability—the protection of natural capital—as its goal. The act requires listing of **endangered** and **threatened** species on a scientific basis and prevents activities that disturb **critical habitats**. The ESA has been criticized because of the costs it may impose on a small number of landholders and rural workers, lack of incentives for participation, and a focus on species instead of ecosystems.

REFERENCES

Arora, Seema, and Timothy N. Carson. 1996. Why do firms volunteer to exceed environmental regulations? Understanding participation in the EPA's 33/50 program. *Land Economics* 72(4): 413–32.

Berrens, Robert, David Brookshire, Michael McKee, and Christian Schmidt. 1998. Implementing the safe minimum standard approach: Two case studies from the U.S. Endangered Species Act. *Land Economics* 74(2): 147–61.

Brown, Michael H. 1989. A toxic ghost town. *Atlantic*, July, 23–28.

Cropper, Maureen L., William N. Evans, Stephen J. Berardi, Marie M. Ducla-Soares, and Paul R. Portney. 1991. The determinants of pesticide regulation: A statistical analysis of EPA decisionmaking. Discussion paper CRM 91–01. Washington, DC: Resources for the Future.

Davies, Terry, and Jan Mazurek. 1997. *Industry incentives for environmental improvement: Evaluation of U.S. federal initiatives*. Washington, DC: Global Environmental Management Initiative.

Easter-Pilcher, Andrea. 1996. Implementing the Endangered Species Act. *Bio-Science* 46(5): 355–62.

The EPA and states found to be lax on pollution law. 1998. *New York Times*, 7 June, A1.

Freeman, A. Myrick. 2000. Water pollution policy. In *Public policies for environmental protection*, ed. Paul Portney and Robert Stavins. Washington, DC: Resources for the Future.

Haigne, Daniel A., James W. Vincent, and Patrick G. Welle. 1992. Benefits of preserving old-growth forests and the spotted owl. *Contemporary Policy Issues* 10(1): 13–26.

Jenkins, Robin, Elizabeth Kopits, and David Simpson. 2009. Policy monitor—"the evolution of solid and hazardous waste regulation in the United States". *Review of Environmental Economics and Policy* 3(1): 104–20.

Jost, Kenneth. 1996. Protecting endangered species. *CQ Researcher* 6(1)5: 339–57.

Metrick, Andrew, and Martin L. Weitzman. 1996. Patterns of behavior in endangered species preservation. *Land Economics* 72(1): 1–16.

Morgan Lewis. 2004. *Environmental deskbook 2004*. Washington, DC: Morgan, Lewis, & Bockius, LLP.

National Research Council. 1991. *Environmental epidemiology: Public health and hazardous wastes*. Washington, DC: National Academy Press.

———. 1995. *Science and the Endangered Species Act*. Washington, DC: National Academy Press.

Portney, Paul R. 2000. Air pollution policy. In *Public policies for environmental protection*, ed. Paul Portney and Robert Stavins, Resources for the Future: Washington DC.

Power, Thomas M., ed. 1996. *Economic well-being and environmental protection in the Pacific Northwest*. Missoula, MT: University of Montana.

Probst, Katherine N., and Paul R. Portney. 1992. *Assigning liability for Superfund cleanups*. Washington, DC: Resources for the Future.

Robinson, James C., and William S. Pease. 1991. From health-based to technology-based standards for hazardous air pollutants. *American Journal of Public Health* 81(11): 1518–22.

Schlickeisen, Roger. 1996. Should the Endangered Species Act be re-enacted without major changes? Yes. *CQ Researcher* 6(15): 339–57.

Schwartz, Mark. 2008. The performance of the Endangered Species Act. *Annual Review of Ecology, Evolution and Systematics* 39: 279–99.

Shapiro, Michael. 1990. Toxic substances policy. In *Public policies for environmental protection*, ed. Paul Portney. Washington, DC: Resources for the Future.

Shistar, Terry, Susan Cooper, and Jay Feldman. 1992. *Unnecessary risks: The benefit side of the pesticide risk-benefit equation*. Washington, DC: National Coalition against the Misuse of Pesticides.

Sigman, Hillary. 2000. Hazardous waste and toxic substances policy. In *Public policies for environmental protection*, ed. Paul Portney and Robert Stavins, Resources for the Future: Washington DC.

Stephenson, John. 2009. United States Government Accountability Office Testimony before the Subcommittee on Commerce, Trade, and Consumer Protection, Committee on Energy and Commerce, House of Representatives "Options for Enhancing the Effectiveness of the Toxic Substances Control Act", 2/26. http://www.gao.gov/new .items/d09428t.pdf

The toxics mess called Superfund. 1992. *Business Week*, 11 May, p. 32.

Videras, Julio, and Anna Alberini. 2000. The appeal of voluntary environmental programs: Which firms participate and why? *Contemporary Economic Policy* 18(4): 449–60.

CHAPTER 14

THE REGULATORY RECORD: ACHIEVEMENTS AND OBSTACLES

14.0 Introduction

Chapter 13 provided an overview of the major environmental legislation in the United States. What has 40 plus years of regulation actually accomplished? Quite a lot, according to one view. Not enough, according to others. We examine some of the evidence in this chapter. We also explore one of the key drivers of regulatory success, the political muscle put behind monitoring and enforcement of the laws on the books. But moving beyond what has been achieved to date, in the face of growing pressure on the environment from rising population and affluence, how can regulation be improved?

Two lines of criticism have been leveled at the current regulatory approach. First, from a normative perspective, efficiency advocates have charged that current legislation often buys relatively small environmental benefits at a substantial cost. Second, regardless of whether the pollution control target chosen is efficiency, safety, or ecological sustainability, the existing regulatory system is more expensive than it needs to be. By building in greater flexibility and harnessing economic incentives, many economists argue that we could buy our current level of environmental quality at a substantially lower cost.

However, assuming we can improve the regulatory process in this way, a final question remains. By their very nature, regulatory approaches are limited to control of narrowly defined pollutants, and work best for stationary and "point" sources; moreover, regulatory gains may be swamped by economic growth. Given the scale of challenges like climate change, does government need to move beyond internalizing externalities through regulation and directly promote the development of clean technology?

14.1 Accomplishments of Environmental Regulation

After more than four full decades of extensive environmental regulation and the expenditure of hundreds of billions of dollars on pollution control, where do we now stand? The record is clearest for air pollution. As Table 14.1 reveals, in absolute terms, ambient concentrations of all of the criteria air pollutants declined over the period from 1980 to 2008. Declines were largest for lead (91%), due largely to a phaseout of leaded gasoline beginning in 1984. Over the period, sulfur dioxide concentrations dropped by 71% and carbon monoxide by 79%. Progress has also been made in reducing concentrations of nitrogen oxides (down 46%) and ground-level ozone (down 25%). Recall that ground-level ozone, or smog, is created from a mixture of nitrogen oxides (NOx), volatile organic compounds (VOCs), and sunlight. The big drops in SO_2 and NOx since 1990 reflect new regulatory standards put in place by the Clean Air Act Amendments of 1990. Powerplant SO_2 emissions are down over 60% from 1980 levels. Post 2008, there were further drops in emissions due primarily to the recession, and a significant switch from coal to natural gas in electricity production. (More on that in Chapter 18.)

Except for ozone, impressive headway toward reducing absolute concentrations of the criteria air pollutants has been made; for lead the gains have been quite spectacular. For most Americans, the air we breathe today is substantially cleaner than it was for our parents' generation. And this is despite economic output in the country more than doubling over the last 40 years.

In many areas, however, some of the National Ambient Air Quality Standards are still violated, at least during parts of the year, and by far the biggest offender is ozone. In 2011, 127 million people lived in counties where at least one NAAQS was violated at some time over the course of the year. Ozone is likely to remain a stubborn and serious air pollution problem, affecting roughly 40% of the population to varying degrees, as long as cities remain dependent on private gasoline-powered autos for transportation.[1]

Air toxic regulation mandated in the 1990 Clean Air Act (CAA) Amendments got under way only in the mid-1990s. Since then, the EPA has issued more than 45 air

TABLE 14.1   Progress in Reducing Air Pollution (average nationwide ambient concentrations)

	Percentage Reduction in Average Ambient Concentrations	
	1980–2008	1990–2008
Particulates	—	31
Sulfur dioxide	71	59
Nitrogen oxides	46	40
Carbon monoxide	79	68
Lead	91	62
Ozone	25	14

Source: U.S. EPA (2009).

---

1. "State of the Air" (2012).

toxics MACT standards, affecting major industrial sources, such as chemical plants, oil refineries, aerospace manufacturers, and steel mills, as well as smaller sources like dry cleaners. Overall, from 1990 to 2002, emissions of air toxics declined by 35%.[2] In 2012, the Clean Air Act celebrated its 40th anniversary, and several major economic studies in recent years have confirmed the dramatic success illustrated in Table 14.1. While motivated by safety goals, the regulations have dramatically improved the efficiency of our economic system. Table 14.2 shows the estimated benefits of the 1990 Clean Air Act amendments—mostly from reduction in premature deaths. Monetized, the benefits through 2020 come close to 2 *trillion* dollars; dwarfing by 30 to 1 the estimated costs of $65 billion.[3]

Turning now to water quality, forward progress has been less dramatic. Table 14.3 illustrates some good news: On average, fewer U.S. rivers and streams were in violation of water quality standards in the 1990s than in the 1970s. At the same time, at the end of the 1990s, about 40% of U.S. streams, lakes, and estuaries were still too polluted to support fishing and swimming, with little progress since.[4] In 2010, there were over 4,000 fish "advisories" nationwide, for which estimated cancer risks from occasional fish consumption (one or two meals per month) were significant. People who depend heavily on fish from inland waters—including some Native Americans and rural populations—faced substantial additional risk.[5] Similar mixed stories emerge from recent data on pesticide and nutrient concentrations in the nations streams and rivers.[6] Overall and on balance, small gains have been achieved in improving water quality nationwide.

Buried within these averages, though, are some clear-cut success stories. Rivers in many urban areas, for example, are dramatically cleaner than they were during the

TABLE 14.2 Benefits of the Clean Air Act as Amended

	Year 2010 (in cases)	Year 2020 (in cases)
The 1990 Clean Air Act Amendments prevent		
Adult mortality—particles	160,000	230,000
Infant mortality—particles	230	280
Mortality—ozone	4300	7100
Chronic bronchitis	54,000	75,000
Heart disease—acute myocardial infarction	130,000	200,000
Asthma exacerbation	1,700,000	2,400,000
Emergency room visits	86,000	120,000
School loss days	3,200,000	5,400,000
Lost work days	13,000,000	17,000,000

Source: U.S. EPA (2012) Benefits and Costs of the Clean Air Act, http://www.epa.gov/air/sect812/prospective2.html.

2. See U.S. EPA (2009).
3. U.S. EPA (2011a).
4. Freeman (2000).
5. U.S. EPA (2000, 2009).
6. See the USGS national assessments at http://water.usgs.gov/nawqa/.

TABLE 14.3   **Trends in U.S. Water Quality**

	Percentage of Streams in Violation of Standards				
	Fecal Coliform	Dissolved Oxygen	Total Phosphorus	Total Cadmium	Total Lead
1975–1980	33.7	6.0	4.5	2.5	9.0
1990–1995	27.2	1.7	2.5	<1.0	<1.0
	Number of Fish Consumption Advisories, Selected Toxins				
	Mercury	PCBs	Chlordane	Dioxins	DDT
1993–1994	995	355	103	59	40
1997–1998	1,857	634	111	62	34
2005–2006	3080	1083	105	125	84
2009–2010	3,710	1,084	60	128	58

Source: U.S. Geological Survey and U.S. EPA, Office of Water, as reported on the Council of Environmental Quality website www.ccq.doe.gov, U.S. EPA (2007), and U.S. EPA (2011b).

1970s. This has facilitated urban waterfront redevelopment in cities across the country. But while some streams and rivers have shown significant improvement, others have deteriorated. Absolute levels of water quality have failed to improve much, in large measure because increases in nonpoint water pollution, particularly agricultural runoff, have offset regulatory gains. Of course, as in the case of air pollution, the achievements of the regulatory program would look better compared to where we would have been in the absence of federal controls.

Regulation *has* had a major effect on point sources of water pollution. Industrial discharges of two conventional water pollutants (suspended solids and dissolved oxygen) declined by more than 90% from 1982 to 1987. This improvement resulted from the installation of BPT and BAT technologies, as well as the diversion of substantial industrial effluent to municipal waste facilities for treatment. In part because of this latter phenomenon and in part due to population growth, the substantial government investment in sewage treatment over the last three decades has merely held the line on surface-water pollution. The bottom line on water pollution is that the United States will be home to another 150 million people by 2050. At the same time, in coastal areas, saltwater intrusion from rising sea levels—and in the western United States, loss of snow melt from global warming—will be reducing water supplies. A new round of tighter industrial regulations, and major and continual upgrades of municipal sewage and domestic septic systems, will be needed to avoid deterioration of the nation's drinking water supplies, streams, lakes, and beaches.

Evaluating the impact of hazardous waste legislation is difficult. The ostensible goal of RCRA (and Superfund liability) has been to prevent future Love Canals. Relatively strict regulations governing land disposal appear to have reduced the flow of hazardous waste into landfills by more than 50% between 1986 and 1995. On net, the volume of toxic waste generated by companies also declined by about 50% from 1986 to 1995, though the overall toxic content of the waste appeared to have stayed constant—implying that the concentration of hazardous chemicals in the waste that is disposed increased. Between 1999 and 2005, hazardous waste generation fell another 23%.[7]

The cleanup of old dump sites has proceeded slowly but steadily; as noted, over 1,000 sites have been cleaned up. However, it is not clear how much of the slow speed and expense of the progress is due to the nature of the beast (the need for careful evaluation and consideration of options) and how much is due to excessive litigation, bureaucratic foot dragging, or insufficient funding.

Unlike air, water, and land disposal laws, pesticides and chemicals are regulated under a benefit–cost standard, and so should be evaluated in these terms. An analysis found that the estimated value of a life saved under the pesticide review process has been $35 million—well above the $5 to $10 million value used in benefit-cost analysis. The authors argue that pesticide regulation has thus been inefficiently strict: marginal costs outweigh marginal benefits. A second source of serious inefficiency in pesticide regulation has been the "grandfathering" of old, more dangerous pesticides that were already on the market at the time the laws were passed. Recent reforms have begun to attack this problem.

Less progress has been made on evaluating the toxicity of new chemicals. Given the limited information on these compounds, whether the EPA's screen for new chemicals successfully achieves its stated goal of efficient regulation is difficult to assess. However, many chemicals known to be toxic at high doses have accumulated at low levels in the body fat of the American population.

Finally, of the species listed in the late 1990s as either threatened or endangered, 41% are stable or improving, 35% are declining, 23% face an uncertain future, and 1%—seven species—have become extinct. Seven species have also been delisted after a successful recovery, and 11 were upgraded from endangered to threatened. A recent study found that of the species with a recovery plan and a target date, 90% were recovering at the speed anticipated.[8]

What are we to make of this record? Let us for the moment take an optimistic view. Even though economic activity more than doubled from 1970 to 2010, the general criteria air pollution picture has improved significantly, dramatically for lead. In addition, large reductions in air toxics have been recorded over the last 15 years. Industrial emissions of some waterborne pollutants have dropped dramatically, and overall water quality has probably improved a bit beyond 1970 levels. Regulation of hazardous waste *is* likely to prevent the development of future "Love Canals." And the rising cost of disposal, along with the "right-to-know" TRI regulation and the potential for Superfund liability, has focused corporate attention on reducing waste through pollution prevention. Particularly nasty new pesticides are not likely to make it through the EPA's initial screen, and under prodding from Congress, the agency has restricted the use of the worst of the existing pesticides. Finally, only a few listed species have slipped into extinction.

Over the last four decades, U.S. environmental regulation has substantially cleared the air, and has essentially held the line against economic growth in the arenas of water, land, and chemical pollution (with a scattering of more dramatic successes). This is a

7. See Sigman (2000) and U.S. EPA (2008).
8. Schwarz (2008) and Suckling et al. (2012).

substantial achievement in a nation in which economic output has more than doubled, and which is now home to an additional 100 million people. In the next section, we explore how environmental gains have been affected by political ups and downs in the monitoring and enforcement of regulations. We then turn to prospects for future success.

14.2 Monitoring and Enforcement: Political Constraints

Monitoring for violations and enforcing the law is, as they say, a dirty job, but one that is essential to the entire regulatory process. As the entire country learned in 2010, with the devastating BP oil blowout in the Gulf of Mexico, tough environmental regulations mean little if society does not have the resources or willpower to back them up. Monitoring and enforcement are particularly important, as we shall see in Chapters 15 and 16, when firms are allowed to have greater flexibility in pursuing innovative—and cost-saving—pollution-reduction options.

The states have the primary responsibility for enforcing most environmental laws. The EPA's role, as characterized by former agency administrator William Ruckelshaus, is to be the "gorilla in the closet," available to back up state efforts. The gorilla's efforts, however, have waxed and waned with the political winds. For example, one measure of enforcement activity is the number of criminal cases referred by the EPA to the Department of Justice (DOJ). Criminal charges during the first Bush administration were about 300 per year. They climbed steadily during the Clinton administration, reaching a peak of almost 600 in 1998. Following the election of President George W. Bush in 2000, enforcement declined substantially; criminal referrals fell below 350. The number of violators actually sent to jail fell from 339 in Clinton's second term to about 240 in Bush's first term. In 2002, the EPA's director of regulatory enforcement resigned, charging that he had been "fighting a White House determined to weaken the laws we are trying to enforce."[9]

These numbers reveal the sensitivity of enforcement efforts to the political climate and **budget pressures**. Because the bulk of enforcement occurs at the state level, variations in enforcement activity across state lines can be substantial. Political struggles between industry and environmental advocates over the size of the environmental agency budget are an annual event in states across the country.

When the EPA gorilla does swing into action, it can impose punishment at three levels. The agency can take an **administrative action** and impose fines directly. These can then be appealed through a quasi-judicial process within the EPA known as administrative review. This approach is by far the most common and accounts for about 90% of the penalties imposed. The agency takes about 4,000 such administrative actions each year, while the states initiate an additional 12,000 or so.[10] The EPA can also refer cases to the DOJ for prosecution as either a **civil case**, where fines can be levied, or a **criminal case**, where a combination of monetary sanctions and incarceration can be obtained. As one moves up the chain, both the standards of proof required for conviction and the available penalties become higher.

---

9. Goodstein (2010: Figure 15.3) and "EPA Official Quits" (2001).
10. U.S. Environmental Protection Agency (1999).

Even at the administrative level of punishment, however, the EPA inspectors are not empowered to impose fines as if they were parking tickets. Typically, a complex process of reporting, documentation, and review will be put in place before any penalty is assessed; once assessed, penalties are typically reduced on appeal or in a bargaining process. Figure 14.1 illustrates the steps in the **enforcement procedure** that have been used at the EPA to impose a penalty once an inspector has uncovered an RCRA violation at a hazardous waste facility.

From inspection (at the top), the most common enforcement path (administrative action) proceeds down the left side of the chart. After several steps, one arrives at a box labeled "Compliance agreement final order, establish compliance schedule." At this point, a monetary penalty may be assessed, although the final order might just as easily include only a timetable for compliance. Yet the ballgame is still not over, because the alleged violator can make an appeal to the EPA administrator and, failing that, to civil court. In the event of further noncompliance, the agency might refer the case to the DOJ for prosecution as a civil or criminal case.

A final political-economic constraint on enforcement is the motivation, training, and experience of the EPA's inspectors. **Turnover** has been a serious problem in its regional offices and in state enforcement agencies. EPA employee and critic William Sanjour provides a particularly blunt assessment of the hazardous waste enforcement program: "The job of inspecting hazardous waste facilities in EPA regions is a dead end job that nobody wants. Turnover is high, training is poor and morale is low. Just as in EPA headquarters, young inspectors soon learn that you don't become a hero by finding major violations in hazardous waste management facilities regulated by EPA. [Due to the revolving door among EPA management and the industry,] It's like the young cop busting the whore house that has been paying off the mayor. As a result, inspectors engage in trivial 'bean-counting' exercises while looking for another job" (Sanjour 1992:11).

Sanjour's characterization of the enforcement process is harsh. Many agency officials work hard under difficult conditions to try to get a tough job done. Nevertheless, on occasion, political favoritism in the enforcement process is exposed to public view. Reports on the BP oil blowout in 2010 suggest widespread corruption in the Minerals Management Service, the agency that was responsible for permitting drilling in the Gulf.

Like any other aspect of the regulatory process, enforcement is subject to **political influence**. This can take the form of budgetary restraints, regulations that are either unenforceable or highly cumbersome, or pressures (informal or direct) placed on field workers to take a "nonconfrontational" approach to their work. The point of this section is *not* to suggest that the EPA and state enforcement agencies are infected by widespread corruption. Rather, the point is merely to recognize the real-world constraints under which the enforcement process operates.

When writing most of the major environmental statutes, Congress recognized that public enforcement efforts might well prove inadequate to ensure full compliance with the new laws. As a result, a provision in most of the statutes allows private citizens to take violators to court. These **citizen suits** became an increasingly important mechanism for enforcing environmental laws beginning in the 1980s.

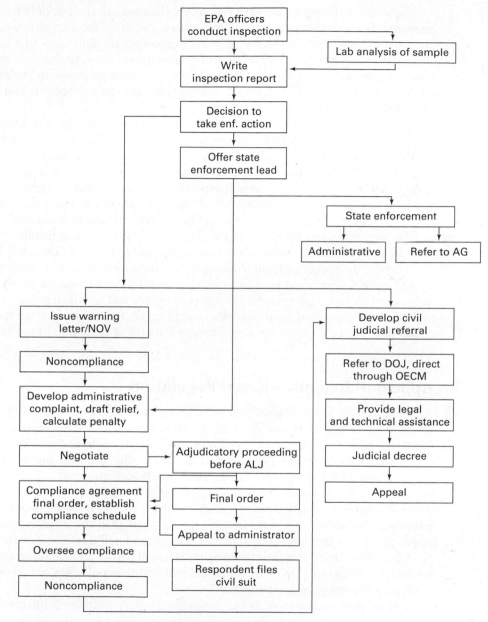

FIGURE 14.1 The RCRA Enforcement Process
Source: Sanjour (1992). Drawn from http://www.epa.gov/airtrends/aqtrends.html#airquality.

Congress limits the enforcement powers of citizens in a variety of ways. Citizens are required to give the alleged violator a 60-day notice period, providing an opportunity to come into compliance. Any settlements must be reviewed by the EPA and the Justice Department, and citizens cannot sue if public officials are already pursuing a "diligent" enforcement effort.

However, citizen suits do have real teeth. Citizens can sue not only to force firms into compliance but also for damage restoration and often the imposition of penalties. Out-of-court settlements increasingly involve corporate financing of the so-called environmentally beneficial expenditures—"donations" to organizations such as the Nature Conservancy, which buy up land for preservation purposes, or the financing of cleanups or environmental studies. Finally, private groups can recover court costs for successful suits.

Given these incentives, why aren't private environmental groups more active in filing suits? The primary problem lies in the difficulty of monitoring emissions and **proving a violation**. The great majority of citizen suits have been filed under the Clean Water Act, where self-reporting of emissions is required. Environmental groups have been able to obtain these self-reported records (at some expense). Proving a violation has thus been as simple as checking emission records against a firm's permit. Citizen enforcement can serve a particularly important role in enforcing compliance at government-owned facilities. If EPA or state officials are reluctant to pursue a government polluter for political reasons, citizen suits provide a fallback.[11]

In spite of ongoing political challenges to enforcement of U.S. environmental law, as we saw in the previous section, over the last 40 years of regulation, real progress has been achieved. That said, future regulatory gains will be constrained by the ability to effectively enforce regulations. We now turn our attention to other fundamental challenges to future regulation, and preview Part III of the book: "How Can We Do Better?"

14.3 The Appeal of Incentive-Based Regulation

As you probably learned when you were about three years old, one of the best ways to discredit someone is to call them a name. Economists have coined a not very flattering label for the current regulatory approach: **command-and-control (CAC)** regulation. CAC involves two parts. The first is the **uniform emission standards** typically mandated under the Clean Air and Water acts and under RCRA. All similar sources are "commanded" to meet identical emission levels. The problem with uniform emission standards is that they fail to achieve **cost-effective** reductions in pollution. Cost-effectiveness means obtaining a given goal—be it safety, sustainability, or efficiency—at the lowest possible cost. The second half of command-and-control is "control." Here, requirements that firms must install particular technologies designated by regulators can discourage technological innovation in pollution reduction and raise the long-run costs of environmental protection.

Let us first take a look at the cost-effectiveness problem with command-and-control.

To use a simple illustration, consider two neighboring oil refineries. Refinery A, which has the ability to reduce emissions of, say, nitrogen oxides at very low cost, is expected to meet the same standard as next-door refinery B, a firm with very high costs of reduction. The reason this policy is not cost-effective is simple: the same overall emission reduction (and local air quality) could be achieved at lower cost by having

---

11. On citizen suits, see Cohen (1999).

the low-cost firm meet a tighter emission standard, while relaxing the standard for the neighboring high-cost firm. Chapters 15 and 16 review a variety of mechanisms—collectively known as *incentive-based regulation*—that harness market incentives to achieve this kind of **cost-saving, pollution-neutral** result.

However, there is one area in which current legislation does not require uniform standards: new sources and old sources are generally treated much differently. The Clean Air Act requires more stringent control technologies for new sources (the New Source Performance Standards), RCRA allows for regulations to differ between existing and new hazardous waste facilities, and FIFRA and TSCA regulate the introduction of new pesticides and chemicals on a preemptive basis but challenge existing substances only on case-by-case review.

The reason for this type of "grandfathering" (providing special protection for existing sources) is not hard to understand. It is politically much easier to pass pollution control laws that have their largest impact on firms not currently around to object. However, regulating new sources more stringently introduces a **new-source bias**. Because higher costs are now attached to new investment, firm managers and consumers will hold on to their old polluting technologies longer than they otherwise would. For example, rather than build new, cleaner electricity-generating facilities, firms may stretch out the lives of older, dirtier ones. Similar effects have been observed for new cars.[12] Or, to consider another case, some new pesticides that have been denied registration are actually safer than substitutes already approved for use on the market.

A new-source bias reduces the cost-effectiveness of a given policy in both the short and long run. In the *short run*, regulators impose tougher standards on new sources that are likely to be cleaner already, while ignoring existing and potentially more severe problems. For example, in some places, one cost-effective way of reducing urban air pollution may be buying up and junking old, highly polluting cars.[13] The *long-run* cost effect, however, is probably more severe. By slowing down investment in new technology, the pace of technological change itself slows down. With less technological progress, long-run pollution-control costs fall slower than they otherwise would.

To review, the first aspect of CAC regulation is the emission standards that the government "commands": uniform for all similar areas and sources, with the often perverse exception that new sources are more stringently regulated than old ones. Both uniformity and the new-source bias serve to reduce the cost-effectiveness of regulation.

The second, "control" part of the name refers to the **technology-based regulatory approach** employed by much current regulation. NSPS, BACT, RACT, MACT, LAER, BPT and BAT: defining all these acronyms involves regulators in a highly detailed process of specifying precisely which technologies firms will employ. There are two cost-effectiveness problems here. First, in the short run, a uniform technological mandate is unlikely to provide the cheapest pollution-control solution for different firms all over the country. This lack of flexibility inherent in centralized, technology-based regulations raises costs.

---

12. See Gruenspecht and Stavins (2002).
13. Old cars are very polluting. Whether a purchase program is cost-effective depends upon (1) whether the cars purchased are heavily driven *and* are not likely to be soon retired anyway and (2) the purchase price. See, for example, Alberini, Harrington, and McConnell (1993).

Again, however, long-run cost effects are probably more important. Technology-based regulation works against technological improvements in several ways. First, once a firm has installed BACT (best available control technology), for example, it has no incentive to do better. Second, the firm actually has a positive incentive *not* to do better. If, for example, it discovered a better technique for pollution reduction, and the EPA then decided to deem this new technology BACT, the firm might legally be required to upgrade its pollution-control technology at other new facilities. Firms have a distinct incentive to keep the agency from upgrading the state-of-the-art technological standard. Finally, if despite these obstacles firms do seek an innovative, non-BACT approach, they must first obtain regulatory clearance to do so.

What would be an alternative to technology-based regulation? Again, we explore this issue further in Chapters 15 and 16, but in essence, the regulator might simply specify a pollution goal for each firm and then let each firm achieve its goal as it sees fit. Provided that *monitoring and enforcement resources were adequate* to ensure that firms were complying, such a flexible system could result in the same emission levels at much lower cost in the short run and provide substantially better incentives for cost-reducing technological progress in pollution control in the long run.

To summarize, many economists would argue that the current command-and-control regulatory strategy is not cost-effective. We could achieve the same goals—whether safety, efficiency, or ecological sustainability—at much lower cost by shifting to more flexible, incentive-based approaches.

Incentive-based regulation, however, is still regulation. Firms must be punished for exceeding allowable emissions of pollutants. Some have argued that this kind of "stick" strategy of forcing firms and consumers to internalize externalities—no matter how flexibly it is designed—will face an increasingly difficult task in holding the line on environmental quality.

14.4 Beyond Regulation? Promoting Clean Technology

As documented earlier in this chapter, regulation has scored substantial successes. However, some hold a pessimistic view of the prospects for future regulatory success. This outlook rests on three assumptions. First, economic growth can eventually swamp the regulatory process. As noted, relatively little recent progress has been made in reducing ozone levels. While cars get cleaner and cleaner, more and more cars are on the road. Despite tremendous investment in sewage treatment facilities, emissions from these sources have improved only marginally. And while regulation may forestall particularly egregious insults such as Love Canal, the fact remains that as the economy grows, industry continues to generate hazardous wastes and toxic chemicals, and *these must go somewhere*. Even if these materials are stored according to best practice, it is argued that general exposure levels must ultimately increase along with the greater and greater volumes of waste.

Second, regulation has already picked off the "easy" targets—stationary air pollution sources and point water pollution sources. In fact, urban smog is due largely to automobiles, while nonpoint pollution has become the dominant water quality problem. Regulating these diffuse sources will prove much more difficult. In economic terms, the marginal costs of a regulatory approach to controlling pollution are likely to rise significantly for the next generation of problems.

We can see how these two issues interact using the IPAT equation from Chapter 9. Increases in economic growth (A) increase environmental impacts, unless offset by improvements in technology (T). The argument is that if the marginal costs of pollution control are rising, then this will undercut the ability of new technology to counterbalance an ever-growing increase in material affluence.

As a final point, even if regulation is successful in one media, say improved air quality, the "reduced" pollution is likely to squeeze out somewhere else. For example, coal power plants reduce sulfur dioxide by "scrubbing" the sulfur out of the gaseous emissions. However, this process produces a hazardous sulfur sludge, which must be disposed of on land. Or, limits on industrial discharge of water pollutants have caused an increase in discharge through municipal sewage facilities. Or, RCRA's tough regulations for land disposal, focused on a handful of sites, are likely to increase the rate of on-site incineration of hazardous waste. This will occur at thousands of points across the country, spawning an additional regulatory headache.

Economists call this the **leakage problem**. Regulating the environment a piece at a time will lead firms to seek out substitute media for disposal. Under these circumstances, regulation ultimately boils down to channeling dangerous substances into areas where they do the least environmental harm.

Our 45-year experience with regulation has not been futile. While we may not have achieved our ambitious target of creating a safe and clean environment, and despite the many political-economic obstacles faced, regulation has made a major difference in the environmental quality experienced by Americans. The real question is, can regulation continue to at least hold the line against continued economic growth and even begin to improve the state of the environment?

Economic growth clearly requires increasingly strict emission standards in order to maintain the same level of environmental quality. If (1) tightening regulation leads to ever-rising marginal costs of reduction or if (2) the pollution "reduced" squeezes out elsewhere, regulatory strategies will clearly fail over the long run.

Is there a way out of this trap? Yes. Our standard assumption is that firms reduce pollution using an **end-of-the-pipe** strategy. That is, faced with a regulation requiring lowered emissions, firms make small adjustments to their production process: say, adding a scrubber at the "end of the pipe" or switching to a cleaner and more expensive fuel. Consider an example of a firm trying to reduce particulate emissions, measured in parts per million (ppm). Under these circumstances, the marginal cost of reduction curve takes on the familiar look of Figure 14.2A; that is, it becomes increasingly difficult (expensive) to clean up emissions as the standard tightens from 100 to 0 ppm.

However, one effect of regulation might be to induce firms to seek out whole new technologies that avoid emitting the pollutant of concern in the first place—call this **clean technology** strategy. (This is the strategy that lies at the core of the sustainable business vision discussed in Chapter 3.) In this case, the marginal cost curve takes on the shape of Figure 14.2B. Here, if the firm bears an initial expense to significantly alter its production process (z), the marginal costs of reduction, and consequently pollution emissions, go to zero. Because the firm no longer emits the pollutant in question, there are no marginal costs of reduction below a level of 90 ppm. Note that *once the new*

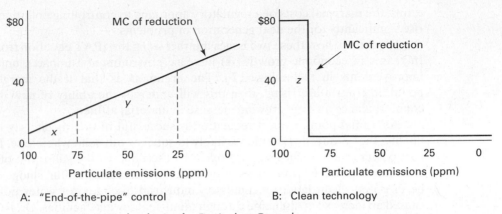

A: "End-of-the-pipe" control   B: Clean technology

FIGURE 14.2 Two Technologies for Particulate Control

technology is in place, both the leakage problem and the problem of rising marginal cost disappear.

Which technology will the firm adopt? That depends on a comparison of the total costs of the two options. In this simple example, the firm will go with an end-of-the-pipe solution if the area under the marginal cost curve is smaller for Figure 14.2A, as opposed to Figure 14.2B. This is true for a standard of 75 ppm ($x < z$), but as the required cleanup increases to 25 ppm the clean technology becomes the cheaper approach ($x + y > z$).

Unfortunately, the story is not this simple. The real-world problem is that firms have little incentive to invest in developing the clean technology in the first place until regulatory costs become very high, especially because regulations are easier to fight politically as they become more stringent and costly. Investment in the cleaner technology, of course, would have led to reductions in cost—through research and development, "learning by doing," and economies of scale.

But a lack of investment means that the cleaner technology seldom exists as an easy, reliable, or low-cost alternative. A chicken-and-egg problem thus emerges: stricter emission standards are too costly (not politically feasible) using end-of-the-pipe approaches, but new pollution-prevention technologies will not be developed by industry until stricter emission standards are required. This in turn implies that the "stick" of regulation—no matter how flexible—may never be strong enough to prod firms into investing in pollution-prevention strategies.

In Chapter 17, we explore further why normal market processes tend not to generate clean technologies of this type—which involve major rather than marginal changes in production processes. But as a preview: to achieve sustainability, it may be necessary to supplement the stick of regulation with the carrot of direct government investment in, and promotion of, clean technologies.

The take-home message of this section is that, unless regulation induces major technological change, we cannot escape the logic of IPAT. That is, if the marginal costs of control continue to rise, then technology simply cannot offset the impact of increased growth. This means that the quality of the environment must deteriorate over time. The key issue then becomes, can regulation alone drive technological innovation, or must the government take a more active role investing in clean technology?

14.5 Summary

This chapter has looked back at the 45-year pollution control record in the United States. In summary, our air is much cleaner, and in other sectors, regulation has managed to hold the line against economic growth. It is, of course, possible to view these accomplishments either as a cup that is half full or half empty. One of the ongoing challenges to regulation is the monitoring and enforcement of existing laws, and the strength of enforcement clearly waxes and wanes depending on the philosophy of the political party in power.

Normative criticisms of the existing laws have been directed both at safety standards (too costly) and efficiency standards (insufficiently safe). These criticisms are important and were dealt with at length in the first part of this book. However, we now want to leave our discussion of the goals of environmental policy behind and begin to consider more effective implementation. The question we move on to address in Part III of the book is: How can we improve the cost-effectiveness and technological dynamism of environmental protection?

Whether our goal is safety, efficiency, or ecological sustainability, this chapter has identified three features of the current command-and-control regulatory system that tend to work against cost-effectiveness: uniform emission standards, a new-source bias, and a technology-based approach. By contrast, we argue in Chapters 15 and 16 that much more flexibility could be built into the regulatory process and incentives harnessed to improve overall cost-effectiveness. However, for a more flexible approach to succeed, careful emissions monitoring is required and adequate enforcement resources must be available.

While a switch to more flexible regulation is, in many cases, a good idea, more flexible regulation is still regulation, and beyond monitoring and enforcement, faces three obstacles to continued success. First, economic growth is a real challenge to effective regulation. As the volume of activity increases, so does the volume of harmful externalities. Second, nonpoint, mobile, and other widely dispersed sources, difficult to regulate by traditional methods, have all become more important players in the pollution story. Finally, the leakage problem—in which pollution regulated in one media squeezes out into another—places a limit on the level of overall environmental cleanup that regulation can ultimately provide. In short, technological innovation that continually lowers the marginal cost of clean-up is critical to achieve ongoing progress. These factors imply that beyond regulation, the direct promotion of clean technology is another important role for government. How to do this wisely is an issue addressed in Chapters 17 to 19.

APPLICATION 14.0

Command-and-Control in the Real World

What are the two features of command-and-control regulation? Go back and reread Section 13.1, 13.2, or 13.3 and explain to what degree the national legislation covering air, water, and land has these two features. Give examples.

APPLICATION 14.1

Regulating Nukes

The first civilian nuclear reactor began operation in 1957. Yet the agency in charge of overseeing the nuclear industry "had fewer than a dozen active regulations in 1970."[14] One explanation for fairly lax safety regulation was the (mistaken) belief that a threshold existed below which exposure to radiation was safe. Why did this belief persist? One reason was that "centralized [government] funding of radiation research ... encouraged a methodological inbreeding which underestimated the scope of nuclear hazards."

1. Use the concepts of the *revolving door* and *agenda control*, explained in Chapters 4 and 11, to explain how the regulatory establishment could persistently underestimate health risks from exposure to radiation.
2. In the 1970s, the laissez-faire regulatory attitude shifted from a hands-off approach in 1970 to "several dozen [active regulations] by 1972, and several hundred by 1977." Is this burst of regulatory activity in the 1970s consistent with the pattern we saw in other areas? What do you think explains it?
3. In the nuclear area, it is possible to view regulatory achievements in either a positive or a gloomy light. From 1974 to 1984, reported emissions of four of six radioactive elements either declined or remained stable, despite a tripling of electrical output from the nuclear industry over the period. However, even with constant or declining emission levels, the *total amount* of these four radioactive materials in the environment was substantially higher in the mid-1980s than the mid-1970s. How can you explain this?

APPLICATION 14.2

Environmental Crime and Punishment

Economists tend to view the decision by an individual to comply with an environmental law in terms of economic motivations. While good citizenship—obeying the law simply because it is the law—certainly plays a role in affecting behavior, it is also useful to analyze compliance decisions in terms of benefits and costs.

---

14. Quotes in this application are from England and Mitchell (1990).

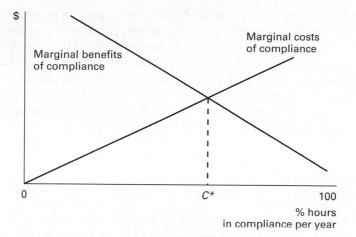

FIGURE 14.3 The Private Compliance Decision

Figure 14.3 illustrates a hypothetical marginal cost–marginal benefit analysis for a manager in a coal-fired power plant who has to decide what percentage of the time he or she plans to be in compliance with the sulfur dioxide emission standards on his or her state permit.

The benefits that come from complying with environmental laws are essentially the avoided costs of punishment: monetary costs (fines and penalties), a damaged reputation (both for corporations and individuals), and the fear of jail terms. The expected benefits depend on two factors: the magnitude of the punishment if imposed and the likelihood of getting caught and convicted. The costs of compliance, on the other hand, are simply the additional outlays needed to install, service, and maintain pollution-control equipment and complete the relevant paperwork.

1.   Why are the marginal benefits of compliance high at low compliance rates? Why are they low at high compliance rates?
2.   Why are the marginal costs of compliance high at high compliance rates?
3.   If C^* is the economically efficient compliance rate, what are two different policy changes that would shift the marginal benefits curve to increase that rate?
4.   Over one seven-year period, Weyerhaeuser—a major international paper company—racked up 122 penalized violations at its three Washington State plants, paying $721,000 in fines, bargained down from an initial $1 million. "In many cases, Weyerhaeuser continued over the years to illegally discharge the same pollutant into the same waterway . . . paying the fine with little protest."[15]

     Based on a model like that in Figure 14.3, would you conclude that, as it repeatedly paid fines, Weyerhauser was taking no steps to clean up its operations?

---

15. "Penalties" (1992).

5. Here are two hard ones. The EPA officially supports a policy of setting fines to eliminate all monetary gain from noncompliance with regulations. Assume that any violation by a firm will be detected with certainty. In this case, try to figure out what the MB curve of compliance in Figure 14.3 looks like under the EPA's recommended policy. (The MC curve stays the same.) Will the plant manager choose full compliance?

6. In the real world, detection does not occur with certainty. In this case, will the manager choose full compliance under the EPA policy?

KEY IDEAS IN EACH SECTION

14.0   This chapter assesses the achievements of environmental regulation in the US; the importance of monitoring and enforcement, and the prospects for future success of regulatory strategies to protect the environment.

14.1   This section provides a progress report. There has been success in reducing criteria air pollutants, though forward movement in several areas has stalled out. However, tighter regulation for particulates and ozone may lead to more improvement over the next decade. On the air toxic front, large emission reductions have been driven by a combination of regulation and bad publicity from the TRI. A major 2012 review of US air regulation found benefits exceeded costs by 30 to 1. Gains in water quality from point-source regulation have been balanced by increases in nonpoint pollution. The impact of regulation on land disposal of waste and chemical safety is hard to evaluate. One study indicates that pesticide regulation is inefficiently strict, though not strict enough to be safe. Finally the Endangered Species Act has also had mixed success—generally preventing extinction, but failing to promote recovery.

14.2   Most enforcement is done by the states. The principal political constraint on enforcement is **budgetary pressure**. Enforcement measures take the form of **administrative action** (by far the most common) or can proceed as **civil or criminal cases**. **Enforcement procedures** are lengthy and complex. There is also high **turnover** among inspectors and some evidence of **political influence** in the enforcement process. **Citizen suits** to enforce environmental laws have become increasingly important. Suits are most common where it is easiest to **prove a violation**.

14.3   The current regulatory approach, dubbed **command-and-control (CAC)**, is not **cost-effective**. **Uniform emission standards** and a **new-source bias** (the "command" aspects), along with **technology-based regulation** (the "control" aspect), mean that the regulatory system has little short-run flexibility to adapt to local conditions. Provided that monitoring and enforcement are adequate, increased flexibility can allow firms to pursue **cost-saving, pollution-neutral** measures. In addition, the CAC system discourages long-run technological innovation in pollution-control technology.

14.4   Is regulation alone sufficient? Obstacles to further regulatory progress include economic growth, the increasing importance of nonpoint and mobile pollution sources, and the **leakage problem**. These three factors imply that the marginal cost of **end-of-the-pipe** regulation will rise; unless regulation induces rapid innovation, leading to **clean technology** development, the quality of the environment must deteriorate. But the chicken-and-egg relationship between regulation and new technology development suggests a critical role for the direct government promotion of clean technology.

REFERENCES

Alberini, Anna, Winston Harrington, and Virginia McConnell. 1993. Determinants of participation in accelerated vehicle retirement programs. Paper presented at the Eastern Economic Association Meetings. Boston, MA, 16 March.

Cohen, Mark A. 1992. Environmental crime and punishment: Legal/economic theory and empirical evidence on enforcement of environmental statutes. *Journal of Criminal Law and Criminology* 82(4): 1053–108.

England, Richard, and Eric P. Mitchell. 1990. Federal regulation and environmental impact of the U.S. nuclear industry. *Natural Resources Journal* 30: 537–59.

EPA official quits, chastises White House. 2001. *Portland Oregonian*, 1 March.

Freeman, A. Myrick. 2000. Water pollution policy. In *Public policies for environmental protection*, ed. Paul Portney and Robert Stavins. Washington, DC: Resources for the Future.

Gruenspecht, Howard, and Robert Stavins. 2002. New source review under the Clean Air Act: Ripe for reform. *Resources* 147: 19.

Penalties aren't stopping land, water pollution. 1992. Associated Press Story reported in the Spokane *Spokesman-Review*, 12 December.

Sanjour, William. 1992. *What EPA is like and what can be done about it*. Washington, DC: Environmental Research Foundation.

Schwartz, Mark. 2008. The performance of the Endangered Species Act. *Annual Review of Ecology, Evolution and Systematics* 39: 279–99.

Sigman, Hillary. 2000. Hazardous waste and toxic substances policy. In *Public policies for environmental protection*, ed. Paul R. Portney and Robert N. Stavins. Washington, DC: Resources for the Future.

State of the Air. 2012. American Lung Association Annual Report. http://www.stateoftheair.org/.

Suckling, Kieran, Noah Greenwald, and Tierra Curry. 2012. How the Endangered Species Act is saving America's wildlife. Washington, DC: Center for Biological Diversity.

U.S. Environmental Protection Agency. 2000. *Taking toxics out of the air*. www.epa.gov/air/toxicair/takingtoxics.

———. 2007. *Fish advisories*. www.epa.gov/waterscience/fish/advisories/2006/index.html#synopsis.

———. 2008. *Report on the environment*. No. EPA/600/R-07/045F. Washington, DC: Author.

———. 2009. *Air trends*. www.epa.gov/airtrends/aqtrends.html#comparison.

———. 2011a. *The benefits and costs of the Clean Air Act from 1990–2020*. http://www.epa.gov/air/sect812/feb11/fullreport.pdf.

———. 2011b. *National listing of fish advisories: General Fact Sheet 2010*. http://water.epa.gov/scitech/swguidance/fishshellfish/fishadvisories/general_factsheet_2010.cfm.

HOW CAN WE DO BETTER?

In Part II of this book, we reviewed the current regulatory picture and discovered that after more than four decades of dedicated national efforts to control pollution and expenditures of hundreds of billions of dollars, our accomplishments are decidedly mixed. Outside of the success stories in air pollution, and with a few exceptions, regulation has essentially held the line against economic and population growth, yet it has failed to achieve its stated objective of substantially reducing many pollutant concentrations to "safe" levels.

We also identified three main obstacles to successful government action to control pollution. First, hampered by imperfect information and motivated by either material gain, peer approval, or ideological commitment, regulators may pursue policies that deviate from their legislative mandate whether that mandate is safety or efficiency. Second, the current command-and-control (CAC) regulatory structure often discourages cost-effective pollution control in the short run and innovation in new technology in the long run. Finally, the difficult yet vital job of monitoring and enforcing compliance with regulations is often underfunded.

Given this background, Part III explores the question "How can we do better?" Doing better is defined as achieving a specified pollution goal at lower cost and with greater certainty.

INCENTIVE-BASED
REGULATION: THEORY

15.0 Introduction

In the late 1960s, when major new environmental legislation was being contemplated, economists had a bit of advice to offer: why not harness market incentives to control pollution? The basic idea was twofold. First, make polluting an expensive activity. This would both reduce pollution directly and induce a search for less-polluting substitutes. Second, lower the costs of pollution control by leaving decisions about how specifically to reduce pollution up to firms and individuals.

Two schemes were widely discussed. The first was a **pollution tax** (also known as an *effluent* or *emission charge* or a *Pigovian tax*).[1] For example, to reduce the acid rain caused by sulfur dioxide emissions from power plants, one could institute a tax on emissions of, say, \$200 per ton of SO_2. Alternatively, one might achieve a rollback through a **cap-and-trade system** (also known as tradeable permit or marketable permit systems). Here permits would be issued only up to a certain target level of emissions. These permits could then be bought and sold, again putting a price tag on pollution. These two regulatory approaches—pollution taxes and cap-and-trade systems—are referred to as **incentive-based (IB) regulation**, because they rely on market incentives to both reduce pollution and minimize control costs.

As we saw in Chapter 13, the recommendations of economists were largely ignored in the drafting of the major environmental legislation of the early 1970s. Instead, the nation opted for what we have called the command-and-control (CAC) approach to regulation, requiring uniform emissions across sources and mandating the adoption of particular pollution-control technologies. Since that time, economists have maintained a steady drumbeat of support for the more flexible incentive-based approach. The mid-1990s saw the first wide-scale test of this type of regulation in air pollution control. Since 1995, sulfur dioxide emission credits have been traded among coal-burning

---

1. After the economist who first proposed pollution taxes, A. C. Pigou.

electric facilities nationwide. At the same time, tradeable permit systems have been introduced in the Los Angeles basin and the Northeastern United States, covering two urban air pollutants: sulfur oxide and nitrogen oxide, and also Northeast utilities are trading under a carbon dioxide cap. Meanwhile, California is moving ahead with the first state-wide trading system for CO_2, and across the globe, from China to Canada to the EU, pollution taxes and cap-and-trade systems are increasingly taking hold.

From a theoretical perspective, incentive-based systems offer several advantages over a CAC approach. First, IB systems will promote more cost-effective regulation in the short run. (Recall that cost-effectiveness is defined as achieving a given pollution target at the lowest possible cost.) More importantly, over the long run, IB systems provide incentives for firms to seek out new technologies to lower pollution-control costs. Finally, in theory, an IB approach reduces the costly burden of information gathering for regulatory bureaucrats—rather than having to choose which technology is to be deemed BACT or BAT or LAER, regulators need only to specify the tax level or the number of permits and then let private incentives take over. Because control over information is a primary means of political influence, as we saw in Chapter 12, IB approaches can reduce such influence in the regulatory process.

However, IB approaches are not without their theoretical drawbacks, including problems of monitoring and enforcement, hot spots (high local concentrations of pollutants), thin markets, price volatility, and the possible exercise of market power, among others. Overcoming these obstacles to realize the potential of IB regulation is the challenge facing policymakers today.

This chapter examines in some detail the theoretical advantages and disadvantages of IB regulation. Chapter 16 then takes a closer look at the lessons to be learned from our practical experience with IB systems and the way that potential problems with the IB approach are being dealt with in the ongoing cap-and-trade and pollution-tax experiments.

15.1 The Cost-Effectiveness Rule

One defining aspect of the stereotypical CAC regulatory approach is its prescription of *uniform standards* for all pollution sources. Economists have widely criticized this requirement, as it essentially blocks any effort to achieve cost-effective pollution control.[2] To see why, we need to understand the following rule:

> **Cost-effectiveness rule**. Cost-effectiveness is achieved if, and only if, the marginal cost of reduction is equal for each pollution source.

It is easy to show that this is true. Consider a town called Grimeville, which hosts an oil refinery, A, and a coal plant, B. The Grimeville City Council wants to control total emissions of harmful gunk at 20 tons per day and is considering a uniform standard of 10 tons per day for each plant. Suppose that when refinery A emits 10 tons of gunk, it has marginal reduction costs of $10 per ton, while at an emission level of 10 tons, coal plant B has marginal reduction costs of only $2 per ton. Here's the question.

---

2. Uniform standards are also typically inefficient. For example, they mandate the same level of protection for densely and sparsely populated areas. However, uniform standards are easier to defend on safety grounds.

PUZZLE

If the Grimeville City Council imposes a uniform, 10-ton-per-plant standard, will it be achieving its pollution target cost-effectively?

SOLUTION

No, because there is a less expensive way of keeping pollution at 20 units total in Grimeville. Suppose that plant B decreased its pollution level from 10 tons to 9 tons. This would cost $2. If plant A then increased its pollution from 10 tons to 11 tons, it would save $10. Overall, industry in Grimeville would save $8 and still achieve the desired pollution target.

Whenever the marginal cost of pollution reduction at one source is greater than that at another, overall costs can be reduced *without changing the pollution level* by decreasing pollution at the low-cost site and increasing it at the high-cost site. Thus cost-effectiveness is achieved *only* when the marginal costs of reduction are equal at all sites.

Let us expand the Grimeville example to illustrate how the city council might identify the cost-effective method of reducing pollution to 20 tons. Table 15.1 lists

TABLE 15.1   Marginal Cost of Gunk Reduction in Grimeville

Pollution at Each Plant (tons/day)	MC of Reduction ($/ton)	
	Plant A	**Plant B**
20	1	0
19	2	0
18	3	0
17	4	0
16	5	0
15	6	0
14	7	0
13	8	0
12	9	0
11	10	0
10	11	2
9	12	4
8	13	6
7	14	8
6	15	10
5	16	12
4	17	14
3	18	16
2	19	18
1	20	20
0		

the complete marginal reduction cost schedules for the two plants, assuming that the $MC_a = 20 - x_a$ and $MC_b = 20 - 2x_b$, and x_a and x_b are the respective levels of pollution.

Table 15.1 reveals that it will cost $1 for plant A to reduce pollution from 20 tons to 19 tons per day, $2 to move from 19 to 18, and so forth. Marginal reduction costs thus rise as pollution falls. Plant B, on the other hand, faces zero marginal reduction costs all the way back to 10 units of gunk. Below 10 units, however, pollution reduction becomes increasingly costly for plant B as well. Of the two, plant B clearly has lower overall emission reduction costs.

The council has a two-part problem to solve: choose pollution levels at the two plants so that (1) total pollution equals 20 tons and (2) marginal reduction costs are (roughly) equal. We already know that cost-effectiveness will require plant A to pollute more than 10 tons, while plant B pollutes less. The simple way to identify the cheapest solution is to try a few combinations. Table 15.2 rearranges the information in Table 15.1 to examine pollutant combinations that add up to a total of 20 tons per day.

We can use the table to find the cost-effective regulatory option. We have already discovered that moving from (10, 10) to (11, 9) lowers total costs by $8. Similarly, moving on to (12, 8) generates savings of $9 at a cost of only $4. Finally, moving to (13, 7) saves an additional $2 ($8 − 6$). However, the (14, 6) option increases net costs by $1, because the additional savings ($7) are less than the additional costs ($8). Moving on to (15, 5) is an even worse idea, as the savings are only $6 for an additional expense of $12. Thus, the cheapest regulatory option that achieves total pollution of 20 is plant A: 13 and plant B: 7. Note, as our rule predicts, that at this point marginal reduction costs are roughly equal.

We can confirm this guess-and-check result using a more general algebraic approach. Recall that the data in Table 15.1 relating pollution levels to the marginal costs of reduction at the two plants are based on these MC relationships: $MC_a = 20 - x_a$ and $MC_b = 20 - 2x_b$. Thus the marginal cost of reduction at plant A, assuming that it is polluting 11 units, would be $20 - 11$, or $9. We also have the constraint that total pollution must equal 20: $x_a + x_b = 20$, all of which, of course, suggests another question.

TABLE 15.2   Identifying the Cost-Effective Option

Plant A		Plant B	
Pollution (tons of gunk/day)	Marginal Savings ($) as Pollution Rises	Pollution (tons of gunk/day)	Marginal Cost ($) as Pollution Falls
10		10	
11	>—— 10	9	>—— 2
12	>—— 9	8	>—— 4
13	>—— 8	7	>—— 6
14	>—— 7	6	>—— 8
15	>—— 6	5	>—— 10

PUZZLE

What is the exact cost-effective allocation of pollution across the two plants that achieves a cleanup back to 20 tons?

SOLUTION

We have three equations and two unknowns:

1. $MC_a = 20 - x_a$
2. $MC_b = 20 - 2x_b$
3. $x_a + x_b = 20$

We know that for cost-effectiveness, the two MC equations should be set equal to each other. This gives us a place to begin.

Step 1. Set $MC_a = MC_b \rightarrow 20 - x_a = 20 - 2x_b$

Step 2. Use equation 3 to solve for $x_a \rightarrow x_a = 20 - x_b$

Step 3. From step 2, plug the value for x_a into the equation from step 1 $\rightarrow$
$20 - (20 - x_b) = 20 - 2x_b$

Step 4. Solve the equation in step 3 for $x_b \rightarrow +x_b = 20 - 2x_b \rightarrow 3x_b$
$= 20 \rightarrow x_b = 6.666$

Step 5. Use equation 3 to solve for $x_a \rightarrow x_b = 20 - 6.666 = 13.333$

This exercise ratifies our eyeballed result for the cost-effective allocation of pollution at 13 tons and 7 tons. As a final bonus, the MC equations allow us to confirm that the marginal cost of reductions are indeed exactly equal at both plants: $20 - 2 \times 6.666 = 20 - 13.333 = 6.66$ per ton.

We can compare total costs at the uniform standard option (10, 10) and the cost-effective option (13, 7) to see how much money we save from the latter choice. Total costs can be calculated as just the sum of all the marginal costs, so total costs at (10, 10) are $1 + 2 + 3 + 4 + 5 + 6 + 7 + 8 + 9 + 10 = 55$. Total costs at (13, 7) are $1 + 2 + 3 + 4 + 5 + 6 + 7 + 2 + 4 + 6 = 40$, for a net savings of $55 - 40 = 15$.

This example illustrates a principal reason why, in general, CAC systems that require uniform standards do not achieve cost-effectiveness. Because both high- and low-cost plants must meet the same standard, in our example 10 tons per day, opportunities for reducing overall costs are ignored. But why are uniform standards set in the first place? Couldn't the Grimeville City Council achieve a cost-effective solution by going through the earlier exercise and choosing (13, 7) in the first place?

In general, the answer is no. In the real world, the council might well founder on a lack of information—what economists refer to as **imperfect information**.[3] Only the firms have access to the pollution-control cost information in Table 15.1, and they

---

3. See Appendix 15A for a discussion of regulation under imperfect information.

would be unwilling to share these data with the public. Of course, the regulators might still recognize in a qualitative way that refinery A has higher reduction costs than coal plant B, and thus incorporate some concern for cost savings into their regulatory design. As we shall see, some CAC systems do just this.

Yet such a rough approach would not capture all cost savings. In addition, in the political arena, plant B's owners and residents around plant A might argue against such a move on the grounds of equity or safety. The next section illustrates that, in theory, incentive-based regulation will achieve cost-effectiveness "automatically" through a market mechanism.

15.2 IB Regulation and Cost-Effectiveness

Back in the Grimeville City Council offices, the village economist proposes a tax system for controlling pollution and claims that the tax will deliver cost-effective pollution control. To prove her point, she draws graphs of the two marginal cost of reduction curves, reproduced in Figure 15.1. (Note that she has switched the direction of the horizontal axis—it now shows *increasing* pollution rather than pollution reduction. The reason for this is that, as we will see, it is easier to illustrate cleanup costs and tax revenues when the marginal cost of reduction curve is drawn sloping downward.) She then proclaims, "Consider, if you will, the effect of a tax on gunk emissions of $7.50 per ton on the pollution situation in our fair city. Faced with such a tax, plant A will reduce its pollution level from 20 to 13 units. It won't go below 13 tons because for these units it is cheaper for it to pollute and pay the tax than it is to reduce pollution. By a similar logic, plant B will reduce pollution down to 7 tons per day. Because at the final pollution levels (13, 7) the marginal cost of reduction for both firms will be just less than the tax and thus equal to each other, my plan will be cost-effective."

"Moreover," the economist continues, "because pollution now has a 'price,' every day they pollute the firms will pay for the privilege, 20 * $7.50, or $150 in all (areas *w* and *x* in the figure). This will provide them with a tremendous long-run incentive to

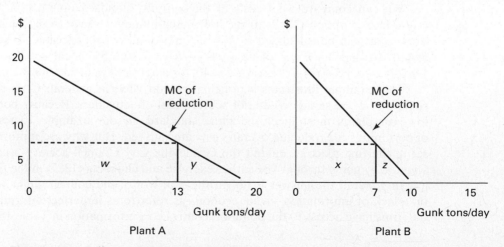

FIGURE 15.1 Pollution Taxes Are Cost-Effective

search out new, less polluting ways of doing business. But best of all, Grimeville will be rich! We'll earn tax revenue from the 20 units of pollution equal to $150 per day!"

For a moment, the audience is awed by the overwhelming clarity and logic of the economist's argument. But only for a moment. "Wait a minute," objects the oil refinery lobbyist. "Grimeville won't earn a dime. Those steep taxes will drive both plants out of business. Not only are you making industry pay to reduce pollution from current levels back to 20 units (areas y and z), but now you're imposing additional taxes as well!"

"Hmmmm," mumbles the village economist. "We can solve this problem. You'll still have to pay the pollution tax, but we'll give the industry an income tax rebate based on the average pollution tax to make the whole thing 'revenue neutral.' [So much for Grimeville's tax windfall!] As long as the size of the rebate is not connected to your individual firm's efforts to reduce pollution, the pollution tax will still give you an incentive for further reductions."

"But, how will we know where to set the tax?" the village environmentalist demands. "If we set it too low, gunk pollution will be more than 20 tons per day. Then we'll have to adjust the tax upward, and he," pointing at the refinery lobbyist, "is bound to complain about taxes being raised again. Besides, inflation will erode the value of the tax. And even if the tax is inflation adjusted, pollution levels will keep going up as population and production levels grow."

"Valid points," the economist concedes. "But here's another idea. Suppose, instead of the pollution tax, we institute a cap-and-trade system."

"A what?" asks the mayor.

"A cap-and-trade system. Let me explain. We're interested in reducing total pollution to 20 tons per day, correct? Suppose we give each firm ten 1-ton permits allowing them to pollute, but we also allow the firms to buy or sell these permits. What will be the outcome?"

"I'm all ears," says the mayor.

"Plant A, facing high marginal reduction costs, would dearly love to have an 11th permit. In fact, from Table 15.2 we know it would be willing to pay up to $10 per day to get its hands on one. Plant B, on the other hand, would be willing to sell one permit, reducing to 9, for anything over $2 per day. Thus, a deal will be made. By a similar logic, A would be willing to pay up to $9 for a 12th permit, and B would sell another for anything over $4. Finally, A would buy the 13th for a price of up to $8, while B would part with an additional permit for a price greater than $6. However, the firms would stop there. Plant A would be willing to pay only $7 for the 14th permit, while B would have to be paid $8 to reduce down to six permits. So, *voila!* Market incentives will generate trade in permits until a cost-effective solution (13, 7) is reached.

"Note that the final price for a permit in this bargaining scenario is between $6 and $8 per day, which is very close to our $7.50 tax. As in the tax case, pollution now has a 'price,' giving firms long-run incentives to develop new, less pollution-intensive techniques so that they can sell their excess permits. Moreover, if new firms enter the area, they can do so only by buying existing permits. Total pollution will be *fixed* at 20 units."

"Wait a minute," objects the environmentalist. "Why should we give away the 'right to pollute'?"

"Well," says the economist, "we do that already whenever we set legal pollution standards. But one alternative would be for the government to sell the permits, instead of giving them away. A price of $7.50 or so would clear the market—because at that price plant A would demand 13, and plant B would demand 7. [Take a minute to check this.] Certain types of auctions would in fact generate such a price. But if you think about it, government sale of permits is really identical to a tax system! Selling permits to pollute one unit at $7.50 per day is the same thing as charging a tax of $7.50 per day for any units of gunk emitted."

"Which is exactly why we oppose permit sales by the government," pipes in the oil refinery lobbyist. "Once again you're asking industry to cough up areas w and x in taxes, in addition to paying areas y and z in cleanup costs. But this permit giveaway idea sounds interesting...."

Now the conversation in Grimeville went on well into the night, but at this point we would like to interrupt and summarize the main points. First, both tax systems and marketable permit systems will achieve cost-effective pollution control "automatically," at least on the chalkboard. In either case, *government regulators do not need to know anything about control costs at different sources*. In the case of a tax, regulators merely specify a tax level, observe the market response, and if the induced pollution reduction is too little (or too great), adjust the tax upward (or downward). In the permit case, the government merely specifies the number of permits desired and distributes them by either sale or giveaway.

The discussion also highlights one of the political drawbacks of taxes (and permit sale systems). Polluters, whether firms or consumers, object strenuously to having to pay the government for the right to pollute up to the legal limit, in addition to the cleanup costs they face. For example, if the government were to impose a CAC standard of 13 units for plant A, the firm would have to pay area y in Figure 15.1 to clean up from 20 tons back to 13 tons. Under a $7.50 per ton tax (or permit-sale system), the firm would have to pay, in addition to these cleanup costs, $13 \times 7.50 = 97.50$, or area w. Such additional costs might in fact drive a firm out of business, and thus they impose a **bankruptcy constraint** on the imposition of tax or permit policies.

In principle, pollution taxes or permit sales can be made **revenue neutral** by rebating the revenues to the affected firms or individuals in the form of income tax cuts. Parties paying the tax would not receive a rebate exactly equal to their pollution tax, as that would negate its effect. Instead, each polluter would receive an average rebate. In this way, average incomes remain the same, but the price of pollution still rises. Such tax rebates have been widely discussed as a way to reduce both the political opposition to, and the regressive impact from, any substantial carbon tax imposed to combat global warming. (Recall the Sky Trust idea from Chapter 1.)

Substituting pollution tax revenues for a tax on labor (the income tax) would enhance **labor market efficiency**, because in this particular case, people would work harder if they faced lower income taxes. This is the "double dividend" hypothesis discussed in Chapter 6.

In the case of a cap-and-trade system, rather than permit sales by government, permit giveaways substantially reduce the cost to, and political opposition from, industry.

In the example provided earlier, where each firm was endowed with 10 permits, plant A ultimately had to pay for only 3 of its 13 permits, while plant B actually reaped a windfall from the giveaway policy.

The Grimeville discussion of the permit system also demonstrates that, in theory, *the final outcome doesn't depend on whether the permits are sold or distributed free of charge*; in either case a cost-effective solution will be achieved, though who pays how much to whom will vary. This is an important application of the Coase theorem discussed in Chapter 4. A **Coase theorem corollary** can be stated as follows:

> If there is a well-functioning permit market, a cost-effective outcome will be achieved by a marketable permit system *regardless* of the initial ownership of the permits.

Take a minute to convince yourself that even if all 20 permits are initially given to plant A, the cost-effective solution (13, 7) will ultimately result. (Because we have only two firms, market power may be present. You have to assume that plant A isn't interested in driving plant B out of business by refusing to sell any permits!)

Having convinced the Grimeville City Council that, at least in theory, incentive-based systems achieve short-run cost-effectiveness, a final question to the village economist might be, "So what?" How much could we, as a society, really save from a shift to an IB approach? At least a dozen studies have compared the compliance costs of CAC regulation with the costs of a hypothetical cost-effective approach. These studies provide a median CAC cost that is four times as high as the least-cost approach. Does this mean that we should expect overall savings of about 300% from a shift to IB regulation?

The answer is no. In practice, IB systems have not performed as well as they do on paper. For a variety of reasons discussed later, real-world pollution tax or tradeable permit approaches do not achieve truly cost-effective regulation. What the studies cited earlier suggest is that in some markets it is technically feasible to reduce pollution-control costs to a quarter of their current level and substantially further in other markets. Thus there is clearly room for doing better. While an IB approach is likely to reduce compliance costs, it will not operate perfectly or capture 100% of the potential cost savings.[4]

15.3 IB Regulation and Technological Progress

The magnitude of short-run cost savings from incentive-based regulation, while uncertain, is probably substantial. However, potentially more important are the cost savings from long-run technological improvements in pollution control and waste reduction induced by the IB approach.

Taxes and permits generate important incentives for **long-run technological progress** in pollution control. Both systems put a "price" on pollution, so that every unit of pollution emitted represents a cost to the firm or individual. In the tax case, the cost is direct: less pollution would mean lower taxes. In the permit case, pollution

---

4. See Tietenburg (1990).

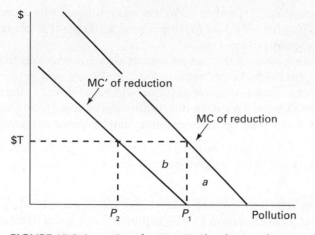

FIGURE 15.2 Incentives for New Technology under IB and CAC

bears an *opportunity cost* as less pollution would free up permits for sale. In both cases, because pollution is now costly to firms, they are provided with the motivation to continuously seek out new ways of reducing pollution.

Figure 15.2 illustrates the benefits of introducing new pollution-control technology for a firm under an IB approach. The improved pollution-control system lowers the MC of reduction curve to MC′, generating savings in two areas. First, the firm pays less for the units it was already cleaning up, area *a*. Second, the firm also pays less in taxes (or earns money from the sale of permits) by reducing pollution from P_1 down to P_2, area *b*.

Compare these savings with those achievable under our stereotypical CAC system. First, the CAC systems are standard based. Once the firm has achieved the delegated emission standard (P_1), it gains relatively little by improving pollution-control technology. Introducing an improved system gains the firm only area *a*, as there is no incentive to reduce pollution below P_1.

In addition, because the CAC approach specifies individual technologies as BACT, LAER, and the like, firms face regulatory obstacles in experimenting with new processes. To do so, they must convince regulators that the new process will be superior to the industry standard, something the firm may not be able to demonstrate before installing the technology. In addition, firms may be reluctant to raise the industry standard by introducing new technologies that may then become the new BACT. This would force them to adopt the new technology in any new construction.

Finally, the CAC system dampens incentives for innovation due to the new source bias discussed in Chapter 14. By regulating new sources more stringently than old ones, the CAC system encourages firms and individuals to concentrate their energies on making old, high-pollution technologies last longer, rather than developing new, less pollution-intensive substitutes. For example, one study found that the average age of electrical generating capacity in the states with nine of the highest environmental enforcement budgets was 16.5 years to 15 years, compared to 11.5 years for the rest of the states. It is difficult to sort out how much of the age increase was in fact due to higher regulation, because most of the nine were also "rust-belt" states, hit with declining demand for electrical generation in the same period. Yet some of the increase was undoubtedly due to a heightened new source bias.[5]

By putting a price on every unit of pollution, by reducing specific technology requirements, and by leveling the playing field between new and old sources, IB regulation on paper appears to do a better job of promoting long-run investment in new pollution-control technologies and waste reduction than does the CAC system. How important are these potential cost savings? This would depend on how fast the pace of technological innovation was accelerated by a switch to IB, and it is a difficult effect to forecast. However, as we saw in Chapter 6, small changes in productivity have large long-run effects on costs, due to the cumulative nature of economic growth. Thus it is safe to say that heightened incentives for technological progress in pollution control generated by IB regulations are probably more important than the short-run savings available from achieving cost-effectiveness.

15.4 Potential Problems with IB Regulation

There are several potential problems with implementing IB regulation. The first two—hot spots and monitoring and enforcement—apply to both tax and permit systems. Cap-and-trade systems have their own peculiar problems: the potential for thin markets, market power, and price volatility. Finally, pollution taxes have the special drawback that they are taxes—and thus are generally fiercely opposed by industries liable to be regulated. In addition, and unlike cap-and-trade systems, taxes do not ensure a particular amount of pollution control, and they must be raised over time to account for both economic growth and inflation. These advantages and disadvantages are summarized in Table 15.3, and discussed further later.

TABLE 15.3   Taxes and Marketable Permits Compared

Advantages of Permits	Advantages of Taxes
If permits are given away, lower cost to firms	If revenues are used to cut income taxes, labor market efficiency will be improved
More certain pollutant level	If revenues are partially retained by enforcement agencies, enforcement incentives are strengthened
No need for adjustment to account for economic growth or inflation	Issues of thin markets, market power, and price volatility are avoided

5. Maloney and Brady (1988) try to account for demand effects on capacity age in a regression context, but their demand variables are poor proxies for expected growth and fail to perform well.

PROBLEMS WITH IB IN GENERAL

Turning our attention first to potential problems associated with both marketable permits and pollution taxes, Grimeville can be used to illustrate the **hot-spot** issue. Hot spots are high local concentrations of pollutants. The IB system would, indeed, keep total pollution in Grimeville at 20 tons per day. However, residents living near plant A, which would pollute 13 tons per day under either a tax or a marketable permit scheme, would view the IB system as unacceptable *if* the higher level of emissions translated into a higher health risk.

Different pollutants display a different relationship between the sites at which emissions and damages occur. To illustrate this principle, suppose that Grimeville was divided into two air-quality regions, one containing plant A, the other plant B. If gunk were a **uniformly mixed pollutant**, 1 ton of emissions from either plant would translate into an even concentration of gunk, and its associated health risk, across the two areas. By contrast, if gunk were a **concentrated pollutant**, all the damage done by emissions from plant A would occur in the area adjacent to A. The more general case is that of a **nonuniformly mixed pollutant**, where the bulk of the damage is done locally, but effects do drift into other areas.

IB approaches work best for uniformly mixed pollutants, those evenly dispersed over fairly broad areas. Two examples are chlorofluorocarbons (CFCs), which deplete the ozone layer, and carbon dioxide, which contributes to global warming. An IB approach would clearly not work for a concentrated pollutant such as nuclear waste, for which uniform safety standards are demanded on equity grounds. To deal with the hot-spot problem in the intermediate case of nonuniformly mixed pollutants, economists have recommended trades (or taxes) based on the contribution of emissions to *ambient* air or water quality. (Recall from Chapter 13 that ambient air quality is the concentration of pollutants actually in the air.)

Implementing such a scheme requires a means of estimating the impact of emissions from specific plants on regional air or water quality. Consider the hypothetical situation in Grimeville, illustrated in Figure 15.3. Suppose that due to prevailing wind patterns, 1 ton of gunk emissions from plant A pollutes 70% in area A and 30% in area B. On the other hand, emissions from plant B are split 50/50 between the two areas. At the (13, 7) solution, a hot spot will indeed emerge in area A. In numerical terms, residents in A will face ambient pollution of $13 \times 0.7 + 7 \times 0.5 = 12.6$ tons, while residents in area B will face ambient pollution of $13 \times 0.3 + 7 \times .05 = 7.4$ tons.

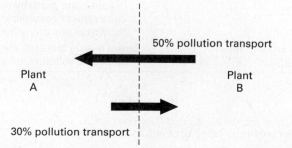

50% pollution transport

Plant A

Plant B

30% pollution transport

FIGURE 15.3 Nonuniformly Mixed Pollutants in Grimeville

In this case, the Grimeville authorities would need to impose an ambient air-quality standard (like the NAAQS discussed in Chapter 13) of 10 tons for each region, and then control emissions in the two regions to meet the ambient standards. To do so using a tax approach would require higher pollution taxes in area A than in area B. Alternatively, if marketable permits were to be used, a given permit would allow lower emissions in area A than in area B.

Carrying this idea beyond Grimeville, taxes would also have to be higher (or the emissions value of a permit lower) in already polluted areas, where new sources are more likely to result in a violation of ambient standards. The exact tax levels, or terms of trade for permits between areas, can be determined as long as the relationship between emissions and ambient standards is known.

As we will see in Chapter 16, trades of this type have occurred under the EPA's "bubble" policy for air pollution control. However, if hot-spot problems proliferate, tax or permit systems can quickly become quite complex and, thus, lose their primary advantage to regulators—simplicity. In addition, the transactions costs for firms are raised if they need to employ complicated air-quality models to demonstrate that emission trades will not violate ambient standards.

Beyond hot spots, the next, and potentially quite serious, problem with IB regulation arises in the area of **monitoring and compliance**. One of the primary monitoring techniques used under the CAC system is simply to ensure that firms have actually installed the required abatement technology. For example, in about 20 states, cars are required to have catalytic converters yet are not required to pass emissions tests. This monitoring system is clearly imperfect as the control equipment may break down and actual emissions are not checked. It does, however, provide regulators with a relatively straightforward tool for ensuring at least initial compliance.

Unlike the CAC case, however, IB regulation does not specify particular pollution-control technologies with known abatement impacts. Thus regulators must rely even more heavily on (currently inadequate) monitoring of emissions to ensure compliance with permits or to collect taxes. As illustrated in Chapter 14, monitoring budgets are a soft political target for regulated industries. Thus, for an IB system of regulation to achieve its potential of reducing pollution at lower cost, a commitment to strict monitoring and stiff enforcement that is insulated from the budgetary axe must be made.

From the enforcement perspective, taxes have an advantage over permit systems because they generate a revenue stream for the government based on emissions. Thus regulators have an economic incentive to monitor emissions closely to ensure maximum government revenues. The introduction of taxes on water pollutants in Germany has led government to require better monitoring technologies and to become more aggressive in enforcement.[6]

PROBLEMS WITH PERMIT SYSTEMS

Both cap-and-trade and pollution tax systems share problems of hot spots and a need for strict enforcement. A major problem unique to the marketable permits approach is that many proposed users face **thin markets**—markets with only a few buyers and sellers. The thin market problem is essentially this: why go to the trouble of "going

---

6. Brown and Johnson (1984).

to the market" when due to the small number of traders, there is a low probability of getting a good deal? In the Grimeville case, in order to trade permits, plants A and B would have to go to considerable trouble and expense to calculate with some precision their respective marginal cost of reduction curves and then employ brokers to engage in a face-to-face bargaining process. Is it worth the bother if there is only one other plant in town, which may well not have anything to offer?

As the Grimeville case illustrated, CAC regulation is seldom cost-effective because regulators do not have access to the control cost information necessary to impose least-cost regulation. In thin markets where trades are infrequent and prices not easily defined, IB systems are also hampered by *imperfect information*. Under such conditions, private firms know little about potential permit trades and face large transactions costs in completing such deals. As we see in the next chapter, many of the small-scale experiments with permit systems in the United States have foundered on the thin market problem. By contrast, acid rain pollution permits are traded on the futures markets in Chicago. Plant managers can read in the newspaper the going price for an SO_2 credit, greatly reducing informational barriers to trade.

A second problem with permits is the potential for the development of **market power**. Concerns here typically focus on access to permits as a barrier to entry. What if existing firms refuse to sell to new entrants in the market as a way to limit competition? This may be a problem when both of the following circumstances hold: (1) new firms are forced to buy permits from direct competitors and (2) a single dominant firm faces new entrants with higher pollution-control costs.[7]

Condition (1) does not generally hold. Under the acid rain program, for example, SO_2 trades are nationwide; thus, a utility in Massachusetts would have a hard time blocking the entry of a new power producer that could purchase credits from a noncompetitor in Ohio. Why is condition (2) necessary? If there are several existing large firms in the industry, the benefits of excluding new rivals to any given firm are lower. Moreover, the existing firms must maintain an informal agreement not to sell. As the price new entrants are willing to pay for permits rises, each firm will have an incentive to cheat on this agreement.

Economists disagree on how significant this market power problem is. However, few would argue that the problem is big enough to seriously undermine the appeal of IB regulation. Indeed, the CAC approach has its own entry barriers associated with high cost of compliance for new sources. Nevertheless, concern should be focused on designing IB systems to minimize these problems. In particular, permit giveaways that endow large firms with a substantial share of the permits should be avoided.

A third and, in real life, more serious problem with cap-and-trade systems relates to **price volatility**. The annual stock of permits is in fixed supply: in the absence of banking (discussed later), it is perfectly inelastic. Thus any changes in demand can lead to large swings in permit prices. As we will see in Chapter 16, a rapid run-up in demand by fossil fuel electricity generators during the West Coast electricity shortages in the early 2000s sent NOx permit prices skyrocketing and led to the temporary cancellation of the program. In Europe, prices for carbon permits have also been fairly volatile, though in the opposite direction, and have undergone repeated periods of collapse.

---

7. Misiolek and Elder (1989).

Volatility is a problem for two reasons. When price goes unexpectedly high, it makes it hard for firms to rely on market purchases to cover unexpected compliance needs. As a result, in volatile markets, firms will hang on to all their permits to make sure that they have enough for compliance. At the high end, volatility thus discourages market participation and the cost savings that might arise from permit sales. On the other side, when prices unexpectedly collapse, firms' incentives to invest in long-term pollution-reduction measures are undercut. Rather than the costly investments, firms might reckon they will be better off just buying permits.

One way to dampen volatility is to allow **banking**: if firms can carry over unused permits from year to year, then during periods of low prices, firms are likely to hold onto permits (helping firm up the market price), for use or sale during high price periods (helping to moderate those price increases). On the down side, banking does raise the possibility of *temporal* hot spots. If all the banked permits were used in a short time, pollution rates during that period would skyrocket. Bearing this in mind, banking can be a very useful tool to reduce price volatility.

A second tool is a "price collar," or in other words, a government-set **price floor** combined with a government-set **price ceiling**. Under this scenario, government buys permits when the price falls below the floor and then bids prices back up to the minimum. If the government then banks these permits, they can hold them to periods when the price rises above the ceiling. By selling their excess stock, they can drive the price down below the ceiling. For more on these so-called hybrid approaches, see Appendix 15B.

A final objection to cap-and-trade systems generally has been raised by some environmentalists: Granting pollution permits "legalizes" pollution and thus takes the social stigma away from pollution as an activity. (An analogy here could be made to the legalization of recreational drugs.) This, it is argued, will lead to a long-run increase in pollution as individual moral codes against polluting weaken. One might counter that existing regulations already mandate some level of pollution as acceptable. Perhaps more importantly, the formal legal status of pollution is probably not one of the primary determinants of social attitudes toward pollution.

PROBLEMS WITH TAXES

Although taxes and tradeable permit systems are quite similar in many respects, there are also important differences, again, summarized in Table 15.3. First, when permit systems are initiated through permit giveaways, they are much less costly than pollution taxes for the affected firms. For this reason, at least until recently, pollution taxes (and auctioned permit systems) have largely been off the real-world policy table in the United States. Because permit giveaways can actually *increase* the profitability of some firms, this is the type of IB regulation that we have generally seen implemented.

Firms profit from receiving permits free of charge in two ways. First, if they face low-cost reduction opportunities, they can sell permits and make money. Second, because IB regulation raises the marginal cost of pollution produced, these increased marginal costs get passed on to consumers in the form of higher prices. As a result of these price increases, with permit giveaways, firms can make windfall profits. This is an important point. *Even when the permits are given away for free*, in unregulated competitive markets, the opportunity cost of those permits gets passed on to consumers.

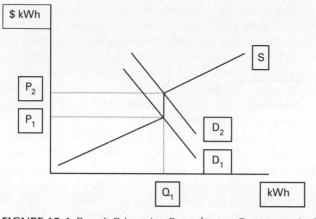

FIGURE 15.4 Permit Prices Are Passed on to Consumers in Competitive Markets

How does this work? Consider the effect of a permit giveaway in the electricity market. Any new firm entering that market will not get any permits, so it will have to buy permits from existing firms. Because this new firm will enter the market only if there is sufficient demand for it to make a profit and cover its marginal costs, the market price of electricity will ultimately rise to cover the marginal costs of the permit.

This process is illustrated in Figure 15.4. Recall that in a competitive market, the supply curve reflects the sum of the marginal costs of production of the firms in the industry. The supply curve in the figure has a curious kink in it at Q_1; all the firms to the left of Q_1 receive permits for free, and all the new entrants into the market to the right of Q_1 must purchase permits for a price equal to the vertical line segment at the kink: $(P_2 - P_1)$. This increases the marginal costs for new entrants and pushes the supply curve up for these producers. As demand rises to D_2, the new entrant supplying the very first additional power now must cover this extra marginal cost in order to operate profitability, so price jumps to P_2. Note that at the new higher price, the producer surplus (or profits) flowing to the existing firms have increased. They got the permits for free, so their costs have not gone up, and yet they benefit from the induced increase in price. When firms earn money through no additional effort on their part, the extra revenues are referred to as *windfall profits*.

Of course these profits come at the expense of electricity consumers. Recently, as economists have become aware of the costs of permit giveaways to consumers in the form of higher prices for dirty goods, and as citizens have begun to notice the large wealth transfers that giveaways create, pressure has been building for "Sky Trust" type systems of auctioned permits (sometimes called "cap and dividend," discussed further in Chapter 1), and the auction revenues are rebated to consumers.[8] Recent U.S. legislation covering global-warming pollutants was a hybrid that included initial permit giveaways to get buy-in from industry, but converted to auction over time. More on this in Chapter 16. The bottom line, however, is that industry will always choose permit

---

8. Burtraw, Kahn, and Palmer (2005).

giveaways over pollution taxes, even if the giveaways eventually morph into permit auctions that function very much like pollution taxes.

Regardless of whether permits are auctioned or grandfathered, there are two fundamental differences between pollution taxes and cap-and-trade systems. First, permits are "quantity instruments": they set a specified level of pollution, and a price emerges through trading. By contrast, taxes are "price instruments": they put a price on pollution, and that price initiates a reduction in the quantity of pollution as firms clean up in response to the price incentive. But with taxes, regulators do not know ahead of time how much pollution will result. They can only guess. In principle, they could raise the taxes after observing the pollution level and finding it still too high, but altering tax rates isn't easy, to say the least. A final, related problem with pollution taxes as opposed to permits is that, to be effective over time, taxes have to be periodically raised to account for inflation or population increases and economic growth.

Given these problems, why use taxes instead of permits? One answer is to avoid the transactions costs associated with monitoring trades. As trading systems grow large and complex, there is a fear that loopholes and lax enforcement will provide opportunities for fraudulent reductions and counterproductive speculation, although both problems can be addressed with good system design. A second reason to prefer taxes is to provide insurance against price volatility and to guard against high costs from an overly ambitious pollution cap. (More on that issue in Appendix 15A.) In addition, the existence of tax revenues provides government a strong incentive for marketing and enforcement, and tax revenues, if used to cut existing labor taxes, can both increase labor market efficiency and make environmental policy less regressive by cushioning the impact of price increases for dirty goods on low-income workers.

Of course, both rebates and stronger enforcement incentives are possible if cap-and-trade relies on 100% auction of the permits. In fact, with 100% auction the major difference between cap-and-trade and taxes is that with the former, the government sets a *quantity target* for allowable pollution, and the market determines the price of pollution. In the latter case of pollution taxes, the government sets a *price target* for pollution, and the market responds by reducing quantity. If the final prices work out to be the same, then the two policies should generate identical impacts in terms of both pollution reduction and government revenues.

IB VERSUS CAC

To conclude this section, it is useful to point out that although economic theory is very useful in thinking through environmental problems, the real world is always messier than our theory. Indeed, CAC and IB systems are seldom found in their pure forms, and their advantages and disadvantages must be weighed in the context of each specific situation. For example, a close look at CAC regulation of particulate air pollution in Baltimore revealed that the CAC approach is often not as clumsy as it is made out to be by the economist's stereotype.

In Baltimore, regulators specified different uniform standards for different categories of sources—"industrial coal-fired boilers, grain shipping facilities, etc."—so that all areas in the city achieved a standard of at least 100 parts per million (ppm). Thus, while CAC regulators did impose uniform standards across categories of sources and mandated the use of specific abatement technologies, they also cast "at least one eye on cost savings." This was reflected in their decision to regulate low-cost categories of sources more stringently than high-cost source categories.

This attention to cost greatly reduced any possible benefits from moving away from CAC and toward an IB system. The conclusion: "A carefully designed and implemented CAC system may stack up reasonably well relative to a feasible IB counterpart."[9]

In our 30-year struggle to influence the pollution-control debate, economists originally concentrated on singing the praises of a chalkboard form of IB regulation, as against an equally theoretical enemy characterized as CAC. In the process, we have somewhat oversold our product. This section has focused on problems that real-world IB regulation either has faced or is likely to face in its implementation.

The existence of these problems, however, does not mean that the shift to IB regulation is a bad idea. On the contrary, pollution taxes and marketable permit systems have a very important role to play in reducing short-run compliance costs, and especially in encouraging long-run innovation in pollution control and waste reduction. The policy challenge is to capture this potential in the face of real-world constraints.

15.5 Summary

As a partial answer to the question "How can we do better?" this chapter has focused on the theoretical arguments in favor of shifting to an IB system of pollution regulation. The economic advantages are twofold: (1) a reduction in the short-run costs of complying with regulations and (2) greater incentives for long-run cost savings and pollution reduction through technological progress. There is also a political-economic argument to be made in favor of IB schemes. By reducing the information necessary for regulators to make intelligent decisions, IB approaches reduce the influence that political actors can wield in the process.

Incentive-based approaches work by putting a price on every unit of pollution produced by a firm. Short-run cost-effectiveness (equality of marginal reduction costs across all sources) is then achieved "automatically," as firms cut back (or increase) pollution levels until marginal reduction costs are just less than the tax or price of a permit. Because all firms do this, marginal costs of reduction equalize across the economy. Moreover, because any level of pollution costs the firm money, the pollution price also generates a long-run incentive for further pollution reduction through technological innovation.

Although taxes and tradeable permit systems are quite similar in many respects, there are also important differences.[10] When permit systems are initiated through permit giveaways, they are much less costly than pollution taxes for the affected firms. Permits also generate a much more certain level of pollution control than taxes and do not need to be adjusted for inflation or population increases and economic growth. However, permit systems have the drawbacks associated with market power,

---

9. Oates, Portney, and McGartland (1989, 1240).
10. Taxes and permits also differ in their effects when there is cost or benefit uncertainty. This discussion is deferred to Appendix 15A.

thin markets, and price volatility. In addition, taxes generate strong incentives for monitoring and enforcement, and if used to replace income taxes, can increase labor market efficiency. Of course, revenues from government permit sales could serve these same two functions.

Potential problems with both types of IB systems include the generation of hot spots and greater reliance on direct performance monitoring to ensure compliance. Despite these potential problems, IB approaches deserve, and are receiving, broader attention as mechanisms for reducing pollution-control costs and pollution at the same time. The next chapter reviews the record on IB systems to date and discusses some of the challenges in implementation faced in the ongoing experiments.

APPLICATION 15.0

Cost-Effective Gunk Control

Two plants are emitting a uniformly mixed pollutant called gunk into the beautiful sky over Tourist-Town. The city government decides it can tolerate total emissions of no more than 100 kg of gunk per day. Plant G has marginal reduction costs of $100 - 4x$ and is currently polluting at a level of 25, while plant K has marginal reduction costs of $150 - y$ and currently pollutes at a level of 150 (x and y are the level of emissions at each plant).

1. What is the cost-effective pollution level for each plant if total pollution must equal 100? Suppose the city government knows marginal reduction costs at the two plants. In this case, could the city obtain cost-effective pollution reduction using a CAC approach? If so, how?
2. In reality, why might the city have a hard time getting this information? What are the two "incentive-based" policies that could be used to get a cost-effective reduction of pollution to 100 units, without knowing the MC of the two firms? Be specific. Discuss two advantages each method has over the other.
3. Suppose the authorities are considering either a tradeable emission permit system, in which they give half the permits to each firm, or a tax system. If both systems work perfectly, how much will the firms have to pay, in total, for pollution reduction under the two schemes? (Assume permits are bought and sold by firms at a price equal to the tax.) Could this explain why Tourist-Town would be more likely to adopt a permit giveaway system?
4. Several theoretical studies have shown that incentive-based policies might generate huge cost savings, and the IB approach could be as much as 22 times cheaper than a CAC approach. Discuss at least three reasons why Tourist-Town might not get such substantial savings in moving from CAC regulation to a marketable permit system.
5. Would a CAC system in Tourist-Town generate benefits in the form of a reduction in hot spots, relative to an incentive-based approach?
6. **(Review of Efficiency)** Suppose the marginal benefits of pollution reduction in Tourist-Town are constant and equal to $64. (Each unit of pollution reduction brings in one more tourist, who spends $64.) Is 100 units of pollution, obtained

cost-effectively, an efficient level? If not, will efficiency be achieved through more or less pollution? Why?

APPLICATION 15.1

Paper Mill, Oil Refinery, and Fishers Trade Permits

On the banks of the Great Fish River sit an oil refinery and a paper mill.[11] Both generate a water pollutant called gunk that kills fish, thus reducing the profits of local fishing boats. But it is costly for the mill and the refinery to clean up. The Environment Ministry needs to step in with a solution. (One way to solve this problem is to break up into three teams of two or three: one team represents the mill, one the refinery, and one the fishing folks.)

The following table shows the marginal and total costs to the polluters for cleanup. They also show the marginal and total benefits of cleanup to the fishing community.

GUNK REDUCED	PAPER MILL Costs of Reduction ($)		OIL REFINERY Costs of Reduction ($)		FISHERS Profit from Reduction ($)	
(tons/day)	Total	Marginal	Total	Marginal	Total	Marginal
0	66.70	16.70	40.00	26.70	197.00	0.70
1	50.00	10.00	13.30	5.30	196.30	0.90
2	40.00	6.70	8.00	2.30	195.30	1.10
3	33.30	4.80	5.70	1.30	194.20	1.40
4	28.60	3.60	4.40	0.80	192.80	1.80
5	25.00	2.80	3.60	0.60	191.00	2.20
6	22.20	2.20	3.10	0.40	188.80	2.80
7	20.00	1.80	2.70	0.30	186.00	3.40
8	18.20	1.50	2.40	0.20	182.60	4.30
9	16.70	1.30	2.10	0.20	178.30	5.30
10	15.40		1.90		172.90	6.70

There is one trick to reading this table. Recognize that the fishers' profits are a function of the total pollution in the system (gunk produced by both the mill and the refinery), while the table shows the cleanup costs to each polluter as a function only of *their own* waste.

a. What is the marginal cost to the refinery of cleaning up from 5 to 4? For the mill of cleaning up from 5 to 4? If both the refinery and the mill are at 5, then what is the benefit to the fishers of the refinery cleaning up to 4?

b. Suppose that the ministry puts in place a pollution tax of $3 per ton of gunk. How much pollution will the mill generate? The refinery?

---

11. Thanks to Gunnar Knapp at the University of Alaska for this problem.

c. Suppose instead that the ministry decides on a cap-and-trade system, limiting total pollution to seven units. And to compensate fishers for damages, the ministry gives the fishers all seven permits, allowing them to either hold them or sell them. Thus, no pollution is allowed initially. With the refinery starting out holding zero permits, how much would the refinery be willing to pay to get one permit from the fishers? Similarly, the mill starts out with zero permits. How much would the mill be willing to pay the fishers to get one permit? Finally, how much would the fishers need to be paid to sell one permit to the refinery? To sell a second permit to the mill?

d. Follow the logic in part c to its conclusion, and determine if the fishers would be willing to sell a third, fourth, fifth, and so on permit for less than the refinery or mill would be willing to pay for these additional permits. What will be the final distribution of permits between the mill, the refinery, and the fishers? At approximately what price will the final permit that changes hands sell for?

e. How does the outcome in part d compare with the outcome in part b?

KEY IDEAS IN EACH SECTION

15.0 Economists have argued that **incentive-based (IB) regulation** can both lower the short-run costs of pollution control and provide better incentives for long-run technological improvements than the current CAC approach. The two types of IB regulation are **pollution taxes** and **cap-and-trade systems**.

15.1 This section illustrates that **cost-effective pollution control** can be achieved only when the marginal costs of reduction at each source are equal. Due to **imperfect information**, regulators have a hard time mandating cost-effectiveness.

15.2 The Grimeville City Council meeting is used to illustrate how IB regulation can help achieve cost-effective pollution control "automatically." Three additional points are stressed. (1) Pollution taxes, if used to replace taxes on labor, would increase **labor market efficiency**. (2) Although pollution taxes can be made **revenue neutral** (and **non-regressive**) in theory, in practice they seldom are, so firms prefer permit giveaways. (3) The **Coase theorem corollary** indicates that, in a well-functioning market, cost-effective pollution control can be achieved regardless of the initial distribution of permits.

15.3 More important than short-run cost-effectiveness, IB regulation provides better incentives than CAC does for **long-run technological progress** in pollution control.

15.4 This section discusses some of the disadvantages of IB regulation. Disadvantages of both systems include **hot spots** for the case of **nonuniformly mixed** and **concentrated pollutants**, and **monitoring** and **compliance** problems. Disadvantages specific to permits include **thin markets**, **market power**, and **price volatility**. Price volatility can be addressed via banking and the imposition of **price floors** and **price ceilings**. Disadvantages specific to taxes include higher costs for firms as well as the need to increase taxes over time to account for inflation and economic growth.

REFERENCES

Brown, Gardener W. Jr., and Ralph W. Johnson. 1984. Pollution control by effluent charges: It works in the Federal Republic of Germany, why not in the U.S.? *Natural Resources Journal* 24: 929–66.

Burtraw, D., D. Kahn, and K. Palmer. 2005. CO_2 allowance allocation in the regional greenhouse gas initiative and the effect on electricity investors. *Electricity Journal* 19(2): 79–90.

Maloney, Michael T., and Gordon L. Brady. 1988. Capital turnover and marketable pollution rights. *Journal of Law and Economics* 31(1): 203–26.

Misiolek, W. S., and H. W. Elder. 1989. Exclusionary manipulation of markets for pollution rights. *Journal of Environmental Economics and Management* 16: 156–66.

Oates, Wallace E., Paul R. Portney, and Albert M. McGartland. 1989. The net benefits of environmental regulation. *American Economic Review* 79(5): 1233–42.

Tietenberg, T. H. (1990). Economic instruments for environmental regulation. *Oxford Review of Economic Policy* 6(1): 17–33.

APPENDIX 15A

Imperfect Regulation in an Uncertain World

The discussion in the previous chapter, comparing permits and taxes, was based on the assumption of **perfect information**: that is, regulators were assumed to know *everything* about both the benefits and cost of pollution control. However, we know from our discussion of the real-world practice of regulation in Chapter 12 that this assumption is far from the truth. In this appendix, we introduce uncertainty into the analysis to highlight an important difference between taxes and permits, based on the costs of regulatory mistakes. Mistakes on the cost side may loom large in controlling greenhouse gas emissions. For that reason, some economists have recommended a hybrid tax/permit system as an alternative to the international cap-and-trade approach negotiated under the Kyoto Protocol.

15A.0 Minimizing the Costs of Being Wrong

We noted earlier that permits have the advantage of providing a more certain level of pollution control than do emission taxes. This is because taxes have to be adjusted if regulators find pollutant levels resulting from a given tax are lower or higher than expected. Let us explore this issue a bit more fully, with the aid of Figure 15A.1.

Figure 15A.1 illustrates the marginal costs and marginal benefits of pollution reduction for two particular cases. This diagram differs from the ones used previously in the book because the horizontal axis is flipped around. Instead of measuring pollution reduction (cleanup) as we have done before, it now measures pollution emitted. As a result, the MC of reduction curve now slopes downward, reflecting that, at high pollution levels, per unit cleanup is cheaper. Similarly, the MB of reduction curve now slopes upward: at high pollution levels, the per-unit benefits of cleanup are also high.

The first panel, with a steep marginal benefit curve, illustrates a pollutant with a **safety threshold**. Cleanup need not be pursued above C', even on safety grounds,

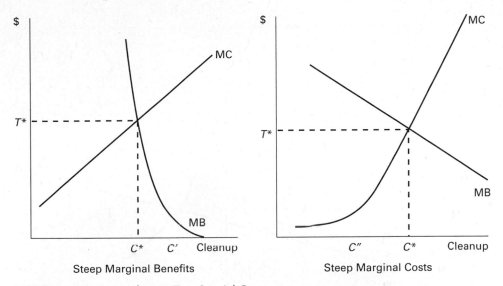

FIGURE 15A.1 IB Regulation, Two Special Cases

because the additional benefits are low. But for cleanup levels below C', damages from additional pollution begin to mount steeply. An example of a pollutant with a safety threshold is the ozone-depleting CFC, discussed in Chapter 21. Because the ozone layer has already been saturated with long-lived CFCs released in the past, any *additional* CFC production generates high marginal damages in the form of skin cancers and eye disease.

The second panel of Figure 15A.1, by contrast, illustrates a situation where *costs* are quite sensitive to the level of cleanup. Pollution reduction to a level of C'' can be pursued relatively cheaply, but beyond C'', costs begin to mount rapidly. Global warming probably fits this picture: carbon dioxide emissions can be reduced at fairly low cost by pursuing energy efficiency and switching to natural gas, but once these opportunities are exhausted, more expensive options have to be exercised.

If regulators knew with certainty the location of the curves in Figure 15A.1, then they could achieve efficient pollution reduction to C^* using *either* form of incentive-based regulation. They might issue just enough marketable permits to achieve the desired cleanup or, alternatively, charge a pollution tax of T^*. However, in the real world, regulators seldom, if ever, have such perfect information. The point of this appendix is to determine, following Weitzman (1974), the approach regulators should use when they are uncertain about the location of the curves *and* are pursuing efficiency as their goal. We will see that when the marginal benefit curve is steep, regulators should use a marketable permit system. By contrast, when the marginal cost curve is steep, a pollution tax system is preferred.

When the marginal benefit curve is steep, regulators will want to keep tight control over the actual quantity of pollutant released into the environment to ensure that the threshold is not far exceeded. Under these circumstances, a marketable permit system is preferred to a pollution tax because of the costs of being wrong. We can see this graphically in Figure 15A.2.

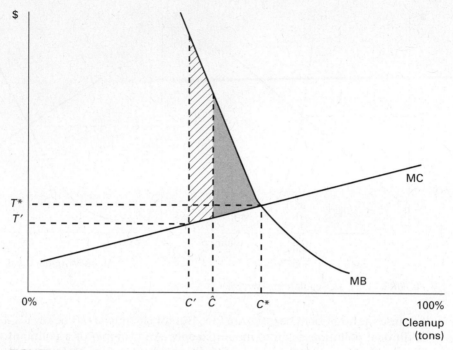

FIGURE 15A.2 Case 1: Permits Preferred

In Figure 15A.2, the efficient level of cleanup is C^*. However, suppose that regulators miss the mark and issue 20% more permits than they should, so that firms clean up only to $\hat{C}$. Then the monetary loss to society is represented by the gray area—the difference between the forgone benefits and increased costs of cleaning up to C^*. By contrast, suppose regulators opted for a pollution tax. Efficiency requires a tax of T^*, but if the regulators are too low by 20%, we get a tax of T'. Facing this tax, firms clean up only to C', and society loses net benefits equal to the gray area *plus* the hatched area as a result. The basic idea here is that a permit approach, because it allows for greater control over actual cleanup levels, keeps pollution relatively close to the safety threshold.

By contrast, when the social costs of being wrong arise more from increased compliance costs and less from the benefits of reduction, a tax policy will be preferred. We can see this in Figure 15A.3.

If regulators undershoot the efficient tax by 20% and set it at T', firms will decrease cleanup only a little, to C'. Because the marginal cost of reduction curve is so steep, firm behavior will not be very responsive to the lower tax. As a result, monetary losses to society will be restricted to the gray area—the difference between lower control costs and higher forgone benefits from cleanup to only C'. By contrast, if regulators mandate a cleanup level that is 20% too low, then firms are forced to make bigger changes in their behavior, thus reducing pollution to $\hat{C}$.

In this case, overall monetary losses to society become the gray area *plus* the hatched area. The intuition here is that, with a steep marginal cost curve, firms will not

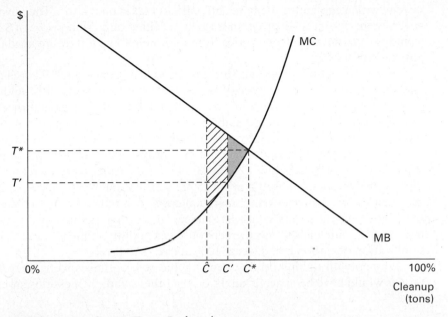

FIGURE 15A.3 Case 2: Taxes Preferred

change their pollution behavior much with decreased (or increased) pollution taxes. As a result, losses to society from either underregulation or overregulation using taxes will be minimized.

What if both the marginal benefit and marginal cost curves are steep? Then a clear-cut advantage for either method, based on the costs of being wrong, disappears.

15A.1 An Application to Greenhouse Gas Emissions

As we discussed in Chapter 1, in 1997, the industrial nations of the world signed the Kyoto global warming treaty. The treaty required developed nations to reduce emissions of global warming gases; for the United States, the target was 7% below 1990 levels by about 2010. The U.S. Senate refused to ratify the treaty, arguing it was potentially too costly to achieve the targets.

To deal with this cost uncertainty, two economists, McKibbin and Wilcoxen, had an idea.[1] They offered a hybrid scheme: the United States should issue annual permits to greenhouse gas polluters that are *tradeable within the country* up to, say, Kyoto-level emissions. The country should then sell additional annual permits for, say, $25 per ton.

We saw in the previous chapter that permit sales are in fact equivalent to pollution taxes. So the McKibben and Wilcoxen (1997) approach can be thought of as a hybrid

---

1. McKibben and Wilcoxen argue for a permit sufficient to achieve 1990 emission levels and a $10 per ton tax. Variations on this proposal have also been advocated by economists at Resources for the Future, as well as a nonprofit organization, which has dubbed it "Sky Trust," and proposes returning permit sale revenue on a per-capita basis to the public, following the model of the Alaska Permanent Fund. See Barnes (2001).

system, with a cap-and-trade base and pollution taxes on the top. The advantage of the government permit sales program is to put a ceiling on permit prices of $25, as no one would buy permits at a higher price from their neighbors if they are available from the government for $25.

In defending their proposal, McKibben and Wilcoxen argue: "There is tremendous uncertainty about what the price of an international carbon permit would be, but $100 per ton is well within the range of estimates and some studies have projected prices of $200 or more" (1997). (Other credible studies put project carbon permit prices to meet the Kyoto targets as low as $25 per ton.) Figure 15A.4 illustrates this situation.

Under the hybrid proposal, permit giveaways would allow firms to pollute up to the Kyoto target, 7% below 1990 levels. If the marginal costs of reduction are low, then permit prices would settle in at $25 per ton, and the Kyoto target would in fact be achieved. If, on the other hand, marginal costs turn out to be high, firms would turn to the government to buy excess allowances. In this hypothetical diagram, the $25 per ton sale program leads to more greenhouse gas pollution than allowed under Kyoto: a stabilization of carbon emissions at 10% above 1990 levels.

Why go with the hybrid approach? If the cost optimists were correct, the Kyoto targets would have been achieved. If, on the other hand, the pessimists were right, and

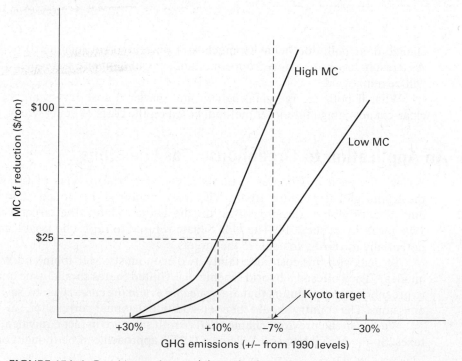

FIGURE 15A.4 Cost Uncertainty and the Hybrid Proposal

marginal reduction costs were high, the economy would have avoided an expensive crash reduction in greenhouse gas emissions. Avoiding this kind of socially disruptive outcome will be politically important in the deeper cuts that will be needed in the future if we seek to stabilize the climate.

15A.2 Summary

This appendix has considered an important distinction between marketable permits and pollution taxes when regulators are uncertain about the precise location of the marginal benefit and cost of pollution reduction curves. (Virtually always!) In such a case, regulators will not be able to correctly specify either the efficient tax or number of permits. If efficiency is the regulatory goal, then regulators should be concerned about minimizing the costs of any mistakes.

When the marginal benefit curve for cleanup is steep, regulators should opt for a tradeable permit system to keep the actual quantity of pollution close to the threshold. When the marginal cost of reduction curve is steep, a tax system is preferred as a firm's pollution behavior will not be particularly responsive to a tax set too high or too low. If these rules are followed, the efficiency costs arising from imperfect regulation in an uncertain world will be minimized.

APPLICATION 15A.0

Still More on Efficient Gunk Control

Suppose that gunk has marginal benefits of reduction equal to $20 - 2x$, and marginal costs of reduction equal to $5 + x/2$, where x is the tons of gunk reduced.

1. Graph the MB and MC curves to find the efficient level of gunk reduction.
2. As a result of imperfect information, regulators are considering two inefficient policies: a tax 10% below the efficient tax level and a marketable permit system with the number of permits to be issued 10% below the efficient reduction level. Use your graph to show the monetary loss to society as a whole of the different policies. Which is more efficient?
3. Suppose regulators did not know exactly where the MB curve lay, but did know that gunk was a threshold pollutant. Should they use a tax or permit system if they are interested in efficient regulation? Why?

REFERENCES

Barnes, Peter. 2001. *Who owns the sky?* Washington, DC: Island Press.

McKibben, Warwick, and Peter Wilcoxen. 1997. A better way to slow global climate change. *Brookings Policy Brief* 17. Washington, DC: Brookings Institution.

Weitzman, M. L. 1974. Prices versus quantities. *Review of Economic Studies* 41: 447–91.

APPENDIX 15B

Incentive-Compatible Regulation

In Chapter 12, we identified imperfect information as one of the primary obstacles to effective government regulation of the environment. We noted that, due to budget limitations, the Environmental Protection Agency gathers or generates less than full information about most problems before acting. In particular, the agency can sponsor only limited research of its own; as a result, it must often turn to industry for data about the expected compliance costs of regulation. Yet, asking for information about costs from the very industry one is regulating has elements of asking the fox to guard the henhouse. The incentives for cheating are rather high.

In Chapter 12, we also discussed two potential solutions to this problem. One was to build up the EPA's institutional capability so as to increase its ability to detect inaccurate reports of compliance costs. The second was to design regulatory policy so as to minimize any gains from lying. The so-called incentive-compatible regulation ensures that the *incentives* faced by the regulated parties are *compatible* with the regulator's goal. This appendix illustrates how incentive-compatible regulation can work.

15B.0 Incentives to Lie

To motivate the problem, consider the EPA's efforts to regulate sulfur dioxide (SO_2) emissions from power plants. Suppose the agency seeks to regulate SO_2 at the efficient level, where the marginal benefits of reduction just equal marginal costs. *If* the EPA knew the costs and benefits, it might then achieve the efficient pollution level in one of two ways. First, it could issue or auction off marketable permits up to the SO_2 target. Or, it could set an emission tax to achieve the same goal. However, as we show next, if firms are expecting a marketable permit system, they have an incentive to overstate compliance costs. By the same token, if they expect a tax, an incentive exists to understate compliance costs.

Figure 15B.1 illustrates a marginal cost–marginal benefit diagram for analyzing pollution control. The true marginal benefits and costs of SO_2 reduction are reflected by the curves labeled MB and MC. If the EPA had access to this information, efficiency would require a pollution level of P^*. This, in turn, could be achieved by either auctioning off P^* marketable permits (at a market-clearing price of T^*) or setting a pollution tax at T^*.

However, suppose the EPA must rely on power companies for information about how much it will cost firms to switch to less-polluting production methods. If faced with a marketable permit system, industry has a clear incentive to lie and *overstate* the cost (MC′). If the industry does so and the EPA uses the industry estimates, the agency will increase the number of permits it sells to P'. This will drive down the price of permits to T' and allow an inefficiently high level of pollution, thus reducing the firm's cleanup costs.

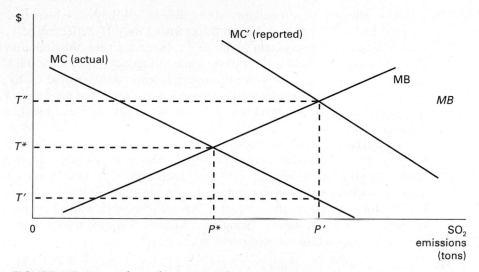

FIGURE 15B.1 Imperfect Information and Permits

By contrast, suppose the agency is planning to use a pollution tax to control SO_2 emissions, and firms know this. Then, as illustrated in Figure 15B.2, companies have the incentive to *understate* their costs, for example, claiming MC″. The EPA will then consider the efficient pollution level to be P'' and set what it *thinks* is the appropriate tax at T''. This, will reduce the emission tax (from T^*). However, with a low tax of T'', *actual* pollution will rise to P'''. Again, pollution levels will be inefficiently high and a firm's cleanup costs will be reduced.

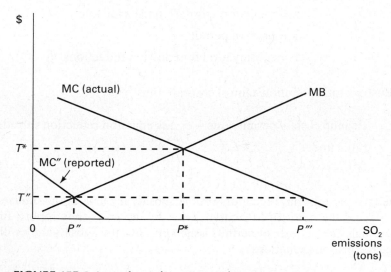

FIGURE 15B.2 Imperfect Information and Taxes

Now, after the fact, regulators will be able to tell they have been lied to. How? In the marketable permits case, permit prices will be only T', reflecting real control costs, when the agency expects them to rise to T''. In the tax case, the pollution level will be P''', again reflecting real control costs, when the agency expects it to be P''. Thus, one approach to solving the problem of imperfect information would be to adjust either the number of permits or the tax level based on the observed outcomes. For example, if the observed pollution level is higher than the regulator predicted, he can raise the pollution tax.

Through such a process, called **iteration**, the regulator might be able to arrive at the efficient tax level or number of permits. However, in practice, it is not easy to adjust either the number of permits or the tax level once they have been established. As detailed in Chapter 12, setting regulatory policy is a cumbersome and politically charged process not amenable to trial and error. Are we then stuck with a recognition that firms will tend to overstate costs if facing a marketable permit system and understate them if facing pollution taxes? Fortunately, no.

15B.1   Incentives to Tell the Truth

An incentive-compatible approach developed by Kwerel (1977) can be used to encourage truthful behavior.[1] This approach mixes a marketable permit system with a tax system to precisely balance the different incentives firms have to lie about compliance costs. It works in the following way. Regulators tell firms that they will combine an auction of marketable permits with a subsidy payment for any pollution reduced over and above the number of permits the firm holds (an **excess emission reduction subsidy**). To see this clearly, we need to use a little mathematical notation. So, let

$$p = \text{industry pollution level}$$
$$L = \text{number of permits made available}$$
$$z = \text{price of permits}$$
$$e = \text{subsidy level for emission reductions}$$

The industry's total pollution control costs are thus

cleanup costs + permit costs − excess emission reduction subsidy
(area under $z * L$ $e * (L - p)$
MC curve)

The trick here is that regulators set the subsidy level, e, at the intersection of the MB curve and the *reported* MC curve. Thus, by the costs they report, firms directly affect not only the number of permits issued but also the subsidy they will receive for any excess emission reductions.

---

1. Gruenspecht and Lave (1989) provide a more general review of the literature on environmental regulation under imperfect information.

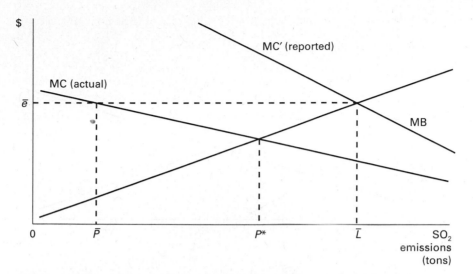

FIGURE 15B.3 Incentive-Compatible Regulation, Case 1

With this setup, we can see how the incentive-compatible mechanism works to encourage truth telling. First, let us consider what happens if firms overstate their costs. At first glance, this seems like a good strategy. Figure 15B.3 illustrates the situation. By overstating their costs, the firms know that regulators will provide a large number of permits $(\overline{L})$ and set a high emission reduction subsidy at $\overline{e}$. Both of these seem favorable. The catch is that, unlike the case of a straight marketable permit system, the large supply of permits will not cause their price to fall. Instead, the high emission subsidy will cause the permit price that firms have to pay to be driven *up*. As long as e is greater than the price of permits, z, each firm would do better buying another permit, holding emissions constant, and collecting the subsidy for the extra "reduction." But this high demand for permits will cause permit prices to get bid up to $\overline{e}$.

As a result, in equilibrium, the permit price z must just equal $\overline{e}$. Because the price of an additional permit just equals the emission subsidy, firms will not come out ahead financially from the subsidy policy and, thus, do not benefit from a high $\overline{e}$. However, as long as the true MC of reduction is less than the subsidy, firms would lose money if they did not reduce pollution and receive the subsidy. As a result, they *will* cut back pollution to $\overline{P}$ even though they hold $\overline{L}$ permits.

Thus the final equilibrium will look like this: L permits auctioned off at a price just equal to the emission subsidy $\overline{e}$, with firms polluting at a level of $\overline{P}$. But $\overline{P}$ is a lower level of pollution and one more costly to achieve than P^*. Thus, overstating compliance costs will lead firms to bear higher pollution reduction costs than they would if they told the truth.

Is there an incentive to understate costs? Figure 15B.4 illustrates this possibility. If firms underreport costs, then $\hat{L}$ permits will be available, and firms will receive a subsidy for emission reductions below $\hat{L}$ of $\hat{e}$. However, because the true marginal costs of reduction exceed the subsidy for excess emission reductions, firms will pollute up to

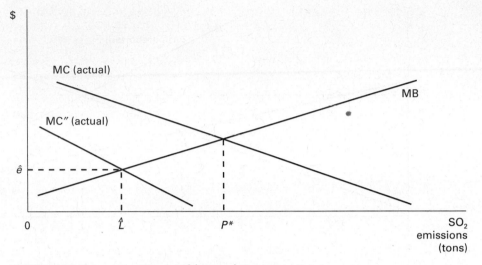

FIGURE 15B.4 Incentive-Compatible Regulation, Case 2

the limit of $\hat{L}$ and not take any subsidies. But, again, this is a stricter and more costly standard than they would have faced if they had told the truth. Understating costs is clearly not a good strategy for firms.

We have just demonstrated that both overstating and understating compliance costs ultimately lead to higher costs for firms than telling the truth. Thus, under this hybrid regulatory mechanism, firms have no incentive to lie. In a nutshell, the advantages to inflating costs that accrue under a straight marketable permit system are here negated by the emission reduction subsidy, which forces up permit prices.

15B.2 Summary

This appendix has provided an introduction to incentive-compatible regulation. We first established that firms have an incentive to overstate compliance costs when faced with marketable permit regulation and to understate costs when faced with pollution taxes. A mechanism was then suggested that precisely balanced these offsetting tendencies by combining a tax-based subsidy policy with a marketable permit system. This hybrid regulatory structure is incentive compatible, because firms are provided an incentive to tell the truth, which is compatible with the regulatory goal of efficient regulation.

APPLICATION 15B.0

CAC and Incentives for Truth Telling

Before passing regulations on Coke ovens in the steel industry, the EPA estimated that the costs of controlling hazardous air pollutant emissions would be about $4 billion; four years later, that estimate had fallen to between $250 and $400 million. Similarly, projections for benzene emission control were on the order of \$350,000 per plant; in actuality, chemical companies found they were able to use substitutes, which "virtually eliminated control costs."[2]

We showed in this appendix that industry has an incentive to overstate costs if faced with marketable permit regulation. Does the same incentive hold for CAC regulation, which was used in Applications 15.0 and 15A.0?

1. Assume (1) that the EPA's initial cost estimates provided earlier were based on industry sources and (2) that the EPA sought to regulate these pollutants at the efficient level.[3] Use a diagram to provide a possible explanation for why the cost estimates were so high. (Show that under CAC regulation, where a uniform emission standard is set, industry has an incentive to overstate true costs.)

REFERENCES

Gruenspecht, A., and L. Lave. 1989. The economics of health, safety and environmental regulation. In *Handbook of industrial organization*, Vol. II, ed. R. Schmalansee and R. Willig. New York: North Holland.

Kwerel, Evan. 1977. To tell the truth: Imperfect information and optimal pollution control. *Review of Economic Studies* 44(3): 595–601.

Mason, Keith. 1991. The economic impact. *EPA Journal*, January/February, 45–48.

---

2. Mason (1991).
3. In fact, these air pollutants are typically regulated under a safety standard. However, control costs still enter agency decisions as to the stringency of regulation.

16

INCENTIVE-BASED REGULATION: PRACTICE

16.0 Introduction

Pollution taxes. Cap-and-trade systems. Theoretical economic arguments about both the cost and environmental effectiveness of incentive-based (IB) regulation have been instrumental in shifting government policy more and more in these directions and away from command-and-control (CAC) over the last three decades. Has the economists' case been proven?

In the United States, we now have substantial experience with IB regulation, primarily with marketable permit systems. Cap-and-trade programs clearly helped reduce the costs of national efforts designed to phase out both leaded gasoline and the production of ozone-destroying CFCs. But victory has been slower to emerge in programs aimed at reducing urban air pollution—from the early EPA Emission Trading Program to the more recent and ambitious RECLAIM trading system in the Los Angeles Basin, to a similar interstate nitrogen oxide trading system on the East Coast. Finally, the national sulfur dioxide (acid rain) cap-and-trade program has been under way since 1995, and the results have been quite favorable. Bottom line from this experience? Permit systems can work very well, but the two big bugaboos that have emerged so far have been thin markets and price volatility.

One new trading program in the United States has recently gotten under way: a group of northeastern states instituted the first domestic controls on the global-warming pollutant carbon dioxide via a cap-and-trade system with the friendly name of RGGI (pronounced Reggie). Controversy here relates to the balance between permit giveaways and auctions. Following these multiple experiments, the United States debated a move toward a national, economy-wide cap-and-trade system for carbon dioxide—a dramatic, high-stakes test of economic theory in all its complexity. In the summer of 2009, the U.S. House passed a cap-and-trade bill, but it was defeated in the Senate. Despite this, California is moving ahead with a statewide carbon cap-and-trade system. Here the U.S. is substantially behind the Europeans, who instituted their own EU-wide CO_2 cap-and-trade system back in 2005.

In contrast to our broad experience with marketable permits, classic pollution taxes—charges tied directly to emissions—are used very infrequently globally, and in particular, in the United States. This may change in the coming years, as there is some bipartisan interest in using carbon tax revenues to reduce the deficit. And carbon taxes have recently emerged in British Columbia, Australia, and some European countries.

In the United States, there are approximations to pollution taxes, such as fees levied on wastewater (sewage) and solid and hazardous waste (pay-by-the-can garbage fees, tipping charges at landfills). There is also a grab bag of incentive mechanisms in place that rely on prices to affect environmental quality, ranging from the bottle deposits and mining bonds to user fees on federal lands, to insurance and liability requirements for hazardous materials handlers, to subsidies for new technologies. European nations historically also have had much higher taxes on energy—electricity, oil, and gasoline. Although energy taxes are not pollution taxes because they do not tax emissions directly, they reduce many important pollutants indirectly.

This chapter reviews the record of IB regulation, with an eye toward lessons learned. As we contemplate the need for dramatic global reductions in carbon dioxide to address global warming, it is doubly important that we glean all we can from the existing track record.

16.1 Lead and Chlorofluorocarbons

Lead is a particularly nasty pollutant that generates developmental problems in children and heart disease and stroke in adults. Lead in gasoline becomes airborne when the fuel is burned in an automobile engine. Unleaded gas is required for most new cars, because lead also damages the catalytic converters used to control other auto pollutants. However, in the mid-1980s, leaded gas was still widely used in older vehicles. Early in 1985, the EPA initiated a phase-in of lower lead standards for leaded gasoline, from an existing 1.1 grams per gallon standard to 0.5 grams per gallon by July 1985 to 0.1 grams per gallon by January 1986. To ease the $3.5 billion compliance costs associated with such a rapid changeover, the EPA instituted its **lead banking** program.

Under this program, gasoline refiners that reduced the lead content in their gasoline by more than the applicable standard for a given quarter of the year were allowed to bank the difference in the form of lead credits. These credits could then be used or sold in any subsequent quarter. In addition, the lead credits had a limited life, because the program ended on schedule at the end of 1987, when all refiners were required to meet the new standard.

Despite its short life, the program proved quite successful. More than 50% of refiners participated in trading, 15% of all credits were traded, and about 35% were banked for future trading or use. Cost savings were probably in excess of $200 million.[1]

What factors underlay the success of lead trading? First, because all refiners were granted permits based on their performance, market power did not emerge as an issue.

---

1. Hahn (1989).

(In addition, new entrant access was not a problem in this declining market.) Markets were not thin, as trading was nationwide, and firms were already required to develop considerable information about the lead content of their product. Because the permits were shrinking, the issue of permit life did not emerge, and hot spots, although they might have developed on a temporary basis, could not persist. Finally, monitoring and enforcement did not suffer, as the lead content in gasoline was already reported by refiners on a regular basis. In one instance the agency fined a company $40 million for spiking 800 gallons of gas with excess lead.[2] Thus none of the theoretical problems identified in Chapter 15 was present in the lead trading market.

In 1988, the EPA introduced a scheme similar to the lead trading program for chlorofluorocarbons (CFCs), which contribute both to depletion of the earth's protective ozone shield and to global warming. Like lead in gasoline, CFCs were being phased out, this time globally, as we discuss further in Chapter 21. The market appears to have functioned relatively well. Congress also imposed a tax on all ozone-depleting chemicals used or sold by producers or commercial users of these chemicals. By increasing the price of the final product, the tax has also encouraged consumers to switch to substitute products.

16.2 Trading Urban Air Pollutants

In contrast to the successes of lead and CFC trading, both national programs, attempts to implement tradeable permit systems at the local level for criteria air pollutants have a mixed record. The nation's first marketable permit experiment, the EPA's Emissions Trading Program, foundered because of thin markets and concerns about hot spots. And hot spots have emerged as a potential problem with the L.A. Basin's RECLAIM and mobile emissions trading programs, which have also suffered from dramatic price instability. Finally, while a multi-state NOx trading program in the eastern United States got off to a strong start, recent regulatory uncertainty has lead to major price fluctuations, discouraging firms from making long run investments based on steady permit prices.

The Emissions Trading Program, initiated in 1976, allows limited trading of **emission reduction credits** for five of the criteria air pollutants: VOCs, carbon monoxide, sulfur dioxide, particulates, and nitrogen oxides. Credits could be earned whenever a source controls emissions to a degree higher than legally required. Regulators certify which credits can then be used in one of the program's three trading schemes or banked for later use. The degree of banking allowed varies from state to state.

The three trading programs are the offset, bubble, and netting policies. **Offsets** are designed to accommodate the siting of new pollution sources in nonattainment areas. Under the offset policy, new sources may locate in such regions if, depending on the severity of existing pollution, they buy between 1.1 and 1.5 pollution credits from existing sources for each unit they anticipate emitting. For example, the March Air Force Base near Los Angeles absorbed the staff and equipment of another base that was closing. The March Base anticipated doubling its pollution emissions from power and heat generation, and aircraft operation and maintenance.

---

2. "Trades to Remember" (1992).

March recruited pollution-credit brokers that acted as middlemen in trades between polluters. Officers also scoured local newspapers and hunted for potential sellers among public documents of previous pollution-credit trades. They made cold calls to refineries and utilities.... Eventually, March managed to buy the credits it needed from five sellers, for a total of $1.2 million. They even found a bargain or two, including the right to emit 24 pounds of nitrogen oxide and six pounds of carbon monoxide a day for the rock-bottom price of $975 a pound—from a machinery company that got the credits by closing down a plant. "This company didn't know what it had," says Air Force Lt. Col. Bruce Knapp.[3]

The offset policy was designed to accommodate the conflict between economic growth and pollution control, not to achieve cost-effectiveness. Thousands of offset trades have occurred, but as suggested by the above-mentioned example provided earlier, the markets still do not function smoothly. High transactions costs remain a serious obstacle to new firms seeking offsets to locate in a nonattainment area. This is reflected in the fact that, at least in the program's early years, about 90% of offset transactions involved trades within a single firm.

The **netting policy** also focuses on accommodating economic growth and has had a significant impact on compliance costs. This program allows old sources that are expanding their plant or modifying equipment to avoid the technological requirements for pollution control (the new source performance standards discussed in Chapter 13) if any increase in pollution above the standard is offset by emission reduction credits from within the plant. Tens of thousands of netting trades have taken place, saving billions of dollars in reduced permitting costs and abatement investment while having little if any negative effect on the environment. The netting program has been the most successful of the three, primarily because it has involved only internal trades.

In contrast to the offset and netting trades, the **bubble policy** was designed primarily to generate cost savings and, of the three programs, is most similar to the theoretical marketable permits model discussed in Chapter 15. "Bubbles" are localized air quality regions with several emission sources; a bubble may include only a single plant or may be extended to include several sources within a broader region. Under the bubble policy, emission reduction credits can be traded within the bubble. In its simplest form, a firm may violate air quality emission standards at one smokestack, provided it makes up the difference at another. Of course, trades between plants within a regional bubble can occur as well.

Bubbles were introduced in 1979, three years after offsets, with high expectations of cost savings. One study, for example, predicted that the cost of nitrogen dioxide control in Baltimore might fall by 96%. However, in the first few years, few trades actually occurred with estimated cumulative savings of less than $0.5 billion. Only two of these trades were thought to have involved external transactions.[4] Analysts have stressed the role of imperfect information and thin markets to explain the relative

---

3. "New Rules Harness Power" (1992).
4. See Hahn (1989). Hahn also describes another disappointing application of marketable permits for water pollutants in Wisconsin. This program appeared to founder on the thin markets problem, as well as limitations on permit life.

failure of the EPA's bubble policy. Because of the difficulty in locating potential deals, most firms simply did not participate. Also, each individual trade between firms must satisfy the constraint of no increase in pollution. This results in much less activity than traditional models of IB regulation, which unrealistically assume that the constant pollution constraint is met as all feasible deals are consummated simultaneously.

Finally, the lack of interfirm trading can be explained in part by the nonuniformly mixed nature of the pollutants. Because the NAAQ standards relate to ambient air quality, not emissions, trades of such emission permits require firms to demonstrate through (costly) air quality modeling that ambient standards will not be violated by the trade.[5]

In short, many economists underestimated real-world complications associated with designing permit markets when they generated rosy predictions for bubbles and offsets. Of the theoretical issues discussed in Chapter 15, the problem of thin markets greatly reduced the effectiveness of emissions trading. In addition, the hot-spot problem with nonuniformly mixed pollutants has been vexing. The technical complications involved in demonstrating that emissions trades will not affect ambient air quality substantially raised the transactions costs for firms engaged in external trades under the bubble program.

Hot spots are largely ignored in southern California's two trading programs—a "clunker" purchase program and the **RECLAIM** (Regional Clean Air Incentives Market) cap-and-trade system. Under the mobile source trading (or clunker) program, stationary sources such as refineries and chemical factories, working through licensed dealers, can purchase and then scrap highly polluting old vehicles (clunkers) and use the pollution credits to avoid clean-air upgrades at their plants. Similar to the EPA's offset program, the system saves companies money, but it can lead to hot spots. As one critic notes, the program "effectively takes pollution formerly distributed throughout the region by automobiles and concentrates that pollution in the communities surrounding stationary sources." And in the L.A. case, these communities are often disproportionately Latino or African American.

The mobile source trading program has been criticized from a monitoring and enforcement perspective as well. The program assumes that clunkers purchased would otherwise be on the road, and driven 4,000 miles, for three years. However, there is an obvious incentive for people to turn in cars that were driving on their last gasp, and would have been scrapped soon anyway. Licensed dealers are supposed to prevent this kind of fraud, but the program has nevertheless been hobbled by these kinds of problems.[6] In 2009, the Obama administration ran a large-scale, national cash-for-clunkers program, this one designed as a stimulus for the car industry rather than as an environmental initiative. This program, too, was criticized as being quite expensive, as many of the cars taken off the road under the program would have been retired in the next year or two regardless.[7]

---

5. Atkinson and Tietenberg (1991).
6. Drury et al. (1999) and Steinzor (2005). The clunker program has also had some incidences of outright fraud, as well as another type of hot-spot problem: the VOC composition from cars varies from that released by stationary sources, such as marine oil terminals. Critics argue that the latter are substantially more toxic than the former. For a general economic analysis of clunker programs, see Alberini, Harrington, and McConnell (1993).
7. Harshaw (2009).

In contrast to the clunker program, RECLAIM is a textbook cap-and-trade system. In operation since 1993, the program requires about 330 stationary sources to hold (tradeable) permits for each ton of sulfur dioxide (SO_2) and nitrogen oxide (NOx) emitted. Figure 16.1 illustrates both the number of allowances issued and the actual emissions by RECLAIM companies for NOx. Note that the total number of allowances granted to firms shrinks every year up until 2003. The initial allocation of allowances was quite generous—well above historical pollution levels. It was not until 1998 and 1999 that actual reductions below pre-RECLAIM levels were required for SO_2 and NOx, respectively. (The high initial allowances were apparently a political concession to promote industry buy-in.)

The tremendous excess supply of permits led to a slow start for the permit market: in 1994 and 1995, many could not be sold even at a zero price. Moreover, though RECLAIM required continuous emissions monitoring and electronic reporting, it took a couple of years for monitors to be installed and certified at some firms. However, by the end of the decade, the monitoring bugs were mostly worked out, and the allowance constraints were beginning to bind. In fact, in 1998, 27 firms violated the regulations by polluting more than their permitted levels. As supply diminished, permit prices rose while trading accelerated; in 1999, 541 trades occurred, valued at $24 million.[8]

RECLAIM was severely tested during the California energy crisis of 2000–2001. At the same time that the number of allowances were shrinking, energy prices went through the roof, and existing California power plants began operating on overtime schedules. As a result, demand for NOx permits in particular shot up, and prices rose almost tenfold—from $4,300 per ton in 1999 to around $39,000 per ton in 2000. (These higher prices for NOx permits fed back into higher electricity prices.) During the crisis, NOx emissions broke through the cap by about 6% (see Figure 16.1). As a result, California regulators fell back to CAC strategies, pulling power plants out of the RECLAIM program to stabilize emission prices.

After a four-year hiatus, in which power producers were required to install technologies capable of reducing NOx emissions by 90%, in 2005 the plants rejoined

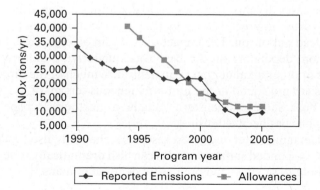

FIGURE 16.1 Reported Emissions and Allowances under RECLAIM
Source: Luong, Tsai, and Sakar (2000); Harrison (2006) and Fowlie, Holland, and Mansur (2009).

8. Luong, Tsai, and Sakar (2000).

the trading program. RECLAIM scheduled an additional round of cuts in the NOx allocations: 20% below the 2004 levels in Figure 16.1 by 2008. To guard against future price surges, California regulators now have the discretionary authority to issue additional permits if prices rise above $15,000 per ton, allowing pollution levels to rise up to 2004 levels in the following year.[9]

As with the clunker program, RECLAIM ignores hot-spot issues. This may pose little problem if NOx and SO$_2$ are regionally mixed. However, critics have argued that toxic co-pollutants may be associated with the criteria pollutants, so SO$_2$ and NOx hot spots may, in fact, also generate toxic hot spots. It is not currently known if RECLAIM trading patterns have increased exposure around particular plants.[10]

To recap the U.S. experience with trading urban air pollutants: The EPA's early experiments were effective at promoting internal trades, but external trades were hampered by thin markets. Los Angeles's clunker program has experienced both monitoring and hot-spot problems, and RECLAIM fell victim to unanticipated price volatility.

On a more optimistic note, the East Coast NOx trading system got off to a good start. Initiated in 1999, the first round of trading included 11 states, and by 2002, large electrical generators and industrial boilers were trading credits equal to only 46% of their 1990 emissions. In 2005, the Bush administration federalized the trading program expanding it to 25 states under the Clean Air Interstate Rule (CAIR). CAIR has since been challenged by price volatility, due to uncertainty over court challenges, and later the impact of climate regulation on NOx emissions.[11]

16.3 Marketable Permits and Acid Rain

To date, the defining "grand experiment" with cap-and-trade in the United States has been the sulfur dioxide trading program designed to reduce acid rain. **Acid rain** is formed when sulfur dioxide, primarily released when coal is burned, and nitrogen oxide, emitted from any kind of fossil fuel combustion, are transformed while in the atmosphere into sulfuric and nitric acids. These acids return to the earth attached to raindrops or in some cases dry dust particles. Acid deposition harms fish and plant life directly and also can cause indirect damage by leaching and mobilizing harmful metals like aluminum and lead out of soil. The impact of acid rain on ecosystem health varies from region to region, depending on the base rocks underlying the area. Naturally occurring limestone or other alkaline rocks can neutralize much of the direct impact of the acid. Such rocks are not found in the primarily igneous terrain of the Adirondack Mountains in New York State, southeastern Canada, or northern Europe, so damage to lakes in these regions has been extensive.

In addition to damaging water and forest resources, the acids also erode buildings, bridges, and statues. Suspended sulfate particles can also dramatically reduce visibility. Finally, they contribute to sickness and premature death in humans.[12]

---

9. Burtraw et al. (2005). For more on this kind of "safety value mechanism," see Appendix 15A.
10. Drury et al. (1999) and Fowlie, Holland, and Mansur (2009).
11. Burtraw and Szambelan (2010).
12. Technically, the offending pollutants are suspended acidic aerosols of several types. Acidic sulfates appear to dominate these acrosol mixes. See NAPAP (1991, 132).

Pollution from sulfur dioxide was at one time concentrated around power plants and metal refineries. The area around Copper Hill, TN, for example, is so denuded of vegetation from now-closed copper-smelting operations that the underlying red clay soil of the region is clearly visible from outer space. In an attempt to deal with these local problems, and with the encouragement of the ambient standards mandated by the Clean Air Act of 1970, smokestacks were built higher. And yet, dilution proved not to be a pollution solution. Sulfur and nitric oxides were picked up by the wind and transported hundreds of miles, only to be redeposited as acid rain. The acid rain problem in the northeastern United States and Canada can thus be blamed on regional polluters—coal-fired utilities and nitrogen oxide emitters ranging from the Midwest to the Eastern seaboard. Similarly, Germany's forest death and acidified lakes in Sweden and Norway required a Europe-wide solution.

Increasing environmental concerns, along with the large health risks from sulfate pollution discussed earlier, finally led to action on acid rain in the 1990 Clean Air Act. The legislation created the **SO_2 trading system**, requiring a 10-million-ton reduction of sulfur dioxide emissions from 1980 levels, down to an annual average of 8.95 million tons per year, and a 2.5-million-ton reduction of nitrogen oxide emissions by the year 2000.[13]

The first stage of the SO_2 rollback was achieved in 1995 by issuing a first round of marketable permits to 110 of the nation's largest coal-burning utilities, mostly in the East and Midwest; the second stage, begun in 2000, imposed tighter restrictions and included another 2,400 sources owned by 1,000 other power companies in the country. To reduce the financial burden on, and political opposition from, utilities and rate payers, most of the permits are not sold by the government. Instead, utilities are simply given permits based on their emission levels in 1986. Each utility receives permits equivalent to 30–50% of its 1986 pollution.[14]

Trading is nationwide, although state legislators and utility regulators do have the authority to restrict permit sales. Given such a broad market, a utility in, say, Ohio has little power to prevent a competitor from setting up shop in the neighborhood merely by refusing to sell permits. Such a firm could simply go shopping in Texas. And finally, to safeguard against potential market power problems arising if new entrants are forced to buy permits from incumbent competitors, the government distributes 2.8% of the permits by auction and sale.

Because sulfur dioxide and nitrogen oxides emitted from the tall stacks of power plants are more or less uniformly mixed on a regional basis (and because midwestern plants are net sellers), major geographical hot spots have not emerged from the acid rain program.[15]

The program creates an 8.9-million-ton cap on SO_2 emissions from power plants after the year 2000. However, Congress has the authority to reduce the number of permits even further without buying them back from the firms. The states' authority to impose tighter regulations has also not been affected. Thus the permits confer no

---

13. NOx control will be by means of technology-based uniform emission standards, that is, a CAC approach.
14. A good discussion of the mechanics of the program can be found in Claussen (1991).
15. Burtraw et al. (2005). In addition, the possibility of a *temporal* hot spot exists. Because firms are allowed to bank their permits, the 8.9-million-ton sulfur dioxide limit might easily be exceeded in a given year, if many firms should choose to use their banked permits simultaneously.

tangible property rights, although firms certainly expected at least a decade's trading before the emission cap is reconsidered.

On the enforcement front, the acid rain program mandated the installation of continuous monitoring equipment, which is required to be operative 90% of the time and to be accurate to within 10–15% of a benchmark technology. The EPA certifies the monitors at each plant; thus, the monitoring process itself retains a CAC flavor. Once a plant's monitoring units are certified, the EPA records all trades and then checks allowances against emissions on an annual basis to ensure compliance.

Violators face a $2,000-per-ton fine for excess emissions and must offset those emissions the following year. The fine level was set substantially above the expected market price and yet not so high as to be unenforceable. Thus it represents a very credible threat to firms. In addition, once a violation is established, the fine is nondiscretionary. These factors have led to very high compliance rates.

As a last note, the acid rain legislation contained measures to compensate high-sulfur coal miners and others who lost their jobs. Funding for support while in job-retraining programs was authorized at a level of up to $50 million for five years. Job-loss estimates through the late 1990s were on the order of 7,000 in total, almost all of them eastern coal miners.[16]

Before the program was introduced, economists were optimistic that the legislated acid rain trading program, expected to cost about $4 billion annually, would result in savings of between 15% and 25% over a stereotypical CAC option.[17] This optimism arose because the theoretical objections to an IB approach raised in the last chapter, some of which contributed to the disappointing performance of bubbles, did not appear likely to emerge in this case.

To begin with, the existence of a national market with hundreds of participants (including the Chicago Board of Trade) minimizes transactions costs and the thin market problem. Because of the approximately uniformly mixed nature of the pollutants, major hot spots were unlikely to emerge. The potential exercise of market power and speculative behavior was mitigated by the set-aside and auction of a limited number of permits. The issue of permit life has been settled by providing firms with an indefinite guarantee—a cap of 8.9 million tons in 2000 with Congress holding the authority to restrict emissions further. And finally, an up-front commitment to better monitoring technology and streamlined enforcement has been made.

From an economic point of view, the acid rain program was one of the best-laid regulatory plans. Nevertheless, to paraphrase Shakespeare, reality often reveals more complications than are dreamt of in our philosophy. This experiment has been worth monitoring closely as it unfolds; to date, the results have been quite positive.

First, both SO_2 and NOx emissions from the power plants participating in the program have fallen sharply since 1995. Ambient (airborne) levels of sulfur dioxide have declined as well. This decline has been linked to both improvements in visibility in national parks, and significant health benefits—reductions in both sickness and premature death. Based largely on these health benefits, the acid rain program easily

16. Goodstein (1999).
17. NAPAP (1991, 510).

passes an efficiency test; the measurable benefits of the acid rain program far exceed the costs.[18]

On the downside, the reduction in NOx from power plants has been countered by increases elsewhere, mostly from automobiles. Some lakes in New England are showing reductions in acidification, but the Adirondack lakes are displaying little sign of recovery—in part because NOx emissions have failed to decline. Some scientists believe that a second round of cuts will be needed to restore the health of the Adirondack aquatic systems.[19]

The big positive surprise from the program has been the dramatic cost savings: utilities achieved the cutbacks by spending less than one quarter of what the cap-and-trade system was originally predicted to cost, which in turn was well below the forecast costs for a traditional CAC system. Before the program went into effect, the EPA estimated that compliance costs for the cap-and-trade system would be $4 billion annually; that estimate has now fallen to less than $1 billion. Most analysts thought that marginal control costs (and thus permit prices) for SO_2 would settle in at between $750 and $1,500 per ton. Instead, for the first few years of the program, permits sold for between $100 and $150 per ton, though they have recently climbed as high as $700 per ton.[20]

During the first two years of the program, relatively few trades between different firms actually occurred; in 1995, less than 5% of the permits in circulation traded hands. Both the phenomena of dramatically lower costs and fewer-than-expected trades can be explained in retrospect by the increased flexibility that firms were given under the acid rain program. Rather than install expensive scrubbers (or buy extra permits), most firms met their early SO_2 targets by switching to low-sulfur coal or developing new fuel-blending techniques. Railroad deregulation led to an unexpected decline in low-sulfur coal prices. And with the increased competition from coal, scrubber prices fell by half from 1990 to 1995.

Recall that a stereotypical CAC regulation has two features that raise costs: uniform standards (which block short-run cost-reducing trades) and technology-based regulations (which discourage long-run cost savings by restricting firm-level compliance options). In the acid rain case, almost all of the initial cost savings came from increased flexibility *within* the individual firm. This included the ability to engage in intrafirm trading (so that any single firm's different plants don't face uniform standards) as well as the ability to use a mix of control technologies.

However, as Figure 16.2 illustrates, interfirm trading picked up dramatically after year 3. Environmental managers at utilities took a while to exhaust internal cost savings from trade, and then began to look outward.[21] Thus even greater costs savings emerged as interfirm trading accelerated. All in all, the acid rain program is a case where economic theory has done a very good job guiding government policy. Emissions have been reduced at low cost and with a high degree of certainty.

---

18. Burtraw et al. (2005).
19. U.S. EPA (1999).
20. See Burtraw et al. (1996). Not all of these price differences reflect "real" cost savings: Permit prices are lower than anticipated because early bonus allowances added to the near-term supply, thus driving down

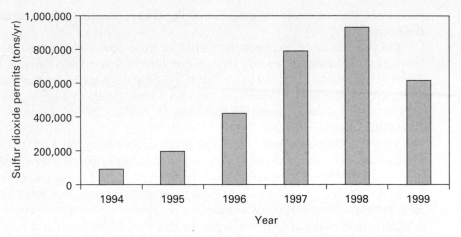

FIGURE 16.2 Interfirm Permit Trade under the Acid Rain Program
Source: U.S. EPA Acid Rain Program, www.epa.gov/docs/acidrain.ats/qlyupd.html.

16.4 Carbon Trading in the Northeast and California

In 2005, seven Northeastern U.S. governors signed on to the **Regional Greenhouse Gas Initiative**, better known as RGGI. In the absence of any federal controls on global-warming pollutants, these states decided to act on their own, agreeing to stabilize carbon dioxide emissions from the electric power sector at *projected* 2009 levels, and then reduce by 10% from there through 2018. From a short-run efficiency perspective, this effort makes no sense. State residents will bear some costs for the reduction, primarily in the form of higher electricity prices, and because the emission reductions proposed are so tiny relative to world emissions, the effort on its own will have no noticeable impact on future global temperatures. Why do it, then?

One reason was to provide leadership in an attempt to overcome the free-rider problem; the states hoped to set an example that the U.S. federal government would soon follow. And under the assumption that this would eventually happen, Northeast states hoped to then capitalize on technology leadership established as they began to reshape their economies to rely less on inputs of fossil fuels. In addition, by reducing the use of out-of-state coal, and investing permit proceeds in weatherizing homes and other energy efficiency measures, the states hoped to keep more of their energy dollars at home, boosting in-region growth.

RGGI trading began at an unfortunate moment: late 2008, just as the economy was sliding into a recession. Due to sluggish economic growth and also the unexpected surge in natural gas generation at the expense of coal (see Chapter 18), by 2012, carbon emissions from the region were already *30% below* the initial cap. Thus, RGGI permits

---

prices (Burtraw 1996). Real cost savings have been on the order of 4 to 8 times greater than predicted, not 4 to 15.

21. The last three paragraphs are drawn from Burtraw (1996).

have been trading at very low prices, around $2 per ton, with many of the auctioned permits going unsold. In 2012, regulators were debating tightening the cap.[22]

Even as initially envisioned, RGGI would not have cost individual consumers much, because the emission cuts it proposed were relatively small. By 2015, RGGI might raise electricity prices by around 1% or less, with annual costs ranging from $3 to $16 per family. As auction revenues from the program are used to invest in energy-efficiency measures, *net* energy payments by many New England residents might actually decline. Much of the policy discussion around RGGI has been devoted to this issue of permit sales revenues. First, how much money is at stake? Second, how many permits should be given away and how many auctioned? Third, what should be done with the auction revenues?

Although not a lot of money for an individual household, the total auction revenues that RGGI might generate are large: around $1 billion over the first three years of operation, and as much as $1 billion per year going forward. After significant debate, the RGGI states now auction 90% of the total permits. States are using RGGI dollars to fund energy-efficiency measures, to fund renewable energy, to assist low-income consumers with electricity bills, and in some cases, to cover general expenses. One study has argued that, on net, these recycled revenue dollars have indeed boosted the regional economy.[23]

Finally, an interesting feature of RGGI is that it allows electricity producers to obtain some of their mandated reduction in carbon dioxide via the purchase of **offsets**—reductions in greenhouse gasses achieved offsite by third parties and then packaged and sold. RGGI specifically allows offsets from the following sources:

- Natural gas, heating oil, and propane energy efficiency
- Landfill gas capture and combustion
- Methane capture from animal operations
- Forestation of nonforested land
- Reductions of sulfur hexafluoride (SF_6) emissions from electricity transmission and distribution equipment
- Reductions in fugitive emissions from natural gas transmission and distribution systems

Offsets from non-RGGI states are allowed, but at a 1-ton credit for each 2 tons of verified reductions.[24]

Since around 2000, offsets have also been available for purchase by companies and individuals not required to reduce their emissions. Several nonprofit organizations around the country offer individual consumers the opportunity to voluntarily offset their personal carbon dioxide emissions and become "carbon neutral" or "carbon cool." (See www.carboncounter.org, for example.) In 2003–2004, the school where one of us used to teach, Lewis and Clark College, became the only school in the world to be (temporarily) compliant with the Kyoto treaty through the purchase of $17,000 of offsets; the money was voted out of student fees, at about $10 per student. The

---

22. "Regional Cap-and-Trade Effort Seeks Greater Impact by Cutting Carbon Allowances" (2012).
23. Hibbard et al. (2011).
24. Data on RGGI are from Regional Greenhouse Gas Initiative (2005).

student funds helped to support new wind-power development in Oregon, among other projects.

The offset market has grown up around voluntary initiatives to reduce greenhouse gases; initiatives like RGGI will help this market grow. A serious problem with offsets is quality control. In particular, to have real value, offset projects must be **additional**. This means that the project—reforestation, reduction in fugitive emissions from pipelines—would not have already occurred under a business-as-usual scenario.

With the RGGI experiment, large-scale carbon trading got under way in the United States in 2009, years before trading is likely to kick in across the nation. California is set to follow the Northeast, with a more ambitious economy-wide cap-and-trade initiative set that will launch in 2013. If California were a nation, it would be the eighth biggest greenhouse gas emitter in the world, so the effort is internationally significant.

California's program, known as AB32 for the law that created it, requires that the state economy roll back greenhouse gas emissions to 1990 levels by 2020. This is a 22% reduction compared to forecasts of what business-as-usual emissions would be. Most of this reduction will not actually be driven by cap-and-trade, but rather by complementary policies (discussed in Chapters 17 and 18) including a renewable portfolio standard for the electricity sector, a clean-car mandate, a low-carbon fuel standard, and the million solar roofs program. The trading system is designed to achieve about 20% of the total CO_2 reductions.[25]

Starting in 2013, around 450 electricity generating plants (including plants that import electricity into California) and large industrial facilities will face carbon caps. In 2015, another 100 distributors of transportation fuels and natural gas will come into the system. Together these facilities account for about 85% of total California greenhouse gas emissions. Each year the total number of permits that will be available to these businesses will decline, reaching 1990 levels by 2020.

Industrial facilities will start out with free allowances to provide them time to adjust to lower emissions, and also to protect trade-exposed industries. Other sectors must purchase permits at auction. By 2015, over 80% of the permits will be sold by the state. By California law, any revenues generated through fees—such as permit auctions—must be used to further the purpose of the fees, in this case greenhouse gas reduction. Auction revenues raised in the utility sector must be used to benefit rate-payers—through measures such as rebates on their bills, energy efficiency investments, or renewable investments.

There is currently a robust debate underway in California as to what to do with the remaining revenue—a fund that will start at $0.6–$1.8 billion, but by 2015 could be five times that amount. The money might be rebated back to households, "skytrust" style; invested in high-speed rail connections between San Francisco and Los Angeles; used to support renewable or efficiency investments; or used in any of a variety of other options consistent with the goal of equitably cutting greenhouse gas emissions. Whether those funds are invested productively will be key both to the economic impact of the law in California, as well as the state's ability to meet deeper emission reductions it might pursue post-2020.

---

25. The discussion of AB32 is drawn from Burtraw et al. (2012).

Firms can meet up to 8% of their pollution limit through the use of offsets, which must be "permanent, verifiable, enforceable," and, of course, additional. Offsets must be certified through third-party, employ-approved protocols and are currently limited to the United States.

The program has a price-collar, with a floor of $10 per ton, and a set of ceiling triggers at $40, $45, and $50 in 2012, rising at 5% each year plus inflation. To keep prices below the triggers, the state is authorized to issue up to 4% additional permits at each trigger point, for a total increase in supply of up to 12%. There is unlimited banking, and compliance is measured over a three-year average period. Firms pay a fine for non-compliance, by being required to purchase four additional tons for every ton for which they are over their limit.

California's AB32 system is benefiting from 25 years of experience with cap-and-trade systems. By moving quickly to an auction system, the state is avoiding the problem of windfall profits accruing to producers (see Chapter 15, Section 15.4) while still providing some period for adjustment; offsets are limited and regulated to ensure high quality; and the price-collar is designed to protect the system from the price volatility at both ends that has plagued other programs. In addition, the legal mandate requiring that auction revenues be used to further the purposes of the program may help ensure productive investment of auction proceeds—the resource rent generated by restricting access to common property.

The California system faced a serious political challenge on the 2010 ballot, when two Texas oil companies funded an initiative that would have repealed the law. California voters were treated to a rare TV ad war: "cap-and-trade will kill jobs" said one side; "cap-and-trade is creating jobs in a clean energy economy" said the other. At the end of the day, AB32 was reaffirmed by the voters 2–1. Political challenges may re-emerge post 2015, when the visible-to-consumer effects on fuel prices kick in. The cap-and-trade system might lead to gas price increases of $.18 to a high of $1.45 per gallon. However, by that time, the California clean car standards will have boosted the average mileage of new cars, helping to substantially offset household expenditures on gasoline.

16.5 Two Failed U.S. Efforts: Mercury and Carbon

Two major federal cap-and-trade systems were proposed but did not advance during the last decade, and the reasons for their failure are instructive. During the George W. Bush presidency, the United States tried to launch a trading system for mercury emissions from coal plants. It is one of the glaring failings of the U.S. regulatory system that mercury emissions remained unregulated until 2012. Airborne mercury from fossil fuel combustion winds up in lakes, rivers, and oceans, where it bioaccumulates in fish. Through this and other exposure routes, perhaps 10–20% of pregnant women in the United States have elevated mercury levels; the figure doubles for Native American and Asian American women. Not all of this contamination comes from U.S. emissions; ocean deposition and contamination of fisheries is a global, transboundary problem.

Mercury originally escaped regulation under the original Clean Air Act. It was categorized as a hazardous pollutant or air toxic, not a criteria pollutant, and thus fell prey to regulatory gridlock discussed in Chapter 13. Following the air toxics mandate of the 1990 CAA amendments, in 2000, the Clinton EPA finally announced its intent to impose maximum achievable control technology (MACT) requirements for mercury, a CAC regulatory approach that would have required emission reductions at all sources on the order of 90% by 2009. The Bush administration EPA, however, did not follow through on this finding. Instead, in 2005, the EPA recategorized mercury as a criteria pollutant and announced plans for a mercury cap-and-trade program designed to reduce emissions 20% by 2010 and 70% by 2018. The reductions up to 2010 were anticipated as "co-benefits" resulting from existing SO_2 and NOx regulations and would not have imposed additional costs on industry.

Efficiency and safety advocates sparred over the very different stringency levels recommended by the Bush and Clinton EPAs. But the particular issue of interest here is the question of **hot spots**: is this a case in which a CAC uniform emission reduction requirement is needed or will trading be acceptable? The Bush EPA argued that no hot spots would emerge from the proposed trading program. Yet many analysts were not convinced: local and regional hot spots appear possible in the upper Great Lakes states of Michigan, Minnesota, and Wisconsin, potentially imposing high costs on rural and Native American populations.

Because of concerns about both hot spots and pollution levels, the Obama administration scrapped the Bush plan and returned to regulating mercury emissions as air toxics, using a CAC approach like that proposed by the Clinton EPA. In 2012, more than 40 years after the original passage of the Clean Air Act, mercury emissions are finally on the verge of becoming regulated.[26]

The Obama administration also supported its own, ultimately unsuccessful national cap-and-trade system, this one for global warming pollutants, primarily carbon dioxide. The system would have been authorized by the American Clean Energy and Security Act (the Waxman-Markey Bill) which passed the House of Representatives in June 2009. However, the Senate was unable to pass a comparable bill, and with the 2010 elections and the rise of Tea Party politics, the political coalition supporting cap-and-trade collapsed.

The House Bill is worth examining because of the way it tried to solve key obstacles: the law sought to insulate residential consumers from price increases and also controlled costs through generous offset provisions. The bill proposed a goal of reducing global-warming pollution emissions from fossil fuel combustion of 17% below 2006 levels by 2020 and 80% by 2050. Covered sectors include electricity producers, oil refineries, natural gas suppliers, and energy-intensive industries: steel, cement, chemical, and paper manufacturers. Combined, these sectors account for 85% of economic activity.

Around 75% of the permits would have been given away to polluters, based on their past emissions of global-warming pollution; 10% given to states to be sold for efficiency, renewables, and other investments; and 15% auctioned by the federal government. Beginning in 2025, giveaways to industry would be phased out, and the program would have moved toward 100% auction by about 2030. Note that relative to RGGI and California's AB32, the proposed federal program was much more generous

---

26. The discussion of mercury is drawn from Steinzor and Heinzerling (2004), O'Neill (2004), Gayer and Hahn (2005), and Steinzor (2005).

to industry, and for many business sectors, would actually have provided windfall profits (as discussed in Chapter 15). This reflected the weakness of the political coalition supporting cap-and-trade at the national level, and the need for greater industry buy-in.

Around 5–10% of the federal government revenue would be used to help developing countries cut deforestation and implement clean technology solutions. Also the bill mandated that a big chunk of government auction revenues—rising over time—would go to weatherization and other efforts to reduce household energy consumption. Finally, as in California, the value of permits given to regulated electric power distributors was required to be passed on to consumers in the form of rebates or other measures.

These kinds of conservation and efficiency efforts were predicted to have a major effect. The EPA estimated that demand would be cut so far that "energy consumption levels that would otherwise be reached in 2015 without the policy are not reached until 2040 with the policy." Overall—through this demand reduction and the mandated rebates to households from their utilities—the EPA believed that households would largely be shielded from increases in their monthly payments for electric power.

Finally, very generous offset provisions also contained the estimated overall cost of the program. The House bill allowed up to 2 billion tons of offsets per year with the possibility of more than 50% of these being international. This number was large: currently around 30% of total emissions. But the relative size of this offset pool would have grown in importance over time, as U.S. domestic emissions shrank. By 2050, this 2 billion tons of offsets—if fully utilized every year—would have meant that instead of "real" emissions reductions of 80% by companies, U.S. producers would have cut only 60%.

The availability of international offsets in particular, and especially in the later, "deep cut" years of the program, reduced expected CO_2 prices a lot—by close to 90%. Why is this so important? It would be much cheaper to clean up inefficient, dirty coal plants in India, or to plant new forests in Ecuador, than it would be to squeeze an additional 20% out of the U.S. economy, for example, by shutting down remaining coal-fired power plants or converting them to biomass. At the same time, of course, these offsets would also be much harder to monitor, and they raised real concerns about the possibility of fraud.

Finally, transition assistance would have been provided in the form of free allocation of permits to energy-intensive and/or trade-exposed industries. As in California, these firms could use the "windfall profits" from their free permits to cushion the increased compliance costs, and any international competitive disadvantage, that they might face. (Unlike California, however, the U.S. system proposed continuing the permit giveaway program to *all firms* for more than a dozen years.) Workers in heavily affected sectors—certainly in coal mining, and potentially in rail shipping of coal—would have access to extended unemployment benefits and support for health care payments (up to three years), job-search expenses, and some relocation allowances.[27]

As noted, support for the cap-and-trade bill disappeared after the 2010 elections. And Tea Party opposition to national global warming legislation means that a national

---

27. The discussion of Waxman-Markey is drawn from Sheppard (2009) and U.S. EPA (2009).

cap-and-trade program (or a carbon tax) is likely off the table for the next few years. Nevertheless, with high probability, the world will continue to heat up. As a result, political support for national action on climate change will undoubtedly resurface. At that point, analysts will look back to Waxman-Markey for guidance.

In the meantime, as noted earlier and in Chapter 13, carbon dioxide is being regulated through state and regional cap-and-trade systems, and nationally under the Clean Air Act, with the EPA pursuing the CAC strategies for stationary and mobile sources that are enabled by that legislation. And elsewhere in the world, China and Korea are moving ahead with their own plans for carbon cap-and-trading systems.

16.6 The European Emissions Trading System

Europe is far ahead of the United States, having kicked off a comprehensive carbon cap-and-trade system in 2005. European nations all ratified the 1997 Kyoto treaty, which required reductions of global-warming pollution in Europe to about 7% below 1990 levels between 2010 and 2012. In anticipation of the treaty going into force, the EU established the **European Trading System** (**ETS**). Under Kyoto, each country has a carbon cap, and each country must develop an implementation plan to achieve the required emission reductions. Typically, the nationwide caps are translated into sector or firm-specific caps. The ETS then allows continent-wide trading of carbon between companies, so that companies (and countries) that have a hard time making their mandated targets can purchase excess emission reduction credits from companies that have beaten their targets. The ETS covers over 12,000 major emitters from the power sector—oil refiners, cement producers, iron and steel manufacturers, glass and ceramics, and paper and pulp producers, accounting for about 40% of Europe's global-warming pollution.[28]

Of the 15 western European countries, by 2009, five countries—The United Kingdom, Germany, Sweden, France, and Greece—were below their Kyoto targets. With the global recession, other western European countries are now also under the cap. In addition, most eastern European countries, as a result of the collapse of their Communist-era heavy industry, are below the Kyoto limits. Thus the EU as a whole has come in under the cap. (This is in contrast to the United States, where emissions are currently about 11% *above* 1990 levels.) Western European countries have purchased some credits from the east, including Russia. But original fears that Kyoto would lead to no real reductions in western Europe but instead rely solely on this "hot air" from the former Communist countries have not been borne out.[29]

Challenges to the system have included problems of price volatility and concerns about offset provisions. Figure 16.3 traces the evolution of European carbon prices on the year-ahead futures market. Prices started out at about 15 euros, as the ETS provided a generous initial allocation of permits to get people used to the system. After a year, as permit allocations began to shrink, prices rose and settled in at around 20 to 30 euros per tonne. But notice three distinct periods of price collapse: a steep one-day

---

28. See the website of the EU ETS: http://ec.europa.eu/environment/climat/emission/index_en.htm.
29. European Environment Agency (2009).

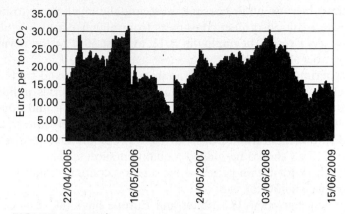

FIGURE 16.3 Carbon Prices in Europe
Source: ECX EUA Futures Contract: Historic Data 2009, http://www.ecx.eu/EUA-Futures.

drop at the end of April 2006, followed by a steady decline into 2007, and another drop again beginning in 2008.

The April 2006 collapse is interesting: this was the first time that ETS traders had to fully report their emissions. This information made it clear to traders that they had collectively overestimated demand, and so the market reacted with a sharp correction. The slump in prices in 2007 resulted from poor policy design; a transition from Phase I to Phase II did not allow banking, so Phase I permits became worthless. Finally, the drop in 2008 reflects the global recession. As with RGGI, European nations are now well within the cap, so there is an excess supply of permits and prices are quite low. Note that the "price stability problem" in Europe is the opposite of what occurred in Los Angeles: not excessive prices, but instead, repeated periods of prices so low that firms had little incentive to undertake long-run investments in emission reductions. There is also concern that, because so many permits have been banked—purchased but not used—that prices will take a long time to recover.[30] The European experience speaks to the need not only for a price ceiling but also for a price floor.

In addition to trading within Europe, the Kyoto treaty and the ETS allow companies to meet their targets via offset purchases from developing countries that do not face caps under the accords. The so-called Clean Development Mechanism (CDM) allows, for example, a German electric power company to gain credit for carbon dioxide reductions by replacing a proposed coal power plant in India with a new wind farm. Here again concerns have been raised about the quality of these offsets and ensuring that they are indeed additional. Reforestation efforts in particular raise quality issues: how will investors be assured that the trees will not later be harvested—or even burn down? Third-party certifiers and government oversight mechanisms have begun to arise as an attempt to ensure both additionality and quality.[31]

In 2009, the ETS was updated along two significant dimensions. First, a new 2020 target was adopted: 20% below 1990 levels for the EU as a whole. Second, the ETS

30. "EU's Hedegaard Says CO_2 Auctions Review Is Short-Term Fix" (2012).
31. Lecocq and Ambrosi (2007).

had been criticized because all the permits were initially given away to industry, and few attempts were made to protect consumers from higher prices for "dirty" (CO_2-intensive) goods. As a result, beginning in 2013, at least 50% of the permits must be auctioned by member states.[32]

The ETS experiment—featuring both an international cap-and-trade system with the CDM offset market thrown in—is by far the most ambitious pollution-control system ever put in place. Given its complexity, some economists and other observers are concerned that the European Trading System may ultimately falter on the critical monitoring and enforcement front. But so far, early problems have been identified and corrected, and the ETS should be judged a qualified success. The current challenge, as with RGGI, is how to sustain prices when, due to economic conditions, emissions unexpectedly fall well below the cap.

In the last few years, some U.S. states and Europe have taken initial, significant steps toward 80% by 2050 reduction. If these policies are effective, and if the rest of the world goes along, these efforts will hold the thickness of the carbon blanket to between 450 and 650 ppm. If we stabilize at the low end of 450 ppm, this in turn, provides some insurance (about a 30% chance, according to the Stern Review) that global temperatures will not rise by more than 2 degrees C (4 degrees F).[33] Is this good enough? Over the next ten years, it may be that the nations of the world may begin to pursue more aggressive measures.

16.7 Pollution Taxes and Their Relatives

In contrast to numerous global applications of cap-and-trade, pollution taxes are relatively rare, and are emerging primarily to attack global warming. A textbook example recently emerged in British Columbia. Since 2008, residents there have been paying a levy slated to rise to $30 per ton of CO_2 by 2012—which will add about $0.10 to a gallon of gasoline. When the tax was instituted, the government gave each household a lump-sum rebate of $85 and cut a number of other taxes to ensure that the policy was "revenue neutral." Despite these measures, the **carbon tax** became a major issue in the 2009 provincial elections, but—this time, going against the general trend—the public actually endorsed the tax, returning its political architect back into office. British Columbia's is the only regional CO_2 tax in North America. Other countries that have instituted carbon taxes (or close relatives) include Sweden, Norway, Britain, and The Netherlands. Carbon prices have been a political football in Australia in recent years. A tax of $24 per ton of carbon that went into effect in 2012, paid initially by the biggest few hundred businesses and government entities, may or may not survive.

In the United States, there are a number of price policies in place that affect the environment, though no real pollution taxes: fees levied per pound, liter, or ton of pollutant emissions. In this section, we examine several of these incentive instruments, and also look at "indirect" pollution taxes—energy taxes—in Europe. We will start with waste disposal fees.

---

32. See "EU ETS Post 2012" at http://ec.europa.eu/environment/climat/emission/index_en.htm.
33. Stern (2006).

Homeowners typically pay by the gallon for sewage disposal, and waste haulers pay by the ton to dispose of hazardous and solid waste. These closely resemble textbook pollution fees, which in theory should result in conservation measures as disposal costs rise.

However, at least in the case of solid waste, this has not been the general result because the incentives for waste reduction are not always passed on to consumers. Historically, much residential, commercial, and industrial municipal solid waste disposal is financed through a lump-sum fee. Thus residential consumers may pay, say, $10 per week for garbage service regardless of how much garbage they produce. In some communities, city government handles waste disposal, and the fee is included in property taxes; in others, private firms charge for disposal on a weekly or monthly basis.

This presents us with a curious problem:

PUZZLE

Why don't private garbage haulers provide their customers with a unit-pricing option? **Unit pricing** refers to paying for garbage disposal by the bag rather than in a lump sum. The lump-sum pricing system in effect generates a subsidy from small to large garbage producers. A "smart" garbage firm could offer a unit-pricing scheme to small garbage producers. By getting rid of (dumping?) its large garbage customers, the firm could service more customers per trip to the landfill and generate a higher profit margin.

SOLUTION

Sorry, I'm not a garbage hauler, so I don't know the answer to this one. However, it might have to do with the higher transactions costs associated with unit pricing. To implement this approach, a garbage firm might face a considerable challenge marketing its idea, then would have to sell bags to its customers, and finally have to keep track of the number of bags used per customer per week. Perhaps these added costs are enough to offset the extra profit opportunity that a unit-pricing scheme offers. Some evidence to support this view comes from a study that found that in 15 of 17 communities with unit pricing, collection was organized as a municipal monopoly, and in one of the exceptional cases, unit pricing was legally mandated. At any rate, this example again reminds us that markets that emerge on a chalkboard sometimes have a harder time in the real world.[34]

In the past, solid waste disposal fees have been relatively low. However, as landfills around the country close and political resistance to new construction has arisen, solid waste disposal costs have been rising rapidly. This has led an increasing number of municipalities to switch to unit pricing, often in combination with curbside recycling programs, as a way to reduce waste flows.[35]

---

34. See the EPA's "Pay as You Throw" website at www.epa.gov/epaoswer.
35. Morris and Byrd (1990).

In a study of unit pricing in suburban Perkasie, PA, semirural Ilion, NY, and urban Seattle, Washington, the introduction of unit pricing in the first two communities reduced waste actually generated by 10% or more, while the flow to the landfill was reduced by more than 30%. In addition, these two communities reduced their waste management costs by 10% or more, and passed on the savings to households through reduced fees. At the same time, unit pricing was adopted, both of these communities also introduced or expanded curbside recycling.

By contrast, Seattle's unit-pricing program was evaluated *before* the introduction of curbside recycling. Seattle had a unit-pricing system in place since 1961 but raised the rates per can substantially over the three years of the study. The response among Seattle residents to the rising rates was to increase trash compaction (locals call it the "Seattle Stomp"), slightly increase recycling rates, and, ultimately, slightly reduce overall waste generated. The study suggests that in the absence of a good substitute (curbside recycling), waste disposal is fairly insensitive to price increases; that is, it is price inelastic.

Of course, a pollution tax will always drive people to look for unintended substitutes. In the Perkasie case, the shift to unit pricing led to an increase in trash burning, which was subsequently banned, and to an increase in out-of-town disposal. However, the town found no increase in sewage disposal of waste. Seattle reported some increase in illegal dumping.[36]

Unit pricing for garbage disposal is about as close as we get to a pollution tax in the United States. However, a variety of other fee-based approaches, while also not classic Pigovian taxes, are in use.

USER FEES FOR PUBLIC LANDS AND ROADS

Hikers, recreational fishers, hunters, logging companies, and ranchers must all pay the federal government permit fees for the use of public resources. Many have argued that some or all of these fees are much too low to discourage overexploitation. Nevertheless, they represent a mechanism by which common property resources are priced and by which marginal damages can, at least in theory, be controlled.

What external costs do hikers impose? Too many hikers can damage trails, and of course, hikers generate congestion externalities—the last hiker crowding the trail reduces the value of the day's hike for all the previous users. Economists have recommended fees as an important component of a land manager's toolbox for rationing access to scarce trails. Similarly, congestion pricing on highways is an economically efficient—though seldom used—way out of urban traffic jams.

ENVIRONMENTAL BONDS

As discussed in Chapter 8, deposit requirements for beverage containers and automobile batteries and bonds posted by strip mines or landfill owners are ways to internalize the social cost of "irresponsible" disposal or development.

---

36. Morris and Byrd (1990). See also Fullerton and Kinnaman (1996).

INSURANCE AND LIABILITY REQUIREMENTS

Under the Oil Pollution Act, oil tankers entering U.S. waters must show proof of insurance of around $1,200 per gross ton of cargo. An insurance requirement of this type is similar to an environmental bond, and if insurers charge higher rates for tanker operators with riskier histories, insurance markets act to help internalize the social costs of risky behavior. (In the tanker insurance market, in fact, insurance rates do go up for carriers that have more oil spills, but probably not at a rate sufficient to fully internalize the environmental damage costs.)[37]

Damage insurance is critical to internalize the environmental costs for businesses likely to suffer low-probability but high-impact accidents. In this regard, the nuclear power industry has long held on to a critical but hidden governmental subsidy. Because nuclear plants would otherwise be unable to obtain private insurance, the Price-Anderson Act limits liability for nuclear accidents. On a per-reactor basis, the subsidy works out to be more than $20 million dollars per year.[38] By shielding the nuclear industry from this cost of operation, the Price-Anderson Act encourages the growth of nuclear power beyond what the market would support.

ENERGY TAXES

Energy taxes can serve as **indirect pollution taxes**. Europe has a long history of high fossil fuel taxes designed to both reduce pollution and improve energy security.

Two weeks before writing this section, I, Eban, returned from a trip to Denmark, where I visited my cousins. They had borrowed a friend's house for us to stay in, and when we departed, my cousins left a little envelope with some money in it "to pay for the electricity," they said. This was a little surprising to me, because in America we are used to thinking of electricity as a virtually free good. But due to high taxes on energy, Danes pay more than twice as much as we do for electricity. As a result, they think about their energy use more carefully than we do.

The production of energy via the burning of carbon-based fuels is a highly polluting process. Most of the criteria air pollutants are generated this way, while upstream mining of oil and coal result in destruction of sensitive habitat and in acid mine pollution. As Table 16.1 illustrates, for uncontrolled pollutants such as carbon dioxide, the relationship between energy use and pollution is fairly clear-cut. The United States, with its high per-capita energy use, also has the highest per-capita carbon dioxide emissions. The table also illustrates a strong negative relationship between energy prices and energy consumption. High prices promote low consumption, and vice versa. Thus one strategy to reduce pollution is to *tax it indirectly* by taxing energy use.

Indeed, since the late 1990s, Great Britain has imposed an energy tax called the Climate Change Levy. It is not, strictly speaking, a global-warming pollution tax, as it taxes energy produced, not carbon emissions. Yet, by exempting renewable power production—and rebating some of the levy revenues to clean power producers—the levy does provide some incentives to help meet Britain's Kyoto targets. (The remainder of the revenues are rebated to power producers in the form of an across-the-board cut in payroll taxes.) Recently the Conservative Party candidate in Britain's election

---

37. Goodstein and Jones (1997).
38. Dubin and Rothwell (1990).

TABLE 16.1   Energy Consumption, Prices, and CO_2 Emissions

Country	Energy Consumption per Capita (kg of oil equiv.)	CO_2 Emissions per Capita (tons)	Gasoline Price ($/gallon)
US	7794	19	3.29
Japan	4040	10	6.70
Germany	4203	10	7.96

Source: World Resources Institute Energy consumption data are from 2003, World Resources Institute; CO_2 data are from 2006, U.S. Department of Energy's Carbon Dioxide Information Analysis Center (CDIAC); gasoline price data are from Randall, Tom (2013) "Highest & Cheapest Gas Prices by Country", Bloomberg, 2/13/13 http://www.bloomberg.com/slideshow/2013-02-13/highest-cheapest-gas-prices-by-country.

was calling for the replacement of the levy with a bona fide carbon tax. Why? By taxing energy instead of carbon emissions, the levy leaves some firms with large bills, regardless of whether they are reducing their carbon footprint. Also, the levy puts the whole burden of energy reduction on power producers—exempting the household and transport sectors, where emissions are growing fastest and could be reduced at the lowest cost.

The potential for these kinds of unintended "perverse effects" means that a direct pollution tax (a charge per ton of carbon) would clearly be preferred to an indirect energy tax (levied on BTUs produced), because the former taxes all sources on the basis of their pollution contribution and promotes a search for all types of cleaner energy sources. Nevertheless, energy taxes do have the advantage of being administratively simpler, particularly if there is no easy formula for assigning pollutant emissions to energy sources.

16.8 Summary

This chapter has reviewed our experience with incentive-based regulation. Cap-and-trade systems can work very well, achieving clear environmental goals with large cost savings (SO_2 trading for acid rain). Or they can fail to achieve much of anything at all (the EPA bubble program). A primary lesson from the existing marketable permit systems is that a permit market can be a delicate thing. In markets with only a few players, potential traders are discouraged from participating, thus prolonging thin market problems. And as the L.A. Basin RGGI and ETS cases illustrate, price volatility has posed an unexpected and thorny problem.

Our experience with hot spots suggests that for nonuniformly mixed pollutants, permit designers face a trade-off between ensuring uniform pollution exposure and achieving a workable permit system. In practice, some compromise of safety has occurred (with the L.A. clunker system) for a permit system to be successfully implemented. For this reason, the proposed cap-and-trade system for mercury in the United States was highly controversial.

In recent permit systems, the choice between auctioning permits and giving them away free to industry has been an important decision. The trend is toward auction, with an initial give-away period to support industry adjustment and to protect trade-exposed industries. Auction revenues can then be devoted to protecting consumers from price increases, through rebates and energy efficiency investments as we have seen with RGGI and anticipate with California's AB32.

Another recent development has been the "politicization" of cap-and-trade. Support for cap-and-trade was initially widely bi-partisan. It was seen as a market-friendly alternative to CAC regulation. Acid rain permit trading in 1990 was supported by the first President Bush, RGGI was supported by a bi-partisan coalition of governors (including then-Massachusetts Governor Mitt Romney); John McCain, the 2008 Republican presidential candidate was a primary Senate co-sponsor of several mid-2000 U.S. carbon cap-and-trade bills; and the California cap-and-trade legislation was championed by Republican Governor Schwarzenegger.

This changed in the 2010 election, with the rise of Tea Party politics, and a tide of blanket Republican opposition—including that by candidate Romney—to all forms of cap-and-trade as a form of unwarranted taxation. Ironically, this has meant that U.S. national carbon policy has fallen back on CAC regulation under the Clean Air Act. For the next few years, the lack of bi-partisan support for cap-and-trade renders unlikely any additional national experiments in this form of regulation.

On the pollution tax side, the main lesson to be learned from our experience is that they are very hard to implement at levels high enough to function as a sole means of pollution control. Thus taxes and other fee-based mechanisms should be viewed as a complement to, not a substitute for, conventional CAC regulation.

Finally, indirect pollution taxes such as gasoline or energy taxes are often a compromise solution when direct pollution taxes prove politically unfeasible or are too hard to administer. In Europe and Japan, high energy taxes, originally imposed as energy security measures, have also functioned to reduce pollution in those countries, and Britain has imposed a specific Climate Change Levy, which is an indirect pollution tax on energy production.

Any type of regulation requires a strong commitment to monitoring and enforcement to be effective. This is especially true of IB regulation, where no special technology is mandated. In the U.S. context, two established marketable permit initiatives (acid rain and the RECLAIM program in Los Angeles) have featured an up-front commitment to better monitoring. However, some economists are concerned that the international complexity of the European Trading System for carbon dioxide (along with the offset option in the CDM) may be setting the system up to fail. The U.S. regional and state carbon cap-and-trade systems also need to confront these issues. If carbon trades are not carefully monitored and enforced, the credibility of the trading system will suffer.

APPLICATION 16.0

Lessons Learned

Consider these cap-and-trade programs discussed in the chapter:

    a. RECLAIM
    b. Bush cap-and-trade proposal
    c. Regional Greenhouse Gas Initiative (RGGI)
    d. Clunker Program

    e. National SO_2 Trading
    f. European Trading System (ETS)
    g. Bubbles
    h. Lead trading
    i. Waxman-Markey cap-and-trade Bill

      1. Of the programs listed above, which were designed to address acid rain? Urban air pollution? Global warming? Mercury pollution?
      2. Which program(s) are known to have suffered (or may suffer) from problems with hot spots? Monitoring and enforcement? Thin markets? Price volatility?

APPLICATION 16.1

CAC versus Direct versus Indirect Taxes

One of the main sources of water pollution is agricultural runoff. Consider three options to control this problem: (1) a CAC requirement prohibiting irrigation ditches from draining directly into streams or rivers; (2) a direct tax on chemical emissions from farms into streams or rivers and (3) an indirect tax placed on pesticide purchases. Evaluate these three options in terms of feasibility, enforceability, and—assuming they could be implemented—cost effectiveness and actual pollution reduction.

KEY IDEAS IN EACH SECTION

16.0 This chapter discusses several real-world applications of incentive-based regulation: marketable permits and direct and indirect pollution taxes.

16.1 An early successful example of a marketable permit system was the **lead banking** program, because none of the obstacles identified in the last chapter proved to be significant. A similar trading scheme also worked for ozone-depleting CFCs.

16.2 In contrast to the lead case, efforts to restrict other criteria urban air pollutants have had mixed success. The **Emissions Trading Program** has been disappointing relative to initial expectations. **Emission reduction credits** for criteria air pollutants are traded in the **offset netting**, and **bubble** programs. Bubbles, in particular, have performed poorly because of thin markets and high transactions costs for nonuniformly mixed pollutants. Hot spots have largely been ignored in California's **RECLAIM** and mobile source ("clunker") trading programs. RECLAIM broke down temporarily under the pressure of the California energy crisis. By contrast, the East Coast NOx trading system seems to be off to a good start.

16.3 The biggest cap-and-trade success story is the **national SO_2 trading system**, designed to reduce **acid rain**. This carefully monitored program achieved its pollution-reduction target and delivered substantial cost savings. Costs were reduced first as firms changed from installing scrubbers to burning low-sulfur coal, scrubber prices declined as a result of competition, and then further cost savings were achieved as interfirm trading gradually picked up.

16.4 The **Regional Greenhouse Gas Initiative** (**RGGI**) in the Northeast is a cap-and-trade program covering only electric utilities. Debates foreshadowed similar issues that have been raised in California and elsewhere: whether to auction or give away permits, how best to spend the auction revenue to maximize the program benefits, and recently, how to run an effective system which is well under the cap—in which there are more permits than emissions and prices have collapsed. In addition, RGGI allows firms to comply with their caps by purchasing **offsets** from inside and outside the region. The main challenge here is ensuring that new offsets are **additional**. California's **AB32** program will be the first economy-wide cap-and-trade system in North America. Mandating 1990 level emissions by 2020, the program covers 85% of the California economy. The majority of permits will be auctioned, and by state law, auction revenues must be used to further the goals of equitably reducing greenhouse gas emissions. The system will attempt to manage price volatility with a **price collar**, and limit the use of offsets.

16.5 During the 2000s, two federal cap-and-trade initiatives were scrapped after failing to gather sufficient political support. The Bush administration's proposal to regulate **mercury** emissions from power plants, using a nationwide marketable permit system, was quite controversial due to the potential for **hot spots**. And in 2010, the United States debated moving forward with a national cap-and-trade system for global-warming pollution. Key features of the bill that passed the House of Representatives: 17% reductions by 2020 and 80% by 2050. Most of the permits would have been given away initially, with the system transition to 100% auction by 2030. Consumers would have been protected by mandated rebates of permit revenues by electric distributors, by large-scale investments in renewables and energy efficiency, and by large offset provisions, including international offsets. **Affected workers** would have received **adjustment assistance**.

16.6 The design of the California and U.S. legislation was influenced by the European experience with the continent-wide **European Trading System** (**ETS**). Europe was on track to meet the Kyoto goal of 7% reductions below 1990 in 2012 prior to the recession; the economic downturn has ensured that the goal was met. Recent ETS reforms include a tightening of the cap—to 20% below 1990 levels by 2020—and a requirement that at least 50% of the permits be auctioned. A controversial feature of the ETS is offset trade with developing countries through the **Clean Development Mechanism** (**CDM**). The ETS market got off to a solid start—billions of dollars of trades have occurred. However, the ongoing global recession has driven permit prices very low. In addition, it has proved difficult to establish verifiability and additionality for CDM offsets, raising worries about poor monitoring and enforcement of the offset component.

16.7 Textbook pollution taxes are infrequently employed to attack pollution, as they are politically difficult to implement. Recently, however, carbon taxes are being implemented in Canada, Australia, and elsewhere. In the United States, the closest major examples are fees for the disposal of solid and liquid waste, both hazardous and nonhazardous. However, even in this sector, **unit pricing** is not always employed and thus incentives for waste reduction have been diluted. Other U.S. pricing policies—while not strictly pollution taxes—include fees for public use of resources, environmental bonds, and insurance and liability requirements. Europe has long had high taxes on fossil fuels and other forms of energy, which serve as an **indirect pollution tax** and induce greater conservation. The theoretical problem with indirect taxes is that they may generate unintended and counterproductive effects on other behavior.

REFERENCES

Alberini, Anna, Winston Harrington, and Virginia McConnell. 1993. Determinants of participation in accelerated vehicle retirement programs. Discussion paper 93–18. Washington, DC: Resources for the Future.

Atkinson, Scott, and Tom Tietenberg. 1991. Market failure in incentive-based regulation: The case of emission trading. *Journal of Environmental Economics and Management* 21(1): 17–31.

Burtraw, Dallas. 1996. Trading emissions to clean the air: Exchanges few but savings many. *Resources* 122 (Winter): 3–6.

Burtraw, Dallas, D. Evans, A. Krupnick, K. Palmer, and R. Toth. 2005. Economics of pollution trading for SO_2 and NOx. *Annual Review of Environment and Resources* 30: 253–89.

Burtraw, Dallas, David McLaughlin, and Sarah Jo Szambelan. 2012. California's new gold: A primer on the use of allowance value created under the CO_2 cap-and-trade program. RFF Discussion Paper 12–23.

Burtaw, Dallas, and Sarah Jo Szambelan. 2010. U.S. Emissions Trading Markets for SO_2 and NOx, In *Permit Trading in Different Applications*, ed. Bernd Hansjürgens. New York: Routledge.

Claussen, Eileen. 1991. Acid rain: The strategy. *EPA Journal* 17(1): 21–3.

Drury, Richard, Michael Belliveau, J. Kuhn, and Shipra Bansal. 1999. Pollution trading and environmental injustice: Los Angeles failed experiment in air quality policy. *Duke Environmental Law and Policy Forum* 9(2): 231–90.

Dubin, Jeffery, and Geoffrey Rothwell. 1990. Subsidy to nuclear power through the Price-Anderson Liability Limit, Contemporary Policy, VII: 3:7, 73–9.

European Environment Agency. 2005. *Greenhouse gas emission trends and projections in Europe 2005* (EEA Report No. 8/2005, Brussels). http://reports.eea.europa.eu/eea_report_2005_8/en/GHG2005.pdf.

European Environment Agency. 2009. *Greenhouse gas emission trends and projections in Europe 2009: Tracking progress towards Kyoto targets* (EEA Report No. 9, Brussels).

Fowlie, Meredith, Stephen P. Holland, and Erin T. Mansur. 2009. *What do emissions markets deliver and to whom? Evidence from Southern California's NOx Trading Program*. Working paper 15082. Cambridge, MA: National Bureau of Economic Research.

Fullerton, Don, and Thomas Kinnaman. 1996. Household response to pricing garbage by the bag. *American Economic Review* 86(4): 971–84.

Gayer, T., and R. W. Hahn. 2005. *Designing environmental policy: Lessons from the regulation of mercury emission*. Regulatory analysis 05-01. Washington, DC: AEI-Brookings Joint Center.

Goodstein, Eban. 1999. *The trade-off myth: Fact and fiction about jobs and the environment*. Washington, DC: Island Press.

Goodstein, Eban, and Robert Jones. 1997. *Testing the market for environment safety: The case of oil tankers*. Lewis and Clark College working paper. Portland, OR: Lewis and Clark College.

Hahn, Robert W. 1989. Economic prescriptions for environmental problems: How the patient followed the doctor's orders. *Journal of Economic Perspectives* 3(2): 95–114.

Harrison, D. 2006. Ex post evaluation of the RECLAIM emissions trading programmes for the Los Angeles Air Basin. In *Tradeable permits: Policy design, evaluation and reform*, 45–69. Paris: OECD.

Harshaw, Tobin. 2009. Weekend opinionator: Was the car rebate plan a clunker? *New York Times Online*, 30 October. http://opinionator.blogs.nytimes.com/2009/10/30/weekend-opinionator-was-the-car-rebate-plan-a-clunker/.

Heinzerling, L., and R. I. Steinzor, 2004. A perfect storm: Mercury and the Bush administration (Parts I & II). *Environmental Law Reports* 34(10297).

Hibbard, Paul, Susan F. Tierney, Andrea M. Okie, Pavel G. Darling. 2011. The economic impacts of the Regional Greenhouse Gas Initiative on ten Northeast and Mid-Atlantic states. Review of the use of RGGI auction proceeds from the first three-year compliance period. 15 November. Boston: Analysis Group.

Krukowska, Ewa. 2012. 'EU's hedegaard says CO_2 auctions review is short-term fix'. *Bloomberg*. 10 May. http://www.bloomberg.com/news/2012-05-10/eu-s-hedegaard-says-co2-auctions-review-is-short-term-fix.html.

Luong, Danny, Susan Tsai, and Dipankar Sakar. 2000. *Annual reclaim audit report for the 1998 compliance year.* Los Angeles: South Coast Air Quality Management District.

Morris, Glenn E., and Denise G. Byrd. 1990. *Charging households for waste collection and disposal.* EPA 530-SW-90-047. Washington, DC: U.S. Environmental Protection Agency.

National Acid Precipitation Program (NAPAP). 1991. *National Acid Precipitation Program, 1990 integrated assessment report.* Washington, DC: Author.

Navarro, Miryear. 2012. Regional cap-and-trade effort seeks greater impact by cutting carbon allowances. *New York Times*, 26 January.

O'Neill, C. A. 2004. Mercury, risk and justice. *Environmental Law Reports* 34(11070).

Regional Greenhouse Gas Initiative. 2005. Frequently asked questions. http://www.rggi.org/docs/mou_faqs_12_20_05.pdf.

Sheppard, Kate. 2009. Everything you always wanted to know about the Waxman-Markey energy/climate bill—In bullet points. *Grist*, 3 June. www.grist.org/article/2009-06-03-waxman-markey-bill-breakdown/.

Steinzor, R. 2005. "Market-based" regulatory tools: Toward better bubble. *Center for Progressive Reform.* www.progressiveregulation.org/perspectives/emissions.cfm.

Stern, Nicholas Herbert. 2006. *The economics of climate change.* Oxford: Cambridge University Press.

Taylor, Jeffrey. 1992. 'New rules harness power of free markets to curb air pollution'. *Wall Street Journal*, 14 April, 1.

U.S. Environmental Protection Agency. 1999. *Progress report on the EPA Acid Rain Program.* Washington, DC: EPA Office of Air and Radiation.

Whiteman, Lily. 1992. Trades to remember: The lead phase-down. *EPA Journal* 18(2): 38–39.

17

PROMOTING CLEAN TECHNOLOGY: THEORY

17.0 Introduction

Since the 1960s, environmental economists have made the case for a switch away from command-and-control (CAC) regulation toward incentive-based (IB) approaches. Their response to the question "How can we do better?" was to reply: "We can achieve the same pollution-reduction goals at much lower cost." The last chapter illustrated how, slowly, through a series of increasingly complex policy experiments, the cap-and-trade idea in particular has taken hold. Today, this concept is triumphant, and IB approaches dominate new regulatory initiatives across the planet. To attack global warming, global carbon trading—under a shrinking cap—has become a fact of life in Europe and is being implemented more widely in North America.

While IB advocates prescribed better regulatory design for our environmental problems, a more fundamental criticism has been leveled at *any* regulatory approach to pollution control, including *both* CAC and IB. As discussed at the end of Chapter 14, regulation faces three generic problems: (1) rapid economic growth, (2) rising marginal costs of control (the "easy" point and stationary sources are already controlled), and (3) leakage (pollution regulated in one medium squeezing out elsewhere). As a result, regulation alone, even when incentive based, may not be sufficient to achieve environmental goals.

Moreover, we have seen that regulation is highly susceptible to political influence due to its information-intensive nature. Thus industry spends tens of millions of dollars to influence and defuse the process, and yet still finds itself saddled with burdensome and seemingly irrational regulatory requirements mandated by a frustrated Congress. At the same time, environmentalists charge that the actual regulations have no teeth and are enforced only erratically. As one observer puts it, "the classical sense of law is lost in sliding scales of targets and goals, accepted tolerances and negotiated exceptions, discretionary enforcement and discretionary compliance."[1]

As indicated in Chapter 14, the regulatory approach taken over the last 45 years *has* made a difference. Pollution levels are well below what they would have been in the absence of regulation, although relative to the initial goal of a "clean and safe" environment, the results have been disappointing. Nevertheless, the widespread perception is that the effectiveness of the regulatory approach is limited by the complexity of the issues at stake and the related opportunities available for political influence. In addition, there is no doubt that the regulatory approach, with its associated need for detailed bureaucratic decision making, has been costly.

Finally, with climate change, "environmental protection" has suddenly become a civilizational challenge. The scale of the energy transformation that will be needed to hold global warming to the low end is staggering. As noted in the introduction, many economists believe that by 2050, the developed countries will need to reduce emissions of carbon dioxide and other global-warming pollution by 80% or more—effectively, a rewiring of the entire planet with clean energy over the next four decades. To meet this challenge, simply mandating that private companies in rich countries cut their emissions to get under a shrinking national cap is inadequate. Without complementary government initiatives supporting the rapid development and diffusion of clean energy alternatives, the private sector simply would be unable to deliver the needed cuts at acceptable costs.

Given these factors, recent economic thinking has focused on the development of clean technologies as a critical complementary strategy to regulation. Rather than relying solely on controlling pollutants at the "end of the pipe," advocates of this approach argue that government should promote the use of technologies that *reduce polluting inputs and processes in the first place*.

Waste reduction in manufacturing, recycling of wastes, low-input agriculture, energy and water efficiency, renewable resource use, and renewable energy production are often cited as candidates for governmental promotion on environmental grounds. Collectively they may be referred to as **clean technologies (CTs)**.

However, this simple formulation begs at least three questions: (1) How can we identify a clean technology? (2) If the technology is so clearly superior, why isn't the market adopting it in the first place? (3) If the market is failing to develop the CT rapidly, how can the government successfully "pick winners" and promote certain types of technologies over others? This chapter explores in more detail the theory of clean technology, focusing on these three questions, and it ends with two case studies: alternative agriculture and recycling. Chapter 18 concludes the CT discussion with a comprehensive look at the dominant technology challenge of our time: a rapid global transition to clean energy.

17.1 Path Dependence and Clean Technology

In 1977, just as I was entering college, an early and influential book arguing for a clean technology approach to energy hit the bookshelves. *Soft Energy Paths: Towards a Durable Peace*, was written by American physicist Amory Lovins. Lovins viewed the

---

1. Greider (1992, 109).

United States as being at a crossroads from which two paths diverged. The first was the road then being followed—a society based on the promotion and production of cheap electricity, via an increased reliance on coal, oil, and nuclear power. Lovins labeled this the "hard" path. By contrast, the "soft" path involved a conscious governmental effort to redirect the economy toward efficient use of energy and the promotion of renewable energy technologies, especially solar power.

Because the soft path depends on decentralized power production and greater reliance on locally available resources, it promised many social benefits: "A soft path simultaneously offers jobs for the unemployed, capital for businesspeople, environmental protection for conservationists, enhanced national security for the military, opportunities for small business to innovate and for big business to recycle itself."[2] But best of all, according to Lovins, it was cheaper.

From a theoretical point of view, government efforts to influence the direction of technological progress can be justified by what economists call **path dependence**.[3] This theory maintains that current production technologies—for example, U.S. reliance on private automobiles for urban transportation—represent only one possible path of development. A potentially cost-competitive alternative in this case might be mass transit, which is dominant in many European and Japanese cities.

The path a society chooses depends on a variety of factors, including the relative political strength of the conflicting interests, chance historical circumstance, and of course consumer preferences and relative production costs. In the auto example, the U.S. government's decision to construct the interstate highway system beginning after World War II, which in turn promoted suburban development, provided the decisive advantage to private transport.

However, once a path has been chosen, other paths are closed off; this happens for three reasons. First, infrastructure and research and development (R&D) investments are increasingly directed toward supporting the chosen technology and diverted from the competing path. Second, the chosen technology is able to exploit economies of scale to consolidate its cost advantage. Third, complementary technologies develop that are tailored to the chosen path, further disadvantaging the competing path. In the transportation example, this would include the sprawling retail and housing patterns of U.S. cities, which now virtually require a private vehicle for access.

Path dependence theory suggests that once a path is chosen, there is no easy way to switch tracks. However, in retrospect, we can see that technological choices have social consequences—the adoption of private transport, for example, has borne a substantial environmental cost. Thus the role of government is to try to influence the current market-driven process of technological development toward a path consistent with a sustainable future. Note that this theory assumes that governments in modern capitalist societies already necessarily play a major role in shaping technological change through infrastructure decisions and subsidy policies; the key here is to ensure that role is a positive one.

Lovins's original argument—that government should actively promote a shift to a clean energy economy—developed intellectual force over the ensuing decades, and

---

2. Lovins (1977, 23).
3. For an accessible introduction to path dependence theory, see Arthur (1991).

as global climate change moved to center stage, has recently begun to shape U.S. policy. Under the Obama administration, as part of the 2009 stimulus bill, many of the policy tools explored in this chapter—R&D spending, infrastructure investment, commercialization subsidies, technology-forcing regulation—were greatly expanded in an effort to build a "Green Economy." Behind all these initiatives lies a theory of path-dependent economic development.[4]

17.2 Clean Technology Defined

For the purposes of this book, a clean technology has three characteristics:

1. It generates services of similar quality to existing technologies.
2. It has minimum long-run *private* marginal costs comparable to existing technologies.
3. It is environmentally less destructive than existing technologies.

1. *CTs provide comparable-quality services.* Judging quality can be a difficult task. For example, in sunny climates, a cost-saving and convenient way to preheat water for a dishwasher is to install a 50-gallon drum, painted black, on the roof. However, early attempts to market such a simple and cost-effective technology foundered on consumer resistance—the barrels looked ugly to most people. On the other hand, some consumers were proud to have an energy-saving barrel on their roof.[5] Judgments about "similar quality" are necessarily subjective. Nevertheless, a governmental decision to promote one certain technology over another requires some judgment about the relative quality of service. Bad choices will ultimately be rejected by consumers, leading to failure of the CT policy.

2. *CTs are cost competitive on a market basis.* Cost comparisons between technologies should be made on the basis of long-run private marginal costs, including taxes and regulatory costs. Why not include external social costs in the comparison? A comparison of private plus social costs does indeed provide the true measure of which technology is theoretically "efficient." However, *if CTs cannot compete on the basis of private costs*, then they will not be adopted, regardless of government efforts to promote them.

For example, consider photovoltaic (PV) cells that produce solar electricity. On the environmental scale, PVs clearly pass the CT screen. Yet if PV prices cannot be brought down to levels competitive in the private market within a few years' time (and many believe they can), their use will not spread rapidly, regardless of governmental efforts to promote them. Clean technologies must be competitive in the marketplace to succeed.

What is meant by **long-run marginal costs**? Simply the cost of producing an additional unit once the technology is mature. CTs can be divided into two categories, based on whether they are achieving the high-volume production needed to reach the long-run minimum marginal cost. **Late-stage CTs** are cost competitive with existing

---

4. An excellent blog that develops this path-dependent perspective on clean energy is www.climate progress.org. The blog is written by Dr. Joe Romm, a physicist and former Clinton Administration official at the Department of Energy. Romm also worked with Lovins during the early 1990s.
5. Thanks to Dallas Burtraw for this example.

technologies at low-volume production. Examples would include the installation of housing insulation or low-flow showerheads, the on-farm adoption of less chemical-intensive pest control, or "housekeeping" measures by manufacturing firms to reduce the generation of hazardous waste. While late-stage CTs are by definition currently cost competitive, they may still experience economies of scale through marketing.

Early-stage CTs, by contrast, require additional R&D or high-production volumes to achieve minimum long-run costs. Examples include start-up recycling operations, photovoltaic or solar thermal electricity production, and the manufacture of the next generation energy-efficient consumer durables such as cars, refrigerators, lights, and air conditioners.

Figure 17.1 illustrates an estimated long-run average cost curve for electricity produced by wind power. Wind electricity costs started out at more than $0.25/kWh in the early 1980s. By 2013, with global wind capacity at more than 200,000 megawatts, the price had fallen to less than $0.04/kWh. At favorable sites, wind has now become competitive with the cheapest new fossil fuel plants.

Per-unit costs fall for three reasons. First, as the firms invest in R&D and gain experience, they generate new and lower cost methods of organization and production. Second, as the market size increases, firms can take advantage of **economies of scale**: lower cost production arising from the ability to use specialized machinery and personnel at high volumes. Third, as complementary industries and markets develop, input costs fall.[6]

As drawn, the average cost curve eventually flattens out as opportunities for technological advancement and specialization are exhausted. This portion of the curve is the minimum long-run average cost, and because the average is constant, marginal cost

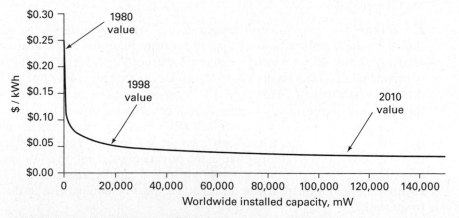

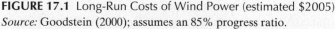

FIGURE 17.1 Long-Run Costs of Wind Power (estimated $2005)
Source: Goodstein (2000); assumes an 85% progress ratio.

---

6. You may recall from an earlier course that short-run average costs also fall as firms spread out their fixed costs. Initial investments in plant and equipment, advertising, and service and sales networks do mean that for a given plant size, costs per unit are high at low output levels. However, in the long run, average fixed costs need not fall as an industry grows, because overhead expenses may grow proportionately. In addition, decreasing returns to scale, resulting from managerial breakdown, may set in at some point and cause long-run average costs to actually rise.

as well. This long-run cost, to the degree it can be estimated, should be the baseline for a comparison between two technologies, for example, wind- and coal-powered electricity.

The history of cost forecasting is replete with major disasters, such as the famous prediction that nuclear power would one day be "too cheap to meter." Thus credible forecasts stay as far as possible from scenarios relying on unproven or speculative technologies, and depend instead on the expected costs of implementing known production methods within a relatively short time frame.

3.   *CTs are environmentally superior.* Point three in the definition of clean technology ensures that it is indeed clean, which is in fact more difficult to establish than it appears. First, it is necessary to account, at least in a rough way, for all of the major environmental impacts of a technology: in manufacturing, use, and disposal. This kind of cradle-to-grave approach is known as **life-cycle analysis**. A second problem arises because different technologies have various types of environmental impacts. This leads to an **adding-up problem**, in which the superiority of one technology over the other may not be clear-cut. The "diaper wars" debate illustrates both the life-cycle and adding-up problems. Each year, American babies use about 17 billion disposable diapers made of paper and plastic. These diapers, which account for between 1% and 2% of material entering the solid waste stream, ultimately wind up in landfills or incinerators. Green entrepreneurs saw an opportunity, and argued that cloth diapers, provided through diaper services, offered a clean alternative—comparable in quality of service (including convenience) and price, and better for the environment. With consumer demand spurred by this "green" marketing claim, the diaper service business was booming.

However, as a counter to the solid waste concern, Procter & Gamble (maker of Pampers and Luvs) sponsored a study and related PR campaign, which maintained that reusable cloth diapers generate substantially more water pollution in the washing process than throwaways do in manufacturing. In response, the National Association of Diaper Services sponsored its own research, which undertook a life-cycle analysis of the environmental impact of the two products. The authors of this study found that, in general, liquid effluent from the manufacturing process was less harmful for cotton than disposable diapers, and that the overall water pollution advantage of disposables did not hold for cotton diapers laundered commercially.

At this point, it appears that cotton diapers have an edge in areas with solid waste problems, and overall in terms of manufacturing effluents, although disposables may be preferable in areas where municipal water treatment facilities are overloaded or inadequate. However, the scientific details have not mattered much in the marketplace. Thanks in some large measure to P&G's ad campaign, cloth diaper services lost their environmental luster and have been virtually eliminated as a competitive threat.[7]

Life-cycle accounting of environmental impacts is an emerging science that, in certain cases, is capable of identifying the relative pollution impact of different technologies with more or less precision. However, as the diaper case illustrates, a given technology need not dominate another in all pollution areas, and depending on how the life-cycle boundaries are drawn, conflicting results may arise. At this point,

---

7. See A. D. Little (1990); Hershkowitz (1990); and Lehrburger, Mullen, and Jones (1991).

TABLE 17.1 **Private and Social Costs of Electricity Production (Cents/KWh)**

	Solar PV	**Conventional Coal**
Private costs	14.4	10.1
Externality costs	0.00–0.002	04–18
Total costs	14.40–14.42	14.10–28.10

Source: Levelized private costs are from U.S. EIA (2013); coal externality costs are from Muller et al. (2011) and Epstein et al (2011); and PV externality cost is from Ottinger (1990).

a policy commitment to support one technology over another must often rely on "commonsense" judgments. This in turn means that "close calls," like cloth diapers, should *not* be considered candidates for governmental promotion as clean technologies.

A natural way to solve the adding-up problem and compare two technologies is to monetize and total the expected life-cycle environmental damages from each source. Such a value could be used to compare the social costs of the two technologies, as is done in Table 17.1 for electricity generation from coal and solar power. Note that the clean technology, photovoltaics (PVs), does impose some externality costs on society. However, the pollution generated in the manufacture of PVs does substantially less damage than that arising from the burning of coal. By monetizing damages in this way, a CT's environmental superiority can be judged. However, as discussed in point two earlier, adding environmental damages should not be part of an assessment of a CT's *cost* competitiveness. Clean technologies will diffuse rapidly only if consumers face costs that are comparable to those of dirty alternatives.

This section has provided a working definition of clean technology. We have found that both small- and large-scale technologies can qualify; there is no up-front bias toward "small is beautiful." However, all of the clean technology candidates discussed in this chapter—PVs and other renewable energy technologies, energy efficiency, diaper services (in some areas), recycling, waste reduction, and alternative agriculture—achieve their environmental advantage by being relatively labor-intensive and/or relying to a greater extent on locally produced resources. As discussed in Chapter 6, these features can sometimes generate higher *local* employment levels.

17.3 If You're So Smart, Why Aren't You Rich?

The first objection raised to the clean technology approach is this: if these technologies are close to commercial development, generate a quality of service and have long-run production costs comparable to existing technologies, *and* are environmentally superior, why aren't private entrepreneurs developing them in the first place? In other words, if CT advocates are so smart, why aren't they rich?

The first response is that, in some cases, they are. For example, tens of thousands of American farmers have adopted various forms of low-input farming; recycling has emerged as an economic form of waste disposal in many communities; service corporations that identify cost-effective energy savings for firms and households are growing rapidly. Thus market forces do provide some support for clean technologies. Yet the market share for many of these CTs, while growing, remains tiny.

TABLE 17.2   Obstacles to the Rapid Diffusion of Clean Technologies

Market Obstacles	Government Obstacles
A. Lack of profit advantage to overcome: • Poor information • Thin resale markets • Limited access to capital • High discount rates	**A. Subsidy policies** favoring dirty technologies **B. Failure of regulation** to internalize all externalities

A variety of obstacles can discourage the market deployment of environmentally superior, cost-effective technologies. Table 17.2 provides a summary. The principal market obstacle is the **lack of a substantial profit advantage** for CTs. There is little incentive for private firms to undertake the marketing efforts necessary to overcome marketplace barriers to rapid diffusion: poor information, thin resale markets, poor access to capital, and high discount rates.

A second substantial barrier arises from current governmental policy: subsidies tilted in favor of existing competitor technologies. These subsidies range from R&D funding to price supports to tax credits to efforts on behalf of industry by state and federal agency personnel. Finally, of course, market prices for the competitor technology fail to reflect externality costs.

MARKET OBSTACLES FACING CLEAN TECHNOLOGIES

Simply because CTs are potentially cost competitive does not mean they are *more* profitable than existing technologies. Entrepreneurs tend to introduce products to fill a "market niche" and provide at least temporary monopoly profits: think iPods or smart phones. Clean technologies, by contrast, generally are not offering a new product; rather, they go head-to-head with an existing, well-established technology in a mature industry. Thus they must enter an already competitive field, where only normal profits can be expected. The only clear-cut advantage CTs have is in their environmental impact. While this may provide some marketing leverage, it generally will not guarantee high profitability.

Under normal market circumstances, new technologies often take substantial time to develop a widespread following. This is due to consumers' lack of knowledge (again, imperfect information) about the advantages of the new technology as well as to differences in consumer needs. The transition to any new technology requires a *marketing commitment* to overcome this lack of information. Marketing expenses are **sunk costs**, those that cannot be recovered if an investment fails. The higher the sunk costs associated with an investment, the riskier it becomes.

Clean technologies face particularly high sunk costs (and thus high risk) because they do not "market themselves" by offering a service consumers do not already have. Instead, CTs need to woo consumers from the use of the existing technology. While CTs offer comparable services, they also tend to require users to learn new consumption habits. This requires a big investment in marketing, which cannot be recovered if the business fails.

Moreover, existing firms do not take inroads into their markets lightly. Witness, for example, Procter & Gamble's massive public relations effort to convince consumers that the disposable diaper is not environmentally inferior to cotton. This type of counter-marketing campaign from powerful incumbent firms can make large-scale entry into a CT market even riskier or can deter it entirely.

As we saw in the case of marketable permits, imperfect information also generates a **thin market problem**. For example, a homeowner may be reluctant to shoulder the high up-front costs of outfitting his or her home with energy- and money-saving LED lightbulbs because most prospective home buyers know little about them. Thus she would probably not be able to recoup her initial investment if she decided to sell the house within a few years. Thin markets for durable technologies (those with resale value) tend to dampen the rate of adoption.

Access to capital is a problem for both small- and large-scale technologies. Small-scale CTs often entail an initial up-front investment, which is compensated for by lower operating costs. Returning to our homeowner, a bank might extend her a home improvement loan to purchase energy-efficient lightbulbs, although such loans are certainly not common; however, the interest rate charged would be much higher than a utility faces when it borrows several hundred million dollars to build a new power plant. The bank would justify its differential lending practices on the basis of increased transactions costs associated with small loans and, perhaps, increased risk.

At the other extreme, clean technologies with major scale economies—for example, solar electric power—require large amounts of capital for R&D, production, marketing, and service efforts. They also need a pool of specialized human capital—management and technical expertise familiar with the market. In the solar field, the "natural" organizations with access to this kind of capital and expertise are the large corporations in the energy and utility fields. Why, by and large, do these companies ignore clean technologies?

As we learned in Chapter 8, private discount rates are often higher than socially appropriate for environmental investments. **High discount rates** mean that profits made in the future are less valuable than profits earned today. And, as was stressed earlier, because CTs compete with mature, conventional technologies, a major investment in CTs is not likely to be a profit center in the near term—say a decade or more. Yet, a 20% before-tax rate of return, a common requirement in many U.S. industries, implies roughly a five-year payback on any investment.

This central fact has kept interest in solar, and other early-renewables on the back burner for most large energy and utility corporations; few have interest in R&D investments with long-term payoffs. In addition, these tend to be the very firms with a strong vested interest in the status quo. Why develop products that will compete with already profitable electricity and fuel sales? European and Japanese businesses, facing higher conventional fuel prices, are naturally more interested in energy CTs.

In the absence of commitments to technologies such as solar electricity by large firms, small firms enter to serve niche markets. However, neither substantial R&D nor economies of scale in production can be achieved by these firms. Thus costs remain high, and the market widens only slowly.

Finally, consumers also appear to require high rates of return for investments in durable CTs. Observed discount rates of 50–100% are not uncommon for the purchase of energy-efficient air conditioners, refrigerators, or lightbulbs. This unwillingness to commit funds to highly profitable investments reflects a combination of poor information, restricted access to capital, risk aversion, and thin resale markets.

GOVERNMENT OBSTACLES TO CLEAN TECHNOLOGIES

In addition to market barriers, CTs are often disadvantaged by government action in the form of **direct or indirect subsidies** to highly polluting competitors. Consider agriculture, for example. As you may have learned in an introductory economics course, due to the high variability in agricultural prices, the government has historically provided farmers with a guaranteed price floor. If the market price falls below the price floor, say $2.80 per bushel for corn, the government makes up the difference. However, as illustrated in Figure 17.2, the price floor also guarantees an excess supply of corn (q_d to q_s) that the government must stockpile. One consequence of the surplus production is of course greater pesticide use. The Conservation Foundation estimates that the *surplus* wheat and corn grown in a single year in the United States required the application of 7.3 billion pounds of fertilizer and 110 million pounds of pesticides.

In addition to promoting excess pesticide use, however, subsidy programs can directly penalize cleaner agricultural practices. Until recently, price supports were primarily available for a limited number of crops, and these crops (coincidentally?) were very high users of chemical fertilizers and pesticides. Moreover, the subsidy payments for a given year were based on past yields of the crop in question, effectively tying farmers to the production of subsidy crops. A farmer desiring to adopt a CT based on diversification into less chemical-intensive crops and crop rotation as a method of fertilization and weed, pest, and erosion control thus might find herself doubly damned. Not only would she lose her subsidy this year, but subsidies for any future program crops she grew would also be reduced.[8]

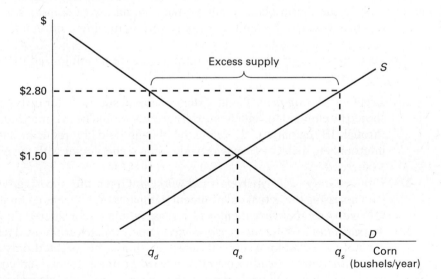

FIGURE 17.2 The Impact of Agricultural Subsidies

---

8. Curtis (1991) cites the Conservation Foundation study.

While farm subsidies provide a very visible example, most CTs face competitor technologies that receive important governmental aid, either direct or indirect. As we discussed in the last chapter, for example, solid waste disposal is often paid for through lump-sum tax payments, not by unit pricing. This provides a subsidy for large garbage producers, disadvantaging recycling. Chapter 18 focuses on subsidies for polluting technologies in the energy field.

This section has provided a look at both market and government obstacles to clean technology adoptions. We now consider how government policymakers can in fact select and promote CTs in the most cost-effective manner.

17.4 Picking the Winning Path

Recently, a prominent government critic was on the radio. He made the argument that many of the environmental problems in the western United States could be traced directly to bad government decisions reflecting industry's influence: subsidies for ranchers leading to overgrazing; subsidies for timber companies leading to clear-cuts; subsidies for mining companies leading to water contamination and the destruction of wilderness areas; and radiation leaks and releases from nuclear facilities owned, leased, or subsidized by the government.

There are two responses to these governmental efforts at industrial promotion. One is to despair of government's ability to intervene rationally in economic affairs. Traditional conservatives would adopt this position and argue that, despite possible market obstacles to the rapid adoption of clean technology, the only thing government should do is to level the playing field by eliminating all subsidies.

Progressives adopt an alternative response. While acknowledging government failures, they argue that a blanket call for the elimination of subsidies is naive. The challenge is to recognize the limitations of government intervention and, taking this into account, implement policies to promote CTs.

How can bureaucratic errors and political influence be minimized in this process? A three-step procedure should be followed.

1. *Level the playing field*. To the extent possible, subsidies for dirty technologies should be eliminated, and their external costs should be internalized, preferably through IB regulation. "Leveling the playing field" by reducing subsidies and internalizing social costs may provide clean technologies with the edge needed to succeed.
2. *Promote only clear environmental winners*. Given the uncertainty associated with assessing the actual environmental impacts of different technologies, only CTs with a clear environmental advantage should be considered for promotion.
3. *Tie subsidies to least-cost performance*. When the government does decide to promote a technology actively, subsidies should be directed only to projects that either are *already* cost-effective or promise to deliver cost-effective services within a relatively short period of time, say a decade or less. Subsidies to the latter category should be conditioned on observable cost reductions. In sum, government planners should focus attention on **least-cost** technology options, subject to an environmental screen.

This least-cost approach is consistent with path dependence theory; the government is looking for environmentally friendly "infant" industries that need only time-limited support to attain a sufficiently large scale to be self-supporting. The rationale for government subsidies under path dependence theory is to jump-start an industry for its environmental benefit, not provide indefinite promotion efforts. Least-cost planning of this type thus achieves two goals. First, government's objective is to speed up, not replace, the market process of adoption of CTs. Market forces will naturally spread technologies with a greater profit advantage faster. The faster the technology spreads, the greater the environmental benefits society reaps. Second, by using a least-cost approach, bureaucrats can avoid making expensive commitments to technological white elephants.

A good example of government "picking losers" has been the support of nuclear fusion. Fusion is an approach to energy production based on fusing two atomic nuclei together. By contrast, commercial reactors today generate power through fission, the splitting apart of particles. The government commitment to fusion research began in 1952, spurred on by the scientific cold war with Russia. Today, after at least six decades of federal funding in the hundreds of millions per year, fusion is nowhere near commercialization.[9]

Why do such subsidies persist? A steady flow of federal dollars created a "fusion community"—physicists and engineers at university and federal labs, and bureaucrats in the Departments of Defense and Energy. This community cultivated ties with key members of Congress and relied on concerns about national security to maintain funding. This is a general story: subsidies, once instituted, create "communities" that organize to protect the subsidies, and they can thus take on a life of their own.

In contrast to the open-ended support of fusion, path dependence theory suggests that a CT program can and should focus on technologies with a clear environmental advantage that will stand on their own relatively quickly. Government can then make only time-limited or performance-based commitments to the technology, and thus avoid the development of vested political interests attached to a particular technology. Fusion would have neither passed an environmental screen nor survived subsidies conditioned on rapid cost reductions.

Following a least-cost strategy ensures that policy concentrates on "picking the low-hanging fruit." Doing this gets more environmental protection for a lower investment with less risk and a lowered probability of prolonged government involvement.

17.5 Promoting Early-Stage Clean Technologies

It is useful to divide clean technologies into early- and late-stage groupings, as the market obstacles they face are somewhat different. Early-stage technologies need policy assistance to ramp up production to high volumes before they can be cost competitive. Late-stage technologies, by contrast, have already achieved high enough production levels to lower their costs, and they have reached cost parity with dirty technologies. The barriers these late-stage technologies face are primarily a function of imperfect information: consumers must "learn" to adopt these alternatives and capitalists to finance them.

---

9. Herman (1990).

The primary barrier facing early-stage CTs is achieving high-volume production. As illustrated in Figure 17.1, this lowers per unit costs through R&D, learning by doing, and scale economies. The key policy issue is to provide some incentive for existing or new firms to enter these markets. This section discusses four policies to encourage such interest: (1) R&D funding, (2) technology-forcing standards, (3) infrastructure investment, and (4) producer subsidies.

RESEARCH AND DEVELOPMENT FUNDING

In general, economists argue that basic R&D funding will be undersupplied in a free market because R&D has many characteristics of a public good. The spillover effects of fundamental technological breakthroughs are large, and so, even with patent protection, private parties can't capture the full benefits of privately funded research. For these reasons, the private sector will underinvest in R&D. Therefore, federal and state governments provide funding for R&D in the sciences and engineering. Some of this funding is channeled through the Departments of Energy and Agriculture, the EPA, the National Science Foundation, and the National Institutes of Health. In the United States, the Department of Defense is the major funder of basic R&D.

The rationale for funding CT research is also spillover benefits: the environmental advantages associated with adopting a new technology path. However, in the United States, in the decade prior to 2008, "dirty" industry in energy production and agriculture continued to pull in the bulk of federal R&D money. For example, Department of Energy (DOE) spending on fossil fuel R&D was consistently at least twice the level for renewables, and both were fairly low. Annual DOE renewables R&D spending was on the order of $300 million, about the cost of two F-22 fighter planes.[10] In the late 2000s, a change from conservative to progressive politics in Washington, the massive global recession fueling stimulus spending, and the passage of new-energy legislation all led to large increases in government R&D expenditures for clean energy technology—increases in the billions of dollars per year. However, history provides a note of caution. A similar surge in clean energy R&D followed the election of President Carter in 1976—indeed, those research dollars laid the foundation for the emergence of the now-competitive global wind and solar thermal industries (more on this story in Chapter 18). Whether Washington will continue to support high R&D levels beyond this current political window remains an open question.

TECHNOLOGY-FORCING STANDARDS

Beyond the carrots of R&D funding and producer subsidies, government policymakers can also employ sticks. The primary tool here is to make access to the market subject to meeting a **technology-forcing standard**. In contrast to policies for small-scale CTs, such as building energy codes for lighting efficiency, technology-forcing standards set a deadline for firms to deliver technology that is *not yet* marketed.

Perhaps the best-known technology-forcing standards are the Corporate Average Fuel Economy, or **CAFE**, standards. In 1975, Congress mandated that car companies had to achieve an average of 18 miles per gallon by the 1978 model year and 27.5 miles

---

10. U.S. Department of Energy (2002).

per gallon by the model year 1985. Stiff fines were to be levied on corporations that failed to comply, although a one-year "carryover" was permitted. Firms that exceeded the standard in one year could credit the excess miles per gallon (mpg) savings for the next year.

From the viewpoint of increasing the mileage of passenger cars, the CAFE policy was a success. Average fleet mileage did increase to around 28 mpg by 1987; since then, fleet-wide fuel economy has actually declined. The CAFE standards had an unintended consequence: encouraging car companies to shift production to SUVs. SUVs—considered in 1975 to be light trucks, not cars—were exempt from CAFE mileage standards. As a result, the effectiveness of the CAFE system fell apart beginning in the mid-1990s. As detailed further in Chapter 18, after a long political battle, and motivated by both global-warming and energy-security concerns, the CAFE standards were finally increased again by President Obama in 2009. Automakers will be required to boost the fuel efficiency of their fleet (including SUVs this time) to 35.5 mpg by 2016 and to 54.5 mpg by 2025. The new CAFE standards are expected to save consumers an average of $3,000, by cutting oil consumption by 1.8 billion barrels for the vehicles sold between 2012 and 2016. This is more oil than the United States imports in a year from Saudi Arabia, Venezuela, Libya, and Nigeria combined.[11]

A second important example of a technology forcing regulation is a Renewable Portfolio Standard (RPS). During the 2000s many states passed an RPS, requiring utilities to purchase a set percentage, say 15%, by a set date, say 2015, of electric power from qualifying renewable power sources. Utilities failing to achieve that percentage would face fines and other penalties. An RPS does not specify what type of renewable power must be purchased. Rather, it sets up a competition between the different renewables to see which ones will win. An RPS is an unparalleled tool for building the markets that support economies of scale and learning by doing, thus driving down renewable costs. This kind of "demand-pull" policy provides confidence to investors.

A final example of technology-forcing regulation is appliance energy standards, which were pioneered in California for refrigerators beginning in the 1970s. Federal standards were introduced in 1988. Between 1978 and 1995, energy consumption standards for new refrigerators dropped by more than half, from 1,500 to 700 kWh, and the annual cost to a consumer of running a refrigerator also fell by more than $65.[12]

From a theoretical perspective, sufficiently high pollution taxes can always achieve the same result as technology-forcing standards. Any inefficiencies are reduced due to greater consumer and manufacturer flexibility. However, as in many other cases, technology-forcing standards appear to be easier to legislate than do high taxes.

INFRASTRUCTURE INVESTMENT

A third tool available to government to influence the adoption of CTs is perhaps the most powerful. As we noted in the introduction to this chapter, the overwhelming dominance of the automobile in American life has much to do with the government-funded interstate highway system. Infrastructure investment, whether roads, pipelines,

---

11. Department of Transportation, DOT, EPA Set Aggressive National Standards for Fuel Economy, http://www.dot.gov/affairs/2010/dot5610a.htm
12. Fickett, Gellings, and Lovins (1990).

dams, or electric lines, has major long-run impacts on both local economic development and environmental quality. An additional new role for government is early stage investment in the **smart grid**. The smart grid relies on information technology to reduce waste and this avoids the need for additional supply.

PRODUCER SUBSIDIES

Another approach to encouraging commercial development is to provide subsidies to producers—tax credits, loans or loan guarantees, grants, or purchase guarantees. One form of purchase guarantee is a **price preference**. Many state governments will pay a premium of up to 5% or 10% for recycled products. Government **procurement contracts** are another way of providing infant CT industries with guaranteed markets.

Loan guarantees are provided by the government to promising start-up firms to help them access capital from private sources. If the firms succeed and pay back their loans, there is no cost to the government. If the firm goes bankrupt, then the government pays the loan back to the bank. In 2011, a high-profile solar firm, Solyndra, was driven out of business and defaulted on a $500 million loan guarantee, generating a political firestorm. But loan guarantee programs are in fact designed to support a portfolio of risky investments: some companies will succeed, and some will fail. In the DOE program that funded Solyndra (actually initiated under President Bush), 33 loan guarantees were provided, and as of 2012, only 2 had defaulted on the loans: 31 leading-edge technology companies successfully accessed private sector funding through the program. Congress provided over $2.5 billion to the program to cover defaults, but DOE paid out less than 1 billion.[13] We look more closely at subsidy issues in our discussion of energy policy in the next chapter.

This section has looked at government polices designed for early-stage clean technologies: helping them scale up production and achieve economies of scale and learning by doing with the goal of reaching cost parity with existing dirty technologies. Once this goal has been achieved, however, the battle is not yet won. Consumers must be persuaded to give up old habits and make the switch.

17.6 Promoting Late-Stage Clean Technologies

Consumer and business resistance to late-stage CTs reflects a natural inclination to stick with "what works," rather than adopt an unknown and possibly risky alternative. As we have seen, the relatively low profit advantage of many CTs discourages private sector marketing initiatives to overcome this resistance. Government policy should therefore be directed at providing information to consumers and reducing perceived risks of adoption. Informational barriers can be dealt with through (1) product labeling and certification requirements, (2) flexible design standards, (3) the reorientation of utility regulation, and (4) technical assistance programs. A program of (5) subsidies for consumers also can attack the information problem as well as compensate for higher capital costs.

---

13. "Report: Most Energy Dept. loan support is low-risk" (2011).

PRODUCT LABELING AND CERTIFICATION

The simplest policy step is to require product labeling. For example, the EPA has developed a standard method for testing the miles per gallon that automobiles can achieve and requires firms to publicly report this information. Similar energy-efficiency reporting is required for consumer durables such as refrigerators and air conditioners, and most recently computers, under the EPA's Energy Star program. This list could be expanded to lamps, motors, and other durables. Product labeling requirements provide consumers with ready access to information on the environmental consequences of their purchases.

Poll results indicate that many people are willing to pay a small premium for environmentally friendly products. During the 1990s, niche markets for recycled paper, organic agricultural products, and even "green" electric power began to develop. To speed up the process, the U.S. government issued regulations governing the use of marketing terms such as *recyclable* and *organic*.

In Germany and Canada, the government went further and issued "environmentally friendly" certifications for whole products. In the United States, by contrast, the trend has been for nongovernmental third-party organizations to act as product certifiers. For example, Green Seal is the major nonprofit organization working to develop this kind of private labeling scheme. The program has taken a while to get under way due to the complexity of identifying "clean" products in a life-cycle framework. Green Seal's approach has been to identify the "major" environmental impacts of a given product and then publish a draft standard for review and comment by affected industries. Green Seal has developed certification standards for several dozen products, including tissue and writing paper, re-refined engine oil, compact fluorescent lighting, and water-efficient fixtures. (*Question:* Have you ever seen the Green Seal on a product you bought? If not, why do you think you haven't?)

Another important private labeling initiative is run by a nongovernmental, international organization called the Forest Stewardship Council (FSC). The FSC develops different certification standards for each region and country of the world and then certifies lumber products as meeting certain minimum environmental standards. The FSC achieved a major victory, when Home Depot became the first major U.S. hardware chain to agree to sell certified lumber.[14]

MINIMUM DESIGN STANDARDS

Product labeling programs leave some choice in consumer hands. However, in markets where complex purchases are made infrequently, consumers have a hard time judging the relative merits of available technologies. Here *flexible* design standards, requiring a minimum level of environmental performance, can be introduced. The most well-known example of a design standard is a building code; many local governments have established energy-efficiency requirements for new homes.

The purchase price for an energy-efficient house is typically more than that for a leaky alternative. Because consumers are reluctant to absorb larger loans, and because banks are hesitant to make them, people naturally opt for the energy-inefficient choice.

---

14. See the Green Seal website at www.greenseal.org. The FSC is at www.fscoax.org.

However, the savings in monthly heating bills from energy efficiency will quickly cover the initial up-front expense, and homeowners will save money in the long run. Thus, from an economic point of view, banks should provide and consumers should shoulder larger loans for an energy-efficient house.

However, neither banks nor consumers are particularly well equipped to evaluate energy cost-saving opportunities on a case-by-case basis. By mandating minimum design standards, government closes off the option of the leaky alternative. The risk to all parties of opting for the CT is thus reduced. Banks will soon learn that, due to lower utility bills, they can offer higher loans on new houses, and all parties, including the environment, are better off in the long run.

Energy-efficiency requirements are included in many local building codes. In addition, federal law now requires banks to offer lower rate, energy-efficiency mortgages, though this regulation is not well known. Several cities and counties in the United States, including San Francisco and Ithaca, NY, have retrofit energy standards that must be met for old buildings whenever they are sold, leased, or renovated. The increased cost is passed on to the buyer, who can then qualify for an energy-efficient mortgage.[15]

Design standards have also been required for lighting, appliances, and electric motors, as a way to promote adoption of these CTs. Design standards provide a "free lunch" when the product's quality is quite generally perceived to be comparable to the conventional technology and its long-run private cost is less. In this case, government is simply mandating the choice that most people would make on their own if given the information. However, design standards become more costly if individual opinion differs substantially as to the CT's quality, or if its cost rises above that of the conventional technology. Nevertheless, even in this case, design standards may still be justifiable as a cost-effective way to control pollution.

UTILITY MARKETING

Another approach to the marketing problem facing late-stage CTs is to have the technologies marketed by large firms, and provide lower cost access to both financial and human capital. In the energy field, many states have restructured their regulation of utilities so that the firms can earn a profit on energy conservation. Until recently, utilities had no incentive to promote efficiency—every kilowatt saved was a reduction in their revenue. However, the new regulations recognize that energy saved is also energy freed up for other uses. Thus investments in energy efficiency are increasingly treated like investments in new generating plants, on which firms are allowed to make a normal profit.

The last few years have seen an increasing level of utility marketing for energy-efficiency efforts. For example, your local utility might retrofit your house's water heater, give you a low-flow showerhead and some pipe and outlet insulation, and conduct an energy audit, all free upon request. Utilities have also been involved in rebate programs for lightbulbs and appliances, and "refrigerator roundups" where the utility buys up and then junks ancient energy-hog refrigerators. These services are paid for through higher electricity bills. From both an economic and environmental

---

15. Geller et al. (1991).

viewpoint, these are all good investments, because by freeing up electricity, they allow the utility to avoid building expensive, polluting power plants.

TECHNICAL ASSISTANCE PROGRAMS

A fourth approach to marketing late-stage CTs is a direct one. Here, government technicians provide advice to firms interested in undertaking CT investments. This direct approach is used by the EPA to promote waste-reducing CTs in manufacturing. It also is the logical way to promote CTs in agriculture, as the government already has a technical assistance program—the state agricultural schools and extension services—in place.

CONSUMER SUBSIDIES

Efforts to provide consumers with information through labeling, standards, utility marketing, and technical assistance can be supplemented by subsidies for CTs. The presence of subsidies gives consumers an incentive to educate themselves about the product; they can also overcome obstacles to rapid diffusion associated with higher capital costs. For example, the New York State government used a pool of funds obtained in a court settlement with oil companies that were overcharging, and provided matching grants to public and nonprofit institutions interested in energy-efficiency projects. The projects must have paycheck periods of no more than 10–15 years. In a similar move, the city of Berkeley has loaned money to homeowners who install rooftop solar units, with the loans being paid back over 20 years in the form of higher property taxes.[16]

Subsidies can take several forms: **tax credits**, **low-interest loans**, or **grants**. To encourage late-stage CTs, loans and grants are preferable because they are easier to target. Loan applications and grants require groups to justify their investment, thus discouraging nonserious applicants, and they also provide government officials a means to allocate funds on a least-cost basis.

In addition, a problem with any subsidy program is that it may provide "windfalls" for people planning to adopt the technology anyway (**free riders**). To deal with this problem, loans and grants can be targeted to working- and middle-class individuals, small businesses, and nonprofit corporations. These groups, being resource-constrained, are least likely to adopt the CTs in the first place. Finally, tax credits are typically used by wealthier individuals and corporations, thus skewing the benefits of the policy in a regressive direction. If tax credits are used, one way to avoid promoting windfalls and tax cuts for the wealthy is to put an income limit on the claim.

Table 17.3 provides a summary of policy tools that government can use to promote CTs and suggest CTs for which their use may be appropriate. Of course, all these tools can be abused; a successful CT program requires that government policy focus on promoting only cost-effective, environmentally superior technologies. In particular, as argued in Section 17.3, government subsidies should support only (1) cost-effective late-stage technologies and/or (2) early-stage technologies that demonstrate substantial progress toward competitive pricing.

---

16. New York State Energy Office (1992) and DeVries (2008).

TABLE 17.3   Policy Tools for Promoting CTs

Early-Stage CTs	
Policy	**CTs**
R&D	Solar electric, wind power, fuel-cell vehicles, biomass fuels, hydrogen fuels, alternative agriculture, waste reduction in manufacturing
Producer subsidies: price preferences, procurement contracts, loan guarantees	Solar electric, hybrid electric vehicles, alternative agriculture, waste reduction in manufacturing
Technology-forcing standards	Energy efficiency, hybrid electric vehicles, fuel-cell vehicles, recycling
Infrastructure investment	Mass transit, recycling

Late-Stage CTs	
Policy	**CTs**
Product labeling	Energy and water efficiency, recycling, alternative agriculture
Design standards	Energy and water efficiency
Utility marketing	Energy efficiency
Technical assistance	Waste reduction in manufacturing, alternative agriculture, passive solar, wind power
Consumer subsidies: grants, loans, tax credits	Energy and water efficiency, recycling, passive solar

17.7 Clean Technology: Two Case Studies

Having explored the theory of path dependence and the tools for clean technology promotion, we now turn our attention to two case studies: agriculture, and solid waste management.

ALTERNATIVE AGRICULTURE

Each year, American farmworkers, landscapers, and homeowners apply over 1 billion pounds of pesticides to crops, fields, lawns, and gardens. Specifically designed to be toxic to insects and other pests, these chemicals unfortunately affect the broader environment as well. Pesticides show up as residue in foods, harm wildlife, contaminate groundwater, and are a significant nonpoint source of surface water pollution in the United States today.

In the face of these problems, farmers have increasingly been experimenting with CTs in agriculture, stressing biological methods of promoting soil fertility and reducing pests and disease. These include crop rotation to disrupt pest cycles, biological and mechanical weed control and fertilization, reducing pesticide use through scouting, use of resistant species, use of natural predators, and control over planting time. While building on traditional methods, the techniques are thoroughly modern, computer assisted, and in fact, management intensive. These techniques are collectively known as "low-input," "sustainable," or simply **alternative agriculture**. They all share a reduced reliance on chemical fertilizers and pesticides, and they are generally environmentally more benign than conventional approaches.

Assuming alternative agriculture is "cleaner" and produces a crop of comparable (or superior) quality, is it also cost competitive? The answer appears to be yes. Decades of documented field experience suggests that farmers can successfully reduce pesticide use and still remain profitable. While adoption of alternative agricultural methods may reduce yields (though it need not), it also reduces costs. The cost reduction is often sufficient to offset any lost production, and price premiums for organic items can also help make up the difference.[17]

Having argued that alternative agriculture is a CT based on our definition earlier in the chapter, what obstacles stand in the way of its widespread adoption? The primary barrier, as usual, is a low-profit advantage coupled with substantial **adjustment costs**. A successful transition from conventional chemical-intensive farming is a complex and risky undertaking for an individual farmer. To begin with, farmers need to invest substantial resources in learning new techniques. In addition, successful techniques are highly region-specific. Finally, a period of two or three years may be necessary to convert a field worked with conventional methods into a productive alternative field. These factors mean that a substantial up-front investment is necessary to redirect a farm onto an alternate path. And while such a farm may experience comparable profitability to a chemical-intensive one, in the highly competitive agricultural field, it is unlikely to be substantially more profitable.

Alternative agriculture illustrates perfectly the CT dilemma. On one hand, we appear to have available a technology capable of holding its own in the market, once adjustment costs have been overcome, with clear environmental benefit. On the other, adoption of the technology is slow primarily due to lack of a profit advantage sufficient to overcome costs associated with a transition. What is to be done?

Step 1: Identify the agricultural CTs with clear environmental benefits and those with the greatest cost advantage.

Step 2: Reduce subsidies to dirty technologies and begin to internalize environmental costs, preferably through IB regulation. As was discussed earlier, price supports for chemical-intensive crops have been an important obstacle to the spread of CTs. Access to water subsidies also has encouraged pollution-intensive agriculture, because agricultural chemicals and water tend to be complements in production. The farm sector also has traditionally been subject to very light environmental regulation of the CAC variety.

Step 3: Promote CTs directly. Here, agriculture is unique among American businesses in that the government already is deeply involved in the pace and direction of technological change in the industry. Because farming is highly competitive and thus a low-profit industry, government has traditionally financed much of the R&D in the field. In addition to this R&D function, the government has taken a leading role in disseminating information about new techniques through the state-funded agricultural colleges and agricultural extension services. Hence,

---

17. See Halweil (2006).

a sensible CT strategy would be first to increase government R&D funding for region-specific strategies to reduce pesticide use and then to increase the budget for technical assistance, to promote the diffusion of these technologies. Increases in these funds could be financed either through reductions in research on conventional farming techniques, which the private sector now covers adequately, or by modest taxes on agricultural chemicals.

Recent federal legislation includes some movement on all the fronts just identified. However, the government has by no means adopted a CT approach wholeheartedly. R&D funding for on-farm research into alternative agriculture remains a small percentage of the Department of Agriculture's R&D budget, and extension services in alternative agriculture have not been significantly expanded. At this point, alternative agriculture has a relatively low level of market penetration, and the major impetus to its growth has been the expanding consumer market for organics.

SOLID WASTE MANAGEMENT

In contrast to alternative agriculture, recycling has received widespread governmental promotion. Largely as a result of local government mandates, the number of curbside collection programs grew from 600 in 1989 to over 9,000 a decade later and now, recycling is widespread across the United States. Is recycling a clean technology?

Americans generate more than 232 million tons of garbage each year. Depending on your perspective, that is (1) enough garbage to fill a fleet of trucks stretching halfway to the moon, or alternatively, (2) garbage that can be landfilled in a space equivalent to less than 0.00001% of the continental United States (but preferably not in my backyard). On a per-person basis, it works out to about three quarters of a ton, twice as much per capita as in many European countries.[18]

Recycling this solid waste yields two types of environmental benefits. The most obvious is a **direct benefit**: cleaner waste disposal. Because recycled products are not sent to landfills or incinerators, they do not pose environmental problems in the disposal process. Recall that environmental hazards from state-of-the-art landfills are not as great as from many other pollution sources, primarily because the only significant exposure route is local, via groundwater. Nevertheless, hazards from leachate do exist. New incinerators, although generally complying with most air pollution regulations, still generate residual hazards from regulated pollutants as well as from some that are still unregulated. Incinerator ash must be disposed of. If this is done via landfilling, the ash also presents a leachate problem.

Indirect benefits constitute the second type of environmental benefit. Table 17.4 compares the production cycle for products made from recycled and virgin materials. The recycling process is, of course, not pollution-free. In all production stages, recycling generates significant pollution. Unique recycling waste, for example, de-inking sludge from paper recycling, also poses serious disposal problems. However, relative to production from virgin material, recycling often yields two important indirect environmental benefits: **energy savings** and **upstream pollution** avoided.

18. Data are from the EPA's Office of Solid Waste website, www.epa.gov/epaoswer. Both the "alarmist" and "don't worry" characterizations of the solid waste problem appeared in *The EPA Journal*. See "A Strategy to Control the Garbage Glut" and "Will the U.S. Recycling Approach Work?" July–August 1992.

TABLE 17.4   Production from Recycled and Virgin Materials

Virgin	Recycling
1. Raw material production	**1**. Collection/processing
2. Transport	**2**. Transport
3. Manufacturing	**3**. Manufacturing
4. Distribution	**4**. Distribution

Because secondary materials are already "preprocessed," it generally takes much less energy to convert them into finished products. Energy savings in turn often translate into significant environmental benefits. Figure 17.3 shows the energy requirements to produce a variety of products from both virgin and recycled materials. Particularly for plastics, the energy savings are impressive: recycled plastic requires only about one-fourth the energy of plastic made from virgin material. In addition to energy savings, the collection and processing of recycled materials can be less environmentally damaging than the production and transport of raw materials from virgin sources.

Recycling can thus have local (direct waste management) and global (indirect) benefits. From an environmental point of view, global benefits have often been

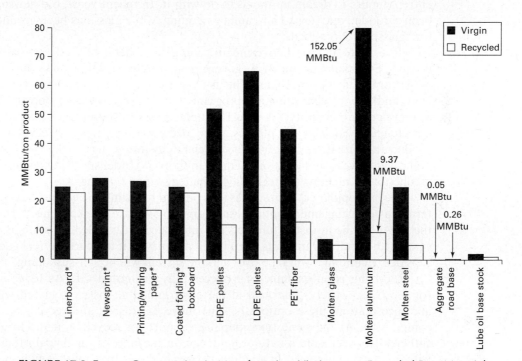

FIGURE 17.3 Energy Consumption in Manufacturing: Virgin versus Recycled Raw Materials
* Using recycled feedstock in paper production while reducing total energy use can actually increase use of purchased (generally nonrenewable) energy, as production from virgin materials uses waste wood to produce energy.
Source: New York State Energy Authority (1994, Figure 35).

thought to dwarf the local benefits. As a result, the latter attribute has motivated popular enthusiasm for recycling. "Think globally, act locally" was the slogan adopted by community groups who first promoted recycling in the 1970s. In its early days, recycling was urged as an environmental duty, and even today most of its political impetus derives from broad support for a cleaner environment. In addition, some of its cost advantage lies in voluntary citizen efforts to sort and/or collect recyclable material. However, recycling did not take off until the local advantages of recycling as a *cost-competitive* waste management strategy became apparent in the late 1980s. As conventional disposal costs began to rise, along with EPA regulations forcing landfills and incinerators to internalize externalities, some communities began to make money off their recycling programs.

Is recycling cost competitive today? Yes, up to a point. The explosive growth in recycling has generally kept prices for recycled materials down, because new supplies have outstripped the growth in end-use markets. Volatile prices in end-use markets mean that recycling programs will "pay" some years and require operating subsidies in others. It is difficult to assess whether communities in general are overinvesting in recycling on purely economic grounds.[19]

The key to the long-term success of recycling has been, and will be, the development of end-use markets. Of course, the mere existence of cheap sources of junk will inspire entrepreneurs to dream up things to do with it. In recent years, old newspapers have been shredded and turned into animal bedding, while glass has been ground up to use for "glassphalt" roadbed.

Here, state and local government actions have been very effective at technology forcing. For example, the U.S. government purchases large quantities of recycled paper for use in copy machines. The increase in mandatory recycling, recycled content laws, and government purchase programs have all dramatically boosted investment in recycled mill capacity. Chemical manufacturers, responding in part to actual and threatened local bans on plastics, have been working hard to develop recyclable products and create end-use markets. Technology forcing has worked well here because of the wide diversity of locations of these initiatives. Under such circumstances, industry was better off meeting the technology challenge than fighting it.

Recent popular enthusiasm has thus pushed recycling to become a dominant, long-term waste management option. According to William Ruckelshaus, former head of the EPA, "If the infrastructure gets put into place, with collection systems, processing centers and end-user markets, then it will not matter if the current 'feel good' attitude subsides. Economics will take over and the system will be self-sustaining."[20]

Recycling is an example of a successfully promoted CT. As federal regulation (of the CAC variety) internalized the environmental costs associated with landfills and incineration, these options became more expensive, and recycling became cost competitive. At the same time, popular support for recycling at the local level was sufficient to overcome a natural tendency on the part of municipal officials to stick with proven technologies. In addition, carrots in the form of market guarantees, as well

19. Ackerman (1996) calculates that the typical recycling program raised disposal costs by $21 per household in 1993 (when prices were low) and saved $5 per household in 1995 (when prices were high).
20. "In Solid Waste" (1991).

as sticks in the form of product bans and content laws, both emerging simultaneously in dozens of locales, have generated substantial investment by the private sector in developing end-use markets for recycled products.

17.8 Summary

This chapter identifies government promotion of CTs as a potentially attractive complement to regulation for controlling pollution. By internalizing social costs, regulation provides a more level playing field on which clean technologies can compete. Yet, with the easy "point and stationary source" regulatory gains already achieved, in the face of pressures from population and economic growth, and with the unprecedented challenge of climate change, rapid development and diffusion of CTs will become an increasingly important means of improving environmental quality.

Regulating waste once it is produced exacerbates short-run conflicts between economic growth and environmental quality. While in the long run, environmental regulation spawns new technologies and creates new industries and jobs, "in the long run," as the economist John Maynard Keynes once said, "we are all dead." As a supplement to the stick of pollution taxes (or other IB regulation), the CT approach offers a carrot of government-promoted, substitute technology. Thus the short-run trade-off between material well-being and the environment becomes much less stark.

Moreover, path dependence theory suggests that a continued exclusive government focus on end-of-the-pipe regulation of pollutants will lead to technological progress in end-of-the-pipe waste management, rather than in waste-reducing CTs. Concerned primarily with regulatory compliance, and provided with the funding to do so, environmental managers in industry and government will continue to develop expertise in emissions monitoring and enforcement, risk analysis, and benefit-cost analysis; engineers will focus on cheaper ways of scrubbing and filtering emissions and on safer ways of incinerating or burying wastes. While these skills and technologies are important for making regulation work better, they are not primarily the skills and techniques needed for a transition to CTs.

Finally, in practice, we have seen that regulation is an adversarial process in which environmentalists and industry compete in an information-intensive conflict over the drafting and enforcing of standards. A regulatory approach in one sense sets government up to fail, because the affected parties have many opportunities, and much to gain, from influencing the process. The political economy of a CT approach promises to reduce the day-to-day conflict between regulators and firms as well as limit the opportunities for political influence.

Promoting CTs, of course, is certain to have its own bureaucratic problems associated with implementation. Conservative critics would charge that the "light-handed" planning process described here, while nice in theory, would dissolve as soon as a CT agency were established. Once provided a budget, CT promotion would devolve into "heavy-handed" restrictions on industries arbitrarily judged to be "dirty" by environmentally motivated bureaucrats, coupled with expensive crash programs to develop completely ludicrous technologies, located in the districts of powerful members of Congress.

Yet a political-economic case can also be made that a CT strategy would be an effective complement to regulation, reducing both costs and regulatory conflict with industry. Because CT development does not involve rule making at the level of individual pollutants, or extensive monitoring and enforcement, informational requirements are diminished. As the need for information falls, so do opportunities for political influence, delay, and indecision. Once funded, technology subsidies are a win-win situation; firms are rewarded for reducing pollution, rather than punished for not doing so.[21] Thus CTs can transform an adversarial relationship into a partnership. Finally, path dependence theory suggests that government subsidy commitments can and should be time-limited and/or performance-based, thus reducing both the probability of picking losers and the development of vested interests. We now turn our attention to an area often seen as critical ground for clean technology promotion: energy.

APPLICATION 17.0

Pests and Path Dependence

Biological pest control has high fixed costs associated with machinery and predator rearing; farmers experience substantial "learning by doing"; and farmers also depend on "network externalities"—information gained from fellow farmers and extension agents. Finally, if neighboring farmers are spraying pesticides, the pesticides will also kill off natural predators. Given these factors, assume we can write an average cost function per ton of output for an individual farmer using biological methods that looks like this:

$$AC_b = \$200 - 01X_b - 1y_b + 0.01X_c$$

where:

X_b = tons of biological farm production in the region
X_c = tons of chemical farm production in the region
y_b = tons of the farmer's production

1. Fill in the chart below.

AC_b	y_b	X_b	X_c
	100	1,000	0
	100	1,000	500
	100	1,000	1,000
	100	500	1,000
	100	100	1,000

2. Why do the farmer's costs rise from the top to the bottom of the table (two reasons)?

3. Suppose that chemical-intensive farmers have constant average costs equal to $185 per ton and that prices in this market are driven down to the cost of the

21. You may recall that in Chapter 4, it was claimed that subsidies for emission reductions were a bad idea, because in the long run this would simply draw other polluters into the business. By contrast, CT subsidies are for better technologies, not for reductions in emissions.

lowest cost producer. Define a long-run equilibrium as one in which there is no incentive for entry or exit by one more farmer of either type. Which of the following are long-run equilibria? Of these, which are stable equilibria?

a. Ten biological farmers, each producing 100 tons. No chemical farmers.

b. Ten biological farmers, each producing 100 tons. Five chemical farmers, each producing 100 tons.

c. One biological farmer producing 100 tons. Ten chemical farmers, each producing 100 tons.

d. No biological farmers. Ten chemical farmers, each producing 100 tons.

4. Which of these is the most efficient outcome? If prices fluctuate over time between $200 and the cost of the lowest-cost producer, which will be the likely long-run free-market equilibrium?

5. In the late 1960s, after cotton pests developed pesticide resistance, cotton growers in Texas successfully made a shift to biological pest control methods. Government infrastructure support (predator rearing, education) was critical in this effort. In Mexico, with no similar support, the cotton industry collapsed. How could this phenomenon be explained using the cost function above?[22]

APPLICATION 17.1

Is Recycling Really a Clean Technology?

Some critics have argued that recycling of old newspapers yields few environmental benefits. First, much pulpwood used in the United States is grown on tree plantations, not in old-growth forests. Second, newspaper cannot be repeatedly recycled, so any upstream reductions in tree harvest are limited. Third, recycling systems cannot displace garbage collection completely, and the extra collection trucks thus add to urban air pollution. Fourth, de-inking newspaper is a highly toxic process; it is better to isolate that ink in a landfill where it is unlikely to leach anywhere. Finally, much of the new recycled mill capacity is being built as expansions to existing mills, close to forests and away from cities, which are the source of the raw materials. Thus there is little raw material transport savings associated with recycling. Response?

APPLICATION 17.2

Low-Hanging Fruit

In an EPA-funded project, teams conducted waste minimization assessments of several medium-sized manufacturing plants. Table 17.5 provides a breakdown of the measures for two plants, the first a paint factory and the second a factory producing oil coolers for heavy equipment. The engineering teams' recommendations ranged from simple "housekeeping" measures, such as putting a lid on a degreasing tank, to more complex process innovations, such as switching from a solvent-based to a vacuum-cleaning

---

22. These examples are drawn from Cowan and Gunby (1996).

TABLE 17.5 Waste Reduction in Two Manufacturing Plants

Plant	Problem	Recommendation	Annual Waste Reduced	Annual Savings ($1,000/yr)	Payback Period (yrs)
1	Pipe rinse water	Use foam plugs for dry wipe	1,780 gal/yr	11	0.2
1	Solvent disposal	Recycling	3,300 gal/yr	5	0.9
1	Mercury in bactericide	Use organic substitute	3,100 gal/yr	6	0.0
2	Vapors from degreaser	Install cover or	50%	17	0.0
		use ultrasonic cleaning	99%	20	2.4
2	Recycling contaminants	Reduce lubricants	20%	1	0.3
2	Sludge from salt baths	Use mechanical method or	4%	20	2.1
		use vacuum method	80%	203	3.5
2	Paint-contaminated cardboard	Reduce paint loss with air jets	22%	4	0.6
2	Paint-contaminated filters	Electrostatic spray control	36%	11	1.2

Source: Kirsch and Looby (1990, Tables 2 and 3).

method. For the two plants, waste reduction ranged from 4% to 99%, while the average payback period was well under one year. The biggest waste reducers also generate the largest annual savings—for example, using ultrasonic degreasing in plant. And even though such measures have the longest payback periods, they are probably the most profitable investments because of the large cost savings.

1. Is "waste reduction" a clean technology?
2. If we believe the evidence in this table, why are these manufacturing firms leaving money on the table? Why don't waste reduction survey companies make a living consulting with companies to show them how to cut pollution and make money at the same time?

APPLICATION 17.3

Designing Subsidies

Governor Blabla has decided that, rather than build a new nuclear power plant to service power needs, the state should save an equivalent amount of energy. As one component of an efficiency plan, he has turned to you, his top aide, to design a policy to encourage adoption of low-emitting diode (LED) lightbulbs. Recall from Chapter 8 that although LEDs save a tremendous amount of money (and energy) over their lifetime, they are quite expensive initially ($5–15 or so per bulb). You've thought up three possibilities:

Utility Rebates Have publicly regulated electric companies provide "rebates" of 75% of the purchase price to consumers who install LED bulbs. Allow utilities to cover the cost of the program through higher electricity rates.

Government Procurement Contract   Have the state government agree to purchase, using general tax revenues, a large quantity of bulbs from an in-state supplier (at competitive rates). The bulbs would be used to retrofit government buildings.

R&D Subsidies   Provide funds from general tax revenues to in-state firms to develop LED bulbs that can be sold at lower cost and/or are more comparable to standard incandescent bulbs. Continued receipt of such subsidies should be conditional on cost reductions or performance enhancements.

1.   For each of the three plans, answer the following questions:
   a.   What obstacles to successful implementation might arise?
   b.   If you had to pick one policy to push for, which would it be? Why?

KEY IDEAS IN EACH SECTION

17.0   This chapter focuses on government efforts to promote clean technology as an alternative to regulation.

17.1   Government intervention in the early stages of technology development and promotion may be justified to achieve environmental goals under a theory known as **path dependence**.

17.2   **Clean technology (CT)** is defined as having three components. CTs must (1) deliver services of a comparable quality and (2) do so with **long-run marginal costs** comparable to existing dirty technologies. (**Early-stage CTs** must achieve **economies of scale** before low-price production can be achieved, while **late-stage CTs** are already cost-competitive.) Finally, CTs must (3) be environmentally superior to existing options. Determining this requires considering all major impacts using **life-cycle analysis** and addressing the **adding-up problem**.

17.3   Two general obstacles to rapid diffusion of CTs are (1) a **lack of substantial profit advantage** in the marketplace and (2) government **direct or indirect subsidies to competitors**. The lack of high profits means there is little private pull to overcome barriers such as high **sunk costs** (R&D and marketing), **thin markets, access to capital**, and **high discount rates**.

17.4   Government can help pick winners if it (1) levels the playing field. This entails removing subsidies for competitor technologies and internalizing social costs, preferably through IB regulation. It must also (2) focus on environmentally superior options only and (3) engage in **least-cost planning**. Under a least-cost approach, all subsidies are either time-limited or conditioned on cost-reducing performance.

17.5   Early-stage CTs can be promoted by (1) R&D funding, (2) producer subsidies such as **price preferences**, **procurement contracts**, and **loan guarantees**, (3) **technology-forcing standards** like the **CAFE** and Renewable Portfolio Standards (RPS), and (4) infrastructure investment including the **smart grid**.

17.6   This section discusses tools for promoting late-stage CTs. These include (1) product labeling, (2) flexible design standards, (3) utility marketing of energy efficiency, (4) technical assistance programs, and (5) consumer subsidies. Subsidy programs must be carefully designed to avoid **free riders**.

17.7   **Alternative agriculture** and solid waste recycling are explored as examples of clean technologies. The primary obstacle to the former is, as usual, an insignificant profit advantage that is unable to overcome **adjustment costs**. Policy here could focus on R&D and technical assistance. Solid waste recycling gains an environmental edge over landfilling and incineration, largely through **indirect benefits**: lowered upstream impacts and reduced energy use in processing. Recycling is a successfully promoted CT. As a result of government support over the last few decades, recycling has become a major waste management option.

REFERENCES

Ackerman, Frank. 1996. *Why recycle? Markets, values and public policy*. Covelo, CA: Island Press.

A. D. Little, Inc. 1990. *Disposable versus reusable diapers: Health, environmental and economic comparisons*. Washington, DC: Author.

Arthur, Brian W. 1991. Positive feedbacks in the economy. *Scientific American*, February, 92–99.

Cowan, Robin, and Philip Gunby. 1996. Sprayed to death: Path dependence, lock-in and pest control strategies. *Economic Journal* 106: 521–42.

Curtis, Jennifer. 1991. *Harvest of hope: The potential of alternative agriculture to reduce pesticide use*. San Francisco: Natural Resources Defense Council.

DeVries, Cisco. 2008. Everything you need to know about Berkeley's innovative rooftop solar program. *Grist*, 3 November. http://grist.org/article/berkeley-rules/.

Epstein P. R., J. J. Buonocore, K. Eckerle, M. Hendryx, B. M. Stout III, R. Heinberg, R. W. Clapp, et al. 2011. Full cost accounting for the life cycle of coal. *The New York Academy of Sciences* 1219: 73–98. doi: 10.1111/j.1749-6632.2010.05890.x.

Fickett, Arnold P., Clark W. Gellings, and Amory B. Lovins. 1990. Efficient use of electricity. In *Readings from Scientific American*. New York: W. H. Freeman.

Geller, Howard, Daniel Lashoff, Alden Meyer, and Mary Beth Zimmerman, eds. 1991. *America's energy choices: Investing in a strong economy and a clean environment*. Cambridge, MA: Union of Concerned Scientists.

Geman, Ben. 2011. 'Report: Most Energy Dept. loan support is low-risk'. *The Hill*. 12 February. http://thehill.com/blogs/e2-wire/e2-wire/196917-report-most-energy-dept-loan-financing-is-low-risk.

Goodstein, Eban. 2000. Prices or policy? The low-cost path to clean technology. In *Advances in the economics of environmental resources*, ed. Darwin Hall. New York: Elsevier.

Greider, William. 1992. *Who will tell the people?* New York: Simon & Schuster.

Halweil, B. 2006. Can organic farming feed us all? *World Watch Magazine*, May–June, 18–24.

Herman, Robin. 1990. *Fusion: The search for endless energy*. Cambridge: Cambridge University Press.

Hershkowitz, Allen. 1990. *NRDC Diaper letter*. New York: Natural Resources Defense Council.

In solid waste, it's the breakdown that counts. 1991. *New York Times*, 31 March.

Lehrburger, Carl, Jocelyn Mullen, and C. V. Jones. 1991. *Diapers: Environmental impacts and lifecycle analysis*. Philadelphia: National Association of Diaper Services.

Lovins, Amory. 1977. *Soft energy paths: Towards a durable peace*. New York: HarperCollins.

Muller, Nicholas Z., Robert Mendelsohn, and William Nordhaus. 2011. Environmental accounting for pollution in the United States economy. *American Economic Review* 101(5): 1649–75.

New York State Energy Authority. 1994. *Energy implications of integrated solid waste management systems*. Albany, NY: Author.

New York State Energy Office. 1992. *Hydro-Quebec economic study, draft report*. Albany, NY: Author.

U.S. Department of Energy. 2002. *DOE Energy resources portfolio: FY 1999–2001*. Washington, DC: Author.

US EIA. 2013. Annual Energy Outlook. Energy Information Administration Report Number DOE/EIA 0383.

18

ENERGY POLICY AND THE FUTURE

18.0 Introduction

Of all economic activities, energy production and use present the biggest challenge to the quality of the environment. This book began with an extended discussion of the challenge of global warming, due to the release of carbon dioxide from the combustion of fossil fuels. But beyond global warming, energy consumption also yields as by-products acid rain and sulfate pollution, urban air pollution and traffic jams, oil spills, oil drilling and strip mining in sensitive habitats, acid mine drainage, hazardous mine tailings and oil drilling muds, occupational diseases such as black lung, and exposure to radioactivity in the mining, transport, and disposal of nuclear fuel and waste. Our three main energy sources—oil, coal, and nuclear—each have their own environmental drawbacks.

Yet reliable access to reasonably priced energy is the lifeblood of any economic system, and the American economy relies more heavily on it than most. This chapter presents an overview of the current energy picture and then considers the prospects for a cleaner energy path, one based on a combination of renewable energy (solar, wind, and biomass electricity), energy efficiency, and electric, hybrid, and biofuel vehicles. The basic message is that the future is up for grabs. Depending on the interaction of technology, economics, and government policy, the energy system could follow the current fossil fuels path or switch to either a renewable/efficiency path or, less likely, a high nuclear path.

How costly is a clean energy future likely to be? As was suggested in the introductory chapter on global warming, there is substantial disagreement among economists about the economic impacts of the different options. Some argue that combating global warming by adopting clean energy options will be expensive, while others have maintained that, through aggressive energy-efficiency measures, we might actually be able to reduce global warming at a profit. This chapter looks more closely at these arguments and evaluates energy options via the clean technology (CT) approach developed in Chapter 17.

What is clear is that to hold global warming to the low end of 4 degrees F will require a staggering, rapid, and wholesale transformation of the global energy system. To meet the energy needs of 3 billion more people, address the rising aspirations of the developing world, and at the same time move quickly away from the global workhorse for baseload electricity—coal combustion—will be the work of a generation.

18.1 Technology Options: Electricity and Heat

Every day, each American consumes the energy equivalent of 6.5 gallons of oil. This section looks at the heat and power side of that equation—how can we satisfy our growing demands for electricity to run our gadgets and the heat we need to stay warm in the winter? The first way is to get efficient. It turns out that the cheapest and cleanest power is the power we save and don't have to produce. Turning next to the supply side of the market, coal (38%), natural gas (28%), and nuclear (20%) are the three main sources of electricity production in the United States. Hydropower (7%) is the primary renewable power source, while other renewables comprise 6%.[1] However, one renewable alternative, wind power, is the fastest-growing source of new power production, and another—solar power—holds substantial promise.

Efficiency. How do Americans stack up against the rest of the world in energy use? Unfortunately, as Figure 18.1 illustrates, we are close to the top of the heap among wealthy countries. What explains the wide variation in international demand for energy illustrated in the figure? National income, of course, but climate, population density, energy prices, transportation infrastructure, and government conservation

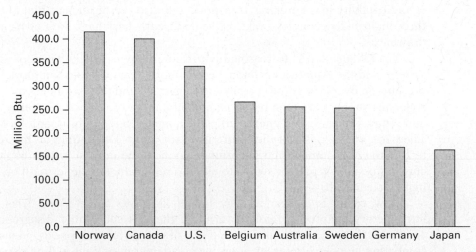

FIGURE 18.1 Energy Consumption per Capita, International Comparisons
Source: U.S. Department of Energy.

---

1. For current data, see the website for the U.S. Energy Information Administration, Electric Power Monthly.

policy are all also important factors.[2] Canada loses on all fronts—cold climate, low population density, low energy prices, a transport system geared to the automobile, and a government with a relatively laissez-faire attitude, by international standards, toward energy conservation.

Germany and Japan, each of which uses about half as much energy per capita as we do in the United States, have comparable climates. However, both are much more densely populated and have urban and interurban transport systems designed heavily around mass transit. Of the two, Japan has pursued energy efficiency most aggressively. Before the first oil shock in 1974, Japan already had one of the most energy-efficient economies; over the next two decades, the nation improved its efficiency by one-third, compared to a 25% improvement in other industrial countries. One reason is that Japanese factories are required to have at least one energy conservation engineer on site who must pass a rigorous national test.[3]

The good news reflected in Figure 18.1 is that there is clearly a lot of room for Americans to save energy without compromising lifestyles. **Demand-side management (DSM)** involves promoting technologies that use energy more efficiently. Note that many conservation measures, such as turning down the thermostat from 68 to 65 degrees or driving 55 mph on the highway, are not efficiency measures as they involve some sacrifice in consumption. By energy efficiency we mean technologies that generate a comparable quality of service using less energy. Such DSM measures "produce" energy by freeing up supply. Amory Lovins calls this power "negawatts."

In earlier chapters, we have discussed many DSM options: compact fluorescent and LED lighting (Chapters 6 and 8), energy-efficient building codes, and standards for refrigeration and lighting (Chapter 17). Other DSM measures include using waste energy from electricity production to heat buildings (cogeneration) as well as adopting energy-efficient industrial motors and cooling and cleaning appliances.[4]

Coal. On the supply side of the market, the dominance of coal in electric power generation to date has been due to one primary factor—a reliable, low-priced fuel source. The technology for producing electricity from coal is well developed, and because domestic coal resources are abundant, the supply of fuel is not subject to the disruption and price fluctuations associated with oil.

On the other hand, the environmental and social problems of using coal are well known. In addition to problems of acid rain, mercury, and criteria air pollutants discussed in Chapters 13 and 16, underground mining for coal is quite dangerous, while strip mining and "mountaintop removal" destroy natural ecosystems. Both can generate acid drainage problems. Coal transport also has a major impact on the nation's roads. But coal's long-run outlook hinges mostly on the progress of efforts to stop global warming. Electric power contributes about 33% of America's carbon dioxide emissions, mostly from coal. Any serious effort to control the greenhouse effect will require that conventional coal-burning power production be restricted, if not ultimately eliminated.

Recent technological advances now allow coal to be gasified before combustion; this process reduces the carbon emissions substantially, but more importantly, allows

2. Electric power in Norway is cheap because of abundant hydropower.
3. "How Japan Became So Energy Efficient" (1990).
4. Choi Granade et al. (2009).

carbon dioxide to be filtered out of the stack. Coal advocates argue that carbon dioxide can be captured and injected into chambers that used to hold natural gas, through a process called underground **sequestration**. Several new coal gasification plants are under construction in the United States, but no one is yet sequestering carbon. Will sequestration work, and can it be made cost competitive? This is the question that hangs over coal's future as a primary fuel for electric production.

Although coal is still the primary source of electricity in the United States, its primacy is being challenged. In the last three years, coal's share of generation has fallen dramatically from 48 to as low as 36%. Few new coal plants are being built, and old ones are being retired, under a combination of pressures: cheap natural gas (more on this later), the growth of renewable generation, a new round of pollution control focused on mercury emissions and criteria air pollutants (see Chapter 16), and the threat of future liability associated with carbon dioxide emissions.

Nuclear. Atomic power faces both economic and environmental challenges. On the economic front, **nuclear power** is competitive only as a result of heavy subsidies, some deeply hidden. From an environmental perspective, nuclear power is hindered by three concerns that must be resolved: meltdowns, waste storage, and terrorism. There are currently about 110 plants operating in the United States.

Recently proposed and canceled nuclear power plants—in Turkey and Quebec—have been extraordinarily expensive, with power prices above $0.20 per kWh. A Finnish plant recently under construction has seen cost overruns greater than 50%. Most plants under construction around the globe are in China and Russia, and little activity is seen in capitalist countries. France, the world leader in nuclear power, has not built a domestic plant since 1999. And despite large, explicit financing subsidies from the U.S. government, none have been built in this country since the 1970s.[5] Why so little activity?

Nuclear is inherently a highly centralized technology, and because each plant is so expensive, requiring many years to build before any returns are realized, the financial risks are great. Advocates argue that if enough orders are placed, economies of scale will kick in, and the costs of later plants will fall, but this argument has so far failed to attract investors. An important issue is construction delays. Intense safety concerns, permitting, failed inspections, and public opposition can further slow plant construction and reduce the profitability of investment. This adds another layer of risk. For these reasons, private-sector investors remain very wary of nuclear power.

Much debate has centered on the safety of nuclear facilities, and the most concern is focused on a Chernobyl-type core failure, or meltdown, with worries reinforced by the 2011 tragedy at the Fukushima plant in Japan. Estimates of cancer-induced fatalities from meltdowns have ranged from 0 (Three Mile Island) to as high as 500,000 for Chernobyl, though most fatality estimates for Chernobyl are much lower. A worst-case disaster in a populous area of the United States might generate casualties of more than a hundred thousand. Based on these figures, nuclear power presents a social gamble: the possibility of accidents generating either a small or very large number of fatalities.[6]

---

5. Kanter (2009).
6. Lisbeth Gronlund, How Many Cancers Did Chernobyl Really Cause? All Things Nuclear (Union of Concerned Scientists, 17 April 2011).

At the same time, people die regularly, but more anonymously, from coal pollution. On the basis of lives lost per kilowatt hour, nuclear power production may well stack up favorably compared to coal. But the risks to those living close to a nuclear power plant will be higher, explaining intense local opposition to siting. Moreover, a risk assessment looks only at the relative probability of death, without assessing the magnitude of the potential disaster—whole communities destroyed overnight. As we noted in Chapter 5, people will buy insurance to avoid very risky situations that occur with low probability. Stronger opposition to nuclear power facilities may thus reflect simple risk aversion.

A new obstacle for nuclear is increasing concern that reactors could somehow become terrorist weapons, either through a triggered meltdown or through the use of waste materials to assemble "dirty bombs." Terrorism and nuclear proliferation also ensure that even if atomic power experiences a comeback in developed countries, it will not present a desirable solution to the energy needs of developing countries with less stable governments. The potential global-warming benefits of nuclear power are thus inherently self-limiting. Finally, public distrust of scientific risk assessment in the nuclear field—whether by government or industry officials—is very high. (Witness *The Simpsons*!) In part, this distrust is attributable to the widespread perception that the NRC, which enforces safety standards for nuclear power, has been captured by the industry. In part, it is because of uncertainty in the science. Official estimates of "safe" exposure to radiation have been repeatedly lowered.

Beyond meltdowns and radiation releases, the other major environmental issue facing the nuclear industry is waste disposal. Nuclear waste is divided into two categories: high-level and low-level waste. **High-level waste** consists of spent fuel rods and waste from weapons production; it remains toxic for hundreds of thousands of years. **Low-level waste** includes contaminated clothing and equipment from nuclear power plants and defense establishments, and wastes from medical and pharmaceutical facilities. Nuclear power accounts for about 80% of the radioactivity found in low-level civilian waste. The radioactive elements in most low-level waste decay to levels the NRC considers harmless within 100 years, although about 3% of this waste needs to be isolated for longer periods.

Currently, there are no operating permanent waste storage facilities for high-level waste in the United States, although a facility for defense waste is being built in Carlsbad, New Mexico, and one is planned for civilian waste at Yucca Mountain in Nevada. At this point, Yucca still remains in the research and design phase, and it may not begin accepting waste until 2015 or 2020, if ever.[7] There are currently three commercial waste facilities for low-level waste, although these sites are increasingly reluctant to accept out-of-state waste. As a result of the unresolved storage question, both high- and low-level waste have been piling up in temporary facilities at commercial power plants and government installations.

The main waste disposal options are burial in geologically stable formations or aboveground storage. Given the extraordinarily long-term nature of the waste's toxicity, the scientific community is divided on the safety of various permanent waste disposal options. Regardless of the technical issues at stake, however, political opposition to the siting of waste facilities has essentially put a brake on nuclear power. Solving the

7. Follow the Yucca story at www.yuccamountain.org/new.htm.

disposal problems—technical and political—for existing waste is essential before we move on to produce more of it.

Unlike other energy sources, production of nuclear power inherently requires expensive, ongoing government supervision. First, the possibility of nuclear terrorism has meant that government must closely monitor shipments of fuel and waste. Second, the need for intense regulation of reactor safety has led to extensive bureaucratic involvement in reactor design, operation, and maintenance. Finally, public opposition to siting, as well as the long-lived nature of waste, has meant that government has taken over the responsibility for trying to solve the disposal problem.

Nuclear power is a significant player in the energy field today as a result of ongoing government support. As we will see in our discussion of subsidy policy, nuclear power in the United States has been aggressively supported by government funds. In France, the country with the world's biggest commitment to nuclear power, the industry is state-owned and heavily subsidized. Yet this remains nuclear power's principal advantage—thanks to the substantial investment of public funds, it is today a proven source of large-scale electricity production, albeit somewhat expensive. Nuclear's best hope in the United States is that global warming becomes recognized on a bi-partisan basis as a serious environmental threat, requiring an immediate reduction in coal-fired power production. Only then will intense local opposition to facility siting, leading to construction delays and high costs, have significant chance of being overcome.

Natural Gas. This fuel source has emerged as a major competitor to coal. The reason: large domestic deposits of natural gas, composed primarily of methane, have recently become accessible because of the development of a new technology called horizontal hydrofracturing, or "fracking." In the fracking process, gas companies drill down to reach shale deposits that hold widely scattered concentrations of natural gas. From a single vertical well, they then drill arms out horizontally. Into these arms they inject fracking fluid, containing a variety of chemicals, at very high pressures, which fractures the shale. When the fluids are removed, the natural gas flows through the fractures in the rock back into drill holes and out of the well.

Natural gas has one major environmental advantage. In terms of air pollution, it is the cleanest of fossil fuels: It has a low sulfur content, emits far fewer particulates and less mercury when burned, and yields about 70% more energy for each unit of carbon dioxide emitted than does coal. However, methane itself is a greenhouse gas. Thus, for natural gas to have any advantage over coal in terms of avoided global warming, careful controls must be implemented to prevent the release of the so-called fugitive emissions—methane that escapes into the atmosphere during production or transport, or from abandoned wells.

In addition, fracking has sparked major concerns over potential contamination of groundwater in the drilling process, contamination of surface water through the disposal of fracking fluids, excessive withdrawals of fresh water from streams and rivers for drilling, fragmentation of habitat, air pollution in the vicinity of the wells, earthquake risk, and general industrialization of rural landscapes. The conflict has become heated because many of the promising gas deposits are in populated areas. It is thus common to have drillers seeking sites quite close to houses and drinking water wells.

In spite of this controversy, since 2008 fracking has generated a large increase in the U.S. natural gas supply. This, along with the leveling out of U.S. demand due to the recession, has led to a period of low cost natural gas, likely to persist for a few years. Unlike highly centralized coal and nuclear plants, natural gas plants can also be built cheaply, at relatively small scale. These factors have led to a rapid rise in the share of natural gas in electricity production: up from 20% at the beginning of 2009, to 28% three years later, largely displacing coal, and also slowing the growth of the solar and wind industries.

How far will the rush to gas go? This depends on the degree to which citizen pressure imposes greater regulatory control over the industry—with respect to global warming, water contamination, and habitat protection. In addition, the fracking technology itself is new enough that it is hard to judge whether recent estimates of large U.S. (and global) reserves are realistic. For the medium term, however, low natural gas prices are likely to continue to promote increased investment in gas-fired electric generation capacity.

Renewables. The final major energy category includes hydroelectric, solar, wind, geothermal, and biomass energy.[8] **Hydroelectric power** currently contributes about 7% of the nation's electricity. Although from a pollution perspective, hydroelectric energy is relatively clean, dam projects can have significant environmental impacts, ranging from the flooding of ecologically valuable lands to negative impacts on aquatic life, such as salmon.

Solar energy is divided into two categories: **active solar**, which produces electric power (and heat as a by-product), and **passive solar**, which produces heat. The major use of passive solar is for heating water for direct use, but it can also be used to heat and cool homes. The two principal active solar technologies are **solar thermal** power, produced by focusing the sun's energy to heat a fluid that is then used to create electricity, and **photovoltaic (PV)** power, produced from solar cells.

Solar thermal is already being deployed on a commercial scale: a recently announced Arizona plant will employ 3,500 mirrors to produce 300 MW of power—about one-third the power production from a large nuclear plant. The last section of this chapter tells how solar thermal technology developed as a result of U.S. government subsidies in the 1980s. As a result of this support, and a second round of European subsidies, the technology is now cost competitive, and expected to deliver power at under $0.10 per kWh.

Solar thermal has tremendous potential as a near-term baseload technology in desert environments, as plants can store power for several hours in heated liquids and thus supply power 24 hours a day, all year long. Arizona, Mexico, Northern Africa, and Middle Eastern countries are looking to become major electricity exporters on the back of this technology.[9]

The better known solar technology, photovoltaic (PV) cells, or solar cells, produce electricity directly from sunlight and do not face the limited geographic range of solar thermal. In fact, cloudy Germany is a world leader in PV technology and installed capacity. In spring of 2012, Germany was meeting 10% of their electric load from solar

8. Other renewable sources of energy with less near-term economic potential include tidal, and wave power.
9. Pool, Sean and John Dos Passos Coggin (2013) *Fulfilling the promise of concentrating solar power*, Center for american Progress: Washington, DC). http://www.americanprogress.org/wp-content/uploads/2013/06/PoolSolarPower-report-3.pdf

alone, up from 3% the year before. Germany is moving rapidly to build solar PV into a major player in their base-load generation capability.[10]

PV is a classic large-scale clean technology. First developed as part of the space program in the 1960s, the technology has advanced slowly but steadily, based on government R&D and subsidy programs. Until recently, PV remained too expensive for more than niche applications. However, as the German case demonstrates, in the second half of the 2000s, PV has begun to see rapid price declines. These cost gains have been driven by technology advances in turn sparked by global and U.S. subsidy policy, growing markets, especially in Europe and China, and finally, the entry of Chinese manufacturers. In 2012, U.S. commercial customers were receiving offers to install solar cell systems on site for prices as low as $.10 per KWh guaranteed over a ten year contract.

PV can be a distributed source of power, installed on rooftops, covered parking garages, or in fields and fed back into the grid via "smart meters." It can also be developed to support a centralized, utility-scale plant. One of the world's largest plants, in Yuma, Arizona—at 290 MW set to deliver power equivalent to one-third of a nuclear power plant—will be fully operational in 2014. The Yuma plant received a $290 million federal loan guarantee (see Chapter 17) to support its construction.[11]

In addition, photovoltaic systems are very low–risk projects: fuel sources are assured at a constant (zero) price, and there is no danger of increased environmental regulation in the future. For this reason, utilities can require a lower rate of return from solar projects than others. The discount rate used to evaluate a PV project matters, because PV systems have very high up-front investment costs and very low operating and maintenance costs.

PVs hold the allure of clean, low-cost power. (Most of the negative environmental effects of PVs can be traced to the manufacture of silicon chips.) PV supporters envision a decentralized power system with PV roofing tiles producing independent power for each household. Low-cost PVs would certainly be one important link in the technological chain necessary to promote sustainable development in poor countries.

To date, however, the most successful renewable electric technology is **wind power**. In 2012, global installed wind capacity was greater than 200,000 MW, equivalent to 200 large nuclear plants, and growing at a rate higher than 20% per year. Costs were competitive with new coal plants—given access to a good site, with accessible transmission—where wind power comes in as low as $0.04 per KWh.

While economies of scale and technology improvements have driven the costs of wind power production down to levels competitive with fossil fuels, wind faces two major economic obstacles. The main one is access to transmission lines. While in theory, wind production could satisfy all U.S. electricity needs, in practice, transmission lines to get this power from windy regions to urban users are often not in place. A related problem is storage. Both wind and active solar technologies produce power on an intermittent basis when the wind blows or the sun shines. Thus effective long-run development of these resources will require storage. The current solution is to use the electricity grid; PV and wind power now supply electricity to the existing system for

10. Solar Provides 10 Percent of Germany's Electricity in May (2012).
11. "Largest Solar PV Plant in North America Comes On-Line" (2012).

distribution. However, because electricity is lost in the transmission process, grid storage and transport are limited. A variety of technologies, primarily improved batteries, are being explored. Other options include using electricity to pump water behind a dam, compress air, or create hydrogen, all to be used for future power production.

The major environmental concern about wind is aesthetic: recent high-profile battles have been fought over locating wind farms off scenic (and wealthy) Cape Cod, and on mountaintops in New England. Despite a common belief that wind farms are dangerous to birds, avian mortality has been quite low at recent wind farm developments though concerns remain regarding bats.[12]

Geothermal power is used residentially and commercially to heat and cool buildings. Ground-source heat pumps take advantage of the fact that the ground is cooler than the buildings it supports in the summer and warmer than the buildings in the winter. Beyond this, as a potential utility-scale electricity source, advanced drilling technologies, similar to fracking discussed previously, now make it possible at many sites across the world to create steam to drive turbines by injecting water deep underground. A recent study argued that a significant fraction of U.S. power might come from this source by 2050. However, one early experiment using this technology in Europe was shut down after generating small earthquakes![13]

Finally, an immediate way to reduce CO_2 emissions from coal plants is to "co-fire" the plants using a mix of coal and **biomass**. Burning biomass reduces the global-warming pollution from the power plants, because the woody material that is burned grows back and recaptures the carbon.

Renewable energy has gotten a lot of good press lately, but it is important to realize that in the United States, non-hydro renewables from all sources remain a small player—only 6% of the nation's electricity supply. State and federal policy aims to up that level to 20% or more by 2020, biting into the 38% share currently held by coal.

18.2 Policy Options: Electricity and Heat

Now that we understand the energy players, we can begin to think through energy solutions for heat and power. If we are going to stop global warming, how, exactly, could we shake our coal dependence in the next couple of decades? Chapter 17 provided a three-part approach for evaluating decisions like this:

1. Pick the clean, low-cost technology.
2. Increase CT profitability by eliminating subsidies and/or internalizing social costs for competitor technologies, preferably through IB regulation.
3. Promote the technology directly.

STEP 1—PICKING WINNERS

On the environmental scale, efficiency comes in first, wind power and solar are tied for second, geothermal is third, co-fired biomass fourth, new natural gas fifth, nuclear is sixth, and coal is in last place. Ranked in terms of current costs, efficiency measures are

---

12. Mazza and Heitz (2006).
13. MIT Panel (2007).

the cheapest. Natural gas is second, wind third. Solar thermal, new coal, and biomass co-firing are tied for fourth, solar PV is fifth, nuclear sixth, and geothermal brings up the rear. (New coal is relatively expensive in this ranking in part because of the risk associated with carbon-control legislation for plants with expected lifetimes stretching out to 50 years.) However, in terms of long-run potential, both PV and geothermal have a decent shot at competing with new coal.

The low-hanging fruits in this case are clearly efficiency, wind, and solar thermal. Photovoltaics present a good bet, and geothermal looks to be a decent investment. Is there a case for aggressive promotion of nuclear? Probably not. While nuclear plants can undoubtedly be made safer, it will be hard to reduce nuclear costs in the United States below their current range and still provide a politically acceptable margin of safety. Efficiency, wind, solar, and geothermal offer more feasible, cleaner, and cheaper alternatives to fossil fuels than does nuclear.

STEP 2—LEVEL THE PLAYING FIELD

The current U.S. energy market is far from the ideal of a free market; government intervention is widespread through both regulation and subsidy. One recent estimate of annual federal energy subsidies ranged from $37 to $64 billion. Tax breaks alone for the oil industry amount to an estimated $7 billion annually. To provide a feel for the type of expenditure undertaken by government agencies, Table 18.1 details the agencies involved in supporting just the exploration phase of oil production—efforts range from subsidies for procurement of resources to R&D to infrastructure development to risk reduction. One of the biggest subsidies to the oil industry that was included in the study is spending by the military to protect shipping in the Persian Gulf; analysts put that cost at between $12 and $20 billion. But the subsidy estimates do not include the costs of the two Gulf wars.[14]

A major subsidy for the nuclear industry is a legal liability limit in the event of a meltdown. As noted in Chapter 17, because nuclear plants would otherwise be unable to obtain private insurance, the Price-Anderson Act limits liability for nuclear

TABLE 18.1 Federal Agency Subsidies for Oil Exploration

Support Activity	Agency Involvement
Procurement	U.S. Geological Survey, National Oceanic and Atmospheric Administration, and Bureau of Indian Affairs all provide survey, mapping, and development support
Technological development	Department of Energy finances R&D on oil extraction
Industry infrastructure	Bureau of Land Management provides low-cost access to leases
Risk reduction	Fish and Wildlife Service conducts environmental impact assessment of arctic drilling

Source: Koplow. 1993. *Federal energy subsidies: energy, environmental and fiscal impacts.* Washington, DC: Alliance to Save Energy, 46, Appendix A-2. Used with permission.

---

14. Koplow (2005) and "Eliminating Tax Subsidies for Oil Companies" (2010).

accidents. On a per-reactor basis, the subsidy works out to be more than $20 million per year.

Who wins and who loses from the federal subsidies? Figure 18.2 provides a breakdown of subsidies between the major energy sources. Efficiency and non-hydro renewables, the two clean technologies identified previously, received only 5.4% of the total. The major beneficiaries of subsidy policies were clearly the conventional fuel sources—nuclear and fossil fuels received 88.5% of all energy subsidies. The fact that coal, oil, and fission (nuclear) technologies have received the bulk of subsidies is not surprising; they also supply the bulk of the country's power (and have important political constituencies). In addition, research to find ways to mitigate the impact of coal burning on global warming is certainly reasonable. However, even on an energy-adjusted basis, one study found that coal and nuclear fission received the highest subsidies calculable, and efficiency came in last.[15]

This discussion of subsidy policy highlights two points. First, energy markets are not free markets; government intervention to promote technologies has been and continues to be substantial. Thus our current energy mix, in which coal dominates electricity production and low gas prices dominate transport, is not a "natural" outcome of market forces. Coal has received tremendous federal subsidies, including large R&D expenditures, to develop cleaner coal technologies that have allowed the industry to expand. Second, federal policy currently tilts the playing field heavily against renewables and energy efficiency. The government's substantial support of conventional technology works against market penetration of inherently clean alternatives.

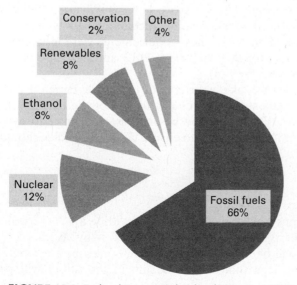

FIGURE 18.2 Federal Energy Subsidies by Sector, 2005
Source: Data are from Koplow (2007).

---

15. Koplow (2007).

Reducing the subsidies for conventional options, or at least leveling the playing field by boosting subsidies for clean technologies, is necessary for their promotion. What about internalizing externalities associated with conventional fuels? The major externalities associated with fossil fuels used for heat and electricity are urban air pollution, acid rain, and global warming. As we discussed in Chapter 17, new mercury emission rules, as well as tightening regulations for SO_2 and NOx, have recently come into force.

In 2008, the U.S. Supreme Court made it clear that the EPA has the authority to regulate CO_2 as a global-warming pollutant under the Clean Air Act. This ruling, combined with the potential for U.S. cap-and-trade legislation, has made it very likely that the price of coal-fired electricity from new plants will rise by half-a-penny per kilowatthour in the short run and by as much as $0.05–$0.06 in the long run. Because coal plants are built to last 100 years, the long run matters. Due to this enhanced regulatory action on conventional pollutants and regulatory risk on climate, interest in building new coal plants has plummeted.

Nuclear advocates often maintain that on safety grounds, the industry is over-regulated, which explains its cost disadvantage. Yet given public opposition to facility siting, regulation may well need to tighten if new nuclear facilities are built. Realistic assessments of waste disposal, insurance, and decommissioning expenses should also be built into cost per kilowatthour estimates for any new facilities. Having evaluated measures to level the playing field for clean energy, we now consider the final policy option.

STEP 3—DIRECT PROMOTION OF CLEAN TECHNOLOGIES

The most powerful and widespread policy tool for promoting clean electric power is a renewable portfolio standard (RPS). As we noted in Chapter 17, by 2009, close to half the states had introduced RPS legislation, including major wind producers: Texas, California, Oregon, and Minnesota. These requirements were instrumental in driving very fast U.S. wind power growth from 2000 to 2012, and were also incentivizing solar thermal plant development.

Beyond an RPS, let us take a brief look at more targeted subsidy policies directed at the principal late-stage clean energy technology (efficiency), and one early-stage alternative (solar PV power). The basic message is that, to avoid waste and counterproductive incentives as well as to ensure equity, subsidies should be carefully targeted. Begin with a

PUZZLE

Suppose that Octopus Power is considering providing a weatherization service to about a quarter of its customers "free of charge." Why? Because, by reducing energy demand, it will be able to avoid building a new power plant. However, because there is no such thing as a free lunch, the utility will pay for the weatherization by charging higher electricity rates for all its customers. Is the weatherization subsidy a good idea?

SOLUTION

Probably not. The problems with the plan highlight a variety of pitfalls facing all efforts to promote energy efficiency. These include equity issues, strategic behavior, free riding, and rebound effects.

Here is the **equity issue**. By providing the weatherization service free of charge, Octopus would provide dramatic benefits to a quarter of its clients at the expense of the rest. While the company and ratepayers will save money in total, most of Octopus's clients will be worse off than if the power plant were built.

Another possible problem is **strategic behavior** by subsidizing one portion of the population, Octopus may inadvertently discourage others from weatherizing on their own. This group may hold back until more subsidies become available. Octopus may also be paying more than it needs to for conservation due to the potential for **free riding**. Some who would have otherwise weatherized on their own may take advantage of the subsidy.

Finally, there is the problem of **rebound effects**. Because electric bills for weatherized homes are now lower, residents will spend some of their increased income on keeping their house warmer or buying new appliances, which uses more electricity. The size of the rebound effect in the electricity field is the subject of current debate. It is probably around 10%.[16]

An alternative plan helps resolve all these issues: have the residents whose buildings are weatherized pay the bill. Consider a house with pre-weatherization electricity use of 12,000 kWh per year; weatherization reduces it to 10,000 kWh. The residents could thus afford a substantial rate increase (e.g., from $0.05 up to $0.06 per kWh) and still come out with the same overall electricity bill ($0.06 per kWh * 10,000 kWh = $600; $0.05 per kWh * 12,000 kWh = $600).

If energy-efficiency measures are truly cost-effective, then in theory it will always be possible to design a financing mechanism by which *the recipient ultimately pays* for a substantial portion of the service *and still comes out ahead*. That is, cost-effective efficiency investments can be designed to generate something close to a Pareto-improving situation.

In practice, the government or utility ratepayers at large may still need to absorb the risk and marketing costs necessary to overcome poor information and access to capital on the part of its clientele. For example, one utility found that requiring participants to pay for insulation to cover hot-water heaters, *even though the clients would save money at zero risk*, reduced program participation substantially. Lowered participation, in turn, increased the cost per kilowatthour saved by 350% due to scale economies in operating the program.

---

16. Kenneth and Van Dender (2007).

Yet *minimizing* the subsidy level by requiring recipients to pay at least a portion of the cost will reduce problems of inequity, strategic behavior, free riding, and rebound effects. This general rule will be true for any subsidy policy designed to encourage small-scale CTs.

Two recent policy innovations are moving us toward this goal of beneficiaries paying program costs. New York's **On-Bill-Recovery** program allows residents to borrow money for energy efficiency upgrades through their utilities, and then pay the loans back as part of their utility bill. Because the energy savings are greater than the repayments, customers both get the energy upgrades and pay less on their monthly bills—a true win-win. The policy is just underway. A similar policy called **PACE (Property Assessed Clean Energy)** allowed homeowners to pay for energy efficiency upgrades or solar investments through their property tax bill. When first instituted in Berkeley and on Long Island, the policy created mini solar booms, but PACE has been at least temporarily derailed by federal loan agencies.

Efforts to promote large-scale solar power through subsidies should be crafted with a similar eye toward the potential for waste. In the photovoltaic field, the challenge remains to reduce PV costs. As discussed in Chapter 17, there are essentially two ways to do this: (1) develop better technology through R&D and (2) capture cost savings through economies of scale and learning by doing. In the early 1980s, government policymakers prematurely took the latter route, funding flashy but uneconomic solar demonstration projects at the expense of basic R&D. At the same time, tax credits for the purchase of solar units were instituted to encourage the purchase of PVs; however, because PV was still not a competitive technology, when the credits expired, the PV market collapsed.[17]

Throughout the 1990s, PV developed further through a combination of low-level U.S. R&D subsidies and aggressive policies to promote solar installation in Europe, especially Germany. A steady decline in prices brought PV down through 2000–and then came a sudden boom in demand, supported by state-level incentives in the United States. In Oregon, for example, households could get a residential tax credit for installing rooftop solar, and the number of these installations exploded. But this demand boom—unlike that of the early 1980s—was not primarily subsidy driven. With surging global demand, the PV market in the late 2000s began to attract substantial investment.

The fast and furious pace of German deployment was fed by a **feed-in-tariff** policy. With a feed-in-tariff, electric companies must buy back electricity produced by households and businesses at a set rate. In the German case, the rate was favorable, and it sparked a massive boom in solar installments, leading to some cutbacks in the program to cool it off in 2012.

Germany is both moving to phase out nuclear and simultaneously reduce carbon footprint—this requires the very rapid pace of renewables deployment that they have been pursuing. In the United States, feed-in-tariffs, and their kin, **purchase power agreements**, are sparking renewables development in California, Florida, New York, Oregon, and other states. Purchase power agreements are long-term contracts for power negotiated with small producers—say a household or business. In this case, the

---

17. Zweibel (1990).

producers do not have the choice of utilizing the power themselves, but instead sell it all at a pre-determined rate.

After a good run in the 2000s—first at the state level, and then via the Obama stimulus—U.S. solar subsidies are now likely to decline for a few years. But regardless, a combination of private sector interest along with continued European and Chinese support means that PV prices will continue to fall. Path-dependence theory tells us that, if PV arrives later rather than sooner, in the interim we will continue to invest in long-lived infrastructure to support our fossil fuel economy. Thus attempts to maximize environmental benefits through a transition to PV will become more difficult. The "who" question is also important from an economic point of view. Industry follows the money, and so we should expect to see faster growth in Europe and Asia than in the United States through 2015. Photovoltaic power is so attractive that, in the long run, it is likely to be developed by private industry regardless of U.S. government policy.

To summarize this subsection: CT-promoting subsidies need to be carefully tailored. Consumer subsidies need to minimize pitfalls such as equity problems, strategic behavior, rebound effects, and free riding. Subsidies targeted at large-scale technologies should strike an appropriate balance between R&D and market building.

At the end of the day, clean energy alternatives ranging from energy efficiency to solar PVs hold out the promise of a low-cost replacement for fossil fuels in the generation of heat and power—in the process, reducing problems of urban air pollution, destruction of upstream habitat, and global warming. Smart government policy can help explore how real those promises are. However, electric power production and heat are only one part of the bigger energy picture.

18.3 Technology Options: Transport

Our transportation system relies almost exclusively on oil and accounts for the bulk of petroleum use. The United States currently consumes about 17 million barrels of oil (about 3 gallons per person) per day, about 40% imported. Close to 30% of U.S. imports come from the Persian Gulf. The Organization of Petroleum-Exporting Countries (OPEC), whose members are primarily Middle Eastern nations, control three quarters of the world's proven oil reserves.

The social costs of oil use fall into three categories: (1) taxpayer subsidies (discussed in Section 18.2), (2) environmental externalities, and (3) energy security. In developed countries, motor vehicles are a major source of urban air pollution, accounting for half of the nitrogen oxide (NOx) and volatile organic compound (VOC) emissions, and nearly two-thirds of the carbon monoxide (CO) emissions. (Recall from Chapter 13 that nitrogen oxide causes airborne acid pollution and, in combination with VOCs, ground-level ozone. CO reduces the oxygen content of the blood.) While autos contribute to local pollution problems, they are also a major source of carbon dioxide, the principal greenhouse gas. Worldwide transportation accounts for 14% of CO_2 emissions from fossil fuels, and this figure rises to around 35% in the United States.[18]

---

18. For the current data, see U.S. Energy Administration Monthly Energy Review, "Carbon Dioxide Emissions from Energy Consumption," http://www.eia.gov/totalenergy/data/monthly/#environment.

The **energy security** issue arises from the impact that dramatic oil price swings have had on the U.S. economy over the last 30 years. Oil price shocks, the latest from the period of heavy, sustained Chinese and Indian demand that first peaked in 2008, have been associated with and have deepened our last four economic recessions. In addition, such price shocks substantially boost inflation. Estimates of the economic costs of dependence on oil have ranged from $1 to $20 a barrel. Related to the energy security issue is the fact that high U.S. demand (about 25% of world consumption) for oil props up the price. As a result of our major presence in the market, we have what economists call **monopsony power** over the price; a unilateral cut in U.S. demand would lower oil prices around the world.

The major technology options for replacing oil can be divided into two categories. The first includes those options compatible with continued reliance on private auto transportation: increased fuel efficiency and switching to cleaner fuels, especially electricity. The second involves a switch to alternative transportation modes: urban mass transit, intercity and long-haul rail, carpooling, and bicycling and walking.

FUEL EFFICIENCY

Of all the options, increased fuel efficiency comes closest to being a simple clean technology as defined in Chapter 17. In the late 1990s, Japanese automakers began to introduce the so-called hybrid vehicles. Hybrids run on batteries in the city, and on gasoline engines on the highway. The batteries recharge while the vehicles are running on gas, so there is no need to plug in the car at night. These vehicles get between 40 and 70 mpg, twice the fuel efficiency of conventional vehicles. Do they save the consumer money? In 2001, I (Eban) bought a Toyota Prius for about $2,000 more than a comparable conventional vehicle would have cost. The Prius had about a 15-mpg advantage. With gas at $3.50 a gallon, the Prius saves me around $450 a year—meaning it took about five years to pay off the $2,000 premium, and begin realizing net savings.

General Motors took the next leadership step, introducing the Chevy Volt in 2011, the first plug-in hybrid. The idea behind a plug-in hybrid is that the owner charges the vehicle's battery from the electricity grid at night, so that in the morning, he or she will have the ability to drive, say, 30 miles on the charge. As with current hybrids, should the battery run out, then the vehicle operates off of an efficient backup gasoline motor, which also serves to recharge the battery. Because many drivers often travel fewer than 30 miles in a day, the vehicles will use no gas at all on those days. But isn't this just a leakage problem? Aren't reductions in gasoline use being offset by increases in coal combustion to produce electricity? Not necessarily. The beauty of plug-in hybrids is that many coal-fired (and all nuclear) power plants do not power down at night, and the electricity they produce is simply wasted. So little additional pollution is generated when the cars plug in at night. Overall, plug-ins are estimated to cut global-warming pollution in half, relative to a conventional compact car, and by more than 30% relative to a nonplug-in hybrid. Plug-in's could even act as grid storage devices. Owners could sell battery-stored power back to the grid at times of high demand.[19]

19. Markel (2006).

Beyond plug-in hybrids, more radical efficiency gains are imaginable; Amory Lovins of the Rocky Mountain Institute has been an advocate of ultralight, aerodynamic vehicles he calls "hypercars." He argues that complete redesign and re-engineering—rather than the marginal modifications now pursued by automakers—could boost fuel efficiency by a factor of 10 without compromising safety or performance.[20]

Safety and performance have indeed been the major concerns raised about fuel-efficient cars. One way to achieve better fuel performance is through "downsizing"—building smaller, lighter cars. However, in the past, lighter cars have proven less safe in a collision with a heavier vehicle. Based on these factors, a National Academy of Sciences panel concluded (with some dissent) that the fleet downsizing between 1975 and 1990 led to an increase of perhaps 2,000 traffic fatalities per year in the early 1990s.

Critics have charged that this is a substantial overestimate, as it fails to take into account that smaller cars pose less danger to others, as well as that the disparities between car sizes—another factor in accidents—shrank as the fleet downsized through 1990. (Of course, disparities grew dramatically again in the 1990s with the SUV fad; and SUVs themselves face safety concerns relating to rollovers.) Moreover, small cars have become safer in recent years, as engineers have focused increasing attention on crash problems and new, high-strength, lightweight materials have been developed. The true impact on safety of increased fuel performance could, in fact, be zero. Nevertheless, to the extent that fuel efficiency is achieved through downsizing, there is likely to be some safety impact.[21] In addition, American consumers have a taste for many energy-intensive features: large size, four-wheel drive, and rapid acceleration. Increased fuel efficiency may require giving some of this back.

In addition to safety and performance concerns associated with improved fuel economy, in the long run, increased fuel efficiency can be swamped by increases in "population" and "affluence" (P&A vs. T in the IPAT equation!). Total vehicle miles traveled increased at a rapid rate of 3.3% per year between 1990 and 2000; this rate was much faster than population growth. The average American car now travels over 12,000 miles a year, up from 10,000 in 1970. Total miles rose even faster as the number of cars per person increased from less than 0.50 to more than 0.65 (the average American household now has more cars than drivers) and population also increased. Interesting, vehicle miles travelled growth declined in the 2000s, and stopped growing from 2008–2012. Population growth, however, continues to fuel increased car ownership and oil consumption.[22]

There is also the possibility of a rebound effect—better fuel efficiency leading to cash savings, some of which will be spent on increased driving. Estimates of the rebound effect in auto transport are in the 10% range. Finally, until 2008, American drivers were shifting from cars to light trucks and SUVs, which got much poorer mileage. As a result of all these factors, during the period in which the fuel efficiency of the *auto* fleet increased by about one-third—1970 to 1988—total U.S. fuel consumption by cars, trucks, and buses still grew by 40%. And since then, with the shift to SUVs and

20. Lovins (1995).
21. National Academy of Sciences (2002).
22. U.S. Department of Transportation, Federal Highway Administration, http://www.fhwa.dot.gov/ohim/tvtw/tvtpage.cfm.

light trucks, the average efficiency of the fleet has actually declined. With the recent tightening of fuel economy standards, discussed later, expect this trend to reverse.[23]

FUEL SWITCHING

The second technology option in the transport sector is to run vehicles (cars, trucks, and airplanes) on fuels other than petroleum. The three main contenders are biofuels, electric batteries, and hydrogen fuel cells. **Biofuels** are fuels derived from vegetable matter. Biofuels in commercial use today include ethanol (primarily from corn, about 2% of the market) and biodiesel (primarily from soybeans, still much less than 1% of the market). It is also possible to convert diesel cars to run on straight vegetable oil, including used fry oil, but there is not a lot of that to go around!

Biofuels are typically cleaner in terms of conventional urban air pollutants, although not always. In its comparison of the emissions of vehicles that can run on either 85% ethanol or straight gasoline, the EPA judged the ethanol option to have roughly half the pollution impact.[24] However, recent concern has surfaced that ethanol vaporizes more easily than gas, contributing to smog problems. And both ethanol and biodiesel can have somewhat higher emissions of nitrogen oxides than does petroleum fuel. On the global-warming front, biofuels do emit carbon dioxide when burned. However, the next year's crop pulls that carbon back out of the atmosphere, so over their life cycle, biofuels have the potential to reduce global warming pollution substantially.

Biofuels face several obstacles to large-scale adoption. First, fuels from agricultural crops are still often more expensive than conventional gas or diesel—though the price gap shrinks, and in places disappears, when gas is around $3 per gallon. More significantly, crop supplies that can be devoted to fuel production are limited. Ethanol from corn could displace only 6% of the U.S. gasoline market before corn costs would start to rise. Concerns about this kind of "food versus fuel" conflict emerged during the biofuel boom of the first half of the 2000s, before the industry crashed along with oil prices in 2009. Thus serious commercialization of biofuels requires R&D to drive down the cost of ethanol and biodiesel produced from non-food-crop sources. The target feedstock for ethanol is cellulose—the woody material found in the leaves and stems of plants. Department of Energy analysts believe that the United States has sufficient surplus acreage to grow enough perennial crops like switchgrass to eventually supply more than 50% of today's U.S. petroleum needs. If at the same time, biodiesel could be economically distilled from algae grown in animal waste ponds, biofuels could clearly supply a large percentage of the nation's transport fuel.[25]

A second fuel-switching option is to use electricity in battery-powered cars. In fact, when plug-in hybrids, like the Volt, run mostly on electricity, then they really represent a fuel-switching option as much as a fuel-efficiency option. A precondition for **electric vehicles** to make global environmental sense is the development of clean electricity. Otherwise, use of electric vehicles will result in little overall reduction in pollutants. However, because they have essentially zero on-site emissions, cars powered

---

23. Center for Sustainable Systems (2006).
24. See www.fueleconomy.gov/feg/byfueltype.htm.
25. Mazza and Heitz (2006).

by batteries charged from coal or nuclear plants do improve urban air quality. In effect, the air pollution is exported from the city to the vicinity of the electricity-generating facility. That said, there is concern that the use of lead-based batteries will generate environmental problems.

Estimates of the potential cost-competitiveness of battery-powered cars range widely. Chevy's Volt and the all-electric Nissan Leaf cost substantially more than comparable conventional vehicles, and will be slow to pay for themselves. As production scales, costs will fall, but it is hard to judge how long it will be for electric vehicles to be truly cost-competitive.

The final alternative to the internal combustion engine is the **hydrogen fuel cell**. You may remember from a high school physics experiment that if you run electricity through water, it splits the molecules into hydrogen and oxygen. Fuel cells do the reverse. They combine hydrogen and oxygen in the presence of a catalyst to produce electricity; the only immediate by-product is water vapor!

In the short term, fuel-cell vehicles will be powered either by liquid fuels (gasoline or ethanol derived from biomass) or by natural gas. These fuels will be converted onboard into hydrogen. In the longer run, car tanks are likely to get filled up directly with hydrogen gas. This may sound dangerous, but because hydrogen vents quickly, in the event of a crash, hydrogen vehicles will be less likely to explode than gasoline-powered ones. If the hydrogen gas were to be produced using renewable energy (electric current from wind, solar, or biomass run through water), fossil fuel combustion and pollution would be eliminated completely from the transport sector.

Fuel cells are used in a few metropolitan bus systems and to produce electricity in some boutique applications. They are currently too expensive for private vehicles. However, all the major auto companies are pursuing fuel-cell research. Cars with fuel cells are currently available in limited commercial release, but the vehicles remain quite expensive.

To summarize this section, and previewing the next: Strategy 1 for reducing the environmental impact of vehicles is to change what is under the hood. Strategy 2 is to get some of these vehicles off the road.

MODE SWITCHING

Urban mass transit—rail or bus—has considerable environmental advantages over private transport. First, because these options are more energy-efficient, they reduce both local and global air pollution problems. For example, a busload of 40 commuters on a 10-mile trip to work emits 1,140 pounds less carbon dioxide than if the commuters had driven their cars to work. In addition to increased efficiency for a given passenger mile traveled, mass transit helps slow the growth in total miles traveled. With good transit, even when people use their cars, they travel shorter distances, because the greater residential and retail densities that develop along with the mass transit system reduce the need for auto travel.

America's high reliance on private auto transport clearly illustrates the importance of **path dependence** in technological development, discussed in Chapter 17. Some cities depend heavily on cars while others have well-developed transit. Toronto has North America's best public transportation system, in part because of a decision not to invest in a freeway infrastructure; the Toronto city government has also kept mass transit a viable long-run option through zoning laws that encourage relatively dense residential neighborhoods, as well as business development, in the area of mass transit stations.[26]

However, the dominance of private auto transport is not based solely on accidents of history or on public-policy measures. Cars clearly have an edge in convenience and greater mobility. Thus, as incomes have risen in both developed and developing countries, people have tended to opt for auto travel. The decline of mass transit has occurred even though in the United States, private transport—including vehicle purchase, finance charges, insurance, and fuel—costs the average commuter about twice as much as using public transport.[27]

The suburban sprawl that now characterizes most American cities means that private transport is a virtual necessity for shopping, getting to work and school, and recreation. In addition, many residents of developed countries have shown an evident preference for auto travel. Thus any rapid switch to mass transit will be difficult. Nevertheless, given the potential environmental benefits from mass transit—greater efficiency and reduced passenger miles traveled—a gradual transition to this mode could be promoted where economically feasible.

A more attractive short-run form of mode switching may involve interurban travel; roughly one-third of air travel involves trips of fewer than 600 miles. **High-speed rail** is a potentially attractive alternative for this market in terms of convenience and cost. From an environmental perspective, rail uses substantially less energy than does air travel.[28]

18.4 Policy Options: Transport

The social case against petroleum-based transportation by land, sea, and air is becoming stronger: mounting global warming, urban air pollution, habitat destruction, and energy security. The CT framework developed in Chapter 17 suggests two steps to promote clean alternatives. First, level the playing field by internalizing externalities; second, directly promote clean alternatives.

POLICY OPTIONS FOR FUEL EFFICIENCY AND FUEL SWITCHING

Fuel efficiency clearly qualifies as a CT. Under a variety of scenarios, achieving greater fuel efficiency standards passes a benefit-cost test. The National Academy of Sciences concluded that, using known technologies, fuel economy could be raised substantially over a decade at no net cost to consumers. SUV mileage, for example, could be improved by 25–40%, and the increased vehicle costs are more than offset by the (discounted) fuel savings. Moreover, the Academy agreed that these improvements could be achieved with no compromise in safety or performance. Taking into account the external benefits from both reduced greenhouse gas emissions and increased oil security, the committee recommended that "the federal government [take action] to ensure fuel economy levels beyond those expected to result from market forces alone."[29]

26. Friskin (1991).
27. Friskin (1991).
28. Chester and Horvath (2010).
29. National Academy of Sciences (2002, 5).

The best way to achieve greater fuel efficiency would be through an incentive-based approach; raising the cost of petroleum products (or emissions) would simultaneously drive the market toward more fuel-efficient choices and encourage the prospects for alternative fuels. Several types of emissions-related fees might be considered: gas taxes, "feebates," emission taxes, and the adoption of pay-by-the-mile auto insurance. Gas taxes have the advantage of both forcing fuel efficiency improvements and attacking the growth in vehicle miles.

However, gas taxes would have to be fairly high to force efficiency improvements of 10 mpg—a 30–35% increase over the current average of 28 mpg. As casual evidence, European cars are not much more efficient than American cars of a similar size, though gas prices are at least double and in some cases are four times as high. The elasticity of fuel usage with respect to gasoline price is about 0.21, meaning that a 1% increase in price leads to a 0.21% increase in fuel economy. This suggests that prices would have to rise from $3.50 per gallon to $5.00 per gallon to achieve only a 10% increase in miles per gallon.

Several other fee-based approaches to encourage fuel efficiency and switching have been proposed. One interesting possibility is an **auto emissions tax**. When cars go in for their annual inspection, owners could be required to pay a tax based on their total emissions: the product of emissions per mile and yearly mileage. This would have the effect both of encouraging cleaner fuels (based on market criteria) and reducing miles driven. The tax could be tailored to suit regional needs.

Another widely discussed possibility has earned the nickname **feebates**. Feebates combine a fee on gas-guzzling cars with a rebate on fuel-efficient cars. A feebate policy would thus be revenue-neutral in an obvious way, have the politically attractive feature of punishing evildoers and rewarding the good, and probably not be regressive, as poor folks would opt for the subsidy. Feebates appear to be a better alternative to high gas taxes for encouraging a market-driven shift to fuel efficiency. However, by lowering the cost of fuel-efficient automobiles, feebates might increase the growth in vehicle miles.

A final suggestion has been reforming auto insurance so as to provide a **pay-by-the-mile** option. Auto insurance is quite expensive but is currently paid in a lump sum. Yet this unfairly penalizes drivers who are on the road less frequently. If accident rates correlate with miles driven, then people who drive less should have lower payments. Billing could be based on odometer checks or electronic monitoring of miles driven. Converting an annual insurance bill to a per-mile basis works out to an equivalent charge of about $1.50 per gallon of gas—certainly a big enough charge to affect people's driving habits! One study estimates that this would reduce miles traveled by 10–20% and suggests that a very small tax credit of $100 per year would be sufficient to start a stampede in the direction of pay-by-the-mile insurance on the part of low-mileage drivers.[30]

All of these policies—higher gas taxes, feebates, emission taxes, and pay-by-the-mile insurance—would also help promote a switch to cleaner cars: hybrid, electric, and fuel-cell vehicles. However, none of these policies is currently in widespread use. In the absence of these incentive-based approaches, the federal government, and in recent years the state of California, have instead relied on technology-forcing

---

30. Baker and Barret (2000).

regulation to increase fuel efficiency. (Recall that a technology-forcing regulation mandates that industry deliver technology meeting some environmental standard by some future date.)

The federal technology-forcing tool for fuel efficiency is the CAFE **(Corporate Average Fuel Economy) standard**, discussed in Chapter 17. However, until spring 2009, CAFE standards had not been substantially tightened since 1978! With federal policy sidelined, California stepped in with two initiatives—one in the 1990s and another in the mid-2000s. Under the Clean Air Act, California is unique among the states in its ability to set air quality standards that are more stringent than the federal standards. Other states can then either follow California's lead or stick with the federal regulations.

In the mid-1990s, concerned about smog, the state instituted a **zero-emissions vehicle (ZEV)** requirement that 10% of all vehicles sold in 2003 in the state must have "zero" (later modified to include "ultra-low") emissions. This means that a car company selling in California must not only produce a qualifying vehicle but also price it low enough to satisfy the 10% requirement. Massachusetts and New York introduced similar policies. The California requirement, combined with growing concerns about global warming, sparked a research race among car companies. The first commercial fruits of this effort were the Japanese hybrids that hit the market in the early 2000s.

California struck again in 2003 with its **Clean Car** law mandating that, beginning in model year 2009, car companies had to begin reducing emissions of global-warming gases—primarily carbon dioxide—so that by model year 2016, a 30% reduction in the fleetwide average would be achieved. Most of the emission reductions in California are projected to come from improvements in fuel efficiency. Therefore, the California mandate is likely to save consumers money! Higher up-front vehicle costs are likely to be more than offset by fuel savings. Several other states, as well as Canada, adopted California-style regulations, And then in 2009, President Obama stepped in with a national mandate. The administration updated the CAFE standards (see Chapter 17), essentially duplicating the California requirements nationwide.[31] Nationally, fleetwide averages are required to rise to 34.1 mpg by 2016 and 54.5 mpg by 2025.

Relative to an incentive-based approach like a gas tax, the problem with CAFE or California's Clean Car mandates is the potential for a rebound effect: by reducing customers' gas bills, vehicle miles may increase. And technology forcing of this kind does little to promote alternative fuels. Nevertheless, technology forcing regulations like CAFE can be a powerful tool for driving R&D and investment in clean technology. Indeed, for fuel switching, all of the major options—biofuels, electric vehicles, and hydrogen fuel cells—remain at a stage where they require R&D expenditures to bring down costs. One study suggests that cellulosic ethanol could achieve the scale economies needed for competitive pricing with expenditures of about $200 million per year for 10 years—about the cost of two to three days of U.S. oil imports.[32]

POLICY OPTIONS FOR MODE SWITCHING

Mass transit is often viewed as a highly subsidized, noncompetitive option vis-à-vis private transport. Indeed, transit does receive substantial government subsidies,

---

31. CARB (2005).
32. Mazza and Heitz (2006).

typically 30–80% of fares.[33] Less often recognized is that private auto transport also receives public subsidies that can rival those of transit systems. These include expenses for roadway construction and maintenance (not covered by gas taxes), police and emergency services, the costs of accidents (not covered by auto insurance), congestion costs, and the costs of pollution. One study puts the annual cost from these categories at $1.76 per gallon of gasoline consumed, roughly $800 per year per car. This figure does not include tax subsidies for parking construction, the energy security costs of oil dependence, and military expenditures to defend Persian Gulf oil transport.[34] Subsidies for private auto transport thus range upward from around 20% of the total private costs of operation.

As noted earlier, the primary advantage of transit is the way that it "naturally" reshapes urban and suburban densities. With denser living patterns, transit does much more than simply replace auto trips in and out of the city. It also substantially reduces vehicle transport for shopping and entertainment. At the same time, cities dominated by urban and suburban sprawl have a hard time providing competitive mass transit. Thus, **zoning laws** are needed to lay the groundwork for a successful transit or bicycle system.

Most economists have focused on promoting mode switching by removing subsidies for private transport (e.g., tax-free and employer-provided parking) and internalizing externalities, particularly those associated with congestion. Congestion generates a variety of problems: wasted commuting time, increases in vehicle operating costs, pollution and accident rates, lowered productivity through worker fatigue and stress, and slowed delivery of products. While most of these costs are borne by vehicle travelers as a group, the commuting decision is a classic open-access problem (discussed in Chapter 3). The individual commuter may recognize that, by taking her car to work, she will slow down average traffic by 15 seconds. This is a small amount of time to her and a cost she is willing to bear. But 15 seconds times several thousand commuters quickly adds up to large social costs. With each commuter viewing the problem in the same way, the result is a "tragedy of the commons" quite similar to an overfished ocean.

With the highways being common property, some kind of rationing system is necessary. One rationing system is price: many economists have advocated toll systems to internalize congestion externalities. These systems can be quite sophisticated, using sensors in the roadbed to monitor passing traffic equipped with electronic identification, and generating monthly bills. One way to attack congestion is **congestion** or **peak-load pricing**: charging higher tolls for travel during congested hours. However, this may have the effect of shifting work habits and commuting times without reducing overall vehicle use. While this may be useful for reducing certain urban air pollutants, it would not have much impact on greenhouse gases. Congestion pricing would tend also to be regressive unless the funds raised were used to compensate for this problem.

A non-price-rationing scheme involves **dedicated traffic lanes**. These lanes are reserved for (or dedicated to) buses and multi-occupant vehicles and effectively lower the price of carpooling or bus travel. To those interested in mode switching, dedicated lanes offer a carrot that could be combined with the stick of congestion pricing and

33. Parry and Small (2009).
34. Parry and Ian (2002).

higher parking fees. In addition, because poorer people tend to take the bus, the overall income impact of dedicated lanes would be progressive.

Of course, any serious effort to promote mode switching would require large-scale **infrastructure investment** in urban light rail and intercity high-speed rail.

18.5 Slowing Global Warming at a Profit?

Having provided a review of energy technology choices and policy options, we can now return to an important question posed in the introduction to this book: How much will it cost to slow down and eventually halt global warming? Recall that estimates ranged from a high of tens of billions of dollars per year in costs to possible net profits for the economy from increased efficiency.

Progressive economists see the government moving in a rational manner to implement cost-effective demand-side measures while funding R&D in renewable energy sources to bring their costs down to a level competitive with coal and gasoline by the second decade of the 21st century. Optimists are not overly concerned about government failure due to the existence of very obvious "low-hanging fruit," especially in the heat and electricity field and hybrid-electric or biofuel-powered vehicles for transport. Because they see these governmental demand and supply-side efforts as ultimately delivering energy services at lower cost than the technologies in use today, global warming can actually be reduced at low cost, or even yield a net economic benefit.

Conservative economists, on the other hand, do not believe that government efforts to promote renewable energy and energy efficiency will be very successful. First, they fear that technology-forcing standards (like the CAFE) will generate self-defeating problems, such as new source bias, that poorly thought-out design standards will retard rather than promote technological change, or that money will simply be wasted by bureaucrats promoting cost-ineffective measures. Second, government must bear the real marketing costs necessary to speed up the slow diffusion of energy-efficient technologies, reducing the net savings. Third, they argue that easy efficiency measures will soon be exhausted, meaning that even a successful, short-term government effort to promote efficiency cannot be sustained. Finally, pessimists tend to feel that renewable energy options do not have the dramatic economic promise that optimists claim.

Despite their disagreements, however, economists largely agree on one point: First, there should be an increased commitment of government R&D funds to non-carbon-based and renewable energy sources. The earlier that cost-competitive technology alternatives become available, the lower will be the cost of reducing greenhouse gases. As we noted in Chapter 6, early cost savings become especially important over time because they free up capital for investment, which raises future productivity.

Beyond R&D funding, however, there is disagreement over whether government should make efforts to promote clean energy sources. However, again most economists feel that if it does so, to the extent possible such efforts should rely on an incentive-based approach. Where possible, government should not try to sort out whether photovoltaic-powered electric vehicles or biomass-based ethanol fuels will be a cheaper, greenhouse-friendly transportation option and then develop and implement a promotional strategy; the better approach is simply to impose a non-regressive carbon price on all energy sources and then let the issue be decided in the market. However, as we have stated repeatedly, taxes (or tradeable permit systems) are not always politically feasible or easy to implement at the level needed to drive change. Thus a role will remain for direct promotion of clean technologies in attacking the global-warming problem.

This section ends with a history lesson suggesting two things. First, a more or less optimistic outcome to the global-warming problem is achievable. Second, major pitfalls need to be avoided along the way.

The late 1970s marked the first serious debates about energy policy in the United States. Following OPEC's oil price increases, the U.S. Congress became concerned about energy security. It took three principal measures: (1) funding substantial R&D in renewable technologies, (2) instituting a 15% tax credit for energy investments, and (3) requiring public utilities to purchase any power produced by qualifying independent facilities at the utility's "avoided" or marginal cost of production.

The state of California took the most aggressive stance toward developing alternative energy sources, instituting its own 25% energy investment tax credit and a property tax exemption for solar facilities, and requiring utilities to provide ten-year, avoided-cost contracts to independent power producers. These contracts were based on the high energy prices of the early 1980s. At the time, they appeared to shield ratepayers from further fuel increases; in retrospect, they protected alternative energy producers from the dramatic decline in oil prices.

This attractive environment fueled a rush of investors, some looking only for lucrative tax shelters. In fact, at the height of California's efforts to promote alternative energy, investors were guaranteed a return on their investment *through the tax benefits alone*. The federal credit required only that the project be in service (even limited service) for five years, while the California tax credits could not be recovered by the government if the project failed to generate any power after its first year.

Into this environment, a variety of technology and design options were introduced, most of dubious value, and most failed. Many of the better ideas, however, were based on work that had begun under the federal R&D programs. Eventually, two success stories emerged: wind and solar thermal electricity. Figure 18.3 illustrates the dramatic progress made in reducing costs for these two technologies over a 15-year period. Solar thermal is now close to competitive; wind power has achieved this goal, at good locations, selling at an unsubsidized price of less than $0.05 per kWh.

There is little doubt that, without aggressive governmental action in the early 1980s, wind and solar thermal electricity today would not be commercial options for producing power. Both industries were highly concentrated in California. The world's first solar thermal power was produced in the state, and California led the world in wind technology: in 1990, it produced about 80% of the world's wind power. Denmark, with strong governmental support, has since captured that technology leadership role. Spain, meanwhile, has taken the lead in solar thermal installation; the world's biggest solar thermal plant, now being built in Arizona, is using Spanish technology. Nevertheless, California today still has more than enough wind capacity to meet the needs of the city of San Francisco.

The optimistic moral of this story is that government policy can be quite effective in promoting clean technology. The pessimistic moral is that it can spend much more money than necessary to do so. The R&D and tax credit policies of the late 1970s

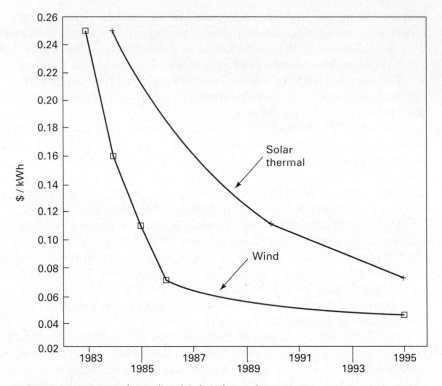

FIGURE 18.3 Costs of Wind and Solar Thermal
Source: Data for this figure are mid-range estimates in Williams. 1990. low-cost strategies for coping with CO_2 emission limits. *The Energy Journal* 11(2): 51–74. Wind figures for 1995 are estimated. The solar thermal estimated for 1995 is from SEG X, which has now been canceled, and the 1995 estimate includes a portion of natural gas-fired power. See A bright light goes out. 1990. *Nature*, 5 December, 345.

were untargeted and poorly designed. Spurred on by fears of high oil prices, as well as unrealistic promises from the supporters of renewable energy, the programs set out to secure new sources of energy soon at any price. As a result, a lot of money went for uneconomic demonstration projects and into the hands of tax farmers rather than wind farmers.

Yet, as a result of these programs, we now have two competitive, clean technologies on the shelf to address pollution control. To put a last optimistic spin on the story: if a shotgun approach to technology promotion like that applied in the 1970s nevertheless yielded competitive, clean options within two decades, a more focused approach can probably achieve similar results at lower cost.

18.6 Summary

The last four chapters have examined the question "How can we do better?" in protecting the quality of our environment, where doing better has been defined as achieving a given level of pollution reduction at lower cost and with greater certainty.

We have explored two ideas: incentive-based regulation and clean technology promotion. We have argued first that IB regulation, where technically and politically feasible, provides more cost-effective pollution control and better incentives for technological change than does the dominant command-and-control system.

However, we have also seen that the regulatory process itself—whether CAC or IB—can be challenging to implement effectively. Moreover, climate stabilization policies—if they are to be effective—demand a rapid transition to cleaner technologies, not end-of-the-pipe fixes. As a result, recent economic attention has been focused on policies designed to promote technologies that reduce pollution in the first place. Path dependence theory suggests that government can and should use selective subsidies tied to cost reductions as a cost-effective complement to regulation. By tying subsidies to performance, a means is provided to avoid government failure in promoting clean technology.

The next section of the book turns to global problems. An optimistic view of the world sees rapid economic development in poor countries based on clean technologies, leading to a stabilization in the world population as living standards rise and birth rates fall. But even under this scenario, the global population will increase by close to half, to close to 10 billion, before it stabilizes. Can the global ecosystem survive this impact? Clearly, the rapid development of clean technology is a prerequisite to a sustainable future. My own view is that without cheap, readily available solar and wind energy, it will be difficult for poor countries to achieve rapid enough economic growth to stabilize population growth without imposing high environmental costs in the process—and in particular, pushing the globe toward a very dangerous, high-end warming. In my mind, *the most important task for environmental economists* is to help design and implement policies to speed up the diffusion of clean technologies.

APPLICATION 18.0

Promoting Electricity Conservation

Suppose that you are in charge of the demand-side management program at Megabucks Power, and your state public utility commission has just decided that you can now count energy-efficiency measures as equivalent to investments in new generating capacity. This means you can recover efficiency investment costs plus a normal profit through higher electric rates for your customers.

You have the following information at your fingertips: Megabucks currently produces 1 billion kWh and anticipates needing another 100 million next year to service new residences. You are currently charging $0.05 per kWh; new generating capacity (a coal plant) would come in at $0.06 per kWh. Buying the coal plant would mean Megabucks could sell 1.1 billion kWh for an average price of $0.0509 per kWh [$0.0509 per kWh = (1 b kWh * $0.05 per kWh + 0.1 b kWh * $0.06 per kWh)/1.1 b kWh].

Fortunately, there is a CT at hand. It is possible to *reduce demand* by 100 million kWh through a program that weatherizes one-quarter of the (identical) houses in your service area. Best of all, weatherization can be obtained at a cost of only $0.03 per kWh or an overall investment of $3 million [$3 m = 0.1 b kWh * 0.03 per kWh].

Your challenge: Which of your customers pays for the $3 million program? Your assistant, Mr. Offthecuff, has a plan. "Let's select one-quarter of the houses at random and provide the weatherization service for free. We can recover the costs by raising electricity rates for everybody. Overall, our customers will be better off as collectively they will save $3 million" [($0.06 − $0.03) per kWh ∗ 0.1 b kWh].

Good idea?

KEY IDEAS IN EACH SECTION

18.0   This chapter looks at technology options and government energy policy in the areas of electric generation and transport. The energy path that the United States follows over the next few decades will depend on the interaction of technology, economics, and government policy.

18.1   Technology options for electricity (and heat) break down into eight main categories. (1) **Demand-side management (DSM)** (**energy efficiency**) has substantial cost-effective savings potential. (2) Coal is the dominant U.S. power plant fuel, but it is also the heaviest global-warming polluter; carbon dioxide capture and underground **sequestration** may provide a solution to this problem. Coal emissions can also be reduced through **biomass** co-firing. (3) **Nuclear power** faces unresolved **high- and low-level waste** storage issues, as well as widespread political opposition. (4) **Natural gas** is the most greenhouse-friendly fossil fuel but has a somewhat limited supply. (5) **Hydroelectric** supply can be expanded, but at a cost to flooded ecosystems. (6) **Solar power** can be divided into **passive** and **active** categories, with the latter including **photovoltaics** and **solar thermal**. (7) **Wind** is a very attractive candidate, while (8) **geothermal** also has considerable potential as a baseload power source. Wind and solar will require improved means of **electricity storage**.

18.2   Based on environmental advantage and cost-effectiveness, clean technology candidates for electric power generation include efficiency, wind power, and solar power. Two steps to promote these CTs are (1) level the playing field by reducing subsidies for "dirty" technologies and/or internalizing externalities through IB regulation and (2) invest in the new technologies directly. For PVs, **feed-in-tariffs** and **purchase-power-agreements** have been important policy drivers. Subsidies need to be designed to deal with **equity issues**, **strategic behavior**, **free riding**, **and rebound effects**, and the right mix between R&D and market development. Two attractive policies that can align these incentives for residential and commercial energy efficiency and solar are **on-bill-recovery** and **PACE financing**.

18.3   Technology options for transport break down into three categories. (1) On net, **fuel efficiency** appears to be relatively cheap. In particular, **hybrid vehicles** including plug-in hybrids hold great promise for cost-effective improvements. Economic benefits include increased **energy security** and lower oil prices through the **monopsony effect**. Costs include possibly reduced performance and safety. (2) **Fuel-switching** options include **biofuels**, hydrogen **fuel cells**, and **electric vehicles**. In the medium term, fuel cells will be powered by gasoline, or biomass-derived ethanol, or natural gas. Electric vehicles remain limited by range. (3) **Mode switching**, from autos to mass transit, yields as a significant benefit an **increase in residential density**, reducing the **growth in vehicle miles traveled. High-speed rail** is a CT alternative to short-haul air travel.

18.4 Fuel efficiency appears to be a CT under our definition. Incentive-based tools to promote efficiency would include **gas taxes**, **feebates**, **emissions fees**, and insurance reforms promoting **pay-by-the-mile**. In the absence of these polices, Federal **CAFE standards** (late 1970s and late 2000s) and California's **ZEV** (mid-1990s) and **Clean Car** (mid-2000s) technology-forcing regulations are pushing fuel efficiency. R&D funding is required to promote a more fundamental switch to alternate fuels. Finally, in the area of mode switching, when subsidies to auto transport are considered, transit systems may be considered CTs, which would justify **infrastructure investment** and **zoning** supporting rail and buses. To encourage mode switching, tools such as **congestion (peak-load) pricing** and **dedicated traffic lanes** can be used.

18.5 Economists are divided in their evaluation of the costs of slowing global warming. Progressives and conservatives differ both on the existence of clean energy technology and the extent to which government can effectively promote it. At a minimum, however, an increased government commitment to R&D in non-carbon fuels, a reduction in subsidies for fossil fuels, and more effective IB regulation are agreed on. The development of solar thermal and wind power in California supports an optimistic view regarding a government energy policy and also illustrates the potential for government to waste available funds.

REFERENCES

Baker, Dean, and James Barret. 2000. Energy insurance. *The American Prospect* 11(17): 18–9.

Buntin, James. 2000. Breakdown lane. *The American Prospect* 11(17): 16–8.

California Air Resources Board (CARB), Sacramento. 2005. *Climate change emission control regulations, fact sheet.* www.arb.ca.gov/cc/factsheets/cc_newfs.pdf.

Center for Sustainable Systems. 2006. *Personal transportation fact sheet.* Ann Arbor: University of Michigan. http://css.snre.umich.edu/css_doc/CSS01-07.pdf.

Chester, Mikhail, and Horvath, Arpad. 2010. Life-cycle assessment of high-speed rail: The case of California. *Environmental Research Letters* 5: 014003.

Choi Granade, Hannah, Jon Creyts, Anton Derkach, Philip Farese, Scott Nyquist, and Ken Ostrowski. 2009. Unlocking energy efficiency in the US economy. McKinsey & Company. http://www.mckinsey.com/client_service/electric_power_and_natural_gas/latest_thinking/unlocking_energy_efficiency_in_the_us_economy.

Energy Information Administration. 2009. *Electric Power Monthly.* May.

Friskin, Francis. 1991. The contributions of metropolitan government to the success of Toronto's public transit system. *Urban Affairs Quarterly* 27(2): 227–48.

Ghandi, Sima. Eliminating Tax Subsidies for Oil Companies. 2010. Center for American Progress, 13 May. http://www.americanprogress.org/issues/2010/05/oil_company_subsidies.html.

How Japan became so energy efficient: It leaned on industry. 1990. *Wall Street Journal*, 10 September, A1, A4.

Kanter, James. 2009. In Finland, nuclear renaissance runs into trouble. *New York Times*, 28 May. http://www.nytimes.com/2009/05/29/business/energy-environment/29nuke.html?pagewanted=all.

Koplow, Douglas. 2007. Subsidies in the U.S. energy sector: Magnitude, causes, and options for reform. In *Subsidy reform and sustainable development: Political economy aspects.* Paris: Organization for Economic Cooperation and Development.

Lacey, Stephen. 2012. Solar provides 10 percent of Germany's electricity in May. Climate Progress. http://thinkprogress.org/climate/2012/06/12/497984/solar-provides-10-of-germanys-electricity-in-may/.

Lovins, Amory. 1995. Hypercars: The next industrial revolution. In *Transportation and energy: Strategies for a sustainable transportation system*, ed. Daniel Sperling and Susan Shaheen. Washington, DC: American Council for an Energy Efficient Economy.

Markel, Tony. 2006. Plug-in hybrid electric vehicles: Current status, long-term prospects and key challenges, NREL/PR-540-40239. *National Renewable Energy Laboratory Presentation at Clean Cities Congress and Expo*, Phoenix, Arizona, 8 May.

Mazza, P., and E. Heitz. 2006. *The new harvest: Biofuels and windpower for rural revitalization and national energy security*. Olympia, WA: Climate Solutions.

MIT Panel. 2007. *The future of geothermal energy*. Idaho Falls: Idaho National Laboratory.

Mouwad, Jad. 2009. Estimate places natural gas reserves 35% higher. *New York Times*, 17 June. http://www.nytimes.com/2009/06/18/business/energy-environment/18gas.html?gwh=5EDCF07B14DDC559A886A5B87CFE5CBB.

National Academy of Sciences. 2002. *Effectiveness and impact of Corporate Average Fuel Economy (CAFE) standards*. Washington, DC: National Academy Press.

Ottinger, Richard L., et al. 1990. *Environmental costs of electricity*. New York: Oceana Publications.

Parry, Ian. 2002. Is gasoline undertaxed in the United States? *Resources* 28(148).

Parry, Ian, and Kenneth A. Small. 2009. Should urban transit subsidies be reduced? *The American Economic Review* 99(3): 700–24.

Romm, Joe. 2008. The technology that will save humanity. *Salon*, 14 April. http://www.salon.com/2008/04/14/solar_electric_thermal/.

Small, Kenneth A., and Kurt Van Dender. 2007. Fuel efficiency and motor vehicle travel: the declining rebound effect. *The Energy Journal, International Association for Energy Economics* (1): 25–52.

Wesoff, Eric. 2012. Largest solar PV plant in North America comes on-line. greentechmedia.4/26/2012. http://www.greentechmedia.com/articles/read/Largest-Solar-PV-Plant-in-North-America-Comes-On-Line/.

Zweibel, Ken. 1990. *Harnessing solar power: The photovoltaics challenge*. New York: Plenum Press.

HOW CAN WE SOLVE
GLOBAL CHALLENGES?

To this point, this book has focused primarily on environmental quality within a single wealthy country, the United States. We have explored the normative debate over the "right" level of pollution; considered political-economic realities that can constrain the effectiveness of government action to achieve these goals; and in the last four chapters, analyzed two broad approaches to "doing better"—incentive-based regulation and clean technology promotion. In this final part of the book, we extend the lessons learned to resolving issues of global environmental concern: global warming, ozone depletion, loss of species diversity, and management of the global commons—the ocean and Antarctica.

As one steps outside the national border of a developed country, two things are immediately apparent. First, we are an awesomely wealthy people. A personal example brought this home to me. When I was in Africa, my driver was admiring my work boots, and wanted to know what they cost. I admitted that the salary he earned in three months, and on which he supported his entire family, would barely be enough to buy them.

The second fact: As significant as our environmental problems are, they pale in comparison to those faced by people in poor countries. Hardship and suffering from water and air pollution, soil erosion and degradation, and deforestation and flooding are serious, dramatic, and widespread in the less developed world.

This part of the book explores the complex links between widespread poverty in poor countries (working in part through high population growth rates), high levels of consumption in rich countries, and environmental degradation at both the global level and in the less developed world. We also consider a variety of policies that governments in both rich and poor countries can take to reverse this environmental decline. Finally, we end with a look at the economics of global environmental agreements.

The stakes are high. By the year 2100, our grandchildren may be living on a planet supporting a stable population of 9 billion people, in an environmentally sustainable manner. On the other hand, our grandchildren may be sharing the globe with a population of 12 billion people (and rising), in a world where environmental life-support systems will surely be stressed beyond recovery. The ultimate outcome depends in large measure on the actions of those of us who have sometimes bought boots at $150 a pair.

CHAPTER 19

POVERTY, POPULATION, AND THE ENVIRONMENT

19.0 Introduction

In John Steinbeck's famous book *The Grapes of Wrath*, the main character Tom Joad returns to the family farm in Oklahoma during the dust bowl of the early 1930s to find his family evicted by the local land company, and their house abandoned. He asks his now-crazy neighbor, Muley, "What's the idear of kickin' folks off?" Muley replies:

> You know what kinda years we been havin'. Dust coming up and spoilin' ever'thing so a man didn't get enough crop to plug up an ant's ass.... An' the folks that owns the lan' says, "We can't afford to keep no tenants." An' they says, "The share a tenant gets is just the margin a profit we can't afford to lose." An' they says, "If we put all our land in one piece we can jus' hardly make her pay." So they tractored all the tenants off the lan'.[1]

Joad's family hits the road for California, the promised land, only to arrive midwinter with thousands of others, finding "no kinda work for three months," misery, and starvation. In the final scene of the book, one of the women, whose baby has just been born dead from malnourishment, breast-feeds a starving 50-year-old man.

Joad's story illustrates the process of economic development in a nutshell. The United States in the 1930s, 1940s, and 1950s saw a transition from small-scale, labor-intensive farming to highly mechanized, chemical-intensive, large-scale agriculture. In the process, with particular force during the great depression and dust-bowl times, tens of thousands of farmers were pushed off the land through evictions, as large landowners consolidated small plots of land into larger, technically more efficient units. From 1950 to 1990, the number of farm residents in the United States dropped from 23 million to 4.5 million. Many of these farmers were African Americans from the South, who subsequently migrated to industrial cities in the North and Midwest.

---

1. John Steinbeck, *The Grapes of Wrath* (New York: Viking Press, 1939), 64.

This **agrarian transition** away from an economy based on traditional small farming to one based on large-scale, market-oriented agriculture has to date been a universal feature of market-driven economic development. The **traditional economic development** challenge is to productively absorb the millions of workers—holding now-useless farming skills, often illiterate or semiliterate—who are "freed up" from agriculture. In the traditional model, increases in agricultural productivity keep food prices low, benefiting urban consumers. At the same time, surplus labor from the agricultural sector fuels growth in other areas, leading to a rise in general living standards and "successful development."

The worldwide depression of the 1930s, the backdrop for *The Grapes of Wrath*, made this a difficult task. In the United States, we were rather fortunate. For a period of about 30 years after the Depression ended, much of the displaced, unskilled agricultural labor was absorbed by the booming manufacturing economy of the 1950s and 1960s. But the tragic experience of Joad's family is unfortunately a common one in many developing countries. On the one hand, traditional agriculture has become less and less viable, in part because of government policies such as subsidized credit favoring large-scale agriculture. On the other hand, many (but not all) poor countries have been stuck in a virtual depression for the last three decades. Large-scale, capital-intensive agriculture has displaced tens of millions of Third-World farmers. These workers then either migrated onto less suitable, ecologically sensitive land, became landless agricultural laborers (often able to find "no kinda work" for many months), or else moved to urban shantytowns in search of jobs in the stagnant industrial or state sectors.

The central point of this chapter is that "solving" the economic development problem—providing productive work and income for displaced farmers and their children—is part and parcel of addressing local and global environmental concerns. **Sustainability**, defined in Chapter 8 as *preventing the deterioration* of average living standards for future generations, cannot be achieved unless poverty is directly addressed, because poverty and environmental degradation go hand in hand. Yet the environmental consequences of economic growth can no longer be ignored; overall living standards do not rise automatically with economic growth as conventionally defined.

The specter of rapid population growth hanging over this entire picture is intimately connected with desperately high rates of poverty. As we discuss later, poor people have rational economic reasons for preferring large families. A basic lesson is thus that providing cheap birth control—throwing condoms at the problem—is only one part of a successful strategy for reducing birth rates in developing countries. Providing health, education, and employment opportunities for the poor majority, especially for young women, and then coupling this with comprehensive family planning services must be part of an effective package for reducing population growth rates.

Beyond poverty and population, the environmental damage people do depends not only on our absolute numbers but also on the natural capital depleted and waste products generated by each person. The average person born in the United States, Europe, or Japan has a dramatically larger impact on the global environment than does a child from a poor country. Yesterday—spent driving my daughter to school, writing this book at my computer (with occasional trips to the refrigerator), taking the family out for a burger at dinnertime, and watching TV in my nice warm house—I arguably contributed more to global warming, ozone depletion, *and* tropical deforestation than a typical Brazilian would in a month or two. As an upper middle class American, I consume more than *100 times the resources* used by the average individual from a poor country.

This of course is just another way of restating the IPAT equation from Chapter 9. Total environmental damage can be decomposed into three parts: the number of people, consumption per capita, and the damage done by each unit of consumption. The "population" problem is indeed concentrated in poor countries; 90% of world population growth in the next century will occur in the developing world. However, through legal and illegal immigration, poor country population pressure spills over into affluent countries. For example, largely as a result of legal immigration, the U.S. population is expected to increase by 33% (to 403 million) by the year 2050.[2]

By contrast, the "consumption" problem is currently centered in the rich countries. This too has begun to change as a growing number of poor-country residents aspire to the consumption levels found in rich countries. The point here is not to make us feel guilty about our affluent lifestyle. Rather, we need to recognize that to address global environmental challenges, one needs to focus as much attention on reducing the environmental impact of high consumption in rich countries as reducing population growth in poor countries.

This chapter provides an overview of these complex and interrelated topics: poverty, rapid population growth in the South, overconsumption in the North, environmental degradation, and sustainable economic development.

19.1 Poverty and the Environment

In rich countries, it is commonly assumed that environmental quality can be improved only by sacrificing material consumption. Indeed, this is the whole premise behind benefit-cost analysis laid out in the first part of the book. In poor countries, by contrast, a broad-based growth in income will, in many respects, tend to improve the quality of the environment. This section discusses four of the close connections between poverty and the environment.

1.   For poor people, many environmental problems are problems of poverty. The biggest environmental health threat facing most people in poor countries is **unsafe drinking water**, compounded by **inadequate sewage** facilities. About 1 billion people are without access to improved water, and more than 2.6 billion are without adequate sanitation. Billions of illnesses and millions of deaths each year are attributed to water pollution.[3]

In developing countries, exposure to **indoor air pollution** (smoke) from cooking and heating sources in fact outweighs urban air pollution as a cause of premature death. Some half a billion people are exposed to unsafe levels of indoor smoke, and 1.6 million die each year from exposure. Another 800,000 die in developing countries from exposure to urban air pollution.[4]

---

2. UN 2008 estimates; see http://csa.un.org/unpp.
3. World Health Organization (2004).
4. World Bank (2008).

2.   Poor people cannot afford to conserve resources. Out of economic necessity, poor people often put an unsustainable burden on the natural capital in their immediate environment. Urban residents scour the immediate countryside for fuel—firewood or animal dung—and this leads to deforestation or the elimination of fertilizer sources. Landless farmers are pushed into overfarming small plots, farming on steep mountain slopes that soon wash out, or farming in clear-cut rain forests incapable of sustaining agriculture.

While poor people in search of subsistence often stress their immediate environment beyond easy repair, the much higher consumption levels of rich-country residents have a substantially larger global impact. For example, commercial ranching for beef exports to European markets has had a bigger impact on Brazilian deforestation than small farmers have. Similarly, the dust bowl, which helped drive Joad's family out of Oklahoma, resulted in part from improper farming practices driven by a rising urban demand for wheat. We address the impact of rich-country consumption on environmental degradation later. But subsistence needs also play an important role.

3.   Richer people "demand" more pollution control. As per-capita income rises in a country, people begin to express a more effective demand for pollution control. Figure 19.1 illustrates cross-country data for two pollutants—ambient concentrations of particulate matter (PM – 10) and per-capita production of carbon dioxide. The former, a regulated air pollutant, first rises as per-capita income grows, and then it begins to fall. Table 19.1 illustrates the same general relationship observed for PM – 10 with city-specific data for sulfur dioxide from a selection of cities. SO_2 concentrations—reflective of unregulated heavy industry, coal combustion, and auto traffic—are low in the urban areas of low-income countries, tend to rise in fast-growing low- and middle-income cities, then fall again in urban areas in wealthy countries. By contrast, the unregulated or lightly regulated pollutant, carbon dioxide, grows with per-capita income.

The inverted U-shape displayed by the particulate and SO_2 pollution can sometimes be seen in other urban air pollutants and reflects what has been called the **Environmental Kuznets Curve (EKC)** hypothesis. This hypothesis states that as economic growth proceeds, certain types of pollution problems first get worse and then get better. (The original Kuznets curve hypothesized a similar relationship between the *inequality of income and wealth* and economic growth.) What might explain an environmental Kuznets curve? Partly **education**. As income rises, so do levels of awareness regarding environmental threats. Partly, it could be explained by expanding democracy. As income rises, political participation tends to increase. As a result, people are provided the opportunity to express a **political demand for pollution control**. (When data from the former Communist regimes are included, the inverted U-shape disappears.) Partly, it has to do with a **shift in industrial composition**—wealthier countries rely more on services and other relatively "clean" industries, while less developed countries have more basic manufacturing and mining. (Indeed, some of the improvement in air quality in developed countries may simply reflect a leakage of dirty manufacturing industries to poor countries.) Finally, the relationship can be explained by **relative risk considerations**: when life spans are short due to inadequate nutrition or access to basic

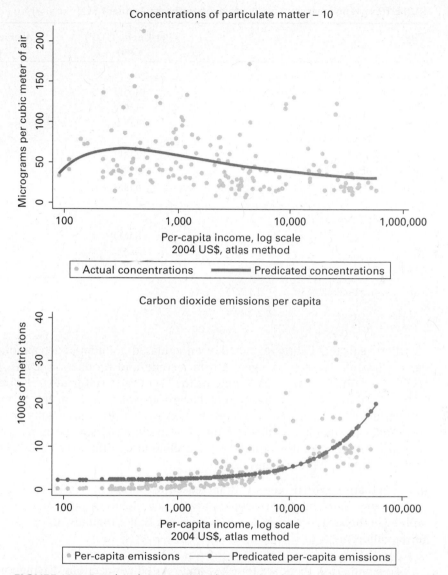

FIGURE 19.1 Regulated (PM − 10) and Unregulated (CO₂) Pollutants by Per-Capita Income
Source: World Bank, Health Nutrition and Population (HNP) Stats. www.worldbank.org.

health care, the concerns about respiratory, neurological, and reproductive diseases, or cancer from pollution, are dampened.

As this discussion indicates, per-capita income in Figure 19.1 and Table 19.1 is in fact "standing in" for a variety of political and economic social changes that accompany economic development. For this reason, the simplistic Environmental Kuznets Curve hypothesis—that growth alone leads to pollution reductions—has not held up to scrutiny, but it has sparked much further research.[5] In addition, Figure 19.1

TABLE 19.1   The Environmental Kuznets Hypothesis: Ambient SO_2

City	(Per-Capita GDP) $2008	Ambient SO_2, 2001 ($\mu g/m^3$)
High Income, Low Pollution		
Los Angeles	46,700	9
Tokyo	34,900	19
Prague	24,000	14
Low to Middle Income, High Pollution		
Mexico City	14,900	74
Rio de Janeiro	10,300	129
Cairo	5,000	69
Beijing	4,900	90
Low Income, Low Pollution		
Quito	8,000	22
Manila	3,500	33
Delhi	2,900	24

Source: World Bank (2008).

clearly reveals that lightly regulated or unregulated pollutants such as solid waste and carbon dioxide increase in tandem with income and production levels. (We should recall, in addition, that at least some of the "reduced" sulfur dioxide documented in Table 19.1 have in fact reemerged as hazardous solid waste in the form of ash and sulfur sludges.) Hazardous waste production is also probably highly correlated with per-capita income. As regulations on these pollutants become more stringent, will their per capita generation also begin to decline in wealthier countries? The graphs in Figure 19.1 cannot predict this.

4.   Population growth slows with increased income. The final link between poverty and the environment lies in income growth as a means of population control. As we will see in the next section, as societies grow wealthier, families almost universally have fewer children.

To summarize, there are four key and related connections driving improvements in environmental quality along with economic development: access to clean water and decent indoor air quality, less pressure on local subsistence resources, the "EKC effect," and a transition to smaller families. The point here is that in poor countries, one need not "trade off" rising material living standards for improved environmental quality. In fact, the *only* effective way to improve environmental conditions is to alleviate the tremendous poverty faced by many of the people in these nations.

---

5. Special issues of both *Ecological Economics* (vol. 25, no. 2, May 1998) and *Environment and Development Economics* (vol. 2, no. 4, October 1997) have been devoted to this topic. See also Stern (2004).

19.2 The Population Picture in Perspective

When my (Eban's) grandparents were born at the turn of the 20th century, there were about 1.6 billion people alive on the planet. When my parents were born, around 1930, that number had risen to 2 billion. On my own birthday in 1960, I joined some 3 billion inhabitants. When my first daughter turned two in 1990, global population had climbed to 5.3 billion. If she has a child, her daughter or son will be born in a world with about 7.5 billion other people. And if my grandchild lives to be 80, he or she will likely die, at the end of the 21st century, on a planet supporting somewhere between 9 and 13 billion people.

Figure 19.2 provides a graphical representation of world population growth spanning these five generations, 200 years. Under the UN's "medium" scenario, effective population control is achieved over the next few decades, with growth rates falling to less than one-half of 1% by 2040. Given these assumptions, global population will stabilize at around 10 billion people. This is about 50% more than the number alive today.

Note that *medium* doesn't mean this prediction will come true without serious changes—in particular, it requires fairly rapid, widespread adoption of birth control. By contrast, a world in which fertility rates fall, but only slowly, leads to a 2050 population

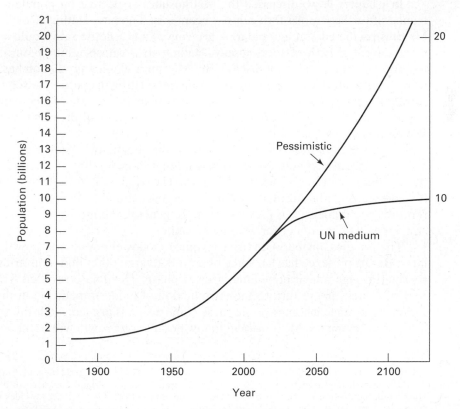

FIGURE 19.2 World Population, 1900–2100

of 10.6 billion and still rising. On the other hand, one could imagine a highly optimistic scenario. If we dip below zero population growth by 2040, this gets us down to 7.7 billion in 2050. The point here is that relatively small changes in fertility over the next two decades will have big impacts on global population by midcentury.[6]

The "pessimistic" population growth line is drawn from a 1992 publication by the World Bank, and is there for illustrative purposes—if fertility rates fail to decline at all, then global population will continue to rise, at the extreme, to 20 billion by the year 2100.[7] The actual number is highly uncertain; at some point, growth would be forcibly checked by large-scale famine, disease, war, or ecological disaster. In an interesting book called *How Many People Can the Earth Support?* the author culled results from some 60 studies (dating back to 1679!) and found answers that tended to range from 4 to 16 billion.[8]

Given the magnitude of the environmental problems we face today, it is challenging to imagine the impact that 10 billion of us will have on the planetary ecosystem, let alone 16 billion. Population pressure must clearly be counted as a major global environmental threat in the medium and long term. At the more local level, population growth is increasingly overwhelming the ability of poor country governments to provide educational, health, and sanitary services. As poverty deepens in these countries, environmental stresses multiply for the reasons discussed in the previous section.

In Chapter 9, we discussed the **Malthusian** perspective on population growth—named after the famous 18th-century economist Thomas Malthus. Reviewing briefly, Malthus predicted that a population growing at a geometric rate would soon outstrip the (slower) growth of food supply, leading to a catastrophic "natural check" on population—war, famine, or disease. But Malthus's gloomy prediction has yet to come true on a global scale; as we saw earlier, population growth continues even in the face of substantial poverty worldwide. To date, we have avoided a Malthusian fate because of impressive technological developments in the field of agriculture—the so-called Green Revolution also discussed in Chapter 9.

Moreover, Malthus's basic assumption, that population growth grows geometrically, does not always hold. Not including immigration, wealthy countries have very low population growth rates, often *below* zero. The availability of effective birth control, not foreseen by Malthus, has meant that families are able to control their "natural" reproductive tendencies if they so desire. In general, the motivation to control family size appears to be greater for wealthier families.

The complex link between rising incomes and lower population growth is discussed later. But its presence has led some observers to argue that poor countries are merely passing through a high-population growth phase. This phase resulted from a decline in death rates, due in turn to the introduction of modern medicine in the 1940s and 1950s. As average incomes rise in these countries, it is argued, birth rates will fall and a "natural" **demographic transition** to low population growth will occur.

---

6. United Nations (2008) estimates, at www.esa.un.org/unpp and see Gillis and Dugger (2011).
7. A 1% growth rate after the year 2000 would generate a year 2100 population of 16 billion; at 1.5%, "projected" population rises to 26 billion. The World Bank (1992, Figure 19.2) provides the pessimistic projection reproduced in Figure 19.2.
8. Cohen (1995).

Indeed, population growth rates worldwide were low, less than 1% from 1900 to 1950. As modern health-care practices spread in the 1950s, however, growth rates in the developing world exploded to well over 2%. After cresting in the late 1960s, population growth rates have fallen in many places including China and India, the middle-income countries, and the developed countries: globally, the rate of population growth fell to 1.3% from 1995 to 2000. The population problem has "taken care of itself" to a remarkable extent in countries like South Korea, which experienced rapid and widely shared economic growth. Population growth rates in that country fell from 2.4% in 1960 to 0.2% in 2011.

The 1990s saw generally good news on the population front. The medium population projections for 2050 presented in Figure 19.2 are *more than 2 billion people lower* than those I presented in the first edition of the book written in the early 1990s. Why? The decade between 1985 and 1995 saw large, unexpected fertility declines in South Central Asia and Africa. During the two-year period from 1994 to 1996 alone, the United Nations lowered its global estimate of the number of children per woman from 3.10 to 2.96. Again, these small changes add up to a big drop in projected numbers over a half century. Nafis Sadik, director of the UN Population fund, credited the fertility decline to the fact that many countries began lifting family planning restrictions in the early 1980s.[9]

At the same time, tragically, population growth in Africa and Southeast Asia slowed due to the devastating impact of the AIDS virus. In Southern Africa, several countries have seen life expectancy more than cut in half, and population growth rates dropped from highs of 2 to 3% in the late 1980s to become slightly negative in recent years. Economic and political decline in Eastern Europe has also reduced life expectancy in that region.

Because more and more couples worldwide are adopting birth control—and because of the devastating impact of AIDS in Africa—Malthusian predictions of runaway global population growth seem significantly less likely than they did ten years ago. Yet in many poor countries, rapid population growth continues to pose an ecological and economic development problem. The United Nations predicts that by 2050, some 67 developing countries will have twice their current population. Some have argued that in these regions, a **vicious cycle** is developing: poverty generating high rates of population growth that generate more poverty, which leads to higher levels of population growth, and so on. For such countries, economic growth alone may not break this cycle; without aggressive measures to control population growth, the demographic transition to low population growth rates experienced by other countries may be delayed for some time.[10]

19.3 An Economic Approach to Family Size

At several points in this chapter, we have asserted that higher incomes tend to be associated with lower population growth rates. As a general rule this is true, both across countries and within countries. In Colombia, Malaysia, and Brazil, for example,

9. Lanza (2006).
10. UN (1998).

the poorest 20% of households support, on average, 30% of the nation's children. By contrast, the wealthiest 20% of households have only 9% of the children.[11] Yet the relationship is not a hard-and-fast one. For example, the high-income oil-exporting countries tend to have high fertility rates, while low-income countries such as Sri Lanka and China have reduced their population growth rates to low levels. In the United States, poor families (including families on welfare) are *not* larger than average.

Many factors determine family size—religious and cultural norms obviously play a prominent role. Yet the strength of the **poverty-fertility relationship** suggests that *economic* factors are quite important as well. Evidently, people choose to vary their family size depending on their income level. So, this suggests the following:

PUZZLE

Suppose you are a farmworker couple, recently married, living in Pakistan. In a good year, you might make $600. Infant mortality rates are high—your children will have a one in ten chance of dying during their first year. The likelihood of your children attending more than a couple of years of school is also very small. Nationwide, only 38% of boys and 27% of girls attend primary school, and you are among the least likely to have access to such services. Systems of public welfare, "social security" retirement pensions, and public health care are very limited.

1. What are the economic benefits and costs to you, the parent, of having children?
2. On strictly economic terms, would you prefer to have two babies or five?

SOLUTION

Economic benefits. In poor countries such as Pakistan, families are the primary social safety net. If you should become too sick or old to work, your children will be your basic source of support. Thus an important motive for having children is for **economic insurance**. A second reason is that children's labor, controlled by the parent, can help provide a direct **income supplement** for the family. Children as young as six or seven can be (and are) employed in agriculture and manufacturing, sometimes to the (meager) economic benefit of their parents.

Economic costs. Raising children is a costly endeavor, both in terms of money and time. In economic terms, parents' child-rearing efforts, and the monetary resources they devote to this endeavor, can be thought of as an investment in the future productivity of their children.

Given this economic calculus, the answer for our farmworker is probably five children rather than two.

---

11. Birdsall and Griffin (1988). These results hold when household poverty is measured on a per-capita basis. Families with more children tend to be "richer" in absolute terms.

Let us look a little more closely at the issue of desired family size. The fact that children provide economic insurance and an income supplement does not *necessarily* mean that a big family is advantageous. Given limited resources, a family could potentially obtain comparable economic benefits following one of two approaches: a **high-investment strategy** with one or two children or a **low-investment strategy** with many children.

The high-investment strategy would involve focusing all available resources on one or two children—ensuring they survived infancy, were provided with a healthy diet, and went on to attend school. Such a child might well land a good job and increase family income substantially. In contrast, the low-investment strategy would be to have many children, recognizing that one or more would likely die young, but that the remainder would survive to contribute a small amount to the family income and insurance network. In short, the low-investment strategy is to substitute quantity for quality.[12]

While in principle both strategies are open to all, for our farm laborer family with their limited resources and restricted access to public services, the high-investment strategy is very difficult to pursue. Moreover, it is tremendously risky; suppose that after five years of intensive investment, a single child dies. Thus they generally prefer five children to two. Yet, as income rises, the high-investment strategy begins to be more attractive. Resources for the long-term (15- to 18-year) investment are more readily available, and access to better health care means that the chances of premature death decline.

The analysis of the poverty-fertility link in this section suggests an effective route to population control: changing parents' economic family plan from a low- to high-investment strategy that focuses on the "quality" rather than the "quantity" of children.

19.4 Controlling Population Growth

The benefit-cost model of family size is a crude one, omitting as it does the important issues of culture, kinship, religion, love, and affection. Yet it does a good job of explaining the strong relationship between poverty and fertility observed in many places around the world. In particular, because there are *good economic reasons* for poor people to have large families, simple provision of low-cost birth control is unlikely to solve the population problem (though it would certainly help). Can we use this benefit-cost model to suggest other effective policies for controlling population growth?

1. BALANCED GROWTH AND REDISTRIBUTION

The poverty-fertility relationship seems to provide a straightforward way to control population: eliminate poverty! Unfortunately, if this were easy to do, nations would have done so already. It does remain true, however, that balanced and rapid economic development that raises the material welfare of the poor majority is one of the most effective population-control measures available. Korea's precipitous drop in

---

12. This basic model was originally proposed by Becker and Lewis (1973). See also Dasgupta (1995).

population growth, noted earlier, can be attributed primarily to the country's dramatic economic success in the 1960s and 1970s. The gains from economic growth, based on labor-intensive manufacturing, were widely shared.

In addition to balanced growth, another way to reduce poverty and thus population growth rates is through **redistribution of wealth** from the rich to the poor. Redistribution often takes the form of publicly provided social services: education, health care, and public pension plans. Another possibility is **land reform**—the breaking up of huge, underutilized estates into smaller units, made accessible to landless farmers. Land reform has long been urged in Latin America and other parts of the developing world. This form of redistribution can help stabilize rural-to-urban migration, increase food production, decrease poverty, reduce population growth rates, and reduce environmental pressure on marginal agricultural lands.

Redistribution can occur between poor and rich classes within countries, or between poor and rich countries. For example, land reform is sometimes financed (involuntarily) by the wealthy landowning class, when their land is taken by the government at below-market prices; land reform can also be financed by the developing nation's taxpayers in general, when the landowners are fully compensated by the government; or it can be financed by international development organizations, with money from rich countries.

At the broad, macro level, rapid and balanced economic development combined with redistributionist policies is clearly the best "contraceptive." Yet both growth and redistribution have been hard to achieve in many parts of the world. Fortunately, it is possible for even poor countries to substantially reduce population growth rates through more targeted policies in the areas of health, education, and family planning.

2. REDUCED INFANT AND CHILDHOOD MORTALITY

Improved public health is an important factor in reducing long-run population growth rates. Our benefit-cost approach to family size suggested that improved health care would help slow population growth for one principal reason: the risk associated with investing in a child's health and education would be reduced, encouraging families to substitute quality for quantity.[13]

In the short run, however, reducing **childhood and infant mortality** accelerates population growth, as parents take some time to adjust their desired number of babies to the new conditions. As noted earlier, during the 1950s and 1960s, population growth rates in poor countries exploded, often doubling, as common diseases were brought under control by modern medicine, but fertility rates remained high.[14] Since then, fertility and thus population growth rates have fallen around the world, though they still remain a severe problem in most poor countries. Part of the demographic transition described in Section 19.2 is reflected in this adjustment on the part of parents to lower childhood mortality rates.

---

13. In addition, in high-mortality areas, only when mortality rates drop do parents have to concern themselves at all with birth control. Falling infant mortality rates thus initiate behavioral changes, which make fertility control more likely (Birdsall and Griffin 1988).

14. The adjustment process is compounded because, as Birdsall and Griffin (1988) report, parents don't replace dead children on a less than one-to-one basis and typically don't fully "insure" against infant mortality by having larger families.

Childhood and infant mortality can be attacked at relatively low cost by providing public health and education services. For example, one of the most common causes of infant death in poor countries is dehydration from diarrhea. This disease can be treated using a simple prescription: clean water with a little sugar.

3. EDUCATION

Our economic model of family size tells us that population growth will slow when parents follow a strategy of "high investment" in their children. A key element making such a strategy possible is **access to education**. This is true for three reasons. First, the availability of education directly lowers the cost of pursuing a high-investment strategy to all parents, educated and uneducated alike. Second, as parents become educated themselves, a strategy of substituting quality for quantity also becomes easier, as the parents can provide guidance to the children.

Finally, as parents become educated, their wages tend to rise. This increases the **opportunity cost of parents' time**, making a low-investment strategy less attractive. This is true because a low-investment, "quantity" strategy requires a bigger commitment of time devoted to child rearing than does a high-investment, "quality" strategy. Another way to look at this is that, as the parents' wages rise, family income and economic insurance are better served by parents working than by raising more children.

For this reason, education is particularly important for women, as they do most of the child rearing. One of the best ways to control fertility is to have women participating in the *modern sector* of the economy. All poor women work. However, employment in agricultural or household labor does not appear to reduce fertility.[15] As the opportunity cost of the woman's time rises, a quantity strategy becomes less and less attractive for the family as a unit.

Education for women appears to have a strong impact on fertility control for other reasons as well. To this point, we have treated the "family" as a homogeneous unit, yet men and women play different roles in the family and may have different ideas about the desirability of limiting family size. In the developing world, as in rich countries, the responsibility for taking birth control measures—whether abstinence, prolonged breast-feeding, or a technological approach—generally falls on the woman. Thus the direct consumers of birth control devices and fertility control information are generally women—providing another argument for improved female education.

More importantly, however, most of the world's societies are male-dominated, **patriarchal cultures**. In such societies, women often must obtain their husband's approval to control their fertility. This distinction is important, because holding all things equal, it is probably true that women prefer to have fewer children than men do. This is likely for a number of reasons: women do the vast majority of the hard work involved in child rearing, child rearing interferes with women's other economic activities, and childbirth represents a significant health risk for many women. Thus policies that strengthen women's status and bargaining position within the family itself—for example, better education or access to paid employment—have important effects on fertility decisions, independent of their impact on *overall* family income and economic insurance.

---

15. Birdsall and Griffin (1988).

4. FAMILY PLANNING

Having argued earlier that poor people may have good reasons for having large families, it is also true that a big obstacle to pursuing a high-investment strategy is lack of access to family planning services. There remains a large unsatisfied demand for birth control worldwide. Outside of sub-Saharan Africa, close to 50% of women in poor countries desire no more children, and about two-thirds of those who want a larger family would prefer to postpone bearing their next child. At the same time, one source estimates that in three-quarters of the world's poor countries, birth control is not affordable for the average individual.[16]

In general, better educated, wealthier urban women are better able to actually achieve fertility control. But effective outreach programs have been able to reduce and, in some cases, almost eliminate urban-rural gaps. Programs that rely on well-trained workers, provide follow-up and support to clients, provide a variety of contraceptive methods, and embed family planning in a more comprehensive system of public health services have proven quite effective in lowering fertility rates. In one well-studied case in Bangladesh, such a program increased contraceptive use from 10 to 31% in two years, thereby reducing the number of births by about 25%.[17]

A comprehensive program of public health, education (especially targeted at women), and family planning can be an effective way to reduce population growth, even in the absence of rapid, balanced growth, and/or explicitly redistributionist policies. Poor countries that have been able to successfully pursue some combination of these policies include Costa Rica, Cuba, Mexico, Colombia, Sri Lanka, Indonesia, China, and the southern Indian state of Kerala. Family planning programs, along with economic growth, have been credited with dramatic fertility declines in Taiwan and Thailand.[18]

The UN estimates that currently around 200 million women worldwide have unmet need for birth control services. Providing these women with access to family planning would cost about $5 billion, and by 2050, would reduce global population by an estimated *half a billion people*—from 9 billion down to 8.5.[19] For comparison, this is about a third of what Americans spend in barbershops, beauty shops, baths, and health clubs each year. Given this, *investment in family planning is one of the most cost-effective measures available for addressing global environmental problems ranging from global warming to loss of biodiversity*.

5. COERCIVE POLICIES

The policies described earlier all function by encouraging parents to *voluntarily* control family size. Some nations, notably China and India, have used coercive birth control methods. China, a country a little larger than the United States in land area but with less good-quality agricultural land, is home to 1.3 billion people, more than four times as many as live in the United States. Even achieving zero population growth today,

---

16. See Birdsall and Griffin (1988) and "Cost Said to Rule Out Birth Control for Many," *New York Times*, 2 July 1991. The study was done by the Population Crisis Committee and defines a supply of affordable birth control as requiring less than 1% of annual income. See also Gakidou and Vayena (2007).
17. Birdsall and Griffin (1988).
18. World Bank (1992) and RAND (1998).
19. Wire (2009).

because of the country's age distribution, the number of people in China is likely to increase to 1.4 billion before stabilizing.

Before 1980, China's government had achieved impressive reductions in fertility primarily by pursuing the noncoercive strategies discussed earlier: raising the status of the poor through growth and redistribution, and providing education, health care, family planning services, and retirement benefits. The number of children per family fell from more than 5.0 in 1970 to 2.7 in 1979.

In 1980, to head off a surge in population as the Chinese baby boom reached childbearing age, the government instituted its so-called One-Child Policy. Urban dwellers were legally limited to a single child, while rural families were allowed to have two or more children. The policy is enforced with a mixture of subsidies, fines, peer pressure, and on occasion physical coercion. Families who have only one child are provided monthly stipends, given access to better schools, and taxed at a lower rate. Economically coercive fines, which might amount to more than a year's salary, are imposed for a child over the legal limit. Pregnant women are sometimes harassed by neighborhood committees, and forced abortions, while not widespread, have been documented.

By 1990, the average number of children per family had dropped to 1.9—zero population growth. The *New York Times* reported in the mid-1990s that the average Chinese viewed the policy as unpleasant but needed, something like income taxes. Public acceptance of the policy has always been much higher in urban than rural areas, and as China's economic and political system began to open up in the 1990s, the policy became increasingly difficult to enforce in the countryside. By 2010, the average fertility was down to 1.1 child per family, well below replacement. Debates about reforming the law continued—in part because of concern about an aging population. But some analysts felt that the new one-child norm would not be dramatically affected should the law be repealed.

One ugly by-product of the One-Child Policy has been a rise in sex selection of male infants through abortions of female fetuses, and probably an increase in female infanticide. Chinese census figures from the late 1980s indicate about half a million anticipated female births are failing to show up on the records each year. However, most of these "missing" girls are probably given up for adoption or raised in secret. In China, sons are especially important from the point of view of economic insurance, as daughters traditionally "marry out" of the family.

China's One-Child Policy—relying on voluntary measures, severe economic and social pressure, and occasional physical coercion—has worked, though sometimes at a tragic human cost. Noncompliance, although evident, was not widespread enough to undermine the policy. Because China is such a huge country, the overall impact of China's family planning and birth control program has been tremendous. If the birth rates evident in 1970 had persisted, over the period from 1980 to 2001 an additional 250 million Chinese—a number somewhat less than the population of the United States—would have been born.[20]

---

20. The information on the One-Child Policy presented here is drawn from these *New York Times* articles: "China, with Ever More Mouths to Feed, Pushes Anew for Small Families" (16 June 1991); "A Mystery from China's Census: Where Have Young Girls Gone?" (17 June 1991); "China's Crackdown on Births: A Stunning and Harsh Success" (25 April 1993); "Births Punished by Fine, Beating or Ruined Home" (25 April

The physically coercive aspects of the Chinese program, while never dominant, have been "accepted" for two mutually enforcing reasons: The Chinese government exercises effective authoritarian political control over the population, *and* the goal of the policy appears to be generally supported. Many Chinese people appear to have accepted a sustainability argument that sacrifice on the part of current generations is necessary to preserve a decent quality of life for the future.

By contrast, in the 1970s, the democratically elected Indian government initiated an aggressive birth control policy that included financial incentives for sterilization. Charges of economic coercion and evidence of forced sterilization brought the program to a halt and generated considerable public suspicion of all government birth control programs.[21]

It is unlikely that, outside of China, coercive population-control methods are likely to be applied. In many parts of the world, they are morally unacceptable. In addition, except under unusual circumstances of an effective, authoritarian regime and widespread if grudging popular support, such policies are unlikely to be effective. Indeed, they are likely to be counterproductive. Luckily, they are also not necessary to stabilize the global population at a sustainable level. Noncoercive, relatively cheap, and in many cases cost-effective measures exist to nudge parents into voluntarily pursuing a high-investment family strategy.

The very good news here is that we need not wait around to see if the near future holds a "natural" demographic transition to a sustainable world population or a vicious neomalthusian cycle of population growth and misery. Neither do we need to follow a coercive path. Instead, policies that raise the material welfare of poor people by promoting balanced growth and redistribution, as well as targeted policies in the areas of health care, education, and family planning, should be sufficient to reach the goal of stabilizing the planetary population by the middle of the century.

19.5 Consumption and the Global Environment

Population-control advocates (like us) are sometimes accused by people in poor countries of racism or even genocide. Why, they ask, do you recommend aggressive, if noncoercive, steps to limit the numbers of (mostly) black or brown people in poor countries, when, in fact, the vast majority of global ecological damage can be traced directly or indirectly to the affluent lifestyles of the (mostly) white people in rich countries?

There are two elements to the **consumption-pollution link**. The first is straightforward. Because inhabitants of rich countries are responsible for over two-thirds of global economic activity, at least two-thirds of global pollution can be laid at our doorstep. The richest 20% of the world's population—including the developed countries—consumes 76% of the world's output.[22] As a result, rich-country consumption has to date been responsible for most of the global atmospheric pollution—global warming, ozone

---

1993); "Rural Flouting of One Child Policy Undercuts China's Census" (14 April 2000); "China Sticking with One Child Policy" (11 March 2008); and "Reports of Forced Abortions Fuel Push to End Chinese Law" (22 July 2012).

21. Jacobson (1987).

22. World Bank (2008).

depletion, acid rain, and radioactive contamination. Rich countries have had by far the biggest impact on polluting and overfishing the oceans. And rich-country inhabitants have generated mountains of toxic wastes that are now, on occasion, finding their way to poor countries for disposal.

In addition to generating global pollution problems, there is a second element to the consumption-pollution link. High levels of consumption demand in rich countries have been responsible for an unsustainable drawdown in environmental quality and the stock of natural capital in many poor countries. One prominent example is the so-called hamburger connection to rainforest depletion. The expansion of beef ranching for export in Latin America has led to a destruction of the region's rainforest resource without sufficient compensating investment in created capital.

Many poor countries rely on the export of primary resources or agricultural commodities to earn money for imported fuel, food, consumer goods, and weapons. In principle, this trade is environmentally sustainable. However, sustainability requires that any drawdown in the stock of natural capital—whether oil or mineral reserves, rainforest resources, topsoil, or air and water quality—be compensated for by investment in created capital. As we discussed in Chapters 8 and 9, if a nation's natural capital is depleted faster than new capital is created, then unsustainable development occurs.

The overwhelming demand for resources in rich countries—ranging from gasoline to steel to bananas to beef—has in many cases depleted the natural capital stock in poor countries, *without* commensurate investment in created capital. Why has this occurred? Historically, colonial governments tended to drain resource-generated wealth from their colonies, investing little in human capital or infrastructure. In the postcolonial period, falling relative prices for primary resources, low taxes on politically powerful resource-based industries, and high levels of spending on military and imported consumption goods by ruling elites have constrained investment in created capital. Finally, the burden of debt repayment has led to a flow of created wealth *from* poor to rich countries over the last few decades.

During the 1970s, First-World banks loaned tremendous sums of money to government agencies and private companies in poor countries around the world. Latin America's external debt, for example, rose from $7.2 billion in 1960 to $315.3 billion in 1982. It is not fully clear what motivated this irresponsible lending binge; however, little of the money was productively invested. Much of it financed imports of consumer goods from First-World countries or else disappeared into private bank accounts. Since the 1980s, a series of rescheduling and compromises have been worked out. Most recently, debts are in the process of being canceled for some of the poorest, highly indebted countries in the world, a move resulting in part from public pressure such as U2 singer Bono's high-profile antipoverty campaign. But most developing countries remain deeply in debt, and over the last three decades tens of billions of dollars of capital have continued to flow from the poor to the rich. Under these circumstances, some developing countries have been liquidating natural resources to pay off debts and have been unable to reinvest the resource rents productively.[23]

The point here is not to assign blame to rich countries or ruling elites for the poverty in the former colonies. Rather, the point is simply to recognize that high levels

---

23. For empirical confirmation of the debt overhang effect on investment, see Cohen (1993).

of rich-country demand can have as much to do with environmental damage in poor countries as do high population growth rates. Thus growing, transporting, and cooking a year's worth of today's breakfast—a banana (Ecuador), a cup of coffee (Guatemala), and a chocolate donut (cocoa, Ghana; sugar, Honduras) uses up about $400 of market resources. This process contributes much more to environmental degradation in those countries—pesticide contamination of water, loss of topsoil, deforestation, and global warming—than does providing breakfast for a person whose *entire yearly income* is $400 or less.

This is also not to say that trade in agricultural commodities or any other goods are, on balance, bad for the environment. We take up the issue of trade policy in the next chapter. Rather, to ensure sustainability, the gains from trade must be invested in created capital sufficient to offset the drawdown in natural capital. *If they are not*, then rich-country consumption leads to unsustainable development in poor countries as surely as does rapid population growth.

This section has discussed the two ways in which high levels of consumption in rich countries and environmental problems, both global and those in poor countries, are linked. At the global level, an obvious and direct correspondence exists between consumption of resources like fish, timber, and oil, and global pollution issues like climate change. But in addition, high levels of demand in rich countries have indirectly promoted a drawdown of the stock of natural capital and environmental quality in poor countries. If natural capital depleted through resource or pollution-intensive exports is not being replaced by investment in created capital, high consumption levels in rich countries can fuel unsustainable resource depletion in poor countries. Many argue that this kind of unsustainable development has in fact been occurring. Given these links, are the critics of population control right? Are neomalthusians, perhaps motivated by unconscious racism, focusing on the wrong problem?

We argue instead that *both* overpopulation and overconsumption pose serious threats to the global environment and sustainable development in poor countries. There is mounting evidence that rapid population growth dramatically compounds the problem of economic development, thereby putting tremendous pressure on local environments. Moreover, as the poor both grow in number and aspire to living standards found in the developed world, their impact on global environmental problems becomes more and more significant. In 2010, for example, China surpassed the United States as the main contributor to global warming.

Yet we are indeed being shortsighted, at best, if we insist solely on blaming the reproductive behavior of poor people in poor countries both for their own environmental problems and for the global ones to which they contribute. High levels of consumption in affluent countries are primarily responsible for the global environmental crisis, including global warming, and have indirectly promoted an unsustainable drawdown of natural capital in many poor countries.

Earlier in the book (Chapter 11) we discussed a variety of tools for addressing the overconsumption problem in wealthier countries. So far in this chapter, we have examined theoretical links between poverty, population growth, and northern consumption. Is there a path to sustainable development?

19.6 Envisioning a Sustainable Future

When one surveys the often overwhelming and interrelated problems of environmental degradation, poverty, population growth, overconsumption, and political powerlessness in poor countries, hopes for a future brighter than the present can seem dim. Yet, what promise does exist comes from an increasing ecological recognition that the earth is genuinely a single spaceship. In the last several decades, citizens in rich countries have started to become aware that the life-support systems of our own affluent lifestyles, and those of our children, are critically affected by the economic security of poor children in São Paolo, Brazil, in the Ghanaian countryside, and indeed throughout the world. Global environmental threats such as global warming, ozone depletion, and biodiversity loss due to deforestation, as well as increasing legal and illegal immigration by the poor, remind us that we ignore our less fortunate sisters and brothers at our own peril.

This recognition is indeed recent. The term *sustainable development* itself gained widespread currency only in 1987 with the publication of a book by the United Nations called, suitably, *Our Common Future*. Also known as the **Bruntland Commission Report**, after the commission's chair Gro Bruntland, the report sought to serve warning—a brighter future can be imagined, but it will not come without hard and conscious work on our part.

The report called for urgent national and international action on four key **sustainability steps**. Although written more than 25 years ago, the key challenges laid out by the Bruntland Commission remain the same today.[24] Underlying all the discussion is one common thread: together, developing and developed countries must undertake real investments to achieve a sustainable future.

1. POPULATION AND HUMAN RESOURCES

Rapid population growth clearly undercuts sustainable development efforts. Between 1985 and 2000, cities in developing countries grew by nearly three-quarters of a billion. Thus just to maintain current—and in many cases desperately inadequate—infrastructure, shelter, and educational facilities, poor countries had to increase investment in these areas substantially in the short term. Fortunately, we are learning how to effectively control population growth. But the process itself—focusing on reducing infant deaths, providing education services, and effective family planning—costs money.

2. FOOD SECURITY

Joad's story in *The Grapes of Wrath* illustrates the agrarian transition underlying the traditional model of economic development: low-productivity, labor-intensive small farmers driven off the land by high-productivity, capital-intensive agriculture. And, to the extent that industrial jobs are available in the urban centers to absorb displaced farmworkers, the process "works," despite tremendous hardships suffered by families like Joad's.

---

24. World Commission on Environment and Development (1987, overview). We take some liberties with the commission's format. The authors place the urban challenge on par with population growth. We subsume the former under the latter. They also subdivide technology needs into energy and clean manufacturing.

Unfortunately, such industrial jobs are not emerging in many poor countries. Instead, the cities are teeming with unemployed and underemployed workers. As a result, there is little rationale for governments to actively promote capital-intensive agriculture in poor countries to displace even more farmworkers; instead, policy should focus on improving the productivity of small farmers. In addition, much of the "modern" farm sector has focused on the production of export crops, rather than food production for domestic consumption. Poor countries need to boost domestic food production to improve food security and basic nutrition.

One of the best ways to both encourage small farmers and increase food output is to reduce subsidies that keep urban food prices artificially low. (Higher food prices are necessary to keep farmers in business.) Yet this can be achieved politically only if money is available to cushion the blow to poor urban residents of food price hikes. Such a policy again will require resources that poor countries may not have.

3. IMPROVED TECHNOLOGY

The Bruntland Commission's third focus was on the need for cleaner technology. Under the UN's medium assumptions, world population is liable to grow to 10 billion people before stabilizing in the 21st century. Consumption per capita could easily triple. Thus our children will grow into middle age on a planet supporting a much larger population, each consuming two or three times as many goods and services. Now imagine tripling or quadrupling the world's stock of conventional automobiles, coal-fired power plants, hazardous and nuclear waste, or land devoted to housing and agriculture. Under this kind of scenario, sustainability is simply impossible.

Thus the development of clean energy and manufacturing technologies (as discussed in Chapters 17 and 18) is a fundamental prerequisite for a sustainable future. This is true because population growth cannot be stabilized without improving the material welfare of poor people in poor countries. Affordable energy, food, and basic manufactured goods are essential to achieve a sustainable global population. Yet, unless this material production can be achieved with substantially less environmental impact than it generates today, ecological degradation will undermine sustainability directly.

In essence, poor countries will have to leapfrog the dirty, resource-intensive development pattern successfully pursued by the rich countries, to both raise incomes and stabilize population growth. Technology leadership is now emerging from India, China, Korea, and Brazil, as well as the developed countries. But rich nations still have the lion's share of resources to drive rapid development of clean technology, forcing down costs, and enabling global deployment.

4. RESOURCE CONSERVATION

Because of open access to common property and high market discount rates, natural resources are often depleted at an unsustainable rate. Thus there is a need for action to preserve much of the stock of natural capital remaining in poor countries, for the benefit of future generations. However, given massive poverty in these countries, even when national preserves are set aside, few resources are available for preventing their immediate, if technically illegal, exploitation. Here again, high-, middle- and low-income countries need to work together to protect our common heritage.

In summary, the Bruntland Commission Report yields two lessons. First, through the vision it provides of a sustainable planetary future, it suggests a framework for analyzing national and international environmental policy. In the next chapters, we look at a variety of tools available for coping with the worldwide environmental crisis. We now have four questions to ask of such policies: What are the impacts on population growth and human resource development? On improving food security? On promoting the development and diffusion of clean technology? On resource conservation? The answers, of course, will be complex and often contradictory, but these sustainability steps are the four fronts on which simultaneous progress must be made.

The second lesson of *Our Common Future* is that it truly is our common future. Whether the planet will ultimately accommodate 10 billion people in a sustainable fashion, or 13 billion in a downward spiral of environmental degradation, conflict, and impoverishment, is a decision entirely in our hands. And by our hands, we mean the people who are reading this book. We are the beneficiaries of 400 years of "dirty" development; we are also the richest people ever to walk the face of the earth. As such, we are the ones with the ability to design policies to channel global resources into resolving these four problems, and we are the ones who will determine whether our favored historical position is ultimately sustainable or not.

Where are the resources to come from? Successful developing countries are the ones who channel resource rents and gains from trade into their own economies. Globally, a major potential course of capital is military spending. The world spends well over a trillion dollars a year on arms, and in many cases, the poor countries are buying from the rich ones. For just a few weeks of global military expenditure, substantial progress could be made in addressing problems of population growth and resource conservation.

The political challenge involved in diverting resources from military to social and environmental spending is formidable. Equally challenging are policies such as debt relief to invest in sustainable development in poor countries. And yet, we are personally more optimistic that the challenge can be met today than we were 35 years ago, when as students we first confronted the relentless mathematics of population growth and its intimate relationship with the desperate poverty found worldwide.

In the 1970s and 1980s, a belief sometimes prevailed that the rich could grow richer while the poor grew poorer, that we in the wealthy countries could in some sense wall off the poverty and population problems of the developing world.[25] Today, worldwide environmental threats—global warming, ozone depletion, and loss of biological diversity—have made this position less and less tenable. For the first time in history, rich countries now have a direct and increasingly important economic stake in helping poor countries to stabilize their population growth rates. Because this can be done most effectively by improving the lives of the poorest on the planet, achieving a sustainable future is a real possibility.

---

25. See, for example, Lucas (1976).

19.7 Summary

This chapter has outlined the fundamental connections between poverty, population growth, overconsumption, and sustainable development. The first step was to characterize the general challenge of economic development as productively absorbing labor freed up in the agrarian transition from small-scale, labor-intensive farming to large-scale, capital-intensive agriculture. It is important to note that, while the agrarian transition has to date been a universal feature of development, the speed at which it occurs is greatly affected by government policies, such as subsidized credit for large farmers, or subsidies that depress food prices and thus discourage food production by small farmers.

Due to an increasing awareness of the importance of natural capital as an input into economic growth as well as of negative environmental externalities as an outcome of economic growth, interest has shifted away from traditional development models to those focusing on sustainable development. Because sustainability is defined in terms of the welfare of the average individual over time, and the average individual in less developed countries is quite poor, sustainable development must concentrate attention on the status of the poor.

Sustainable development will tend to increase environmental quality for four reasons. First, exposure to two of the most pressing environmental problems in poor countries—polluted water and indoor air pollution (smoke)—are a direct result of poverty. Second, poor people cannot afford to conserve resources, and so they often put unsustainable pressure on their local environment. Third, as incomes rise, for a variety of reasons, certain regulated pollutant concentrations decline. Finally, income growth is one of the most effective population control measures available.

There is a debate over the extent of the population problem. On one side are those who foresee a "natural" demographic transition to a stable global population as economic progress proceeds in poor countries. By contrast, neomalthusians have argued that a vicious cycle is developing, in which poverty leads to high population growth rates that engender more poverty. Such a cycle, they argue, has already begun to overwhelm the beneficial effects of economic growth in many places. As a result, they are worried that the demographic transition is stalling out and that global population will rise far above the 10 billion figure before being checked by physical or social limits.

The debate between neomalthusians and proponents of a natural demographic transition is about whether the global population will rise in the next 100 years to 9 to 10 billion, or 13 to 15 billion. From a policy point of view, however, there is little disagreement. Both sides agree that effective, noncoercive population control methods can speed up the demographic transition and should be implemented.

Controlling population growth is not as simple as dispensing low-cost birth control devices, though this certainly helps. Poor people often have good economic reasons for having large families. Parents around the world depend on children for economic insurance and income supplements. Because of limited opportunities, and risk, poor families tend to pursue a low-investment, "quantity" strategy when choosing family size. Encouraging families to adopt a high-investment, "quality" strategy is the crux of an effective population-control program.

Balanced economic growth and/or general economic redistribution are the most effective ways to alleviate poverty and thus make a high-investment strategy feasible for many families. However, such outcomes, desirable for many reasons, have often been difficult to achieve. Yet even poor countries have had success in achieving lower birth rates by pursuing a mixture of three policies: (1) reducing infant and childhood mortality; (2) improving access to education, especially for women; and (3) providing comprehensive family planning services. (Of course, these policies are also a form of redistribution of income and can help promote balanced growth.) Finally, coercive measures, both economic and physical, have been employed by China to control population growth. Aside from important moral issues, outside of China such programs are likely to be counterproductive.

The pressure that people place on their environment depends not only on absolute numbers but also on the number of goods they consume and the damage that each good does. While in some poor countries overpopulation is the primary threat to both local and global environmental quality, in rich countries consumption behavior is the problem. The consumption-pollution link arises from both the disproportionate share of global consumption engaged in by rich countries and the *potential* for an unsustainable drawdown of natural capital and environmental resources fueled by rich country consumption. High levels of debt are among the factors that have made it difficult for poor countries to productively reinvest the resource rents that are generated from trading away their natural capital.

Is a sustainable future possible? The Bruntland Commission provided an outline of the steps necessary to get us from here to there. They include controlling population growth, creating food security, improving technology, and conserving natural capital. All these options will be expensive and ultimately must be funded to some degree by rich countries. The increasing recognition that rich-country welfare depends on sustainable progress in poor countries makes this program at least potentially feasible from a political perspective. One possible pool of resources to finance the sustainable development program can be found in current world expenditures on military hardware and personnel.

APPLICATION 19.0

High-Income Counties and Hazardous Waste

Some recent evidence shows that hazardous waste sites in the United States display an inverted U-shaped relationship with county income.[26] That is, as income in a county rises, the number of hazardous waste sites at first increases and then decreases, with a turning point of between $17,000 and $21,000 per capita. (The authors also find evidence of "environmental racism" [Chapter 7]. Controlling for income, a higher white population saw a significant drop in the number of hazardous waste sites.)

Do you take the evidence on income to mean that richer counties ultimately generate less hazardous waste? Why or why not?

---

26. Bohara et al. (1996).

APPLICATION 19.1

Childhood Mortality and Population Growth

Reducing the rate of infant and childhood mortality in poor countries clearly leads to a short-run increase in population growth. Use the economic model of family size developed in this chapter to explain why population growth experts nevertheless advocate improved public health measures as an important component of a population control strategy.

KEY IDEAS IN EACH SECTION

19.0   In large measure, successful **traditional economic development** means productively absorbing the labor freed up in the **agrarian transition**. Because poverty and environmental degradation go hand in hand, economic development is required for **sustainability**; however, sustainable development must also recognize the environmental costs of economic growth.

19.1   There are four connections between poverty and environmental quality. (1) Poor people suffer from **unsafe drinking water, inadequate sewage**, and **indoor air pollution**. (2) Poor people degrade local resources because they cannot afford not to. (3) Some regulated pollutants display an inverted U-shape as a function of income. This relationship has generated the **Environmental Kuznets Curve** hypothesis, and may be due to **education-relative risk considerations political demand for pollution control**, and a **shift in industrial composition**. (4) Wealthier people tend to have lower rates of **population growth**.

19.2   Median and "highly pessimistic" **population growth scenarios** are laid out in this section. Under the former, world population will stabilize at 10 billion people; under the latter, it will quadruple over the next century to 20 billion. Growth predictions change rapidly with small changes in fertility rates. To date the **Malthusian** population trap, resulting from an arithmetic growth in food supply and a geometric growth in population, has been avoided. This is due in part to the Green Revolution and in part to the **demographic transition** to low birth rates in rich countries. However, a **vicious cycle**, in which population growth leads to poverty that sustains high population growth, remains a concern in some developing countries.

19.3   The **poverty-fertility relationship** is explained by an economic model in which all parents seek **economic insurance** and an **income supplement** from children. Due to lack of resources and risk, poor parents choose a **low-investment (quantity) strategy**, rather than a **high-investment (quality) strategy**.

19.4   Based on the model, population growth can be controlled in the following ways: (1) balanced economic growth and/or **redistribution of income** (perhaps via **land reform**), (2) reduced **infant and childhood mortality**, (3) **access to education** (educated parents have a **higher opportunity cost of time** education can also enhance women's status and decision-making ability in a **patriarchal culture**), and (4) comprehensive

family planning. These measures, designed to change parental behavior by increasing opportunity, have proven successful. In addition to such measures, China has employed more **coercive** forms of population control in its **One-Child Policy**.

19.5   There are two elements to the **consumption-pollution link**. (1) Because rich countries consume most of the world's resources, we are responsible for most of the world's global pollution problems. (2) Rich country demand can lead to an unsustainable drawdown in natural capital in poor countries.

19.6   The **Bruntland Commission Report** for the United Nations identified four **sustainability steps** necessary to achieve sustainable development. (1) Slow **population growth** (2) boost **food security** by improving the productivity of small farmers, (3) develop and diffuse **clean technology**, and (4) engage in effective **resource conservation**. Each of these steps will cost money, some of which will have to come from rich countries. One source of funding would be to divert funds from global military spending.

REFERENCES

Becker, Gary S., and H. G. Lewis. 1973. Interaction between quality and quantity of children. *Journal of Political Economy* 81: 279–88.

Birdsall, Nancy M., and Charles C. Griffin. 1988. Fertility and poverty in developing countries. *Journal of Policy Modeling* 10(1): 29–55.

Bohara, Alok, Kishore Gawande, Robert Berrens, and Pingo Wang. 1996. *Environmental Kuznets Curves for U.S. hazardous waste sites.* Working paper. Albuquerque: University of New Mexico.

Cohen, Daniel. 1993. Low investment and large LDC debt in the 1980s. *American Economic Review* 83(3): 437–49.

Cohen, Joel. 1995. *How many people can the earth support?* London: W.W. Norton.

Cost said to rule out birth control for many. 1991. *New York Times*, 2 July. http://www.nytimes.com/1991/07/02/science/cost-said-to-rule-out-birth-control-for-many.html.

Dasgupta, Partha. 1995. Population, poverty and the local environment. *Scientific American* 272(2): 40–46.

Gakidou, Emmanuela, and Effy Vayena. 2007. Use of modern contraception by the poor is falling behind. *PLOS Medicine*, February.

Gillis, Justin, and Celia W. Dugger. 2011. U.N. forecasts 10.1 billion people by century's end. *New York Times*, 3 May.

Jacobson, Jodi L. 1987. *Planning the global family.* Washington, DC: Worldwatch.

Lanza, Robert. 2006. *One world: The health and survival of the human species in the 21st century.* Santa Fe, NM: Health Press.

Lucas, George (ed.). 1976. *Lifeboat ethics.* New York: Harper and Row.

RAND. 1998. International family planning. *Population Policy Briefing*. www.rand.org/pubs/research_briefs/RB5022/index1.html.

Stern, David I. 2004. The rise and fall of the environmental Kuznets Curve. *World Development* 32(8): 1419–39.

United Nations Population Division. 1998. *The world at six billion.* New York: Department for Economic and Social Information and Policy Analysis. www.un.org/esa/population/.

Wire, Thomas. 2009. *Fewer emitters, lower emissions, less cost: Reducing future carbon emissions by investing in family planning.* London: London School of Economics; sponsored by Optimum Population Trust.

World Bank. 1992. *World development report 1992: Development and the environment.* New York: Oxford University Press.

World Bank. 2008. *World development indicators.* Washington, DC: Author.

World Commission on Environment and Development. 1987. *Our common future.* New York: Oxford University Press.

World Health Organization. 2004. *Water, sanitation and hygiene links to health.* Online fact sheet. www.who.int/water_sanitation_health/publications/facts2004/en/.

CHAPTER 20

ENVIRONMENTAL POLICY IN POOR COUNTRIES

20.0 Introduction

At the end of Chapter 19, we identified four interrelated **sustainability steps** that need to be pursued in developing countries if the ultimate vision of a sustainable future for human beings is to be realized. These four policy goals are (1) stabilizing population growth and investing in education, (2) achieving food security, (3) promoting the development and adoption of clean technology, and (4) conserving natural capital. This chapter moves on to consider a variety of actions that poor and rich countries can take to promote the four policy goals.

As in our discussion of environmental policy in the United States, we need to be fully aware of the constraints that government policymakers in poor countries face. Because the potential for government failure in poor countries is large, due in part to much stronger business influence over policy, the first half of this chapter analyzes measures designed to harness the profit motive in pursuit of sustainable development. First, poor-country governments should eliminate environmentally destructive subsidy policies. Second, by strengthening property rights, governments can reinforce profit-based motives for conservation.

While government can do a lot by selectively disengaging itself from market transactions and improving private incentives for conservation, government ultimately must be counted on to take an effective, proactive role in promoting sustainable development. This chapter thus goes on to examine the role that regulatory and clean technology strategies must play.

Finally, we end with a trio of related topics: resource conservation, debt relief, and international trade. In each case, resource rents that should form the foundation for economic development are not being captured by poor countries. The basic message of the chapter is that achieving the four sustainability steps is not cheap; without effective capture and investment of resource rents, sustainable development is not possible.

20.1 The Political Economy of Sustainable Development

Before jumping into specifics, we need to pause to consider the constraints under which government policy operates. Part II of this book focused considerable attention on the obstacles to effective government action in the United States, raised both by imperfect information and the opportunity for political influence.

The United States is a wealthy country with a fairly efficient marketplace and government. By contrast, the average person in a less developed country is a very poor person, and this poverty undermines the efficiency of both markets and governments. Per-capita annual income in low-income countries is about $600, or about $1.75 per person per day. But even these abysmal figures disguise the true extent of poverty, as there is considerable wealth inequality *within* countries.

In general, most countries have a small **political-economic elite** who control a disproportionate share of national income and wield disproportionate influence over political events. This kind of tremendous economic and political disparity often has a historical basis in the period of colonial rule. For example, throughout Latin America, the current, dramatic concentration of land ownership in the hands of a small percentage of the population can be traced to the *hacienda* system established by the Spanish colonists. Or, consider another example: Britain granted Zambia independence in 1964 after exploiting that nation's rich copper deposits for 40 of its 70 years of colonial rule. At independence, only 100 Africans out of a population of 3.5 million had received a college education, and fewer than 1,000 were high school graduates.[1]

At the risk of grossly oversimplifying, the typical class structure in a developing country can be represented by the pyramid in Figure 20.1. At the top are a small group of wealthy landholders, industrialists, and military officers, often educated in

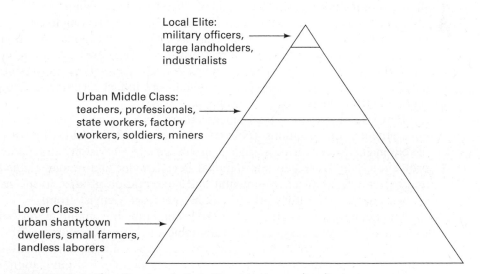

FIGURE 20.1 Class Structure in Poor Countries (generalized)

---

1. Musambachime (1990).

Western universities. Businessmen in this group include both local capitalists and local managers of multinational corporations. Below them come the urban middle class: teachers, professionals, state employees, factory workers, miners, and soldiers. The vast majority of the population are the poor: urban shantytown dwellers subsisting on part-time work, rural small farmers, and landless laborers.

Sustainable development—increasing net national welfare (NNW) for the average individual—by definition requires focusing on the lower class, as they are the average individuals. Moreover, it is this group who, out of brute necessity, often run down the local stock of natural capital in an unsustainable manner. As we begin to evaluate development and environmental policy in poor countries, the question we thus need to ask is, "Does the policy improve or exacerbate the position of the poor?"

Unfortunately, because the lower class generally has little political power in developing countries, this question is seldom central to policy design. Elite-dominated governments, often maintaining their power through military force, rarely provide democratic avenues for those adversely affected by government policy to register their protests. Yet, for environmental progress, the ability to protest is vital.

As argued in Chapter 12, the primary environmental lesson from the Communist experience is that a lack of democracy stifles the recognition of environmental problems. Absent substantial pressure from those affected, government will have neither the power nor the inclination to force economic decision makers—whether state bureaucrats, managers of private corporations, or ordinary citizens—to recognize and internalize the external environmental costs generated by their actions.

In addition to nonrecognition of important problems, when government leaders are not democratically accountable, opportunities for corruption multiply. This is especially true when even top government officials in poor countries fail to achieve a standard of living common to the middle class in Western countries. Not surprisingly, given their very low pay and level of training, corruption among low-level bureaucrats in poor countries is not uncommon. Thus, as a general rule, government bureaucracies in poor countries are not particularly efficient. (The few developing countries for which this is not true tend to be economically quite successful.) As a result, even when development and/or environmental problems are in fact recognized, and policies are set up to attack them, progress may be quite slow.

Partly in response to government failures in poor countries, the so-called nongovernmental organizations (NGOs) have emerged to deal with issues of rural development, small farmers' rights, urban service provision, and natural resource protection. NGOs include international development and human rights groups, the international arms of environmental and conservation groups, local environmental groups, peasant and rural workers' unions, and urban activist groups.

Unlike in wealthy countries, the "environmental movement" is very small in poor countries. Thus progress toward sustainable development must spring from either environmental concern on the part of ruling elites or a nonenvironmental interest on their part in population control, food security, technological innovation, or resource conservation. No strong groundswell drives the political process in a sustainable direction.

To summarize, for a variety of reasons including colonial history, small political-economic elites, undemocratic governmental structures, and poorly trained and paid bureaucrats, factors leading to government failure are compounded in poor countries. Given this potential, policies that depend on sophisticated analytical capabilities or aggressive monitoring and enforcement are not likely to succeed in many parts of the developing world.

Weak governments and the lack of popular environmental counterpressure means that business interests have a much freer hand in affecting environmental policy in poor countries. Both **domestic** and **multinational businesses** operate in the developing world. Domestic firms are owned and operated by residents of the poor country; multinational firms operate in many countries around the globe and are typically headquartered in a developed country. Multinationals have a dominant presence in most extractive and resource-processing industries, as well as sectors such as chemicals and paper.

The influence of business, whether domestic or multinational, on environmental policy goals can be positive. For example, businesses can create jobs leading to balanced growth and a subsequent reduction in population growth rates. Or they can import or develop new clean technology. However, the influence can also be negative. Businesspeople may bribe officials to obtain subsidized access to timber or other resources and may understate profits to avoid taxation. Or businesses might promote subsidized credit programs, allowing them to import capital-intensive agricultural technologies that displace farmworkers—on net, leading to an increase in unemployment and poverty. Or business might use its resources to discourage the passage and/or enforcement of environmental or resource-protection legislation.

The point here is neither to condemn nor praise business as an agent of environmental change in poor countries. Rather, the point is simply to remind that business managers, whether multinational or domestic, are generally not interested in sustainable development. They are interested in profit. To the extent that profit opportunities promote sustainable development, business will do so as well. However, businesses will just as eagerly pursue profit-driven options that are ultimately unsustainable.

Likewise, the point is not to condemn governments in poor countries as hopelessly corrupt or inefficient. There are many examples of government success as well as failure in the developing world. Ultimately, we *must* rely on poor-country governments to undertake greater effective action if we seek to achieve a sustainable future. There is simply no other choice.

20.2 Ending Environmentally Damaging Subsidies

Both rich and poor countries around the world maintain a broad array of **subsidies** for particular industries with the purported intent of promoting economic development. Some of the forms these subsidies take include special tax breaks, privileged access to imported parts and materials, protection from international competition, low-cost access to natural resources, the provision of subsidized or interest-free loans, and investment in infrastructure.

Unfortunately, many of these subsidy policies have had the effect of undermining the four steps to sustainability discussed earlier. This section looks closely at the forest industry, where government policy has often worked to promote a rapid and unsustainable exhaustion of the resource. To begin with, governments often sell public timber to logging companies at prices that are "too low." By this we mean that governments **fail to capture all the resource rent** associated with the timber. As discussed in Chapter 9, for timber harvesting to be sustainable, *all* of the resource rent must be retained in the host country and invested in created capital.

In the recent past, the governments of Ghana, Indonesia, and the Philippines have received less than 38% of the total rents from timber production in the form of sales revenue and taxes.[2] By failing to capture all the rents, governments make logging artificially profitable, and this speeds up the depletion of the resource. In addition, once timber sales have been consummated and roads built, it has proven very difficult for governments to enforce environmental contract terms in remote areas, or to monitor illegal cutting and smuggling of timber.

Many governments also engage in **infrastructure development** to support forestry — building roads and ports, and surveying and grading timber. In the extreme, taxpayers actually pay firms to harvest timber. This has occurred in the United States, where the Forest Service sells timber at prices that do not cover its administrative and road-building expenses. This direct subsidy from the Forest Service has been as high as $230 million per year. Comparable problems exist in the developing world.

Poor countries have also **subsidized "downstream" industries**, which process raw timber into lumber and other finished wood and paper products. Subsidies include substantial tax breaks and subsidized credit, as well as placing bans on the export of unfinished logs. Many of these policies have not succeeded, however, due to high tariffs in rich countries designed to protect *their* wood-processing industries. Moreover, due to a lack of domestic competition, wood-processing industries in poor countries tend to be inefficient and require continuous subsidies. In addition, their existence puts further pressure on the government to artificially lower timber prices to maintain employment.

Governments have also sponsored **colonization projects** to resettle landless farmers in rainforest areas. Such conversion efforts have been judged a sustainable success in peninsular Malaysia, where since 1950 about 12% of the country's forest has been converted to permanent tree crops such as rubber and palm oil.[3] However, efforts in Brazil and Indonesia have failed, and the land is sometimes abandoned after deforestation. In part, this failure has resulted from poor soil quality. In addition, the policies have been hampered by inadequate, though still substantial, government efforts to develop distribution and marketing channels for small farmers in remote areas. Subsidies for these programs, from the government and the World Bank, ranged as high as $10,000 per household in Indonesia, where GNP per capita is $560.[4]

Finally, governments have been quite active in promoting the spread of **cattle ranching** in forested areas. This process has advanced furthest in the Brazilian Amazon, where cattle ranching has been a primary driver of deforestation. Under the theory that ranching would serve as a spur to the general economic development of the Amazon, and concerned about securing its national borders through settlement, the Brazilian government pumped more than a billion dollars into beef industry subsidies.

To summarize, with the ostensible goal of supporting resource-based economic development (and influenced by factors as diverse as national defense and personal

2. Repetto (1988).
3. Gillis (1988).
4. Repetto (1988).

gain), policymakers in poor countries have established an array of subsidies for logging companies, forest product industries, small farmers, and large ranchers. With a few exceptions, such policies have failed to generate stand-alone industries and have continually drained capital from other sectors. With limited economic progress, population growth has not declined. Because of the policy emphasis on ranching instead of basic foodstuffs, and the failure of small farm programs to take root, food security has not improved. And little clean technology has been developed or introduced.

At the same time, subsidy policies have led to unsustainable declines in natural capital—the forest resource. In addition, they have generated environmental damage ranging from siltation and flooding to forest fires to a tremendous loss of biodiversity. Finally, native inhabitants of the forests have lost access to their means of subsistence, and their cultural survival is threatened.

This section has explored in detail some of the subsidy policies that promote rapid deforestation around the world, for little if any net economic benefit to poor countries. Subsidies for other products that aggravate environmental damage include energy, pesticides and fertilizer, and irrigation water. In Egypt, India, Brazil, China, and Mexico, for example, electric power has been sold at less than 60% of production cost, and the government makes up the difference through tax revenues.[5] The increased demand for power sparked by lower prices has brought with it associated environmental damages from hydroelectric, coal, and nuclear power plants.

Environmentally damaging subsidies are not unique to poor countries, as our discussions of the U.S. Forest Service and of energy and agricultural subsidies in Chapters 17 and 18 make clear. And just as subsidy elimination is difficult in rich countries, so it will be in poor countries. Subsidies can seldom be eliminated without some form of compensation for the losers.

On political and sometimes equity grounds, removing environmentally damaging subsidies requires resources to compensate people who lose out. Nevertheless, eliminating such subsidies often presents a cheap way to improve environmental quality in poor countries. Removing subsidies requires no ongoing governmental expense, and sustainability can be enhanced through the productive use of the resources freed up.

20.3 Establishing and Enforcing Property Rights

Way back in Chapter 3, we identified one of the primary causes of pollution and resource degradation—open access to common property. Recall that the **open-access problem** arose when individuals considered only the private benefit and costs from exploiting a shared resource—air, land, or water—without considering the external social costs imposed on others. Recall also that traditional societies managed common property problems through informal social controls and moral sanctions.

However, as traditional control mechanisms have broken down, and both population and consumption pressures have risen, the free access problem has emerged as a major underlying source of environmental degradation worldwide. When the **property rights** or titles to resources such as land or fisheries are not clearly defined, the people who exploit the resource have little incentive to engage in profit-based conservation

---

5. World Bank (1992, 68–69).

or invest in long-lived environmental protection measures such as erosion control. To improve this situation, government has three options.

1. COMMUNAL OWNERSHIP

Where an existing community is managing the property sustainably, government policy can protect and enforce the existing communal property right. Often this will mean restricting access to outsiders and may require imposing limitations on the use of sophisticated technology. For example, in one case, cooperative fishing agreements in southern Brazil broke down when nylon fishing nets were adopted by some members of the group, giving them an "unfair" advantage. In addition, under Brazilian law, the group could not exclude outsiders, who also used such nets. The primary advantage of communal ownership patterns, when they can be supported by cohesive communities, is that they tend to be quite sustainable.[6]

One of the most successful modern experiments in communal ownership rights was Zimbabwe's CAMPFIRE (Communal Areas Management Programme for Indigenous Resources), which reached its heyday in the mid-1990s. Rural district councils, on behalf of communities on communal land, were given the right to market access to wildlife in their district to safari operators. The district councils would then make payments to communities. CAMPFIRE was successful in promoting both community development and conservation, for villages saw their elephant herds and other game species as resources to be protected rather than as agricultural nuisances to be eliminated.

From 1989 to 2001, CAMPFIRE produced some $20 million of revenue for participating communities, 89% of which was generated by sport hunting. Sadly, the CAMPFIRE program lost effectiveness as a result of political turmoil in Zimbabwe,[7] CAMPFIRE is an example of community ownership that relies on **payment for ecosystem services**, or PES. For more on this notion, see Section 20.6.

2. STATE OWNERSHIP

Government can declare the land a national forest, reserve, or park, or it can regulate an ocean fishery. However, a simple declaration is inadequate. Government must also devote the necessary resources to protecting the boundaries of the reserve in order to prevent unauthorized uses. This kind of enforcement task can be extremely difficult for most poor countries. Even in a country with a relatively efficient bureaucracy such as Costa Rica, illegal deforestation on state-owned reserves continues to be a major problem.

Economists often compare Zimbabwe's successful CAMPFIRE experience for maintaining elephant herds against Kenya's less successful National Park Strategy. The Kenyans designate refuges, with access controlled by the central government, and attempt to rely on a police force to prevent poaching. Compared to CAMPFIRE, this strategy is expensive, creates resentment among the populace, and provides no incentive for local people to protect wildlife. However, the recent collapse of Zimbabwean government is a telling reminder that no strategy for conservation can succeed in the presence of a failed or failing state.

---

6. The Brazilian example is from the World Bank (1992, 70). Katz (2000) emphasizes the role of "social capital" in resource management. See also Hanna and Munasinghe (1995).
7. Frost and Bond (2008) and Balint and Mashinya (2008).

3. PRIVATE OWNERSHIP

The final option to overcome the common property problem is to assign property rights to private individuals. However, this process also is more difficult than it seems on the surface. First, it is not free, as government resources must be put to work delineating and enforcing private property rights. Moreover, privatizing forested land can also have ambiguous environmental impacts. For example, as a way to clearly establish ownership uses, many poor countries require that settlers clear the land in order to take title (as was the practice on the U.S. frontier). This process of course encourages deforestation. Yet without actual occupation and use of the land, settlers and government officials would have a hard time validating whose claim to a piece of land is legitimate. Even where clearance is not required, establishing legal title to land in many poor countries can take years. As a result, farmers tend to clear the land anyway in order to establish de facto control.

Yet, because they risk losing their land, farmers who have not attained legal title tend to underinvest in profit-based conservation measures like erosion control, as well as investments that increase farm output. To encourage such measures, governments can speed up the titling process, for example, by employing more surveyors and land clerks and by providing better law enforcement to prevent illegal evictions. This will increase the security of farmers' private property rights and should encourage them to invest more in their land. Privatization is most useful for promoting sustainable development when it serves as a safeguard against the taking of small farmers' land by the politically powerful.

Privatizing commonly held property often hurts those who previously had access under traditional law. For example, privatization of rural land in Kenya led to married sons and wives losing their traditional land rights, because they were not represented in the process. And in many instances, privatization schemes provide an advantage to wealthy and/or educated individuals to increase their wealth at the expense of the poor.[8] This type of privatization is counterproductive from a sustainability point of view as it tends to increase poverty and downgrade women's social status, thus increasing population growth rates while reducing food security. Privatization efforts designed to boost profit-based conservation must therefore be conducted carefully so as to increase rather than decrease both the social status of women and general employment opportunities.

To summarize, clarifying and strengthening property rights is a way to directly reduce environmental damage by "internalizing externalities." When property rights are clearly defined, then the owner—a community, the government, or an individual—bears a larger part of the social costs of environmental resource degradation or depletion. Individual and community ownership schemes have an advantage in this respect over government ownership, because people at the local level are directly affected by resource degradation. As a result, they have a greater incentive than do government managers to maintain the productivity of the piece of the environment they "own."

Ownership at the individual or community level thus tends to promote profit-based conservation, while conservation under state ownership depends on the strength of

---

8. Barrows and Roth (1990).

environmental concern within the governing elite. As we have argued previously, such concern may be quite weak, and even where it is strong, the enforcement capabilities of poor-country governments can make resource conservation and environmental protection difficult.

The first two sections of this chapter have focused on ways that poor-country governments can improve environmental quality: either by selectively reducing environmentally damaging subsidies or by strengthening communal and private property rights in order to promote profit-based conservation. We now move on to a consideration of more proactive government policy: regulation and clean technology promotion.

20.4 Regulatory Approaches

Environmental regulation is a new phenomenon in the developed world. Most of the major laws were passed within the last 45 years. Regulation is even more recent in developing countries: Mexico, for example, passed its comprehensive federal environmental law in 1988. In this section, we argue that a mix of direct regulation and indirect pollution taxes will generally be most effective in a developing country context.

Chapters 15 and 16 have already provided an in-depth look at the theory of regulation. It was argued there that, in general, an **incentive-based** system (pollution taxes or marketable permits) is both more cost-effective in the short run, and better at encouraging technological advancement in the long run, than a so-called command-and-control approach to pollution control. Recall that a stereotypical command-and-control system features (1) uniform emission standards for all sources and (2) the installation of government-mandated pollution-control technologies. The inflexibility in the approach means that cost-saving opportunities that can be captured by incentive-based systems are not exploited, and that incentives for improved technology are limited. This lesson holds for poor countries as well, with a couple of caveats.

First, monitoring and enforcement is the weakest link in the regulatory process in rich countries. This observation holds even stronger in poor countries. Mexico, for example, has been trying to beef up its enforcement efforts, partly in response to the North American Free Trade Agreement, discussed later in this chapter. Yet despite some highly publicized efforts, including plant shutdowns, enforcement remains quite weak by U.S. standards. Thus the primary focus of regulatory policy in the developing world must be **enforceability**.

Pollution taxes can improve enforcement, because government benefits materially from enforcing the law. This is especially true if the enforcement agency is allowed to keep some portion of the fines. Command-and-control systems also have some enforceability advantages, when regulators can force firms to install low marginal cost ("automatic") pollution-control technologies. However, recall that even such automatic technologies, like catalytic converters or power plant scrubbers, break down and require maintenance.

The second rule that poor-country governments must heed in selecting regulatory instruments is to seek **administrative simplicity**. For example, the city of Dalian in China has a comprehensive regulatory strategy to deal with severe problems of water, air, and chemical pollution. Dalian government officials have shut down old, inefficient, and highly polluting plants; required the relocation of some plants from central city areas to the suburbs, with new pollution control requirements; and imposed command-and-control upgrades on others. While a pollution tax or tradable permit system might have been considered, pollution problems in the city were not subtle, and relatively straightforward command-and-control strategies have achieved substantial improvements in local air and water quality. On the other hand, China is considering regional cap-and-trade systems for carbon dioxide, which poses no immediate health threat, but rather long-term negative impacts from climate change.[9]

In practice, avoiding administrative complexity and ensuring enforceability means that pure incentive-based systems (pollution taxes or marketable permit systems) may not be feasible. However, in conjunction with command-and-control systems, the use of **indirect pollution taxes** is often a good approach. In contrast to direct pollution taxes, which tax the emission of pollutants directly, indirect pollution taxes impose fees on inputs to, or outputs from, a polluting process. Examples include energy or fuel taxes (discussed in Chapter 18) or taxes on timber production.

The example of taxes on timber sold to mills (called **royalties**) is an interesting one, as it illustrates some of the problems raised by indirect taxation of pollution. The idea is that taxing rainforest timber production will make logging less profitable, thus leading to a reduction in this activity. This in turn may be desirable because logging contributes to environmental damage ranging from siltation and flooding to loss of biodiversity to an aggravation of global warming. The situation is illustrated in Figure 20.2.

In a classic supply-and-demand analysis, increased royalties raise costs to firms, causing some to drop out of the market. This shifts the supply curve up to S', and the timber brought to market drops to T'. This appears to be the desired result of the policy. However, an offsetting effect may in fact lead to a much smaller reduction in the actual area logged. As royalties are raised, fewer tree species become profitable to harvest. Yet to get the remaining profitable species, firms may still need to clear-cut the same acreage. Firms then remove the profitable species, leaving much of the timber that would formerly have been brought to market behind; this process is called *high grading*. Thus, although increased royalties will have a big effect on the timber brought to market, they may have a smaller impact on the acreage logged.

To solve this problem, one might suggest a more direct pollution tax—a royalty based on the acreage logged. Such a tax would get at the problem in an up-front way. But monitoring logging activity is much harder than slapping a tax on logs as they come to the mill, so the indirect tax wins out on enforceability grounds. Another alternative would be to vary royalties by species and impose higher taxes on high-value trees, as is done in the Malaysian state of Sarawak. This reduces high grading and thus can have a bigger impact on acreage reduction.[10] In summary, the lesson from the timber royalty case is that indirect pollution taxes *are not* direct pollution taxes, and their ultimate effect on pollution or resource degradation cannot be taken for granted. The impact of indirect taxes on the environmental problem at hand must be carefully considered.

---

9. Shin (2004) and World Bank (2012).
10. Though it need not. In fact, which system reduces overall logged acreage more will depend on which system reduces logging profitability more. Repetto (1988a) provides the information on the royalty structure in Sarawak.

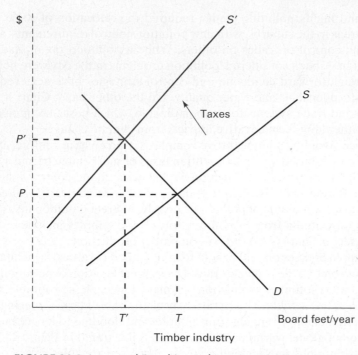

FIGURE 20.2 Increased Royalties and Logging Activity

This is not to say, however, that indirect pollution taxes are a bad idea. Well-designed indirect taxes can substantially affect environmental problems. In addition to such measures, cost-saving flexibility can be built into command-and-control regulatory structures wherever possible. To see how the use of an indirect tax combined with flexibility in a command-and-control regulatory approach can reduce the costs of pollution control, we turn to the case of air pollution control in Mexico City.

Mexico City is home to both 20 million people and more than half of Mexico's non-oil manufacturing output. Air pollution in the city is among the worst in the world. One study suggested that simply breathing the air had a health effect comparable to smoking 40 cigarettes per day.[11] During the winter of 1991, the pollution problem was at an all-time high: athletes were warned not to train outside, birds dropped dead out of the trees, and vendors began selling oxygen on the street. The government began taking steps to control the problem, including the shutdown of some major private and public-owned industrial facilities and incentive-based measures such as increased parking fees in the central city. By the year 2000, significant improvements had been achieved but globally, the city still ranks among the bottom 10 in terms of overall air quality.[12]

A World Bank study constructed a marginal cost of reduction curve for air pollution from motor vehicles in the city; this curve is reproduced in Figure 20.3. The curve

---

11. The study was done by the U.S. Embassy and is cited in Lepkowski (1987).
12. "Smog City" and "Pay to Breathe," *The Economist*, 18 May 1991 and 16 February 1991, and "Terrific News in Mexico City," *New York Times*, 5 January 2001, A1.

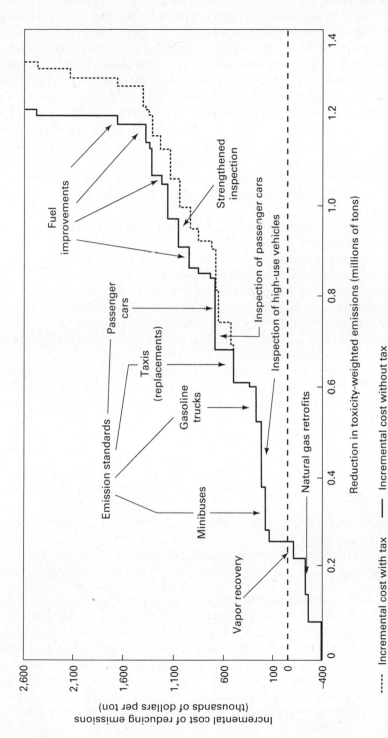

FIGURE 20.3 Air Pollution Control in Mexico City, Marginal Costs from Vehicles

Source: From WORLD DEVELOPMENT REPORT 1992 by World Bank. Copyright © 1992 by The International Bank for Reconstruction and Development/The World Bank. Reprinted by permission of Oxford University Press. Inc.

starts out at the left with measures that actually save money: retrofitting some high-use public vehicles to natural gas and recovering refueling vapors. However, the options for further improvement—first emission standards, then strengthened inspection, and then improvements in fuel—become increasingly costly. The author estimated that by using these command-and-control measures alone, pollution could be reduced by 1.2 million tons per year, at a cost of about $1,800 per ton for the last unit removed.

However, as indicated by the dotted line, if the measures were coupled with a relatively low **gasoline tax** (of about $0.05 per liter), the same pollution reduction could be achieved at lower cost. As you can see in the graph, there are estimated marginal savings of about $300 per ton of air pollution for the last ton reduced. The reason: the gas tax would reduce overall driving, and forestall the need for more expensive command-and-control measures to achieve a given reduction in pollution. In fact, the government has since raised gasoline taxes by a substantially higher margin than the study recommended.

However, because a gasoline tax is not a direct emission tax, it is not fully cost-effective. For example, both dirty and clean cars are taxed at the same rate. The equal marginal cost of reduction principle necessary for cost-effectiveness (Chapter 15) is thus not satisfied. As a result, the World Bank study recommended that cleaner cars receive a rebate of some of their gas tax when they are inspected, thus encouraging their purchase. In another move toward cost-effectiveness, the Mexican government required taxi drivers to buy new, cleaner vehicles every three years. This measure generated a large environmental bang for the buck because taxis are driven ten times as far per year as are private cars.

The government also pursued one symbolic but highly cost-ineffective regulatory policy: the Day Without a Car program. Under this program, travel by car, depending on the license plate number, is banned on a specified workday. This brief description provides a good opportunity to present a

PUZZLE

Will the Day Without a Car program necessarily cause families to reduce overall driving?

SOLUTION

By now, you have probably figured out that the answer to these puzzles always seems to be no. First, car travel is unlikely to fall by one-fifth, because people will simply drive more on other days of the week to accomplish their shopping and recreational tasks. This substitution effect will cause the overall decline in driving to be small. Moreover, some families, for whom compliance with the regulation is very costly, will likely buy a second car. Access to a second vehicle would actually *increase* driving for such a family. Of course, the program may yield other benefits; in particular, it might raise public awareness.

This section has argued that for reasons of enforceability and ease of administration, poor countries will most often rely on command-and-control regulatory methods, combined with indirect pollution taxes. Often, the two measures can complement one another. In addition, careful analysis often reveals fairly simple ways to increase the cost-effectiveness of both indirect pollution taxes and command-and-control regulatory systems. Examples from Mexico City include gas tax rebates for clean cars at inspection time, and tight regulation of highly polluting sources like taxi cabs.

20.5 Sustainable Technology: Development and Transfer

In addition to regulation, promoting the adoption of more sustainable technology is the other proactive tool that poor-country governments have to improve environmental quality. Chapters 17 and 18 provide a general discussion of **clean technology**. There we defined a clean technology as one capable of delivering comparable services at comparable long-run private costs to existing technology, *and* doing so in an environmentally superior manner. In poor countries, we need to tack on another condition. In the interests of controlling population growth by reducing poverty, technologies that the government promotes should also (1) not reduce employment and/or (2) improve the economic position of the poor, especially women. The so-called sustainable technologies are clean technologies that also help reduce poverty.[13]

This section addresses three questions about promoting sustainable technology. First, how can sustainable technologies be identified? Second, how are they developed? Third, what steps can be taken to promote their diffusion?

Technologies can be judged sustainable only after field testing and may be sustainable only under certain conditions. For example, one study examined the introduction of irrigation pumps and a new type of rice into a drought-stricken region of northern Mali. The new technology increased yields dramatically *and* increased employment. Overall food security thus rose. The increased yields also made it possible for the communities to afford the imported capital necessary for production, at least in principle. (Outside support from the United Nations had not yet been withdrawn.) However, the greater centralization of production fostered by the pumps concentrated economic power in the hands of males of a wealthier ethnic group, thus increasing both gender and income inequality.[14]

Is this technology sustainable? At this point, it is hard to tell. Over time, one would need to answer the following two questions. First, in the absence of outside aid, can the villagers afford to operate and maintain their more capital-intensive production method? In other words, is the technology really profitable and thus self-sustaining? Second, do the income and food security benefits of higher yields outweigh the increase in inequality? In other words, are women and the ethnic minority group on balance better off after the introduction of the new technology? If the answer to both of these questions is yes, then we would judge the technology sustainable.

---

13. Sustainable technologies differ from appropriate or intermediate technologies in that they need not be small-scale or locally produced. Sustainable technologies can *include* traditional, intermediate, conventional, or emerging technologies, or any blend.
14. Ton and Jong (1991).

Sustainable technologies need not be sophisticated. Examples include erosion control methods such as building rock or clay dikes or planting trees, and efficient cooking stoves, which reduce charcoal use by several hundred percent. These technologies can dramatically improve environmental quality while boosting the material well-being of people in poor countries. The short-term cost-effectiveness of these technologies is essential. Poor people cannot afford to adopt new techniques unless their advantages are clear-cut and substantial.

How are sustainable technologies developed? Chapter 19 stressed that rich countries must bear much of the cost of research and development of technically sophisticated clean technologies—photovoltaic cells are a good example. However, external aid is often needed to establish and promote simple sustainable technologies as well. An **NGO** called Plan International financed a project in the African country of Burkina Faso, which serves as a good example. The NGO found that reintroducing traditional erosion control techniques, using mostly locally crafted implements, boosted yields of peanuts and grains by over 100%. Later, outside agronomical assistance was gradually withdrawn, and the project became self-sustaining. Unfortunately, this success story was not widely replicated. The Burkina Faso government, while supportive of the project, simply had no money to invest in it.[15]

While potentially beneficial technologies often have to be developed with assistance from the rich countries, the actual users of the technology must be closely involved in the design process. This is true first because poor-country residents, particularly farmers, often have the greatest knowledge of potential solutions to a given problem. Second, if the technologies do not suit the needs of the users, they will never be adopted, no matter how "sustainable" they are in theory.

Poor-country governments, sometimes in combination with international development agencies and NGOs, can employ a wide range of tools to promote sustainable technologies—from design standards for technology to technical assistance programs to consumer and producer subsidies to research and development grants. The advantages and disadvantages of these options, summarized in Table 20.1, were discussed in detail in Chapter 17 and are not further reviewed here.

While government efforts to promote technologies are important, the private sector and **multinational corporations** in particular will typically play an important role in diffusing new techniques of production and consumption. Sometimes these technologies are sustainable, sometimes not. One beneficial influence of direct foreign investment by multinational corporations in manufacturing is that they may bring with them cleaner production technologies. For example, multinational investment has promoted the diffusion of relatively clean technology in the paper and pulp industries.[16] In addition, international product quality standards such as ISO and sustainable supply chain initiatives by companies like Nike have affected labor and environmental practices in developing countries.

---

15. Wardman and Salas (1991). Yield increases were measured vis-à-vis the surrounding countryside. Yields were also improved by importing a superior variety of sorghum. In addition, the project included agroforestry and husbandry components.
16. Wheeler and Martin (1993).

TABLE 20.1   Policies for Sustainable Technology

Policy	Late-Stage Sustainable Technologies
Design standards	Energy and water efficiency
Technical assistance	Waste reduction in manufacturing, alternative and agroforestry, passive solar, wind power, energy and water efficiency
Small grants/loans/ tax credits	Energy and water efficiency, active solar, passive solar, agriculture and agroforestry, wind power

Policy	Early-Stage Sustainable Technologies
R&D	Agriculture and agroforestry
Infrastructure investment	Mass transit, agriculture and agroforestry, active solar, wind power, telecommunications

On average, multinationals, with higher profits, higher visibility, and easier access to technology, probably have somewhat better environmental and safety records than do domestic firms in poor countries. Nevertheless, and not surprisingly, multinational operations in the developing world are generally dirtier and more dangerous than are their similar facilities in rich countries.

The most tragic example of this so-called double standard was illustrated in the wake of a 1984 chemical explosion in Bhopal, India, at a plant owned by a subsidiary of Union Carbide. More than 2,000 people were killed and up to 200,000 injured, many severely, by a toxic gas cloud. While the Bhopal plant was technologically similar to a sister plant in West Virginia, safety systems in Bhopal werc very poorly maintained.[17]

More gencrally, manufacturing and agricultural production methods imported from rich countries by multinationals tend to be fairly capital intensive. A chemical plant in Mexico is very much like a chemical plant in Ohio. If taxes on these firms are low and/or their profits are not reinvested locally, the use of this capital-intensive technology may lead to little net increase in employment or reduction in poverty, while at the same time aggravating environmental problems. This is yet another example of the critical need to capture and invest domestically the economic surplus from foreign investment.

This section has defined a sustainable technology as a clean technology, which also helps reduce poverty. The rapid diffusion of such technologies in poor countries is crucial if they hope to outrun a neomalthusian cycle in which increased poverty leads to high rates of population growth, thus generating more poverty, and so on. Such technologies must also alleviate poverty in a clean way, because environmental degradation in many poor countries is already quite severe. With both their populations and per-capita consumption of resources likely to increase substantially over the next 50 years, dramatically exacerbating environmental decline, poor countries must leapfrog the path of dirty development followed by their rich neighbors. Sustainable technology may deliver the means to do so.

---

17. Lepkowski (1987).

However, developing, identifying, and diffusing sustainable technologies are expensive tasks that will not be accomplished without a major and ongoing commitment of resources. At the same time, the recipient communities must be full partners in the process. On one of our desks is a beautiful picture of a modern windmill on a hilltop in eastern Zimbabwe, built there by a Danish aid group to electrify a remote village. Unfortunately, the windmill had been inoperative for over a year when we took the picture. The village was unable to raise the money to buy spare parts, which had to be imported from Denmark. The lesson: a successful sustainable technology depends much more on the social needs, capabilities, and organizations of the people it is intended to serve than it does on the provision of hardware.

20.6 Resource Conservation and Debt Relief

Several times over the last few chapters we have remarked that it has proved difficult for poor countries to successfully conserve natural resources—forests, wetlands, rangelands, and fisheries—by simply setting aside reserves and parks. Problems are faced both in establishing such protected areas and in managing the regions once they have been created.

Over the last few decades, we have seen fierce battles in the United States over wilderness set-asides to protect the habitat of the spotted owl in the Pacific Northwest, to reduce logging in the Tongass National Forest in Alaska, and to prohibit oil development in the Arctic National Wildlife Refuge. Similar **development-environmental struggles** are played out in poor countries, but the stakes there are more dramatic. Failure to develop will mean that many millions of people will continue to face hardships with inadequate food, housing, health care, and other necessities. But rapid development also threatens to degrade ecosystems. Many poor countries are rich in biodiversity. Poor countries are located disproportionately in tropical areas that tend to contain many more species than temperate areas. Both desperately poor people and wealthy development companies desire access to the resources, and together they can form a potent anticonservation political force.

Even when a protected area has been established, the government faces the daunting task of **enforcement** to prevent game poaching, illegal logging, and the invasion of landless farmers. These governments often have very limited budgets and simply cannot meet the challenges they face. Given these facts, there has been an increasing recognition that protecting natural resources in poor countries requires directly addressing the economic needs of the poor people who depend on, and threaten, those resources. This section explores three related policy options for strengthening the link between resource protection and economic opportunity—sustained-yield resource development, payments for ecosystem services (PES), and debt-for-nature swaps.

Sustained-yield resource development means using available renewable natural capital in an ecologically sustainable way. Under a sustained-yield rule, harvests cannot exceed the regenerative capacity of the land or fishery (see Chapter 10). To illustrate this concept, let us consider the economics of deforestation in the Amazon rain forest in Brazil.

As illustrated in Figure 20.4, three primary forms of commercial resource-based activity exist in the Amazon, and they sometimes occur in sequence. First, the rain

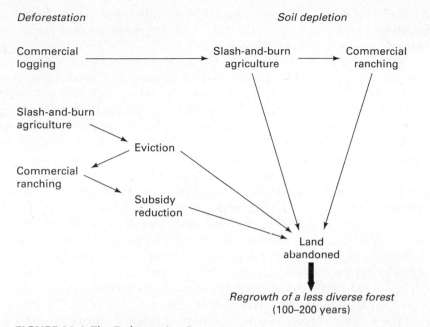

FIGURE 20.4 The Deforestation Process

forest is clear-cut by logging companies, small farmers, or commercial ranchers. The latter two groups tend to simply burn the fallen timber. Small farmers, sometimes following roads built by loggers, grow crops for a few years. However, these early migrants often move on, either abandoning their land or selling out to cattle farmers. This technology is known as shifting cultivation or slash-and-burn agriculture.

When populations and farm plots are small, slash-and-burn agriculture can generate a sustained yield because the rain forest is given time to recover. However, as population pressure has increased, and ranchers have moved in to follow the farmers, the system has in some cases become ecologically untenable.

There is ongoing debate as to the motivation for land abandonment by both small farmers and cattle ranchers. Some argue that the poor-quality tropical soils make rainforest farming unsustainable; others maintain that poor and politically powerless pioneers are unable to hold onto the property that they farm as a second wave of wealthier migrants move in. Finally, in some cases, reductions in subsidies have led to some abandonment by ranchers.[18]

How could sustained-yield resource development proceed in the Amazon? As we will see, the rain forest *does* have substantial economic value that might be exploited in an ecologically sustainable manner. Doing so will require applying a successful mix of the policies described previously: eliminating unsustainable subsidies, clarifying property rights, and promoting sustainable technologies via measures such as technical assistance programs, infrastructure development, and subsidized credit programs. The problem is compounded, however, because much of the benefit of sustained-yield

18. See Schneider (1993).

development accrues to people outside of the rain forest, particularly to those in rich countries. Getting us to pay "our share" for the public good of rainforest protection becomes an added policy challenge.

What sustained-yield values do the rain forest hold? First, experience has shown that there are profitable, **sustained-yield farming and ranching methods**, suitable for tropical forest soils, that do not require shifting cultivation. Governments can encourage farmers to adopt these sustainable technologies both by promoting them directly through technical assistance programs and targeted credit subsidies and by eliminating subsidies for unsustainable practices. Deforestation will be slowed if farmers and ranchers can eliminate their voracious need for more land.

More generally, the *standing* forest is increasingly viewed as a resource with substantial economic value. From a commercial perspective, the **harvesting of wild products** such as meat and fish, and primates (for medical research), could generate an annual income of $200 per hectare, more than is earned either by one-time clear cutting or by unsustainable cattle ranching.[19] Developing this potential would require nurturing a marketing and transportation infrastructure as well as clarifying property rights within the rain forest. Some kind of communal or private ownership would be necessary to avoid the overharvesting of profitable wild resources such as nuts, meat, or vegetable oils on commonly held property.

The rain forest holds two other important products: **medicine** and a **gene pool for agriculture**. Tropical forest species form the basis for pharmaceutical products whose annual sales are valued at well over $12 billion.[20] The forest undoubtedly contains many more valuable species, thousands of which may be lost each year. However, the medical value of the rain forest lies not only in its biodiversity; the native Amazon people have a medical knowledge base that is also being threatened by deforestation. Finally, the huge gene pool represented by the forest is economically important for breeding disease-resistant and high-yield agricultural crops.

In addition to these commercial benefits, the forest yields a variety of other ecosystem services. One of these is carbon sequestration; a substantial portion of the world's carbon dioxide is tied up in the rainforest biomass. When the forests are burned, the CO_2 is released into the atmosphere, contributing to global warming. Deforestation contributes an estimated 6–17% of total global CO_2 emissions from human sources.[21] In addition, the rain forest serves as a **rainfall regulator** by recycling much of its own moisture. As deforestation proceeds, the Amazon basin may well dry out as large parts of the forest are burned down and convert to savanna. This would release a huge pulse of carbon dioxide into the atmosphere, further warming the planet and affecting rainfall patterns throughout Brazil.

Finally, many people have expressed considerable moral interest in protecting the rain forest, its natural species, and its human cultures. From an economic point of

---

19. Pearce and Myers (1990). They report that commercial logging returns about $150 per hectare, while Browder (1988) finds ranching income to average $112.50 per hectare. Balmford et al. (2002) also found that low-impact logging generated higher returns than conventional logging or plantations in forested ecosystems in Malaysia and Cameroon (see Chapter 10). See also the special issue of *Environmental Development Economics* 4(2), May 1999.
20. Pearce and Myers (1990).
21. Balcini et al. (2012).

view, this concern represents an **existence value** for the rain forest (see Chapter 5). Especially in rich countries, people have expressed a willingness to pay for rainforest preservation independent of the material economic services that the tropical forest might provide.

The benefits from medical, agricultural, environmental, and existence value services provided by the rain forest accrue primarily to those living outside of the Amazon, and indeed, Brazil. Thus rainforest protection is a classic **public good**, as described in Chapter 3. Many of us have been solicited by environmental groups to contribute money to efforts to "save the rain forest." While each of us has a material stake in such a project, we also have an incentive to **free ride** on the efforts of others to provide the public good. As a result, economic theory predicts that rainforest protection groups will raise less than the amount of money we as a society are really willing to pay for such efforts.

This in turn means that private sector efforts to promote sustained-yield development in the Amazon will be inefficiently low on a simple benefit-cost basis. Traditionally, economists have argued that government needs to step in and use its power to tax in order to provide an efficient quantity of public goods—whether this involves a national park, clean air, or national defense. In an international context, this implies that to protect the narrow economic interests of their citizens, rich-country governments will have to raise aid money for rainforest protection. Of course, such aid might also be justified on the grounds of economic sustainability and fairness to future generations.

One method of generating funds in rich countries to use in poor countries to provide funds for conservation is to institute programs of **payments for ecosystem services (PES)**. Around the world, dozens of such efforts have been launched in recent years. An ambitious recent initiative is the UN's REDD (Reducing Emissions from Deforestation and Forest Degradation) program. REDD is working to provide incentives to forest landholders in developing countries to retain and restore their forests so as to keep the carbon sequestered in the trees and soils. But like most of these programs, REDD is currently underfunded. Because rich countries are often major beneficiaries of resource preservation, an efficient level of conservation will be achieved only if a mechanism is established by which rich-country residents pay for the benefits they receive.

In other cases, low- or middle-income countries themselves have initiated ambitious PES programs. Costa Rica launched a PES program in 1996, *Pago por Servicios Ambientales* (PSA). PSA pays landowners to maintain forests or plant trees in order to provide four ecosystem services: carbon sequestration, water provision, biodiversity conservation, and scenic beauty. The money to pay landowners comes primarily from a tax of fossil fuel use with a lesser amount coming from foreign sources. The program has achieved considerable success. Prior to the start of the PSA, Costa Rica had one of the highest rates of deforestation of any country. Since 2000, Costa Rica has net positive reforestation.

Other successful PES programs in low- or middle-income countries have been instituted in South Africa (Working for Water Program), and the largest program of all in China, the Sloping Lands Conversion Project (or "Grain for Green Program"). The Grain for Green Program pays farmers to plant trees on steep slopes to prevent erosion, better manage runoff to prevent flooding, sequester carbon, and provide other ecosystem services. The program has led to a large increase in the area of forest in China. More local and regional PES programs involve payments by water users to protect watersheds that provide drinking water. Following on the success of such a program in Quito, Ecuador, such "water funds" are now spreading quickly to other cities in Latin America.

Another approach to provide incentives to invest in resource conservation is through a **debt-for-nature swap**. During the 1970s and early 1980s, many developing countries accumulated a huge quantity of debt owed to private banks in rich countries. Merely paying the interest on this debt remains a tremendous burden on poor countries today. The debt burden poses a major obstacle to sustainable development, as it reduces investment in the created capital that poor countries desperately need. Under a debt-for-nature swap, a rich-country group (government, NGO, or bank) pays off a portion of the loan, typically at a deep discount. Banks are willing to sell this debt at a paper loss, because they suspect they will not be repaid in full anyway. In exchange, poor-country governments must agree to invest a certain amount of money into a resource conservation program at home. These programs tend to focus on beefing up enforcement and supporting sustained-yield resource development at existing preserves. The actual ownership of the natural resource does not change hands.

The developing country benefits in several ways. First, the debt is reduced. Second, it can undertake needed conservation measures at home. Finally, the conservation program can be financed using local money, not scarce foreign currency (dollars, yen, or euros). It is thus "cheaper" from the poor country's perspective. Figure 20.5 provides the details of a swap between the Brazilian government and the U.S.-based NGO, the Nature Conservancy.

Debt-for-nature swaps are one way for residents of rich countries to express their demand for resource preservation in poor countries. However, their use has been fairly limited. Consummated deals have reduced total debt in poor countries by only about 1% of total Third-World debt. About one-quarter of these swaps have been financed

1. The Nature Conservancy buys $2.2 million in Brazilian debt owed to a private bank. The bank agrees to a price of $850,000 for the debt, $0.38 to the dollar.
2. The Nature Conservancy donates the debt to FUNATURA, a Brazilian conservation NGO. FUNATURA, in turn, uses it to buy $2.2 million in long-term Brazilian government bonds, paying 6% interest, or $132,000 per year.
3. These funds accrue to a partnership between the Nature Conservancy, FUNATARA, and IBAMA (the Brazilian EPA). Their goal is to manage the Grande Sertão Veredas National Park, in the interior highland of the country. Endangered mammals that have taken refuge in the park include the jaguar, the pampas deer, the maned wolf, the giant anteater, and the harpy eagle.
4. The management strategy includes purchasing "buffer zone" lands around the park, hiring park rangers, and promoting sustained-yield resource development. Early priorities include such basic measures as the purchase of a motor boat and a four-wheel-drive vehicle, and the construction of a park headquarters.

FIGURE 20.5 A Debt-for-Nature Swap in Brazil
Source: Fundaçao Pró-Natureza and the Nature Conservancy (1991).

by private parties, primarily conservation NGOs. The rest of the efforts have been paid for by rich-country governments.[22]

The restricted use of the option reflects, in part, resistance on the part of poor country governments, who are concerned that environmentalists from rich countries will "lock up" their resource base. Probably more significant is the fact that NGOs in rich countries have been able to raise only limited funds for such purposes. Due to the free-rider problem, discussed previously, such an outcome is predicted for private groups that seek to provide public goods. At the same time, government efforts have been limited for lack of political support. If debt-for-nature schemes are in fact effective in conserving resources in poor countries—and the record is too recent to fully judge—a significant expansion could well be justified on benefit-cost grounds.

In summary, in poor and densely populated countries, the only feasible way to conserve natural resources is often to link conservation with enhanced economic opportunity. That conservation often provides valuable ecosystem services is one way to motivate funds for conservation. Successful conservation programs bring together willing buyers (those who benefit from provision of ecosystem services) with willing sellers (typically landowners who take actions to enhance provision of services). The success of PES programs in many low- and middle-income countries provides hope that conservation overall can succeed in poor countries that provide important local and globally valuable ecosystem services.

20.7 Trade and the Environment

In 1999, tear gas wafted through the streets of Seattle, following massive protests by environmentalists and union members at a meeting of the World Trade Organization (WTO). The WTO is an international body that oversees trade and investment agreements negotiated between member states; the mission of the WTO is to promote increased global trade and investment. The protestors' message was that the WTO, through its promotion of free trade, was exacerbating global environmental problems and undercutting workers' rights. Earlier in the decade, similar concerns created headlines during the debate over the **North American Free Trade Agreement (NAFTA)**. NAFTA, a 1993 agreement between Canada, Mexico, and the United States, was designed to reduce tariff and subsidy trade barriers and eliminate restrictions on foreign investment and capital mobility. Passage of NAFTA in the United States was hotly contested, in part because of fears it would exacerbate environmental decline in all three countries.

There are essentially three environmental arguments against freer trade, and one environmental argument in favor, all well illustrated by the NAFTA debate and all summarized in Figure 20.6. The argument for the free-trade act was that, by stimulating investment and economic growth in Mexico, poverty would be reduced and cleaner technologies would be imported and adopted, leading to a "flattening" of the Environmental Kuznets Curve. As we learned in Chapter 19, **poverty reduction** in poor countries can have important environmental benefits as water and air quality improve, pressures on nonrenewable resources decline, more resources are available

---

22. Deacon and Murphy (1997).

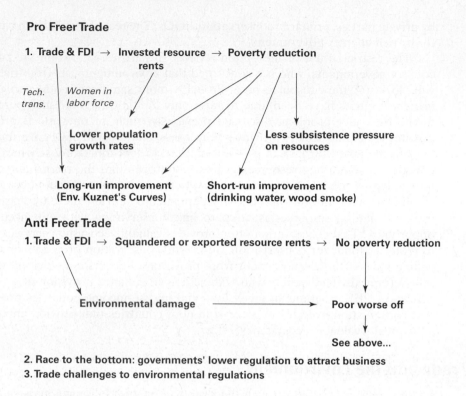

Pro Freer Trade

1. Trade & FDI → Invested resource → Poverty reduction
rents

Tech. trans.

Women in labor force

Lower population growth rates

Less subsistence pressure on resources

Long-run improvement (Env. Kuznet's Curves)

Short-run improvement (drinking water, wood smoke)

Anti Freer Trade

1. Trade & FDI → Squandered or exported resource rents → No poverty reduction

Environmental damage ⟶ **Poor worse off**

See above...

2. Race to the bottom: governments' lower regulation to attract business
3. Trade challenges to environmental regulations

FIGURE 20.6 Trade and the Environment

for investment in health care, education, and family planning, and parents are provided with the option of pursing a quality rather than a quantity strategy for family size. In the case of NAFTA in particular, advocates argued that the agreement process strengthened both democratic and environmental political movements within Mexico.

Environmental critics of the treaty lodged three principal objections. First they argued that, in fact, it would not reduce poverty. For example, NAFTA required the Mexican government to significantly reduce subsidies for corn farmers. It was feared that hundreds of thousands of small farmers might lose their livelihoods, as cheap northern grain entered the market. (Canada and the United States have built up tremendously productive farm sectors through their own subsidy policies.) While urban dwellers in Mexico might benefit from lower corn prices, they would also suffer from substantially increased migration to the cities and downward pressure on wages. As a result, it was possible that they too would be worse off. With greater poverty would come higher birth rates and more pressure on local resources.

Following the passage of NAFTA, U.S. grain exports to Mexico grew rapidly, though urban consumers appeared not to benefit substantially from lower prices due to monopoly pricing. And, somewhat surprisingly, Mexican maize production in subsistence areas appears to have stayed relatively constant. U.S. producers grabbed all of the growth in the market, depressing prices, but rural farmers continued to produce for their own subsistence. The bottom line: U.S., not Mexican, farmers profited from the growing internal market, and U.S. and Mexican wholesalers, not Mexican consumers, appear to have gotten the largest share of the increased surplus.[23] Thus, Mexico's corn farmers have been hit with lower product prices, but they are not low enough to drive the subsistence growers off the land in large numbers.

The second charge against the treaty was that Mexico, with its **weak environmental enforcement** apparatus, would face dramatic and escalating pollution problems as a result of increased investment in manufacturing and vegetable production. There is evidence, for example, that pesticide pollution would increase in Mexico (but decrease in Florida) following a trade agreement. The following judgment was thus made: environmental improvements that accompany reductions in poverty and the import of technology will not compensate for the direct increase in pollution. On balance, it was argued, freer trade will lead to deteriorating environmental conditions in poor countries. Ironically, at least in the maize case, it appears that the reverse is true: as U.S. corn production increased by close to 1% to serve the Mexican market, agricultural pollution shifted from Mexico to the United States.[24]

Again, the response from supporters of trade was strengthen enforcement activities, don't restrict trade. NAFTA does contain a "side agreement" on environmental issues that in principle gives parties the ability to prod businesses that "persistently" violate environmental laws to comply. However, the process is complex and restrictive; the commission set up to oversee complaints has accomplished little.[25]

The final environmental charge against a free-trade agreement is that environmental regulations in rich countries will be weakened as (1) **business mobility increases** and (2) foreign governments and companies issue **trade-based challenges to environmental laws**. This process is known as a **race to the bottom**. In Chapter 6, we learned that differences in the stringency of environmental regulation in fact appear to have little influence on business location decisions. Much more important are wage differences and access to markets. Given this, U.S. lawmakers appear to have little to lose by maintaining strong environmental standards. Indeed, Mexico could begin stringently enforcing its laws without sacrificing investment from the United States.

Unfortunately, it is not always reality but perception that matters in regulatory decisions. Much of the public and many policymakers appear to believe that strong environmental standards discourage investment. Evidence from the few industries in which environmental regulation *has* discouraged investment can be used as a stick by industry to weaken standards.

Free-trade agreements can also lead to a race to the bottom as they give foreign governments and corporations the ability to challenge certain regulations as trade barriers. Table 20.2 provides a list of several recent challenges. One of the most widely cited has been a case in which the U.S. government imposed a ban on the import of Latin American tuna. The embargo was enacted because these countries were not using fishing techniques required by U.S. law to reduce the incidental killing of dolphins and other marine animals. Mexico challenged the embargo under the terms of the General Agreement on Tariffs and Trade (GATT), a predecessor to the WTO. The trade court

23. Ackerman et al. (2003).
24. Ackerman et al. (2003).
25. The body set up by NAFTA, the North American Commission for Environmental Cooperation, has its website at www.cec.org.

TABLE 20.2 Trade Challenges to Environmental Regulation

Measure	Trade Agreement	Challenger	Decision
U.S. ban on Latin American tuna imports	GATT	Mexican govt.	Ban declared illegal
Danish requirement that drinks be sold in reusable deposit containers	Treaty of Rome	U.K. govt., European beer manufacturers	Deposit requirement upheld, reuse weakened
U.S. ban on asbestos	U.S.-Canada FTA	Quebec govt.	Ban overturned on other grounds; trade issue referred to GATT
Canadian requirement that fish must be sampled prior to export, to promote conservation	U.S.-Canada FTA	—	Requirement declared illegal
Canadian review of natural gas export license	U.S.-Canada FTA	U.S. energy companies	Review dropped
U.S. standards for reformulated gasoline	WTO	Venezuelan government	Standards revised
Japanese efficiency standards for auto engines	WTO	U.S. govt., auto manufacturers	Case dropped
California ban on MBTE	WTO	Methanex Corp.	Review dropped on a technicality

Sources: Based on data from Shrybman (1992); U.S. defeated in its appeal of trade case. 1996. *New York Times*, 30 May D1; and Wallach and Sforza (1999).

ruled in Mexico's favor, arguing that member nations were not allowed to dictate production methods beyond their borders. The United States was forced to rescind the ban or face international trade sanctions.

An unanticipated feature of NAFTA that has raised major concern relates not to restrictions on trade, but rather on investment. A clause in the treaty, known as "Chapter 11," prohibits countries from expropriating the property of investors without compensation. Under this clause, companies have started to sue governments that impose environmental regulations, arguing that these regulations are in effect expropriations of profit. For example, a Canadian cattle company has sued the U.S. government for $300 million over closing the border to Canada for beef imports following a mad cow incident. A Canadian mining company has sued the United States for $50 million in damages over a California requirement that open-pit mines be backfilled and restored if they pose a threat to Native American sacred sites. And a U.S. company won its suit against Canada over a ban on the gasoline additive MMT. The Canadian government, after losing in the NAFTA tribunal, lifted the ban and paid the company $13 million in damages.[26] Chapter 11 effectively undermines the

---

26. Public Citizen (2005).

"polluter pays" principle and gives companies the right to pollute, rather than giving governments the right to prevent pollution.

As Table 20.2 illustrates, by prohibiting import and export bans, regulations, and tariffs, free-trade agreements can tie the hands of environmental agencies. In effect, environmental decisions made by democratically elected bodies (congresses and parliaments) can be overruled by a very closed international legal process, of which the primary treaty charge is to promote free trade for the sake of efficiency gains.

This section has provided a look at the debate over the environmental impact of free-trade agreements. Clearly, trade can be a vital component of any strategy to promote sustainable development. When trade works to reduce poverty, it can provide environmental benefits in the form of greater investment in air and water quality, reduced pressure on the local environment, and lowered population growth rates.

However, the economic growth that accompanies free-trade agreements need not reduce poverty. In the Mexican case, the "losers" from NAFTA have been the large class of small corn farmers. More generally, we saw in Chapter 19 that trade in natural-resource-based industries can foster unsustainable development. This occurs when the *full* resource rent is not reinvested in created capital in the developing country. In a world whose poor-country governments are both debt-burdened and have difficulty collecting and productively investing tax revenues from resource-based industries, such an outcome is not unlikely.

Critics have also charged that, despite the environmental benefits that accompany growth, the direct increase in pollution will lead to a decline in environmental quality in poor countries. Finally, they charge that environmental regulations in rich countries will be weakened as business mobility increases and legal challenges are lodged by international competitors.

In the decade-plus since the Seattle WTO protests, there has been a growing response in America and Europe to "localize" economic activity by using the power of government to promote the purchase of, especially, local food. This movement has been spurred on by a belief that shipping the average tomato 1,500 miles from farm to fork simply has to be an inefficient practice! Let's pause to consider a food

PUZZLE

If local food production is in fact more efficient than global agribusiness, why is locally produced food generally much more expensive? And if we were serious about replacing global food production with local production, what policies would be most efficient?

SOLUTION

There are good reasons and bad reasons why agribusiness food is cheap. Good reasons include economies of scale in food production and transport, and comparative advantages in terms of soil, climate, and workforce. Bad reasons would be unaccounted-for social costs: externalities. So, for example, global food production and transport is artificially cheap because oil is artificially cheap (see the global-warming discussion in Chapter 1 and the "peak oil" discussion in Chapter 8); water and topsoil are also artificially cheap (see Chapter 8); undocumented immigrant farm labor is also artificially cheap; and pesticide and chemical runoff from agriculture is largely unregulated (see Chapter 13).

In this case, a policy response that would promote local food production would be to raise the price of these externalized input and output costs through regulation and/or pollution taxes, thereby getting the prices "right." The economist's response in this case is, don't restrict food imports, which deliver real benefits to communities and could beggar our poorer, food-exporting neighbors. Instead, resolve the pollution and labor problems directly, to level the playing field.

An encouraging experiment promoting local food production comes from Brazil's fourth-largest city, Belo Horizonte. There the city government has provided choice retail locations throughout the urban area for farmer's markets, and for "ABC" stores (ABC is the Portuguese acronym for "food at low prices.") These shops are required to sell 20 basic, healthy foods at state-set prices, and then are free to sell other goods at the market rate. The city also serves 12,000 meals a day, made from local foods at low-cost "People's Restaurants." The result of these and other initiatives has been the development of a healthy local food industry and dramatic reductions in hunger: Belo Horizonte has cut its infant death rate by more than 50%. The cost has been quite reasonable: about $10 million each year, around 2% of the city's budget, and about one penny a day per resident.[27]

Is free trade good or bad for the environment? Freer trade is generally championed by economists because it tends to increase efficiency; and as we know from Chapter 4, more efficient production means a bigger overall economic pie. The environmental challenge is to channel the efficiency gains from trade into investment in a sustainable future. From this perspective, freer trade should be viewed as a means to an end—stabilizing population growth and building human capital, enhancing food security, transferring sustainable technology, and conserving resources—not as an end in itself. Yet at this point, trade agreements have only just begun to acknowledge environmental and sustainability concerns.

20.8 Summary

Environmental policy in poor countries cannot be narrowly viewed as "controlling pollution." The complex and conflicting problems of poverty, population growth, and environmental and resource degradation require a broader focus: promoting sustainable development. This task in turn can be broken down into four subareas: controlling population growth, ensuring food security, promoting clean and sustainable technology, and conserving natural resources.

---

27. Lappé (2009).

This chapter has considered several general steps that governments can take in these directions. These include reducing environmentally damaging subsidies, working to clarify and enforce communal or private property rights, regulating pollution in as cost-effective a manner as possible, promoting the development and transfer of sustainable technology, conserving natural capital by encouraging sustained-yield resource development, and ensuring that the gains from trade are funneled into measures promoting sustainable development.

One recurring theme in this chapter has been the question of who will pay for these programs. Until recently, many poor countries have questioned the wisdom of environmental or natural resource protection, reasoning that they could not afford to engage in such measures. There is an increasing recognition, however, that improving environmental quality is often a good economic investment. The financial reality remains unchanged, however. Developing countries still cannot afford to make many of these investments.

As an example, the people of Burkina Faso would benefit greatly if the erosion control measures discussed in Section 20.5 were widely disseminated, boosting agricultural productivity and incomes, and slowing down population growth rates and rural-to-urban migration. Yet the country is desperately poor. As a result, such programs are proceeding at a snail's pace, funded through private donations by people in affluent countries.

Ultimately, sustainable development in low-income countries is unlikely to occur without a substantial commitment of resources by those of us in rich countries. This commitment can take a variety of forms: research and development in clean and sustainable technologies ranging from solar and wind power to biotechnology to improved refrigerators and stoves, funding of family planning efforts, debt relief in the form of debt-for-nature swaps, international aid for rural development projects, financial and technical assistance in the implementation of environmental regulatory programs; the removal of trade barriers to poor-country products, and adjustment aid to help poor countries reduce their own environmentally damaging subsidies.

In some instances, this kind of resource commitment is justified on the basis of narrow self-interest. Global pollution problems such as the accelerated greenhouse effect and ozone depletion *will not* be adequately addressed without such efforts. Natural resources that we in rich countries value—medical products, agricultural gene pools, wild animal species, and wilderness—*will be* rapidly exhausted if we do not pay our share for their protection. Beyond narrow self-interest, however, resources must be committed by those of us in rich countries if we want to ensure a high quality of life for our children and grandchildren.

One environmental impact of continuing population and consumption growth will be simply to intensify the problems of local air and water pollution, disposal of solid and hazardous waste, exposure to toxic chemicals, and the disappearance of green spaces and wild creatures. On the other hand, such trends are leading to new and unimagined changes in the global environment. Within the last decade, two such threats have emerged: ozone depletion and global warming. The final chapter of the book turns to the increasingly critical issue of global environmental regulation.

APPLICATION 20.0

Subsidy Removal: Environmental and Social Impact

Some have argued that removing government controls that keep food prices down is a necessary step to ensure food security.[28] In addition, some maintain, the subsequent increase in price will reduce soil erosion by giving farmers stronger incentives (and access to capital) to invest in long-term erosion control measures.

1. It seems counterintuitive to argue that increasing the price that consumers face for food will, in many cases, actually improve access to food. How can you explain this line of reasoning?
2. In the short run, who would suffer most from lifting price controls on food? How can this problem be addressed?
3. Can you think of a reason why rising food prices might actually increase soil erosion?

APPLICATION 20.1

Environmental Regulation and Nontariff Barriers

In the past, the United States has imposed a ban on the export of unprocessed logs from public lands in the Pacific Northwest, with the purported intent of slowing down deforestation of the spotted owl ecosystem. Japan objected to the ban, arguing that it is a "thinly disguised nontariff barrier" to trade. "The ban does not meet the environmental objective, since it does not apply to processed wood products. [Rather] it will raise the price of unprocessed wood to Japan (the U.S. is the largest timber supplier to Japan) and encourage ailing U.S. wood processing industries."[29]

From the U.S. perspective, of course, aiding our wood-processing industries might seem like a good idea, particularly if the burden of higher prices is borne by a principal competitor. The danger, of course, is that this kind of action might prompt retaliation by the Japanese in the form of trade restrictions on U.S. products.

To sort out whether environmentally motivated regulations or product standards are genuine, or are instead thinly disguised trade barriers, consider the following suggestion: Standards or regulations must not only meet the environmental objective but also do so in a *least-cost* way.

1. Do you think the Japanese objection, as stated, is correct?
2. Do you think the ban is an environmental measure or a trade barrier?
3. If a regulation or product standard does not meet the environmental objective in a least-cost way, then we may be justified in assuming it to be a trade barrier. Do you agree?

---

28. This problem draws in part on an unpublished paper by S. Barret (1990) called "Macroeconomic Policy Reforms and the Third World Soil Conservation," summarized in Dean (1992).
29. This summary of the Japanese objection is found in Dean (1992).

KEY IDEAS IN EACH SECTION

20.0   This chapter considers **sustainability policy** in poor countries. The basic message is that none of these policies is cheap; in many cases, success will require investment aid from wealthy countries.

20.1   We begin with a brief consideration of the possibility of government failure due to imperfect information and political influence, both compounded by a lack of resources and small **political-economic elites**. Both **multinational** and **domestic business** can have substantial political influence in poor countries.

20.2   Removing **environmentally damaging subsidies** in industries such as timber, energy, and agriculture is the first policy considered. For example, tropical deforestation is promoted by (1) **failure to capture resource rents** ("low" timber prices), (2) **infrastructure development**, (3) **subsidized "downstream" industries**, (4) **colonization projects**, and (5) **subsidized cattle ranching**. When subsidies are removed, **compensation** is often required, both on political and fairness grounds.

20.3   Reducing **open access to common property** is a second policy. This can be achieved by strengthening **property rights**, whether **communal**, **state**, or **private**. Once property rights are established, it is at least possible to establish systems of **payment for ecosystem services** (**PES**). When ownership rights are strengthened, owners are more likely to engage in profit-based conservation. Private and communal owners in poor countries often have greater incentives, and more resources, than do state managers for good management. Yet privatization can penalize the poor and is itself a difficult task for poor country governments to manage well.

20.4   The general points made in Chapters 15 and 16 about **incentive-based** versus **command-and-control** regulation hold true in poor countries. However, special attention must be paid to **enforceability** and **administrative simplicity**. **Indirect pollution taxes**, such as **timber royalties** or **gasoline taxes**, are thus appealing; but because they don't tax pollution directly, their environmental effect must be carefully considered. Flexible or targeted CAC measures are also good regulatory strategies.

20.5   A **sustainable technology** is a **clean technology** that also improves the economic position of the poor majority. Government can promote the development and diffusion of sustainable technology using tools such as **subsidies** and **infrastructure investment**. Major sources of technology transfer are **nongovernmental organizations** (**NGOs**) and **multinational corporations**. Poor countries can encourage the transfer of clean technology by instituting environmental regulation and by obtaining adequate tax concessions from multinationals for reinvestment elsewhere in the economy.

20.6   Two obstacles to resource conservation in poor countries are the intensity of the **development-environment conflict** and the difficulty of **enforcement**. One way to address these problems is through **sustained-yield resource development**. Examples from the rain forest include **sustained-yield farming and ranching harvesting of wild products** prospecting for **pharmaceuticals** and **agricultural genes** and tourism. However, the forest also delivers nonmarketable **(public)** goods, such as a **carbon sink rainfall regulator**, and **existence value**. The **free-rider problem** means that, without some collective mechanism for rich countries to pay for preservation, inefficiently low levels of preservation will occur. One such mechanism is a **debt-for-nature swap**.

20.7 Debates over the **North American Free Trade Agreement (NAFTA)** illustrate the environmental pros and cons of freer trade. If it leads to **poverty reduction** in Mexico, NAFTA may improve environmental quality. However, as U.S. corn floods the market, rural poverty may have deepened. In addition, through **weak environmental enforcement** and a **race to the bottom** over regulatory standards (in turn arising from **increased business mobility** and **trade-based regulatory challenges**), trade agreements may undermine environmental quality in both trading countries.

REFERENCES

Ackerman, Frank, Timothy Wise, Kevin Gallagher, Luke Ney, and Regina Flores. 2003. *Environmental impacts of the changes in U.S.–Mexico corn trade under NAFTA.* NACEC. Global Development and Environment Institute, Working paper 03–06. Medford, MA: Tufts University.

Baccini, A., S. J. Goetz, W. S. Walker, N. T. Laporte, M. Sun, D. Sulla-Menashe, J. Hackler, et al. 2012. Estimated carbon dioxide emissions from tropical deforestation improved by carbon-density maps. *Nature Climate Change* 2: 182–5.

Balint, Peter, and Judith Mashinya. 2008. CAMPFIRE during Zimbabwe's national crisis: Local impacts and broader implications for community-based wildlife management. *Society and Natural Resources* 21(9): 783–96.

Balmford, A., A. Bruner, P. Cooper, R. Costanza, S. Farber, R. Green, M. Jenkins, et al. 2002. Economic reasons for conserving wild nature. *Science* 297: 950–3.

Barrows, Richard, and Michael Roth. 1990. Land tenure and investment in African agriculture: Theory and evidence. *Journal of Modern African Studies* 28(2): 265–98.

Browder, John O. 1988. Public policy and deforestation in the Brazilian Amazon. In *Public policies and the misuse of forest resources*, ed. Robert Repetto and Malcolm Gillis. Cambridge: Cambridge University Press.

Deacon, Robert, and Paul Murphy. 1997. The structure of an environmental transaction: The debt-for-nature swap. *Land Economics* 73(1): 1–24.

Dean, Judith. 1992. *Trade and the environment: A survey of the literature*. Policy research working paper WPS966. Washington, DC: World Bank.

Frost, Peter G. H., and Ivan Bond. 2008. The CAMPFIRE programme in Zimbabwe: Payments for wildlife services. *Ecological Economics* 65(4): 776–87.

Fundaçao Pró-Natureza and the Nature Conservancy. 1991. *Grande Sertao Veredas National Park debt conversion proposal, revised draft*. Washington, DC: The Nature Conservancy.

Gillis, Malcolm. 1988. Malaysia: Public policies and the tropical forest. In *Public policies and the misuse of forest resources*, ed. Robert Repetto and Malcolm Gillis. West Nyack, NY: Cambridge University Press.

Hanna, Susan, and Mohan Munasinghe. 1995. *Property rights and the environment: Social and ecological issues*. Washington, DC: World Bank.

Katz, Elizabeth. 2000. Natural resource management in Guatemala. *Land Economics* 76(1): 114–32.

Lappé, Frances Moore. 2009. The city that ended hunger. *Yes!* 49 (Spring). http://www.yesmagazine.org/issues/food-for-everyone/the-city-that-ended-hunger.

Lepkowski, Wil. 1987. The disaster at Bhopal—Chemical safety in the third world. In *Multinational corporations, environment and the third world*, ed. Charles S. Pearson. Chapel Hill, NC: Duke University Press.

Musambachime, Mwelma. 1990. The impact of rapid population growth on economic decline: The case of Zambia. *Review of African Political Economy* 448(2): 81–91.

Pearce, David, and Norman Myers. 1990. Economic values and the environment of Amazonia. In *The future of Amazonia: Destruction or sustainable development?*, ed. David Goodman and Anthony Hall. New York: St. Martin's Press.

Public Citizen. 2005. *NAFTA Chapter 11: Investor-state cases: Lessons for the Central America Free Trade Agreement*. Washington, DC: Public Citizen.

Repetto, Robert. 1988. Overview. In *Public policies and the misuse of forest resources*, ed. Robert Repetto and Malcolm Gillis. West Nyack, NY: Cambridge University Press.

Schneider, Robert. 1993. *Land abandonment, property rights, and agricultural sustainability in the Amazon*. LATEN dissemination note 3. Washington, DC: World Bank, Latin America Technical Department.

Shin, Sangbum. 2004. Economic globalization and the environment in China: A comparative case study of Shenyang and Dalian. *Journal of Environment & Development* 13(3): 263–94.

Shrybman, Steven. 1992. Trading away the environment. *World Policy Journal* (Winter) 93–110.

Ton, Kees, and Kees de Jong. 1991. Irrigation technology and social change: An analysis of social variables of technology. *Journal of Developing Areas* 25: 197–206.

Wallach, Lori, and Michelle Sforza. 1999. *Whose trade organization? Corporate globalization and the erosion of democracy.* Washington, DC: Public Citizen.

Wardman, Anna, and Luci G. Salas. 1991. The implementation of anti-erosion techniques in the Sahel: A case study from Kaya, Burkina Faso. *Journal of Developing Areas* 26(1): 65–80.

Wheeler, David, and John Martin. 1993. *Prices, policies and the international diffusion of clean technology: The case of wood pulp production.* Paper presented at the American Economic Association Meetings, Anaheim, California.

World Bank. 1992. *World development report 1992: Development and the environment.* New York: Oxford University Press.

World Bank. 2012. State and trends of the carbon market report 2012. http://web.worldbank.org/WBSITE/EXTERNAL/TOPICS/ENVIRONMENT/EXTCARBON FINANCE/.

21

The Economics of Global Agreements

21.0 Introduction

This books ends where it began. The reality of global warming burst into human consciousness barely 20 years ago, suddenly and at a scale dwarfing the local and regional pollution problems that defined the 20th century. Incredibly, the human ecological footprint is now disrupting the entire planet's climate control system. Even if we manage to hold further warming to the low end of 4 degrees F, still we will have pushed the earth into a climate that is fundamentally different from the one that has supported human civilization for the last 10,000 years. In the coming decades, human-induced global warming will challenge both humans' adaptability and the survival of perhaps half the species on the planet. Mitigating and adapting to climate change will be the work of your generation.

Since our early introduction to global warming, we have explored four difficult, but general, environmental economic questions. The answers to these questions can help us address the global-warming challenge. First, how much pollution—in this case, global warming—is too much? We considered three broad answers to this normative question: efficiency, safety, and ecological sustainability. Efficiency advocates would have us carefully balance the very real costs of slowing global warming against the obvious benefits. Both safety and ecological proponents find benefit-cost analysis too narrow a basis for choice, and advocate immediate rollback of carbon dioxide emissions, despite the cost.

The second issue is, what are the obstacles to effective governmental action in achieving our goals? Suppose we set a target to cut carbon dioxide emissions 15% by the year 2020? Are we in fact likely to get there? Government policymakers are hampered by imperfect information. In addition, the possibility of political influence over environmental policy emerges when regulators must make discretionary choices. Our 40-plus-year experience with environmental regulation indicates that ambitious pollution reduction goals have proven difficult to achieve. Enforcement in particular has proven a weak link in the regulatory chain.

Our third question asked how can we do better? The book suggested two possible answers: (1) smarter regulation and (2) a shift in government focus to the promotion of clean technology. Incentive-based regulation carries the promise of reducing pollution in a more cost-effective and technologically dynamic manner than the current reliance on command-and-control methods. In the greenhouse case, this means that carbon taxes or marketable permit systems can help us achieve our goals at lower cost than mandating particular types of carbon dioxide emission-reduction technology.

In addition to better regulation, the government can initiate a proactive policy promoting the rapid development and diffusion of clean technology. To qualify as clean, a technology must be found cost-competitive, either immediately or after only a short period of subsidy. If the government follows this selection rule, the policy of promoting clean technology will also be cost-effective. Clean technologies with substantial power to reduce carbon dioxide emissions include energy efficiency, solar power, and wind power.

Here is the fourth and final question: Is an effort to combat global warming consistent with the need for sustainable development in poor countries? On the one hand, boosting the incomes of the poor majority of the planet in order to raise billions of people out of desperate poverty, increase food security, and ultimately reduce population growth rates will work against the goal of CO_2 emission reductions in the short term. Yet consumption by the poorest half of the planet's inhabitants is not the main greenhouse problem. Moreover, reduced population growth is a vital step in any program to control global warming. At the same time, promotion and diffusion of sustainable technology, and greater efforts to conserve forest resources, will directly reduce carbon dioxide emissions.

This chapter of the book considers one last and formidable obstacle toward progress on global environmental issues such as slowing global warming: the need for coordinated international action. Because carbon dioxide pollution arises across the globe, no one country can solve the global warming problem. International action, in turn, will result only from *effective* international agreements. Such agreements are unfortunately hard to achieve, and once reached, can prove difficult to enforce.

We begin by analyzing the incentives that a nation has, first to join an international pollution-control agreement and second to comply with the terms of that agreement once it is signed. We then turn to a discussion of the tools available for enforcing such treaties. The chapter then moves on to analyze two international agreements, one on ozone depletion and the other on biodiversity. We end by coming full circle with a consideration of the prospects for an effective treaty to halt global warming.

21.1 Agreements as Public Goods

Effective international agreements are hard to develop. The basic problem is that agreement on burden sharing is difficult to achieve. In principle, each country might contribute its **true willingness to pay** for a treaty. This willingness to pay in turn would depend on both the benefits received and the ability to pay, which might vary widely between nations. For example, low-lying Bangladesh and Egypt have a tremendous stake in slowing global warming and preventing a sea-level rise. Yet both countries are poor and would have a difficult time financing strong measures to reduce carbon dioxide emissions. On the other hand, a wealthy country like Germany has a high ability to pay but may have fewer immediate interests at stake.

A poor country's willingness to pay to join an agreement will typically be much smaller than a rich country's, simply because it has a much lower national income. Yet poor-country participation is often vital. For example, if China industrializes further, using its vast coal reserves, global warming will accelerate considerably. Given China's low willingness to pay for a reduction in global warming (as a result of its low income), a compensation fund would have to be established for China to sign a greenhouse treaty. Those with a high willingness to pay (typically rich countries) would have to pay to help China adopt, at a faster pace than the nation already is, less-polluting and less-costly energy sources. Otherwise, it would not be in China's interests to sign the treaty.

If each nation did contribute its true willingness to pay, then the agreement process would generate an efficient level of global pollution control. However, a country's underlying willingness to pay for an agreement is not well defined in the first place and is certainly not transparent to negotiators from other nations. Therefore, each nation's bargainers will have an incentive to *understate* their true interest in a treaty in the hopes that others will shoulder more of the burden. In the extreme, a country might not sign a global warming or other environmental treaty at all *but still benefit* from the efforts of other nations.

This is just another form of the **free-rider problem** we have encountered several times in the book, beginning in Chapter 3. From an economic point of view, an international pollution-control agreement is a **public good**, which has to be provided *voluntarily* by the private nations of the world. Reducing global warming is a public good, because there is no way to exclude free riders from enjoying the benefits provided by the treaty.

The public good nature of environmental treaties has two implications. First, treaties will tend to be **too weak** from a benefit-cost point of view, as signatory nations are reluctant to reveal and commit their true willingness to pay in the bargaining process. Second, once signed, nations will have a strong **incentive to cheat** on the agreement. Unilateral cheating is another way to free ride on the pollution-control efforts of others. Of course, if everyone cheats, the agreement will collapse.

While the theory of public goods predicts that international environmental treaties will be both weak and susceptible to enforcement problems, agreements nevertheless do get signed and efforts are made to ensure compliance. Table 21.1 lists some of the most significant environmental treaties now in effect.

21.2 Monitoring and Enforcement

In Chapter 3, we noted two ways to overcome the free-rider problem: government provision of the public good and social pressure. Within a single country, government typically supplies the public good of environmental protection, using its ability to tax, fine, and jail to prevent free riding (pollution) by private individuals and corporations. In the United States, for example, environmental laws are passed by Congress, and the regulatory details are then worked out and enforced by the Environmental Protection Agency and the Justice Department.

TABLE 21.1 Global Environmental Agreements

Formal Name (Common Name)	Year Signed	Prominent Nonmembers, 2010
The Antarctic Treaty System	1959	Self-limited membership
Nuclear Test Ban Treaty	1963	France, China
The Convention on International Trade in Endangered Species of Wild Flora and Fauna (CITES Treaty)[a]	1973	
New Management Procedure of International Whaling Commission (Whaling Moratoria)	1974	Japan
Law of the Sea (not currently in force)	1982	United States, United Kingdom, West Germany
Montreal Protocol on Substances That Deplete the Ozone Layer (Montreal Protocol)	1987	
The Basel Convention on Transboundary Movement of Hazardous Wastes and Their Disposal (Basel Convention)[b]	1989	African nations
Kyoto Global Warming Treaty	1997	United States
Rio Convention on Biodiversity[c]	1992	United States

Treaty websites: www.cites.org/www.ats.aq.
[a]www.wcmc.org.uk/CITES.
[b]www.ban.org.
[c]www.biodiv.org.

At the international level, the treaty is the equivalent of an environmental law. However, *no* international government exists that coerces nations into undertaking the broadly agreed-upon steps, nor is there likely to be one soon. The United Nations has no authority over its member nations in the environmental arena. Nevertheless, each treaty does set up its own **intergovernmental organization** (**IGO**), which is charged with overseeing the agreement. Countries seldom agree to give IGOs the authority to actually enforce treaty agreements; this would be giving away too much sovereignty. However, IGOs can still be given substantive powers. One of these is to set **nonbinding standards** that states are "expected" but not required to meet. The second is to **monitor** compliance with agreements.

For example, under the Antarctic Treaty, an environmental committee has been appointed to which each nation must submit information on its management procedures. Environmental impact statements (see Chapter 8) are also now required for new activities, including tourism, sponsored by a member nation. Social pressure can then be brought to bear on states that either fail to achieve the standards or are out of compliance with the broader terms of the treaty. The environmental group Greenpeace has effectively "shamed" countries with particularly poor environmental records on the continent.

Such **social pressure** is the second way in which free riding has traditionally been controlled. However, a well-orchestrated public relations campaign encouraging the

United States to join with the "community of nations" was insufficient to get it to sign a biodiversity treaty. Such moral pressures are even less likely to be effective in ensuring compliance once treaties have been signed. Nevertheless, bad publicity and community pressure, as in the Antarctic case mentioned earlier, remain among the important tools of international negotiation.

Given the lack of an international pollution-control agency, and the limited effectiveness of social pressure, the burden of enforcement will fall on measures written into the treaty itself. Treaty members must agree in advance on the sanctions to be levied against noncomplying members or nonmembers. In the absence of such sanctions, compliance is liable to be very poor. For example, the CITES treaty regulating trade in endangered species relies primarily on national enforcement efforts. According to the World Wildlife Federation, an environmental group that voluntarily monitors CITES, about one-third of the member nations have never filed the required biennial progress report. Most nations that do report have done so in a very tardy manner. The basic problem is a lack of committed resources. Even in a rich country such as the United States, a lack of trained customs officials means that up to 60,000 parrots have entered the country illegally in a single year.[1]

There are two basic enforcement tools: restricting access to a compensation fund and imposing trade sanctions. The simplest mechanism is to establish a **compensation fund** to act as a carrot for both joining a treaty and complying with its terms. Such compensation funds, however, can induce compliance only by poor countries as high-income countries are the ones who contribute to the fund. **Trade sanctions** are the most powerful tool available. As we shall see, their mere existence played an important part in the success of the agreement to control depletion of the ozone layer. Sanctions tend to be restricted to goods related to the treaty. This is useful, as it minimizes the possibility that the imposition of sanctions for enforcement purposes will degenerate into a trade war. For example, under the CITES treaty, a ban on trade in wildlife products from Thailand was imposed to encourage that country to crack down on illegal exports. Many environmental agreements authorize some form of trade sanction.

21.3 The Ozone Layer and Biodiversity

This section examines two environmental treaties: the 1987 Montreal Protocol to control the depletion of the ozone layer and the 1992 Rio Earth Summit agreement on biodiversity. We focus on the factors that promoted agreement and the enforcement mechanisms built in. In the ozone case, we also have a compliance record to examine.

OZONE DEPLETION

The earth's upper atmosphere is surrounded by a thin shield of a naturally occurring chemical known as ozone. Ozone at ground level is better known as smog and is quite harmful. By contrast, the **ozone layer** surrounding the earth serves a beneficial role by screening out the sun's harmful ultraviolet rays. Exposure to ultraviolet rays causes skin cancer and eye disease, reduces the productivity of agriculture, and can kill small terrestrial and marine organisms at the base of the food chain.

---

1. Heppes and McFadden (1987).

The ozone layer is threatened by the buildup of human-made chemicals in the upper atmosphere. These chemicals, known as chlorofluorocarbons (CFCs), were invented in the 1940s. They have since served as aerosol propellants, coolants in refrigerators and air conditioners, foam-blowing agents, and gaseous cleansers for medical and computer equipment. They are also very long-lived stock pollutants. CFCs released into the atmosphere from discarded refrigerators today will continue to break down the ozone layer for up to 100 years.

The potential for significant ozone depletion by CFCs was first established in 1974. Despite the serious health and ecological effects of ozone depletion, uncertainty about the scientific link between depletion and CFCs slowed international regulatory action. Although the United States unilaterally banned CFCs as aerosol propellants in 1977, few other countries followed suit. In 1982, a benefit-cost analysis published in the prestigious *American Economic Review*, while acknowledging substantial uncertainty, argued *against* regulating CFC use on efficiency grounds.[2] This position was also advanced by CFC manufacturers.

Nevertheless, international concern over the problem was mounting, fueled by a 1985 British study documenting a huge, seasonal **ozone hole** over Antarctica. Less severe, but measurable depletion was occurring throughout the middle latitudes. In 1987, building on six years of United Nations efforts, 24 countries signed the **Montreal Protocol** to Protect Against Atmospheric Ozone Reduction. Just *after* the protocol was signed, a conclusive scientific link between ozone depletion and CFCs was at last established.

The treaty called for a ten-year, 50% reduction in CFC production by each country from a 1986 baseline. The treaty made some concessions to poor countries, which would otherwise be locked into current levels of low consumption, and were hardly responsible for the global problem in the first place. Developing countries were given a ten-year grace period before cutbacks would have to be made. In addition, rich countries were urged, but not required, to set up an assistance fund to ease the transition.[3]

These incentives were insufficient to attract India and China, both of which viewed the benefits of cheap refrigeration from CFCs as too high to forgo. As a result, a 1990 revision of the Montreal Protocol required rich countries to establish a fund of $260 million to finance the adjustment to CFC replacements in poor countries, and that $60 million was to be contributed by the primary CFC producer, the United States. This fund provided a sufficient inducement for most of the remaining nonmember countries to join, including India and China.

As a way to discourage free riding by nonmembers, the treaty mandated trade restrictions on CFCs. Parties to the treaty were required to ban imports and exports of CFCs, many products containing CFCs, products produced with CFCs, and technologies for producing CFCs to nonmember countries. These trade sanctions limited the gains from nonmembership and thus reduced free riding.

The half-dozen companies that produce the great bulk of CFCs worldwide ultimately supported the 1987 Montreal Protocol, although they viewed the goal of a 50%

2. Bailey (1982).
3. Somerset (1989).

reduction as greater than necessary. But by 1988, faced with mounting evidence of ozone depletion, the major producer DuPont announced its intentions to phase out CFCs altogether by the year 2000. In 1990, the Montreal Protocol nations also revised the treaty to call for a complete ban by the year 2000. In 1992, after a finding that an accelerated phaseout might save an additional million lives through reduced skin cancer, the treaty nations agreed to eliminate CFC production by 1996. The compensation fund was also boosted to $500 million.

Compliance with the early terms of the treaty by the rich countries was quite good; the accelerated phaseout adopted in 1992 was possible because several nations were already ahead of schedule. As discussed in Chapter 16, the United States adopted an incentive-based regulatory approach—tradeable permits combined with indirect pollution taxes—to meet its treaty obligations. Developing countries appear to be making good on their commitments as well. The compensation fund in particular has been credited with helping China meet its mandated targets.[4]

The first two sections of this chapter suggested, on theoretical grounds, that the prospects for obtaining enforceable international agreements on the environment were not good. In many ways, the Montreal Protocol contradicts such a gloomy picture. Despite scientific uncertainty, initial international agreement was obtained. The threat of trade sanctions helped overcome the free-rider problem. A sufficient compensation fund was eventually established to bring poor countries on board. The pollution control target was dramatically tightened as scientific knowledge advanced, and compliance has been remarkably good in the developed countries.

Several factors help explain the success of the Montreal Protocol. The dramatic discovery of the ozone hole over the Antarctic provided an initial boost to the treaty process, as did findings of a comparable arctic hole in 1992. Once the agreement had been signed, however, two additional factors worked in its favor. First, because only six main corporations were involved in the production of CFCs, monitoring the progress of the CFC phaseout has been relatively easy. Second, clean technological substitutes for CFCs have developed quickly as a result of the imminent ban. Early predictions of prohibitively high compliance costs proved faulty.

To sum up, the Montreal Protocol has proven to be a stunningly successful environmental treaty. Beginning with initial meetings in 1980, through the 50% cuts agreed to in 1987, and the accelerated phaseout decided on in 1992, it took "only" 16 years to effectively ban the production of CFCs. By 2010. the Antarctic ozone hole had stopped growing, and it should fully repair itself by around 2050.[5] Given the elevation in skin cancers likely to emerge even after the 1996 phaseout, CFCs have already earned their place in the history books as one of the most destructive pollutants released into the environment.

BIODIVERSITY

Protecting **biodiversity** means protecting endangered species—not only cuddly mammals but also the entire ecosystems in which they live. As we discussed in the last chapter on deforestation, preserving the stock of genetic material found in natural

---

4. Zhao (2005).
5. Information on the status of the Treaty is at www.unep.org/ozone/.

ecosystems is important not only for its **existence value** but also for two utilitarian reasons: **pharmaceuticals** and **agricultural breeding**. As an example, a strain of wild Mexican maize had a natural immunity to two serious viral diseases. Hybrid corn seeds based on the genetic material in the maize are now available from U.S.-based seed companies.

The fact that Mexico received no compensation for this profitable innovation helps explain why the valuable resource of biodiversity is threatened.[6] Historically, genetic material has been viewed as an **open access**, common property resource. Seed and drug companies based in rich countries would send prospectors to tropical countries that are host to the vast majority of the world's species. (A single tree in an Amazon rain forest contained 43 species of ants, more than in the entire British Isles!) The prospectors would return with samples to be analyzed for prospective commercial uses. If a plant or animal then generated a profitable return, the country from which it originated would receive no benefit. Host country residents, not being able to realize any of the commercial value of biodiversity, have thus been little interested in conservation.

This situation has begun to change a bit, thanks largely to improvements in technologies that have made large-scale screening and cataloging of species economically attractive. Costa Rica has struck several deals with drug companies as well as with several U.S. foundations and universities to develop a "forest prospecting industry." The long-run goal is to train a Costa Rican workforce capable of regulating biological prospectors. Costa Rica will then grant access to its forests, conditional on receiving a share of profits from any agricultural or pharmaceutical innovations. Building a strong institutional base for this industry is important so that Costa Rica can prevent illegal prospecting, as well as forestall efforts by corporations to synthesize a new drug based on a botanical finding, and then fail to report it.

Essentially what Costa Rica is doing is shifting an open-access, common property resource into a state-owned resource by beefing up its technical **enforcement capabilities**. This in turn greatly strengthens the incentive for profit-based conservation. Costa Rica is well placed to do this on its own, because it has a relatively efficient bureaucracy, has a highly literate population, already has an extensive national park network, and has strong links with U.S.-based conservation groups.[7]

Global efforts to protect biodiversity have taken the form of a treaty signed at the Earth Summit in Rio de Janeiro in 1992. The initiative had three central features. First, nations were required to inventory and monitor their biological assets. Second, conservation efforts centered around sustained-yield resource development were to be pursued, conditional on financial support from wealthy countries. Finally, the treaty specified that a product developed from the genetic resources of a country remained the intellectual property of the host nation, unless a company had agreed to a profit-sharing mechanism in advance.[8] In other words, under the treaty a country like Mexico would have a legal right to block the sale of hybrid corn seeds developed from Mexican maize unless it was guaranteed a share of the profits.

At the Rio Summit, developing nations also tried to get the rich countries to agree to commit 0.7% of their annual GDP to sustainable development projects, up from

6. Sedjo (1992).
7. For details on the efforts in Costa Rica, see www.inbio.ac.cr.
8. Hathaway (1992).

0.4% (from $55 billion to $98 billion annually). However, no such firm commitment was forthcoming. An additional $5 billion in annual aid over the next five years was pledged at the summit: 80% came from Japan, 16% from the European Community, and 4% from the United States. Some of this aid helped finance the conservation programs under the biodiversity treaty.

The Rio agreement was weakened by developing countries that objected to initial attempts to list particular species and habitats as endangered (the approach taken in the CITES treaty on wildlife trade). Ultimately, the agreement was signed by 158 nations, and there was one significant holdout: the United States. The United States had several objections, but primary was the provision that assigned host countries the property rights to genetic resources.

Under the agreement, these rights must be purchased by foreign and domestic firms. As we noted in Chapter 20, whenever common property resources are privatized, those who previously had free access will lose out. In this case, multinational seed and pharmaceutical companies, many of them U.S. based, were the losers. A U.S. biotech industry spokesperson put it this way: "It seems to us highway robbery that a Third World country should have the right to a protected invention simply because it supplied a bug, or a plant or animal in the first place. It's been weighted in favor of developing nations." While Japan and Britain shared some of the U.S. reservations, these two nations ultimately signed on under pressure from domestic environmental groups. However, the U.S. Senate still has refused to ratify.[9]

The Rio agreement is important from a symbolic viewpoint in that the rich countries formally acknowledged the need for a transfer of resources in order to protect biodiversity. However, the treaty has done little to slow down the massive acceleration in species extinction we are currently witnessing.

First, the treaty itself contains no requirement that rich countries contribute to the conservation fund. While significant monies were committed at Rio, no ongoing financial mechanism was established. Second, while the Rio treaty formally assigned to each country the property rights to its genetic resources, no legally binding benefit sharing process has been set up and the United States has opted out. What if biotech companies ignore or circumvent the international law? Without the kind of technical enforcement capability that Costa Rica is building up, the property rights provision of the treaty is liable to be fairly hollow.

The prospects for strengthening the Rio biodiversity treaty are not good, for two related reasons. First, it is very hard to assess compliance with and progress toward an agreement whose goal is to "protect biodiversity." As the treaty acknowledges, the problem of species extinction is a diverse and deeply rooted one, ultimately driven by rapid population growth and desperate poverty in poor countries. In short, effectively preserving biodiversity means *achieving sustainable development* throughout the less-developed world. As related to biodiversity, this will require a substantial increase in the transfer of technology and other resources from wealthy countries to poor ones.

The second obstacle to an effective international agreement is closely related. The loss of biodiversity is unlikely to galvanize the massive aid efforts from the developed

---

9. The quote is from Biodiversity convention a 'lousy deal' says US. 1992. *New Scientist*, 4 July. For an update on the treaty, see Rosendal (2011) and visit the treaty website at www.cbd.int.

world essential to such an effort. The daily extinctions of dozens of species of plants, insects, and animals in the tropical rain forest may deprive our children of important medicines and agricultural products. However, this threat is a negative and distant one. The loss of biodiversity may reduce well-being, but it does not immediately threaten many human lives. By contrast, action to ban CFCs in the ozone case was forthcoming because of the potential for direct and positive harm: massive increases in skin cancer.

To sum up, the framework laid at Rio for protecting biodiversity was certainly helpful, but success on the scale of the Montreal Protocol has not been duplicated. As a result, nongovernmental conservation organizations, some multinational drug and agricultural companies, and host country governments are struggling to protect biodiversity largely on their own. As the next section discusses, however, protecting tropical forests might be an important side benefit of a global-warming agreement.

21.4 Stopping Global Warming: Theory

The prospects for progress on an effective international agreement to control global warming fall midway between the examples of the Montreal Protocol and Rio biodiversity treaty. Like ozone depletion, and unlike the loss of biodiversity, global warming represents a distinct, positive threat to a wide range of nations. Also like ozone depletion, the greenhouse threat arises from several well-defined atmospheric pollutants—primarily carbon dioxide (CO_2) and methane. Thus a treaty can be structured around the concrete goal of controlling these pollutants, instead of an ill-defined target of "preserving ecosystems." These two features—the prospect of **positive harm** to our children and the existence of a **well-defined problem**—improve the prospects for an effective agreement.

However, a **global warming treaty** shares many of the problems faced in the biodiversity case. Foremost among these is the vastly **decentralized** nature of the problem. Unlike the case of CFCs, there are millions of producers of carbon dioxide and methane. Virtually no sector of a modern economy operates without producing CO_2, and methane pollution arises from sources as diverse as natural gas pipelines, rice paddies, and cattle ranches. The CO_2 problem seems a bit less daunting when it is reduced to its two main contributors—coal-fired power plants and gasoline-powered transport. Nevertheless, before clean energy alternatives to these technologies (discussed in Chapter 18) are fully cost competitive, enforcement looms as a major obstacle to an effective treaty.

In addition, as in the loss of biodiversity, both **deforestation** and **economic growth** in poor countries are important drivers of global warming. Although the majority of greenhouse gas emissions are currently generated by the rich countries, sometime over the next two decades, emissions from poor countries will dominate. This means that "solving" global warming is also tied up with the momentous task of achieving sustainable development in the less-developed world.

What does it mean to solve global warming? Under a business-as-usual scenario, by 2100, concentrations of heat-trapping CO_2 will climb well above double their preindustrial levels, to 700, 800, or even 1,000 ppm. This will lead to a likely increase in global temperatures of 6–12 degrees F, with far-reaching, mostly negative consequences for human well-being and for the survival of many of the earth's creatures.

Figure 21.1 outlines a different future. Here, concerted efforts to reduce emissions—beginning globally about ten years ago—would eventually lead to a stabilization of CO_2 concentrations in the atmosphere of 450 ppm by mid-century. This would not stop the warming—with CO_2 at this level, planetary temperatures would still rise by 4 degrees F. But by freezing the thickness of the carbon blanket (and, post 2050, beginning to roll it back down into the 300 ppm), we can buy insurance against truly catastrophic impacts of climate change: rapid sea-level rise from the collapse of the Greenland or West Antarctic Ice Sheets, large-scale methane releases from the tundra, or the fire-driven deforestation of the Amazon and other great forests of the planet.

The figure shows the developed countries meeting the Kyoto targets (roughly 5% below 1990 levels by 2010) and then, by the end of the century, cutting emissions of greenhouse gases by 90%. In this scenario, in the short term, poor countries keep on increasing pollution; but by 2050, they too have to make steep cutbacks, getting 50% below where they are currently. Figure 21.1 also shows clearly that developing countries from the South will soon far outstrip emissions coming from the industrialized North.

As a reference point and reality check, recall that the European countries have met the Kyoto targets, but U.S. emissions in 2011 were 11% above 1990 levels. Going forward, the Europeans have committed to the mid-term trajectory shown in Figure 21.1, with 20% cuts below 1990 by 2020, but recent U.S. proposals—even if passed—would only move our country to around 1990 levels by 2020. Thus, to hit the 450 target would require deeper cuts before 2050 than are shown here, both from developed and developing countries.

Achieving the CO_2 emission reductions in Figure 21.1—on the order of 90% over the next 100 years in the rich countries—may seem like an impossible task. It is helpful

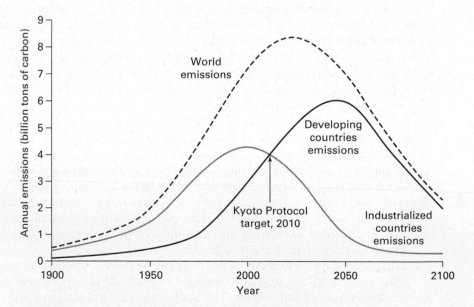

FIGURE 21.1 Stabilizing CO_2 Concentrations at 450 ppm
Source: Bernow et al. (1999). © 1999 WWF (panda.org). Some rights reserved.

to recall that the major pollution source from the transportation sector 100 years ago was horse poop. And we have definitely managed to reduce horse poop in our streets by well over 90%. The diagram simply reflects an assumed phaseout of fossil fuels and a transition to a cheap, clean energy future with electricity provided by wind, solar, and biomass and transportation powered by electric and hybrid vehicles, biofuels, and hydrogen fuel cells. These are not pipe-dream technologies. The uncertain questions, however, are how quickly can their costs drop to competitive levels, and how rapidly can these technologies be transferred to the South, where emissions are growing the fastest?

It is apparent that, unlike the Montreal Protocol, an effective treaty to slow down global warming cannot focus primarily on regulatory control of industries (and consumers) in the rich countries. Instead, it must eventually confront a broad range of interrelated and difficult development issues: poverty, growth in both population and affluence, and deforestation, while quickly rewiring the planet with clean-energy technologies. Fortunately, the ultimate task still remains the narrow and quantifiable one of reducing carbon and methane emissions.

With this background, the bare bones of a successful treaty must do three things: (1) mandate **numerical emission reduction targets** for carbon dioxide and methane, (2) provide a mechanism by which rich countries effectively **transfer technology and resources** to poor countries to finance sustainable development, and (3) provide strong **enforcement** mechanisms. A potential tool for accomplishing these three goals simultaneously would be an international **cap-and-trade** system.

How would this work? Figure 21.2 illustrates one version of the process. An initial treaty would first put an annual cap on targeted global emissions of a greenhouse pollutant, say CO_2. A share of the annual total would then be allocated to each nation. Some have suggested that carbon permits be allocated based on a nation's population, others have suggested an initial fifty-fifty split between rich and poor countries. At any rate, for the system to work, poor countries would have to emerge from the process with an excess supply of permits, while rich countries would have an excess demand.

The next step in the process would be for rich nations to trade expertise and technology to poor nations in exchange for permits. Trade would be authorized only for measures that lead to demonstrable reductions in greenhouse gas emissions. To lessen the opportunity for corruption, trade in cash would be discouraged.

Each country would then be responsible for reducing CO_2 emissions to the level specified by the tradeable permits held. This could be done through an "internal" marketable permit system, carbon taxes, command-and-control regulation, or programs to promote investment in clean technology. An IGO established by the initial treaty would have to have broad compliance monitoring powers. One possibility is **chain monitoring**, in which the countries are ranked by CO_2 emissions, and each nation is monitored by the next biggest emitter. Presumably, such monitors would have an economic incentive to ensure that their (larger) competitors were not cheating on an agreement.

Finally, a permit system could be enforced by restricting trade in permits to countries that were either exceeding their permitted emissions or violating other terms of the agreement. Poor-country sales would be restricted, as would rich-country purchases. One beauty of the permit system is that it gives countries something that can

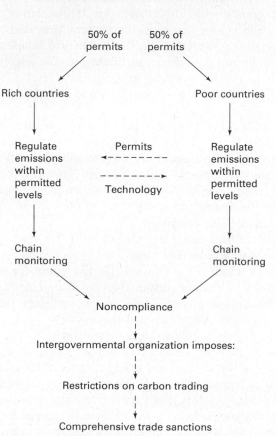

FIGURE 21.2 Model Greenhouse Treaty

then be taken away if they refuse to comply. Finally, the treaty would have to authorize more **comprehensive trade sanctions** against a nation that repeatedly or willfully failed to meet its permitted emissions requirements.

The near-term prospects for this kind of comprehensive agreement, including both rich and poor countries, are not good. First, an effective treaty would both require nations to allow foreign or intergovernmental monitoring of compliance and authorize the imposition of full-scale trade embargoes for willful noncompliance. To date, countries have seldom agreed to give up this much sovereignty. Second, such a treaty might be painted as a large-scale foreign aid program, as resources were transferred to developing countries to support clean energy conversion and forest protection. Such initiations are not particularly popular. Finally, uncertainty as to the magnitude of the problem provides an excuse for inaction. However, as in the ozone case, greenhouse gases are very long-lived. Thus, by the time the magnitude of global warming is confirmed, it may be too late to take any effective action.

21.5 Stopping Global Warming: Reality

International efforts to tackle global warming date back to the Rio de Janeiro Earth Summit in 1992. There, the U.S. government did plead uncertainty, and successfully weakened the **framework global warming convention** that was ultimately signed. The European nations were originally pressing for a schedule of timetables and cutbacks aimed at substantially *reducing* global CO_2 emissions. President Bush, the elder, by threatening to boycott the Rio summit altogether, was able instead to achieve a much weaker agreement. Ultimately, the nations made only a nonbinding commitment to "try" to stabilize carbon emissions at 1990 levels by the year 2000. This effort failed—emissions in the United States, for example, rose about 11% over the period.[10]

The governments of the world reconvened in Kyoto, Japan, in December 1997, and signed a stronger agreement calling for a total reduction in greenhouse gases to 5% below 1990 levels by about 2010. For the United States, the target was 7% below 1990 levels, for Japan, 6%, and for the European Union, 8%. The **Kyoto Protocol** imposed emission targets and timetables on only the industrialized countries. The rationale here was twofold: First, greenhouse gases are long-lived, so although poor countries will soon catch up in terms of annual emissions, the cumulative emissions from developed countries will remain primarily responsible for climate change over the medium term. Second, poor countries don't have the resources to invest in the alternative technologies—electric and biofueled vehicles and solar and wind-powered electricity—that are needed to address the global-warming problem.

Thus the idea behind the Kyoto agreement—explicitly modeled on the Montreal Protocol—was that rich countries would go first and develop low-cost alternatives to gasoline-powered automobiles and coal-fired power plants. These technologies would then spread from the North to the South, allowing poor countries to leapfrog the fossil fuel–based development patterns followed by the rich countries. This progress will be critical: China is currently opening, every week, a new coal-fired power plant big enough to power a city the size of Dallas. At this rate, the increase in emissions over the next quarter century from China alone will be five times larger than the cuts sought by the Kyoto treaty.[11]

Chapter 16 discussed the trading system set up under Kyoto, including the **Clean Development Mechanism**, in which rich countries gain credit for clean investments in poor countries. This is one prototype for the kind of large-scale technology transfer that will be needed to stabilize the climate. If and when Kyoto is expanded to include limits on developing-country emissions, a global carbon **cap-and-trade** system will build on this approach. The trading system should provide excess carbon allowances to poor countries; these could then be "sold" to rich countries in exchange for access to solar power or fuel-cell technologies, or for help in protecting standing forests. Also, as noted in Chapter 16, Kyoto currently does incorporate a more limited marketable permit approach: the **Joint Implementation** procedure, which allows for trade in carbon rights between the industrialized countries that are subject to emission limits.

The Kyoto Accord was ratified by the European countries and by Canada, Japan, Australia, and Russia. The United States is the only major industrial country that has

---

10. "How Bush Achieved Global Warming Pact with Modest Goals" (1992).
11. Bradshaw and Barboza (2006).

failed to ratify. Indeed, in 2001, President Bush withdrew the United States from the Kyoto process.

Conservative opposition in the United States has centered on two arguments: Kyoto would cost far too much for too little benefit and poor countries should be parties to the treaty and forced to reduce emissions on the same timetable as rich countries. Otherwise, it was argued, U.S. industry will be at a competitive disadvantage, leading to large-scale job loss. As we saw in Chapter 6, this kind of widespread jobs-environment conflict, while often predicted in the past, has never materialized.[12]

In December 2009, nations met again in Copenhagen to begin to hammer out a post-Kyoto international framework. No "grand deal" emerged; instead, major nations, including the United States, Europe, Japan, and China, all pledged cooperative action toward a maximum 2 degree C warming target (the 450 ppm outcome modeled in Figure 21.1). Hard decisions on coordinated national emission targets and funds for technology transfer and forest protection were put off. That said, President Obama's commitment to rolling U.S. emissions back to 1990 levels by 2020—a goal that is probably achievable under existing Clean Air Act regulations—along with China's new-found willingness to talk, provided a mild sense of optimism coming out of the meetings.

In 2010, politics in the United States took a hard right turn with the election of dozens of "Tea-Party" affiliated members of the House of Representatives, vociferously opposed to action on climate. This fact, combined with a swing back to the center and Obama's re-election in 2012, suggests that U.S. climate policy through 2016 will be driven largely by U.S. EPA action under the Clean Air Act. The EPA has the authority to develop regulations working toward a "safe" level of CO_2 in the atmosphere, but the agency—facing continued strong opposition from conservatives in the House—is unlikely to move aggressively to regulate CO_2 emissions from existing utility or industrial sources. Given the politics, an optimistic trajectory would see the United States achieving Obama's 17% reduction goal at low economic cost, setting the stage for further legislative action to cut emissions later in the decade.

Strong U.S.-based opposition to climate change action is not surprising. Our nation, along with China, is one of the two biggest greenhouse gas emitters. U.S. opposition to the treaty process up until the current time is thus illustrative of the general problem of forging agreements outlined in the introduction to this chapter. Relative to its much more energy-efficient Japanese and European competitors, the United States includes more actors likely to lose from a global-warming treaty. These include highly profitable oil companies, who have substantial political influence. Thus the opposition to carbon reduction has been strong from our country.

The most surprising development post-Copenhagen has been Chinese openness to pursuing domestic CO_2 restraints. The quality of the urban environment has emerged as a major political issue in China; this, combined with the long-term danger to China's coastal populations and agricultural productivity, has led the Chinese government to announce a number of policy experiments—including both CO_2 taxes and trading systems. Whether such policies will be strong enough to alter the vast momentum of

12. Goodstein (1999).

China's growing carbon footprint will be critical in determining the trajectory of global warming in this century and beyond.

Whether urgent international action on global warming is in fact justified is the subject of an important economic (and ethical) debate, explored in Chapters 1 and 18. Clearly, however, Kyoto compliance would not have bankrupted the U.S. economy. Indeed, from 2002 to 2007, the United States spent more on the war in Iraq than the Kyoto Protocol would have been expected to cost—even at the higher end—over its lifetime.[13] Initial steps to control CO_2 emissions (improved energy efficiency, expansion of wind power, and the control of natural gas leaks) will not be particularly costly. Indeed, as noted in Chapter 1, most of the economists working on global warming issues have publicly called for action—ranging from a modest \$10 per ton tax to full-on Kyoto compliance—based on efficiency arguments. Given this call for action, the U.S. actions over the last decade have been unfortunate from a global benefit-cost perspective.

As the Montreal Protocol case illustrates, a treaty process is a long, drawn-out affair. The Kyoto Protocol, though much stronger than the Rio Convention of 1992, was a far cry from the effective agreement outlined in Figure 21.2. It deals only with step 1, establishing numerical reduction targets, but does not address in a serious way the other two requirements: resources for sustainable development and enforcement. From this perspective, our nation's opposition to action in the 2000s undercut the substantial insurance value that would have been provided by an agreement that at least addressed the first of the three necessary steps. The treaty process must be well advanced in the event that the additional bolder steps are to be seriously contemplated.

We noted earlier that one of the factors favoring a global-warming treaty is that the climate change is liable to inflict positive and significant harm on the citizens of many nations. As an example of a clear and present danger yielding an impressive international response, we can look to the appearance of the ozone hole in 1985, which spurred nations into signing the Montreal Protocol. In the global-warming case, no individual extreme weather event can be attributed to human-induced climate change. However, it is possible that a series of catastrophic events consistent with a warming planet—the deadly heat wave that gripped Europe in 2003, Hurricane Katrina in 2005, massive Midwestern flooding, followed by unprecedented heat and drought across the United States in 2011 and 2012, then followed by superstorm Sandy, and whatever comes next—may provide the impetus to an effective global-warming treaty.

21.6 Summary

This chapter identifies a basic obstacle to effective international action on global environmental problems: the public good nature of an agreement. Free riding means that agreements are likely to be too weak from an efficiency perspective and to be susceptible to noncompliance. International bodies set up to administer agreements may monitor compliance but have few enforcement powers. One informal tool is

---

13. Sunstein (2006).

community pressure. Formal enforcement mechanisms must be written into a treaty and include restricted access to a compensation fund and targeted trade sanctions.

The Montreal Protocol to protect the ozone layer represents the most successful environmental treaty to date. In a period of 16 years, nations moved from skepticism about the need to regulate CFCs at all to banning the bulk of production. The treaty's success can be traced to three factors: (1) the rapidly mounting evidence of a significant health threat; (2) the centralized nature of CFC production, which minimized enforcement problems; and (3) the speedy development of low-cost CFC substitutes.

By contrast, the Rio biodiversity agreement has value primarily as a symbol of concern. The treaty formally recognizes two key points: (1) rich nations must finance sustained-yield resource development projects in poor countries if biodiversity is to be preserved and (2) an important obstacle to profit-based conservation has been open access by multinational firms to genetic resources. However, the treaty is very weak on enforcement mechanisms, and rich nations have little political incentive to pay the necessary price to beef up the treaty.

The prospects for a global-warming treaty are enhanced by the positive threat posed and the focus on a handful of pollutants. However, as in the biodiversity case, solving the problem would in fact require achieving sustainable development in poor countries—increasing incomes in a clean manner while reducing population growth.

An effective treaty would mandate emission reductions, provide a means to transfer technology and resources to poor countries, and have a built-in enforcement mechanism. An international cap-and-trade system has the first two features but may prove difficult to monitor and enforce. Enforcement would ultimately have to be guaranteed by the threat of comprehensive trade sanctions. To date, international action in the form of the Kyoto treaty reflects only the first feature—emission reductions—and even this limited agreement has been plagued by the problem of free riding. The successor to the Kyoto Accord will have to address these challenges.

This book has ended, as it began, with a discussion of global warming. Today, we all compounded this problem by actions as simple as driving to work and turning on our computers. Yet global warming is just one of the pressing environmental problems we will face in the coming years. From the siting of waste facilities at the community level to regulatory policy at the national level to sustainable development around the globe, environmental challenges abound. While these problems are formidable, we have no option but to face them squarely. This book has provided some tools for doing so.

At the risk of repeating ourselves (again!), let us summarize the three-step approach that we have developed:

Step 1. **Set your environmental goal**. Efficiency, safety, or ecological sustainability?

Step 2. **Recognize the constraints on effective governmental action**. Imperfect information, political influence, and inadequate enforcement.

Step 3. **Look for ways to do better**. Incentive-based regulation and clean technology promotion.

Now, get to work.

APPLICATION 21.0

Benefits, Costs, and Kyoto

Yale economist William Nordhaus has done a lot of work on benefit-cost analysis of the Kyoto treaty. Bearing in mind the vast uncertainties associated with estimating both the costs and the benefits of the Kyoto emission reductions, consider his results in Figure 21.3. By 2070, relative to a business-as-usual increase in CO_2 emissions, the original Kyoto Protocol would have led to global emission cuts of 15%, and the efficient policy would lead to cuts of about 10%.

1. Assume that Nordhaus used a 5% discount rate for costs and benefits. Assume also that most of the benefits of reducing emissions today come in 80–100 years, while most of the costs will occur in the next 10–20 years. How would the "efficient" curve look different if he had instead used a 3% discount rate? (Fill in the illustrative chart for the Kyoto Protocol to help you with your answer: Is Kyoto more efficient at the 3% discount rate or the 5% discount rate?)

Year	Costs ($)	Benefits ($)	5%	5%	3%	3%
20	70 b	×		×		×
100	×	800 b	×		×	

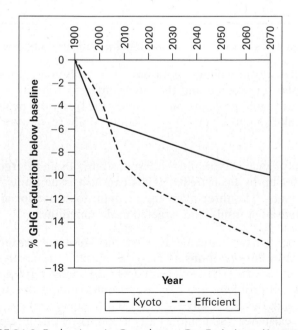

FIGURE 21.3 Reductions in Greenhouse Gas Emissions: Kyoto versus Efficiency
Source: Adapted from Nordhaus (2001).

2.   Nordhaus is generally an efficiency advocate. And yet, following the presentation of the results in Figure 21.3, he concluded: "There is little appreciation of the importance of 'institutional innovations' of this kind, and even less appreciation for the fact that there are no mechanisms for dealing with economic global public goods like global warming. For this reason, the Kyoto-Bonn Accord may be a useful if expensive guinea pig.

Operating the Kyoto-Bonn mechanism will provide valuable insights on how complicated international environmental programs will work. It is hard to see why the United States should not join with other countries in paying for this knowledge."

What does the "global public good" nature of global warming help explain?

3.   In fact, from 2005-2012, the Kyoto Treaty moved ahead without U.S. participation. Referring to this chapter and Chapter 16, what important piece of knowledge do we hope to get from the European Trading System?

4.   Nordhaus also says of Kyoto: "Economic analyses of the accord have pointed to its inefficiencies, especially the shortcomings from using pure quantity-type instruments such as emissions constraints with no price caps or tax instruments … therefore, it might be preferable to redesign the accord along the lines of a globally harmonized carbon tax."

Why might country-specific carbon taxes be preferable to an international cap-and-trade system for carbon? What might be lost by not allowing international trading?

KEY IDEAS IN EACH SECTION

21.0   This chapter discusses the economics of global pollution-control agreements.

21.1   Each country has a true **willingness to pay** for a pollution-control agreement that is a function of both its income and the environmental benefits it is likely to receive. However, because agreements are **public goods**, the **free-rider problem** means they will be both **too weak** from an efficiency (and safety) point of view and provide **incentives for cheating**.

21.2   Monitoring compliance is typically the responsibility of an **intergovernmental organization (IGO)** set up by each treaty. IGOs can also issue **nonbinding standards** and **monitor** compliance. The three main enforcement tools are **social pressure**, restricted access to **compensation funds**, and targeted **trade sanctions**.

21.3   This section describes two agreements. First, the **Montreal Protocol** initiated a global phaseout of **chlorofluorocarbons (CFCs)** to protect the earth's **ozone layer**. The treaty succeeded due to (1) the clear and present danger from the **ozone hole**, (2) a narrowly defined problem, and (3) ease of enforcement due to limited number of producers. Second, the Rio Convention on Biodiversity seeks to protect **biodiversity** (important for **existence value** and as a gene pool) by encouraging member nations to inventory reserves, take conservation measures, and provide host countries with a share in **pharmaceutical and agricultural breeding** profits. The treaty has little more than symbolic value due to (1) a clear but distant danger of negative harm, (2) a broadly defined problem, and (3) inability to take action without funding from rich countries.

21.4   How likely is an effective **global warming treaty?** Pros include the likelihood of **positive harm** and the existence of **well-defined problems**. Cons arise from highly **decentralized** producers and the fact that a greenhouse treaty would have to confront sustainability issues ranging from **deforestation** to **population growth**. An effective treaty would have three components: (1) **numerical emission reduction targets**, (2) **technology and resource transfers**, and (3) **good enforcement**. A global **cap-and-trade**, combined with **chain monitoring** and **comprehensive trade sanctions**, is one model that fits these requirements.

21.5   The UN **Framework Convention on Climate Change** was negotiated in Rio de Janeiro in 1992 and called for voluntary efforts to prevent growth in emissions, which failed. Subsequent meetings led to the signing of the **Kyoto Protocol**, which required the industrial nations collectively to reduce greenhouse gas emissions 5% below 1990 levels by about 2010. The Protocol does incorporate developing countries into a carbon-trading system through the **Clean Development Mechanism**. It also includes a textbook cap-and-trade component for the industrial nations, known as **Joint Implementation**. The United States withdrew from the Kyoto accord; most other industrial countries moved forward with implementation though with varying levels of success. In Copenhagen in 2009, Kyoto was replaced with a system in which individual countries pledged reduction goals, and collectively the nations agreed to try and hold warming to 4 degrees F.

REFERENCES

Bailey, Martin. 1982. Risks, costs and benefits of fluorocarbon regulation. *American Economic Review* 72(2): 247–50.

Bernow, Stephen, Karlynn Cory, William Dougherty, Max Duckworth, Sivan Kartha, and Michael Ruth. 1999. *America's global warming solutions*. Washington, DC: World Wildlife Fund.

Bradshaw, K., and D. Barboza. 2006. The energy challenge: Pollution from Chinese coal casts a global shadow. *New York Times*, World Business, 11 June.

Goodstein, Eban. 1999. *The trade-off myth: Fact and fiction about jobs and the environment*. Washington, DC: Island Press.

Hathaway, Oona. 1992. Whither biodiversity? The global debate over biological variety continues. *Harvard International Review* 15(2): 58–60.

Heppes, John B., and Eric J. McFadden. 1987. The convention on trade in endangered species: The prospects for preserving our biological heritage. *Boston University International Law Journal* 5(2): 229–46.

How Bush achieved global warming pact with modest goals. 1992. *Wall Street Journal*, 27 May.

Nordhaus, W. D. 2001. Global warming economics. *Science* 294: 1283–4.

Rosendal, G. K. 2011. Biodiversity protection in international negotiations: Cooperation and conflict in beyond resource wars scarcity, environmental degradation, and international cooperation, ed. Shlomi Dinar. MIT Press: Cambridge.

Sedjo, Roger A. 1992. Property rights, genetic resources and biotechnological change. *Journal of Law and Economics* 35(1): 199–213.

Somerset, Margaret. 1989. An attempt to stop the sky from falling: The Montreal Protocol to protect against atmospheric ozone reduction. *Syracuse Journal of International Law and Commerce* 15(39): 391–429.

Sunstein, Cass. 2006. It's only $300 billion. *Washington Post*, 10 May.

Zhao, Jimin. 2005. Implementing international environmental treaties in developing countries: China's compliance with the Montreal Protocol. *Global Environmental Policy* 5(1): 58–81.

SELECTED WEB SITES FOR ENVIRONMENTAL AND NATURAL RESOURCE ECONOMISTS

THE NUMBER-ONE SITE:

Resources for the Future (RFF is the premier environmental economics research organization in the country—this should be your first stop for a research project, with top quality papers on virtually every subject you might want to research): www.rff.org

EBAN'S FAVORITE BLOG:

Climate progress at www.climate.progress.org

DATA SOURCES AND ENVIRONMENTAL RESEARCH ORGANIZATIONS:

- Climate Science: www.realclimate.org
- Environmental Working Group Farm Subsidy Database 1996–2001: www.ewg.org/farm
- The EPA Economy and the Environment: www.epa.gov/economics
- The National Bureau of Economic Research: www.nber.harvard.edu
- Real World Results (emission trading site): www.etei.org
- Resources for Economists on the Internet: www.econwpa.wustl.edu/EconFAQ/EconFAQ.html
- The Toxics Release Inventory: www.epa.gov/tri

INTERNATIONAL DATA AND RESEARCH ORGANIZATIONS:

- The World Resources Institute: www.wri.org
- The World Bank: New Ideas in Pollution Regulation: www.worldbank.org/nipr
- The World Trade Organization: www.wto.org

ENVIRONMENTAL ECONOMICS ORGANIZATIONS:

- Association for Environmental and Resource Economics (mainstream): www.rff.org
- International Society for Ecological Economics (ecological): www.ecologicaleconomics.org
- Economics for Equity and the Environment: www.e3network.org
- Environmental Economics (blog): www.env-ecom.net

AUTHOR INDEX

SUBJECT INDEX